Microsoft®

Windows® 7

Comprehensive

Gary B. Shelly

Steven M. Freund

Raymond E. Enger

COURSE TECHNOLOGY
CENGAGE Learning™

Australia • Brazil • Japan • Korea • Mexico • Singapore • Spain • United Kingdom • United States

COURSE TECHNOLOGY
CENGAGE Learning

Microsoft© Windows® 7
Comprehensive
Gary B. Shelly
Steven M. Freund
Raymond E. Enger

Vice President, Publisher: Nicole Pinard

Executive Editor: Kathleen McMahon

Product Manager: Jon Farnham

Associate Product Manager: Aimee Poirier

Editorial Assistant: Lauren Brody

Print Buyer: Julio Esperas

Director of Production: Patty Stephen

Content Project Manager: Matthew Hutchinson

Development Editor: Karen Stevens

Director of Marketing: Cheryl Costantini

Marketing Manager: Tristen Kendall

Marketing Coordinator: Stacey Leasca

QA Manuscript Reviewers: John Freitas,
  Danielle Shaw

Art Director: Marissa Falco

Cover Designer: Lisa Kuhn, Curio Press, LLC

Cover Photo: Tom Kates Photography

Compositor: PreMediaGlobal

Copyeditor: Karen Annett

Proofreader: Kathy Orrino

Indexer: Alexandra Nickerson

Appendix C: C-1 Courtesy of Cisco Systems;
  C-2 Courtesy of Dell Computers, Inc.;
  Courtesy of Cisco Systems; C-3 Courtesy
  of Dell Computers, Inc.; Courtesy of Cisco
  Systems

For product information and technology assistance, contact us at
Cengage Learning Customer & Sales Support, 1-800-354-9706
For permission to use material from this text or product, submit all requests online at **cengage.com/permissions**
Further permissions questions can be emailed to
permissionrequest@cengage.com

Library of Congress Control Number: 2010930484

ISBN-13: 978-1-4390-8103-7

ISBN-10: 1-4390-8103-4

Course Technology
20 Channel Center Street
Boston, MA 02210
USA

Cengage Learning is a leading provider of customized learning solutions with office locations around the globe, including Singapore, the United Kingdom, Australia, Mexico, Brazil, and Japan. Locate your local office at:
international.cengage.com/region

Cengage Learning products are represented in Canada by Nelson Education, Ltd.

Visit our website **www.cengage.com/ct/shellycashman** to share and gain ideas on our textbooks!

To learn more about Course Technology, visit **www.cengage.com/coursetechnology**

Purchase any of our products at your local college store or at our preferred online store **www.CengageBrain.com**

Printed in the United States of America
1 2 3 4 5 6 16 15 14 13 12 11

Contents

CHAPTER FOUR
Personal Information Management and Communication

Appendices

Preface

The Shelly Cashman Series® offers the finest textbooks in computer education. We are proud of the fact that our Microsoft Windows 3.1, Microsoft Windows 95, Microsoft Windows 98, Microsoft Windows 2000, Microsoft Windows XP, and Microsoft Windows Vista books have been so well received by students and instructors. With each new edition of our Windows books, we have made significant improvements based on the software and comments made by instructors and students.

Microsoft Windows contains many changes in the user interface and feature set. Recognizing that the new features and functionality of Microsoft Windows 7 would impact the way that students are taught skills, the Shelly Cashman Series development team carefully reviewed our pedagogy and analyzed its effectiveness in teaching today's student. An extensive customer survey produced results confirming what the series is best known for: its step-by-step, screen-by-screen instructions, its project-oriented approach, and the quality of its content.

We learned, though, that students entering computer courses today are different than students taking these classes just a few years ago. Students today read less, but need to retain more. They need not only to be able to perform skills, but to retain those skills and know how to apply them to different settings. Today's students need to be continually engaged and challenged to retain what they're learning.

As a result, we've renewed our commitment to focusing on the user and how they learn best. This commitment is reflected in every change we've made to our Windows 7 books.

Objectives of This Textbook

Microsoft© Windows® 7: Comprehensive is intended for a ten- to fifteen-week period in a course that teaches Microsoft Windows 7 as the primary component. No experience with a computer is assumed, and no mathematics beyond the high school freshman level is required. The objectives of this book are:

- To offer a comprehensive presentation of Microsoft Windows 7
- To expose students to practical examples of the computer as a useful tool
- To acquaint students with the proper procedures to manage and organize document storage options for coursework, professional purposes, and personal use
- To help students discover the underlying functionality and customization options of Windows 7 so that they can become more productive
- To develop an exercise-oriented approach that allows learning by doing

Distinguishing Features

A Proven Pedagogy with an Emphasis on Project Planning The project orientation is strengthened by the use of Plan Ahead boxes that encourage critical thinking about how to proceed at the beginning of each chapter. Step-by-step instructions with supporting screens guide students through the steps. Instructional steps are supported by the Q&A, Experiment Step, and BTW features.

A Visually Engaging Book that Maintains Student Interest The step-by-step tasks, with supporting figures, provide a rich visual experience for the student. Call-outs on the screens that present both explanatory and navigational information provide students with information they need when they need to know it.

Supporting Reference Materials (Appendices) The appendices provide additional information about Windows 7, such as the security features and networking.

Integration of the World Wide Web The World Wide Web is integrated into the Windows 7 learning experience through step-by-step instruction on Internet Explorer, as well as the Learn It Online section for each chapter.

End-of-Chapter Student Activities Extensive end of chapter activities provide a variety of reinforcement opportunities for students where they can apply and expand their skills through individual and group work.

Instructor Resources CD-ROM

The Instructor Resources include both teaching and testing aids.

INSTRUCTOR'S MANUAL Includes lecture notes summarizing the chapter sections, figures and boxed elements found in every chapter, teacher tips, classroom activities, lab activities, and quick quizzes in Microsoft Word files.

SYLLABUS Easily customizable sample syllabi that cover policies, assignments, exams, and other course information.

FIGURE FILES Illustrations for every figure in the textbook in electronic form.

POWERPOINT PRESENTATIONS A multimedia lecture presentation system that provides slides for each chapter. Presentations are based on chapter objectives.

SOLUTIONS TO EXERCISES Includes solutions for all end-of-chapter and chapter reinforcement exercises.

TEST BANK & TEST ENGINE Test Banks include 112 questions for every chapter, featuring objective-based and critical thinking question types, and including page number references and figure references, when appropriate. Also included is the test engine, ExamView, the ultimate tool for your objective-based testing needs.

DATA FILES FOR STUDENTS Includes all the files that are required by students to complete the exercises.

ADDITIONAL ACTIVITIES FOR STUDENTS Consists of Chapter Reinforcement Exercises, which are true/false, multiple-choice, and short answer questions that help students gain confidence in the material learned.

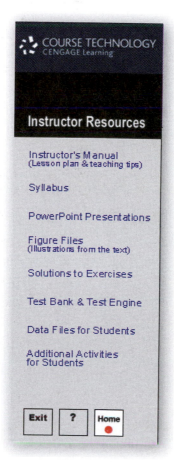

Blackboard

course|notes™
quick reference guide

Content for Online Learning

Course Technology has partnered with Blackboard, the leading distance learning solution provider and class-management platform today. The resources available for download with this title are the test banks in Blackboard- and WebCT-compatible formats. To access this material, simply visit our password-protected instructor resources available at www.cengage.com/coursetechnology. For additional information or for an instructor username and password, please contact your sales representative.

Guided Tours

Add excitement and interactivity to your classroom with "*A Guided Tour*" product line. Play one of the brief mini-movies to spice up your lecture and spark classroom discussion. Or, assign a movie for homework and ask students to complete the correlated assignment that accompanies each topic. "*A Guided Tour*" product line takes the prep-work out of providing your students with information on new technologies and software applications and helps keep students engaged with content relevant to their lives, all in under an hour!

CourseNotes

Course Technology's CourseNotes are six-panel quick reference cards that reinforce the most important concepts and features of a software application in a visual and user-friendly format. CourseNotes serve as a great reference tool during and after the student completes the course. CourseNotes are available for software applications, such as Microsoft Office, Word, PowerPoint, Excel, Access, and Windows 7. There are also topic-based CourseNotes available for Best Practices in Social Networking, Hot Topics in Technology, and Web 2.0. Visit www.cengage.com/ct/coursenotes to learn more!

SAM: Skills Assessment Manager

SAM is designed to help bring students from the classroom to the real world. It allows students to train and test on important computer skills in an active, hands-on environment.

SAM's easy-to-use system includes powerful interactive exams, training and projects on the most commonly used Microsoft® Office applications. SAM simulates the Office 2010 application environment, allowing students to demonstrate their knowledge and think through the skills by performing real-world tasks such as bolding word text or setting up slide transitions. Add in live-in-the-application projects and students are on their way to truly learning and applying skills to business-centric document.

Designed to be used with the Shelly Cashman Series, SAM includes handy page references, so students can print helpful study guides that match the Shelly Cashman Series textbooks used in class. For instructors, SAM also includes robust scheduling and reporting features.

Textbook Walk-Through

The Shelly Cashman Series Pedagogy:
Project-based — Step-by-Step — Variety of Assessments

Plan Ahead boxes prepare students to create successful projects by encouraging them to think strategically about what they are trying to accomplish before they begin working.

Step-by-step instructions now provide a context beyond the point-and-click. Each step provides information on why students are performing each task, or what will occur as a result.

Microsoft **Windows 7**

3 | File and Folder Management

Introduction

In Chapter 2, you used Windows 7 to create documents on the desktop and work with documents and folders in the Documents library. Windows 7 also allows you to examine the files and folders on the computer in a variety of other ways, enabling you to choose the easiest and most accessible manner when working with the computer. The Computer folder window and the Documents library provide two ways for you to work with files and folders. In addition, the Pictures library allows you to organize and share picture files, and the Music library allows you to organize and share your music files. This chapter illustrates how to work with files in the Computer folder, as well as the Documents, Pictures, and Music libraries.

Overview

As you read this chapter, you will learn how to work with the Computer folder window, as well as the Pictures and Music libraries, by performing these general tasks:

- Opening and using the Computer folder window
- Searching for files and folders
- Managing open windows
- Opening and using the Pictures library
- Using Windows Photo Viewer
- Opening and using the Music library
- Playing a music file in Windows Media Player
- Backing up and restoring a folder

Plan Ahead

Working with Files and Folders
Working with files and folders requires a basic knowledge of how to use the Windows 7 desktop.

1. **Be aware that there might be different levels of access on the computer you will be using.** A user account can be restricted to a certain level of access to the computer. Depending on the level of access that has been set for your account, you might or might not be able to perform certain operations.

2. **Identify how to connect a USB flash drive to your computer.** Depending upon the setup of your computer, there might be several ways to connect a USB flash drive to your computer. You should know which USB ports you can use to connect a USB flash drive to your computer.

3. **Determine if your computer has speakers.** Some computer labs do not provide speakers. If you are going to be using a computer in a lab, you need to know if the computer has speakers or if you will need to bring earbuds.

(continued)

To Open the Getting Started Window

If you are new to using Windows 7, you can open the Getting Star... allows you to complete a set of tasks to optimize the computer. The task... transferring files and settings from another computer, and backing up yo... Started window to perform these tasks, but it can assist you with configu... open the Getting Started window. If the Getting Started window alread... without performing them.

1
- Click the Start button on the taskbar to display the Start menu (Figure 1–13).

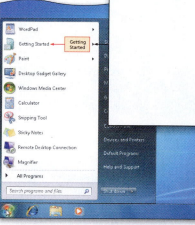

Figure 1–13

2
- Click Getting Started to open the Getting Started window (Figure 1–14).

Q&A
What should I do if the Getting Started command does not display on the Start menu?

Depending upon how your computer is configured, you might find the Getting Started command in the Accessories list instead.

Other Ways
1. Display Start menu, click All Programs, click Accessories, click Getting Started

Figure 1–14

BTW
Screen Shots
Callouts in screenshots give students information they need, when they need to know it. The Series has always used plenty of callouts to ensure that students don't get lost. Now, color is used to distinguish the content in the callouts to make them more meaningful.

Navigational callouts in red show students where to click.

Explanatory callouts summarize what is happening on screen.

Textbook Walk-Through

Q&A boxes offer questions students may have when working through the steps and provide additional information about what they are doing right where they need it.

Experiment Steps within our step-by-step instructions, encourage students to explore, experiment, and take advantage of the features of Windows 7. These steps are not necessary to complete the projects, but are designed to increase the confidence with the software and build problem-solving skills.

To Collapse the Local Disk (C:) List

The following step collapses the Local Disk (C:) list.

1
- Click the arrow next to Local Disk (C:) to collapse the Local Disk (C:) list (Figure 1–30).

Should I keep the list expanded or collapsed?

If you need to use the contents in the list, it is handy to keep the list expanded. You can collapse the list when the information is not needed.

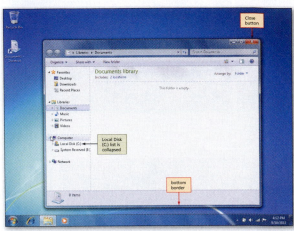

Figure 1–30

...ew to its original size. To return the ...ibrary, complete the following steps.

...uments ...brary is ...ed

...ure 1–31

Windows Chapter 1

To Delete a Desktop Icon by Dragging it to the Recycle Bin

Although Windows 7 has many ways to delete desktop icons, one method of removing an icon from the desktop is to drag it to the Recycle Bin. The following steps delete the Documents - Shortcut icon by dragging the icon to the Recycle Bin.

1
- Point to the Documents - Shortcut icon on the desktop and press the left mouse button to select the icon (Figure 1–32). Do not release the left mouse button.

Figure 1–32

2
- Drag the Documents - Shortcut icon over the Recycle Bin icon on the desktop, and then release the left mouse button to place the shortcut in the Recycle Bin (Figure 1–33).

Experiment
- Double-click the Recycle Bin icon on the desktop to open a window containing the contents of the Recycle Bin. The Documents - Shortcut icon you have just deleted will display in this window. Close the Recycle Bin window.

Why did the Documents - Shortcut icon disappear?

Releasing the left mouse button moved the icon from the desktop to the Recycle Bin.

Figure 1–33

Other Ways
1. Right-click icon, click Delete, click Yes button
2. Right-click icon and hold, drag to Recycle Bin, release right mouse button, click Move Here

Textbook Walk-Through

Other Ways boxes that follow many of the step sequences explain the other ways to complete the task presented.

②
- Click the Restore Down button on the Computer folder window to return the Computer folder window to its previous size (Figure 1–21).

Q&A

What happens to the Restore Down button after I click it?

The Maximize button replaces the Restore Down button on the title bar.

Other Ways

1. Double-click title bar, double-click title bar
2. Right-click title bar, click Maximize, right-click title bar, click Restore
3. Click title bar and drag window to the top of screen, click title bar and drag window down towards the center of the screen

Figure 1–21

To Close a Window

...r of a window closes the window. To close the Computer folder window,

Figure 1–22

Part 6: What's New in Mobile PC Features Area?
1. Click the Laptops link to open the Laptops page.
2. Click the 'Using Windows Mobility Center' link, and answer the following question:
   a. How do you open the Mobility Center?

   _____

3. Click the Close button in the Windows Help and Support window.

Extend Your Knowledge

Extend the skills you learned in this chapter and experiment with new skills. You might need to use Help to complete the assignment.

Using Windows Help and Support to Obtain Help
Instructions: Use Windows Help and Support to perform the following tasks.

1. Find Help about Windows keyboard shortcuts by typing `shortcuts` in the Search Help text box and then clicking the Search Help button (Figure 1–81). Click the result titled Keyboard shortcuts.
   a. What general keyboard shortcut is used to display the Start menu?
   b. What general keyboard shortcut is used to display the shortcut menu for an active window?
   c. What general keyboard shortcut is used to view the properties for a selected item?

Extend Your Knowledge projects at the end of each chapter allow students to extend and expand on the skills learned within the chapter. Students use critical thinking to experiment with new skills to complete each project.

Figure 1–81

Continued >

Textbook Walk-Through

Figure 1–82

The in-depth **In the Lab** assignments require students to utilize the chapter concepts and techniques to solve problems.

3. Play the Picture Puzzle game, by moving the puzzle tiles around by clicking on them when they are near the empty slot. Continue to rearrange the tiles until you have completed the picture (you can show the picture at any time to determine if you are close to the solution). Record your time here: _____

4. Click the Close button on the gadget to remove the gadget from the desktop.

In the Lab

Lab 2: Switching through Open Windows

Instructions: Perform the following steps to launch multiple programs using the Start menu and then use different methods to switch through the open windows (Figure 1–83 on the next page).

Part 1: Launching the Getting Started Window, WordPad, and Internet Explorer
1. Click the Start button, click the All Programs command, and then click the Internet Explorer command to launch Internet Explorer.

[text obscured] ll Programs command, click the Accessories folder, and then click [text obscured] display the Getting Started window.

[text obscured] ll Programs command, click the Accessories folder, and then click

[text obscured] ext open window.

[text obscured] press the TAB key two times to switch to the next open window.

[text obscured] open programs. Press TAB. Click the WordPad window to switch

[text obscured] ew the open programs. Press TAB. Click the Internet Explorer [text obscured] lorer.

[text obscured] ressing ALT+TAB and pressing WINDOWS+TAB? _____

[text obscured] ressing ALT+TAB and CTRL+ALT+TAB? _____

Continued >

Cases and Places

Apply your creative thinking and problem-solving skills to design and implement a solution.

• **EASIER**   •• **MORE DIFFICULT**

• 1 Finding Programs

You are interested in identifying which programs are installed on your computer. To find all the programs, you decide to search the Program Files folder on your computer. Using techniques you learned in this chapter, open the Program Files folder on the C drive. Search for *.exe files. Summarize your findings in a brief report. Be sure to indicate the number of programs you found.

• 2 Filter Searching

Your employer suspects that someone has used your computer during off-hours for non–company business. She has asked you to search your computer for files that have been created or modified during the last week. Search for files in the Windows 7 libraries using the Date modified filter. When you find the files, determine if any are WordPad files or Paint files that you did not create or modify. Summarize the number and date they were created or modified in a brief report.

•• 3 Researching Backups

Backing up files is an important way to protect data and ensure that it is not lost or destroyed accidentally. You can use a variety of devices and techniques to back up files from a personal computer. Using Windows Help and Support, research the Backup and Restore. Determine what backup tools Windows 7 provides. Write a brief report of your findings.

•• 4 Researching Photo Printing Sites

Make It Personal
Now that you know how to work with the Pictures library, you want to find Web sites where you can upload and print your photos. Using the Internet, search for three photo printing Web sites. Find the prices per 4 x 6 photo, which file formats are required, and explore any other photo products that you would be interested in purchasing. Write a brief report that compares the three Web sites and indicate which one you would use.

•• 5 Researching Data Security

Working Together
Data stored on disk is one of a company's most valuable assets. If that data were to be stolen, lost, or compromised so that it could not be accessed, the company could go out of business. Therefore, companies go to great lengths to protect their data. Working with classmates, research how the companies where you each work handle their backups. Find out how each one protects its data against viruses, unauthorized access, and even against natural disasters such as fire and floods. Prepare a brief report that describes the companies' procedures. In your report, point out any areas where you find a company has not protected its data adequately.

Found within the Cases & Places exercises, the **Make It Personal** exercise calls on students to create an open-ended project that relates to their personal lives.

1 Fundamentals of Using Windows 7

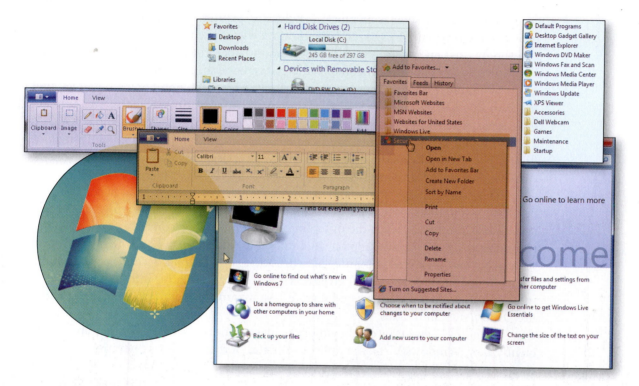

Objectives

You will have mastered the material in this chapter when you can:

- Describe Windows 7

- Explain the following terms: operating system, server, workstation, and user interface

- Log on the computer

- Identify the objects on the Windows 7 desktop

- Display the Start menu

- Add gadgets to the desktop

- Identify the Computer folder window and the Documents library

- Add and remove a desktop icon

- Open, minimize, maximize, restore, and close a window

- Move and size a window on the Windows 7 desktop

- Scroll a window

- Launch a program

- Switch between running programs

- Use Windows 7 Help and Support

- Log off the computer and turn off the computer

1 | Fundamentals of Using Windows 7

What is Windows 7?

An **operating system** is the set of computer instructions that controls the allocation of computer hardware such as memory, disk devices, printers, and optical disc drives, and provides the capability for you to communicate with the computer. The most popular and widely used operating system is the Windows operating system from Microsoft. **Windows 7** is the newest version of the Windows operating system.

Windows 7 is commonly used on desktop computers, notebook computers, including netbooks and Tablet PCs, and workstations. A **workstation** is a computer connected to a server. A **server** is a computer that controls access to the hardware and software on a network and provides a centralized storage area for programs, data, and information. Figure 1–1 illustrates a simple computer network consisting of a server, three workstations, and a printer connected to the server.

Windows 7 is easy to use and can be customized to fit individual needs. The operating system simplifies working with documents and programs, transferring data between documents, interacting with the different components of the computer, and using the computer to access information on the Internet or an intranet. The **Internet** is a worldwide group of connected computer networks that allows public access to information about thousands of subjects and gives users the ability to use this information, send messages, and obtain products and services. An **intranet** is an internal network that uses Internet technologies.

Windows 7 has improved memory management so that it runs faster and more efficiently than Windows Vista, the previous version of the Windows operating system. The user interface also has been enhanced to create a more friendly and customizable experience. Several other improvements over previous versions of Windows make Windows 7 a suitable choice for all users.

This book demonstrates how to use Windows 7 to control the computer and communicate with other computers both on a network and the Internet. In Chapter 1, you will learn about Windows 7 and how to use the Windows 7 user interface.

Overview

As you read this chapter, you will learn how to use the Windows 7 user interface by performing these general tasks:

- Start Windows 7 and log on
- Display the Start menu and expand and close a list
- Work with Windows gadgets
- Launch and switch between programs
- Open, minimize, restore, move, size, scroll, and close a window
- Use the Help system to answer questions
- Log off and turn off the computer

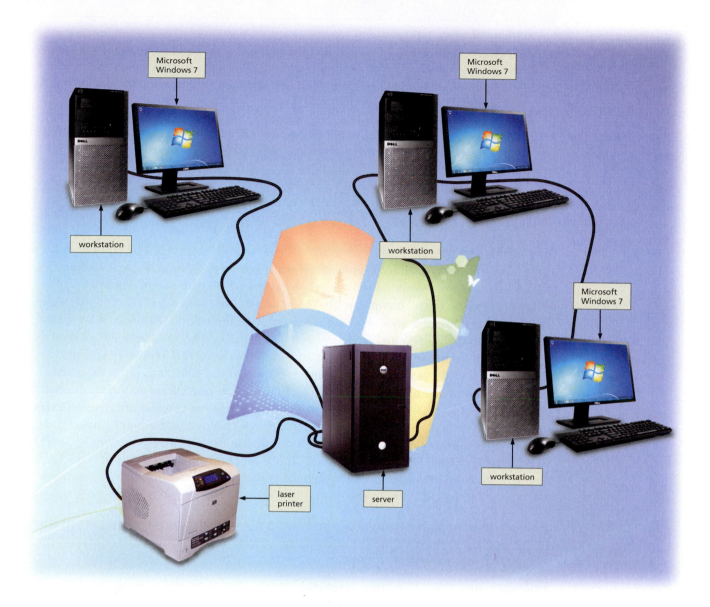

Figure 1–1

Working with Windows 7

Working with an operating system requires a basic knowledge of how to start the operating system, log on and off the computer, and identify the objects on the Windows 7 desktop.

1. **Determine how you will be logging on to computer.** Depending on the setup of the computer you are using, you might need a user account, consisting of a user name and password. If it is a computer provided in a work or education setting, you might be assigned an account.

2. **Establish which edition of Windows 7 is installed.** There are six different editions of Windows 7, each containing different features. You should know which edition is installed on the computer you will be using.

(continued)

Plan Ahead

(continued)

3. **Be aware that there might be different levels of access on the computer you will be using.** A user account can be restricted to a certain level of access to the computer. Depending on the level of access that has been set for your account, you might or might not be able to perform certain operations.

4. **Determine if you have Internet access.** The Internet contains useful material for Windows 7, such as Windows Help and Support. You will want to know if your computer has Internet access and whether anything is required of you to use it.

Multiple Editions of Windows 7

The Windows 7 operating system is available in a variety of editions. The editions that you most likely will encounter are Windows 7 Starter, Windows 7 Home Basic, Windows 7 Home Premium, Windows 7 Professional, Windows 7 Enterprise, and Windows 7 Ultimate. Because not all computers are the same, or used for similar functions, Microsoft offers these various editions so that each user can have the edition that best meets their needs. **Windows 7 Ultimate** is the most complete of all editions and includes all the power, security, mobility, and entertainment features. **Windows 7 Home Premium** contains many of the same features as Microsoft Windows 7 Ultimate, but is designed for entertainment and home use. The Home Premium edition allows you to establish a network of computers in the home that share a single Internet connection, share a device such as a printer or scanner, share files and folders, and play multicomputer games. You can create a home network using Ethernet cable, telephone wire, or wireless technologies. The six editions are briefly described in Table 1–1. For more information about the new features of Windows 7 and the differences between the editions, see Appendix A.

Table 1–1 Windows 7 Editions	
Edition	**Description**
Windows 7 Starter	This edition contains the least number of features and mostly is used for computers with limited capabilities. Windows 7 Starter typically is installed by computer manufacturers and is generally not available in retail outlets.
Windows 7 Home Basic	This edition is designed for use in emerging markets only and lacks several new features. Similar to the Starter edition, Windows 7 Home Basic is installed by computer manufacturers and generally is not available in retail outlets.
Windows 7 Home Premium	This edition is designed for home users and includes features such as Windows Media Center, Windows Aero, and touch screen controls. This edition is available in retail outlets and is installed on new computers.
Windows 7 Professional	This edition is designed for small business users. It includes network and productivity features, backup and restore capabilities, and the ability to join domains. This edition is available in retail outlets and on new computers.
Windows 7 Enterprise	This edition is designed for enterprise customers who plan to install Windows 7 enterprise-wide. This edition includes additional features such as support for Multilingual User Interface packages and BitLocker Drive Encryption.
Windows 7 Ultimate	This edition contains all Windows 7 features and is designed for home and small business users who want all the features Windows 7 offers. This edition is the most expensive of the six Windows 7 editions.

Windows 7

Windows 7 is an operating system that performs the functions necessary for you to communicate with and use the computer. Windows 7 is available in 32-bit and 64-bit versions for all editions except Windows 7 Starter Edition.

Windows 7 is used to run **programs**, which are a set of computer instructions that carries out a task on the computer. **Application software** consists of programs designed to make users more productive and assist them with personal tasks, such as word processing. Windows 7 includes several programs, including Windows Internet Explorer and Windows Media Player. **Windows Internet Explorer**, also known as Internet Explorer, is a Web browser that integrates the Windows 7 desktop and the Internet. Internet Explorer allows you to work with programs and files in a similar fashion, regardless of whether they are located on the computer, a local network, or the Internet. **Windows Media Player** lets you create and play CDs, watch DVDs, listen to radio stations originating from all over the world, and search for and organize digital media files.

Some features of Windows that previously were available within the operating system are now only available online by downloading Windows Live Essentials. **Windows Live Essentials** is a suite of free downloadable programs, including Windows Live Movie Maker and Windows Live Mail. **Windows Live Movie Maker** can transfer recorded audio and video from analog camcorders or digital video cameras, also called DV cameras, to the computer, import existing audio and video files, and distribute finished movies, either in an e-mail message or by posting the movies on the World Wide Web. **Windows Live Mail** is an e-mail program that lets you exchange e-mail messages with friends and colleagues, manage your calendar and contacts, and view RSS feeds.

Windows 7 offers a variety of features that you can customize. Depending upon your personal preferences, you can change the appearance of various components such as the desktop, the taskbar, and the Start menu. As you proceed through this book, you will learn many ways to customize your experience. To use programs with Windows 7, you first should understand the Windows 7 user interface.

BTW

Determining Edition Support
Before you upgrade an existing Windows operating system to Windows 7, you should determine which edition your computer will support by installing and running the Windows 7 Upgrade Advisor. To access the Windows 7 Upgrade Advisor, visit http://www.microsoft.com/windows/windows-7/get/upgrade-advisor.aspx.

User Interface

A **user interface** is the combination of software and input devices that you use to communicate with and control the computer. Through the user interface, you are able to make selections on the computer, request information from the computer, and respond to messages displayed by the computer. Thus, a user interface provides the means for dialogue between you and the computer.

The computer software determines the messages you receive, the means of your response, and the actions that occur based on your responses. The goal of an effective user interface is to be **user-friendly**, which means that the software is easy to use by people with limited training.

A **graphical user interface**, or **GUI** (pronounced gooey), is a user interface that relies on graphics in addition to text to communicate with the user. Windows 7 has two user interfaces: Windows 7 Basic and Windows 7 Aero. The Basic interface appears in all editions of Windows 7. If your hardware configuration supports it, the Aero interface appears in all editions, except for the Starter or Home Basic editions.

BTW

Aero Enhancements
The Windows 7 Aero experience has been improved from the Windows Vista version. It now is designed to be easier to customize and is considered faster and more efficient than before. For example, Aero now allows live preview to display a window preview at full-screen size, along with a thumbnail size.

Windows Aero

The **Aero** interface, also known as the Aero experience, features translucent colors along with various animations. To use Aero, your computer must have a compatible video card and an edition of Windows 7 installed that supports Aero. The first thing you will notice about Aero is **Aero Glass**, which is a translucent glass effect around the borders of the windows that allows you to partially see the items behind the windows. **Aero Flip 3D**, another component of the Aero experience, makes switching between your programs as visual and tactile as flipping through papers on your desk.

Aero provides a simple and entertaining interface for interacting with Windows 7. Figure 1–2 shows examples of the Basic experience and the Aero experience. The figures in this book were created using the Aero interface in Windows 7 Ultimate.

title bars are transparent, allowing you to see contents of background windows

live preview shows contents of minimized window when you point to the program button on the taskbar

(a) Basic experience

(b) Aero experience

Figure 1–2

Launching Windows 7

When you turn on the computer, an introductory screen consisting of the Windows logo and copyright messages is displayed. The Windows logo is animated and glows as the Windows 7 operating system loads. After the Windows logo appears, if your computer is configured to start with **automatic logon**, your desktop will display on the screen without first asking you to type a user name or password. If your computer is not configured for automatic logon, the Welcome screen displays (Figure 1–3).

The Welcome screen shows the user icons and names of every user on the computer. The Ease of Access button, in the lower-left corner of the Welcome screen, allows you to change accessibility options as long as you have permission to change them. In the lower-right corner of the Welcome screen is the Shut down button. The Shut down command shuts down Windows 7 and turns off the computer.

BTW

User Icons

When a user account is created, an icon (picture) can be selected to identify the user. This user icon can be changed by using the Control Panel if you have permission to change it. If your account is on a school or work computer, you might not be allowed to change your user icon.

BTW

User Names and Passwords

A unique user name identifies each user. In the past, users often entered a variation of their name as their user name. For example, Nicki Kennedy might have chosen nickikennedy or nkennedy. Today, most Windows 7 users use their first and last name as the user name. A password is a combination of characters that allows you to access your account on the computer or your account on a network. Passwords should be kept confidential. For security purposes, you might want to, or be required to, change your password on a regular basis.

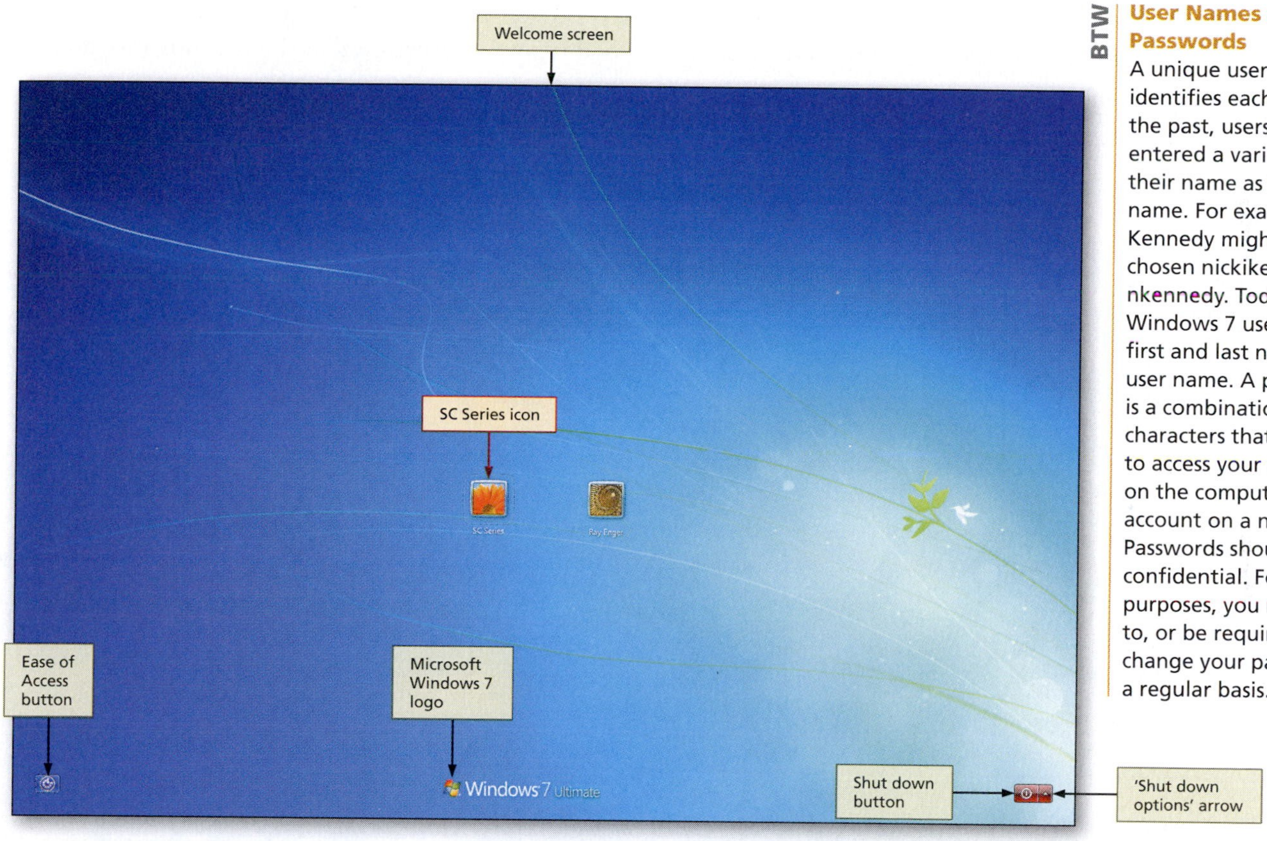

Figure 1–3

At the bottom-center of the Welcome screen is the Windows logo and the name of your Windows 7 edition, for example, Windows 7 Ultimate. In the middle of the Welcome screen is a list of the user icons and user names for all authorized computer users. The list of user icons and user names on the Welcome screen on your computer might be different. Clicking the user icon or user name begins the process of logging on the computer. If the user account you clicked does not require a password, you will be taken to your desktop; otherwise, you will be prompted to enter your password to log on.

BTW

Buttons

Buttons are an integral part of Windows 7. When you point to a button, its function will display in a ScreenTip. When you click a button, it will appear to recess on the screen to mimic what would happen if you pushed an actual button. All buttons in Windows 7 operate in the same manner.

If, after logging on the computer, you leave the computer unattended for a predetermined period of time, the computer might go to sleep automatically. In **sleep mode**, your work is saved and the computer is placed in power saving mode. When you start using your computer again, the Welcome screen will display and you will have to log on the computer again to access your account.

To Log On the Computer

After starting Windows 7 and before working, you must log on the computer. For this section, it is assumed that automatic logon is turned off and that you have to type in a password. Logging on the computer opens your user account and makes the computer available for use. In the following steps, the SC Series icon and the Next button are used to log on the computer and enter a password. When you perform these steps, you will want to log on the computer by clicking *your user icon* on the Welcome screen and typing *your password* in the text box instead of the password shown in the steps.

1

- Click the SC Series icon (or the icon representing your user account) on the Welcome screen to display the password text box.

- Type your password in the password text box (Figure 1–4).

Q&A Why do I not see an SC Series icon?

The SC Series icon is not present as the SC Series account is not a user account on your computer.

Q&A Where is my password text box?

You will not see a password text box if your account does not require a password. You only have to select your user icon to log on.

Q&A Why do I have an icon and a password text box?

If there only is one user account, the password text box automatically displays, as there are no other accounts to select.

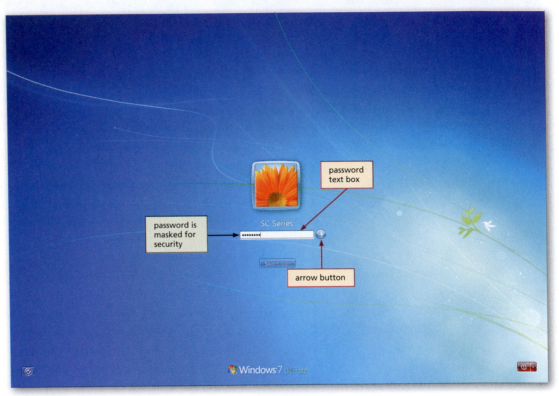

Figure 1–4

2

- Click the arrow button to log on the computer and display the Windows 7 desktop (Figure 1–5).

Q&A

Why does my desktop look different from the one in Figure 1–5?

The Windows 7 desktop is customizable and your school or company might have modified the desktop to meet their needs. For example, some schools customize their computer desktops with a picture of the school and/or the school name.

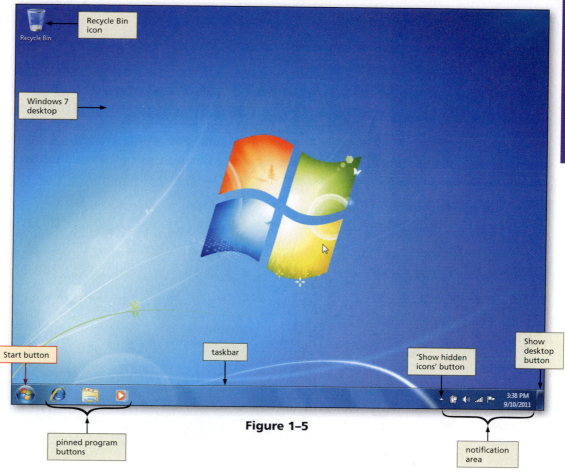

Recycle Bin icon

Windows 7 desktop

Start button

taskbar

'Show hidden icons' button

Show desktop button

pinned program buttons

notification area

Figure 1–5

The Windows 7 Desktop

The Windows 7 desktop, and the objects on the desktop, emulate a work area in an office. You can think of the desktop as an electronic version of the top of your desk. You can perform actions such as placing objects on the desktop, moving the objects around the desktop, and looking at objects and then putting them aside.

Although the Windows 7 desktop can be arranged to meet your needs, it does contain some standard elements. The items on the desktop in Figure 1–5 include the Recycle Bin icon and name in the upper-left corner of the desktop and the taskbar at the bottom. The **Recycle Bin** allows you to discard unneeded objects. Your computer's desktop might contain more, fewer, or different icons, depending on how the desktop was modified.

The taskbar shown at the bottom of the screen in Figure 1–5 contains the Start button, taskbar button area, and notification area. The Start button, which displays the Start menu, allows you to perform many tasks such as launching a program, finding or opening a document, changing the computer's settings, obtaining help, and shutting down the computer. The taskbar button area contains buttons to indicate which windows are open on the desktop. When a program has been **pinned** to the taskbar, a button with the program icon appears, regardless of whether the program is open or closed. You can access the program quickly by clicking the pinned program button. Pinned programs usually are the programs that you use most frequently and appear first in the taskbar button area.

BTW

The Notification Area
The 'Show hidden icons' button displays on the left edge of the notification area if one or more inactive icons are hidden from view in the notification area. Clicking the 'Show hidden icons' button displays all of the inactive icons in a pop-up window. Moving the mouse pointer away from the notification area, or clicking the 'Show hidden icons' button again, hides the inactive icons.

By default, Internet Explorer, Windows Explorer, and Windows Media Player are pinned to the taskbar. **Windows Explorer** is a program that allows you to browse the files and folders on your computer.

The notification area contains the 'Show hidden icons' button, notification icons, and the current time and date. The 'Show hidden icons' button indicates that one or more inactive icons are hidden from view in the notification area. The notification icons provide quick access to programs that are currently running in the background on your computer. A program running in the background does not show up on the taskbar, but is still working. Icons may display temporarily in the notification area when providing status updates. For example, the printer icon is displayed when a document is sent to the printer and is removed when printing is complete. The notification area on your desktop might contain more, fewer, or different icons than shown in Figure 1–5.

To Display the Start Menu

The Start menu allows you to easily access the programs on your computer as well as other frequently used features and files. A **menu** is a list of related commands and the **commands** on a menu perform a specific action, such as launching a program or obtaining help. The following steps display the Start menu.

1

• Click the Start button on the Windows 7 taskbar to display the Start menu (Figure 1–6).

Q&A Why does my Start menu look different?

Depending upon your computer's configuration, the Start menu can look different. In a work or school environment, it might be customized for any number of reasons, such as usage requirements or security policies.

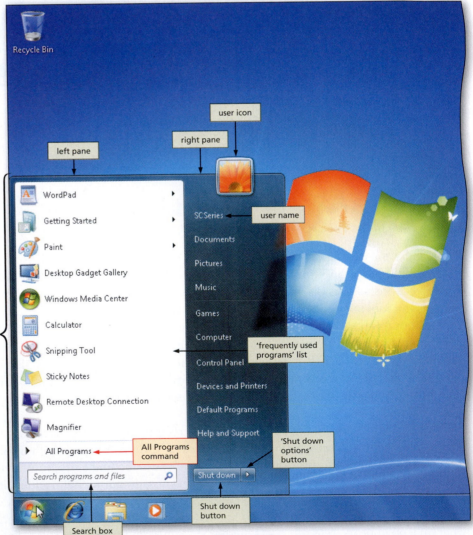

Figure 1–6

2

- Click the All Programs command on the Start menu to display the All Programs list (Figure 1–7).

Q&A

Why does my All Programs list look different than the All Programs list in Figure 1–7?

The programs installed on your computer might differ. Your All Programs list will show the programs that are installed on your computer.

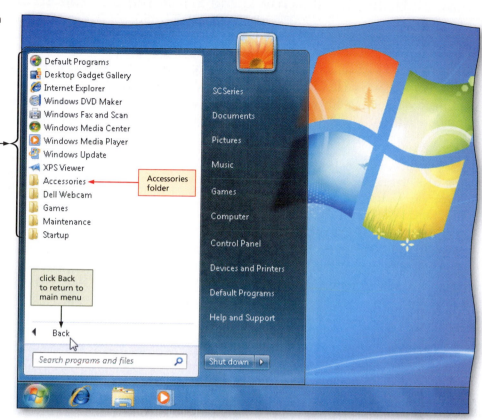

Figure 1–7

3

- Click the Accessories folder to display the Accessories list (Figure 1–8).

Q&A

What can I expect to find in the Accessories list?

The Accessories list contains programs that accomplish a variety of tasks commonly required on a computer. Most of these programs are installed with the Windows 7 operating system, such as Calculator, Snipping Tool, Windows Mobility Center (if you have a portable computer), and WordPad. Your Accessories list might contain additional or fewer programs.

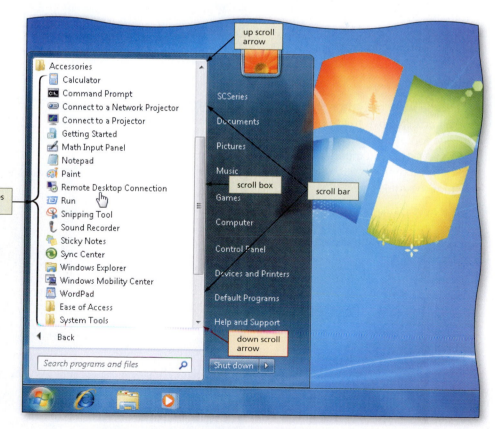

Figure 1–8

To Scroll Using Scroll Arrows, the Scroll Bar, and the Scroll Box

A **scroll bar** is displayed when the contents of an area are not completely visible. A vertical scroll bar contains an up scroll arrow, a down scroll arrow, and a scroll box that enables you to view areas that currently are not visible. In Figure 1–8, a vertical scroll bar displays along the right side of the All Programs list. Scrolling can be accomplished in three ways: (1) Click a scroll arrow, (2) click the scroll bar, or (3) drag the scroll box. You **drag** an object by pointing to it, holding down the left mouse button, moving the object to the desired location, and then releasing the left mouse button. The following steps scroll the items in the All Programs list.

- Click the down scroll arrow on the scroll bar to display additional folders at the bottom of the All Programs list (Figure 1–9). You might need to click more than once to reach the bottom of the All Programs list.

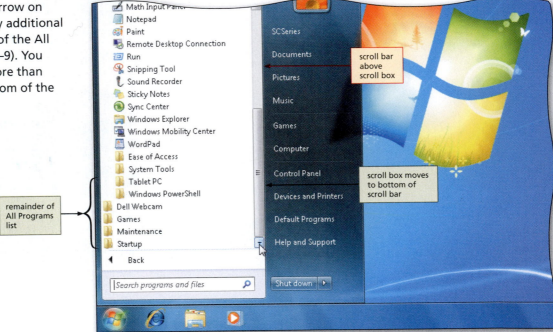

Figure 1–9

- Click the scroll bar above the scroll box to move the scroll box to the top of the All Programs list (Figure 1–10). You might need to click more than once to reach the top of the All Programs list.

Q&A

Why does it take more than one click on the scroll bar to move the scroll box to the top of the scroll bar?

There might be more programs installed on your computer than on the one in the figure. As the number of programs on your computer increases, you might need to click the scroll box multiple times to reach the top of the list.

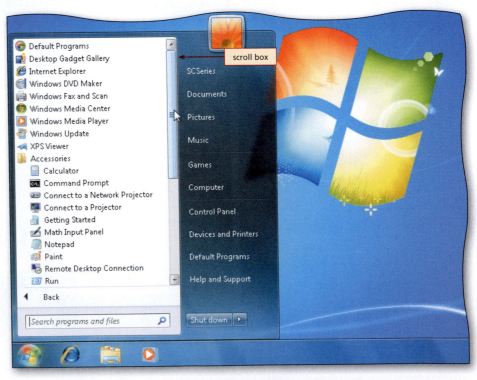

Figure 1–10

3

- Click the scroll box and drag down to the bottom of the scroll bar to display the bottom of the All Programs list (Figure 1–11).

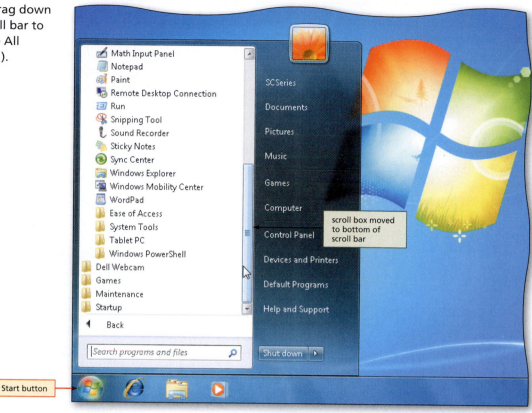

Figure 1–11

4

- Click the Start button to close the Start menu (Figure 1–12).

Figure 1–12

To Open the Getting Started Window

If you are new to using Windows 7, you can open the Getting Started window. The **Getting Started window** allows you to complete a set of tasks to optimize the computer. The tasks might include adding user accounts, transferring files and settings from another computer, and backing up your files. You do not have to use the Getting Started window to perform these tasks, but it can assist you with configuring your computer. The following steps open the Getting Started window. If the Getting Started window already is visible on your desktop, read these steps without performing them.

1
• Click the Start button on the taskbar to display the Start menu (Figure 1–13).

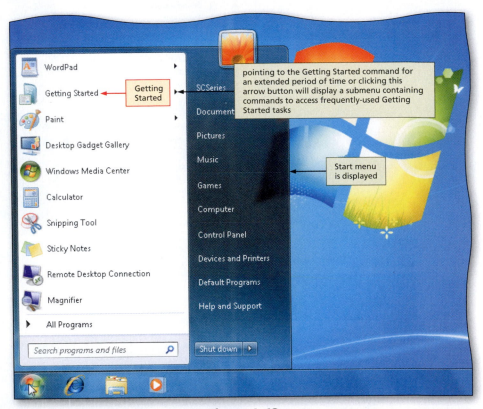

Figure 1–13

2
• Click Getting Started to open the Getting Started window (Figure 1–14).

Q&A
What should I do if the Getting Started command does not display on the Start menu?

Depending upon how your computer is configured, you might find the Getting Started command in the Accessories list instead.

Other Ways
1. Display Start menu, click All Programs, click Accessories, click Getting Started

Figure 1–14

To Close the Getting Started Window

After reviewing the options available in the Getting Started window, you can close it. The following step closes the Getting Started window.

1
- Click the Close button on the Getting Started window to close the Getting Started window (Figure 1–15).

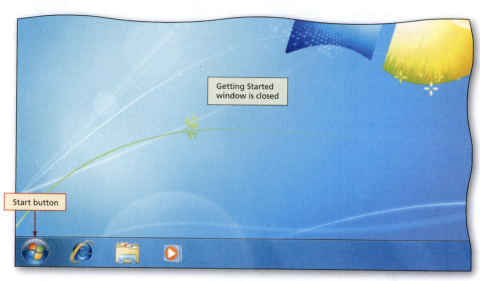

Getting Started window is closed

Start button

Figure 1–15

To Open the Computer Folder Window

The Computer folder is accessible via the Start menu. When opened, the Computer folder opens in a folder window. The Computer folder is the place you can go to access hard disks, optical disc drives, removable media, and network locations that are connected to your computer. You also can access other devices such as external hard disks or digital cameras that might be connected to your computer. The following steps open the Computer folder window.

1
- Click the Start button on the Windows 7 taskbar to display the Start menu (Figure 1–16).

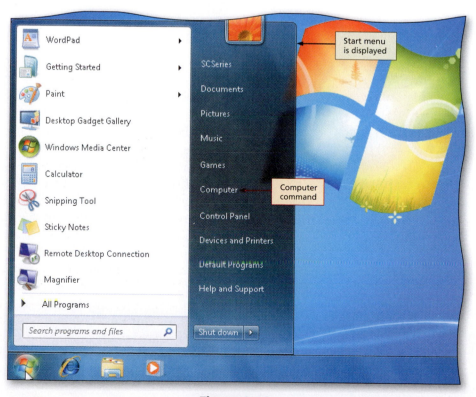

WordPad

Getting Started

Paint

Desktop Gadget Gallery

Windows Media Center

Calculator

Snipping Tool

Sticky Notes

Remote Desktop Connection

Magnifier

All Programs

Search programs and files

SCSeries

Documents

Pictures

Music

Games

Computer

Control Panel

Devices and Printers

Default Programs

Help and Support

Shut down

Start menu is displayed

Computer command

Figure 1–16

2

• Click the Computer command on the right pane of the Start menu to open the Computer folder window (Figure 1–17).

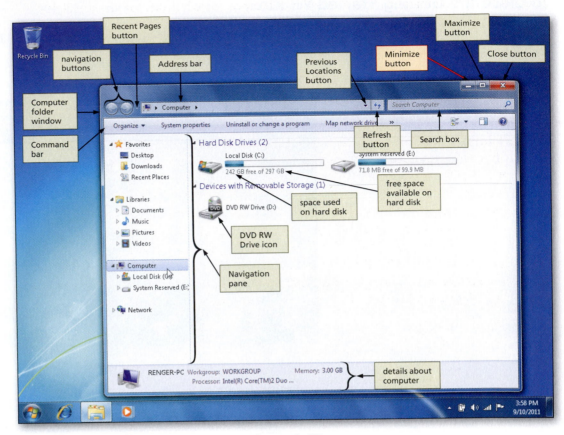

Figure 1–17

Folder Windows

Folder windows are the key tools for finding, viewing, and managing information on the computer. Folder windows have common design elements, as shown in Figure 1–17. The three buttons to the left of the Address bar allow you to navigate the contents of the right pane and view recent pages. The Recent Pages button saves the locations you have visited and displays the locations in a list. On the right of the title bar are the Minimize button, the Maximize button, and the Close button, which can be used to reduce the window to the taskbar, increase the window to the full screen, or close the window.

The Previous Locations button and the Refresh button are on the right side of the Address bar. The Previous Locations button displays a list of recently visited file locations. The Refresh button refreshes the contents of the window. The Search box to the right of the Address bar contains the dimmed word, Search, followed by the location you currently are viewing. For example, in Figure 1–17, the Search box displays Search Computer because the Computer folder window is open. You can type a term into the Search box to search for files, folders, shortcuts, and programs containing that term within the specified location.

The Command bar contains context-specific buttons used to accomplish various tasks on the computer related to organizing and managing the contents of the open window. Depending upon the selections you make in the Computer folder window, the Command bar buttons will change to reflect the selections. If you navigate to an optical disc drive, the Command bar would display the appropriate buttons for an optical disc drive. For example, you might see a Burn button for burning an optical disc. The area below the Command bar is separated into two panes; the left pane contains the Navigation pane and the right pane displays the contents of the location you currently are viewing.

The Navigation pane on the left contains the Favorites section, Libraries section, Computer folder section, Network folder section, and if your computer is connected to a network, the Homegroup section. The Favorites section contains links to your favorite locations. By default, this list contains only links to your desktop, downloads, and recent places. The Libraries section shows links to files and folders that have been included in a library.

A **library** is designed to help you manage multiple folders and files stored in various locations on your computer. It does not store the files and folders, but rather displays links to them so that you can access them quickly. For example, you can save pictures from your digital camera in any folder in any storage location on your computer. Normally, this would make management of the different folders difficult; however, if you add the folders to the Pictures library, you can access all your pictures no matter where they are stored.

Expanding the Computer folder section displays all your folders in the classic folder list, or folder tree, that you might be familiar with from previous versions of Windows. Finally, the Network folder section allows you to browse network locations.

To Minimize and Redisplay a Window

Two buttons on the title bar of a window, the Minimize button and the Maximize button, allow you to control the way a window displays or does not display on the desktop. The following steps minimize and restore the Computer folder window.

1

- Click the Minimize button on the title bar of the Computer folder window to minimize the Computer folder window (Figure 1–18).

Q&A

What happens to the Computer folder window when I click the Minimize button?

The Computer folder window remains available, but no longer is an active window. It collapses down to a button on the taskbar.

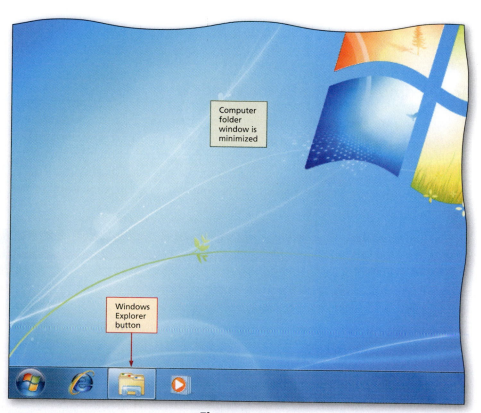

Computer folder window is minimized

Windows Explorer button

Figure 1–18

2

- Click the Windows Explorer button on the taskbar to display the Computer folder window (Figure 1–19).

Q&A Why does the Windows Explorer button on the taskbar change?

The button changes to reflect the status of the Computer folder window. A highlighted button indicates that the Computer folder window is active on the screen. An unhighlighted button indicates that the Computer folder window is open but not active.

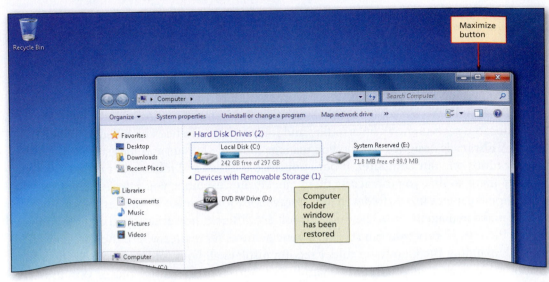

Figure 1–19

Q&A Why do I see a picture when I point to the Windows Explorer button?

Whenever you move your mouse over a button or click a button on the taskbar, a live preview of the window will be displayed. This is a new feature of the Aero user experience with Windows 7.

Other Ways

1. Right-click title bar, click Minimize; in taskbar button area, click taskbar button
2. Press WINDOWS+M, press WINDOWS+SHIFT+M

To Maximize and Restore a Window

Information sometimes is not completely visible in a window. One method of displaying the entire contents of a window is to enlarge the window using the Maximize button. The Maximize button increases the size of a window so that it fills the entire screen, making it easier to see the contents of the window. When a window is maximized, the Restore Down button replaces the Maximize button on the title bar. Clicking the Restore Down button will return the window to the size it was before it was maximized. The following steps maximize and restore the Computer folder window.

1

- Click the Maximize button on the title bar to maximize the Computer folder window (Figure 1–20).

Q&A When a window is maximized, can you also minimize it?

Yes. Click the Minimize button to minimize the window to the taskbar. Clicking the button on the taskbar will return the window to its maximized size.

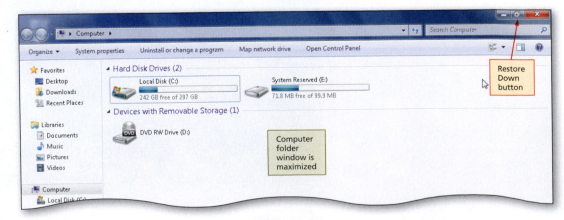

Figure 1–20

2

- Click the Restore Down button on the Computer folder window to return the Computer folder window to its previous size (Figure 1–21).

What happens to the Restore Down button after I click it?

The Maximize button replaces the Restore Down button on the title bar.

Figure 1–21

To Close a Window

The Close button on the title bar of a window closes the window. To close the Computer folder window, complete the following step.

1

- Click the Close button on the title bar of the Computer folder window to close the Computer folder window (Figure 1–22).

Figure 1–22

To Add a Shortcut to the Desktop

Once you start doing more work on your computer, you might want to add shortcuts to the desktop. For example, you might want to add the Documents library shortcut to the desktop so that you can access the Documents library quickly. The **Documents library** is a central location for the storage and management of documents. This library is optimized for faster searching and organizing. The following steps add a shortcut to the Documents library to your desktop.

• Click the Start button to display the Start menu.

• Point to the Documents command in the right pane, and then click the right mouse button (right-click).

• Point to the Send to command on the Documents shortcut menu to display the Send to submenu (Figure 1–23).

Q&A What is a shortcut menu?

A shortcut menu contains commands specifically for use with that object. Shortcut menus often appear when you right-click an object. Using shortcut menus can speed up your work and add flexibility to your interaction with the computer by making often-used items easily accessible.

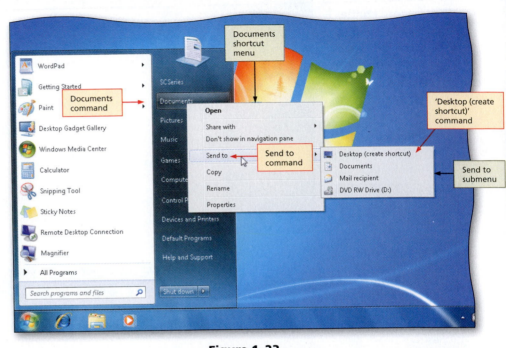

Figure 1–23

• Click the 'Desktop (create shortcut)' command on the Send to submenu to place a shortcut to the Documents library on the desktop (Figure 1–24).

Q&A Why am I unable to add an item to my desktop?

On some work or school computers, users are not allowed to add items to the desktop.

Q&A How many icons should I have on my desktop?

Icons can be added to your desktop by programs or by users; however, it is considered a best practice to keep your desktop as clutter free as possible. If you are not using an icon on the desktop, consider removing it from the desktop.

• Click the Start button to close the Start menu.

Figure 1–24

To Open a Window Using a Desktop Shortcut

The following step opens the Documents library using the shortcut you have just created on the desktop.

1

- Double-click (click the left mouse button twice, in rapid succession) the Documents - Shortcut icon on the desktop to open the Documents library (Figure 1–25).

Q&A

Why are the contents of my Documents library different from Figure 1–25?

The Documents library in the figure is empty because there are no files or folders added. Because you might have different documents and folders on your computer, the contents of your Documents library might be different from the one in Figure 1–25.

Figure 1–25

Other Ways

1. Right-click desktop icon, click Open on shortcut menu

Double-Clicking Errors

When double-clicking an object, it is easy to click once instead of twice. When you click an object such as the Documents - Shortcut icon once, the icon becomes active and highlighted. To open the Documents library after clicking the Documents - Shortcut icon once, double-click the icon as if you had not clicked it at all.

Another possible error occurs when the mouse moves after you click the first time and before you click the second time. In most cases when this occurs, the icon will appear highlighted as if you had clicked it just one time.

A third possible error is moving the mouse while you are pressing the mouse button. In this case, the icon might have moved on the screen because you inadvertently dragged it. To open the Documents library after dragging it accidentally, double-click the icon as if you had not clicked it at all.

To Move a Window by Dragging

You can move any open window to another location on the desktop by dragging the title bar of the window. The following step drags the Documents library to the center of the desktop.

- Drag the title bar of the Documents library so that the window appears at the center of the screen, as shown in Figure 1–26.

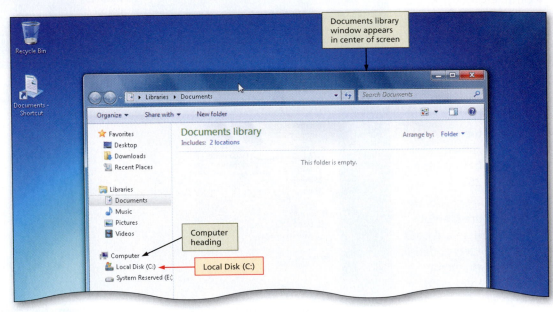

Figure 1–26

Other Ways

1. Right-click title bar, click Move, drag window

To Expand the Contents of Local Disk (C:)

In Figure 1–26, the Local Disk (C:) list in the Documents library is collapsed. The Navigation pane displays arrows that can be used to expand and collapse the different sections in the Navigation pane. Clicking the arrow that appears next to Local Disk (C:) expands and reveals the contents of Local Disk (C:). The following steps expand the Local Disk (C:) list.

- Point the mouse to the arrow next to Local Disk (C:) below the Computer heading in the Navigation pane (Figure 1–27).

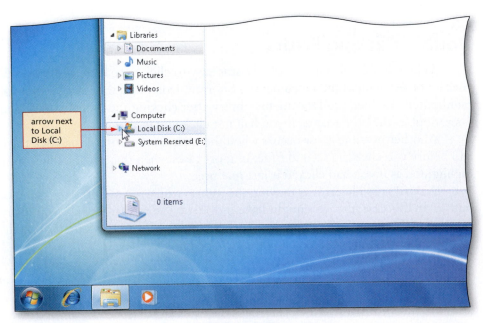

Figure 1–27

2

- Click the arrow to expand the contents of Local Disk (C:) in the Navigation pane of the Documents library (Figure 1–28).

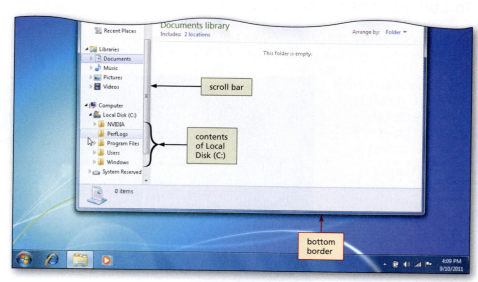

Figure 1–28

To Size a Window by Dragging

Sometimes information is not completely visible in a window. You have learned how to use the Maximize button to increase the size of a window. Another method to change the size of the window is to drag the window borders. The following step changes the size of the Documents library.

1

- Point to the bottom border of the Documents library until the mouse pointer changes to a two-headed arrow.

- If necessary, drag the bottom border downward to display more of the Navigation pane so that your screen looks similar to Figure 1–29.

Q&A Can I drag other borders besides the bottom border to enlarge or shrink the window?

Yes, you can drag the left, right, and top borders and any window corner to resize the window.

Q&A Will Windows 7 remember the new size of the window after I close it?

Yes. Windows 7 remembers the size of the window when you close the window. When you reopen the window, the window will display at the same size as when you closed it.

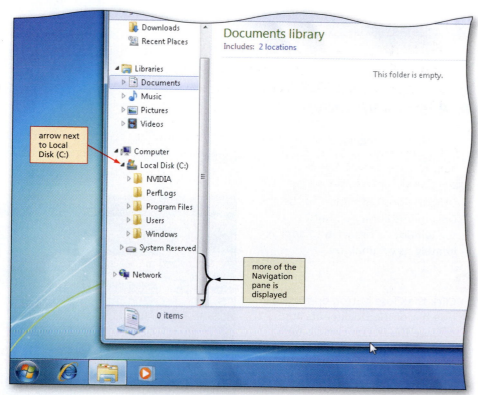

Figure 1–29

To Collapse the Local Disk (C:) List

The following step collapses the Local Disk (C:) list.

• Click the arrow next to Local Disk (C:) to collapse the Local Disk (C:) list (Figure 1–30).

Q&A

Should I keep the list expanded or collapsed?

If you need to use the contents in the list, it is handy to keep the list expanded. You can collapse the list when the information is not needed.

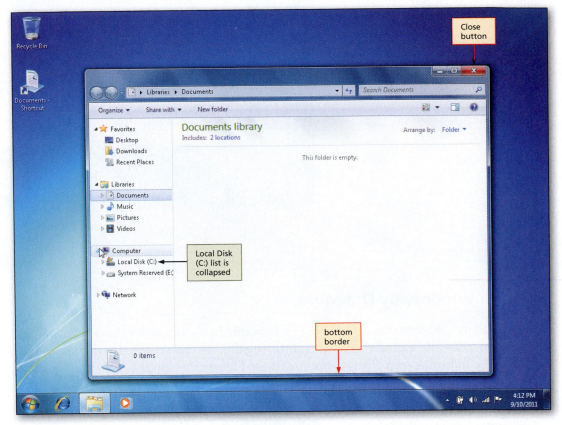

Figure 1–30

To Resize a Window

After moving and resizing a window, you might want to return the window to its original size. To return the Documents library to approximately its original size and close the Documents library, complete the following steps.

• Drag the bottom border of the Documents library up until the window is returned to approximately its original size.

• Click the Close button on the title bar of the Documents library to close the Documents library (Figure 1–31).

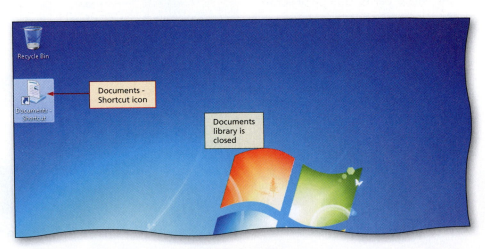

Figure 1–31

To Delete a Desktop Icon by Dragging it to the Recycle Bin

Although Windows 7 has many ways to delete desktop icons, one method of removing an icon from the desktop is to drag it to the Recycle Bin. The following steps delete the Documents - Shortcut icon by dragging the icon to the Recycle Bin.

1

- Point to the Documents - Shortcut icon on the desktop and press the left mouse button to select the icon (Figure 1–32). Do not release the left mouse button.

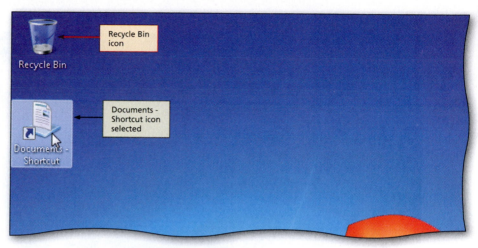

Figure 1–32

2

- Drag the Documents - Shortcut icon over the Recycle Bin icon on the desktop, and then release the left mouse button to place the shortcut in the Recycle Bin (Figure 1–33).

Experiment

- Double-click the Recycle Bin icon on the desktop to open a window containing the contents of the Recycle Bin. The Documents - Shortcut icon you have just deleted will display in this window. Close the Recycle Bin window.

Q&A

Why did the Documents - Shortcut icon disappear?

Releasing the left mouse button moved the icon from the desktop to the Recycle Bin.

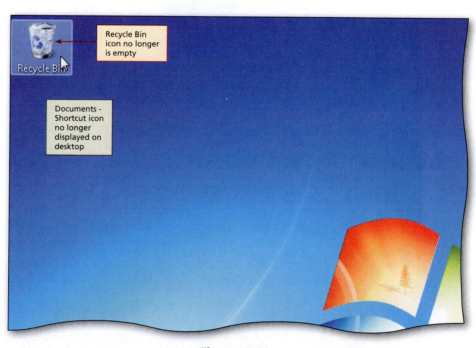

Figure 1–33

Other Ways
1. Right-click icon, click Delete, click Yes button
2. Right-click icon and hold, drag to Recycle Bin, release right mouse button, click Move Here

To Empty the Recycle Bin

The Recycle Bin prevents you from deleting files you actually might need. Until you empty the Recycle Bin, you can recover deleted items from it. The following steps empty the Recycle Bin. If you are not sure that you want to permanently delete all the files in the Recycle Bin, read these steps without performing them.

1

- Right-click the Recycle Bin to display the shortcut menu (Figure 1–34).

2

- Click the Empty Recycle Bin command to permanently delete the contents of the Recycle Bin.

- Click the Yes button to confirm the operation.

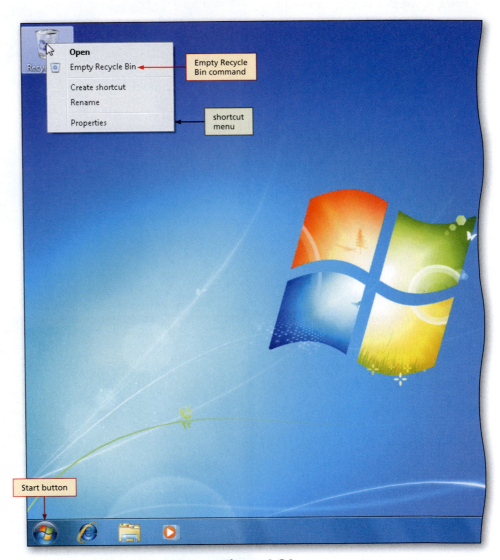

Figure 1–34

Other Ways

1. Right-click Recycle Bin icon, click Open, click Empty the Recycle Bin, click Yes button, click Close button

2. Double-click Recycle Bin icon, click Empty the Recycle Bin, click Yes button, click Close button

To Add a Gadget to the Desktop

Gadgets are miniprograms that display information and provide access to various useful tools. Gadgets can be found in the Gadget Gallery or you can download gadgets from the Internet. Gadgets can include games, viewers for RSS feeds, and even online auction updates. The first step when using a gadget is to add the gadget to the desktop. One way to add a gadget to the desktop is to double-click the gadget in the Gadget Gallery. The following steps open the Gadget Gallery and add a gadget to the desktop.

1

- Click the Start button to display the Start menu.

- Click All Programs to display the All Programs list (Figure 1–35).

Figure 1–35

2

- Click the Desktop Gadget Gallery command to open the Gadget Gallery (Figure 1–36).

Q&A

Where can I find more gadgets?

You can download additional gadgets by clicking the Get more gadgets online link, by downloading gadgets from `http:// gallery.live.com`, or by searching online to locate other gadget collections.

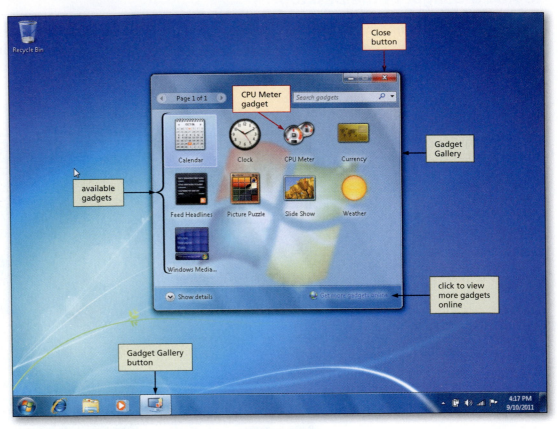

Figure 1–36

3

- Double-click the CPU Meter gadget in the Gadget Gallery to add the gadget to the desktop and display the performance measurements for your CPU (Figure 1–37).

- Click the Close button to close the Gadget Gallery.

Q&A

Can I change the position of gadgets on the desktop?

Yes, you can move them to any location you desire on the desktop by clicking and dragging them to your preferred location.

Figure 1–37

To Remove a Gadget from the Desktop

In addition to adding gadgets to the desktop, you can remove gadgets. The following steps remove the gadget from the desktop.

- Point to the CPU Meter gadget to make the Close button visible (Figure 1–38).

- Click the Close button to remove the CPU Meter gadget from the desktop.

Close button

Figure 1–38

Launching a Program

One of the basic tasks you can perform using Windows 7 is to launch a program. Recall that a program is designed to perform a specific user-oriented task. For example, a **word-processing program** allows you to create written documents; a **presentation program** allows you to create graphical presentations for display on a computer; and a **Web browser** allows you to explore the Internet and display Web pages.

Internet Explorer, the default Web browser in Windows 7, appears as a pinned program on the taskbar. Because you can change which Web browser is the default, the Web browser on your computer might be different. For example, you could install another frequently used Web browser such as **Mozilla Firefox** and set it as the default Web browser.

BTW

Programs
Many programs (for example, Internet Explorer, WordPad, Paint) are installed with Windows 7. Most programs, however, such as Microsoft Office or Adobe® Photoshop®, must be purchased separately. Other programs, such as Mozilla Firefox or OpenOffice, are available to download for free.

To Start a Program Using the Start Menu

The most common activity performed on a computer is using a program to accomplish tasks. You can start a program by using the Start menu. **Paint** is a popular program available with Windows 7 that allows you to create and edit simple graphics. The following steps start Paint using the Start menu.

1

- To display the Start menu, click the Start button.

- Display the All Programs list.

- Display the Accessories list (Figure 1–39).

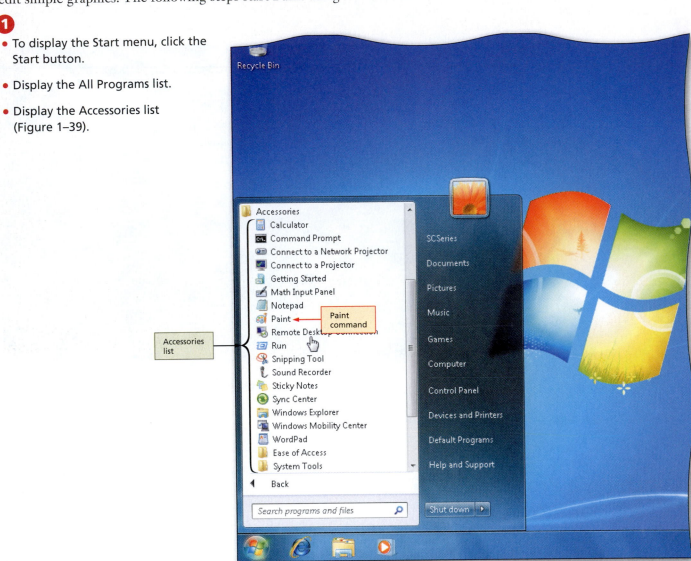

Figure 1–39

2

- Click the Paint command to start Paint and display the Untitled - Paint window (Figure 1–40).

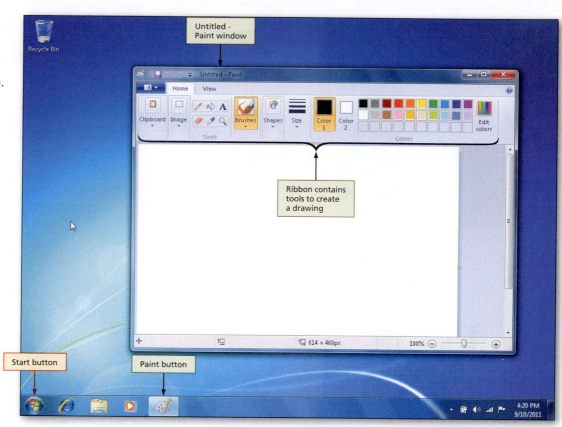

Figure 1–40

To Start a Program Using the Search Box

If you are unsure of where to find the program you want to open in the Start menu, you can use the Start menu Search box to search for the program. The following steps search for the WordPad program using the Search box.

1

- Display the Start menu.

- Type `wordpad` in the Search box to have Windows 7 look for WordPad (Figure 1–41).

Q&A

Why did different items display as I typed in the Search box?

As you type in the Search box, Windows 7 automatically tries to find items matching the text you type.

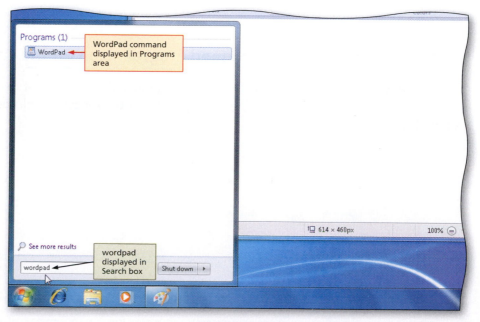

Figure 1–41

2

• Click the WordPad command in the Programs area to start WordPad and display the Document - WordPad window (Figure 1–42).

Q&A

Do I have to type the entire word before clicking the result?

No. As soon as you see the result you are looking for in the Programs area above the Search box, you can click it.

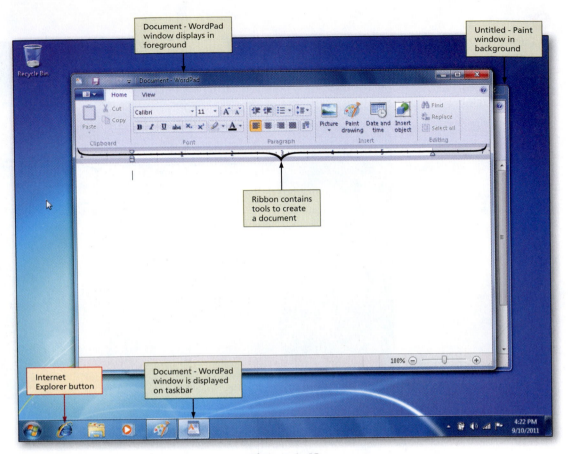

Figure 1–42

Other Ways

1. Open Start menu, type wordpad in Search box, press ENTER

2. Open Start menu, click All Programs, open Accessories list, click WordPad

To Start a Program Using a Pinned Program Icon on the Taskbar

Windows 7 allows users to access selected programs with one click of the mouse button when the program icon is pinned to the taskbar. The following step launches the Internet Explorer program using the pinned program icon on the taskbar.

1

• Click the Internet Explorer button on the taskbar to start Internet Explorer (Figure 1–43).

Q&A What if the Internet Explorer icon does not appear on my taskbar?

The pinned items on the taskbar are customizable, and yours might differ. Use one of the previous methods to open Internet Explorer instead.

Figure 1–43

Other Ways

1. Display Start menu, click All Programs, click Internet Explorer

To Switch Programs Using Aero Flip 3D

When you have multiple programs open simultaneously, invariably you will need to switch between them. Aero Flip 3D provides an easy and visual way to switch between the open programs on your computer. The following steps switch from Internet Explorer to WordPad using Aero Flip 3D.

1

• Press CTRL+ WINDOWS+TAB to start Aero Flip 3D (Figure 1–44).

Q&A Why does this effect not appear three-dimensional on my computer?

Your computer is set up to use the Basic experience, so you are seeing the basic program switching method, which is not three-dimensional. Aero Flip 3D is part of the Aero experience.

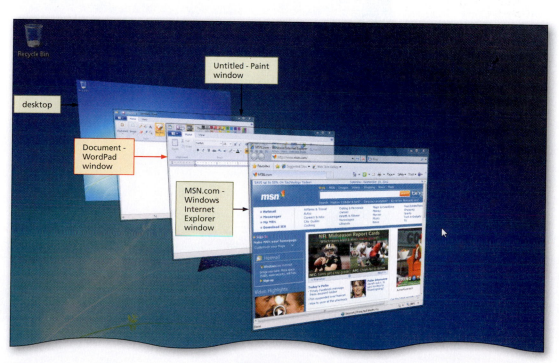

Figure 1–44

2

- Press the TAB key repeatedly until the Document - WordPad window appears at the front of the programs displayed in Aero Flip 3D (Figure 1–45).

Q&A

Do I have to use the TAB key?

You also can scroll the mouse wheel, if your mouse has one, until the WordPad window is at the front.

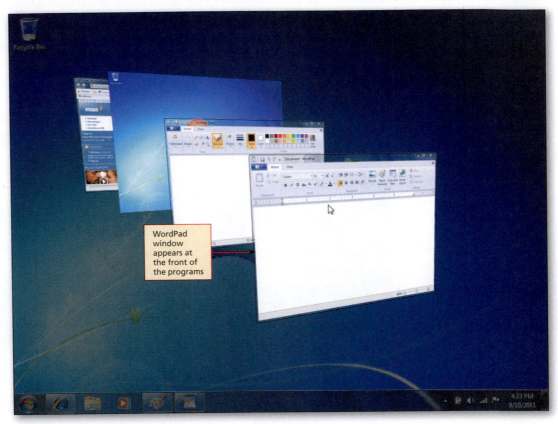

WordPad window appears at the front of the programs

Figure 1–45

3

- Click the WordPad window to exit Aero Flip 3D and make the WordPad window the active window (Figure 1–46).

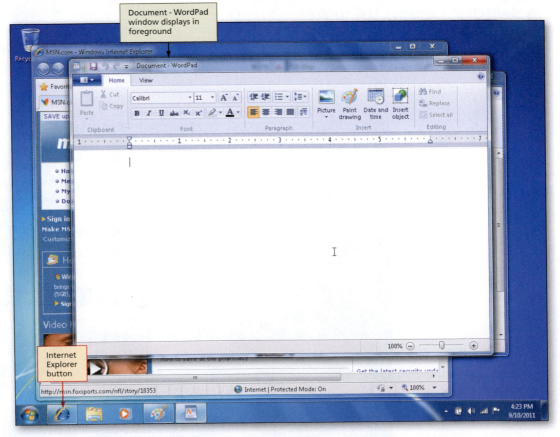

Document - WordPad window displays in foreground

Internet Explorer button

Figure 1–46

To Switch Between Programs Using the Taskbar

You also can switch between programs using the taskbar. By clicking the button for the program, you make that program active by bringing the window to the front. If the button represents multiple windows or there are multiple files open in a program, you will need to click the button for the program and then the particular file or window you want to make active. The following steps switch between programs using the taskbar.

1

- Click the Windows Internet Explorer button on the taskbar to make the MSN.com - Windows Internet Explorer window the active window (Figure 1–47).

Figure 1–47

2

- Click the Untitled - Paint button on the taskbar to make the Paint window the active window (Figure 1–48).

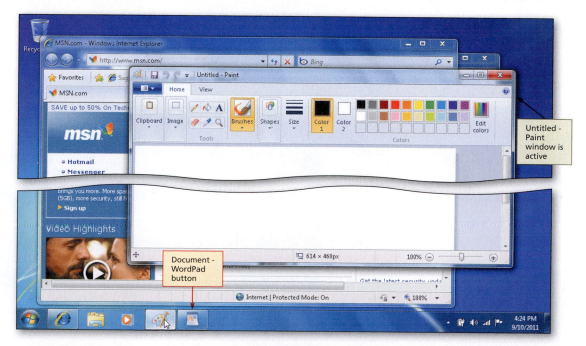

Figure 1–48

3

• Click the Document - WordPad button on the taskbar to make WordPad the active window (Figure 1–49).

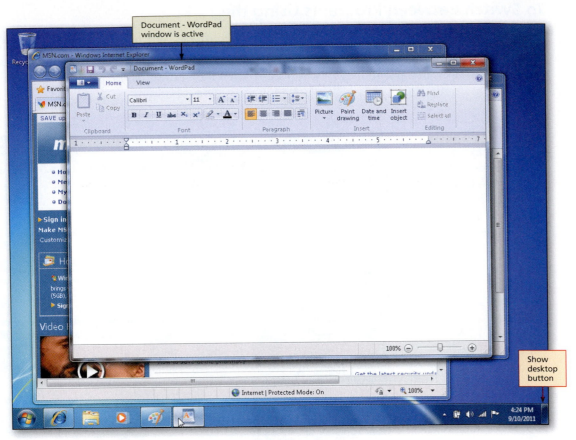

Figure 1–49

To Show the Desktop Using the Show Desktop Button

When you have several windows open at the same time and need to reveal the desktop without closing all of the open windows, you can use the Show desktop button on the taskbar to quickly display the desktop. The following step shows the desktop.

1

• Click the Show desktop button on the taskbar to show the desktop (Figure 1–50).

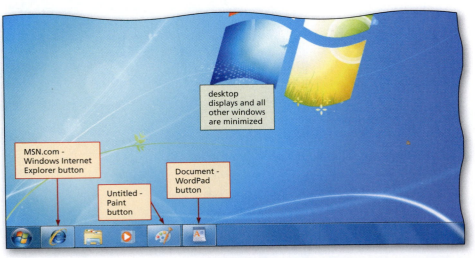

Figure 1–50

To Close Open Windows

After you are done viewing windows or using programs in Windows 7, you should close them. The following steps close the open programs.

1 Click the Document - WordPad button on the taskbar to display the WordPad window. Click the Close button on the title bar of the WordPad window to close WordPad.

2 Click the Internet Explorer button on the taskbar to display the MSN.com - Windows Internet Explorer window. Click the Close button on the title bar to close Internet Explorer.

3 Display the Untitled - Paint window and click the Close button to close Paint.

Other Ways

1. Right-click taskbar button of the program you want to close, click Close window

Using Windows Help and Support

One of the more powerful Windows 7 features is Windows Help and Support. **Windows Help and Support** is available when using Windows 7 or when using any Microsoft program running under Windows 7. This feature is designed to assist you in using Windows 7 or the various other programs. Table 1–2 describes what can be found in Windows Help and Support.

Table 1–2 Windows Help and Support Content Areas	
Area	**Function**
Find an answer quickly	This area contains instructions about how to perform a quick search using the Search Help box.
Not sure where to start?	This area displays three links to topics to help guide users: How to get started with your computer, Learn about Windows Basics, and Browse Help topics. Clicking one of the options takes you to corresponding Help and Support pages.
More on the Windows website	This area contains links to online content from the Windows Web site. Clicking one of the links takes you to the corresponding Web pages on the Web site.

To Start Windows Help and Support

Before you can access the Windows Help and Support services, you must start Windows Help and Support. One method of launching Windows Help and Support uses the Start menu. The following steps start Windows Help and Support.

1

- Display the Start menu (Figure 1–51).

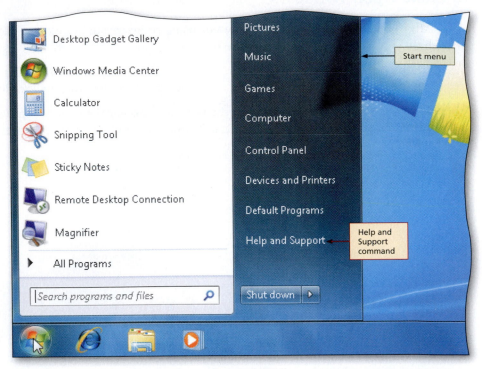

Figure 1–51

2

- Click the Help and Support command to display the Windows Help and Support window (Figure 1–52).

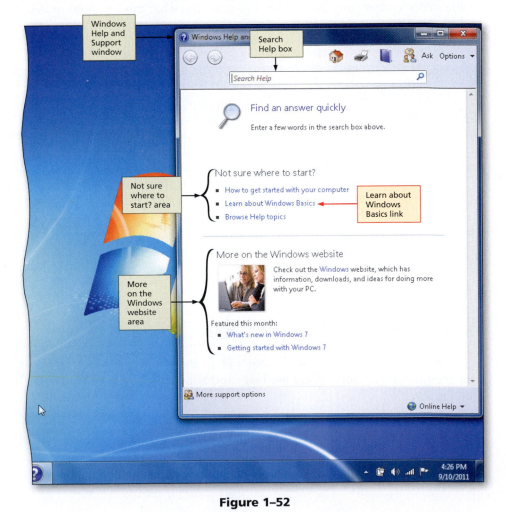

Figure 1–52

Other Ways

1. Press CTRL+ESC, press RIGHT ARROW, press UP ARROW, press ENTER

2. Press WINDOWS+F1

To Browse for Help Topics in Windows Basics

After launching Windows Help and Support, your next step is to find Help topics that relate to your questions. The following steps use the Not sure where to start? area in the Windows Help and Support to locate a Help topic that describes how to use the Windows Help and Support.

- Click the Learn about Windows Basics link in the Not sure where to start? area to display the Windows Basics: all topics page (Figure 1–53).

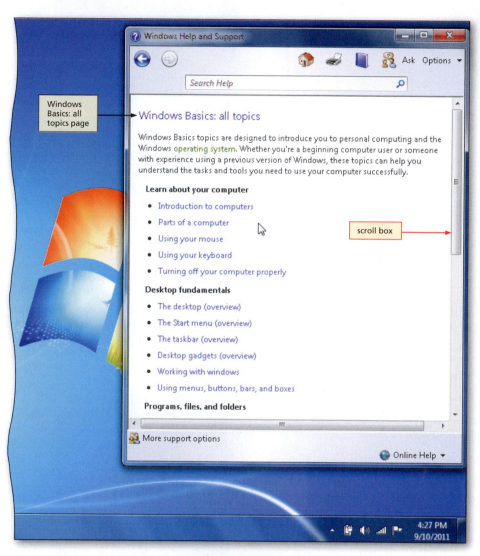

Figure 1–53

2

● Scroll down until you can see the Getting help link under the 'Help and support' heading (Figure 1–54).

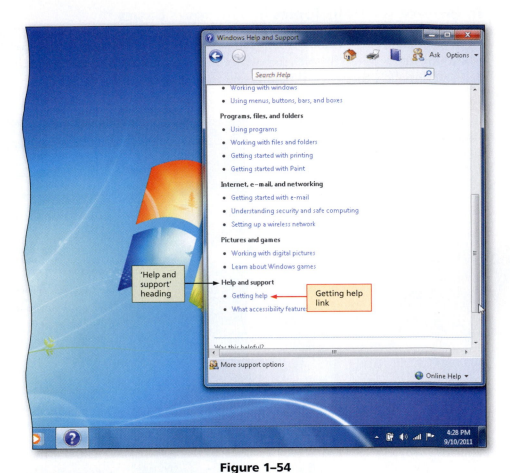

Figure 1–54

3

● Click the Getting help link to display the Getting help page (Figure 1–55).

● Read the information on the Getting help page.

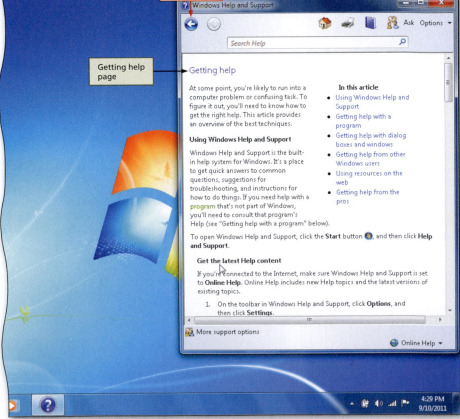

Figure 1–55

4
• Click the Back button on the Navigation toolbar two times to return to the Help and Support home (Figure 1–56).

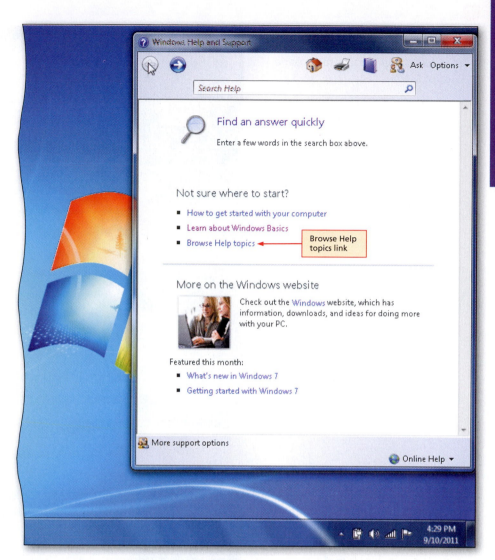

Figure 1–56

To Search for Help Topics Using the Table of Contents

A second method for finding answers to your questions about Windows 7 is to use the Browse Help topics link. Browse Help topics contains a list of categories, organized like a table of contents. Each category contains links to help pages and subtopics, which allow you to refine your search until you find the material that answers your question. The steps on the following pages locate help and information about what you need to set up a home network.

1

● Click the Browse Help topics link in the 'Not sure where to start?' area to display the Contents page (Figure 1–57).

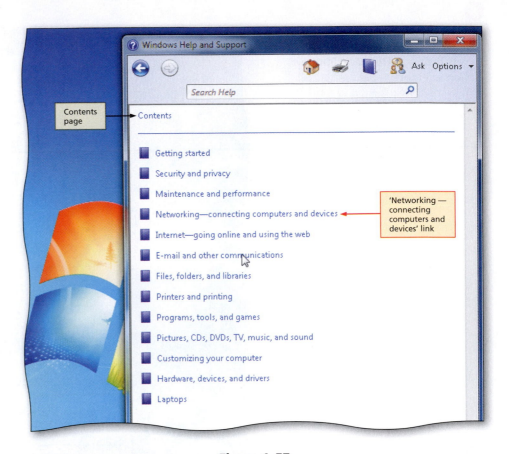

Figure 1–57

2

● Click the 'Networking—connecting computers and devices' link on the Contents page to display the links in the 'Networking—connecting computers and devices' topic (Figure 1–58).

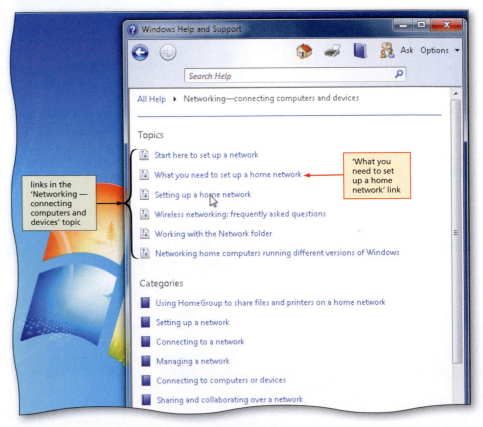

Figure 1–58

3

- Click the 'What you need to set up a home network' link to display the 'What you need to set up a home network' help page (Figure 1–59).

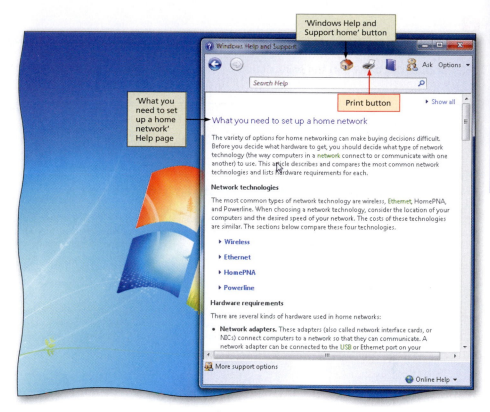

Figure 1–59

To Print a Help Topic

There are times when you might want to print a help topic so that you can have a printout for reference. The following steps show you how to print a Help topic. If you do not have access to a printer, read the following steps without performing them.

1

- Click the Print button on the Help toolbar to display the Print dialog box (Figure 1–60).

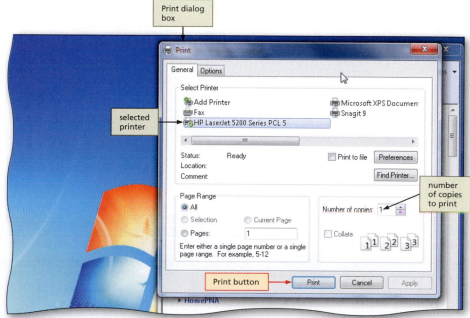

Figure 1–60

2

- Verify that the correct printer is selected, and ready the printer according to the printer instructions.

- Click the Print button in the Print dialog box to print the Help topic (Figure 1–61).

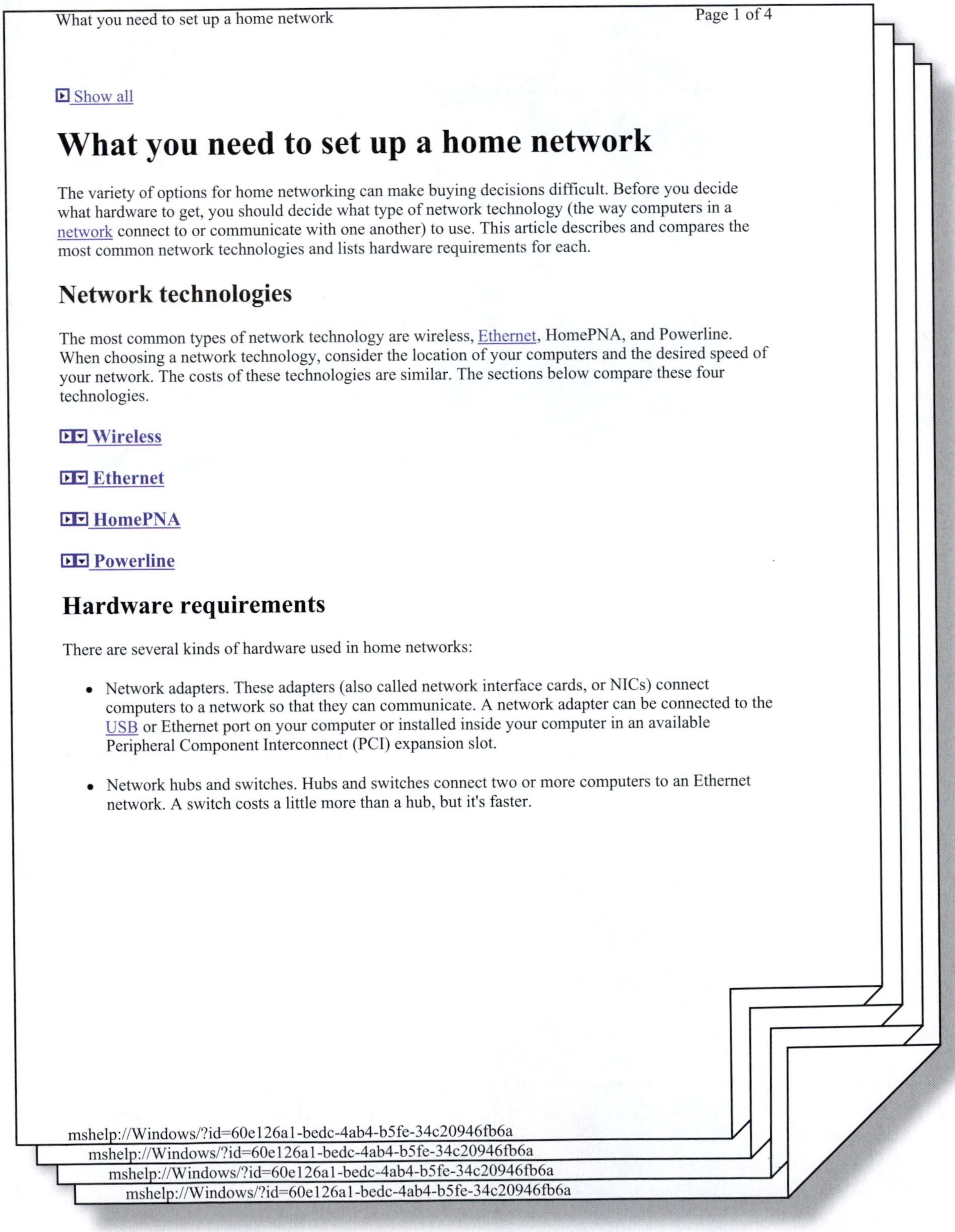

What you need to set up a home network   Page 1 of 4

▶ Show all

What you need to set up a home network

The variety of options for home networking can make buying decisions difficult. Before you decide what hardware to get, you should decide what type of network technology (the way computers in a network connect to or communicate with one another) to use. This article describes and compares the most common network technologies and lists hardware requirements for each.

Network technologies

The most common types of network technology are wireless, Ethernet, HomePNA, and Powerline. When choosing a network technology, consider the location of your computers and the desired speed of your network. The costs of these technologies are similar. The sections below compare these four technologies.

▶▼ **Wireless**

▶▼ **Ethernet**

▶▼ **HomePNA**

▶▼ **Powerline**

Hardware requirements

There are several kinds of hardware used in home networks:

- Network adapters. These adapters (also called network interface cards, or NICs) connect computers to a network so that they can communicate. A network adapter can be connected to the USB or Ethernet port on your computer or installed inside your computer in an available Peripheral Component Interconnect (PCI) expansion slot.

- Network hubs and switches. Hubs and switches connect two or more computers to an Ethernet network. A switch costs a little more than a hub, but it's faster.

mshelp://Windows/?id=60e126a1-bedc-4ab4-b5fe-34c20946fb6a
mshelp://Windows/?id=60e126a1-bedc-4ab4-b5fe-34c20946fb6a
mshelp://Windows/?id=60e126a1-bedc-4ab4-b5fe-34c20946fb6a
mshelp://Windows/?id=60e126a1-bedc-4ab4-b5fe-34c20946fb6a

Figure 1–61

To Return to Windows Help and Support Home

The following step returns to Windows Help and Support home.

- Click the 'Help and Support home' button on the Navigation toolbar to return to Windows Help and Support home (Figure 1–62).

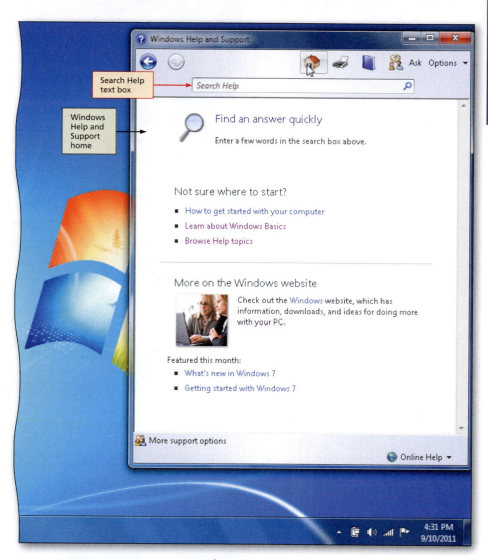

Figure 1–62

To Search Windows Help and Support

A third method for obtaining help about Windows 7 is to use the Search Help text box in the Windows Help and Support window. The Search Help text box allows you to enter a keyword and search for all Help topics containing the keyword.

When you search Help, the results of the search are sorted to produce the best matches for your keyword. When the computer is connected to the Internet, Windows Help and Support also searches the Microsoft Knowledge Base Web site for topics or articles that are relevant to the keyword you enter. If there are 30 results or less, all results are displayed. If there are more than 30 results for your keyword, a link to view more results will appear at the end of the Best 30 results list. The total number of results will depend upon the search keywords. The following steps use the Search Help text box to locate information about computer viruses.

1

- Click the Search Help text box and type `virus` in the Search Help text box to provide a keyword for searching (Figure 1–63).

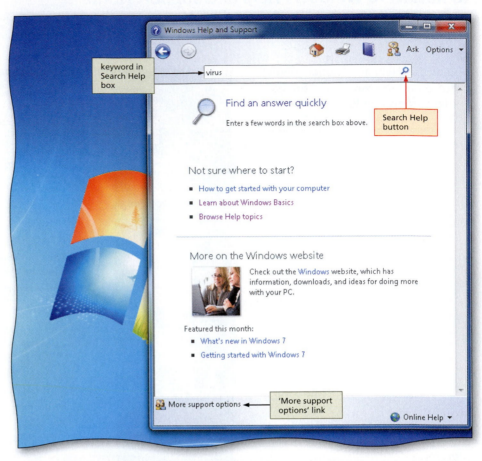

Figure 1–63

2

- Click the Search Help button to search for items matching your keyword (Figure 1–64).

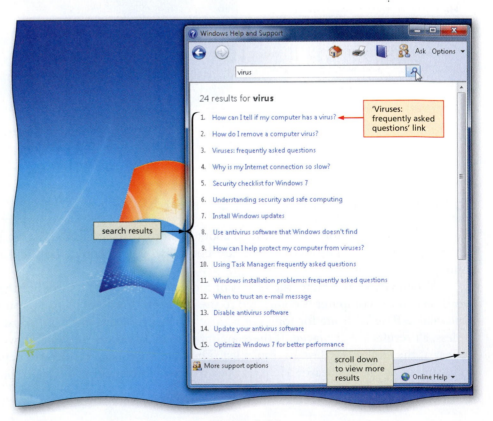

Figure 1–64

3

- Click the 'Viruses: frequently asked questions link' to display the 'Viruses: frequently asked questions' help page (Figure 1–65).

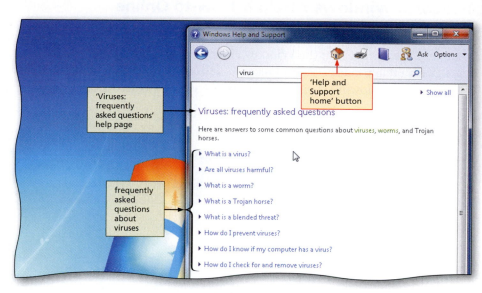

Figure 1–65

Other Ways

1. Press ALT+S, type keyword, press ENTER

To Get More Help

If you do not find the answers you are seeking, the 'More support options' link offers additional methods for asking for and receiving help. The following step opens the 'More support options' area.

1

- Click the Help and Support home button to return to the Windows Help and Support home page.

- Click the 'More support options' link at the bottom of the Windows Help and Support window to open the 'More support options' page (Figure 1–66).

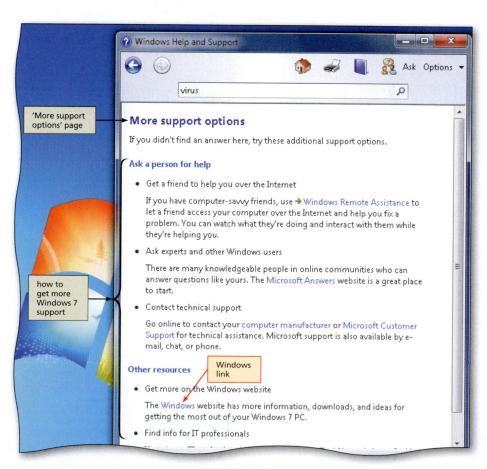

Figure 1–66

To Search Windows 7 Help & How-to Online

The Windows link on the 'More support options' page launches your Web browser and opens the Microsoft Windows Web site. From the Windows Web site, you can search a broader range of content, get help from others, share a Help topic, or save a link to a Help topic for future reference by adding it to your Favorites in Internet Explorer. The following steps open Internet Explorer to access the Windows Web site.

1

- Click the Windows link to open Internet Explorer.

- Point to the Help & How-to link and then click Windows 7 to display the Windows 7 Help & How-to Web page (Figure 1–67).

- If necessary, click the Maximize button on the Internet Explorer title bar to maximize the Internet Explorer window.

Q&A Why am I unable to access Windows Help online?

You must have an active Internet connection to use Windows Help online.

Figure 1–67

2

• Click the Security checklist link on the Windows 7 Help & How-to Web page to display the Security checklist for Windows 7 Web page (Figure 1–68).

Figure 1–68

To Add a Page to Favorites

When you know you will want to return to a Windows Help Web page in the future, you can add it to your Favorites Center in Internet Explorer. The following steps add the Security checklist for Windows 7 page to your favorites.

1

● Click the Favorites button to display the Favorites Center (Figure 1–69).

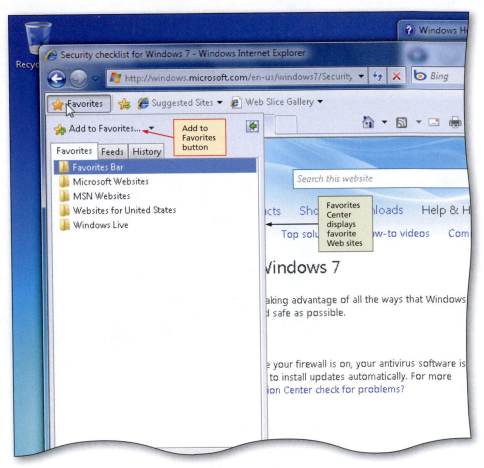

Figure 1–69

2

● Click the Add to Favorites button in the Favorites Center to display the Add a Favorite dialog box (Figure 1–70).

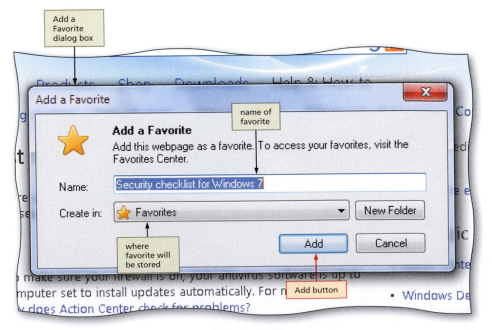

Figure 1–70

• Click the Add button to add the Security checklist for Windows 7 page to your Favorites Center (Figure 1–71).

Figure 1–71

4

• Click the Favorites button on the Favorites bar to display the Favorites Center and view the Security checklist for Windows 7 link (Figure 1–72).

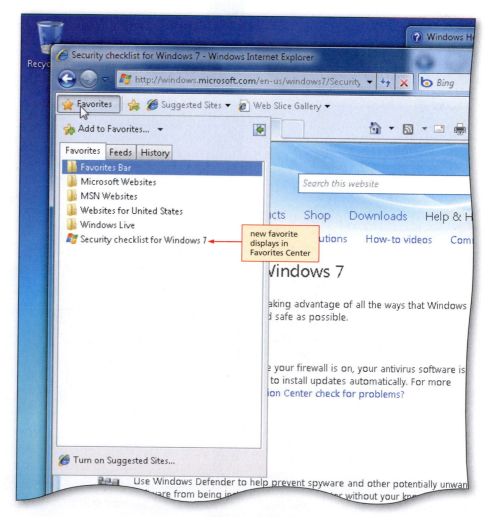

Figure 1–72

To Delete a Link from Favorites

When you are through referring to a Help topic stored in your Favorites Center, you might want to delete the link. The following steps delete the Security checklist for Windows 7 Web page from your Favorites Center.

- Right-click the Security checklist for Windows 7 entry to display a shortcut menu (Figure 1–73).

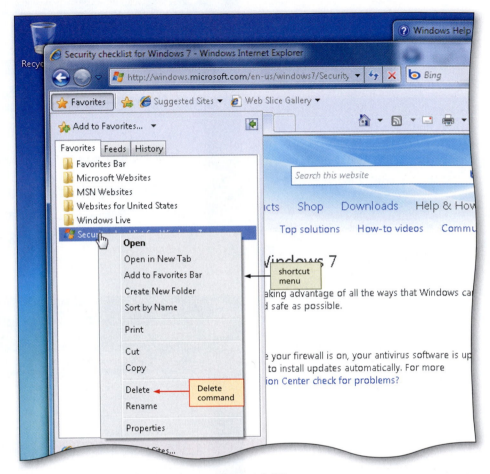

Figure 1–73

- Click the Delete command to close the shortcut menu and display the Delete Shortcut dialog box (Figure 1–74).

- Click the Yes button in the Delete Shortcut dialog box to delete the Security checklist for Windows 7 Favorite from the Favorites Center.

Q&A

Why does the dialog box ask me if I want to delete a shortcut?

Internet Explorer and Windows 7 store your favorites as small text files in a special folder on your computer. When you add a favorite, you are creating a shortcut. When you delete a favorite, you are deleting a shortcut.

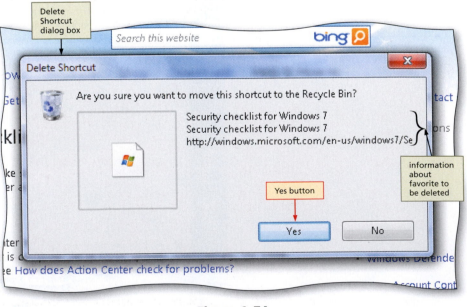

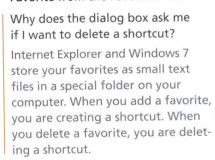

Figure 1–74

To Close Windows Internet Explorer and Windows Help and Support

When you have finished using a program, you should close it. The following steps close Windows Internet Explorer and Windows Help and Support.

1 Click the Close button on the title bar of the Windows Internet Explorer window.

2 Click the Close button on the title bar of the Windows Help and Support window.

To Empty the Recycle Bin

When you decide that you no longer need files located in the Recycle Bin, you can empty the Recycle Bin. The following steps empty the Recycle Bin and permanently delete the files it contains.

1 Right-click the Recycle Bin to display the shortcut menu.

2 Click the Empty Recycle Bin command to permanently delete the contents of the Recycle Bin.

3 Click the Yes button to confirm the operation.

Logging Off and Turning Off the Computer

After completing your work with Windows 7, you should close your user account by logging off the computer. In addition to logging off, there are several options available for ending your Windows 7 session. Table 1–3 describes the various options for ending your Windows 7 session.

BTW

Sleep Command
When a computer has been put to sleep using the Sleep command, you can bring it out of the sleep state in a variety of ways. Depending on the computer, you might press the power button, press a key on the keyboard, click the mouse, or open the lid, if it is a notebook computer.

Table 1–3 Options for Ending a Windows 7 Session	
Option	**Description**
Switch user	Click the Start button, point to the arrow next to the Shut down button, and then click the Switch user command to keep your programs running in the background (but inaccessible until you log on again), and allow another user to log on.
Log off	Click the Start button, point to the arrow next to the Shut down button, and then click the Log off command to close all your programs and close your user account. This method leaves the computer running so that another user can log on.
Lock	Click the Start button, point to the arrow next to the Shut down button, and then click the Lock command to deny anyone except those who have authorized access to log on the computer.
Restart	Click the Start button, point to the arrow next to the Shut down button, and then click the Restart command to close all open programs, log off, and restart the computer.
Sleep	Click the Start button, point to the arrow next to the Shut down button, click the Sleep command, wait for Windows to save your work to memory and then power down your computer to a low-power state. This is useful if you are expecting to return to your computer in a short amount of time.
Hibernate	Click the Start button, point to the arrow next to the Shut down button, and then click the Hibernate command. Windows will save your session to the hard disk and turn off your computer. When you turn the computer on again, Windows restores your session. This is useful if you are expecting to not use your computer for at least several hours.
Shut down	Click the Start button and then click the Shut down button to close all your programs and turn off the computer.

To Log Off the Computer

Logging off the computer closes any open programs, giving you the opportunity to save any unsaved documents, and then makes the computer available for other users. A logging off message displays briefly as Windows 7 logs you off. When the process is finished, the Welcome screen appears. At this point, another user can log on the computer. The following steps log off the computer. If you do not want to end your session on the computer, read the following steps but do not perform them.

• Display the Start menu (Figure 1–75).

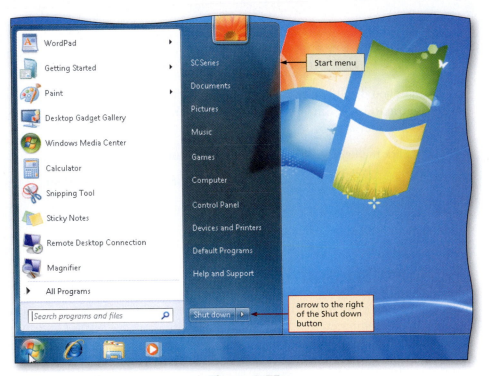

Figure 1–75

2

• Point to the arrow to the right of the Shut down button to display the 'Shut down options' menu (Figure 1–76).

Figure 1–76

3

- Click the Log off command, and then wait for Windows 7 to prompt you to save any unsaved data, if any, and log off (Figure 1–77).

Q&A

Why should I log off the computer?

Some Windows 7 users have turned off their computers without following the log off procedure only to find data they thought they had stored on disk was lost. Because of the way Windows 7 writes data on the hard disk, it is important you log off the computer so that you do not lose your work. Logging off a computer is also a common security practice to prevent unauthorized users from tampering with the computer or your user account.

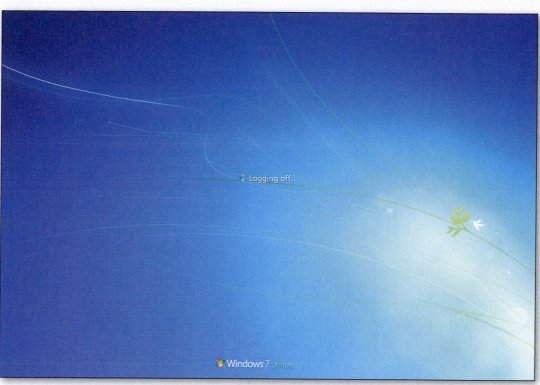

Figure 1–77

Other Ways

1. Press CTRL+ESC, press RIGHT ARROW, press RIGHT ARROW, press L

To Turn Off the Computer

After logging off, you also might want to turn off the computer. Using the Shut down button on the Welcome screen to turn off the computer shuts down Windows 7 so that you can turn off the power to the computer. Many computers turn the power off automatically as part of shutting down. While Windows 7 is shutting down, a message shows stating "Shutting down" along with an animated progress circle. When Windows 7 is done, the computer will shut off. You should not turn off your computer during this process, as you could lose data. The following step turns off the computer. However, if you do not want to turn off the computer, read the step without performing it.

- Click the Shut down button to turn off the computer (Figure 1–78).

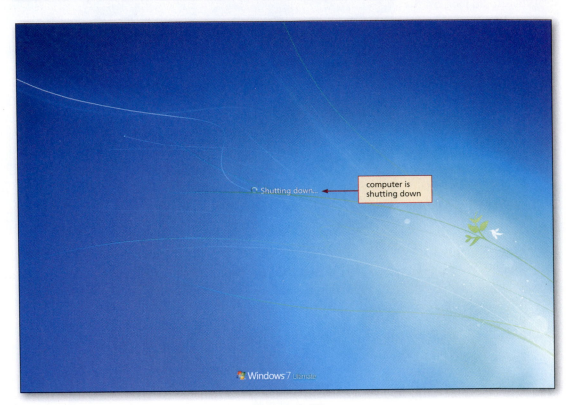

Shutting down... ← computer is shutting down

Windows 7 Ultimate

Figure 1–78

Other Ways
1. Press ALT+F4, select Shut down, click OK

Chapter Summary

In this chapter, you have learned how to work with the Microsoft Windows 7 user interface. You launched Windows 7, logged on the computer, learned about the parts of the desktop, and added and removed a gadget from the desktop. You opened, minimized, maximized, restored, and closed Windows 7 windows. You launched programs and used Aero Flip 3D to switch between them. Using Windows Help and Support, you located Help topics to learn more about Microsoft Windows 7. You printed a Help topic and learned how to find Help topics online. You logged off the computer using the Log off command and then shut down Windows 7 using the Shut down button on the Welcome screen. The items listed below include all of the new Windows 7 skills you have learned in this chapter.

1. Log On the Computer (WIN 8)
2. Display the Start Menu (WIN 10)
3. Scroll Using Scroll Arrows, the Scroll Bar, and the Scroll Box (WIN 12)
4. Open the Getting Started Window (WIN 14)
5. Close the Getting Started Window (WIN 15)
6. Open the Computer Folder Window (WIN 15)
7. Minimize and Redisplay a Window (WIN 17)
8. Maximize and Restore a Window (WIN 18)
9. Close a Window (WIN 19)
10. Add a Shortcut to the Desktop (WIN 20)
11. Open a Window Using a Desktop Shortcut (WIN 21)
12. Move a Window by Dragging (WIN 22)
13. Expand the Contents of Local Disk (C:) (WIN 22)
14. Size a Window by Dragging (WIN 23)
15. Collapse the Local Disk (C:) List (WIN 24)
16. Resize a Window (WIN 24)
17. Delete a Desktop Icon by Dragging it to the Recycle Bin (WIN 25)
18. Empty the Recycle Bin (WIN 26)
19. Add a Gadget to the Desktop (WIN 27)
20. Remove a Gadget from the Desktop (WIN 29)
21. Start a Program Using the Start Menu (WIN 30)
22. Start a Program Using the Search Box (WIN 31)
23. Start a Program Using a Pinned Program Icon on the Taskbar (WIN 32)
24. Switch Between Programs Using Aero Flip 3D (WIN 33)
25. Switch Between Programs Using the Taskbar (WIN 35)
26. Show the Desktop Using the Show Desktop Button (WIN 36)
27. Start Windows Help and Support (WIN 37)
28. Browse for Help Topics in Windows Basics (WIN 39)
29. Search for Help Topics Using the Table of Contents (WIN 41)
30. Print a Help Topic (WIN 43)
31. Return to Windows Help and Support Home (WIN 45)
32. Search Windows Help and Support (WIN 45)
33. Get More Help (WIN 47)
34. Search Windows 7 Help & How-to Online (WIN 48)
35. Add a Page to Favorites (WIN 50)
36. Delete a Link from Favorites (WIN 52)
37. Log Off the Computer (WIN 54)
38. Turn Off the Computer (WIN 56)

Learn It Online

Test your knowledge of chapter content and key terms.

Instructions: To complete the Learn It Online exercises, start your browser, click the Address bar, and then enter the Web address scsite.com/win7/learn. When the Windows 7 Learn It Online page is displayed, click the link for the exercise you want to complete and then read the instructions.

Chapter Reinforcement TF, MC, and SA

A series of true/false, multiple-choice, and short-answer questions that test your knowledge of the chapter content.

Flash Cards

An interactive learning environment where you identify chapter key terms associated with displayed definitions.

Practice Test

A series of multiple-choice questions that test your knowledge of chapter content and key terms.

Who Wants To Be a Computer Genius?

An interactive game that challenges your knowledge of chapter content in the style of a television quiz show.

Wheel of Terms

An interactive game that challenges your knowledge of chapter key terms in the style of the television show *Wheel of Fortune*.

Crossword Puzzle Challenge

A crossword puzzle that challenges your knowledge of key terms presented in the chapter.

Apply Your Knowledge

Reinforce the skills and apply the concepts you learned in this chapter.

What's New in Windows 7?

Instructions: Use Windows Help and Support to perform the following tasks.

Part 1: Launching Windows Help and Support

1. Click the Start button and then click Help and Support on the Start menu.
2. Click the What's new in Windows 7 link in the 'More on the Windows website' area in the Windows Help and Support window.

Part 2: Exploring What's new in Windows 7

1. In the Windows 7 simplifies everyday tasks area, click the HomeGroup link to display the 'Windows 7 features - HomeGroup' page (Figure 1–79), and then click the Play button to watch the video. As you watch the video, answer the following questions:

   a. What is HomeGroup?

   _____

   b. How does HomeGroup protect privacy?

   _____

   c. How do you share files with other computers?

   _____

2. Click the Close button to close the Internet Explorer Window.
3. If necessary, click the Windows Help and Support button on the taskbar to make it the active window.

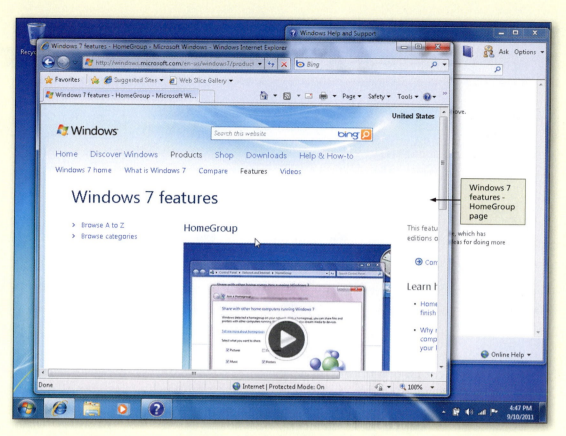

Figure 1–79

Part 3: What's New in Security?

1. In the 'Not sure where to start?' area, click the Browse Help topics link.

2. Click the 'Security and privacy' link to open the 'Security and privacy' page.

3. Click the Action Center link in the Categories area to open the Action Center page.

4. Click the What is Action Center? link to open the What is Action Center page.

5. Read the page, and then scroll down until you see the Click to open Action Center link.

6. Click the Click to open Action Center link to open the Action Center (Figure 1–80 on the next page). Answer the following questions:

   a. What are the main areas shown in the Action Center?

   _____

   b. Are there any issues in the Action Center that you need to review?

   _____

   c. What link should you click if you need to restore your computer to an earlier time?

   _____

7. Close the Action Center and return to the Windows Help and Support window. Click the Back button two times to return to the All Help > Security and privacy page.

8. Browse the topics and look for information about firewalls. What does a firewall do?

9. Click the Back button as necessary to return to the 'Security and privacy' page.

Continued >

Apply Your Knowledge *continued*

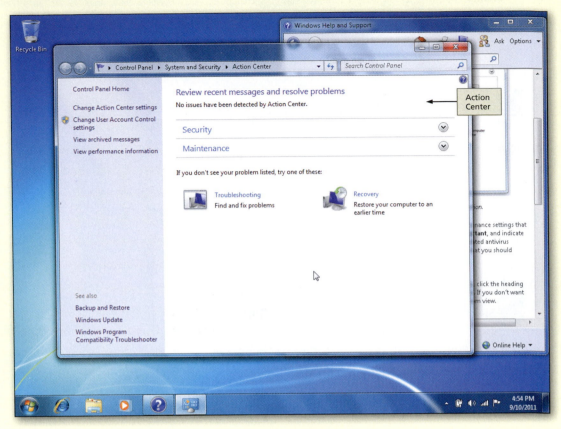

Figure 1–80

Part 4: What are Parental Controls?

1. Scroll down to view and click the Parental Controls link.

2. On the Parental Controls page, click the What can I control with Parental Controls link. Answer the following questions:

   a. What can you do with Parental Controls?

   _____

   _____

   b. After setting up Parental Controls, how can a parent keep a record of a child's computer activity?

   _____

3. Click the Back button as necessary to return to the Contents page in the Windows Help and Support window.

Part 5: What's New in the Picture Area?

1. Click the 'Pictures, CDs, DVDs, TV, music, and sound' link on the Contents page.

2. In the Categories area, click the Pictures link.

3. Click the 'Working with digital pictures' link, and answer the following question:

   a. What are the two main ways to import pictures?

   _____

4. Click the Back button as necessary to return to the Contents page in the Windows Help and Support window.

Part 6: What's New in Mobile PC Features Area?

1. Click the Laptops link to open the Laptops page.

2. Click the 'Using Windows Mobility Center' link, and answer the following question:

   a. How do you open the Mobility Center?

   _____

   _____

3. Click the Close button in the Windows Help and Support window.

Extend Your Knowledge

Extend the skills you learned in this chapter and experiment with new skills. You might need to use Help to complete the assignment.

Using Windows Help and Support to Obtain Help

Instructions: Use Windows Help and Support to perform the following tasks.

1. Find Help about Windows keyboard shortcuts by typing `shortcuts` in the Search Help text box and then clicking the Search Help button (Figure 1–81). Click the result titled Keyboard shortcuts.

   a. What general keyboard shortcut is used to display the Start menu?

   b. What general keyboard shortcut is used to display the shortcut menu for an active window?

   c. What general keyboard shortcut is used to view the properties for a selected item?

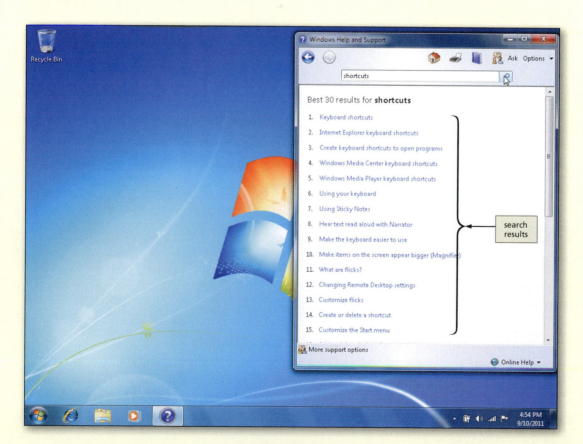

Figure 1–81

Continued >

Extend Your Knowledge *continued*

    d. What dialog box keyboard shortcut is used to move backward through options?

    e. What dialog box keyboard shortcut is used to display Help?

    f. What keyboard shortcut is used to open the Computer folder window?

2. Use the Help and Support Content page to answer the following questions.

    a. How do you reduce computer screen flicker?

    b. What dialog box do you use to change the appearance of the mouse pointer?

    c. How do you minimize all windows?

    d. What is a server?

3. Use the Search Help text box in Windows Help and Support to answer the following questions:

    a. How can you reduce all open windows on the desktop to taskbar buttons?

    b. How do you launch a program using the Run command?

    c. What are the steps to add a toolbar to the taskbar?

    d. What wizard do you use to remove unwanted desktop icons?

4. The tools to solve a problem while using Windows 7 are called **troubleshooters**. Use Windows Help and Support to find the list of troubleshooters, and answer the following questions.

    a. What problems does the HomeGroup troubleshooter allow you to resolve?

    b. List five Windows 7 troubleshooters.

5. Use Windows Help and Support to obtain information about software licensing and product activation, and answer the following questions. To get the most current information, you will need to search Windows Help and Support online.

    a. What is software piracy?

    b. What are the five types of software piracy?

    c. Why should I be concerned about software piracy?

    d. What is a EULA (End-User License Agreement)?

    e. Can you legally make a second copy of Windows 7 for use at home, work, or on a portable computer?

    f. What is Windows Product Activation?

6. Close the Windows Help and Support window.

In the Lab

Use the guidelines, concepts, and skills presented in this chapter to increase your knowledge of Windows 7. Labs are listed in order of increasing difficulty.

Lab 1: Improving Your Mouse Skills with Windows Gadgets

Instructions: Perform the following steps to play a game using a gadget.

1. Open the Start menu and then open All Programs. Click the Desktop Gadget Gallery command. Double-click the Picture Puzzle to add it to the desktop. Close the Gadget Gallery window.

2. Click the Show picture button on the Picture Puzzle to see what the picture will look like once you solve the puzzle (Figure 1–82).

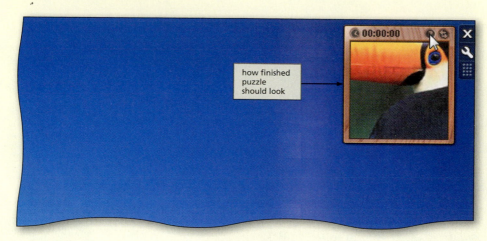

how finished
puzzle
should look

Figure 1–82

3. Play the Picture Puzzle game, by moving the puzzle tiles around by clicking on them when they are near the empty slot. Continue to rearrange the tiles until you have completed the picture (you can show the picture at any time to determine if you are close to the solution). Record your time here: _____

4. Click the Close button on the gadget to remove the gadget from the desktop.

In the Lab

Lab 2: Switching through Open Windows

Instructions: Perform the following steps to launch multiple programs using the Start menu and then use different methods to switch through the open windows (Figure 1–83 on the next page).

Part 1: Launching the Getting Started Window, WordPad, and Internet Explorer
1. Click the Start button, click the All Programs command, and then click the Internet Explorer command to launch Internet Explorer.
2. Click the Start button, click the All Programs command, click the Accessories folder, and then click the Getting Started command to display the Getting Started window.
3. Click the Start button, click the All Programs command, click the Accessories folder, and then click WordPad to launch WordPad.

Part 2: Switching through the Windows
1. Press ALT+TAB to switch to the next open window.
2. While holding the WINDOWS key, press the TAB key two times to switch to the next open window.
3. Press CTRL+ALT+TAB to view the open programs. Press TAB. Click the WordPad window to switch to WordPad.
4. Press CTRL+WINDOWS+TAB to view the open programs. Press TAB. Click the Internet Explorer window to switch to Internet Explorer.

Part 3: Report your Findings
1. What is the difference between pressing ALT+TAB and pressing WINDOWS+TAB? _____
_____

2. What is the difference between pressing ALT+TAB and CTRL+ALT+TAB? _____
_____

Continued >

In the Lab *continued*

Figure 1–83

3. What is your favorite method of switching between windows? _____

_____

4. Besides using the keyboard shortcuts, what other ways can you switch between open windows?

Part 4: Closing the open Windows
1. Close WordPad.
2. Close Internet Explorer.
3. Close the Getting Started window.

In the Lab

Lab 3: Launching and Using Internet Explorer

Instructions: Perform the following steps to Internet Explorer to explore a selection of Web sites.

Part 1: Launching Internet Explorer
1. If necessary, connect to the Internet.
2. Click the Internet Explorer button on the taskbar. Maximize the Windows Internet Explorer window.

Part 2: Exploring CNN's Web Site
1. Click the Web address in the Address bar to select it.
2. Type www.cnn.com in the Address bar and then press the ENTER key.

3. Answer the following questions:

   a. What Web address displays in the Address bar? _____

     _____

   b. What window title displays on the title bar? _____

     _____

4. If necessary, scroll the Web page to view the contents of the Web page. List five links shown on this Web page. _____

5. Click any link on the Web page. What link did you click? _____

    _____

6. Describe the Web page that displayed when you clicked the link. _____

    _____

7. If requested by your instructor, click the Print button to print the Web page.

Part 3: Exploring Universal Studios: Orlando's Web Site

1. Click the Web address in the Address bar to select it.

2. Type www.universalorlando.com in the Address bar and then press the ENTER key.

3. What title displays on the title bar? _____

    _____

4. Scroll the Web page to view the contents of the Web page. Do any graphic images display on the Web page? _____

5. Pointing to an image on a Web page and having the mouse pointer change to a hand indicates the image is a link. Does the Web page include an image that is a link? _____

    _____

   If so, describe the image. _____

    _____

6. Click the image to display another Web page. What window title displays on the title bar?

7. If requested by your instructor, click the Print button to print the Web page.

Part 4: Displaying Previously Displayed Web Pages

1. Click the Back button. What Web page displays? _____

2. Click the Back button twice. What Web page displays? _____

3. Click the Forward button. What Web page displays? _____

Part 5: Exploring the Shelly Cashman Series Web Site

1. Click the Web address in the Address bar to select it.

2. Type www.scsite.com in the Address bar and then press the ENTER key.

3. Scroll the Web page to display the Operating Systems link, and then click the Operating Systems link.

4. Click the Microsoft Windows 7 link, and then click the title of your Windows 7 textbook.

5. Click any links that are of interest to you. Which link did you like the best? _____

    _____

6. Use the Back button or Forward button to display the Web site you like the best.

7. Click the Print button to print the Web page, if requested by your instructor.

8. Click the Close button on the Internet Explorer title bar to close Internet Explorer.

Cases and Places

Apply your creative thinking and problem-solving skills to design and implement a solution.

• EASIER   •• MORE DIFFICULT

• 1: Researching Technical Support

Technical support is an important consideration when installing and using an operating system or a program. The ability to obtain a valid answer to a question at the moment you have the question can be the difference between a frustrating incident and a positive experience. Using Windows Help and Support, the Internet, or another research facility, write a brief report on the options that are available for obtaining help and technical support while using Windows 7.

• 2: Assessing Windows 7 Compatibility

The Windows 7 operating system can be installed only on computers found in the Windows 7 hardware compatibility list. Locate three older personal computers. Look for them in your school's computer lab, at a local business, or in your house. Use the Windows Web site on the Internet to locate the Windows 7 Compatibility Center. Check each computer against the list and write a brief report summarizing your results.

•• 3: Researching Multiple Operating Systems

Using the Internet, a library, or other research facility, write a brief report on the Windows, Mac OS, and Linux operating systems. Describe the systems, pointing out their similarities and differences. Discuss the advantages and disadvantages of each. Finally, tell which operating system you would purchase and explain why.

•• 4: Sharing Your Pictures

Make it Personal

Using Windows Help and Support and the keywords, digital pictures, locate the "Working with Digital Pictures" article. In a brief report, summarize the steps required to send a photo in an e-mail message as well as the different ways to get photos from your camera. Next, research Windows Live Essentials and include a description of how to organize and find your pictures.

•• 5: Researching Operating Systems in Use

Working Together

Because of the many important tasks an operating system performs, most businesses put a great deal of thought into choosing an operating system. Each team member should interview a person at a local business about the operating system he or she uses with his or her computers. Based on the interview, write a brief report on why the businesses chose that operating system, how satisfied it is with it, and under what circumstances it might consider switching to a different operating system.

2 | Working with the Windows 7 Desktop

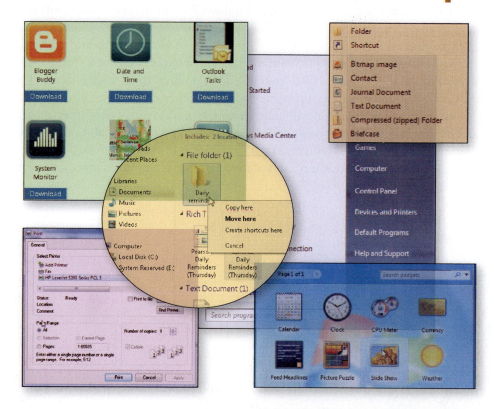

Objectives

You will have mastered the material in this chapter when you can:

- Create, name, and save a document directly in the Documents library
- Change the view and arrange objects in groups in the Documents library
- Create and name a folder in the Documents library
- Move documents into a folder
- Add and remove a shortcut on the Start menu
- Open a document using a shortcut on the Start menu
- Open a folder using a desktop shortcut
- Open, modify, and print multiple documents in a folder
- Store files on a USB flash drive
- Delete multiple files and folders
- Work with the Recycle Bin
- Work with gadgets

2 | Working with the Windows 7 Desktop

Introduction

In Chapter 2, you will learn about the Windows 7 desktop. With thousands of hardware devices and software products available for desktop and notebook computers, users need to manage these resources quickly and easily. One of Windows 7's impressive features is the ease with which users can create and access documents and files. You will organize the lives of two computer users by developing and updating their daily reminders lists. You will create folders, use shortcuts, open and modify multiple documents, and work with gadgets.

Mastering the desktop will help you to take advantage of user-interface enhancements and innovations that make computing faster, easier, and more reliable, and that offer seamless integration with the Internet. Working with the Windows 7 desktop in this chapter, you will find out how these features can save time, reduce computer clutter, and ultimately help you work more efficiently.

Overview

As you read this chapter, you will learn how to work with Windows 7 to create the documents shown in Figure 2–1 and how to perform these general tasks:

- Creating and editing a WordPad document
- Moving and renaming a file
- Creating and moving a folder
- Storing documents on a USB flash drive
- Deleting and restoring shortcuts, files, and folders using the Recycle Bin
- Customizing and rearranging gadgets

Plan Ahead

Working with the Windows 7 Desktop
Working with the Windows 7 desktop requires a basic knowledge of how to use the desktop, insert a USB flash drive, access the Internet, and use a printer.

1. **Be aware that there might be different levels of access on the computer you will be using.** A user account might be restricted to a certain level of access to the computer. Depending on the level of access that has been set for your account, you might or might not be able to perform certain operations.

2. **Identify how to connect a USB flash drive to your computer.** Depending on the setup of the computer you are using, there might be several ways to connect a USB flash drive to your computer. You should know which USB ports you can use to connect a USB flash drive to your computer.

3. **Determine how to access the Internet.** Many gadgets can be found online, free of charge. You will want to know if your computer has Internet access and how to access it.

4. **Ascertain how to access a printer.** To print, you must know which printer you can use and where it is located.

Creating a Document in WordPad

As introduced in Chapter 1, a program is a set of computer instructions that carries out a task on the computer. For example, you create written documents with a word-processing program, spreadsheets and charts with a spreadsheet program, and presentations with a presentation program.

To learn how to work with the Windows 7 desktop, you will create two daily reminders lists, one for Mr. Sanchez and one for Ms. Pearson. Because they will be reviewing their lists throughout the day, you will need to update the lists with new reminders as necessary. You decide to use WordPad, a popular word-processing program available with Windows 7, to create the daily reminders lists. The finished documents are shown in Figure 2–1.

Figure 2–1

To Launch a Program and Create a Document

You will first create the daily reminders document for Mr. Sanchez using WordPad, by launching the WordPad application program, typing the reminders, and then saving the document in your My Documents folder using the Documents library. The Documents library acts as a central location for managing documents and folders. In computing terminology, this method of opening an application program and then creating a document is known as the **application-centric approach**. The steps on the following page launch WordPad and create a daily reminders document for Mr. Sanchez.

1

- Display the Start menu.

- Type wordpad in the Search box to prompt Windows 7 to search for the WordPad program.

- Press the ENTER key to launch WordPad and display the Document - WordPad window (Figure 2–2).

Q&A

Do I have to type the entire word before I press the ENTER key?

No. As soon as you see the result you are looking for at the top of the list in the Programs area above the Start menu Search box, you can press the ENTER key.

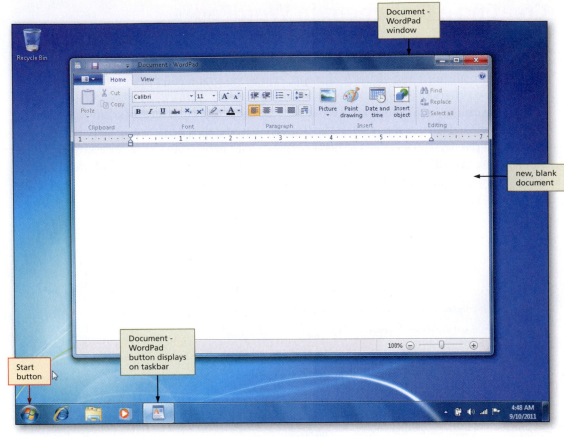

Figure 2–2

2

- Type Sanchez Daily Reminders (Thursday) and then press the ENTER key two times.

- Type 1. Update eBay bid on HP Laptop with Windows 7 and then press the ENTER key.

- Type 2. Add blog entry for Thursday and then press the ENTER key.

- Type 3. E-mail Elma Patterson – update Myspace entry – put me back at top of list! and then press the ENTER key.

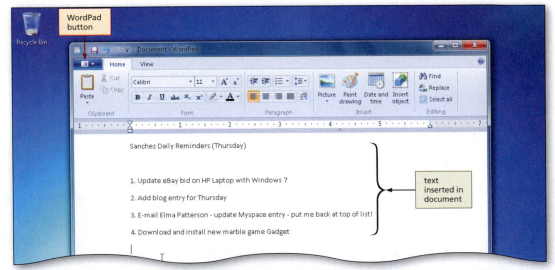

Figure 2–3

- Type 4. Download and install new marble game Gadget and then press the ENTER key (Figure 2–3).

Other Ways

1. Open Start menu, type wordpad in Search box, click WordPad

2. Open Start menu, click All Programs, click Accessories, click WordPad

Saving Documents

When you create a document using a program such as WordPad, the document is stored in the main memory (RAM) of the computer. If you close the program without saving the document or if the computer accidentally loses electrical power, the document will be lost. To protect against the accidental loss of a document and to allow you to modify the document easily in the future, you should save your document. Although you can save a file on the desktop, it is recommended that you save the document in a different location to keep the desktop free from clutter. For example, you can save files to the Documents library or to a USB flash drive.

The **Documents library** displays links to the user's documents as well as any public documents. The files and folders are not stored in the library; instead, the library links to files and folders regardless of where they are stored. You can add items to the Documents library as if you were working in the My Documents folder. A document saved to the Documents library will be easier to find when searching. The **My Documents** folder contains a particular user's documents and folders. The Documents library will show the links, although the actual folders and files will be stored in the My Documents folder. By default, the Documents library shows all files and folders in the My Documents folder.

When you save a document, you are creating a file. A **file** refers to a group of meaningful data that is identified by a name. For example, a WordPad document is a file; an Excel spreadsheet is a file; a picture made using Paint is a file; and a saved e-mail message is a file. When you create a file, you must assign a file name to the file. All files are identified by a file name. A file name should be descriptive of the saved file.

To associate a file with a program, Windows 7 assigns an extension to the file name, consisting of a period followed by three or more characters. Most documents created using the WordPad program are saved as Rich Text Format documents with the .rtf extension, but they also can be saved as plain text with the .txt extension. A Rich Text Format document allows for formatting text and inserting graphics, which is not supported in plain text files.

Many computer users can tell at least one horror story of working on their computers for a long period of time and then losing all of their work because of a power failure or software problem. Consider this a warning: Save often to protect your work.

To Save a Document to the Documents Library

The steps on the following pages save the document you created using WordPad to the Documents library using the file name, Sanchez Reminders (Thursday).

1

- Click the WordPad button to display the WordPad menu (Figure 2–4).

Q&A

Why is there an arrow following the Save as command?

The arrow indicates that there are several preset ways to save the file, which can be accessed by clicking the arrow.

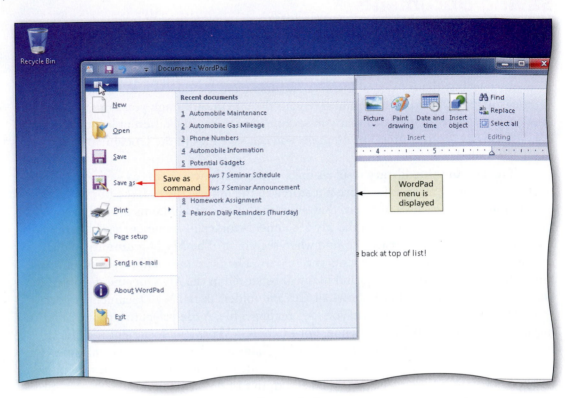

Figure 2–4

2

- Click the Save as command to display the Save As dialog box (Figure 2–5).

- Type Sanchez Daily Reminders (Thursday) in the File name text box.

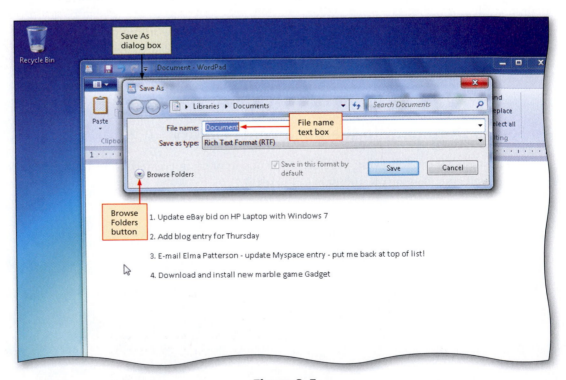

Figure 2–5

3
- Click the Browse Folders button to expand the folders list (Figure 2–6).

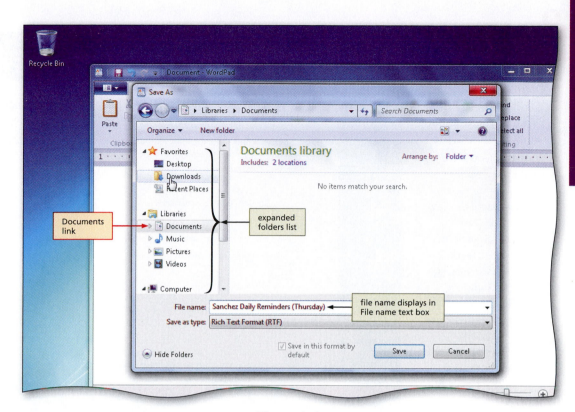

Figure 2–6

4
- Click the Documents link to select the Documents library (Figure 2–7).

Figure 2–7

5

- Click the Save button to save the document and close the Save As dialog box (Figure 2–8).

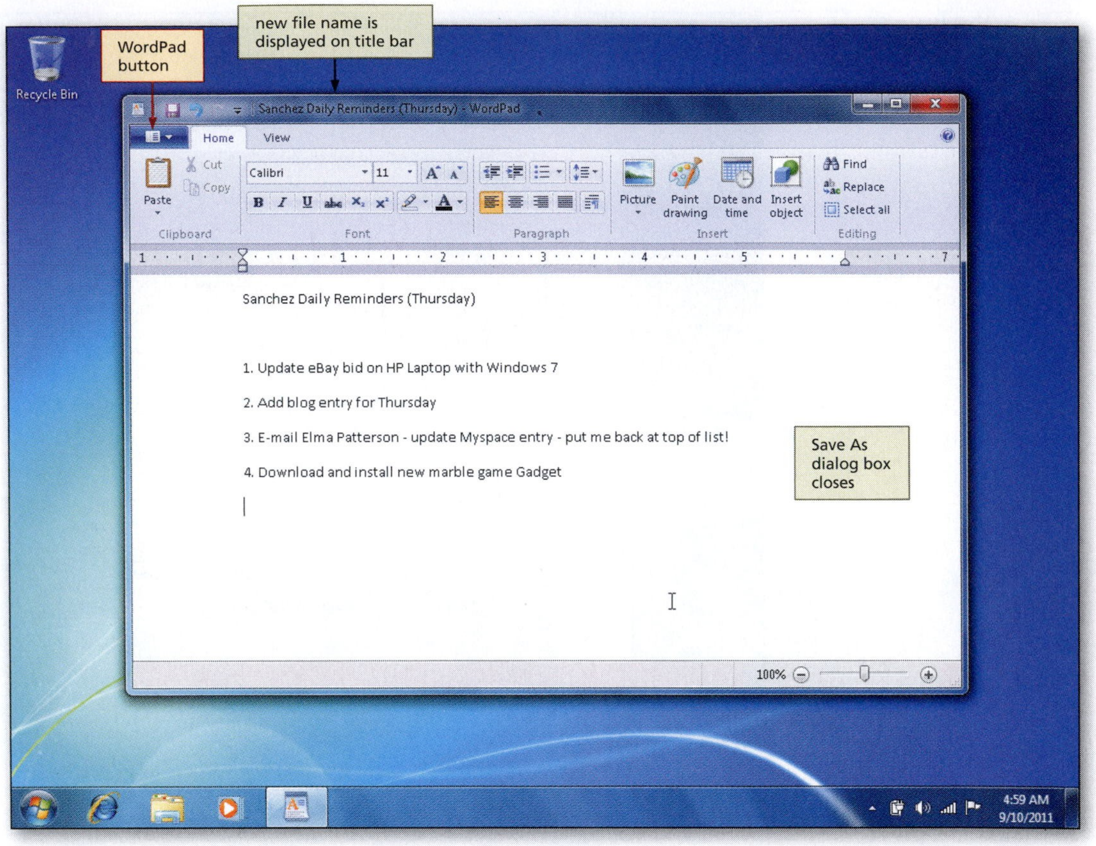

Q&A

Why did the title bar of WordPad change?

Now that you have saved the document with a file name, the file name will display on the title bar. To display a preview of the Sanchez Daily Reminders (Thursday) - WordPad window, point to the WordPad button on the taskbar.

Q&A

Will I have to use the Save as command every time to save?

Now that you have saved the document, you can use the Save command to save changes to the document without having to type a new name or select a new storage location. If you want to save the file with a different name or to a different location, you would use the Save as command. By changing the location using the Address bar, you can save a file in a different folder, library, or drive.

Figure 2–8

To Open the Print Dialog Box from a Program

Paper printouts are and will remain an important form of output for electronic documents. However, many sophisticated programs are expanding their printing capabilities to include sending e-mail messages and posting documents to Web pages on the World Wide Web. One method of printing a document is to print it directly from a program. The following steps open the Print dialog box in WordPad.

1
- Click the WordPad button to display the WordPad menu.

2
- Click the Print command to display the Print dialog box (Figure 2–9).

Q&A

What do the four options in the Page Range area represent?

The option buttons give you the choice of printing all pages of a document (All), selected parts of a document (Selection), current page (Current Page), or selected pages of a document (Pages). The selected All option button indicates all pages of a document will print.

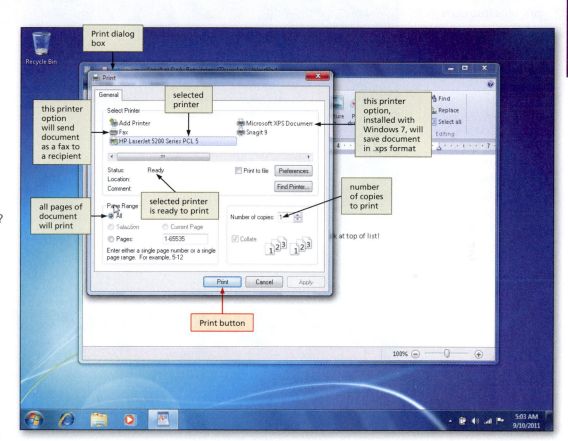

Figure 2–9

Other Ways

1. Press ALT+F, press P

To Print a Document

The following step prints the Sanchez Daily Reminders (Thursday) document.

- Ready the printer according to the printer's instructions.

- If necessary, click the appropriate printer to select your printer.

- Click the Print button to print the document and return to the Sanchez Daily Reminders (Thursday) - WordPad window (Figure 2–10).

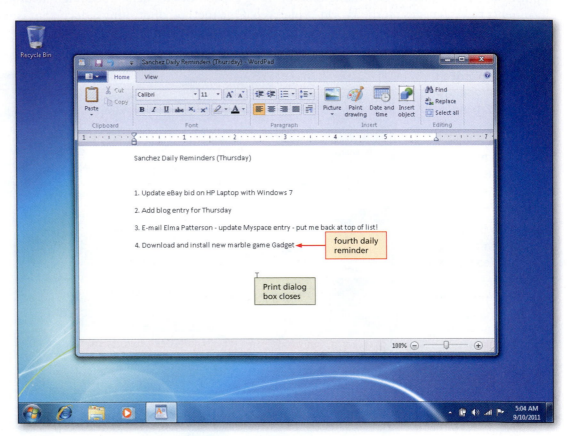

Figure 2–10

Other Ways
1. Click appropriate printer, press ENTER

To Edit a Document

Undoubtedly, you will want to make changes to a document after you have created it and saved it. For any document, your edits can be as simple as correcting a spelling mistake or as complex as rewriting the entire document. The following step edits the Sanchez Daily Reminders (Thursday) document by adding a new reminder.

1
- Click directly after the fourth daily reminder and then press the ENTER key.

- Type 5. Register for next semester's classes and then press the ENTER key (Figure 2–11).

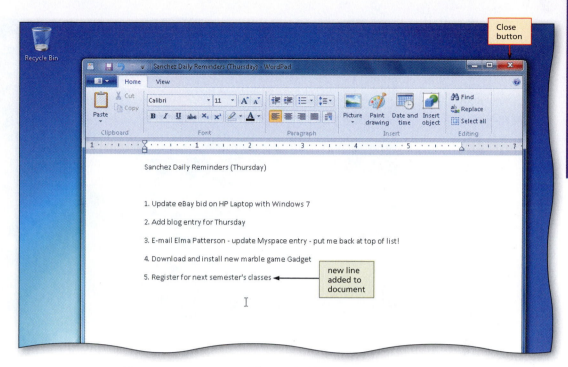

Figure 2–11

To Save and Close a Document

If you forget to save a document after you have edited it, a dialog box will display asking if you want to save your changes. This is how many programs help protect you from losing your work. If you choose to not save your changes, then all edits you made since the last time you saved will be lost. If you click the Cancel button, your changes are not saved, but the document remains open and you can continue working. The following steps close and save the Sanchez Daily Reminders (Thursday) document.

1
- Click the Close button on the title bar to display the WordPad dialog box (Figure 2–12).

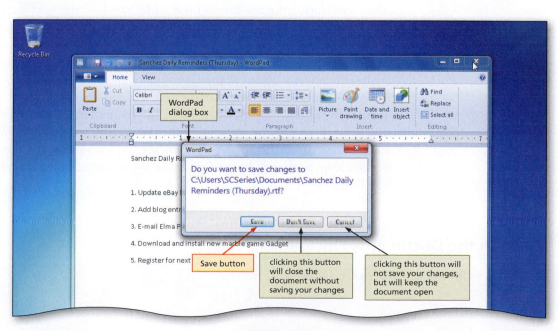

Figure 2–12

2

- Click the Save button in the WordPad dialog box to save your changes to the document and close WordPad (Figure 2–13).

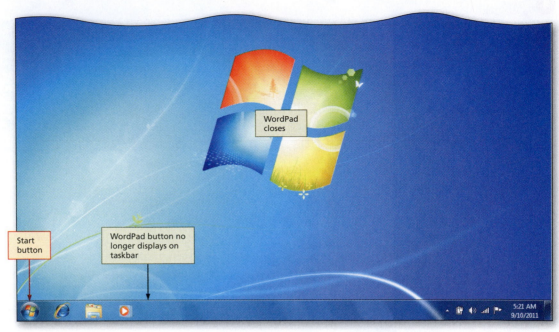

WordPad closes

Start button

WordPad button no longer displays on taskbar

Figure 2–13

Other Ways

1. On title bar double-click WordPad icon, click Save
2. On title bar click WordPad icon, click Close, click Save
3. On WordPad menu click Exit, click Save
4. Press ALT+F, press X; or press ALT+F4, press ENTER

Creating a Document in the Documents Library

After completing the reminders list for Mr. Sanchez, the next step is to create a similar list for Ms. Pearson. Opening a program and then creating a document (the application-centric approach) was the method used to create the first document. Although the same method could be used to create the document for Ms. Pearson, another method is to create the new document in the Documents library without first starting a program. Instead of launching a program to create and modify a document, you first create a blank document directly in the Documents library and then use the WordPad program to enter data into the document. Recall that the document is saved in the My Documents folder, and the link appears in the Documents library. This method, called the **document-centric approach**, will be used to create the document that contains the reminders for Ms. Pearson.

To Open the Documents Library

The following step opens the Documents library.

1

- Display the Start menu.

- Click the Documents command to display the Documents library window (Figure 2–14).

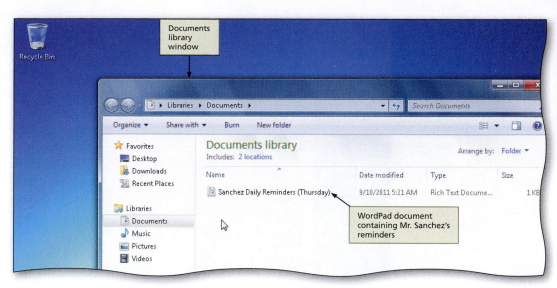

Figure 2–14

To Create a Blank Document in the Documents Library

The phrase, creating a document in the Documents library, might be confusing. The document you actually create contains no data; it is blank. You can think of it as placing a blank piece of paper with a name inside the Documents library. The document has little value until you add text or other data to it. The following steps create a blank document in the Documents library to contain the daily reminders for Ms. Pearson.

1

- Right-click an open area of the Documents library to display the shortcut menu.

- Point to the New command on the shortcut menu to display the New submenu (Figure 2–15).

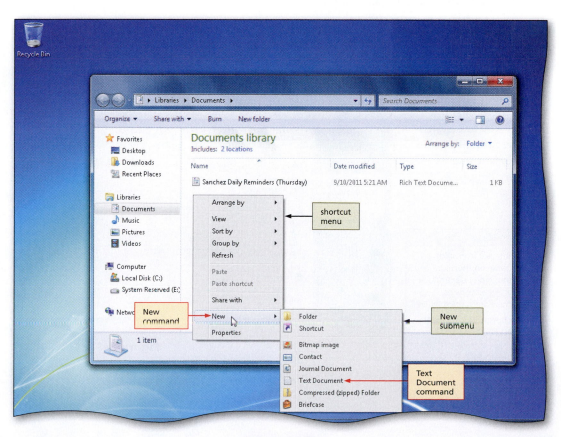

Figure 2–15

2

• Click the Text Document command to display an entry for a new text document in the Documents library window (Figure 2–16).

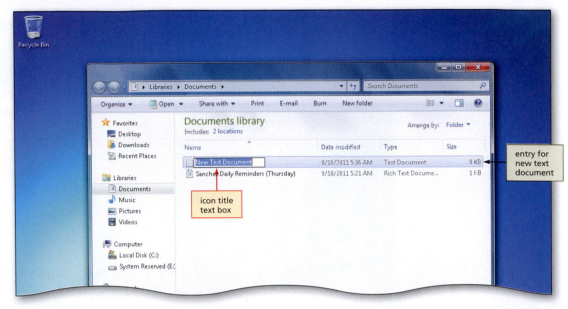

Figure 2–16

To Name a Document in the Documents Library

After you create a blank document, you need to name the document so that it is easily identifiable. In Figure 2–16, the default file name (New Text Document) is highlighted and the insertion point is blinking, indicating that you can type a new file name. The following step assigns the file name, Pearson Daily Reminders (Thursday), to the blank document you just created.

1

• Type `Pearson Daily Reminders (Thursday)` in the icon title text box, and then press the ENTER key to assign a name to the new file in the Documents library (Figure 2–17).

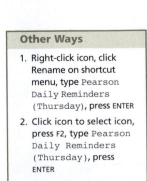

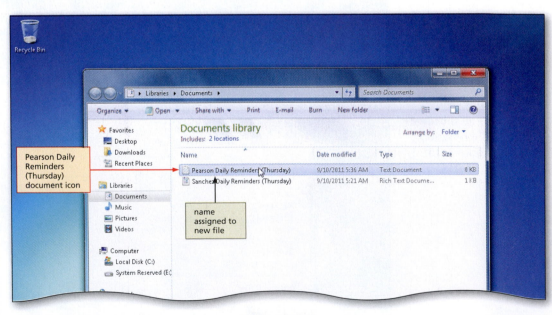

Figure 2–17

Other Ways

1. Right-click icon, click Rename on shortcut menu, type `Pearson Daily Reminders (Thursday)`, press ENTER

2. Click icon to select icon, press F2, type `Pearson Daily Reminders (Thursday)`, press ENTER

To Open a Document with WordPad.

Although you have created the Pearson Daily Reminders (Thursday) document, the document contains no text. To add text to the blank document, you must open the document. Because text files open with Notepad by default, you need to use the shortcut menu to open the file using WordPad. The following steps open a document in WordPad.

- Right-click the Pearson Daily Reminders (Thursday) document icon to display the shortcut menu.

- Point to the Open with command on the shortcut menu to display the Open with submenu (Figure 2–18).

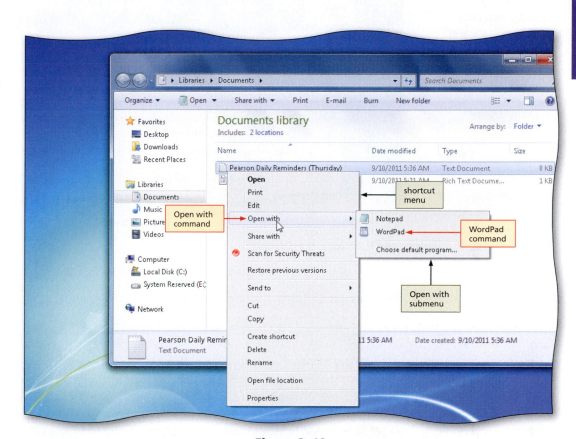

Figure 2–18

- Click the WordPad command on the Open with submenu to open the Pearson Daily Reminders (Thursday) document in WordPad (Figure 2–19).

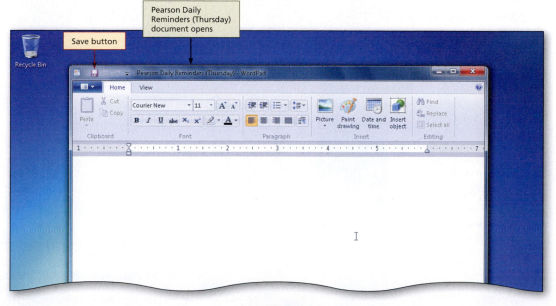

Figure 2–19

To Add Text to a Blank Document

After the document is open, you can add text by typing in the document. The following step adds text to the Pearson Daily Reminders (Thursday) document, and then saves the document.

- Type `Pearson Daily Reminders (Thursday)` and then press the ENTER key twice.

- Type `1. Teleconference Ron Klein – Authentication Problem` and then press the ENTER key.

- Type `2. E-mail Susie Yang – Groove presentation for board meeting Tuesday` and then press the ENTER key.

- Type `3. Lunch with Sam – Noon, Cyber Cafe` and then press the ENTER key (Figure 2–20).

- Click the Save button on the Quick Access Toolbar to save the file.

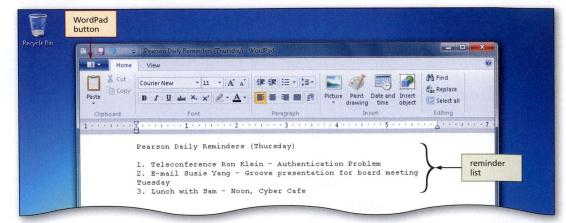

Figure 2–20

To Save a Text Document in Rich Text Format (RTF)

Typing text into the Pearson Daily Reminders (Thursday) document modifies the document, which results in the need to save the document. If you make many changes to a document, you should save the document as you work. When you created the blank text document, Windows 7 assigned it the .txt file name extension, so you will need to use the Save as command to save it in Rich Text Format, which is WordPad's default format. Using the Rich Text Format will allow you to use all of WordPad's features, including formatting options. The following steps save the document in Rich Text Format.

- Click the WordPad button to display the WordPad menu.

- Click the Save as command to display the Save As dialog box.

- Click the 'Save as type' list box arrow to display the 'Save as type' list (Figure 2–21).

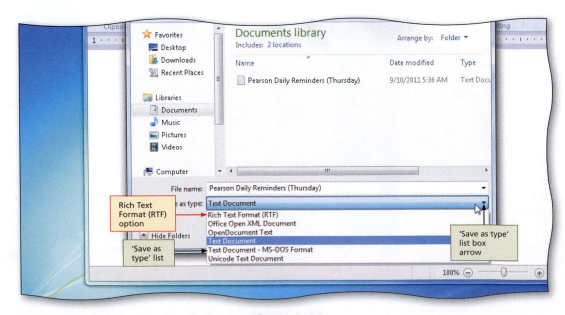

Figure 2–21

2

- Click the Rich Text Format (RTF) option to change the file type to Rich Text Format.

- Type `Pearson Daily Reminders (Thursday).rtf` in the File name text box to change the file name (Figure 2–22).

- Click the Save button to save the document in Rich Text Format.

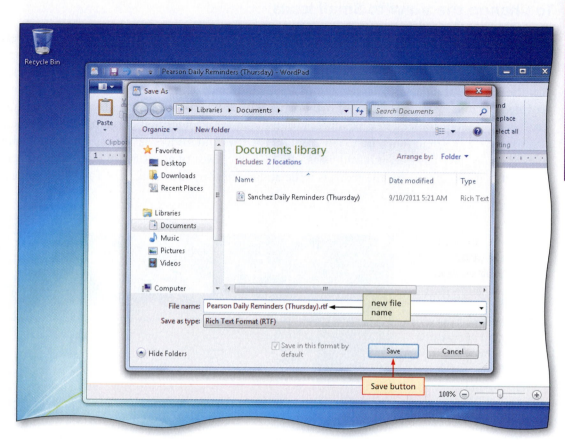

Figure 2–22

To Close the Document

You have saved your changes to Pearson Daily Reminders (Thursday), and now you can close the document.

1 Click Exit on the WordPad menu to close the Document and exit WordPad.

Working with the Documents Library

Once you create documents in the Documents library using either the application-centric or document-centric approach, you can continue to modify and save the documents, print the documents, or create a folder to contain the documents and then move the documents to the folder. Having a single storage location for documents makes it easy to create a copy of the documents so that they are not accidentally lost or damaged.

BTW

The Documents Library
Windows 7 creates a unique Documents library for each computer user. When you have multiple users on a single computer, having a unique central storage area for each user makes it easier to back up important files and folders.

To Change the View to Small Icons

The default view in the Documents library (shown in Figure 2–23) is Details view. Details view shows a list of files and folders, in addition to common properties such as Date Modified and Type. You can use the Change your view button to change to other views. The Small icons, Medium icons, Large icons, and Extra large icons views display the icons in increasingly larger sizes. When Medium, Large, or Extra large icon views are selected, Windows 7 provides a live preview option. With live preview, the icons display images that more closely reflect the actual contents of the files or folders. For example, a folder icon for a folder that contains text documents would show sample pages from those documents. List view displays the files and folders as a list of file names without any extra details. Tiles view displays the files and folders as tiles, which consist of an icon and icon description. With all of these views, the default arrangement for the icons is to be alphabetical by file name. The following steps change the view from the Details view to the Small icons view.

• Click the More options button arrow button next to the 'Change your view' button on the toolbar of the Documents library window to display the 'Change your view' menu (Figure 2–23).

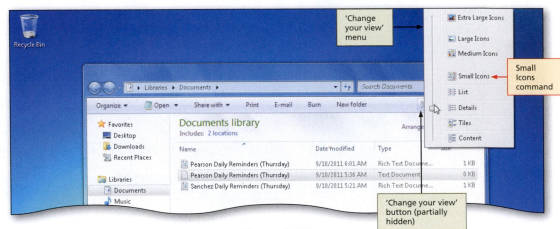

Figure 2–23

• Click the Small Icons command to display the files and folders as small icons (Figure 2–24).

Experiment

• Select each of the options from the 'Change your view' menu to see the various ways that Windows can display folder contents. After you have finished, be sure to select the Small Icons command from the 'Change your view' menu.

Figure 2–24

Other Ways

1. Right-click open space in Documents library, point to View, click Small icons

To Arrange Items in Groups by File Type

There are other methods of arranging the icons in the Documents library. One practical arrangement is to display the icons in groups based upon file type. This arrangement places files of the same type (File Folder, Text Documents, Microsoft Word, Microsoft Excel, and so on) in separate groups. When a window contains many files and folders, this layout makes it easier to find a particular file or folder quickly. The following steps group the icons in the Documents library by file type.

- Right-click the open space below the list of files and folders in the Documents library to display the shortcut menu.

- Point to the Group by command to display the Group by submenu (Figure 2–25).

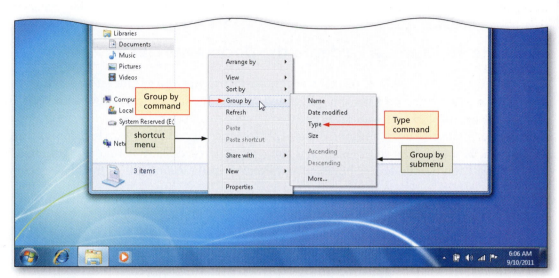

Figure 2–25

- Click the Type command to display the files and folders grouped by type (Figure 2–26).

Can I group the files and folders in other ways?

You can group the files by any of the options on the Group by submenu. This includes Name, Date modified, Type, and Size. To remove the groupings, select (None) on the Group by submenu. The Ascending and Descending options change the order of the groups from alphabetical order to reverse alphabetical order.

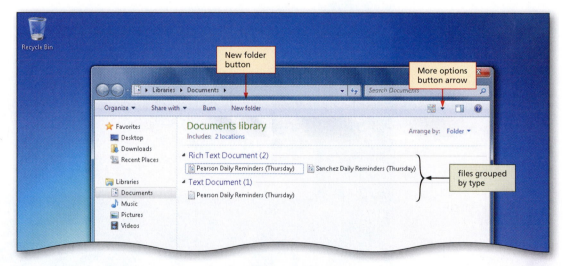

Figure 2–26

Other Ways

1. Press ALT+V, press P, press T

To Change to Medium Icons View

Small icons view is not the best view when creating folders, so you will change the view to Medium icons.

1 Click the More options button arrow button next to the 'Change your view' button on the toolbar and then click the Medium Icons command to change to Medium icons view.

To Create and Name a Folder in the Documents Library

Windows 7 allows you to place one or more documents into a folder in much the same manner as you might take a document written on a piece of paper and place it in a file folder. You want to keep the Sanchez and Pearson documents together so that you can find and reference them easily from among other documents stored in the Documents library. To keep multiple documents together in one place, you first must create a folder in which to store them. The following steps create and name a folder titled Daily reminders in the Documents library to store the Sanchez Daily Reminders (Thursday) and Pearson Daily Reminders (Thursday) documents.

• Click the New folder button on the tool-bar to create a new folder (Figure 2–27).

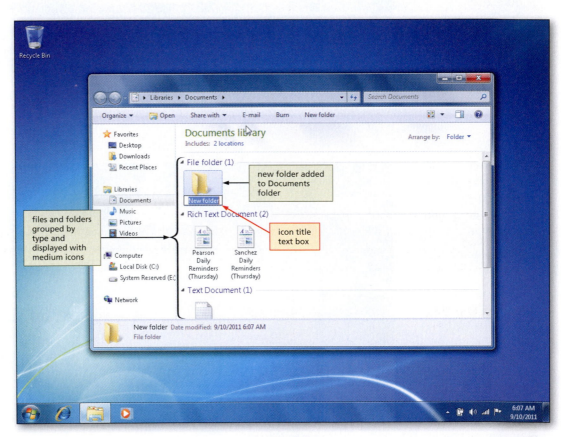

Figure 2–27

2

- Type `Daily reminders` in the icon title text box and then press the ENTER key to name the folder and sort the folder in the Documents library (Figure 2–28).

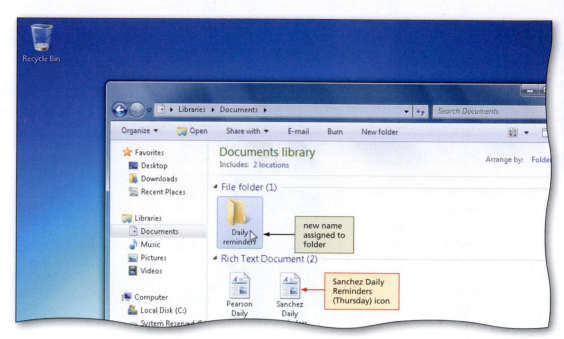

Figure 2–28

Other Ways

1. Right-click open space in Documents library, click New, click Folder, type file name, press ENTER
2. Press ALT+F, press W, press F, type file name, press ENTER

To Move a Document into a Folder

The ability to organize documents and files within folders allows you to keep the Documents library organized when using Windows 7. After you create a folder in the Documents library, the next step is to move documents into the folder. The following steps move the Sanchez Daily Reminders (Thursday) and the Pearson Daily Reminders (Thursday) documents into the Daily reminders folder.

1

- Right-click and drag (also known as right-drag) the Sanchez Daily Reminders (Thursday) icon onto the Daily reminders folder icon to display the shortcut menu (Figure 2–29).

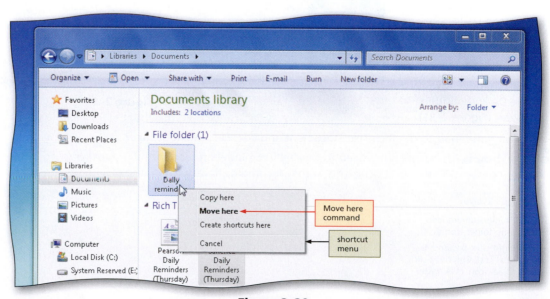

Figure 2–29

2

• Click the Move here command on the shortcut menu to move the Sanchez Daily Reminders (Thursday) icon to the Daily reminders folder (Figure 2–30).

Q&A

What are the other options in the shortcut menu?

When you right-drag, a shortcut menu opens and lists the available options. In this case, the options include Copy here, Move here, Create shortcuts here, and Cancel. Selecting Copy here creates a copy of the Sanchez document in the Daily reminders folder, Create shortcuts here puts a link to the Sanchez document (not the file or a copy of the file) in the Daily reminders folder and Cancel ends the right-drag process. The options in the shortcut menu might change, depending on the type of file and where you are dragging it.

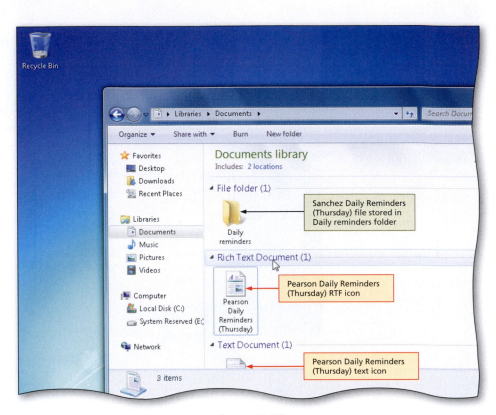

Figure 2–30

3

• Right-drag the Pearson Daily Reminders (Thursday) RTF icon onto the Daily reminders icon to move it to the Daily reminders folder.

• Right-drag the Pearson Daily Reminders (Thursday) text icon onto the Daily reminders icon to move it to the Daily reminders folder (Figure 2–31).

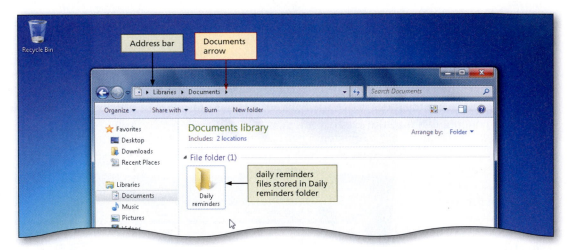

Figure 2–31

Q&A

What happened to the Rich Text Document and Text Document groups?

The documents have been moved to the Daily reminders folder, so the groups were no longer needed. Only if there were other RTF and text documents in the Documents library would the groupings remain.

Other Ways

1. Drag document icon onto folder icon
2. Right-click document icon, click Cut, right-click folder icon, click Paste

To Change Location Using the Address Bar

If you would like to navigate to the folder to see if your files are there, there are several ways to do this. One way in Windows 7 is to use the Address bar. The Address bar appears at the top of the Documents library window and displays your current location as a series of links separated by arrows. By clicking the arrows, you can change your location. The Forward and Back buttons can be used to navigate through the locations you have visited just like the Forward and Back buttons in a Web browser. The following steps change your location to the Daily reminders folder.

1
• Click the Documents arrow on the Address bar to display a location menu that contains a list of folders in the Documents library (Figure 2–32).

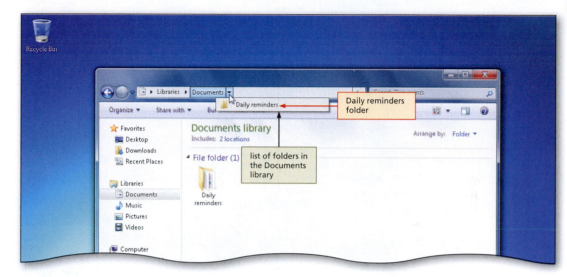

Figure 2–32

2
• Click the Daily reminders folder on the location menu to move to the Daily reminders folder (Figure 2–33).

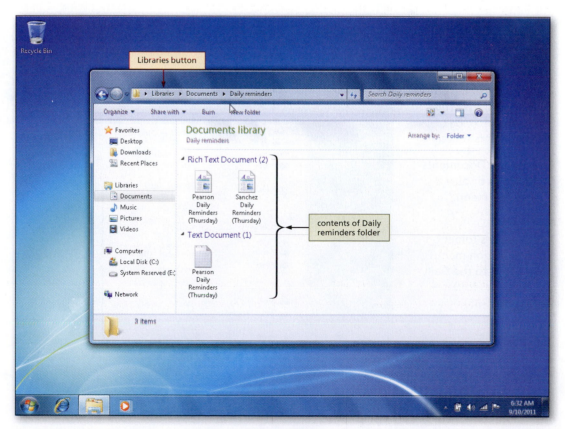

Figure 2–33

3

• Click the Libraries button on the Address bar to switch to the Libraries window (Figure 2–34).

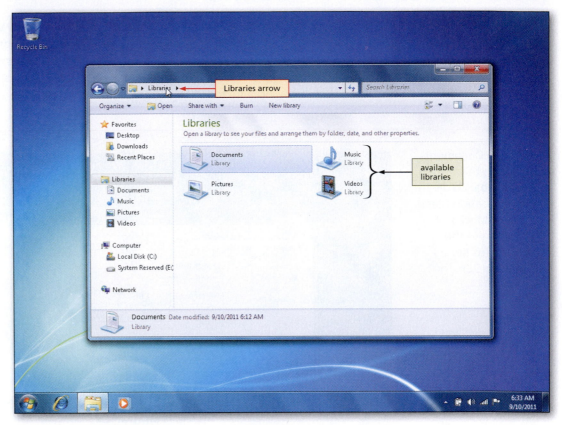

Figure 2–34

4

• Click the Libraries arrow to display a location menu.

• Click Documents on the location menu to move to the Documents folder.

• Click the Documents arrow to display a location menu.

• Click the Daily reminders folder on the location menu to move to the Daily reminders folder (Figure 2–35).

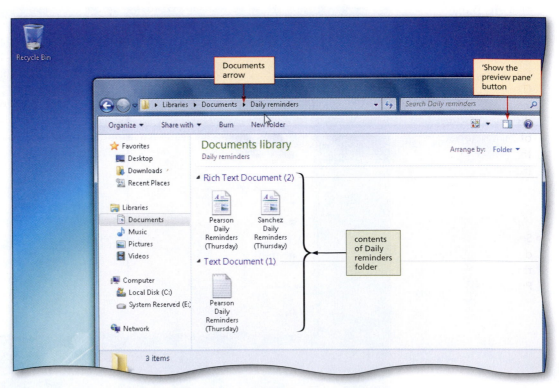

Figure 2–35

To Display and Use the Preview Pane

Now that you are viewing the contents of the Daily reminders folder, you can add a Preview pane to the layout, which will provide you with an enhanced live preview of your documents. When you select a document, the Preview pane displays a live view of the document to the right of the list of files in the folder window. The following steps add the Preview pane to the layout of the Daily reminders folder and then display a live preview of the Sanchez document.

 1

- Click the 'Show the preview pane' button on the toolbar to display the Preview pane (Figure 2–36).

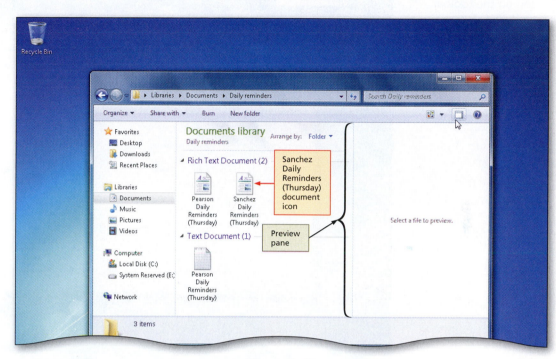

Figure 2–36

 **2**

- Click the Sanchez Daily Reminders (Thursday) document icon on the right to display a preview of the document in the Preview pane (Figure 2–37).

Experiment

- Select different documents to display their preview in the Preview pane.

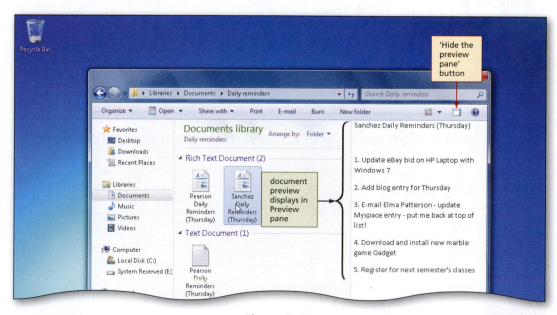

Figure 2–37

Other Ways
1. Click Organize, point to Layout, click Preview pane

To Close the Preview Pane

After verifying that your files are in the Daily reminders folder, you can close the Preview pane and then use the Address bar to return to the Documents library. The following step closes the Preview pane.

- Click the 'Hide the preview pane' button on the toolbar to close the Preview pane (Figure 2–38).

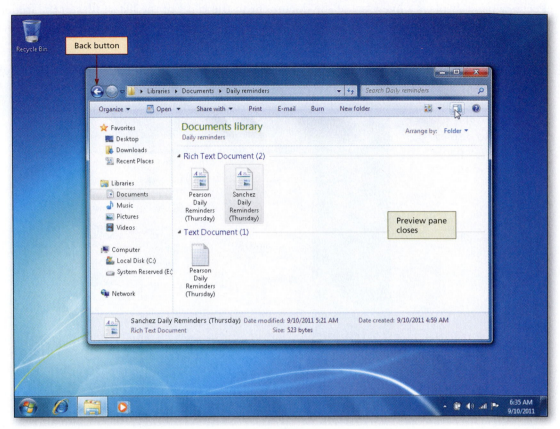

Figure 2–38

To Change Location Using the Back Button on the Address Bar

In addition to clicking the arrows in the Address bar, you also can change locations by using the Back and Forward buttons. Clicking the Back button allows you to return to a location that you already have visited. The following step changes your location to the Documents library.

1

- Click the Back button on the Address bar once to return to the Documents library (Figure 2–39).

Figure 2–39

Creating Folder Shortcuts

One way to customize Windows 7 is to use shortcuts to launch programs and open files or folders. A shortcut is a link to any object on the computer or on a network, such as a program, file, folder, Web page, printer, or another computer. Placing a shortcut to a folder on the Start menu or on the desktop can make it easier to locate and open the folder.

A shortcut icon is not the actual document or program. You do not actually place the folder on the menu; instead, you place a shortcut icon that links to the folder on the menu. When you delete a shortcut, you delete the shortcut icon but do not delete the actual document or program; they remain on the hard disk.

To Add a Shortcut on the Start Menu

The steps on the following pages place the Daily reminders folder shortcut on the Start menu.

1
- Drag the Daily reminders folder icon onto the Start button to begin to add the icon to the Start menu. Do not release the left mouse button (Figure 2–40).

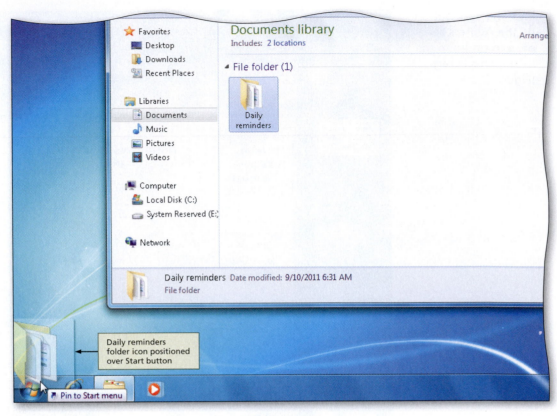

Figure 2–40

2
- Release the left mouse button to add the Daily reminders shortcut to the Start menu (Figure 2–41).

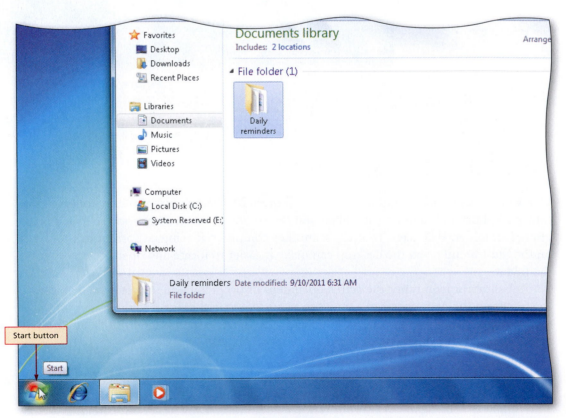

Figure 2–41

3

• Display the Start menu to see the Daily reminders icon pinned to the Start menu (Figure 2–42).

Q&A

Can I add other shortcuts to the Start menu?

In addition to placing a folder shortcut on the Start menu, you also can place a shortcut to other objects (programs, files, USB flash drives, Web pages, printers, or other computers) on the Start menu in a similar manner. First display the object's icon and then drag the icon onto the Start button.

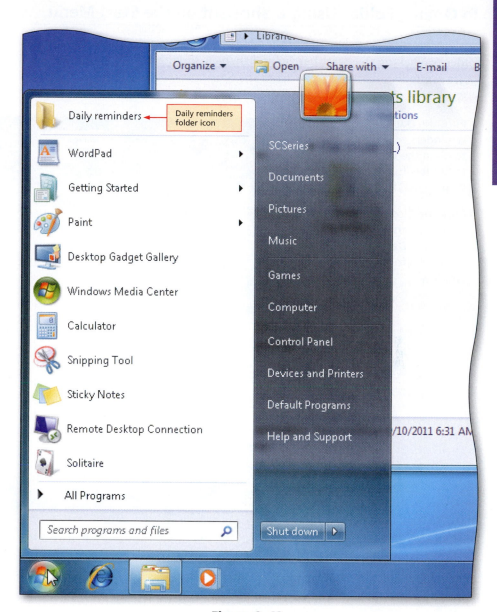

Figure 2–42

Other Ways
1. Right-drag folder icon onto Start button

To Open a Folder Using a Shortcut on the Start Menu

After placing a shortcut to the Daily reminders folder on the Start menu, you can open the Daily reminders folder by clicking the Start button and then clicking the Daily reminders command. The following step opens the Daily reminders folder window from the Start menu, and then closes the window.

- Click the Daily reminders command to open the Daily reminders folder (Figure 2–43).

- Click the Close button on the title bar of the Daily reminders folder window.

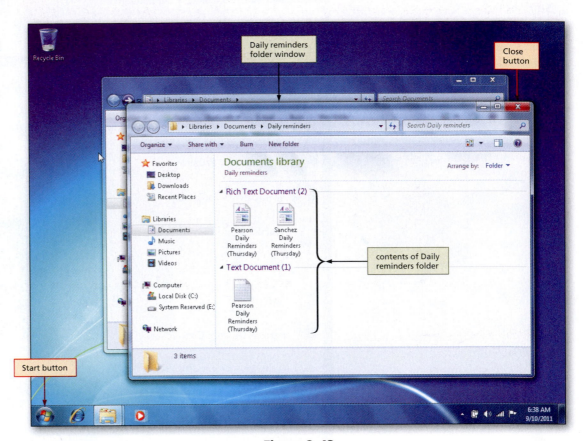

Figure 2–43

To Remove a Shortcut from the Start Menu

The capability of adding shortcuts to and removing them from the Start menu provides great flexibility when customizing Windows 7. Just as you can add shortcuts to the Start menu, you also can remove them. The following steps remove the Daily reminders shortcut from the Start menu.

- Display the Start menu.

- Right-click the Daily reminders command on the Start menu to display the shortcut menu (Figure 2–44).

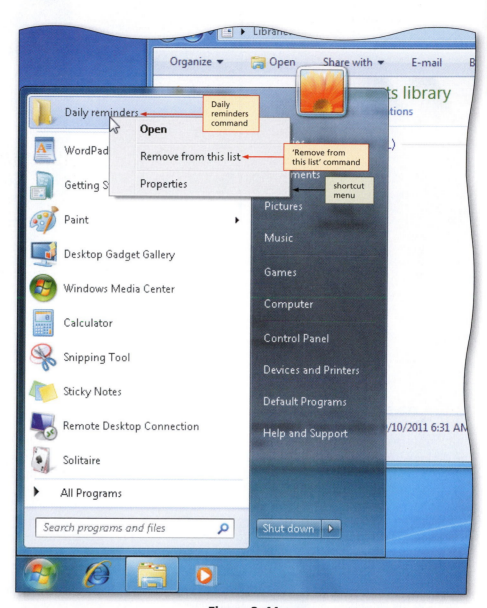

Figure 2–44

2

- Click the 'Remove from this list' command to remove the Daily reminders shortcut from the Start menu (Figure 2–45).

- Close the Start menu.

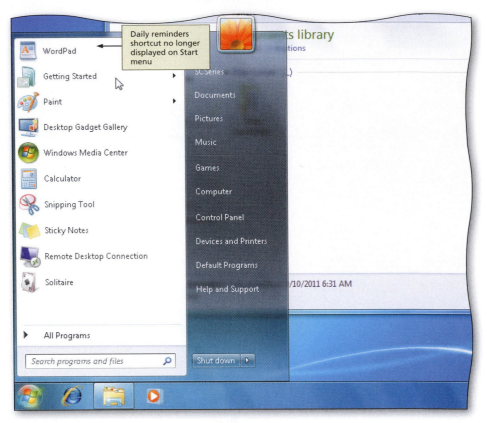

Figure 2–45

To Create a Shortcut on the Desktop

You also can create shortcuts directly on the desktop. Windows 7 recommends that only shortcuts be placed on the desktop rather than actual folders and files. This is to maximize the efficiency of file and folder searching, which will be covered in a later chapter. The following steps create a shortcut for the Daily reminders folder on the desktop.

1

- Right-click the Daily reminders folder to display the shortcut menu.

2

- Point to the Send to command to display the Send to submenu (Figure 2–46).

3

- Click the Desktop (create shortcut) command to create a shortcut on the desktop.

4

- Close the Documents library.

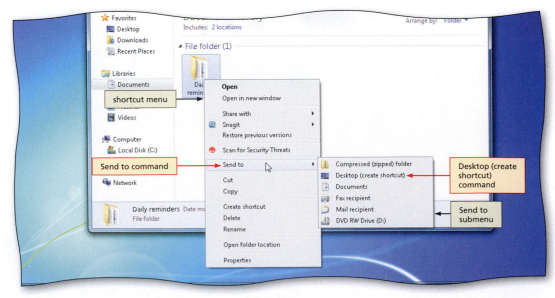

Figure 2–46

Opening and Modifying Documents within a Folder

When editing a document, you can open the document directly instead of first opening the program and then opening the document. You have received new information to add to Mr. Sanchez's daily reminders. An Internet meeting with the Sales Department in the western United States has been scheduled for 3:00 p.m. and the Sales Department must be notified of the meeting. To add this new item to the Daily reminders document, you first must open the Daily reminders folder that contains the document.

To Open a Folder Using a Shortcut on the Desktop

You have created a shortcut on the desktop for the Daily reminders folder, so you can use the shortcut icon to open the Daily reminders folder the same way you opened the Documents library using a shortcut in Chapter 1.

1 Double-click the Daily reminders shortcut on the desktop to open the Daily reminders folder.

To Move the Pearson Daily Reminders (Thursday) Text File to the Recycle Bin

You will not be using the Pearson Daily Reminders (Thursday) text file, so you will move it to the Recycle Bin.

1 If necessary, click the Restore Down button so that the Daily reminders folder is not maximized and the Recycle Bin icon is visible.

2 Drag the Pearson Daily Reminders (Thursday) text icon to the Recycle Bin.

To Open and Modify a Document in a Folder

Now you will edit the remaining document in the Daily reminders folder. The following steps open the Sanchez Daily Reminders (Thursday) document and add new text about the Internet meeting.

- Open the Sanchez Daily Reminders (Thursday) document in WordPad.

- Move the insertion point to the blank line below item 5 in the document.

- Type 6. Notify Sales – NetMeeting at 3:00 p.m. and then press the ENTER key to modify the Sanchez Daily Reminders (Thursday) document (Figure 2–47).

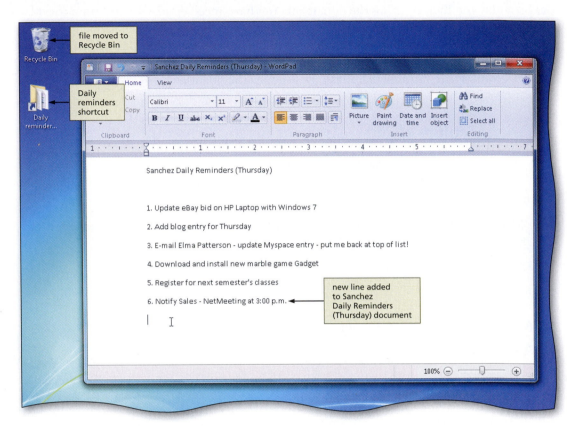

Figure 2–47

To Open and Modify Multiple Documents

Windows 7 allows you to have more than one document and program open at the same time so that you can work on multiple documents. The concept of multiple programs running at the same time is called **multitasking**. To illustrate how you can work with multiple windows open at the same time, you now will edit the Pearson Daily Reminders (Thursday) document to include a reminder to talk to Dan about Carol's birthday party. You will not have to close the Sanchez Daily Reminders (Thursday) document. The following steps open the Pearson Daily Reminders (Thursday) document and add the new reminder.

- Open the Pearson Daily Reminders (Thursday) document in WordPad.

Q&A Why does the font look different in the two documents?

Because the Pearson Daily Reminders (Thursday) document was created as a text file, its font will appear different from that of the Sanchez Daily Reminders (Thursday) document. Remember, Rich Text Format documents allow for more formatting than plain text files.

Q&A Why did the WordPad icon on the taskbar change?

When only one document is open in WordPad, the WordPad icon appears like a single button. If multiple documents are open, the icon changes to appear as a stacked button to indicate there is more than one document open.

2

- Move the insertion point to the end of the document in the WordPad window.

- Type 4. Call Dan – Birthday party for Carol and then press the ENTER key (Figure 2–48).

Opening Windows
In addition to clicking the taskbar button of an inactive window to make that window the active window, you can click any open area of the window. For example, many people click the title bar of a window to activate the window.

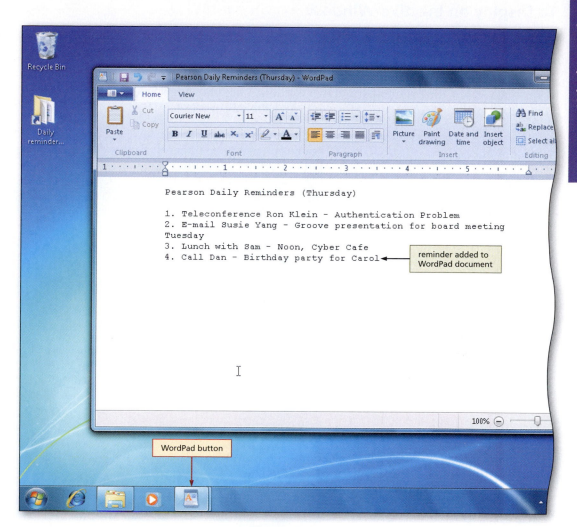

Figure 2–48

To Display an Inactive Window

After you have modified the Pearson Daily Reminders (Thursday) document, you receive information that a dinner meeting with Art Perez has been scheduled for Mr. Sanchez for 7:00 p.m. at The Crab House. You are directed to add this entry to Mr. Sanchez's reminders. To do this, you must make the Sanchez Daily Reminders (Thursday) - WordPad window the active window. The following steps make the Sanchez Daily Reminders (Thursday) - WordPad window active and enter the new reminder.

- Point to the WordPad button on the taskbar to display a live preview of the two documents (Figure 2–49).

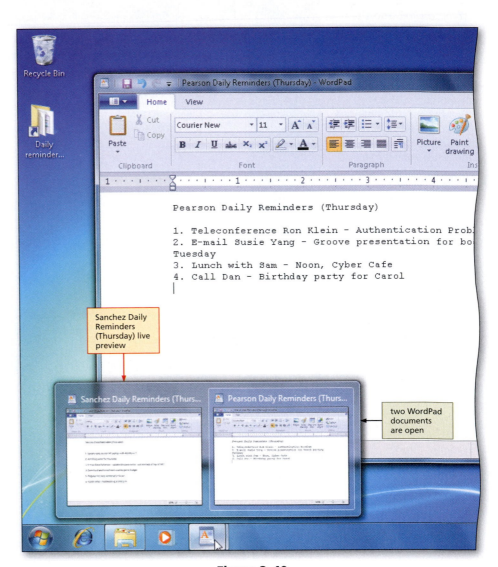

Figure 2–49

2

- Click the Sanchez Daily Reminders (Thursday) live preview to make it the active window (Figure 2–50).

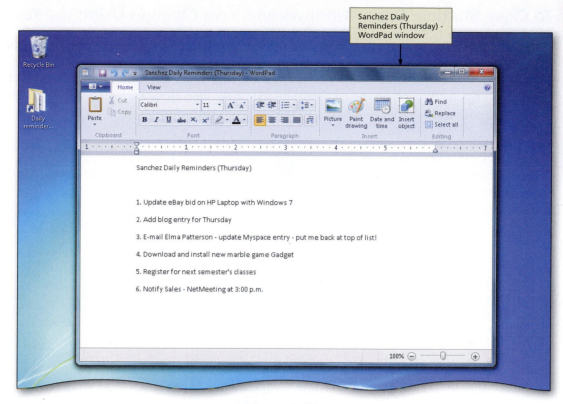

Figure 2–50

3

- When the window opens, type
  `7. Dinner with Art Perez – 7:00 p.m., The Crab House` and then press the ENTER key to update the document (Figure 2–51).

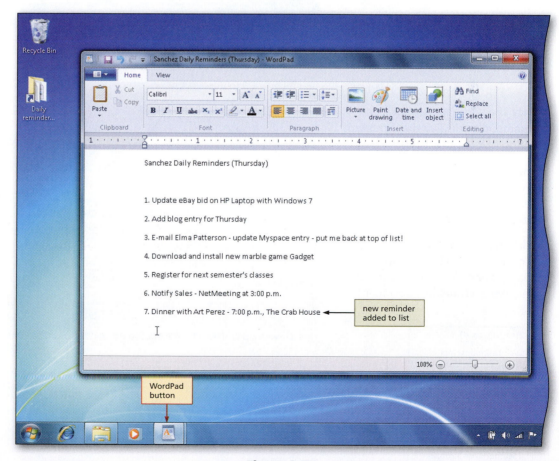

Figure 2–51

To Close Multiple Open Windows and Save Changes Using the Taskbar

When you have finished working with multiple windows, you should close them. If the windows are open on the desktop, you can click the Close button on the title bar of each open window to close them. Regardless of whether the windows are open on the desktop or are minimized using the Show desktop button, you can close the windows using the buttons on the taskbar. The following steps close the Sanchez Daily Reminders (Thursday) - WordPad and Pearson Daily Reminders (Thursday) - WordPad windows using the taskbar.

1

● Right-click the WordPad button on the taskbar to display a shortcut menu (Figure 2–52).

Q&A Why are there multiple instances of the documents in the Recent list?

The list shows the files you recently have edited, and does not remove duplicate listings. As a result, a document might appear in the list multiple times.

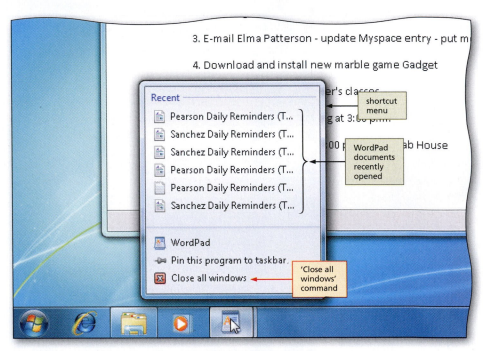

Figure 2–52

2

● Click the 'Close all windows' command to display the WordPad dialog box (Figure 2–53).

● Click the Save button in the WordPad dialog box to save the changes and close the Sanchez Daily Reminders (Thursday) document.

● Click the Save button in the WordPad dialog box to save the changes and close the Pearson Daily Reminders (Thursday) document.

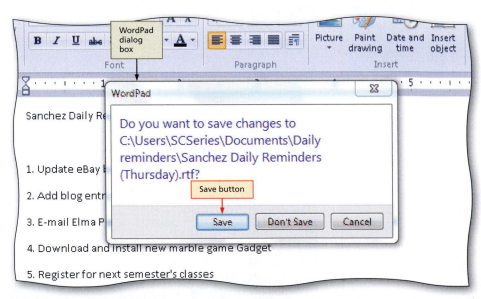

Figure 2–53

Other Ways

1. Click taskbar, select document, on WordPad menu click Save, click Close

2. Click taskbar, select document, on title bar click Close, click Save

3. Click taskbar, select document, on WordPad menu click Exit, click Save

To Print Multiple Documents from within a Folder

After you modify and save documents on the desktop, you might want to print them so that you have an updated hard copy of the documents. Earlier in this chapter, you used the Print command on the WordPad menu to print an open document. You also can print multiple documents from within a folder without actually opening the documents.

Before you can print them, you must select both of them. There are several different ways to select multiple items. You can select the first item, then while holding down the CTRL key, you can select the other items, or you can select the first item, then while holding down the SHIFT key, you can select the other items. The first method works when the items you want to select are not adjacent, whereas the second method (using the SHIFT key) only works if all of the items are next to each other. The following steps print both the Sanchez Daily Reminders (Thursday) and the Pearson Daily Reminders (Thursday) documents from the Daily reminders folder.

- Make the Daily reminders folder window the active window.

- Click the Pearson Daily Reminders (Thursday) icon in the Daily reminders folder to select the icon.

- Press and hold the SHIFT key, click the Sanchez Daily Reminders (Thursday) icon, and then release the SHIFT key to select both items in the Daily reminders folder (Figure 2–54).

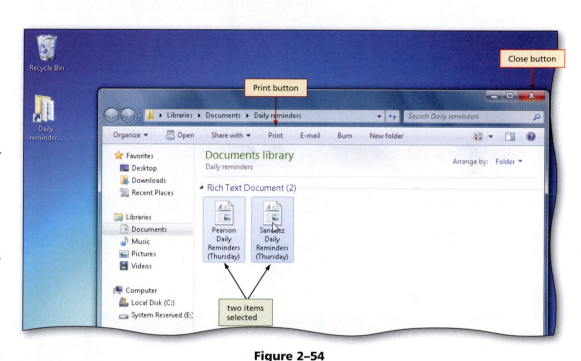

Figure 2–54

- Click the Print button on the toolbar to print the two files.

- Click the Close button in the Daily reminders window to close the Daily reminders window.

Other Ways

1. Select document icons, right-click, click Print

2. Select document icons, press ALT+F, press P

Copying a Folder onto a USB Flash Drive

A shortcut on the desktop is useful when you frequently use one or more documents within the folder. It is a good policy to make a copy of a folder and the documents within the folder so that if the folder or its contents are accidentally lost or damaged, you do not lose your work. This is referred to as making a backup of the files and folders. Another reason to make copies of files and folders is so that you can take the files and folders from one computer to another, for instance if you need to take a file or folder from a work computer to your home computer. A USB flash drive is a handy device for physically moving copies of files and folders between computers.

BTW

Backups
Copying a file or folder to a USB flash drive is one way to create a backup, but backing up files often is a much more elaborate process. Most backup systems use tape or portable hard disks that contain hundreds of gigabytes (billions of characters) or even terabytes (thousands of gigabytes).

To Copy a Folder onto a USB Flash Drive

You want to be able to use the files you have created on another computer. To do so, you will need to copy the files to your USB flash drive. The following steps copy the Daily reminders folder on to a USB flash drive.

- Insert a USB flash drive into an open USB port to display the AutoPlay dialog box (Figure 2–55).

Q&A Why does my USB flash drive have a different letter?

Depending on how many devices you have connected to your computer, your USB flash drive might have been assigned a different letter such as E or G.

Q&A What happens if the AutoPlay dialog box does not appear?

If your computer is not configured to display the AutoPlay dialog box automatically, click the Start button, click the Computer command on the Start menu, and then double-click the icon representing your USB flash drive. Next, skip to Step 3.

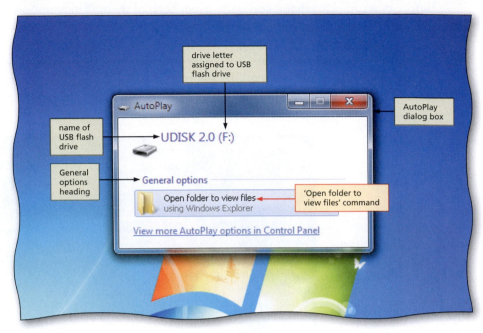

Figure 2–55

- Under the General options heading in the AutoPlay dialog box, click the 'Open folder to view files' command to open a folder window that displays the contents of your USB flash drive (Figure 2–56).

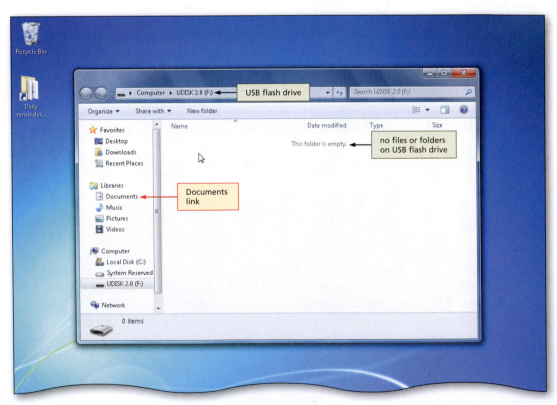

Figure 2–56

3

- Click the Documents link in the left pane to display the contents of the Documents library.

- Right-click the Daily reminders folder to display the shortcut menu.

- Point to the Send to command to display the Send to submenu (Figure 2–57).

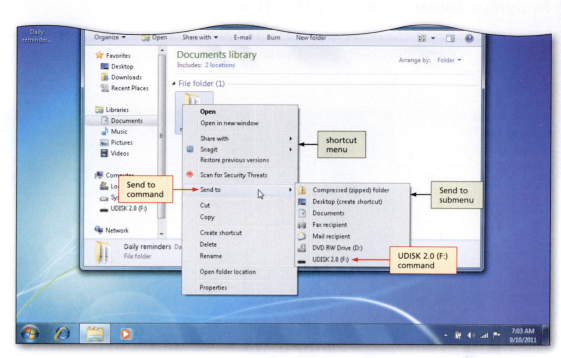

Figure 2–57

4

- Click the UDISK 2.0 (F:) command (or the name and drive letter representing your USB flash drive) to copy the folder to the USB flash drive (Figure 2–58).

Q&A

Can I back up the entire Documents library?

Yes. It is important to regularly back up the entire contents of your Documents library. To back up the Documents library, display the Start menu, right-click the Documents command, click Send to on the shortcut menu, and then click the location of the backup drive.

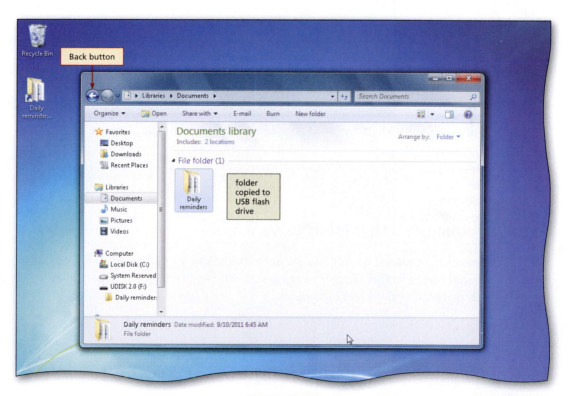

Figure 2–58

Other Ways

1. Press ALT+F, point to Send to, click UDISK 2.0 (F:)

To Open a Folder Stored on a USB Flash Drive

After copying a folder onto a USB flash drive, in order to verify that the folder has been copied properly, you can open the folder from the USB flash drive and view its contents. The following steps open a folder stored on a USB flash drive.

- Click the Back button on the Address bar of the Documents library to return to the USB flash drive window (Figure 2–59).

- Double-click the Daily reminders icon to open the folder and verify the files are in the Daily reminders folder.

- Close the Daily reminders folder window.

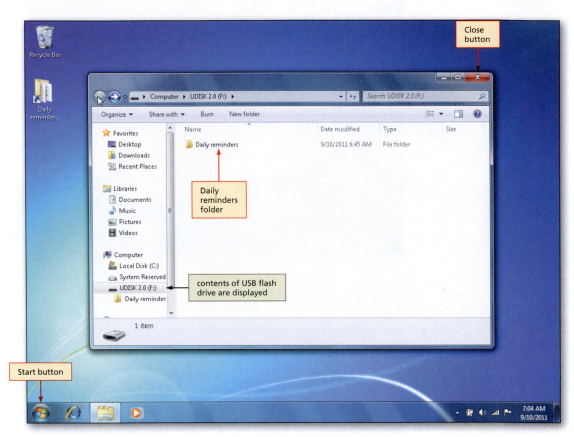

Figure 2–59

To Safely Remove a USB Flash Drive

If you want to open one of the documents in the folder stored on the USB flash drive, you can use one of the methods covered earlier in this chapter to open and edit the file. Once you are finished, you should safely remove the USB flash drive using the Eject command.

1

- Display the Start menu and then click the Computer command to open the Computer folder window (Figure 2–60).

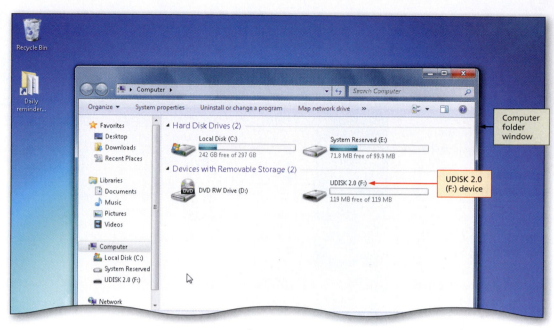

Figure 2–60

2
- Right-click the UDISK 2.0 (F:) device to display the shortcut menu (Figure 2–61).

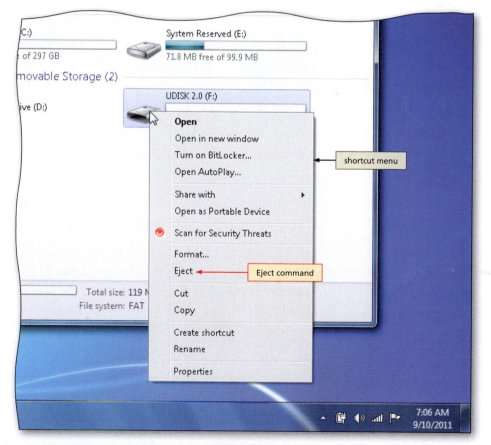

Figure 2–61

3

- Click the Eject command on the shortcut menu to close the USB flash drive and display the Safe To Remove Hardware message in the notification area (Figure 2–62).

- Remove the USB flash drive from the USB port.

- Close the Computer folder window.

Q&A

Why do I need to safely remove the USB flash drive?

Even though you might not have anything open on the USB flash drive, Windows 7 still might be accessing it in the background. Safely removing the USB flash drive tells Windows 7 to stop communicating with the device. If you were to remove it while Windows 7 was still accessing it, you could lose your data stored on it.

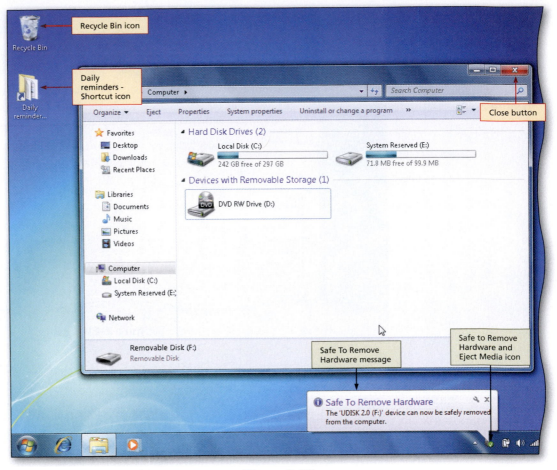

Figure 2–62

The Recycle Bin

Occasionally, you will want to delete files and folders from the Documents library. Windows 7 offers three different techniques to perform this operation: (1) Drag the object to the Recycle Bin; (2) right-drag the object to the Recycle Bin; and (3) right-click the object and then click Delete on the shortcut menu.

It is important to realize what you are doing when you delete a file or folder. When you delete a shortcut from the desktop, you only delete the shortcut icon and its reference to the file or folder. The file or folder itself is stored elsewhere on the hard disk and is not deleted. When you delete the icon for a file or folder (not a shortcut), the actual file or folder is deleted. A shortcut icon includes an arrow to indicate that it is a shortcut, whereas a file or folder does not have the arrow as part of its icon.

When you delete a file or folder, Windows 7 places these items in the Recycle Bin, which is an area on the hard disk that contains all the items you have deleted. If you are running low on hard disk space, one way to gain additional space is to empty the Recycle Bin. Up until the time you empty the Recycle Bin, you can recover deleted files. Even though you have this safety net, you should be careful whenever you delete anything from your computer.

To Delete a Shortcut from the Desktop

The following step removes a shortcut from the desktop.

1 Drag the Daily reminders - Shortcut icon onto the Recycle Bin icon on the desktop to move the shortcut to the Recycle Bin.

To Restore an Item from the Recycle Bin

At some point, you might discover that you accidentally deleted a shortcut, file, or folder that you did not want to delete. As long as you have not emptied the Recycle Bin, you can restore them. The following steps restore the Daily reminders - Shortcut icon to the desktop.

1

- Double-click the Recycle Bin icon to open the Recycle Bin.

- Click the Daily reminders - Shortcut icon to select it (Figure 2–63).

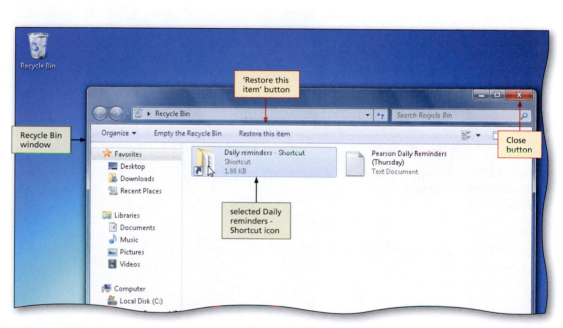

Figure 2–63

2

- Click the 'Restore this item' button to restore the Daily reminders - Shortcut icon to its previous location. In this case, the icon is restored to the desktop (Figure 2–64).

- Close the Recycle Bin window.

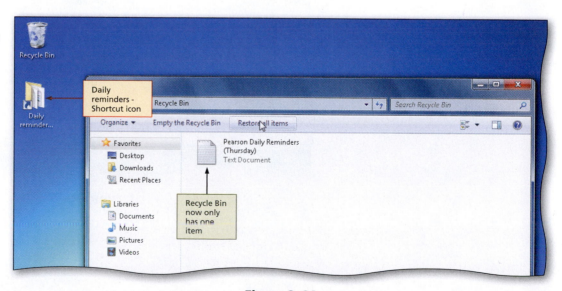

Figure 2–64

To Delete a Shortcut from the Desktop

Now you should delete the Daily reminders shortcut icon again so that you can leave the desktop how you found it.

 Drag the Daily reminders - Shortcut icon onto the Recycle Bin icon.

To Delete Multiple Files from a Folder

You can delete several files at one time. The following steps delete both the Sanchez Daily Reminders (Thursday) and the Pearson Daily Reminders (Thursday) documents.

1

- Open the Documents library.

- Open the Daily reminders folder.

- Click the Sanchez Daily Reminders (Thursday) document to select it.

- Press and hold the CTRL key, and then click the Pearson Daily Reminders (Thursday) document.

- Right-click the documents to display the shortcut menu (Figure 2–65).

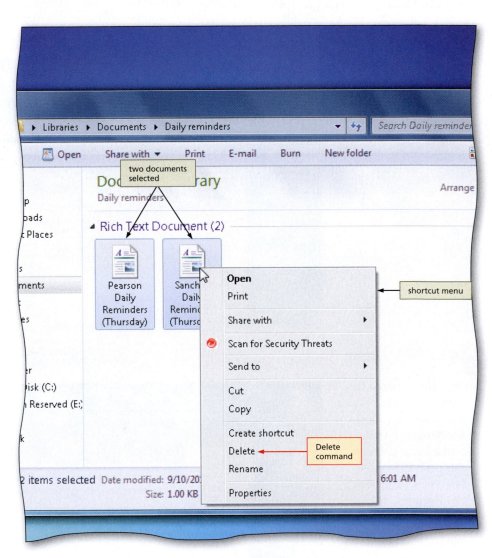

Figure 2–65

• Click the Delete command to display the Delete Multiple Items dialog box (Figure 2–66).

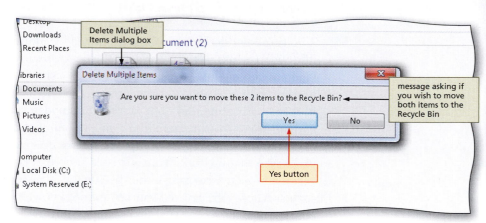

Figure 2–66

3

• Click the Yes button to move the files to the Recycle Bin (Figure 2–67).

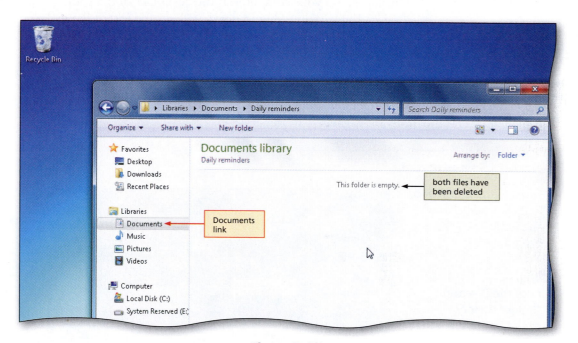

Figure 2–67

To Delete a Folder from the Documents Library and Empty the Recycle Bin

You also can delete folders from the Documents library using the same method.

1 Click the Documents link in the navigation pane.

2 Delete the Daily reminders folder.

3 Close the Documents library.

4 Right-click the Recycle Bin to display the shortcut menu.

5 Click the Empty Recycle Bin command.

6 Click the Yes button in the Delete Multiple Items dialog box to permanently delete the contents of the Recycle Bin.

Desktop Gadgets

The Windows desktop can be customized by adding miniprograms called gadgets. Through the use of these gadgets, the desktop can display useful tools and information. Gadgets can include items such as a clock, a small calendar, the current weather, and news headlines. In addition to the gadgets that come preinstalled with Windows 7, you also can find gadgets online that offer news, sports updates, entertainment, or other useful tools and information. Once you find a gadget online that you are interested in, you can download and install it on your computer. Before downloading and installing a gadget, first make sure that it comes from a trusted source. A **trusted source** is a source that has been verified to be trustworthy either by you, by a trusted friend, or by a trusted organization such as Microsoft. Trusted sources are not known to offer gadgets that contain offensive content or malicious code that could possibly damage your computer or do any other type of harm. If you download from a trusted source, you can feel secure about what you are installing on your computer. If the developer of the gadget you want to download is not a trusted source, you should not download and install the gadget.

To Add Multiple Gadgets to the Desktop

As you learned in Chapter 1, you can add gadgets to the Windows desktop. You also can customize the existing gadgets. Depending on the gadget, different options are available to you for customizing the gadget. You decide to add the Clock and the Slide Show gadgets to the desktop.

1
- Display the Start menu, and click All Programs to display the All Programs list.

2
- Click the Desktop Gadget Gallery command to open the Gadget Gallery.

3
- Double-click the Clock gadget in the Gadget Gallery to add the gadget to the desktop.

4
- Double-click the Slide Show gadget in the Gadget Gallery to add the gadget to the desktop (Figure 2–68).

5
- Close the Gadget Gallery window.

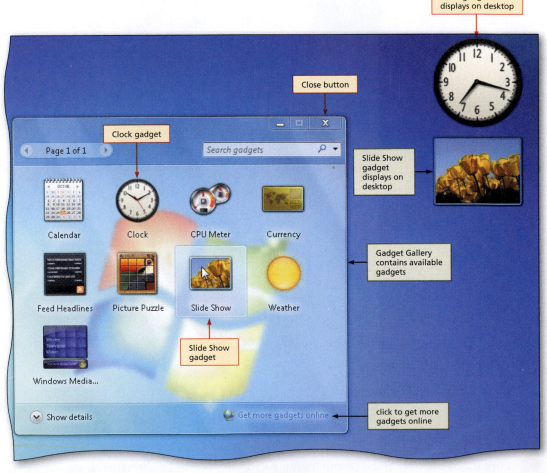

Figure 2–68

To Customize the Clock Gadget

You decide to experiment with the Clock gadget as you would like to see a different clock design, and you would like to add your name to it. The following steps customize and personalize the Clock gadget.

- Right-click the Clock gadget on the desktop to display the shortcut menu (Figure 2–69).

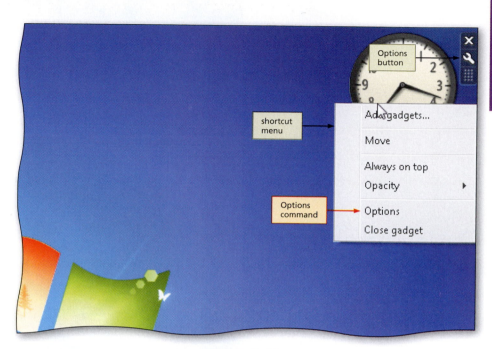

Figure 2–69

- Click the Options command to display the Clock dialog box (Figure 2–70).

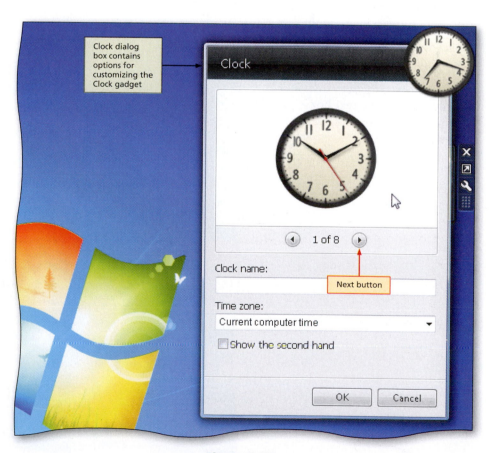

Figure 2–70

3

- Click the Next button three times to display the neon light clock (Figure 2–71).

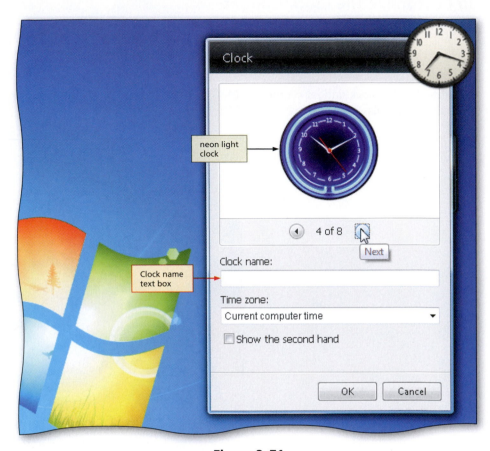

Figure 2–71

4

- Click the Clock name text box to select it.

- Type Steve's (or your own name) in the Clock name text box (Figure 2–72).

Figure 2–72

5

- Click the OK button to apply your changes and close the Clock dialog box (Figure 2–73).

Q&A

Do all gadgets have the same options?

Every gadget has different options. For example, the Calendar gadget can be customized to show a week or a month, instead of just the current day.

new clock style applied to Clock gadget

Figure 2–73

To Undo the Changes to the Clock Gadget

Although you like the new look for the Clock gadget, you decide that the original style was easier to read. You, therefore, want to undo the changes you have made. The following steps undo the changes to the Clock gadget.

1

- Point to the Clock gadget to display the icons associated with the gadget.

- Click the Options button to display the Clock dialog box (Figure 2–74).

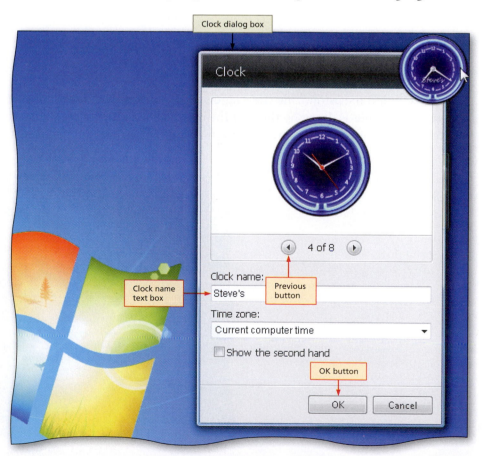

Clock dialog box

Clock

4 of 8

Clock name:
Steve's

Previous button

Clock name text box

Time zone:
Current computer time

Show the second hand

OK button

OK   Cancel

Figure 2–74

2

- Click the Previous button three times to display the original clock.

- Delete the text from the Clock name text box (Figure 2–75).

- Click the OK button to apply your changes and close the Clock dialog box.

Figure 2–75

To Rearrange Gadgets on the Desktop

In addition to customizing the gadgets, you also can rearrange the gadgets on the desktop. Rearranging gadgets is as simple as dragging them to the desired location. You decide to see how the gadgets would look in another arrangement. The following steps rearrange the gadgets on the desktop.

1

- Point to the Drag gadget button located to the right of the Clock gadget (Figure 2–76).

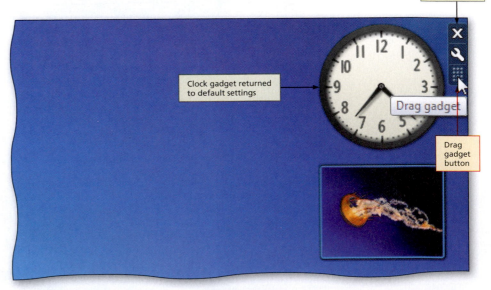

Figure 2–76

2

- Click the Drag gadget button and drag the Clock gadget below the Recycle Bin to reposition it on the desktop (Figure 2–77).

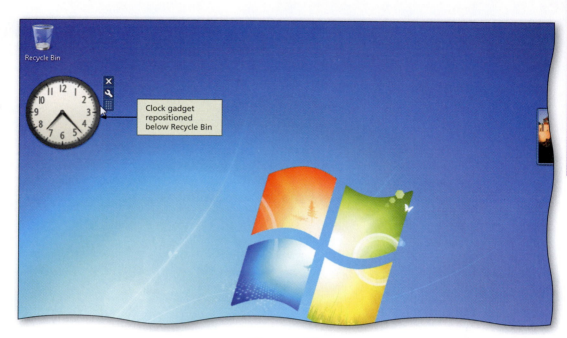

Figure 2–77

To Search for Gadgets Online

Now you decide to browse the Internet for new gadgets, although you are not going to download and install any new gadgets at this time. You want to become familiar with what types of gadgets are available. In fact, because you have been so busy, you want to find some gadgets to provide quick relief from work, without the gadgets becoming too distracting or time consuming. The following steps search for gadgets online.

1

- Display the Start menu, and click All Programs to display the All Programs list.

- Click the Desktop Gadget Gallery command to open the Gadget Gallery (Figure 2–78).

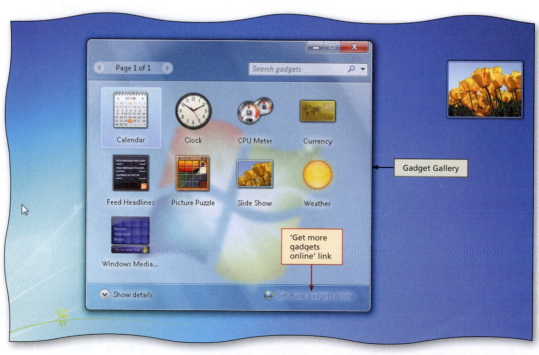

Figure 2–78

2

● Click the 'Get more gadgets online' link to open Windows Internet Explorer and display the Personalization Gallery Web page (Figure 2–79).

Q&A

Why do I see different gadgets on my computer?

The Personalization Gallery Web site is frequently updated. Each time you search for gadgets online, different gadgets might display.

Figure 2–79

3

● Scroll down to view the Desktop gadgets tab.

● Click the Desktop gadgets tab to display the available Desktop gadgets (Figure 2–80).

 **Experiment**

● Click the 'Get more desktop gadgets' link, located below the featured gadgets, to see what gadgets other developers have created. Review the various categories and available gadgets.

Figure 2–80

To Close the Internet Explorer and Gadget Gallery Windows

After having reviewed some of the gadgets available online, you decide to close Internet Explorer. You do not want to download gadgets yet; you want to wait until you have verified that the gadgets you want are from trusted sources. The following steps close Internet Explorer and the Gadget Gallery windows.

1 Click the Close button to close Internet Explorer.

2 Click the Close button in the Gadget Gallery to close the window.

To Remove Gadgets from the Desktop

Not only can you place gadgets on the desktop, you can remove them. The following steps remove the gadgets you added.

1 Point to the Clock gadget and click the Close button to remove the Clock gadget from the desktop.

2 Point to the Slide Show gadget and click the Close button to remove the Slide Show gadget from the desktop.

To Log Off from the Computer

After removing the gadgets from the desktop, you decide to log off the computer. The following steps log off the computer.

1 Display the Start menu.

2 Point to the arrow to the right of the Shut down button to display the Shut Down options menu.

3 Click the Log off command, and then wait for Windows 7 to prompt you to save any unsaved data, if any, and log off.

To Turn Off the Computer

The following step turns off the computer. If you are not sure whether you should turn off the computer, read the following step without actually performing it.

1 Click the Shut down button to turn off the computer.

Chapter Summary

In this chapter, you learned to create text documents using both the application-centric approach and document-centric approach. You moved these documents to the Documents library, and then modified and printed them. You created a new folder in the Documents library, placed documents in the folder, and copied the new folder onto a USB flash drive. You worked with multiple documents open at the same time. You placed a folder shortcut on both the Start menu and on the desktop. Using various methods, you deleted shortcuts, documents, and a folder. Finally, you learned how to customize a gadget, rearrange gadgets on the desktop, search for new gadgets online, and remove gadgets from the desktop. The items listed below include all the new Windows 7 skills you have learned in this chapter.

1. To Launch a Program and Create a Document (WIN 69)
2. Save a Document to the Documents Library (WIN 71)
3. Open the Print Dialog Box from a Program (WIN 75)
4. Print a Document (WIN 76)
5. Edit a Document (WIN 76)
6. Save and Close a Document (WIN 77)
7. Open the Documents Library (WIN 78)
8. Create a Blank Document in the Documents Library (WIN 79)
9. Name a Document in the Documents Library (WIN 80)
10. Open a Document with WordPad (WIN 81)
11. Add Text to a Blank Document (WIN 82)
12. Save a Text Document in Rich Text Format (RTF) (WIN 82)
13. Change the View to Small Icons (WIN 84)
14. Arrange Items in Groups by File Type (WIN 85)
15. Create and Name a Folder in the Documents Library (WIN 86)
16. Move a Document into a Folder (WIN 87)
17. Change Location Using the Address Bar (WIN 89)
18. Display and Use the Preview Pane (WIN 91)
19. Close the Preview Pane (WIN 92)
20. Change Location Using the Back Button on the Address Bar (WIN 92)
21. Add a Shortcut on the Start Menu (WIN 93)
22. Open a Folder Using a Shortcut on the Start Menu (WIN 96)
23. Remove a Shortcut from the Start Menu (WIN 97)
24. Create a Shortcut on the Desktop (WIN 98)
25. Open and Modify a Document in a Folder (WIN 100)
26. Open and Modify Multiple Documents (WIN 100)
27. Display an Inactive Window (WIN 102)
28. Close Multiple Open Windows and Save Changes Using the Taskbar (WIN 104)
29. Print Multiple Documents from within a Folder (WIN 105)
30. Copy a Folder onto a USB Flash Drive (WIN 106)
31. Open a Folder Stored on a USB Flash Drive (WIN 108)
32. Safely Remove a USB Flash Drive (WIN 108)
33. Restore an Item from the Recycle Bin (WIN 111)
34. Delete Multiple Files from a Folder (WIN 112)
35. Add Multiple Gadgets to the Desktop (WIN 114)
36. Customize the Clock Gadget (WIN 115)
37. Undo the Changes to the Clock Gadget (WIN 117)
38. Rearrange Gadgets on the Desktop (WIN 118)
39. Search for Gadgets Online (WIN 119)

Learn It Online

Test your knowledge of chapter content and key terms.

Instructions: To complete the Learn It Online exercises, start your browser, click the Address bar, and then enter the Web address `scsite.com/win7/learn`. When the Windows 7 Learn It Online page is displayed, click the link for the exercise you want to complete and then read the instructions.

Chapter Reinforcement TF, MC, and SA

A series of true/false, multiple-choice, and short-answer questions that test your knowledge of the chapter content.

Flash Cards

An interactive learning environment where you identify chapter key terms associated with displayed definitions.

Practice Test

A series of multiple-choice questions that test your knowledge of chapter content and key terms.

Who Wants To Be a Computer Genius?

An interactive game that challenges your knowledge of chapter content in the style of a television quiz show.

Wheel of Terms

An interactive game that challenges your knowledge of chapter key terms in the style of the television show *Wheel of Fortune*.

Crossword Puzzle Challenge

A crossword puzzle that challenges your knowledge of key terms presented in the chapter.

Apply Your Knowledge

Reinforce the skills and apply the concepts you learned in this chapter.

Creating a Document with WordPad

Instructions: Use WordPad to create the homework list shown in Figure 2–81.

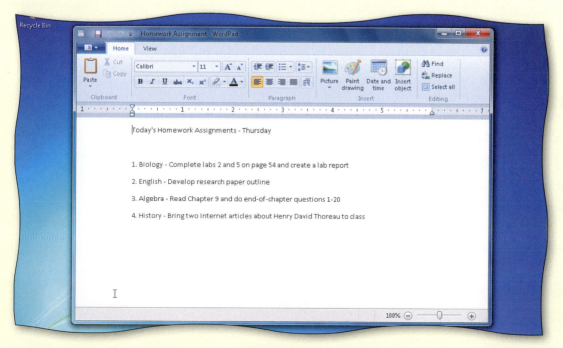

Figure 2–81

Continued >

Apply Your Knowledge *continued*

Part 1: Launching WordPad
1. Click the Start button.
2. Launch WordPad.

Part 2: Creating a Document Using WordPad
1. Type Today's Homework Assignments - Thursday and then press the ENTER key twice.
2. Type 1. Biology - Complete labs 2 and 5 on page 54 and create a lab report and then press the ENTER key.
3. Type 2. English - Develop research paper outline and then press the ENTER key.
4. Type 3. Algebra - Read Chapter 9 and do end-of-chapter questions 1-20 and then press the ENTER key.
5. Type 4. History - Bring two Internet articles about Henry David Thoreau to class and then press the ENTER key.

Part 3: Printing the Today's Homework Document
1. Click the WordPad button and then click Print to display the Print dialog box. Click the Print button to print the document.

Part 4: Saving and Closing the WordPad Window
1. Insert a USB flash drive.
2. Save your document as Homework Assignment to the USB flash drive.
3. Close WordPad and any open windows.

Extend Your Knowledge

Extend the skills you learned in this chapter and experiment with new skills. You might need to use Help to complete the assignment.

Finding File and Folder Help

Instructions: Use Windows Help and Support to learn about files and folders.

Part 1: Creating a Document in the Documents Library
1. Start WordPad and create a WordPad document in the Documents library. Save the document as Working with Files and Folders.
2. Maximize the Working with Files and Folders - WordPad window.

Part 2: Launching Windows Help and Support
1. Click the Start button on the taskbar.
2. Click Help and Support on the Start menu.
3. Click Learn about Windows Basics in the 'Not sure where to start?' area.
4. Scroll down to the Programs, files, and folders area.
5. Click 'Working with files and folders'. The 'Working with files and folders' page displays (Figure 2–82).

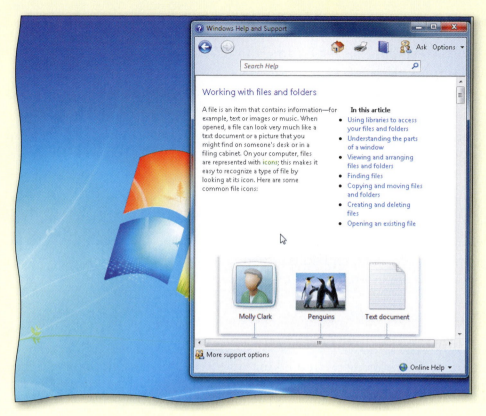

Figure 2–82

Part 3: Copying Selected Text to the WordPad Window

1. Click the 'Creating and deleting files' link.

2. Click and drag from the 'Creating and deleting files' heading through the paragraphs below to highlight them.

3. Right-click the highlighted text to display a shortcut menu.

4. Click Copy on the shortcut menu.

5. Click the Working with Files and Folders button in the taskbar button area to display the Working with Files and Folders - WordPad window.

6. Right-click the text area of the WordPad window to display a shortcut menu.

7. Click Paste. The Creating and deleting files text displays in the window.

8. Click the WordPad button to display the WordPad menu, and then click the Save button to save the document.

9. Click the Windows Help and Support button in the taskbar button area to display the Windows Help and Support window.

Part 4: Copying Additional Text to the WordPad Window

1. Using the method shown in Part 3, scroll up, and copy and paste the following headings and paragraphs to the WordPad window: 'Using libraries to access your files and folders', 'Understanding the parts of a window', and 'Finding files'.

2. Click the WordPad button to display the WordPad menu, and then click the Save button to save the document.

3. Click the WordPad button to display the WordPad menu, click Print on the WordPad menu, and then click the Print button to print the document.

Continued >

Extend Your Knowledge *continued*

4. Close the Working with Files and Folders - WordPad window.

5. Close the Windows Help and Support window.

6. Insert a USB flash drive and copy the Working with Files and Folders document in the Documents library to the USB flash drive.

7. Delete the Working with Files and Folders document from the Documents library and empty the Recycle Bin.

In the Lab

Use the guidelines, concepts, and skills presented in this chapter to increase your knowledge of Windows 7. Labs are listed in order of increasing difficulty.

Lab 1: Windows 7 Seminar Announcement and Schedule

Instructions: A two-day Windows 7 seminar will be offered to all teachers at your school. You have been put in charge of developing two text documents for the seminar. One document announces the seminar and will be sent to all teachers. The other document contains the schedule for the seminar. You prepare the documents shown in Figures 2–83 and 2–84 using WordPad.

Part 1: Creating the Windows 7 Seminar Announcement Document

1. Open a new WordPad document. Save the document as Windows 7 Seminar Announcement on the desktop.

2. Enter the text shown in Figure 2–83.

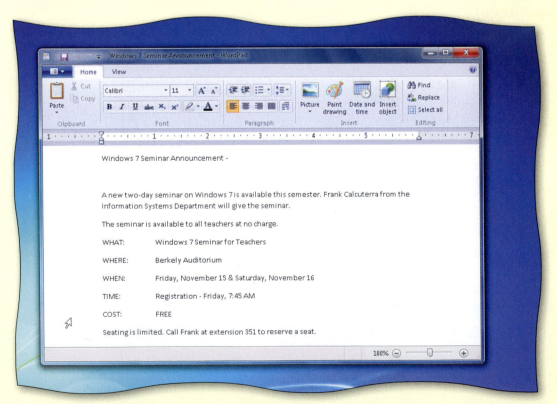

Figure 2–83

3. Save the document.

4. Print the document.

5. Close the document.

6. Move the document to the Documents library.

7. Create a folder in the Documents library called Windows 7 Seminar Documents.

8. Place the Windows 7 Seminar Announcement document in the Windows 7 Seminar Documents folder.

Part 2: Creating the Windows 7 Seminar Schedule Document

1. Open a new WordPad document. Save the document as Windows 7 Seminar Schedule on the desktop.

2. Enter the text shown in Figure 2–84.

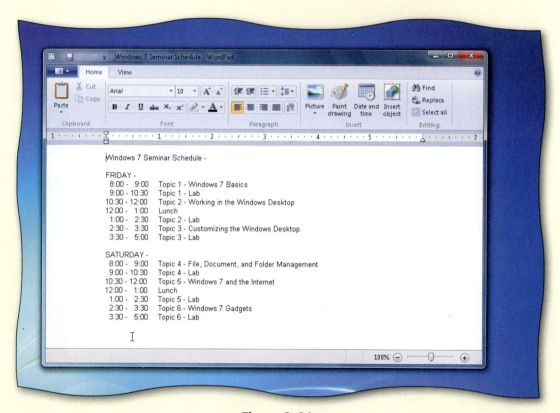

Figure 2–84

3. Save the document.

4. Print the document.

5. Close the document.

6. Move the Windows 7 Seminar Schedule document to the Documents library.

7. Place the Windows 7 Seminar Schedule document in the Windows 7 Seminar Documents folder.

8. Move the Windows 7 Seminar Documents folder to your USB flash drive.

In the Lab

Lab 2: Researching Online Gadgets

Instructions: You are asked to create a list of gadgets that your company might find useful. Using the Personalization Gallery Web site, you will create a gadget list that lists the gadgets and the categories in which they are located. Your boss is interested in four main categories. Create the headings shown in Figure 2–85 using the application-centric approach and WordPad. Then follow the steps to find some potentially useful gadgets online.

Perform the following tasks:

1. Start WordPad.
2. Enter the text shown in Figure 2–85.

Figure 2–85

3. Use Save as to save the document in the Documents library with the file name Potential Gadgets.
4. Right-click an empty area of the desktop and then click the Gadgets command on the shortcut menu to display the Gadget Gallery.
5. Click the 'Get more gadgets online' link to open the Personalization Gallery Web page.
6. Scroll down to display the Desktop gadgets tab. Click the tab to display the Desktop gadgets area. Click the 'Get more desktop gadgets' link.

7. Click the 'News and feeds' link.

8. Find at least three news gadgets that you think a business might use. Write down the name of each gadget you selected and who developed it in the following space.

_____

_____

_____

9. In WordPad, under the News and Feeds heading, enter a numbered list stating the names of the three gadgets and who developed them.

10. In Internet Explorer, click the All categories link. Click on the 'Safety and security' link.

11. Find at least three safety and security gadgets that you think a business might use. Write down the name of each gadget, who developed it, and why it might be of use to a business.

_____

_____

_____

12. In WordPad, under the Safety and Security heading, enter a numbered list that includes the names of the gadgets, who developed them, and why they might be of use to a business.

13. In Internet Explorer, click All categories. Click the Search tools link.

14. Find at least three search tool gadgets that you think a business might use. In WordPad, under the Search Tools heading, enter a numbered list stating the names of the three gadgets and who developed them.

15. In Internet Explorer, return to the main list of gadgets. Click the 'Tools and utilities' link.

16. Find at least three tools or utilities gadgets that you think a business might use. In WordPad, under the Tools and Utilities heading, enter a numbered list stating the names of the three gadgets and who developed them.

17. Save the document.

18. Print the document from WordPad.

19. Close WordPad.

20. Insert a USB flash drive in an open USB port.

21. Right-click the Potential Gadgets icon in the Documents library, click Send to, and then click the USB flash drive.

22. Close the Documents library.

23. Safely remove the USB flash drive.

24. Close the Gadget Gallery.

25. Close Internet Explorer.

In the Lab

Lab 3: Creating, Saving, and Printing Automobile Information Documents

Instruction: For eight months, you have accumulated data about your 2008 Chevy Malibu automobile. Some of the information is written on pieces of paper, while the rest is in the form of receipts. You have decided to organize this information using your computer. You create the documents shown in Figures 2–86 and 2–87 using the application-centric approach and WordPad.

Part 1: Creating the Automobile Information Document

1. Create a new WordPad document. Save the document on the desktop with the file name Automobile Information.

2. Enter the text shown in Figure 2–86.

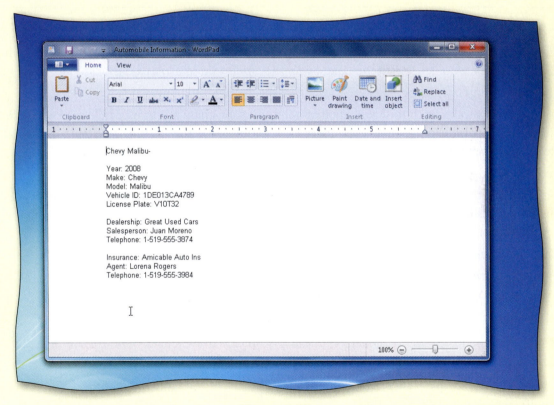

Figure 2–86

3. Save the document.

4. Print the document.

5. Create a folder in the Documents library called Automobile Documents.

6. Place the Automobile Information document in the Automobile Documents folder.

Part 2: Other Automobile Documents

1. Create the Phone Numbers document (Figure 2–87a), the Automobile Gas Mileage document (Figure 2–87b), and the Automobile Maintenance document on the desktop (Figure 2–87c).

2. Move each document into the Documents library.

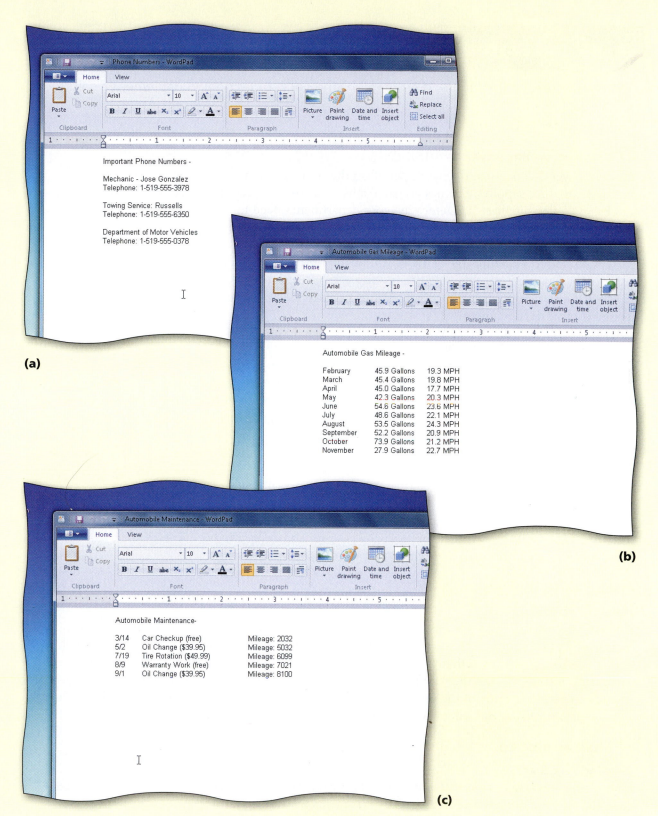

(a)

(b)

(c)

Figure 2–87

3. Print each document.

4. Place each document in the Automobile Documents folder.

5. Move the Automobile Documents folder to a USB flash drive.

Cases and Places

Apply your creative thinking and problem solving skills to design and implement a solution.

• EASIER   •• MORE DIFFICULT

• 1 Creating an Employer Request List

Your employer is concerned that some people in the company are not thoroughly researching purchases of office supplies. She has prepared a list of steps she would like everyone to follow when purchasing office supplies: (1) Determine your department's need for office supplies, (2) identify at least two Internet sites that sell the office supplies you need, and (3) obtain prices for the office supplies from their Web sites.

Your employer wants you to use WordPad to prepare a copy of this list to post in every department. Save and print the document. After you have printed one copy of the document, try experimenting with different WordPad features to make the list more eye-catching. Save and print a revised copy of the document.

• 2 Locating Gadgets Online

As you have learned, you can add useful gadgets to your desktop. You would like to find out more about gadgets and install one for yourself. Visit the Windows 7 Personalization Gallery Web site and locate gadgets that will provide up-to-date weather. Download one and try it out. Write a brief report about what you found online and what you think about weather gadgets. Include the name and developer of the gadget you installed.

•• 3 Researching Retraining Costs

Retraining employees can be an expensive task for a business of any size. Many Windows 7 users believe that the Windows 7 operating system is an intuitive, easy-to-learn operating system that can reduce retraining costs. Using the Internet, current computer magazines, or other resources, research this topic and write a brief report summarizing your findings. Explain those features that you think make the Windows 7 operating system an easy-to-use operating system.

•• 4 Research Gadgets for Personal Use

Make It Personal

Just like for business, there are lots of useful gadgets for you to find and use. Look online for a multimedia gadget that will let you play a radio station, monitor your Facebook account, or watch a television show. Select a few that you find interesting. Download and install them. Write a brief report comparing and contrasting them. Which one is the easiest to use? Which one is the worst? If you decide you do not like any of the ones you downloaded, try more until you find one you like. Include in your report how likely you will or will not download more gadgets to use in the future.

•• 5 Researching Course Registration Procedures

Working Together

Registering for classes can be a daunting task for incoming college freshmen. As someone who has gone through the process, prepare a guide for students who are about to register for the first time next semester. Working with classmates, research and create your guide. Your guide should contain two or more documents, including a schedule of key dates and times, a description of the registration procedure, and suggestions for a smooth registration process. Give the documents suitable names and save them in a folder in the Documents library. Print each document.

3 | File and Folder Management

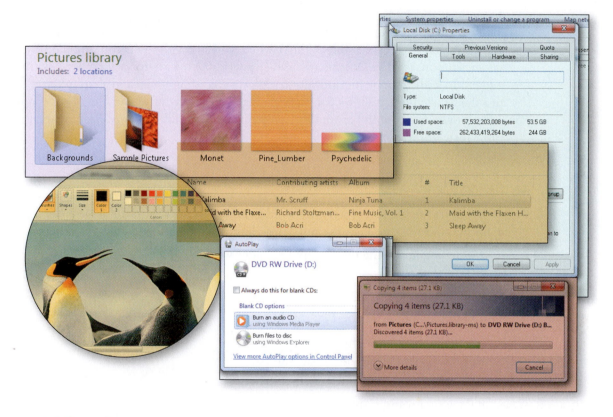

Objectives

You will have mastered the material in this chapter when you can:

- View the contents of a drive and folder using the Computer folder window

- View the properties of files and folders

- Find files and folders from a folder window

- Cascade, stack, and view windows side by side on the desktop

- View the contents of the Pictures library

- Open and use the Windows Photo Viewer

- View pictures as a slide show

- View the contents of the Music library

- View information about an audio file

- Play an audio file using Windows Media Player

- Create a backup on a USB flash drive and an optical disc

- Restore a folder from a backup on a USB flash drive

3 | File and Folder Management

Introduction

In Chapter 2, you used Windows 7 to create documents on the desktop and work with documents and folders in the Documents library. Windows 7 also allows you to examine the files and folders on the computer in a variety of other ways, enabling you to choose the easiest and most accessible manner when working with the computer. The Computer folder window and the Documents library provide two ways for you to work with files and folders. In addition, the Pictures library allows you to organize and share picture files, and the Music library allows you to organize and share your music files. This chapter illustrates how to work with files in the Computer folder, as well as the Documents, Pictures, and Music libraries.

Overview

As you read this chapter, you will learn how to work with the Computer folder window, as well as the Pictures and Music libraries, by performing these general tasks:

- Opening and using the Computer folder window
- Searching for files and folders
- Managing open windows
- Opening and using the Pictures library
- Using Windows Photo Viewer
- Opening and using the Music library
- Playing a music file in Windows Media Player
- Backing up and restoring a folder

Plan Ahead

Working with Files and Folders
Working with files and folders requires a basic knowledge of how to use the Windows 7 desktop.

1. **Be aware that there might be different levels of access on the computer you will be using.** A user account can be restricted to a certain level of access to the computer. Depending on the level of access that has been set for your account, you might or might not be able to perform certain operations.

2. **Identify how to connect a USB flash drive to your computer.** Depending upon the setup of your computer, there might be several ways to connect a USB flash drive to your computer. You should know which USB ports you can use to connect a USB flash drive to your computer.

3. **Determine if your computer has speakers.** Some computer labs do not provide speakers. If you are going to be using a computer in a lab, you need to know if the computer has speakers or if you will need to bring earbuds.

(continued)

(continued)

4. **Determine whether you have access to the sample files installed with Windows 7.** To complete the steps in this chapter, you will need access to the sample pictures, videos, and sounds installed with Windows 7.

5. **Determine if your computer has an optical disc burner.** Some labs do not provide optical disc burners. If you are going to be using a computer in a lab, you should know whether you have access to an optical disc burner to back up your files.

6. **Understand copyright issues.** When working with multimedia files, you should be aware that most pictures, movies, and music files are protected by copyright. Before you use these files, you should make sure that you are aware of any copyright restrictions. Although you can download a picture or music file from the Internet, it does not mean you have permission to use it.

The Computer Folder Window

As noted in previous chapters, the Start menu displays the Computer command. Clicking the Computer command displays a window that contains the storage devices that are installed on the computer. The Computer folder window looks very similar to the Documents library that you worked with in the previous chapter. This is because Windows 7 uses folder windows to display the contents of the computer. A **folder window** consists of an Address bar at the top, a toolbar containing various options, a Navigation pane on the left below the toolbar, a headings bar and list area on the right below the toolbar, and a Details pane at the bottom of the window. Depending upon which folder or library you are viewing—Computer, Documents, Pictures, and so on—the folder window will display the toolbar options that are most appropriate for working with the contents.

BTW

Managing Windows
Having multiple windows open on the desktop can intimidate some users. Consider working in a maximized window, and when you want to switch to another open window, click its button on the taskbar and then maximize it. Many people find it easier to work with maximized windows.

To Open and Maximize the Computer Folder Window

The list area of the Computer folder window groups objects based upon the different types of devices connected to your computer. The Hard Disk Drives group contains the Local Disk (C:) icon that represents the hard disk on the computer. The **hard disk** is where you can store files, documents, and folders. Storing data on a hard disk is more convenient than storing data on a USB flash drive because the hard disk is more convenient and generally has more available storage space. A computer always will have at least one hard disk, which normally is designated as drive C. On the computer represented by the Computer folder window in Figure 3–1, the icon consists of an image of a hard disk and a **disk label**, or title, Local Disk, and a drive letter (C:). The label text can change, and may differ depending upon the name assigned to the hard disk. For example, some people label their drives based upon usage; therefore, it could be called PRIMARY (C:), where PRIMARY is the label given to the hard disk as it is the drive that houses the operating system and main programs.

The steps on the following page open and maximize the Computer folder window so that you can view its contents.

1

- Display the Start menu.

2

- Click the Computer command to open the Computer folder window. If necessary, maximize the Computer folder window.

Q&A

What does the Devices with Removable Storage group contain?

The Devices with Removable Storage group contains the DVD RW Drive (D:) icon, indicating that there is a DVD burner attached to your computer. If the icon displayed a CD RW Drive (D:), it would indicate that your computer has a CD burner instead of a DVD burner. If your computer has a CD or DVD drive that cannot burn to the discs, you would not see the RW. **RW** is an abbreviation for rewritable, which means that the drive can write data onto read/writable optical discs.

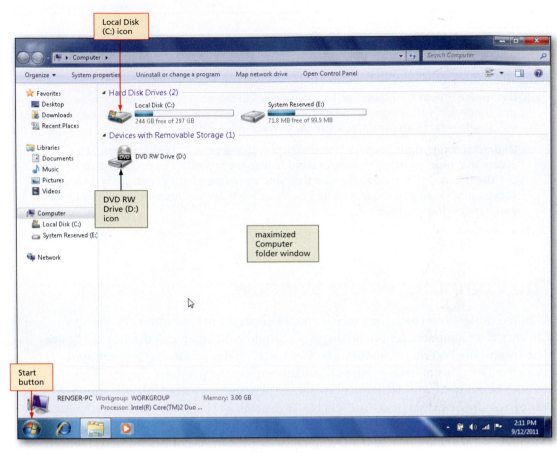

Figure 3–1

Q&A

Why do the icons on my computer differ from the figure?

It is possible that some icons might appear that you do not recognize. Software vendors develop hundreds of icons to represent their products. Each icon is supposed to be unique, meaningful, and eye-catching. You can purchase thousands of icons on a CD or DVD that you can use to represent documents you create.

To Display Properties for the Local Disk (C:) Drive in the Details Pane

The Details pane of a folder window displays the properties of devices, programs, files, and folders, which all are considered to be objects by Windows 7. Every object in Windows 7 has properties that describe the object. A **property** is a characteristic of an object such as the amount of storage space on a storage device or the number of items in a folder. The properties of each object will differ, and in some cases, you can change the properties of an object. For example, in the Local Disk (C:) properties, you could check the Space free property to determine how much space is available on the C drive. To determine the drive's capacity, you would view the Total size property. The following step displays the properties for the Local Disk (C:) in the Details pane of the Computer folder window.

1

- Click the Local Disk (C:) icon to select the hard disk and display the properties in the Details pane (Figure 3–2).

🔎 **Experiment**

- See what properties display for the other disks and devices shown. Click each one and note what properties display in the Details pane. Return to the Local Disk (C:) when you are done.

Q&A

Why do the properties of my Local Disk differ from those in the figure?

The size and contents of your disk will be different from the one in the figure. As a result, the properties of the disk also will be different. Depending upon what has been installed on the disk and how it is formatted, the Space used, File system, Space free, and Total size properties will vary.

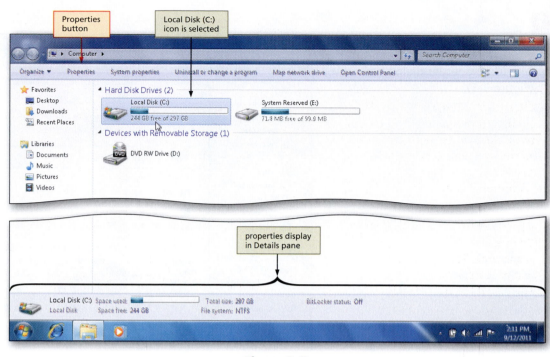

Figure 3–2

To Display the Local Disk (C:) Properties Dialog Box

The properties shown in the Details pane are just a few of the properties of the C drive. In fact, the Details pane is used to highlight the most popular properties of a hard disk: the size of the disk, how much space is free, how much space is used, and how the disk is formatted. However, you can display more detailed information about the hard disk.

The Local Disk (C:) Properties dialog box includes tabs that contain advanced features for working with the hard disk. The Tools sheet, accessible by clicking the Tools tab, allows you to check for errors on the hard disk, defragment the hard disk, or back up the hard disk. The Hardware sheet allows you to view a list of all disk drives, troubleshoot disk drives that are not working properly, and display the properties for each disk drive. The Sharing sheet allows you to share the contents of a hard disk with other computer users. However, to protect a computer from unauthorized access, sharing the hard disk is not recommended. The Security sheet displays the security settings for the drive, such as user permissions. The Previous Versions sheet allows you to work with copies of your hard disk that are created when using backup utilities or from automatic saves. Finally, the Quota sheet can be used to see how much space is being used by various user accounts. Other tabs might display in the Local Disk (C:) Properties dialog box on your computer.

The step on the following page displays the Properties dialog box for the Local Disk (C:) drive.

- Click the Properties button on the toolbar to display the Local Disk (C:) Properties dialog box (Figure 3–3).

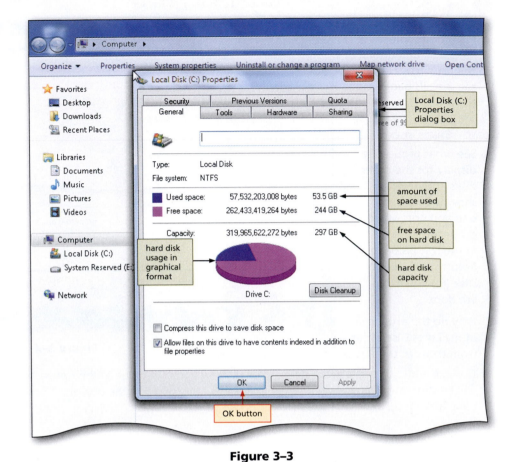

Figure 3–3

Other Ways

1. Right click Local Disk (C:) icon, click Properties
2. Click disk icon, press ALT, on File menu click Properties
3. Select drive icon, press ALT+ENTER

To Close the Local Disk (C:) Properties Dialog Box

Now that you have reviewed the Local Disk (C:) Properties dialog box, you should close it.

- Click the OK button to close the Local Disk (C:) Properties dialog box (Figure 3–4).

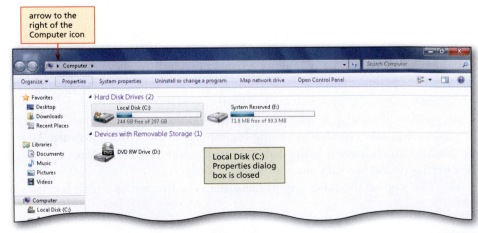

Figure 3–4

Other Ways

1. Click Cancel
2. Click Close
3. Press ESC

To Switch Folders Using the Address Bar

Found in all folder windows, the Address bar lets you know which folder you are viewing. A useful feature of the Address bar is its capability to allow you to switch to different folder windows by clicking the arrows preceding or following the folder names. Clicking the arrow to the right of the computer icon, for example, displays a command menu containing options for showing the desktop in a folder window, switching to the Computer folder, the Recycle Bin, the Control Panel, and other locations and folders that can vary from computer to computer. The following steps change the folder window from displaying the Computer folder to displaying the desktop and then return to the Computer folder.

- Click the arrow to the right of the computer icon on the Address bar to display a menu that contains folder switching commands (Figure 3–5). Depending upon your computer's configuration, the list of commands might differ.

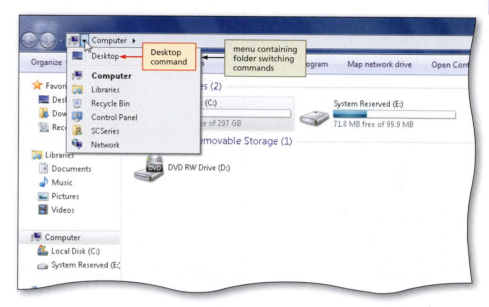

Figure 3–5

❷

- Click the Desktop command to switch to viewing the contents of the desktop in the folder window (Figure 3–6).

Q&A

Why do icons appear in this folder window that do not display on the desktop?

Although these icons do not display on the desktop, Microsoft provides you with convenient access to Libraries, the Control Panel, and the Network folder window (if applicable) by placing these icons in the Desktop folder window.

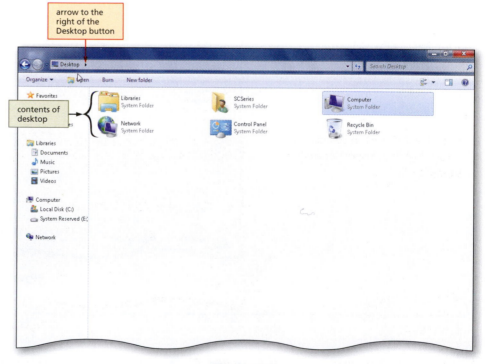

Figure 3–6

3

● Click the arrow to the right of the Desktop button on the Address bar to display a menu containing switching options (Figure 3–7).

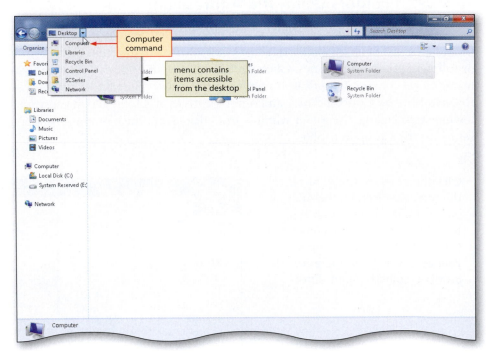

Figure 3–7

4

● Click the Computer command to switch to the Computer folder (Figure 3–8).

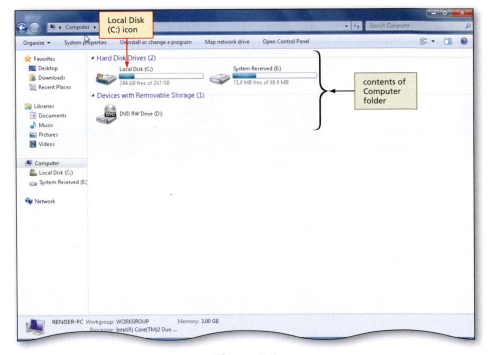

Figure 3–8

To View the Contents of a Drive

In addition to viewing the contents of the Computer folder, you can view the contents of drives and folders. In fact, the contents of any folder or drive on the computer will display in a folder window. By default, Windows 7 uses the active window to display the contents of a newly opened drive or folder. Because only one window displays on the desktop at a time, the clutter of multiple windows on the desktop is eliminated. The following step displays the contents of the C drive in the active window.

1

- Double-click the Local Disk (C:) icon in the Computer folder window to display the contents of the Local Disk (C:) drive (Figure 3–9).

Q&A

Why do I see different folders?

The contents of the Local Disk (C:) window that display on your computer can differ from the contents shown in Figure 3–9 because each computer has its own folders, programs, and documents.

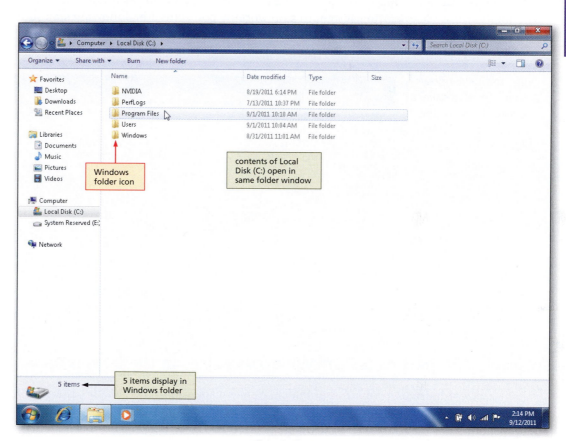

Figure 3–9

<table>
<tr><td>**Other Ways**</td></tr>
<tr><td>1. Right-click Local Disk (C:), click Open</td></tr>
<tr><td>2. Click Local Disk (C:), press ENTER</td></tr>
</table>

To Preview the Properties for a Folder

When you move your mouse over a folder icon, a preview of the folder properties will display in a ScreenTip. A **ScreenTip** is a brief description that appears when you hold the mouse over an object on the screen. A ScreenTip does not appear for every object, but when they do, they provide useful information. The properties typically consist of the date and time created, the folder size, and the name of the folder. The Windows folder in the Local Disk (C:) window contains programs and files necessary for the operation of the Windows 7 operating system. As such, you should exercise caution when working with the contents of the Windows folder because changing the contents of the folder might cause the operating system to stop working correctly. The following step shows a preview of the properties for the Windows folder.

- Point to the Windows folder icon to display a preview of the properties for the Windows folder (Figure 3–10).

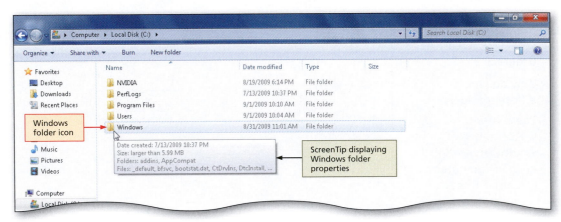

Figure 3–10

To Display Properties for the Windows Folder in the Details Pane

Just like with drives, properties of folders can be displayed in the Details pane. The following step displays the properties for the Windows folder in the Details pane of the Computer folder window.

- Click the Windows folder icon to display the properties in the Details pane (Figure 3–11).

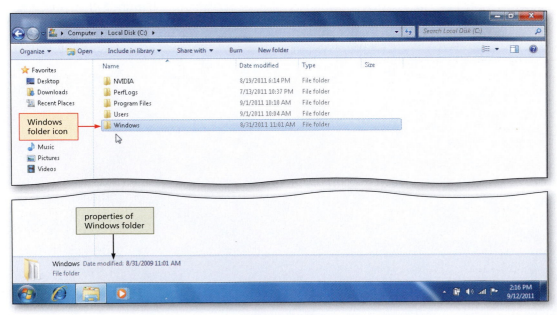

Figure 3–11

To Display All of the Properties for the Windows Folder

If you want to see all of the properties for the Windows folder, you will need to open the Properties dialog box. The following steps display the Properties dialog box for the Windows folder.

1

- Right-click the Windows folder icon to display a shortcut menu (Figure 3–12). (The commands on your shortcut menu might differ.)

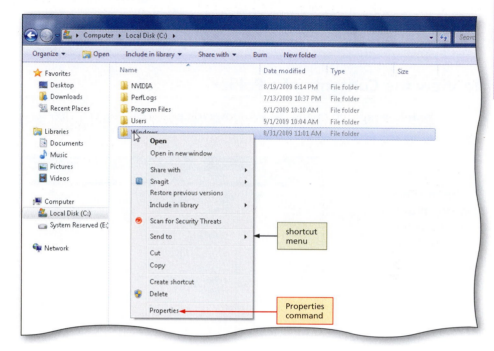

Figure 3–12

2

- Click the Properties command to display the Windows Properties dialog box (Figure 3–13).

 Experiment

- Click the various tabs in the Properties dialog box to see the different properties available for a folder.

Q&A Why might you want to look at the properties of a folder?

When you are working with folders, you might need to look at folders' properties to make changes, such as configuring a folder for sharing over a network or hiding folders from users who do not need access to them. You even can customize the appearance of a folder to be different than the default Windows folder view.

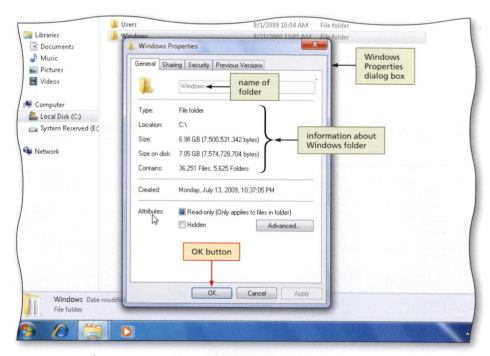

Figure 3–13

Q&A Why are the tabs of the Windows folder properties different from the Local Disk (C:) properties?

Drives, folders, and files have different properties and, therefore, need different tabs. A folder's Properties dialog box typically shows the General, Sharing, Security, and Previous Versions tabs; however, depending upon your Windows 7 version and installed programs, the tabs may differ. The Properties dialog box always will have the General tab, although what it displays also may differ.

To Close the Windows Properties Dialog Box

Now that you have seen the Windows folder properties, you should close the Windows Properties dialog box.

 Click the OK button to close the Windows Properties dialog box.

To View the Contents of a Folder

The following step opens the Windows folder so that you can view its contents.

1
- Double-click the Windows folder icon to display the contents of the Windows folder (Figure 3–14).

contents of Windows folder

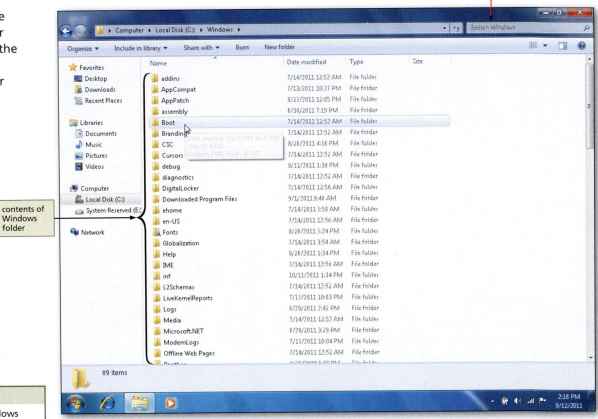

Search box

Figure 3–14

Other Ways

1. Right-click Windows folder, click Open

2. Click Windows, press ENTER

Searching for Files and Folders

The majority of objects displayed in the Windows folder, as shown in Figure 3–14, are folder icons. Folder icons always display in alphabetical order at the top of the list of objects in a folder window, before the icons for programs or files.

Folders such as the Windows folder can contain many files and folders. When you want to find a particular file or folder but do not know where it is located, you can use the Search box to find the file or folder quickly. Similar to the Search box on the Start menu, as soon as you start typing, the window updates to show search results that match what you are typing. As Windows 7 is searching for files or folders that match your search criteria, you will see a searching message displayed in the list area, an animated circle attached to the pointer, and an animated progress bar on the Address bar which provides live feedback as to how much of the search has been completed. When searching is complete, you will see a list of all items that match your search criteria.

If you know only a portion of a file's name and can specify where the known portion of the name should appear, you can use an asterisk in the name to represent the unknown characters. For example, if you know a file starts with the letters MSP, you can type msp* in the Search box. All files that begin with the letters msp, regardless of what letters follow, will display. However, with Windows 7's powerful search capabilities, you would get the same results if you did not include the asterisk. If you want to search for all files with a particular extension, you can use the asterisk to stand in for the name of the files. For example, to find all the text files with the extension .rtf, you would type *.rtf in the Search box. Windows 7 will find all the files with the .rtf extension.

BTW

Hidden Files and Folders
Hidden files and folders usually are placed on your hard disk by software vendors such as Microsoft and often are critical to the operation of their programs. Rarely will you need to designate a file or folder as hidden. You should not delete a hidden file or folder, as doing so might interrupt how or whether a program works. By default, hidden files and folders are not displayed in a file listing.

To Search for a File and Folder in a Folder Window

The following step uses the Search box to search the Windows folder for all the objects that contain "aero" in the file name.

1

• Type aero in the Search box to search for all files and folders that match the search criteria (Figure 3–15).

Q&A How can I stop a search while it is running?

If you decide to stop a search before it is finished running, click the Stop button that appears next to the Address bar in place of the Refresh button. The Stop button only appears while Windows is performing a search. Once a search is complete, the Refresh button is displayed again.

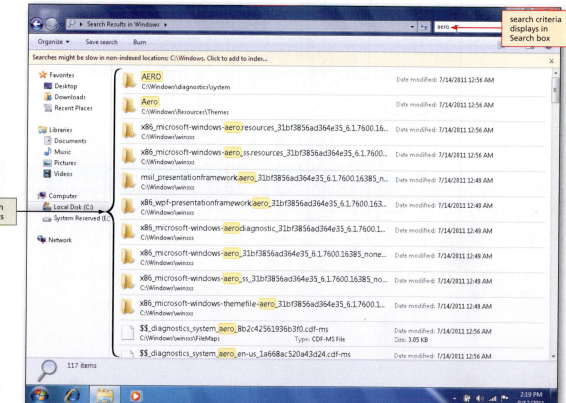

Figure 3–15

Q&A What does the message, "Searches might be slow in non-indexed locations" mean?

Windows 7 maintains an index of certain locations on the computer, such as the libraries, to make searches perform faster. The Windows folder is a very large folder with many items and is not part of the index. This message appears to let you know that the search will take extra time.

To Search for Files Using Search Filters

When searching using the Search box in a folder window, you also can use search filters. A **search filter** is an advanced searching tool that Windows 7 provides from the Search box. Once you select a search filter, you then will be able to select from provided options. For example, if you use the Date modified search filter, you will be shown options such as "Select a date or date range," "A long time ago," or "Earlier this month." The following steps add the Size search filter to the aero search already performed.

1

- Click in the Search box to display search filter options (Figure 3–16).

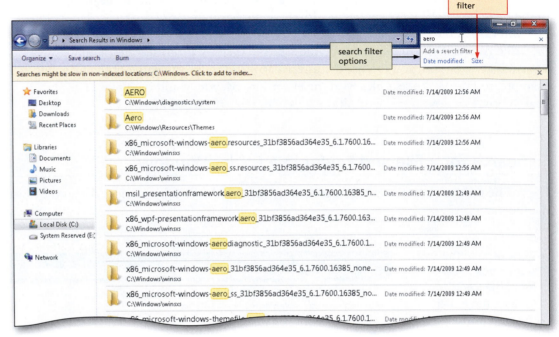

Figure 3–16

2

- Click the Size search filter to add the Size search filter and display filter options (Figure 3–17).

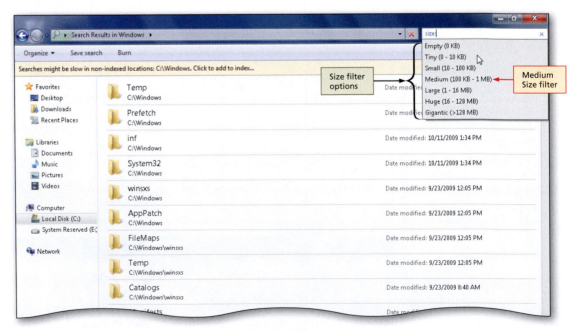

Figure 3–17

3

- Click the Medium size filter to see files between 100 KB and 1 MB (Figure 3–18).

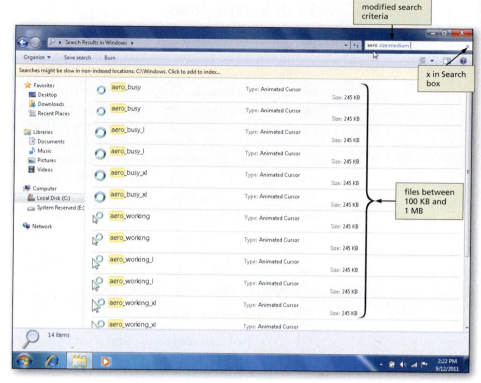

Figure 3–18

To Clear the Search Box

When you finish searching, you can end the search by clearing the Search box. The following step clears the Search box.

1

- Click the x in the Search box to remove the search text from the Search box and redisplay all files and folders in the Windows folder (Figure 3–19).

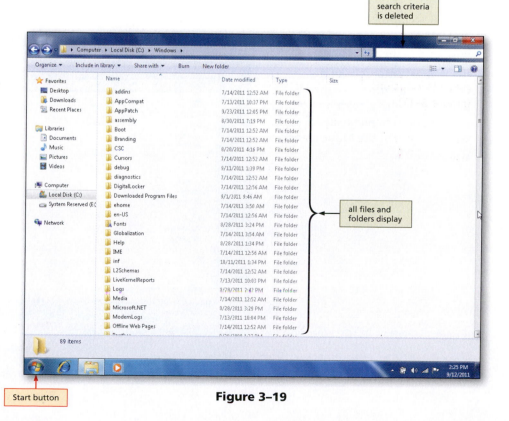

Figure 3–19

To Open Windows

In this chapter, you have been working with one window open. Windows 7 allows you to open many more windows depending upon the amount of RAM you have installed on the computer. However, too many open windows on the desktop can become difficult to use and manage. In Chapter 1, you used Aero Flip 3D to navigate through multiple open windows. However, Windows 7 provides additional tools for managing open windows. You already have used one tool, maximizing a window. When you maximize a window, it occupies the entire screen and cannot be confused with other open windows.

Sometimes, it is important to have multiple windows appear on the desktop simultaneously. Windows 7 offers simple commands that allow you to arrange multiple windows in specific ways. The following sections describe the ways that you can manage multiple open windows. First you will open the Pictures and Music libraries.

1 Display the Start menu.

2 Click the Pictures command to open the Pictures library.

3 Maximize the Pictures library window.

4 Display the Start menu.

5 Click the Music command to open the Music library.

To Use Aero Shake to Minimize and Restore All Windows Except the Active Window

Aero Shake lets you minimize all windows except the active window and then restore all those windows just by shaking the title bar of the active window. The following steps use Aero Shake to minimize all windows except the Music library and then restore those windows.

- Click the title bar of the Music library window, and, holding the mouse button, shake the title bar (drag the title bar back and forth in short, swift motions several times) to minimize all windows except the Music library (Figure 3–20).

Figure 3–20

2

- Click the title bar of the Music library window, and, while holding the mouse button, shake the title bar to restore all the windows (Figure 3–21).

- Maximize the Music library window.

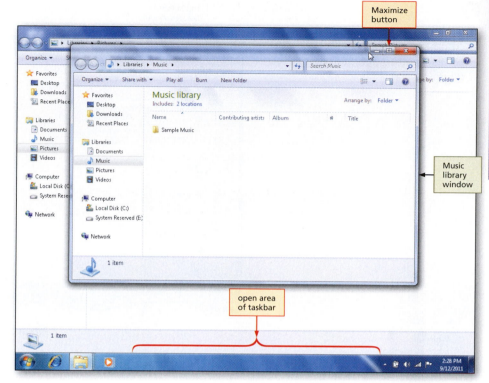

Figure 3–21

To Cascade Open Windows

One way to organize windows on the desktop is to display them in a cascade format, where they overlap one another in an organized manner. In Windows 7, only open windows will be displayed in cascade format: Windows that are minimized or closed will not appear in the cascade. When you cascade open windows, the windows are resized to be the same size to produce the layered cascading effect. The following steps cascade the open windows on the desktop.

- Right-click an open area on the taskbar to display a shortcut menu (Figure 3–22).

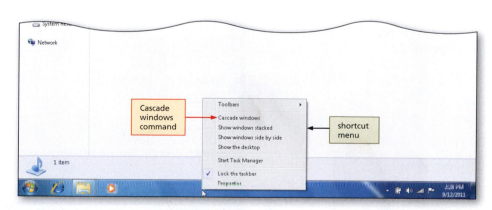

Figure 3–22

2

- Click the Cascade windows command on the shortcut menu to cascade the open windows (Figure 3–23).

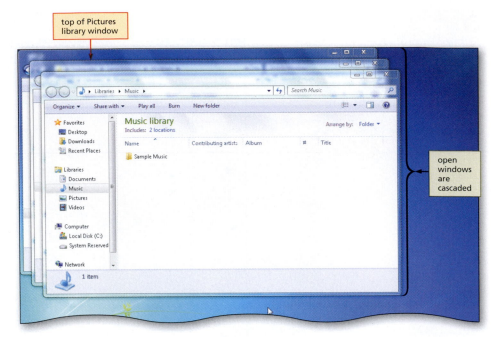

Figure 3–23

To Make a Window the Active Window

When windows are cascaded, as shown in Figure 3–23, they are arranged so that you can see them easily. To work with one of the windows, you first must make it the active window. When you make the Pictures library window the active window, it will remain the same size and remain in the same relative position as placed by the Cascade windows command. The following step makes the Pictures library window the active window.

1

- Click the top of the Pictures library window to make it the active window (Figure 3–24).

Q&A

What happens if I click the wrong window?

Click the remaining windows until the Pictures library window displays in the foreground.

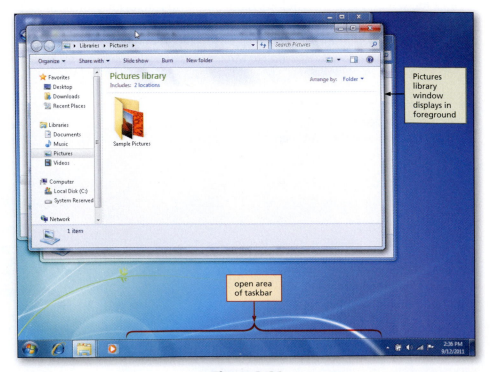

Figure 3–24

To Undo Cascading

Now that you have seen the effect of the Cascade windows command, you will undo the cascade operation and return the windows to the size and location they were before cascading. The following steps return the windows to their previous size and location.

1
- Right-click an open area on the taskbar to display the shortcut menu (Figure 3–25).

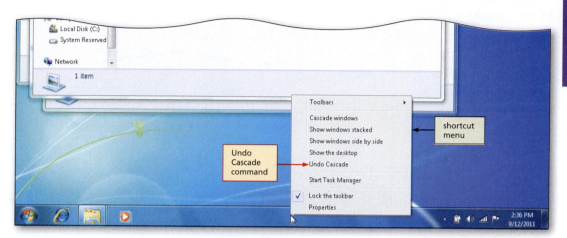

Figure 3–25

2
- Click the Undo Cascade command to return the windows to their original sizes and locations (Figure 3–26).

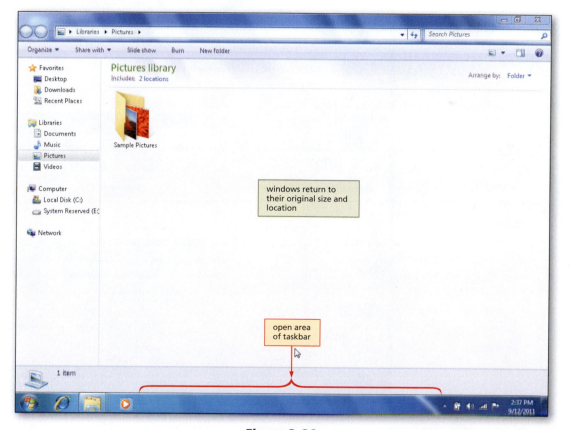

Figure 3–26

Other Ways
1. Right-click open area on taskbar, press U
2. Press CTRL+Z

To Stack Open Windows

Although cascading arranges the windows on the desktop so that each of the windows' title bars is visible, it is impossible to see the contents of each window. Windows 7 also can stack the open windows, which allows you to see partial contents of each window. When stacking windows, the windows will be resized to the full width of the screen and arranged on top of each other vertically. Each window will be the same size, and you will be able to see a portion of each window. The following steps stack the open windows.

1

• Right-click an open area of the taskbar to display a shortcut menu (Figure 3–27).

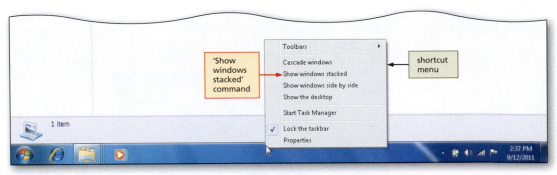

Figure 3–27

2

• Click the 'Show windows stacked' command to stack the open windows (Figure 3–28).

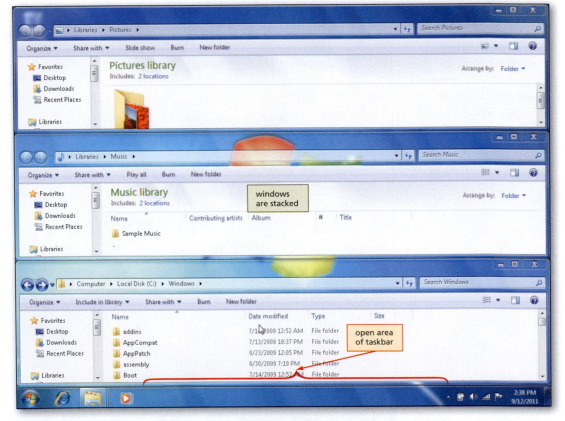

Figure 3–28

Other Ways

1. Right-click open area on taskbar, press T until 'Show windows stacked' is selected, press ENTER

To Undo Show Windows Stacked

Although the stacked windows are arranged so that you can view all of them, you find that the reduced size of an individual window makes working in the window difficult. You will undo the stacking operation to return the windows to the size and position they occupied before stacking. If you want to work in a particular window, you should maximize the window. The following steps return the windows to their original size and position.

1

• Right-click an open area of the taskbar to display the shortcut menu (Figure 3–29).

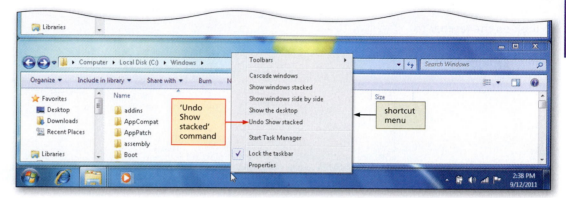

Figure 3–29

2

• Click the 'Undo Show stacked' command to return the windows to their original sizes and locations (Figure 3–30).

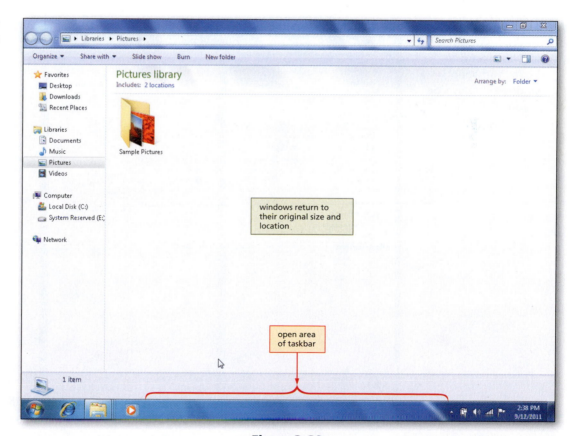

Figure 3–30

Other Ways
1. Right-click open area on taskbar, press U
2. Click CTRL+Z

To Show Windows Side by Side

Although stacking arranges the windows vertically above each other on the desktop, it also is possible to arrange them horizontally from left to right, or side by side, like books on a bookshelf. The 'Show windows side by side' command allows you to see partial contents of each window horizontally. The following steps show the open windows side by side.

1
- Right-click an open area on the taskbar to display the shortcut menu (Figure 3–31).

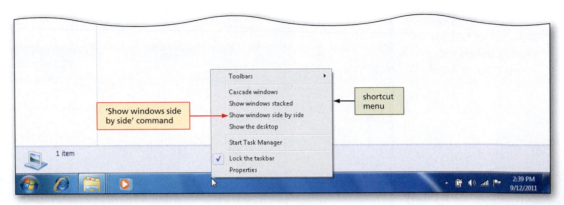

Figure 3–31

2
- Click the 'Show windows side by side' command to display the open windows side by side (Figure 3–32).

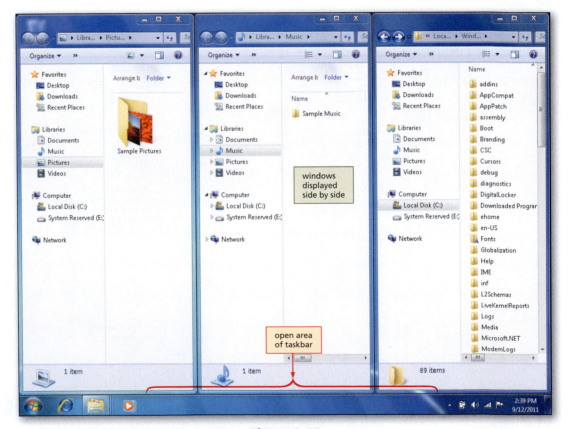

Figure 3–32

Other Ways

1. Right-click open area on taskbar, press I

To Undo Show Windows Side by Side

The following steps undo the side by side operation and return the windows to their original arrangement.

1
- Right-click an open area on the taskbar to display the shortcut menu (Figure 3–33).

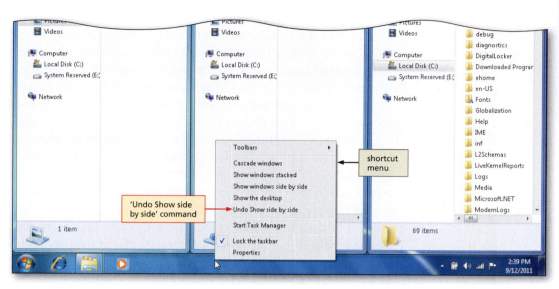

Figure 3–33

2
- Click the 'Undo Show side by side' command to return the windows to their original size and locations (Figure 3–34).

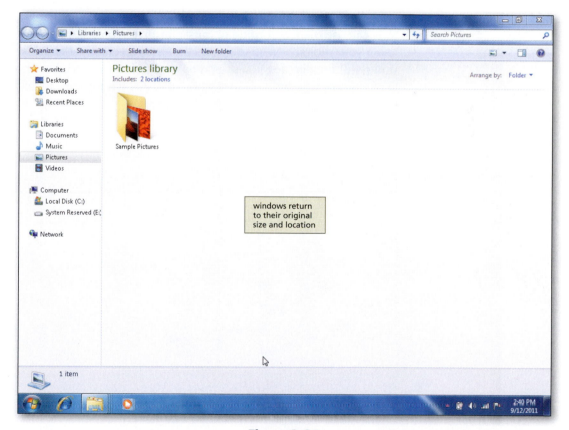

Figure 3–34

Other Ways

1. Right-click open area on taskbar, press U
2. Press CTRL+Z

The Pictures Library

You can organize your pictures and share them with others using the Pictures library. By putting all your pictures in the Pictures library, you will always know where to find them. When you save pictures from a digital camera, scanner, or the Internet, they are saved to the Pictures library by default. More specifically, they are saved to the My Pictures folder. The My Pictures folder is part of the Pictures library and is set as the default save location to be used when working with the library. Recall that when documents were created in the Documents library in Chapter 2, they automatically were saved in the My Documents folder. Each library has a default save location; the default save location for the Documents library is the My Documents folder.

Using the Pictures library allows you to organize pictures, preview pictures, share your pictures with others, display your pictures as a slide show, print your pictures, attach your pictures to e-mail messages, or burn your pictures to an optical disc. You will work with a few of the options now, and the rest will be covered in a later chapter when multimedia files are covered in greater depth.

There are many different formats for picture files. Some pictures have an extension of .bmp to indicate that they are bitmap files. Other pictures might have the .gif extension, which indicates that they are saved in the Graphics Interchange Format. There are too many file types to mention; however, some common types include .bmp, .jpg, .gif, .png, and .tif.

When working with pictures, you should be aware that most pictures that you did not create yourself, including other multimedia files, are copyrighted. A **copyright** means that a picture belongs to the person who created it. The pictures that come with Windows 7 are part of Windows 7 and you are allowed to use them; however, they are not yours. You only can use them according to the rights given to you by Microsoft. Pictures that you take using your digital camera are yours because you created them. Before using pictures and other multimedia files, you should be aware of any copyrights associated with them, and you should know whether you are allowed to use them for your intended purpose.

To View the Save Location for the Pictures Library

To see the default save location for a library, you need to display the properties for the library. You then can change the save location if you so desire. The following steps display the default save location for the Pictures library.

- Right-click an open area in the list area of the Pictures library to display the shortcut menu.

- Click the Properties command on the shortcut menu to display the Pictures Properties dialog box (Figure 3–35).

2

- After viewing the save location, click the OK button to close the Pictures Properties dialog box.

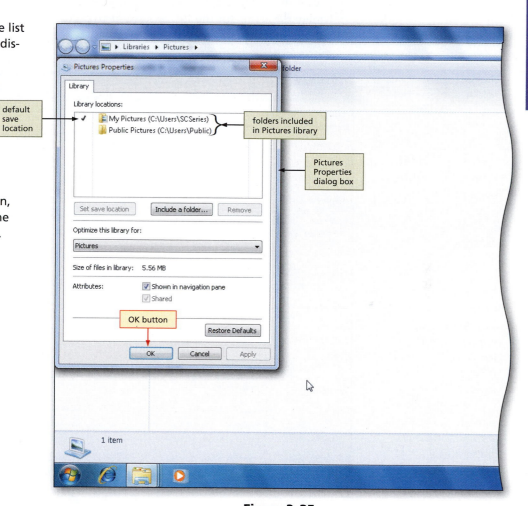

Figure 3–35

To Search for Pictures

You want to copy three files, Monet, Psychedelic, and Pine_Lumber, from the Windows folder to the Pictures library; but first, you have to find these files. Because the three files all have the .jpg extension, you can search for them using an asterisk (*) in place of the file name, as discussed earlier in this chapter. The following steps open the Windows folder window and display the icons for the files you want to copy.

1

• Make the Windows folder window the active window.

2

• Type *.jpg in the Search box and then press the ENTER key to search for all files with a .jpg file extension.

3

• Scroll down the right pane of the Windows folder window until the icons for the Monet, Pine_Lumber, and Psychedelic files are visible in the right pane (Figure 3–36). If one or more of these files are not available, select any of the other picture files.

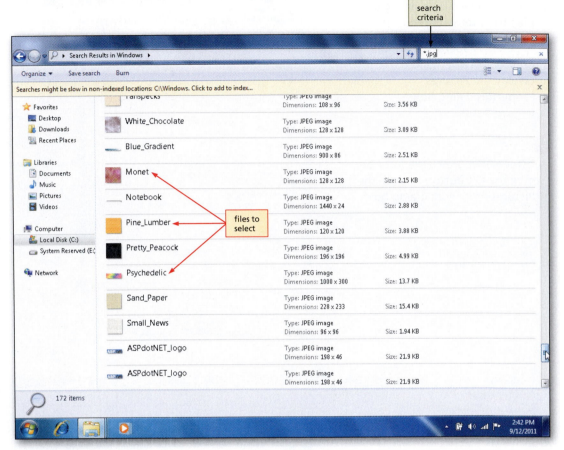

Figure 3–36

To Copy Files to the Pictures Library

In Chapter 2, you learned how to move and copy document files to a folder, how to copy a folder onto a USB flash drive, and how to delete files. Another method you can use to copy a file or folder is the **copy and paste method**. When you **copy** a file, you place a copy of the file in a temporary storage area of the computer called the **Clipboard**. When you **paste** the file, Windows 7 copies it from the Clipboard to the location you specify, giving you two copies of the same file.

Because the search results include the pictures you were looking for, you now can select the files and then copy them to the Pictures library. Once the three files have been copied into the Pictures library, the files will be stored in both the My Pictures folder (the default save location) and Windows folder on drive C. Copying and moving files are common tasks when working with Windows 7. If you want to move a file instead of copying a file, you would use the Cut command on the shortcut menu to move the file to the Clipboard, and the Paste command to copy the file from the Clipboard to the new location. When the move is complete, the files are moved into the new folder and no longer are stored in the original folder.

The following steps copy the Monet, Pine_Lumber, and Psychedelic files from the Windows folder to the Pictures library.

1

- Hold down the CTRL key and then click the Monet, Pine_Lumber, and Psychedelic icons.

- Release the CTRL key.

- Right-click any highlighted icon to display a shortcut menu (Figure 3–37).

Q&A

Are copying and moving the same?

No. When you copy a file, it is located in both the place to which it was copied and in the place from which it was copied. When you move a file, it is located only in the location to which it was moved.

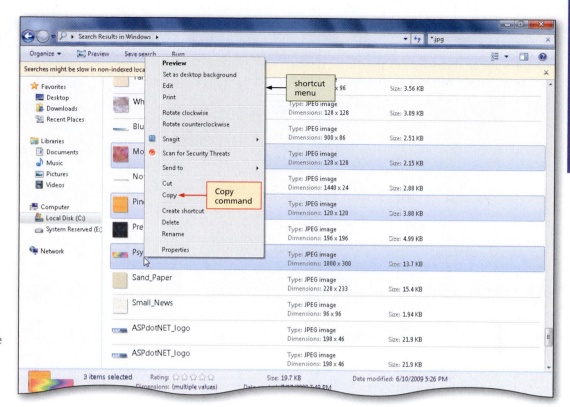

Figure 3–37

2

- Click the Copy command on the shortcut menu to copy the files to the Clipboard (Figure 3–38).

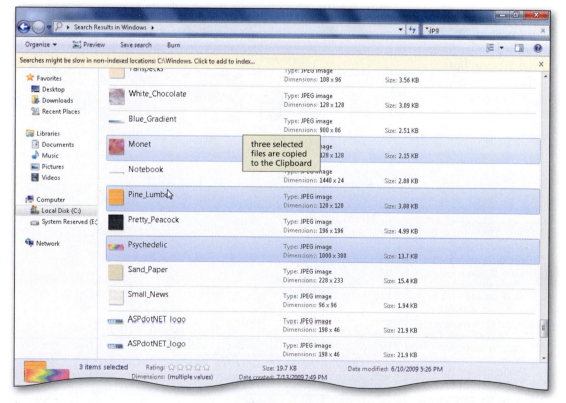

Figure 3–38

3

- Make the Pictures library the active window.

- Right-click an open area of the Pictures library window to display a shortcut menu (Figure 3–39).

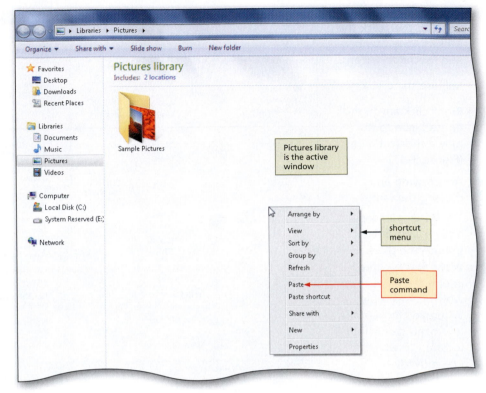

Figure 3–39

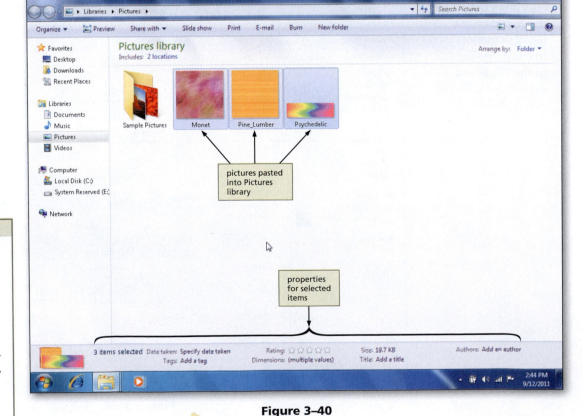**4**

- Click the Paste command on the shortcut menu to paste the files in the Pictures library (Figure 3–40).

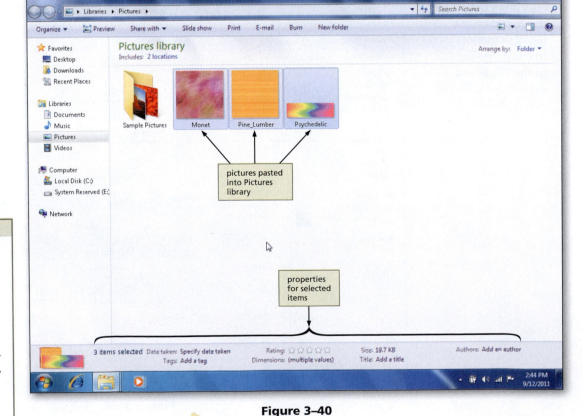

Figure 3–40

Other Ways

1. Select file icons, press ALT, on Edit menu click Copy, display window where you want to store file, press ALT, on Edit menu click Paste

2. Select file icons, press ALT, on Edit menu click Copy to folder, click arrow next to your user name, click My Pictures, click Copy

3. Select file icons, press CTRL+C, display window where you want to store files, press CTRL+V

To Close the Search Results Window

You no longer need the Search Results window open, so you can close it. Whenever you are not using a window, it is a good idea to close it so as not to clutter your desktop. The following steps close the Search Results window.

1 Display the Search Results window.

2 Close the Search Results window.

To Create a Folder in the Pictures Library

When you have several related files stored in a folder with a number of unrelated files, you might want to create a folder to contain the related files so that you can find and reference them easily. To reduce clutter and improve the organization of files in the Pictures library, you will create a new folder in the Pictures library and then move the Monet, Pine_Lumber, and Psychedelic files into the new folder. The following steps create the Backgrounds folder in the Pictures library.

- Make the Pictures library the active window.

- Right-click any open part of the list area of the Pictures library to display a shortcut menu (Figure 3–41). (The commands on the shortcut menu on your computer might differ slightly.)

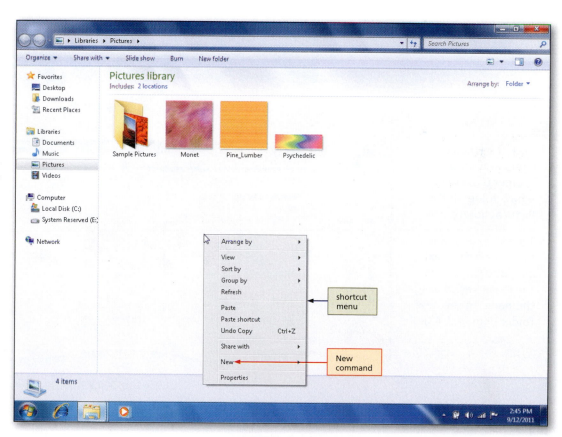

Figure 3–41

2

- Point to the New command on the shortcut menu to display the New submenu (Figure 3–42). (The commands on the New submenu on your computer might differ slightly.)

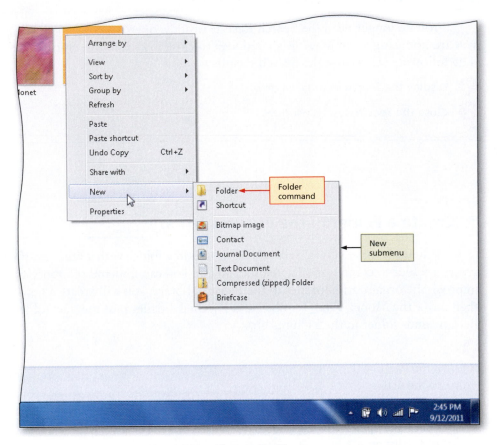

Figure 3–42

3

- Click the Folder command on the New submenu to create a new folder in the Pictures library.

- Type Backgrounds in the icon title text box, and then press the ENTER key to assign the name to the new folder (Figure 3–43).

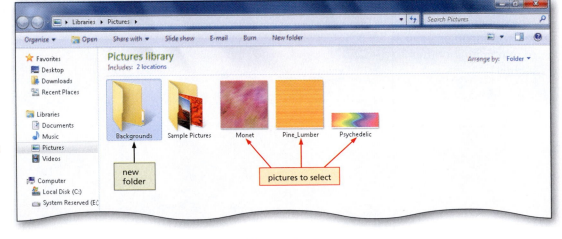

Figure 3–43

Other Ways

1. Click New folder button, type folder name, press ENTER

2. Press ALT, click File menu, point to New, click Folder, type folder name, press ENTER

3. Press ALT+F, press W, press F, type folder name, press ENTER

To Move Multiple Files into a Folder

After you create the Backgrounds folder in the Pictures library, the next step is to move the three picture files into the folder. The following steps move the Monet, Psychedelic, and Pine_Lumber files into the Backgrounds folder.

1

● Click the Monet icon, hold down the CTRL key, and then click the Pine_Lumber and Psychedelic icons to select all three icons (Figure 3–44).

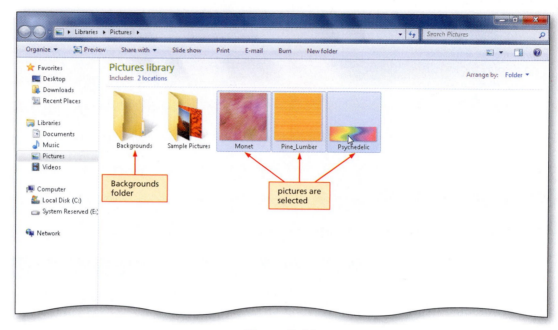

Figure 3–44

2

● Drag the selected icons to the Backgrounds folder, and then release the mouse button to move the files to the Backgrounds folder (Figure 3–45).

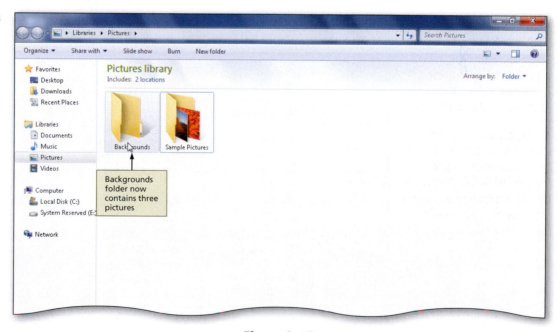

Figure 3–45

Other Ways
1. Drag icons individually to folder icon
2. Right-click icon, click Cut, right-click folder icon, click Paste

To Refresh the Image on a Folder

After moving the three files into the Backgrounds folder, it still appears as an empty open folder icon. To replace the empty folder icon with a live preview of the three files stored in the Backgrounds folder (Monet, Pine_Lumber, Psychedelic), the Pictures library must be refreshed. The following steps refresh the Pictures library to display the live preview for the Backgrounds folder.

- Right-click any open part of the list area to display a shortcut menu (Figure 3–46).

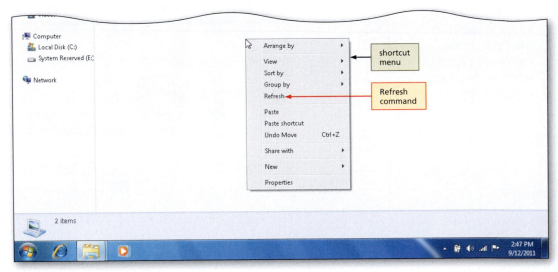

Figure 3–46

- Click the Refresh command to refresh the list area (Figure 3–47).

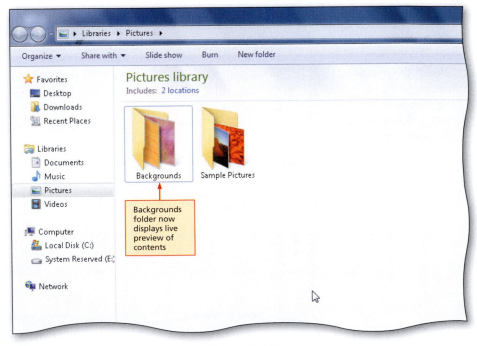

Figure 3–47

Other Ways

1. Press ALT, click View, click Refresh

To View and Change the Properties of a Picture

As mentioned earlier in the chapter, in Windows 7, all objects have properties. You already have explored the properties of a drive, and now you will review the properties of a picture. Picture properties include the Size, Title, Authors, State, Date taken, Tags, Rating, and Dimensions. State refers to whether or not the picture is shared with other users on the computer. Date taken refers to the date the person created the picture.

Tags are keywords you associate with a picture file to aid in its classification. For example, you could tag a family photo with the names of the people in the photo. When you create a tag, it should be meaningful. For example, if you have pictures from a family vacation at the beach and you add a title of vacation; later on, you will be able to find the file using the tag "vacation" in a search. Be aware that you only can search for tags that you already have created. If your family vacation photo was saved as "photo1.jpg" and tagged with the tag "vacation", you will not find it by searching for "beach" as it is not part of the name or tag. Rating refers to the ranking, in stars, that you assign to a picture. You can rate a picture from zero to five stars. Date taken, Tags, and Rating all can be changed using the Details pane. Because you do not know when the Background pictures were created, you only will change the Tags and Rating properties. The following steps display and change the Tags and Rating properties of the Monet image in the Backgrounds folder.

- Display the contents of the Backgrounds folder.

- Click the Monet icon to select it (Figure 3–48).

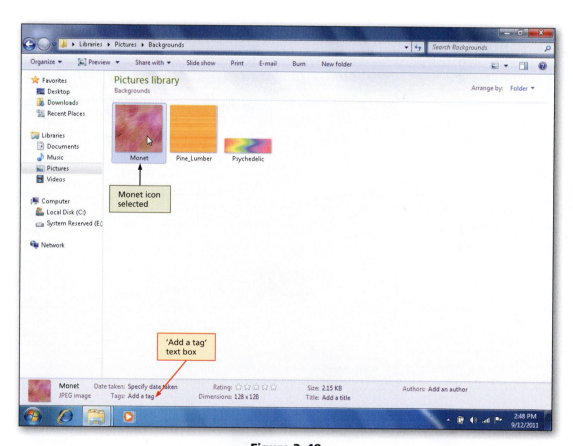

Figure 3–48

2

• Click the 'Add a tag' text box in the Details pane to activate it (Figure 3–49).

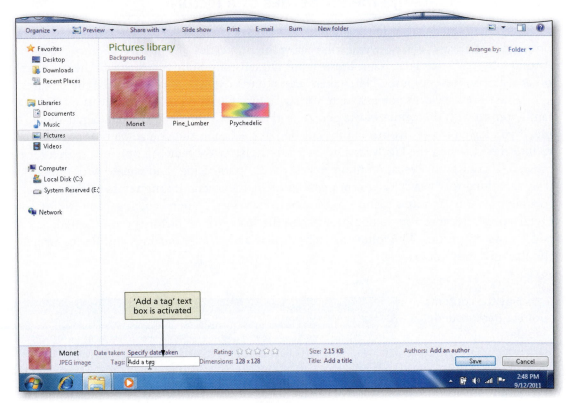

Figure 3–49

3

• Type A Work of Art in the text box to create a tag for the picture (Figure 3–50).

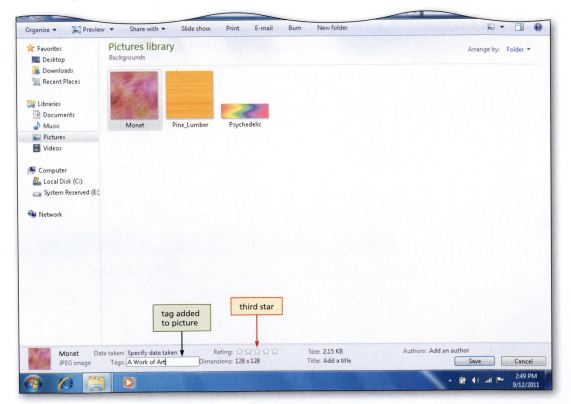

Figure 3–50

4
- Click the third star next to the Rating heading in the Details pane to assign a 3-star rating to the picture (Figure 3–51).

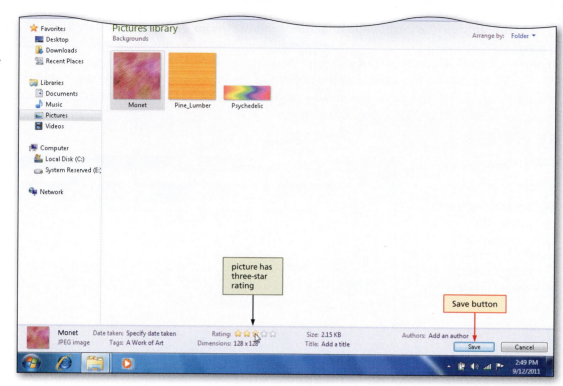

Figure 3–51

5
- Click the Save button in the Details pane to save the changes to the Tags and Rating properties (Figure 3–52).

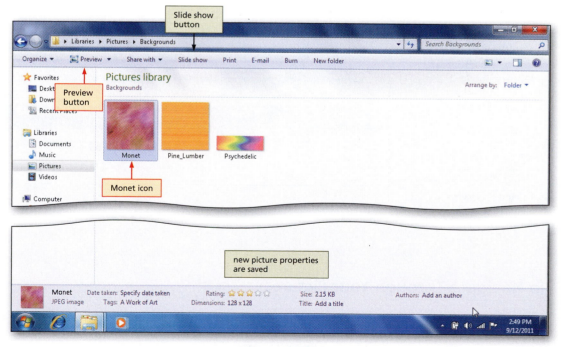

Figure 3–52

Other Ways

1. Right-click icon, click Properties, click Details tab, click third star next to Rating, enter text next to Tags, click OK

To Open a Picture in Windows Photo Viewer

You can view the images in a folder in Windows Photo Viewer or as a slide show. **Windows Photo Viewer** is a program that allows you to view, print, e-mail, burn, and open the pictures in your Pictures library. You can view pictures individually or as part of a slide show.

The buttons on the toolbar at the bottom of the Windows Photo Viewer window allow you to move through the pictures and rotate a picture clockwise or counterclockwise. The following step displays the Monet picture in the Backgrounds folder in Windows Photo Viewer.

1

- If necessary, select the Monet icon.

- Click the Preview button on the toolbar to open the Monet picture in Windows Photo Viewer (Figure 3–53).

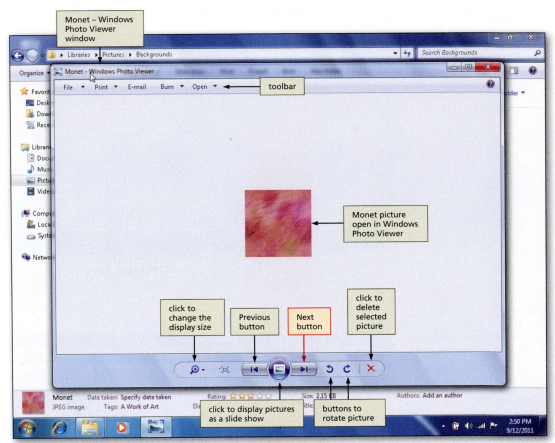

Figure 3–53

Other Ways

1. Right-click icon, click Preview

To Navigate Through Your Pictures

To navigate through your pictures, you use the buttons at the bottom of the Windows Photo Viewer window. The Next (right arrow) button allows you to move to the next picture, and the Previous (left arrow) button allows you to move to the previous picture in the folder. You also can rotate a picture clockwise or counterclockwise using the Rotate buttons, change the display size of a picture, or even delete a picture. The following steps navigate through the pictures in the Backgrounds folder using Windows Photo Viewer.

1

• Click the Next (right arrow) button to view the Pine_ Lumber picture in Windows Photo Viewer (Figure 3–54).

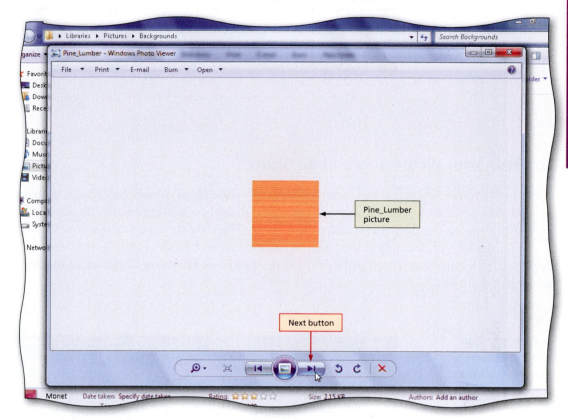

Figure 3–54

2

• Click the Next (right arrow) button to view the Psychedelic picture in Windows Photo Viewer (Figure 3–55).

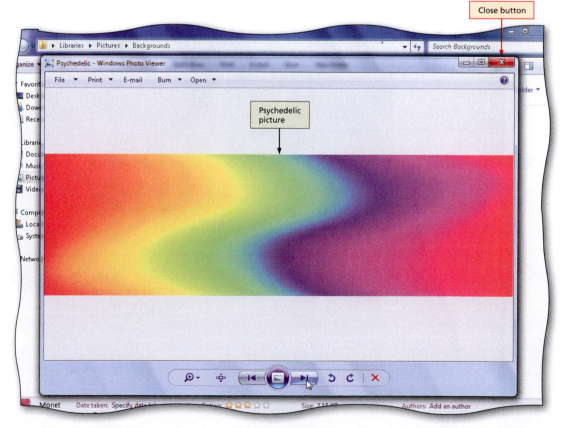

Figure 3–55

To Close Windows Photo Viewer

Now that you have seen all of the pictures, the next step is to close Windows Photo Viewer.

 Click the Close button to close Windows Photo Viewer.

To View Your Pictures as a Slide Show

In Windows 7, you can view your pictures as a **slide show**, which displays each image in the folder in a presentation format on your computer screen. The slide show will automatically display one picture at a time while everything else on the desktop is hidden from sight. The slide show allows you to select whether the pictures will loop in order or will be shuffled to appear in random order. You also can select the speed at which the pictures are displayed, pause the slide show, and exit the slide show. The following step opens the images in the Backgrounds folder as a slide show.

- Click the Slide show button on the Pictures library toolbar to view the selected files as a slide show (Figure 3–56).

- Watch the show for a few seconds while the pictures change.

Q&A Can I change the slide show speed?

Yes, you can right-click and then select speeds of Slow, Medium, and Fast.

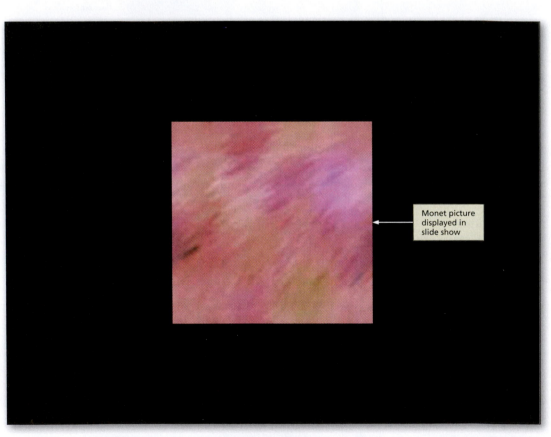

Monet picture displayed in slide show

Figure 3–56

To End a Slide Show

When you are done viewing the slide show, the next step is to end it. The following step exits the slide show.

- Press ESC to end the slide show (Figure 3–57).

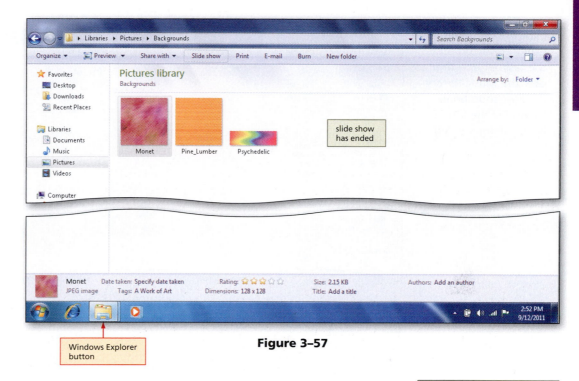

Windows Explorer button

Figure 3–57

The Music Library

The **Music library** can be used to view, organize, and play your music files. If you have a digital music player installed, it will use the default save location of the Music library when you download, play, rip, and burn music. When you **rip** a file, you extract the audio data from a CD and transfer it to your hard disk. After the file has been ripped, it will be in a format that is compatible with your computer as opposed to a CD player. When you **burn** music, you take files that are compatible with your computer and copy them onto a CD in the format that can be played in CD players. When you burn data files to a CD, the contents of the CD cannot be read by a CD player.

You can arrange your music files into organized collections. The Sample Music folder, installed with Windows 7, contains samples of music for you to experiment with so that you can make sure that your sound card and speakers are working properly. If you use a music program such as iTunes or Windows Media Player, you will be able to add additional music files to your collection. Music files come in a variety of formats, similar to how picture files have different formats. Common music file formats include .wav, .wma, .mp3, .mp4, and .mid. For example, audio podcasts often are saved in the .mp3 format.

As with other media files, you should be aware of copyright issues. If you download music from the Internet, make sure that you have permission to do so. To add music files to your Music library, you can obtain permission by paying a small fee to download the song. It is illegal to download and share music that you do not have the rights to download and share.

To Switch to the Music Library

You want to view the contents of the Music library to understand how music is stored and arranged. To see this, you will switch to the Music window. The following step makes the Music library the active window.

- Click the Windows Explorer button on the taskbar and then click the Music library window thumbnail to display the Music library (Figure 3–58).

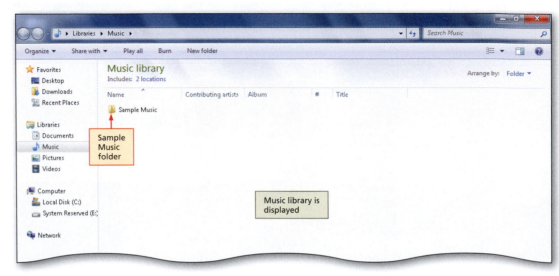

Figure 3–58

To Open the Sample Music Folder

To see the sample music files, you need to open the Sample Music folder. The Sample Music folder is located in the Public Music folder, although a shortcut to the Sample Music folder appears in the Music library. This demonstrates the power of a library; you do not actually need to know where a particular folder is located when working with a library. The library keeps track of that for you. When you view the contents of the Sample Music folder, notice that the Address bar reflects the fact that you are in the library (not the actual storage location). The following step opens the Sample Music folder.

- Double-click the Sample Music folder to display the Sample Music folder contents (Figure 3–59).

Figure 3–59

To View Information about a Music File

Similar to the Pictures library, when you view a folder that contains music files, the folder structure and options are specific to music files. In the Music library, after the column titled Name, all of the remaining columns, Contributing artists, Album, #, and Title, are properties of the music files. The Contributing artists column contains the name or names of the recording artist(s), whereas the Album column contains the name of the album that includes the song. The number symbol (#) indicates the track number of the song on the album, whereas Title displays the full title of the song.

You might see the album cover image in the Details pane. For an album cover to be displayed, your music files must include the album cover image, which usually occurs when the music files are created. If you download music files, they often will have the album art included, but not every music file will have this.

Once you select a file, its properties display in the Details pane. As with picture files, you can use the Details pane to change the properties. The following steps display the properties of the Kalimba music file in the Details pane and change the genre to New Age.

- Click the Kalimba file icon to select the music file (Figure 3–60).

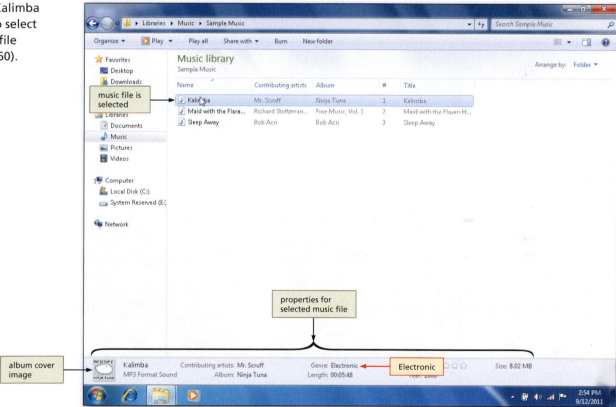

Figure 3–60

2

● Click Electronic in the Genre property to select it.

● Type New Age to change the Genre property (Figure 3–61).

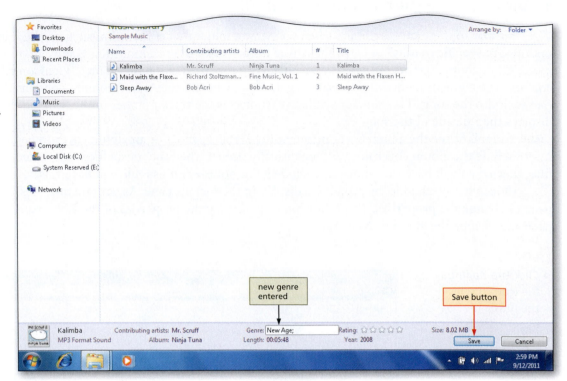

Figure 3–61

3

● Click the Save button to save the changes to the Kalimba music file properties (Figure 3–62).

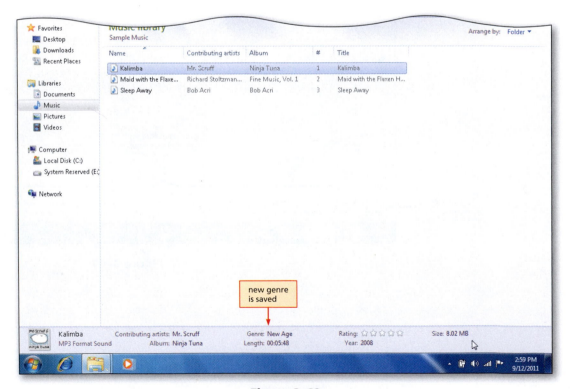

Figure 3–62

To Reset the Genre for a Music File

Because the Kalimba file is in the Sample Music folder that is shared by everyone who uses this computer, you should undo your genre change. However, if you are working on your own computer and you agree with the new genre, you could leave it alone. The following step will reset the genre of the Kalimba file back to its original value.

- Click the mouse at the left edge of the genre info.

- Delete New Age from the Genre list.

- Type Electronic to enter the original genre value.

- Click the Save button to save the changes to the Kalimba music file properties (Figure 3–63).

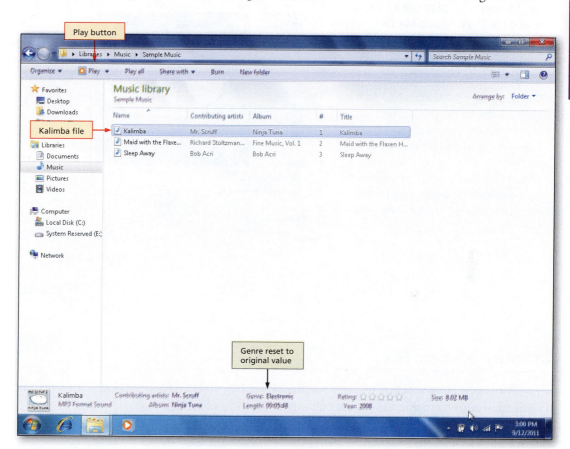

Figure 3–63

To Play a Music File in Windows Media Player

There are several ways to play a music file. The easiest way is to use the Music library toolbar. If you click the Play button, you play the selected song. Clicking the Play all button plays all the music files in the folder. **Windows Media Player** is the default Windows 7 program for playing and working with digital media files such as music or video files.

In addition to playing music files, Windows Media Player can rip and burn music, maintain a music library, sync with portable media players, and even download music. Windows Media Player also works with other multimedia files, including movies. These features of Windows Media Player are discussed in a later chapter.

In Windows Media Player, there are buttons for controlling the playback of the music file. The step on the following page plays the Kalimba music file in Windows Media Player.

- If necessary, select the Kalimba file.

- Click the Play button on the toolbar to open and play the Kalimba music file in Windows Media Player (Figure 3–64).

Q&A Why am I unable to hear any music?

Check the speakers attached to your computer. Your speakers might not be turned on, or the volume might not be turned up on the speakers or on the computer. If you are using a computer without speakers, you will need earbuds to listen to the music file.

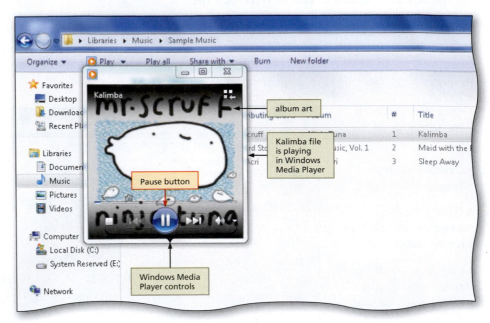

Figure 3–64

To Pause a Music File

After you have listened to the Kalimba music file, you can stop playing the recording. The following step pauses the Kalimba music file that is playing in Windows Media Player.

- Click the Pause button on the toolbar at the bottom of the window to pause the song in Windows Media Player (Figure 3–65).

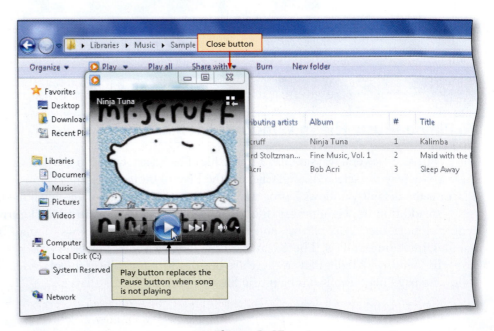

Figure 3–65

To Close Windows Media Player

Now that you are done using the Windows Media Player and the Sample Music folder, you should close them.

1 Close Windows Media Player.

2 Close the Sample Music folder window.

Backing Up Files and Folders

It is very important that you make backups of your important files and folders. A **backup** is a copy of files and folders that are stored at a different location than the originals. Backing up files and folders is a security aid; if something happens to the primary copy of a file or folder, you can restore it from the backup.

Although you can back up files and folders on the same drive where they were created, it is not considered as safe as backing them up to a separate drive. For example, you should not back up your C drive files and folders on the C drive. If something goes wrong with the C drive, it would affect any backups stored there as well. Depending upon the size of the files and folders you are backing up, you might use a USB flash drive, an optical disc, an external hard disk, or any other available storage device to back up your files. You might even consider creating a scheduled backup. A **scheduled backup** is a backup that is made according to predetermined dates and times.

After you have created a backup, you should store your backup away from the computer. Many people store their backups right by their computer, which is not a good practice. If a mishap occurs where the computer area is damaged, someone steals the computer, or any other number of events occurs, the backup still will be safe if it is stored in a different location. Most corporations make regular backups of their data and store the backups off-site.

When you **restore** files or folders from a backup, you copy the files or folders from the backup location to the original location. If your hard disk crashes, a virus infects your computer, or an electrical surge damages your computer, you can restore the files and folders that you have stored on the backup. Before restoring files or folders, make sure that the location to where you are restoring the files is now secure. For example, before restoring files on a hard disk that has been infected by a virus, first make sure the virus is gone.

First, you will back up your files and folders to a USB flash drive. A USB flash drive is handy for backing up files and folders created on a computer in a classroom, computer lab, or cybercafé, where you have to remove your files before you leave.

To Insert a USB Flash Drive and Open It in a Folder Window

First, you need to insert the USB flash drive so that you can back up your data to your USB flash drive. The following steps insert a USB flash drive and open it in a folder window.

1 Insert a USB flash drive into any available USB port on your computer to display the AutoPlay window. If the AutoPlay window does not appear, click the Start button, click the Computer command to open the Computer folder window, and then click the drive letter representing your USB flash drive.

2 Under the General Options heading, click the 'Open folder to view files' command to open a folder window.

To Create a Backup on a USB Flash Drive

With the USB flash drive connected, you are ready to make a backup. You decide to back up your Backgrounds folder. By copying this folder to the USB flash drive, you will be adding a measure of security to your data. The following steps copy the Backgrounds folder from the Pictures library to the USB flash drive.

- Make the Backgrounds window the active window (Figure 3–66).

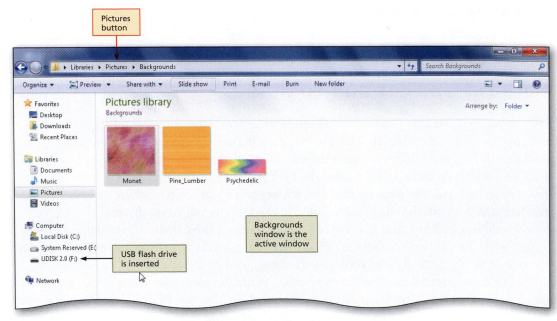

Figure 3–66

2

- Click the Pictures button on the Address bar to change the location to the Pictures library (Figure 3–67).

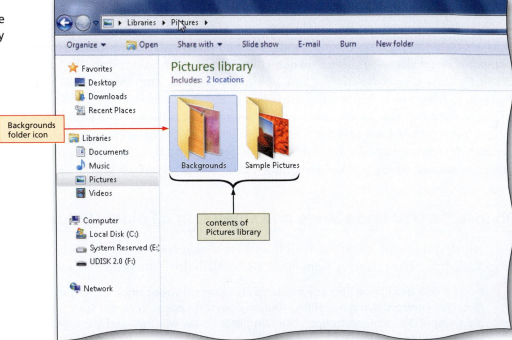

Figure 3–67

3

- If necessary, click the Backgrounds folder icon to select the Backgrounds folder.

- Right-click the Backgrounds folder to display a shortcut menu (Figure 3–68).

- Click the Copy command on the shortcut menu to copy the folder to the Clipboard.

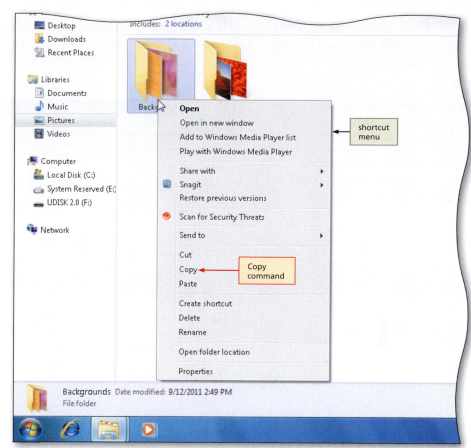

Figure 3–68

4

- Make the UDISK 2.0 (F:) window the active window.

Q&A

Why do I not have a UDISK 2.0 (F:) window?

UDISK 2.0 refers to the name of the USB flash drive, and (F:) refers to the drive letter. If either the name of your USB flash drive or drive letter are different, the window containing your USB flash drive's contents would be named to reflect these differences.

- Right-click an open area in the list area to display a shortcut menu.

- Click the Paste command on the shortcut menu to paste a copy of the Backgrounds folder onto the USB flash drive (Figure 3–69).

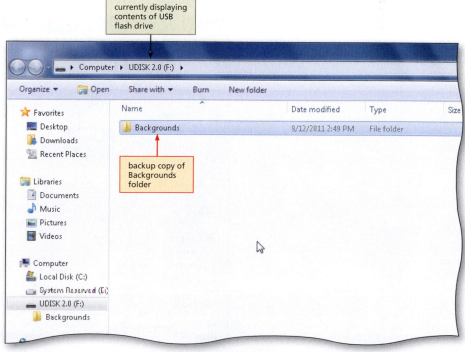

Figure 3–69

To Rename a Folder

The folder on the USB flash drive is a backup copy of the original folder, so it is a good idea to change its name to reflect that it is a backup. The following steps rename the folder on the USB flash drive to indicate that it is a backup folder.

- If necessary, click the Backgrounds folder icon to select the Backgrounds folder.

- Right-click the Backgrounds icon to display a shortcut menu (Figure 3–70).

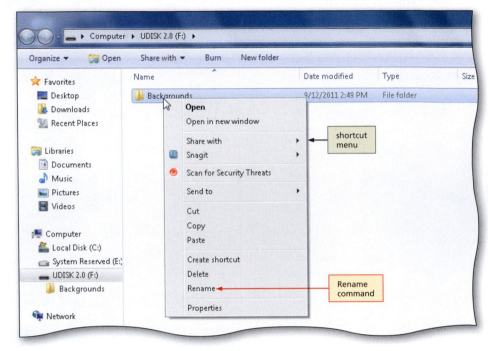

Figure 3–70

- Click the Rename command to open the name of the folder in a text box (Figure 3–71).

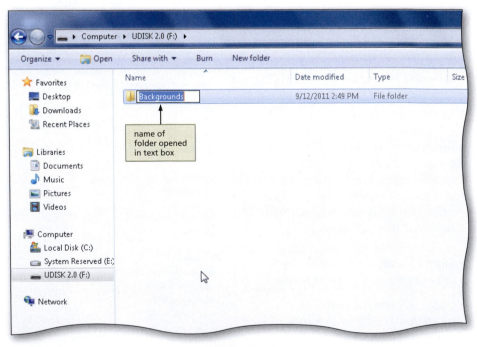

Figure 3–71

3

● Type `Backgrounds - Backup` as the new name for the folder (Figure 3–72).

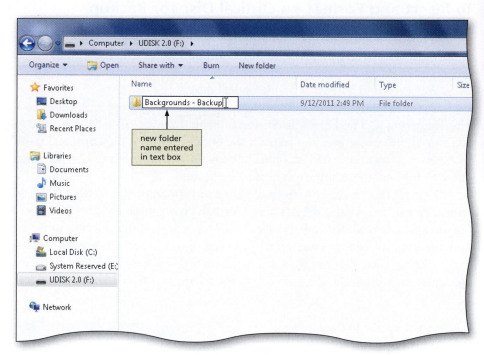

Figure 3–72

4

● Press the ENTER key to apply the new name to the folder (Figure 3–73).

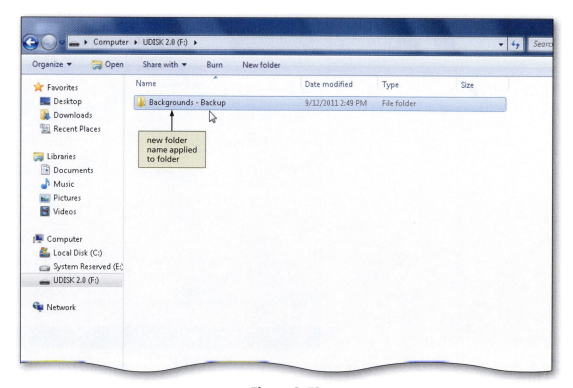

Figure 3–73

To Insert and Format an Optical Disc for Backup

Copying a folder to a USB flash drive is one method of creating a backup. Another way to make a backup is to burn the files to an optical disc. Most computer users who back up to optical discs either use a CD or DVD. The process of backing up files to an optical disc requires that you have an optical disc drive that can write data to optical discs. You also need a blank writable optical disc.

In this backup process, the optical disc can be formatted with the Live File System or formatted with the Mastered format. The **Live File System**, or the 'Like a USB flash drive' option, is a file storage system that allows you to add files each time you reinsert the optical disc into the computer (similar to how you can add files to a USB flash drive). However, when an optical disc is formatted with the Live File System, the files only are readable on other computers that support the Live File System.

Optical discs burned with the **Mastered** format, or the 'With a CD/DVD player' option, are readable on all optical disc drives. Using the Mastered format, you cannot add new files once the optical disc has been finalized. Finalizing an optical disc means that the disc is prepared for later use in your computer or another computer. With both formats, the files are not actually burned onto the optical disc until you eject the optical disc.

The following steps insert and format a CD for creating a backup. If you do not have access to an optical disc burner or do not have a blank disc, read the following steps without performing them.

- Insert a blank CD to display the AutoPlay options (Figure 3–74).

- If the AutoPlay window does not appear, open the Computer folder window and then double-click the drive letter representing your optical disc drive to display the Burn a Disc dialog box. Next, skip to Step 3.

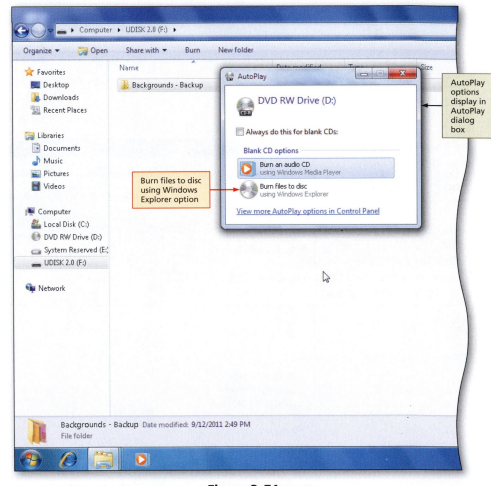

Figure 3–74

2

- Click the 'Burn files to disc using Windows Explorer' option to display the Burn a Disc dialog box.

- If necessary, click the 'Like a USB flash drive' option button to select it (Figure 3–75).

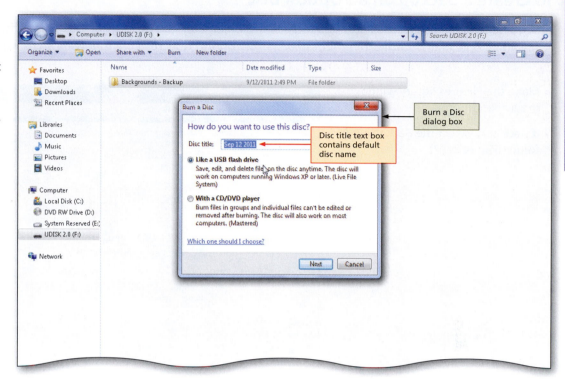

Figure 3–75

3

- Type `Backup – Sep` in the Disc title text box to provide a name for the disc (Figure 3–76).

- Click the Next button to format the disc. If the AutoPlay dialog box displays after the formatting is complete, click the Close button to close the AutoPlay dialog box.

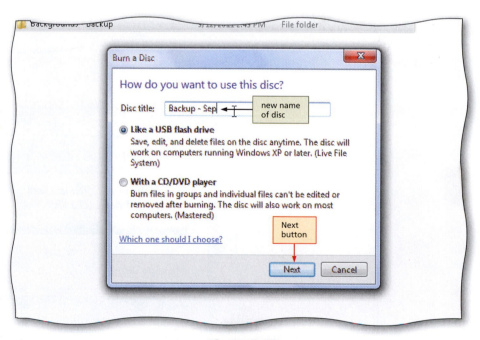

Figure 3–76

To Create a Backup on an Optical Disc

The following steps back up the Backgrounds folder from the Pictures library to the disc. If you do not have access to an optical disc burner or do not have a blank optical disc, read the following steps without performing them.

- Make the Pictures library window the active window.
- If necessary, select the Backgrounds folder (Figure 3–77).

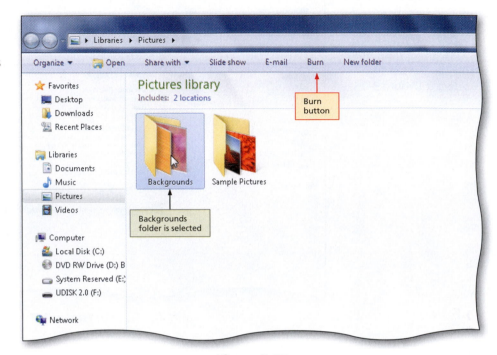

Figure 3–77

- Click the Burn button on the toolbar to begin the process of copying the files to the disc (Figure 3–78).

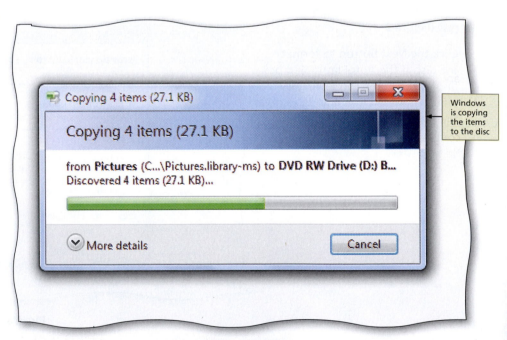

Figure 3–78

● Once the copy process has completed, the contents of the Backup – Sep disc appear in a new folder window (Figure 3–79).

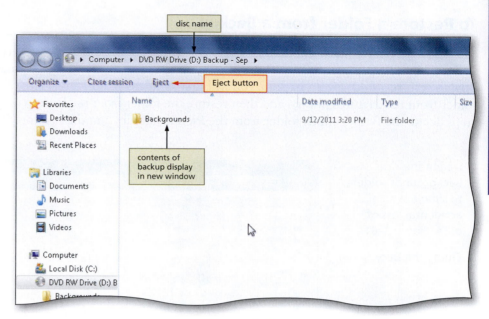

Figure 3–79

To Eject an Optical Disc

Now that the backup process is complete, the Backup - Sep folder is shown in a new folder window (Figure 3–79). You can continue to add files to this disc until you run out of storage space on the disc. Once you are ready to remove the disc, you eject it. Before the computer ejects the disc, it will be finalized. The following step ejects and finalizes the optical disc.

①

● Click the Eject button on the toolbar to have Windows 7 finalize and eject the CD (Figure 3–80).

● Remove the disc from computer's optical disc drive.

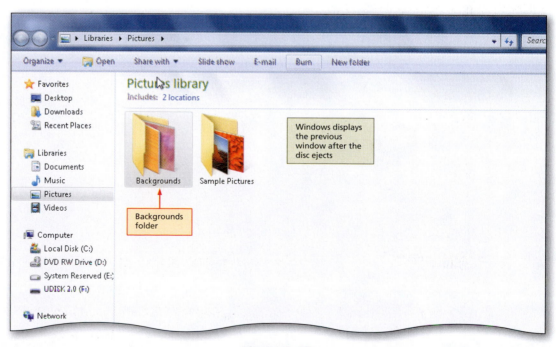

Figure 3–80

To Restore a Folder from a Backup

Whenever you need to restore a file or folder from a backup copy, you need to insert the removable media (where the backup copy was stored), and then you can copy the backup to the destination drive or folder. To learn how to restore a folder from backup, you will first simulate an accidental loss of data by deleting the Backgrounds folder from the Pictures library, and then restore the folder from the backup on your USB flash drive. The following steps delete the Backgrounds folder from the Pictures library and then restore it from your backup copy.

1

- Delete the Backgrounds folder to simulate an accidental loss of data (Figure 3–81).

- Empty the Recycle Bin.

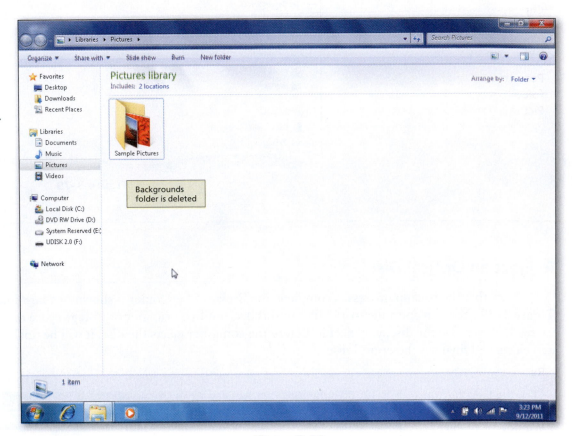

Figure 3–81

- Make the UDISK 2.0 (F:) window, or the window representing your USB flash drive, the active window.

- Copy the Backgrounds - Backup folder to place a copy on the Clipboard.

- Make the Pictures library window the active window.

- Paste the Backgrounds - Backup folder to place a copy in the Pictures library (Figure 3–82).

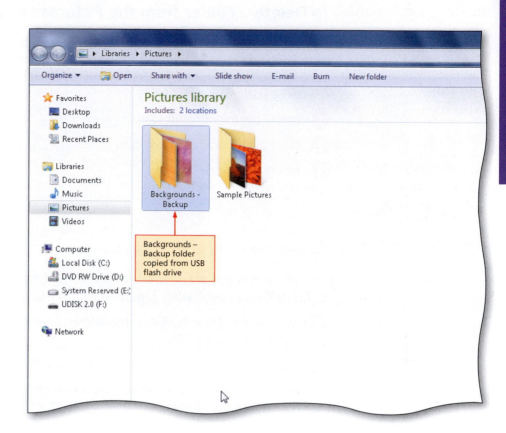

Figure 3–82

3

- Rename the folder Backgrounds to finish the restoration process (Figure 3–83).

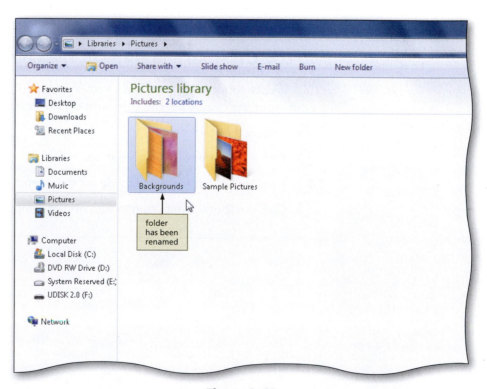

Figure 3–83

To Delete a Folder from the Pictures Library

You now have restored the Backgrounds folder after a mishap. This process would be the same if you were working from an optical disc backup. To return the Pictures library to its original state, you will delete the Backgrounds folder. The following steps delete the Backgrounds folder.

1 Delete the Backgrounds folder.

2 Close the Pictures library window.

3 Empty the Recycle Bin.

To Remove the USB Flash Drive

Now that you are done working with the USB flash drive, you should safely remove it. The following steps safely remove the USB flash drive.

1 Click the Computer button on the Address bar of the UDISK 2.0 (F:) window to display the Computer folder window.

2 Right click the UDISK 2.0 (F:) icon to display a shortcut menu.

3 Click the Safely Remove command to prepare the drive to be removed. If the Safely Remove command does not display on the shortcut menu, click the Eject command.

4 Remove the USB flash drive from your computer.

5 Close the Computer folder window.

To Log Off from and Turn Off the Computer

After completing your work with Windows 7, you should end your session by logging off of the computer, and then turn off the computer.

1 Display the Start menu.

2 Click the Shut down options button.

3 Click the Log off command to log off the computer.

4 Click the Shut down button to turn off the computer.

Chapter Summary

In this chapter, you learned about the Computer folder window. You learned how to view the properties of drives and folders, as well as how to view their content. You worked with files and folders in the Pictures library, reviewed and changed their properties, and viewed images in Windows Photo Viewer and as a slide show. As part of this process, you also learned how to copy and move files as well as how to create folders. Next, you saw how to work with files and folders in the Music library. You changed the genre of a music file and learned how to listen to a music file using the Windows Media Player. Finally, you gained knowledge of how to make a backup of files and restore the files, including how to copy, rename, and delete files and folders. The items listed below include all of the new Windows 7 skills you have learned in this chapter.

1. Display Properties for the Local Disk (C:) Drive in the Details Pane (WIN 136)
2. Display the Local Disk (C:) Properties Dialog Box (WIN 137)
3. Close the Local Disk (C:) Properties Dialog Box (WIN 138)
4. Switch Folders Using the Address Bar (WIN 139)
5. View the Contents of a Drive (WIN 141)
6. Preview the Properties for a Folder (WIN 142)
7. Display Properties for the Windows Folder in the Details Pane (WIN 142)
8. Display All of the Properties for the Windows Folder (WIN 143)
9. View the Contents of a Folder (WIN 144)
10. Search for a File and Folder in a Folder Window (WIN 145)
11. Search for Files Using Search Filters (WIN 146)
12. Clear the Search Box (WIN 147)
13. Use Aero Shake to Minimize and Restore All Windows Except the Active Window (WIN 148)
14. Cascade Open Windows (WIN 149)
15. Make a Window the Active Window (WIN 150)
16. Undo Cascading (WIN 151)
17. Stack Open Windows (WIN 152)
18. Undo Show Windows Stacked (WIN 153)
19. Show Windows Side by Side (WIN 154)
20. Undo Show Windows Side by Side (WIN 155)
21. View the Save Location for the Pictures Library (WIN 157)
22. Search for Pictures (WIN 158)
23. Copy Files to the Pictures Library (WIN 158)
24. Create a Folder in the Pictures Library (WIN 161)
25. Move Multiple Files into a Folder (WIN 163)
26. Refresh the Image on a Folder (WIN 164)
27. View and Change the Properties of a Picture (WIN 165)
28. Open a Picture in Windows Photo Viewer (WIN 168)
29. Navigate Through Your Pictures (WIN 168)
30. View Your Pictures as a Slide Show (WIN 170)
31. End a Slide Show (WIN 171)
32. Switch to the Music Library (WIN 172)
33. Open the Sample Music Folder (WIN 172)
34. View Information about a Music File (WIN 173)
35. Reset the Genre for a Music File (WIN 175)
36. Play a Music File in Windows Media Player (WIN 175)
37. Pause a Music File (WIN 176)
38. Create a Backup on a USB Flash Drive (WIN 178)
39. Rename a Folder (WIN 180)
40. Insert and Format an Optical Disc for Backup (WIN 182)
41. Create a Backup on an Optical Disc (WIN 184)
42. Eject an Optical Disc (WIN 185)
43. Restore a Folder from a Backup (WIN 186)

Learn It Online

Test your knowledge of chapter content and key terms.

Instructions: To complete the Learn It Online exercises, start your browser, click the Address bar, and then enter the Web address scsite.com/win7/learn. When the Windows 7 Learn It Online page is displayed, click the link for the exercise you want to complete and then read the instructions.

Chapter Reinforcement TF, MC, and SA
A series of true/false, multiple-choice, and short-answer questions that test your knowledge of the chapter content.

Flash Cards
An interactive learning environment where you identify chapter key terms associated with displayed definitions.

Practice Test
A series of multiple-choice questions that test your knowledge of chapter content and key terms.

Who Wants To Be a Computer Genius?
An interactive game that challenges your knowledge of chapter content in the style of a television quiz show.

Wheel of Terms
An interactive game that challenges your knowledge of chapter key terms in the style of the television show *Wheel of Fortune*.

Crossword Puzzle Challenge
A crossword puzzle that challenges your knowledge of key terms presented in the chapter.

Apply Your Knowledge

Reinforce the skills and apply the concepts you learned in this chapter.

File and Program Properties

Instructions: You want to demonstrate to a friend how to display the properties of an image, display the image using the Paint program instead of the Windows Photo Viewer program, and print the image. You also want to demonstrate how to display the properties of an application program.

Part 1: Displaying File Properties
1. Click the Start button and then click the Computer command.
2. Double-click the Local Disk (C:) icon. If necessary, click 'Show the contents of this folder' link.
3. Double-click the Windows icon. If necessary, click the 'Show the contents of this folder' link.
4. Search for the Penguins picture file. If the Penguins icon is not available on your computer, find the icon of another image file.
5. Right-click the Penguins icon. Click Properties on the shortcut menu. Answer the following questions about the Penguins file.
   a. What type of file is Penguins?

   _____

   b. What program is used to open the Penguins image?

   _____

   c. What is the path for the location of the Penguins file?

   _____

d. What is the size (in bytes) of the Penguins file?

_____

e. When was the file created?

_____

f. When was the file last modified?

_____

g. When was the file last accessed?

_____

Part 2: Using the Paint Program to Display an Image

1. Click the Change button in the Penguins Properties dialog box. Answer the following questions.

   a. What is the name of the dialog box that displays?

   _____

   b. Which program is used to open the Penguins file?

   _____

   c. List the other program(s) you can use to open the file.

   _____

2. Click the Paint icon in the Open with dialog box.
3. Click the OK button in the Open with dialog box.
4. Click the OK button in the Penguins Properties dialog box.
5. Double-click the Penguins icon to launch the Paint program and display the Penguins image in the Penguins – Paint window (Figure 3–84).

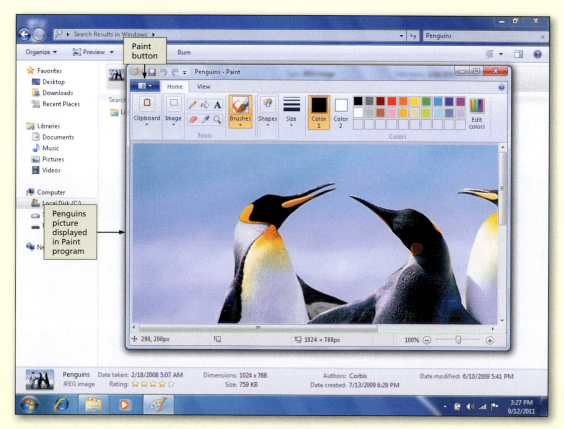

Figure 3–84

Continued >

Apply Your Knowledge *continued*

6. Print the Penguins image by clicking the Paint button on the menu bar, clicking the Print command, and then clicking the Print button in the Print dialog box.

7. Click the Close button in the Penguins – Paint window. Do not save the changes.

Part 3: Resetting the Program Selection in the Open with Dialog Box

1. Right-click the Penguins icon. Click Properties on the shortcut menu. Answer the following question.

  a. What program is used to open the Penguins image?

  _____

2. Click the Change button in the Penguins Properties dialog box.

3. If necessary, click the Windows Photo Viewer icon in the Open with dialog box to select the icon.

4. Click the OK button in the Open with dialog box.

5. Click the OK button in the Penguins Properties dialog box.

Part 4: Displaying Program Properties

1. Return to the Search Results in the Windows folder and clear the Search box.

2. Scroll the right pane of the Windows folder window until the HelpPane icon displays. If the HelpPane icon does not appear, scroll to display another file.

3. Right-click the icon. Click Properties on the shortcut menu. Answer the following questions.

  a. What type of file is selected?

  _____

  b. What is the file's description?

  _____

  c. What is the path of the file?

  _____

  d. What size is the file when stored on disk?

  _____

4. Click the Cancel button in the Properties dialog box.

5. Close the Windows window.

Extend Your Knowledge

Extend the skills you learned in this chapter and experiment with new skills. You might need to use Help to complete the assignment.

Creating a Picture

Instructions: You want to use Paint to design a Congratulations image for a friend and then print the message. The file name of the Paint program is paint, but you do not know the location of the program on the hard disk. You first will use Search to find the paint file on the hard disk.

Part 1: Searching for the Paint Program

1. Click the Start button.

2. Type paint in the Search box.

3. Click the Paint icon.

Part 2: Creating a Bitmap Image

1. Launch Paint and display the Untitled – Paint window (Figure 3–85).

2. Use the Pencil tool shown in Figure 3–85 to write the message Congratulations Graduate! in the Untitled – Paint window. *Hint:* Hold the left mouse button down to write and release the left mouse button to stop writing. If you make a mistake and want to start over, click the Undo button.

3. Click the Paint button on the menu bar and then click Save as. When the Save As dialog box displays, type Congratulations Graduate in the File name text box, click the Pictures library in the Navigation pane, and then click the Save button in the Save As dialog box to save the file in the Pictures library.

4. Close the Congratulations Graduate - Paint window.

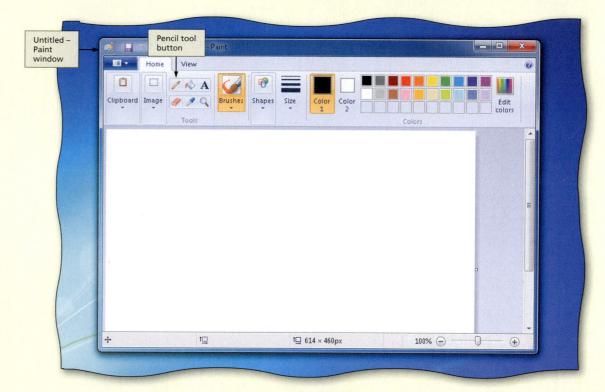

Figure 3–85

Part 3: Previewing and Printing the Congratulations Graduate Image

1. Open the Pictures library folder.

2. Click the Congratulations Graduate icon in the Pictures window to select the icon.

3. Click Preview on the toolbar.

4. After viewing the image in Windows Photo Viewer, click the Print button on the toolbar to view printing options.

5. Click Print to open the Print Pictures dialog box.

6. Click Print to print the image.

7. Close Windows Photo Viewer.

Part 4: Deleting the Congratulations Graduate Image

1. Click the Congratulations Graduate icon to select the file.

2. Click Organize on the toolbar, and then click Delete.

3. Click the Yes button in the Delete File dialog box.

4. Close the Pictures library window.

In the Lab

Use the guidelines, concepts, and skills presented in this chapter to increase your knowledge of Windows 7. Labs are listed in order of increasing difficulty.

Lab 1: Using Search to Find Picture Files

Instructions: You know that searching is an important feature of Windows 7. You decide to use the Search text box to find the images on the hard disk. You will store the files in a folder in the Pictures library, print the images, and copy them to a USB flash drive.

Part 1: Searching for Files in the Search Results Window

1. If necessary, launch Microsoft Windows 7 and log on to the computer.
2. Click the Start button on the taskbar and then click the Computer command. Maximize the Computer folder window.
3. Double-click Local Disk (C:), and then double-click the Windows folder to open it.
4. In the Search box, type `Lighthouse` as the entry.
5. Copy the image to the Pictures library using the Navigation pane.
6. If necessary, close all open windows.

Part 2: Searching for Files from Another Window

1. Click the Start button and then click the Pictures command.
2. Click the Search box.
3. Type `Koala` as the entry.
4. Copy the image to the Pictures library.
5. Close the Pictures library window.

Part 3: Searching for Groups of Files

1. Click the Start button and then click the Computer command.
2. Double-click Local Disk (C:), and then double-click the Windows folder to open it.
3. In the Search box of the Windows folder, type `tu*` as the search term (Figure 3–86).
4. Answer the following question.
   a. How many files were found?

   _____

5. Scroll to find the Tulips icon. Click the Tulips icon to select the icon. If the Tulips icon does not display, select another icon.
6. Copy the image to the Pictures library.

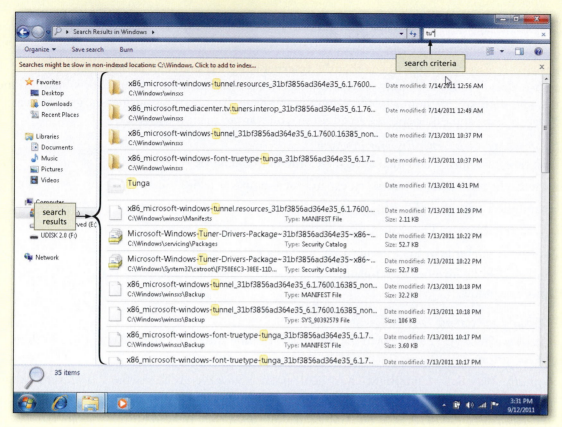

Figure 3–86

Part 4: Creating the More Backgrounds Folder in the Pictures Library

1. Click the New folder button, type `More Backgrounds` in the icon title text box and then press the ENTER key.

2. Select the icons of the images you copied to the Pictures library and then move the images to the More Backgrounds folder.

3. Right-click an open area of the window and refresh the thumbnail image on the More Backgrounds folder.

Part 5: Printing the Images

1. Open the More Backgrounds folder.

2. Select the pictures.

3. Click Print on the toolbar to display the Print Pictures dialog box.

4. Use the scroll bar to select the Wallet option.

5. Type 3 in the Copies of each picture text box.

6. Click the Print button to print the pictures.

Part 6: Moving the More Backgrounds Folder to a USB Flash Drive

1. Insert a USB flash drive into an available USB port and then click the 'Open folder to view files' command.

2. Switch to the Pictures window.

3. Select the More Backgrounds icon in the Pictures window.

4. Right-click the More Backgrounds icon.

5. Click Send to and then click USB flash drive.

6. Close the Pictures library.

7. Safely remove the USB flash drive from the computer.

Continued >

In the Lab *continued*

Lab 2: Finding Pictures Online

Instructions: A classmate informs you that the Internet is a great source of photos, pictures, and images. You decide to launch Internet Explorer, search for well-known candy and drink logos on the Internet, and then save them in a folder. A **logo** is an image that identifies businesses, government agencies, products, and other entities. In addition, you want to print the logos.

Part 1: Launching the Internet Explorer Program

1. Click the Start button and then click the Computer command.

2. In the Navigation pane, if necessary, expand the Computer listing.

3. Expand the Local Disk (C:) list.

4. Expand the Program Files list.

5. Display the contents of the Internet Explorer folder.

6. Double-click the iexplore icon to launch Internet Explorer and display the Windows Internet Explorer window.

Part 2: Finding and Saving Logo Images

1. Type `www.jellybelly.com` in the Address bar in the Internet Explorer window, and then click the Go button.

2. Locate the Jelly Belly icon. Right-click the icon, click Save Picture As on the shortcut menu, and then click the Save button to save the logo in the Pictures library.

3. Type `www.smarties.com` in the Address bar and then click the Go button. Locate the Smarties picture that matches the one in Figure 3–87 and use the file name, Smarties logo, to save the Smarties logo in the Pictures library.

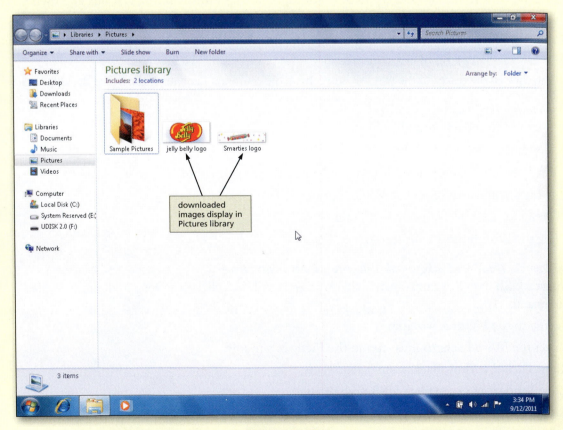

Figure 3–87

4. Close Internet Explorer and close the Internet Explorer folder window.

5. Click the Start button and then click Pictures. The Jelly Belly logo and Smarties image display in the Pictures window (Figure 3–87). The logos in the Pictures library window on your computer might be different from the logos shown in Figure 3–87 if the businesses have changed their logos.

Part 3: Displaying File Properties

1. Right-click each logo file in the Pictures library, click Properties, answer the following question about the logo, and then close the Properties dialog box.

   a. What type of file is the Jelly Belly logo file?

   _____

   b. What type of file is the Smarties logo file?

   _____

2. Click an open area of the Pictures library to deselect the Smarties logo file.

Part 4: Creating the Candy Logos Folder in the Pictures Library

1. Make a new folder in the Pictures library, type Candy Logos in the icon title text box, and then press the ENTER key.

2. Click the Jelly Belly logo, hold down the CTRL key, and then click the Smarties logo.

3. Right-drag the icons to the Candy Logos icon and then click Move here on the shortcut menu.

4. Refresh the image on the Candy Logos folder.

Part 5: Printing the Logo Images

1. Open the Candy Logos folder.

2. Select both of the logos.

3. Click Print on the toolbar to display the Print Pictures dialog box. Choose the option for printing both logos on a single page.

4. Click the Print button to print the pictures.

Part 6: Moving the Candy Logos Folder to a USB Flash Drive

1. Insert a USB flash drive into an available USB port.

2. Copy the Candy Logos folder to the USB flash drive.

3. Safely remove the USB flash drive from the computer.

4. Delete the Candy Logos folder from the Pictures library.

5. Close the Pictures library.

Lab 3: Managing Your Music

Instructions: You want to investigate the different ways you can organize the music stored on your computer. Once you determine which method of organizing your music you prefer, you decide that you want to add to your music collection. First you will learn about the copyright laws that pertain to digital music and then you will research a few Web sites that allow you to download music files.

Part 1: Organizing Your Music

1. Open the Start menu and then open the Music library. Open the Sample Music folder and answer the following questions.

   a. How many files are there?

   _____

   b. To which album does Sleep Away belong?

   _____

Continued >

In the Lab *continued*

c. Which song is the longest running? (*Hint:* Play in Windows Media Player.)

Part 2: Researching Copyright Laws Regarding Digital Music Files

1. Click the Internet Explorer icon on the taskbar. Type `www.copyright.gov` in the Address bar and then press the ENTER key.

   a. What copyright laws exist concerning music files?

   b. What should you know before downloading music files?

   c. What are the legal ramifications of downloading and sharing illegal music files?

Part 3: Finding Music Online

1. Type `www.netmusic.com` in the Address bar and press the ENTER key.

   a. What types of music can be downloaded from this Web site?

   b. What are the fees?

   c. Are there any free, legal downloads available?

   d. Would you use this service?

2. Type `rhapsody.com` in the Address bar of Internet Explorer and press the ENTER key. (Figure 3–88).

   a. What program do you need to download music from this Web site?

   b. What are the fees for using the program? for shopping?

   c. How are music files downloaded from within the program?

   d. Would you use this service?

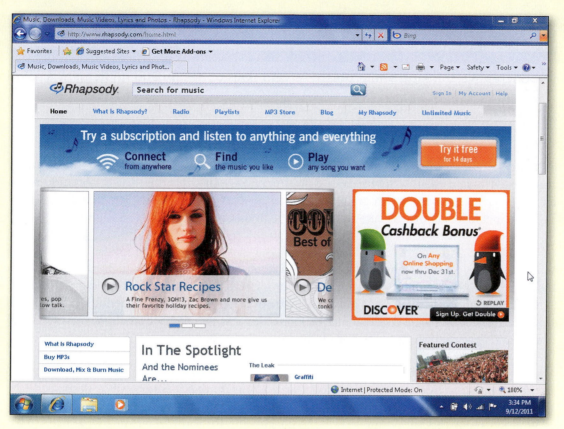

Figure 3–88

3. Type www.apple.com/itunes in the Address bar of Internet Explorer and press the ENTER key. Click the learn how to get started link.

   a. What program do you need to download music from this Web site?

      _____

   b. What are the fees for using the program? for shopping?

      _____

   c. How are music files downloaded from within the program?

      _____

   d. Would you use this service?

      _____

Cases and Places

Apply your creative thinking and problem-solving skills to design and implement a solution.

• EASIER   •• MORE DIFFICULT

• 1 Finding Programs

You are interested in identifying which programs are installed on your computer. To find all the programs, you decide to search the Program Files folder on your computer. Using techniques you learned in this chapter, open the Program Files folder on the C drive. Search for *.exe files. Summarize your findings in a brief report. Be sure to indicate the number of programs you found.

• 2 Filter Searching

Your employer suspects that someone has used your computer during off-hours for non–company business. She has asked you to search your computer for files that have been created or modified during the last week. Search for files in the Windows 7 libraries using the Date modified filter. When you find the files, determine if any are WordPad files or Paint files that you did not create or modify. Summarize the number and date they were created or modified in a brief report.

•• 3 Researching Backups

Backing up files is an important way to protect data and ensure that it is not lost or destroyed accidentally. You can use a variety of devices and techniques to back up files from a personal computer. Using Windows Help and Support, research the Backup and Restore. Determine what backup tools Windows 7 provides. Write a brief report of your findings.

•• 4 Researching Photo Printing Sites

Make It Personal

Now that you know how to work with the Pictures library, you want to find Web sites where you can upload and print your photos. Using the Internet, search for three photo printing Web sites. Find the prices per 4 x 6 photo, which file formats are required, and explore any other photo products that you would be interested in purchasing. Write a brief report that compares the three Web sites and indicate which one you would use.

•• 5 Researching Data Security

Working Together

Data stored on disk is one of a company's most valuable assets. If that data were to be stolen, lost, or compromised so that it could not be accessed, the company could go out of business. Therefore, companies go to great lengths to protect their data. Working with classmates, research how the companies where you each work handle their backups. Find out how each one protects its data against viruses, unauthorized access, and even against natural disasters such as fire and floods. Prepare a brief report that describes the companies' procedures. In your report, point out any areas where you find a company has not protected its data adequately.

4 Personal Information Management and Communication

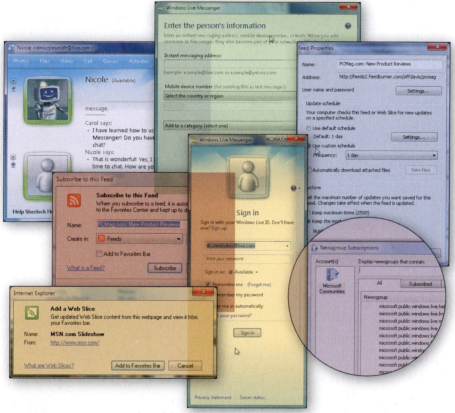

Objectives

You will have mastered the material in this chapter when you can:

- Open, read, print, reply to, and delete e-mail messages

- Open a file attachment

- Compose and format an e-mail message

- Attach a file to an e-mail message

- Send an e-mail message

- Add and modify a Calendar event

- Add and delete a Windows contact

- Display and work with a newsgroup

- Locate and subscribe to an RSS feed

- Identify other communication methods available on the Internet

- Start and sign in to Windows Live Messenger

- Add and remove a Windows Live Messenger contact

- Send an instant message

4 | Personal Information Management and Communication

Introduction

Microsoft Windows traditionally has provided programs that allow you to manage your personal information and communicate with other individuals via the Internet. These programs and features are not installed with Windows 7 but instead are included with Windows Live Essentials. **Windows Live Essentials** is free software that enhances Windows 7 functionality, which can be downloaded from the Microsoft Web site. Windows Live Essentials includes programs such as Windows Live Mail and Windows Live Messenger. Windows Live Mail allows you to send and receive e-mail messages, read and post messages to a newsgroup, keep track of appointments and tasks, and capture detailed contact information for your friends and associates. Windows Live Messenger is a program that allows you to communicate by sending and receiving instant messages. For this chapter, it is assumed that you have Windows Live Essentials installed.

Windows 7 includes Internet Explorer, a Web browser that allows you to visit Web sites, subscribe to RSS feeds, and communicate using blogs, groups, chat rooms, bulletin boards, and forums. In this chapter, you will use Windows Live Mail for personal information management, along with Internet Explorer and Windows Live Messenger to explore other means of Web-based communications.

Overview

As you read this chapter, you will learn how to use Windows Live Mail, Contacts, Calendar, Internet Explorer, and Windows Live Messenger and how to communicate using the Internet (Figure 4–1) by performing these general tasks:

- Sending and receiving e-mail messages
- Scheduling appointments and tasks
- Adding and removing contacts
- Subscribing to and reading newsgroup articles
- Subscribing to and reading RSS feeds
- Sending and receiving instant messages

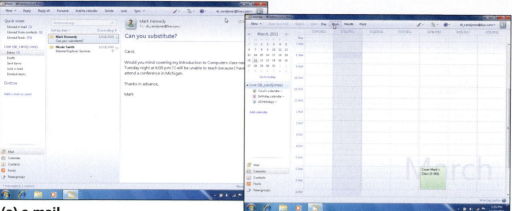

(a) e-mail

(b) calendar

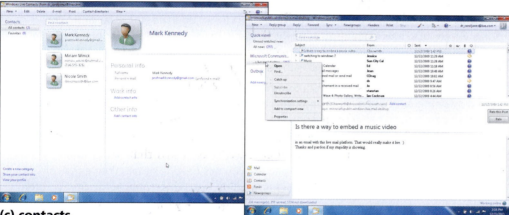

(c) contacts

(d) newsgroups

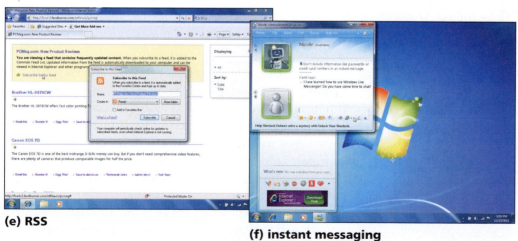

(e) RSS

(f) instant messaging

Figure 4–1

Internet Communication Guidelines

Plan Ahead

To communicate effectively, you should understand the general guidelines for using e-mail and instant messaging programs and other online communications. Before communicating via the Internet, consider these general guidelines:

1. **Determine the information you need.** The Internet provides access to a wealth of information, whether it is current news, a note from a friend agreeing to join you for

(continued)

Plan Ahead

(continued)

dinner Friday, or an instant message from a colleague who is asking a question for a customer at his desk. The type of information and the speed at which you need it will help you choose the most effective method of communication.

2. **Consider who is most likely to have the information you need.** Some programs, such as e-mail or instant messaging, allow you to communicate easily with friends and family, whereas others, such as groups, newsgroups, or chat rooms, provide you with access to people you might not know. If the information you are seeking is not available from those who are close to you, consider using a communication method that enables you to reach a broader audience.

3. **Communicate with people you trust.** The Internet enables anyone to communicate with you. In fact, it is possible to receive a large amount of unsolicited communication as well as harmful e-mail attachments. Communicate with individuals you trust or through exchanges that you initiate, and be cautious when communicating with strangers.

4. **Do not open unsolicited file attachments.** If you receive a file via an e-mail or instant message, do not open it unless you are expecting it from someone you know and trust. Some viruses that travel via file attachments are able to appear as if they originated from someone you know and trust, so it is especially important for you to be careful. If you receive a file that you suspect to be infected with a virus, contact the sender of the file immediately.

5. **Determine whether your communication should be formal or informal.** If you are communicating with a potential employer or a colleague at work, you should use proper spelling, grammar, and etiquette. If you are communicating with friends and family, you can be less formal, and you might not bother checking for spelling and grammatical errors.

6. **Gather e-mail and instant messaging addresses.** Before you can send e-mail or instant messages to your friends, family, and colleagues, you will need to obtain their e-mail or instant messaging addresses. Without this information, you will be unable to communicate with them.

Electronic Mail (E-Mail)

Electronic mail (**e-mail**) is an important means of exchanging messages and files between business associates and friends. Businesses find that using e-mail messages to send files electronically saves both time and money. Parents with students away at college or relatives who are scattered across the country find that exchanging e-mail messages is an inexpensive and easy way to stay in touch with family members. In fact, exchanging e-mail messages is one of the more widely used features of the Internet. E-mail is so popular nowadays that many individuals have multiple e-mail accounts. For instance, you might have an e-mail account for your job and an e-mail address for personal use. It is important to recognize that if your employer supplies you with an e-mail account, all messages sent to and from that account are the property of, and accessible by, your employer. If you plan to send personal e-mail messages, it is recommended that you do not use the e-mail account provided by your employer. Some individuals also find it useful to have multiple personal e-mail accounts. They might give one e-mail address to their friends and family, and use another e-mail address when signing up for mailing lists, filling out registration forms, or entering a sweepstakes. This way, personal e-mail messages are kept separate from bulk or junk e-mail messages.

Windows Live Mail is an e-mail program that allows you to receive and store incoming e-mail messages, compose and send e-mail messages, access your contacts and your calendar, and read and post messages to Web feeds and Internet newsgroups. Windows Live Mail can be downloaded from the Windows Live Essentials home page (download.live.com). The Contacts folder in Windows Live Mail allows you to store information about individuals you contact frequently. This information might include their e-mail address, street address, telephone number, and birthday. The Calendar feature in Windows Live Mail allows you to keep track of appointments and events that you have scheduled.

E-mail can be accessed by using Windows Live Mail, or by other e-mail programs installed on your computer, such as Microsoft Outlook or Mozilla Thunderbird, or by using a Web-based e-mail service. A **Web-based e-mail service** allows you to send and receive e-mail messages by logging on to a Web site, instead of installing an e-mail program on your computer. By using a Web-based e-mail service, you are able to check your e-mail messages on any computer that has an Internet connection and a Web browser. Free Web-based e-mail services include Windows Live Hotmail, Gmail, Yahoo! Mail, and AIM Mail. These companies are able to provide free Web-based e-mail services by placing advertisements on their Web sites or directly in the e-mail messages sent from their Web site. Although all e-mail services offer the same basic functionality, such as sending and receiving e-mail messages and storing contact information, some features, such as the amount of storage space each service offers, might differ. Before choosing a Web-based e-mail service, compare the different features to determine which one might work best for you.

If you work for an employer who provides you with an e-mail account, you most likely access your e-mail account by using an e-mail program installed on your computer. Some companies also provide Web-based access to their e-mail system, enabling employees to send and receive e-mail messages from a location other than the office. It is common for the Web-based interface to resemble the interface of the e-mail program you use in the office to access your e-mail account. Although the interfaces and functionality might be similar between Web-based e-mail services and e-mail programs installed on your computer, some differences do exist. For example, if you are accessing your e-mail account by using an e-mail program installed on your computer, the e-mail messages are transferred to and stored on your computer before you can read them. If you are accessing your e-mail account using a Web-based e-mail service, the e-mail messages are stored remotely on the e-mail server.

BTW

POP Mail
You can configure Windows Live Mail to automatically retrieve e-mail messages from other e-mail accounts, such as Gmail, by using the Post Office Protocol (POP). This feature is useful when you do not want to access your e-mail account using a Web browser.

To Install Windows Live Essentials

As stated previously, Windows Live Essentials includes programs that extend the capabilities of Windows 7. Because Windows Live Essentials is not installed with Windows by default, it might be necessary to install it before completing the remainder of the chapter. To determine whether Windows Live Essentials is installed, display the Start menu, click All Programs, and then look for the Windows Live folder in the All Programs list. If the Windows Live folder is present, Windows Live Essentials is installed and the following steps are for illustrative purposes only. If the Windows Live folder is not present, complete the following steps to install Windows Live Essentials.

1 Display the Start menu.

2 Display the All Programs list.

3 Click Accessories to display the Accessories list.

4 Click the Getting Started command to display the Getting Started window (Figure 4–2 on the next page).

5 Double-click the Go online to get Windows Live Essentials link to display the Essentials - Windows Live Web page.

6 Click the Download button on the Essentials - Windows Live Web page. When the File Download - Security Warning dialog box is displayed, click the Run button to start the download and initiate the install. If the User Account Control dialog box appears, click the Yes button.

7 Follow the instructions on the screen to complete the Windows Live Essentials installation.

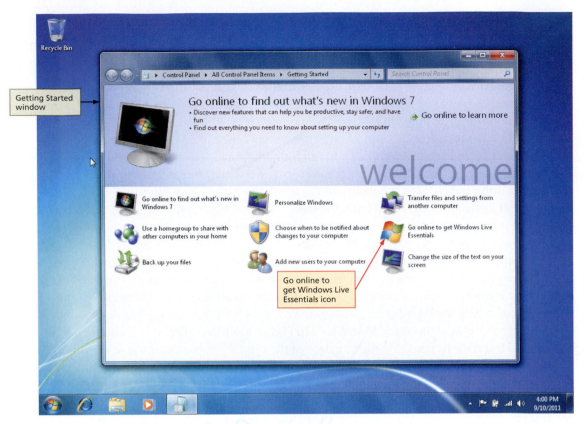

Figure 4–2

To Start Windows Live Mail

The following steps, which start Windows Live Mail, assume that you have an e-mail account configured in Windows Live Mail. For more information about configuring an e-mail account in Windows Live Mail, see your instructor.

1

• Display the Start menu.

• Click All Programs on the Start menu to display the All Programs list (Figure 4–3).

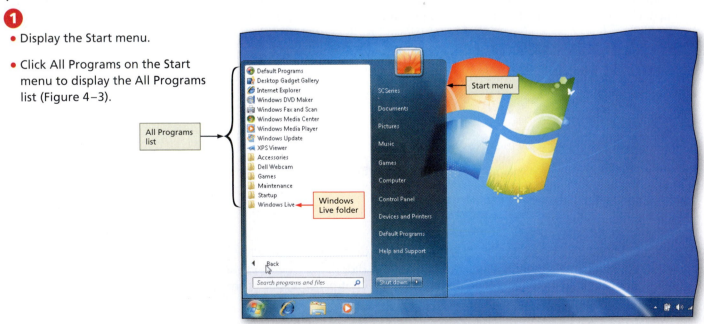

Figure 4–3

2

- Click Windows Live to display the Windows Live list containing the Windows Live programs.

- Click Windows Live Mail to start Windows Live Mail.

- If necessary, maximize the Inbox-Windows Live Mail window (Figure 4–4).

Q&A Why does my screen look different?

Because you are accessing your own e-mail account, Windows Live Mail will display different e-mail messages in the message list. However, you can follow the steps presented in this chapter by using the e-mail messages displayed in your message list.

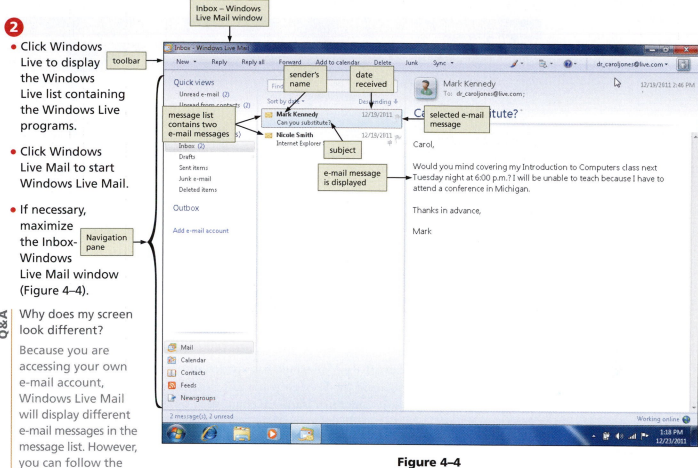

Figure 4–4

Other Ways

1. Press CTRL+ESC, type Windows Live Mail, click Windows Live Mail

The Windows Live Mail Window

The Inbox - Windows Live Mail window shown in Figure 4–4 contains a number of elements. The toolbar below the title bar contains buttons specific to Windows Live. Table 4–1 contains the toolbar buttons and a brief explanation of their functions.

BTW **Formatting E-Mail**
Windows Live Mail, like many other e-mail programs, allows you to change the appearance of an e-mail message by using different fonts and formatting, changing the background graphic, attaching files, and adding links to Web pages.

Table 4–1 Toolbar Buttons and Functions

Button	Function
New ▾	Displays the New Message window used to compose a new e-mail message.
Reply	Displays a window used to reply to an e-mail message. The recipient's name, original subject of the e-mail message preceded by the Re: entry, and the original e-mail message appear in the window.
Reply all	Displays a window used to reply to an e-mail message. The names of all recipients, subject of the e-mail message preceded by the Re: entry, and the original e-mail message appear in the window.

(continued)

Table 4–1 (continued)

Button	Function
Forward	Displays a window used to forward an e-mail message to another recipient. The original subject of the e-mail message preceded by the Fw: entry and the original e-mail message appear in the window.
Add to calendar	Adds the highlighted e-mail message to the calendar.
Delete	Deletes the highlighted e-mail message in the message list.
Junk	Marks the highlighted e-mail message as junk e-mail.
Sync	Synchronizes the e-mail accounts associated with Windows Live Mail.
	Displays options for changing the appearance of Windows Live Mail.
	Displays options for changing the menus of Windows Live Mail.
	Displays Help pages for Windows Live Mail.
	Signs in to a Windows Live account.

BTW

Displaying the Menu Bar
Windows Live Mail includes a menu bar that is not displayed by default. If you click the Menus button and then click the 'Show menu bar' command, the menu bar displays. Several options, such as configuring e-mail accounts and setting safety options, are available from the menu bar, so you might want to consider displaying it.

BTW

Creating New Mail Folders
You can create additional folders in the e-mail account folder list by right-clicking the e-mail account, clicking the New folder command, typing the folder name in the Folder name text box, and then clicking the OK button.

The Inbox - Windows Live Mail window is divided into three areas: the Navigation pane, the message list pane, and the Preview pane. The Navigation pane displays the Quick views list, the email account folder list (for the account used by Windows Live Mail), the Outbox, and links to Mail, Calendar, Contacts, Feeds, and Newsgroups. The Quick views list provides links for you to quickly read unread e-mail messages, unread e-mail messages only from people in your Contacts list, and unread posts from your subscribed RSS feeds.

Below the Quick views list, the Navigation pane displays the mail folders for the active e-mail account. Depending on the e-mail account being used, the folders will vary. For example, because the e-mail account used by Windows Live Mail in this chapter is a Windows Live account, the folders include Inbox, Drafts, Sent items, Junk e-mail, and Deleted items. A Gmail account might include folders including Inbox, [gmail], Follow up, Misc, and Priority.

Mail folders can contain e-mail messages, faxes, and files created in other Windows programs. Folders sometimes might be followed by a blue number in parentheses indicating the number of messages in the folder that are unread.

The contents of the Inbox folder automatically appear in the message list pane, shown in Figure 4–5, when you start Windows Live Mail. The message list pane displays information for each message that contains the sender's name or e-mail address, subject of the message, and date and time the message was received. Collectively, these three entries are referred to as the message heading.

In Figure 4–5, the first e-mail message, from Mark Kennedy, contains an opened envelope icon and a message heading that appears in normal type. The opened envelope icon and message heading indicate that the e-mail message has been read. The second e-mail message, from Nicole Smith, contains a paper clip icon, a closed envelope icon, and a message heading that appears in bold type. The closed envelope icon and bold message heading indicate that the e-mail message has not been read (opened) and the paper clip indicates that the message has an attachment.

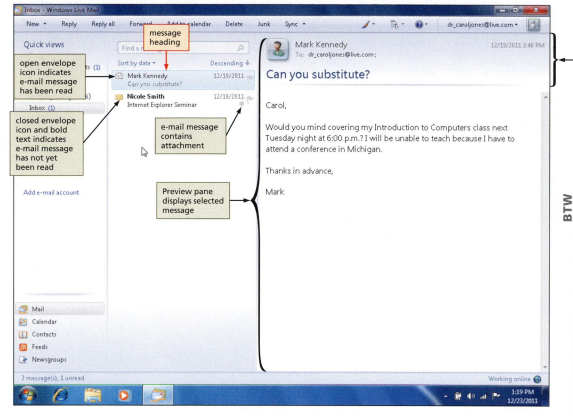

Figure 4–5

BTW

Sorting E-Mail Messages
You can sort e-mail messages in Windows Live Mail by characteristics such as sender, subject, and date received. To sort your e-mail messages by sender, for example, click the Sort by arrow button, and then select From. E-mail messages can be sorted in ascending or descending order.

BTW

Reading E-Mail Messages
Many people minimize the Inbox - Windows Live Mail window when perfoming other tasks on the computer. When they receive a new e-mail message, an envelope icon is displayed in the status area on the Windows taskbar and a notification sound is played.

The closed envelope icon is one of several icons, called message list icons, which display to indicate the status of the e-mail message. For example, an exclamation point icon indicates that the message has been sent with high priority. Message list icons also can indicate if an action was performed by the recipient. The recipient of a message often adds the flag icon to mark an e-mail message as important. Other icons appear when a message has been replied to, forwarded, digitally signed, or encrypted.

The Preview pane in Figure 4–5 contains the text of the e-mail message (Mark Kennedy) highlighted in the message list pane. The message header is displayed at the top of the Preview pane and contains the sender's name, the recipient's e-mail address, and the subject of the e-mail message. The text of the e-mail message appears below the message header.

To Open (Read) an E-Mail Message

In Figure 4–5, the message headings for Mark Kennedy and Nicole Smith are displayed in the message list pane. Double-clicking the envelope icon opens the e-mail message in a separate window, instead of opening it in the Preview pane. The step on the following page opens an e-mail message in a new window so that you can read it.

1

- Double-click anywhere on the message heading of the message from Mark Kennedy, which has the closed envelope icon. If the envelope icon for Mark Kennedy is not displayed in the message list, double-click another message with a closed envelope icon.

- Maximize the opened e-mail message window (Figure 4–6).

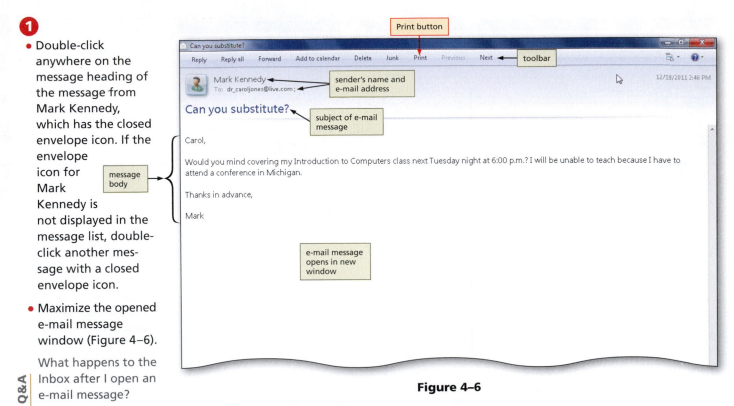

Figure 4–6

 Q&A

What happens to the Inbox after I open an e-mail message?

The closed envelope icon changes to an opened envelope icon, the message heading no longer appears in bold type, and the number of unread e-mails in the Quick views list decreases by one.

Other Ways

1. Right-click message heading with closed envelope icon, click Open on shortcut menu

2. Select message heading, press CTRL+O

To Print an Opened E-Mail Message

You can print the contents of an e-mail message before or after opening the message. The following steps print an opened e-mail message.

1

- Ready the printer according to the printer instructions.

- Click the Print button on the toolbar to display the Print dialog box (Figure 4–7).

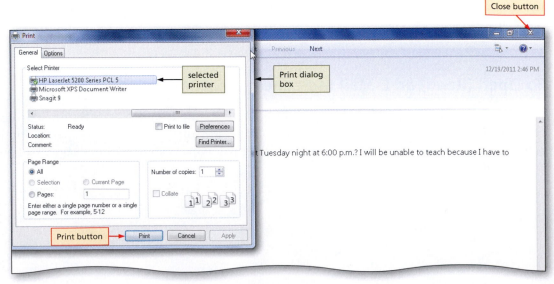

Figure 4–7

2
- Click the Print button in the Print dialog box (Figure 4–8).

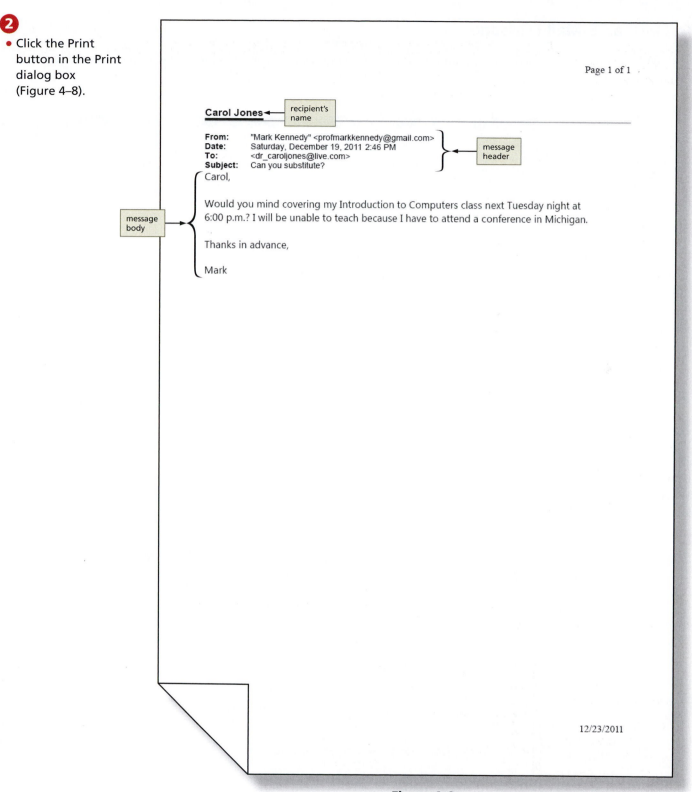

Page 1 of 1

Carol Jones ← recipient's name

From:	"Mark Kennedy" <profmarkkennedy@gmail.com>
Date:	Saturday, December 19, 2011 2:46 PM
To:	<dr_caroljones@live.com>
Subject:	Can you substitute?

message header

Carol,

Would you mind covering my Introduction to Computers class next Tuesday night at 6:00 p.m.? I will be unable to teach because I have to attend a conference in Michigan.

Thanks in advance,

Mark

message body

12/23/2011

Figure 4–8

Other Ways

1. Press ALT, click File, click Print, click Print button in Print dialog box

2. Press ALT+F, press P, press ENTER

3. Press CTRL+P, press ENTER

To Close an E-Mail Message

When you have finished opening and reading an e-mail message, you can close the window containing the e-mail message.

- Click the Close button on the title bar to close the window containing the e-mail message (Figure 4–9).

Reply button

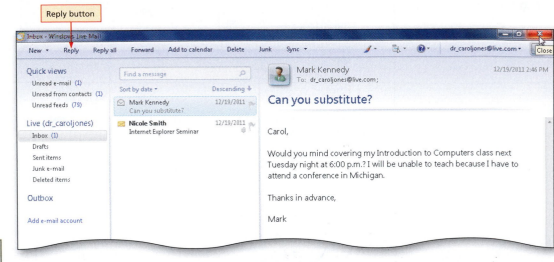

Figure 4–9

Other Ways

1. Press ALT, click File, click Close
2. Press ALT+F4

To Reply to an E-Mail Message

One method of composing and sending an e-mail reply uses the Reply button, located on the toolbar. The Reply button opens a new e-mail message and pre-populates the To text box with the e-mail address of the original sender and the Subject text box with the subject line of the original message preceded by Re: (regarding). The following steps compose and send an e-mail reply to a sender, in this case, Mark Kennedy, using the Reply button.

- Click the Reply button on the toolbar.

- If necessary, maximize the 'Re: Can you substitute?' e-mail message window (Figure 4–10).

Q&A

If I am replying to a message that was sent to multiple recipients, will each recipient see my reply?

No. Your reply only will be sent to the sender of the original message. If you want all recipients to see your reply, click the Reply all button instead of the Reply button.

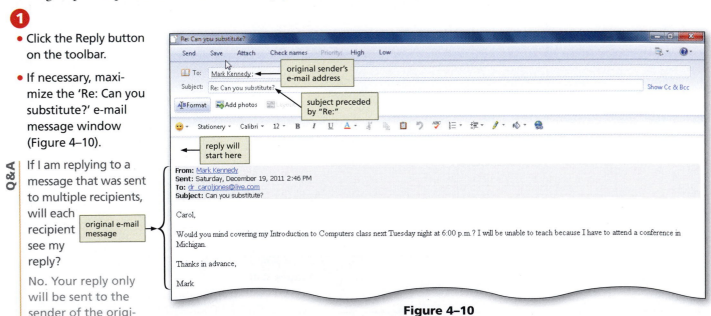

Figure 4–10

Q&A

Can I remove my original e-mail message that appears below the reply?

Yes. To configure Windows Live Mail so that the original e-mail message will not be included in the reply, press the ALT key, click Tools on the menu bar, click Options, click the Send tab, click to deselect the 'Include message in reply' check box, and then click the OK button.

2
- Type I will be happy to cover your class. Please let me know what I will have to cover. (Figure 4–11).

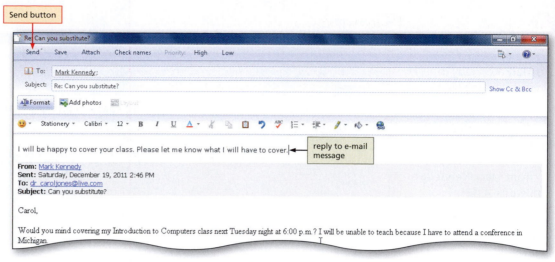

Figure 4–11

3
- Click the Send button on the toolbar to send the message (Figure 4–12).

Q&A
Will my e-mail message be sent immediately?

Although e-mail programs can be configured to send e-mail messages as soon as you click the Send button, they also can be config-

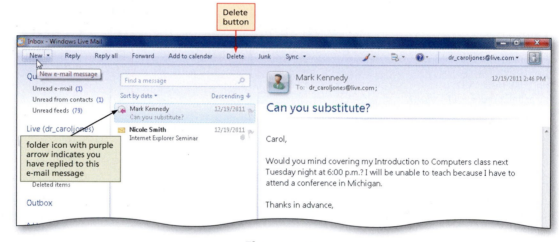

Figure 4–12

ured to send all outgoing e-mail messages at specified intervals, such as every 10 minutes. Once the e-mail program sends the e-mail messages, in most cases, you cannot reverse that action.

Q&A
How can I be sure that the intended recipient will receive my e-mail message?

The best way to verify that the recipient has received your e-mail message is to ask him or her for a response. If an e-mail address is incorrect, you often will receive an e-mail message stating that your message was unable to be delivered. If this happens, confirm the e-mail address of your recipient and try to send the e-mail message again.

Other Ways
1. Right-click message, click 'Reply to sender'
2. Press CTRL+R

To Delete an E-Mail Message

After reading and replying to an e-mail message, you might want to delete the original e-mail message from the message list pane. Deleting a message moves it from the Inbox folder to the Deleted items folder. If you do not delete unwanted messages, the number of messages in the Inbox folder will increase until it becomes difficult to find and read new messages. The step on the following page deletes the e-mail message from Mark Kennedy.

1

- If necessary, click the message from Mark Kennedy in the message list to select it.

- Click the Delete button on the toolbar to delete the message from Mark Kennedy (Figure 4–13).

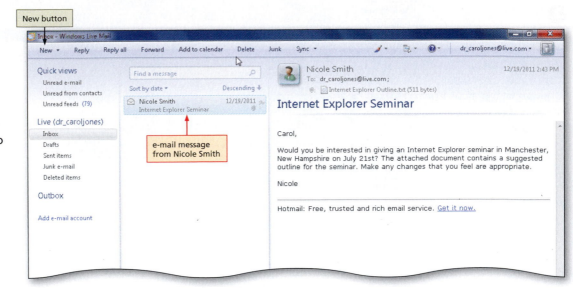

Figure 4–13

Other Ways	
1. Drag e-mail message to Deleted items folder in folder list	3. Press ALT, click Edit, click Delete
	4. Press CTRL+D
2. Right-click e-mail message, click Delete on shortcut menu	5. Press ALT+E, press D

To Open a File Attachment

The remaining message in the message list, from Nicole Smith, contains a file attachment, as indicated by the paper clip icon displayed in the message list item. The following steps open the file attachment.

1

- Double-click the remaining message heading in the message list to display the e-mail message from Nicole Smith in a new window.

- Maximize the Internet Explorer Seminar e-mail message window (Figure 4–14).

Q&A

Should I open a file attachment if I do not know who has sent it to me?

You should never open a file attachment sent from an unknown source. It is usually best to only open file attachments when you are expecting them from a trusted source.

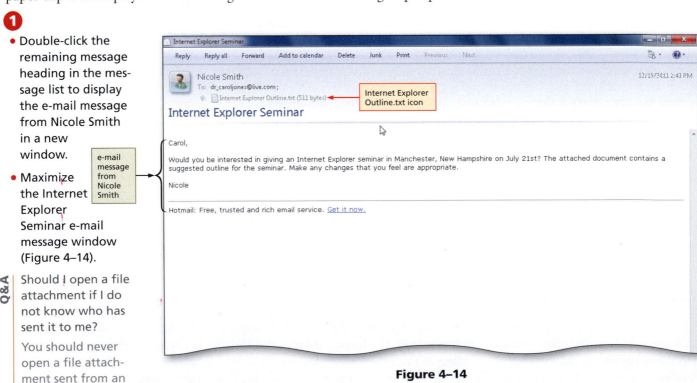

Figure 4–14

2

- Double-click the Internet Explorer Outline.txt attachment icon to open the attachment (Figure 4–15).

Q&A

What should I do if a dialog box opens?

If the Mail Attachment dialog box opens when you attempt to open an attachment, you can open the attachment by clicking the Open button.

Q&A

What types of files can be attached to an e-mail message?

File attachments can be anything from spreadsheets to pictures to programs.

Figure 4–15

Q&A

Why did my attachment open in a different program?

Other programs might be installed on your computer and be set to open certain file types by default. For example, if you have Microsoft Word installed, RTF files will open in Word.

To Save and Close a File Attachment

After reviewing the attachment in Notepad, you decide to save it to your computer to read at a later time. The following steps save and close the attachment.

1 To display the Save As dialog box, click File on the menu bar and then click Save As.

2 If necessary, click the Browse Folders button and then click the Documents link to save the file to the Documents library.

3 Click the Save button.

Q&A

If I make changes to a file attachment before saving it, will the file attached to the original e-mail message also change?

No. If you open the e-mail message containing the attachment again, you will not see any of your changes. However, if you open the file that was saved to your computer, your changes will display.

4 Click the Close button in the Internet Explorer Outline - Notepad window.

5 Click the Close button in the Internet Explorer Seminar window.

Composing a New E-Mail Message

In addition to opening and reading, replying to, and deleting e-mail messages, you also need to compose and send new e-mail messages. When composing an e-mail message, you enter a brief one-line subject that identifies the purpose or contents of the e-mail message in the subject line, and then type your text in the message area. You must know the e-mail address of the recipient before you can send it.

You also can format e-mail messages to enhance their appearance. **Formatting** is the process of altering how a document looks by modifying the style, size, or color of its text or by changing its background. One method of formatting an e-mail message is to use stationery. Using stationery allows you to add a colorful background image, unique text sizes and colors, and custom margins to an e-mail message. For example, if you select the Color Stripe stationery, a narrow multicolor striped border appears on the left edge of your e-mail message and the text of the e-mail message appears using the Calibri 12-point font. The Calibri font is one of many fonts, or typefaces, available to format an e-mail message. In addition, any links within the e-mail message will be underlined and displayed in blue text. It is important to note that in a business environment, it might be inappropriate to apply stationery to e-mail messages. In most cases, work-related e-mail messages use the default background and text colors (black text on a white background). If you are sending a personal or informal e-mail message, using stationery might be more appropriate.

To Compose an E-Mail Message Using Stationery

The next steps compose an e-mail message to Mark Kennedy using the Color Stripe stationery.

1

- Click the New button to compose an e-mail message in a new window (Figure 4–16).

Figure 4–16

2

- Click the Stationery button to display a list of stationery commands (Figure 4–17).

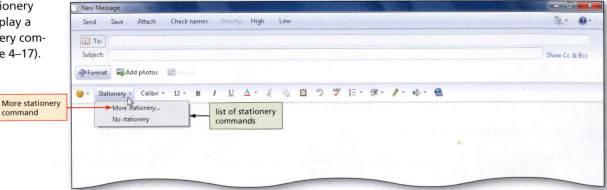

Figure 4–17

3

• Click the More stationery command to display the Select Stationery dialog box, which displays a list of stationery options (Figure 4–18).

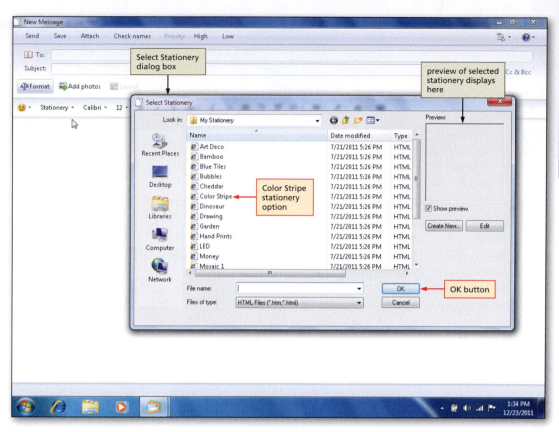

Figure 4–18

4

• Click the Color Stripe option to preview the Color Stripe stationery design.

• Click the OK button to apply the Color Stripe stationery design to the e-mail message (Figure 4–19).

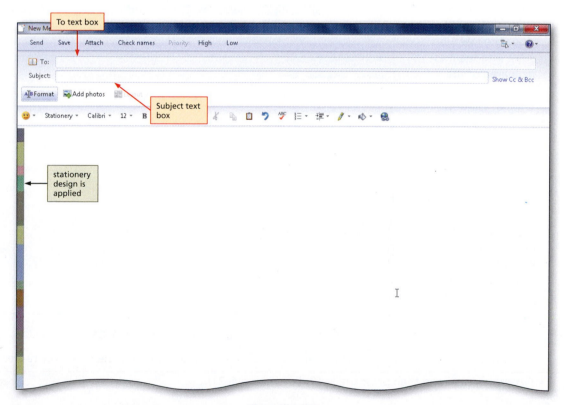

Figure 4–19

5

- Type `ProfMarkKennedy@gmail.com` in the To text box.

- Click the Subject text box.

- Type `Internet Explorer Seminar` in the Subject text box (Figure 4–20).

Q&A
What should I use as a subject for e-mails that I send?

You should choose an e-mail subject that briefly describes the contents of the e-mail message. It is not good practice to leave the Subject blank, as some spam filters will mark your e-mail message as spam and it will not reach your intended recipient.

Q&A
Why did the e-mail address change to Mark Kennedy's name after I typed it?

If you previously have received an e-mail message from someone, Windows Live Mail might remember the name associated with that e-mail address and display the name instead. If you are entering an e-mail address for someone with whom you have not communicated, the e-mail address will display in place of the name.

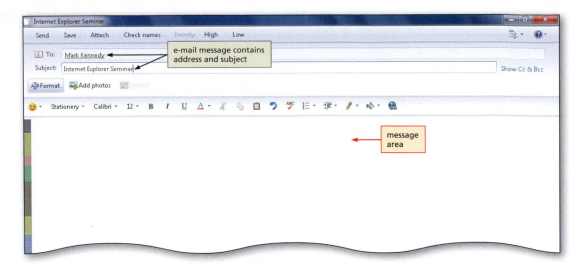

Figure 4–20

6

- Press the TAB key on the keyboard to move the insertion point into the message area of the Internet Explorer Seminar window.

- Type `Internet Explorer Seminar` and then press the ENTER key twice.

- Type `There will be an Internet Explorer Seminar in Manchester, NH on July 21st. Would you like to attend? Please see the attached file for more details.` in the message area and then press the ENTER key twice.

- Type your name and then press the ENTER key (Figure 4–21).

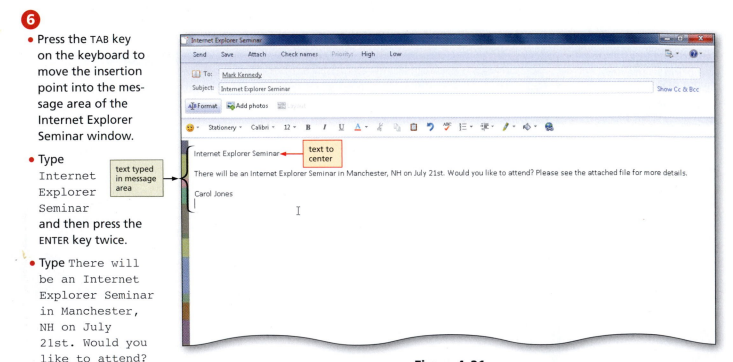

Figure 4–21

Formatting an E-Mail Message

The e-mail message window contains two toolbars. The toolbar containing buttons specific to replying to an e-mail or composing a new e-mail message is displayed below the title bar. The Formatting toolbar is displayed above the message area. The Formatting toolbar (Figure 4–22) contains options for changing the appearance of your e-mail message. Table 4–2 shows the buttons and boxes on the Formatting toolbar and their functions.

BTW

Font Size
You change the size of text by selecting a font size. A font size is measured in points. One inch contains 72 points. Thus, a font size of 36 points is approximately one-half inch in height when printed.

Figure 4–22

Table 4–2 Formatting Toolbar Buttons/Boxes and Functions

Button/Box	Function	Button/Box	Function
	Inserts an emoticon		Copies items in the message
Stationery	Changes the stationery design of the message		Pastes items in the message
Calibri	Changes the font of text in the message		Undoes an action performed in the message
12	Changes the font size of text in the message		Checks the spelling of the message
B	Bolds text in the message		Creates a numbered list or bulleted list in the message
I	Italicizes text in the message		Changes the format of a paragraph
U	Underlines text in the message		Changes the highlight color of text in the message
A	Changes the color of text in the message		Changes the background color of the message
	Cuts items from the message		Inserts a hyperlink in the message

To Format an E-Mail Message

The following steps use the Formatting toolbar to center the text, Internet Explorer Seminar, and format it using the 36-point font size.

1

• Select the phrase Internet Explorer Seminar in the first line of the e-mail message by pointing to any word on the first line and then triple-clicking to se-lect the entire phrase (Figure 4–23).

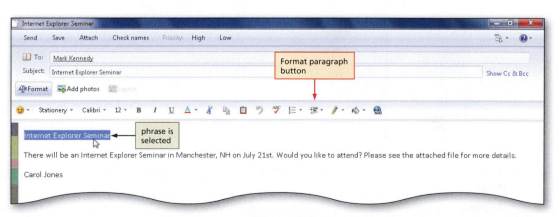

Figure 4–23

Q&A

I have never heard of triple-clicking. What does it mean to triple-click?

Similar to how double-clicking refers to clicking the mouse twice in rapid succession, triple-clicking refers to clicking the mouse three times in rapid succession.

2

- Click the Format paragraph button on the Formatting toolbar to display a list of formatting options (Figure 4–24).

- Click the Center command to center the selected words, Internet Explorer Seminar.

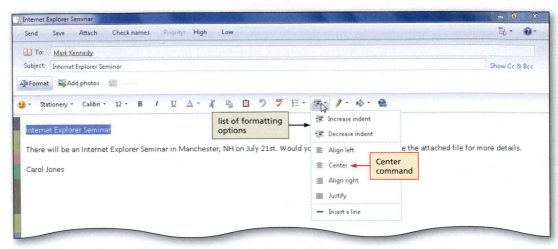

Figure 4–24

3

- Click the Font Size button arrow to display a list of available font sizes (Figure 4–25).

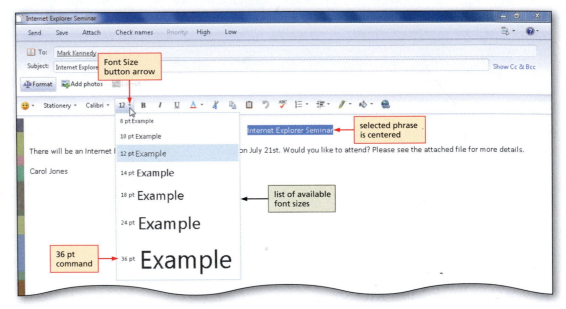

Figure 4–25

4

- Click the 36 pt option in the Font Size list to change the font size of the words, Internet Explorer Seminar, to 36 points.

- Click the selected text to remove the highlight (Figure 4–26).

Q&A

Will the recipient of this e-mail message be able to view the formatting?

Figure 4–26

Many e-mail programs are capable of displaying e-mail messages formatted with various fonts, styles, and backgrounds. If this e-mail message is read with an e-mail program that does not support this formatting, the e-mail message will be formatted as plain text.

To Attach a File to an E-Mail Message

You might find it necessary to supplement your e-mail message by attaching a file. There are many reasons why you might want to attach a file to your e-mail message: Friends and family share pictures, students submit assignments to their instructors, and professionals send important documents to colleagues. The following steps attach a file to an e-mail message.

1
- Click the Attach button on the toolbar to display the Open dialog box (Figure 4–27).

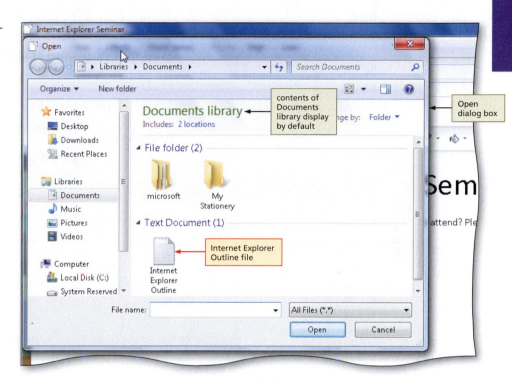

Figure 4–27

2
- Click the Internet Explorer Outline file in the Open dialog box to select it (Figure 4–28). If the Internet Explorer Outline file does not display, navigate to the folder containing the file.

Q&A

What types of files can I attach to my e-mail messages?

You can attach just about any type of file to an e-mail message, but you should make sure that the attachment is not too large in size. If you attach a large file, it might take the recipient a long time to download the attachment, or the recipient's e-mail program might reject the message.

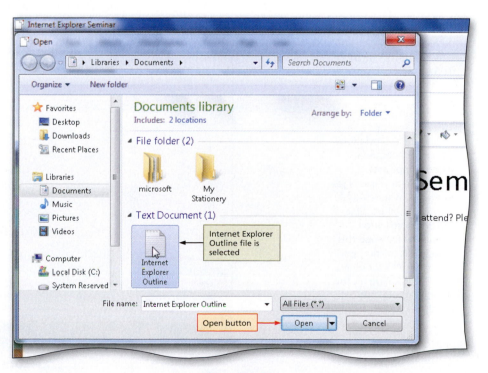

Figure 4–28

- Click the Open button to attach the Internet Explorer Outline file to the e-mail message (Figure 4–29).

Q&A

How do I know that my file has been attached?

After you click the Open button, the name and size of the file should display below the Subject text box. If the file does not display, repeat the previous steps to try again.

Figure 4–29

To Send an E-Mail Message

After composing and formatting an e-mail message, send the message. The following step sends an e-mail message.

- Click the Send button on the toolbar to send the e-mail message to Mark Kennedy. Sending the e-mail message closes the Internet Explorer Seminar window, stores the e-mail message message in the Outbox folder temporarily while it sends the message, and then moves the message to the Sent items folder (Figure 4–30).

BTW

Abbreviations in E-Mail Messages
The use of abbreviations has become popular when composing informal e-mail messages. Examples include ASAP for as soon as possible, CUL8R for see you later, HTH for hope this helps, NRN for no reply necessary, PLS for please, ROTFL for rolling on the floor laughing, and THX for thank you.

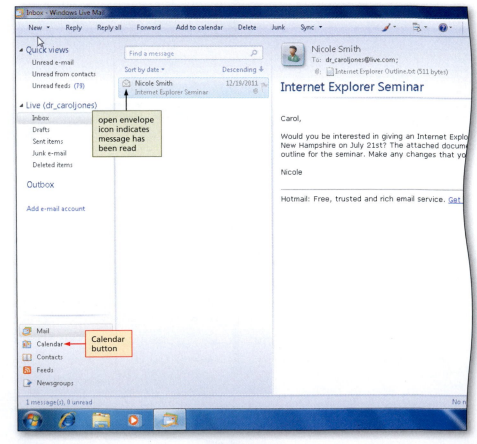

Figure 4–30

Calendar

Another tool accessible from Windows Live Mail is the Calendar. Calendar allows you to manage your schedule by keeping track of your tasks and appointments. In Calendar, you can input important events such as your class schedule, work schedule, birthdays, and anniversaries. When you schedule an appointment, Calendar blocks out the time in your schedule, helping you to avoid scheduling conflicts.

In Calendar, tasks and appointments are added as events. You can schedule events that occur at a particular time and place for a specified duration of time, for example, you might have a meeting on Tuesday in the conference room from 10:00 to 11:00 a.m. You also can schedule events that recur over a period of time. For example, you can add your class that meets Mondays and Wednesdays for the spring semester.

To Add an Event in Calendar

You have agreed to cover the class for Mark, and you need to make an appointment in your calendar so that you do not forget about the class. The following steps open your calendar and add an appointment.

1
- Click the Calendar button to open Calendar.
- If necessary, maximize the Calendar window (Figure 4–31).

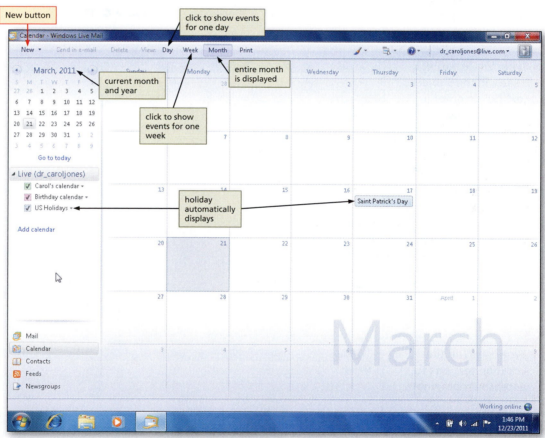

Figure 4–31

2

- Click the New button on the Calendar toolbar to add a new event.

- If necessary, maximize the New Event window (Figure 4–32).

Q&A Why did Calendar assign a time to my new event?

By default, Calendar automatically schedules an event based on the current time. When you specify the details for the event, it is easy to change the time.

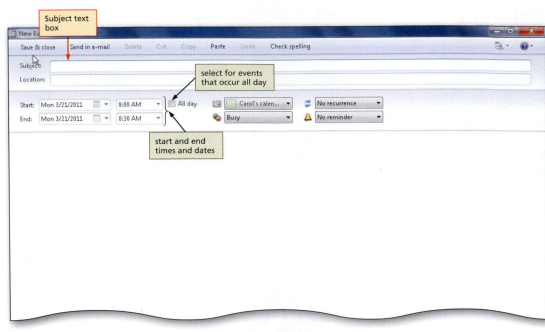

Figure 4–32

3

- Type Cover Mark's Class in the Subject text box to enter a subject for the event (Figure 4–33).

Figure 4–33

4

- Type 3-301 in the Location text box to enter the room number for Mark's class (Figure 4–34).

Figure 4–34

5

- Click the Start arrow to display the mini calendar (Figure 4–35). If necessary, use the arrows to display the month of March.

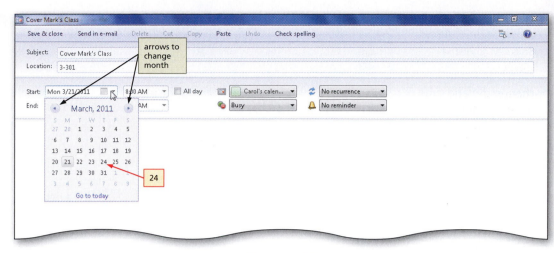

Figure 4–35

6

- Click 24 to select March 24 as the start date for the appointment (Figure 4–36).

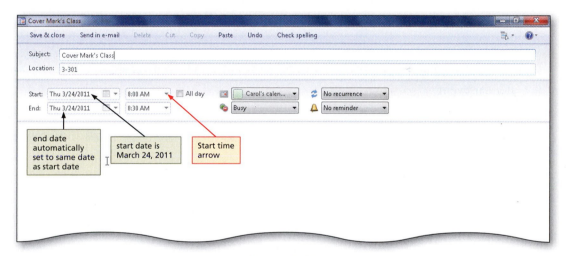

Figure 4–36

7

- Click the Start time arrow to view the Start time options.

- Scroll until you see 6:00 PM (Figure 4–37).

- Click 6:00 PM to set the start time.

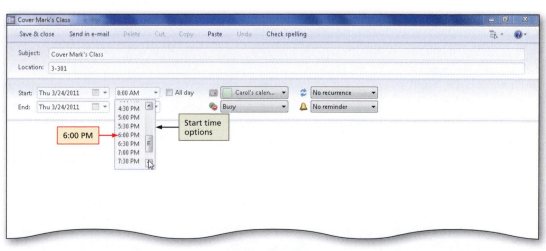

Figure 4–37

8

- Click the End time arrow and scroll until 8:00 PM is visible.

- Click 8:00 PM to change the end time (Figure 4–38).

Other Ways

1. Press ALT, click File, click New, click Event, type event subject, set Start date, set Start time, set End time

2. Press CTRL+SHIFT+E, type event subject, set Start date, set Start time, set End time

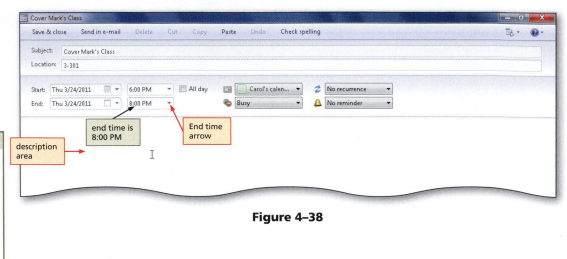

Figure 4–38

To Add a Reminder and Description to an Event

You might want to add a description to remind you to prepare for the class. Besides a description, you can tell Calendar to remind you about the event before it happens. The following steps add a description and a reminder to the Calendar event.

1

- Click the description area in the event window to select it. (Figure 4–39).

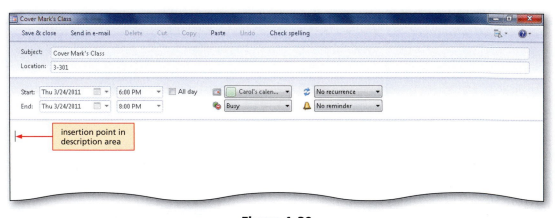

Figure 4–39

2

- Type Prepare for Mark's class by creating a Chapter 4 presentation to enter a description for the event (Figure 4–40).

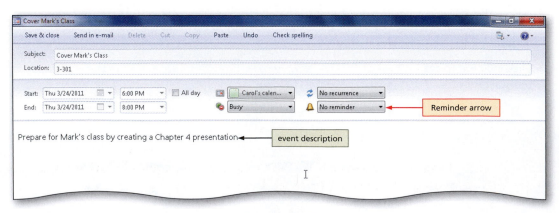

Figure 4–40

3

- Click the Reminder arrow to display the list of reminder options (Figure 4–41).

Q&A

What if I do not see a Reminder arrow?

A Reminder arrow only displays if you are using a Windows Live e-mail account. If you are not using a Windows Live e-mail account, the following steps are for illustration purposes only.

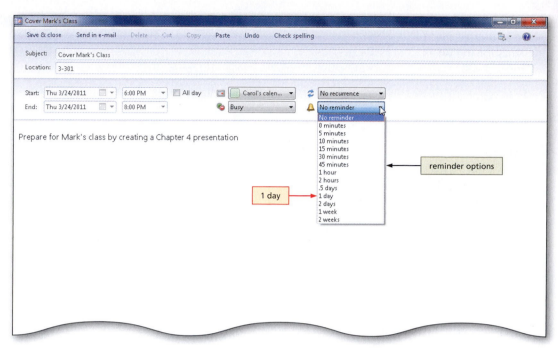

Figure 4–41

4

- Click the 1 day option to select that a reminder be shown one day before the event (Figure 4–42).

- Click the Save & close button on the toolbar to save and close the event.

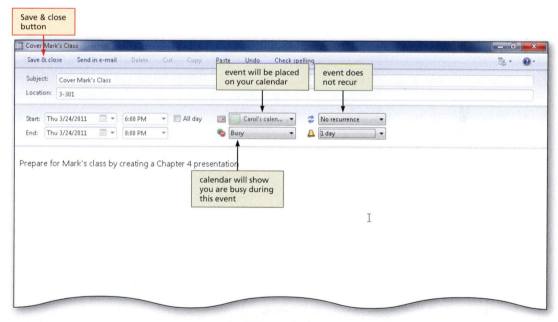

Figure 4–42

To Change the Calendar View

You can change the view in Calendar so that you can see events by day, week, and month. The steps on the following pages change the calendar view to Week view.

1

• Click the Week button to display the events for the week (Figure 4–43).

 Experiment

• There is more than one way to view your calendar. Click the different View buttons to switch to the various views and see what they look like.

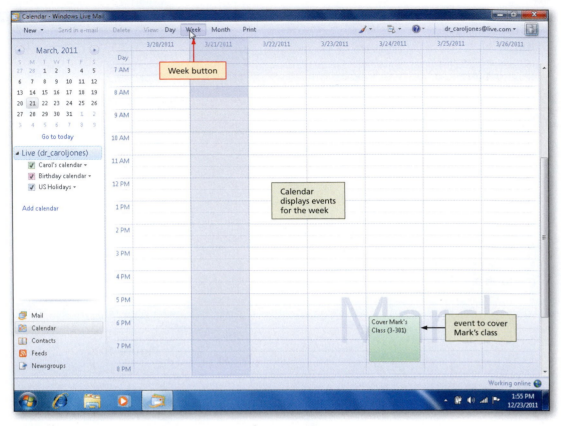

Figure 4–43

2

• Click the Month button to change the calendar view to Month view (Figure 4–44).

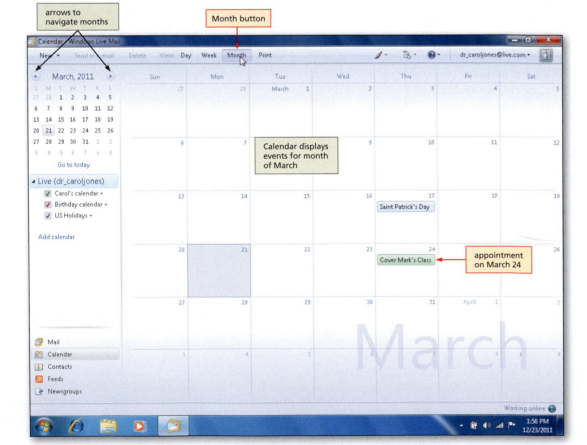

Figure 4–44

3

- Double-click the appointment on March 24 to display the Cover Mark's Class appointment (Figure 4–45). If March is not the current month on your computer, use the right and left arrow navigation buttons on the calendar to navigate to the month of March.

- Click the Close button to close the event window.

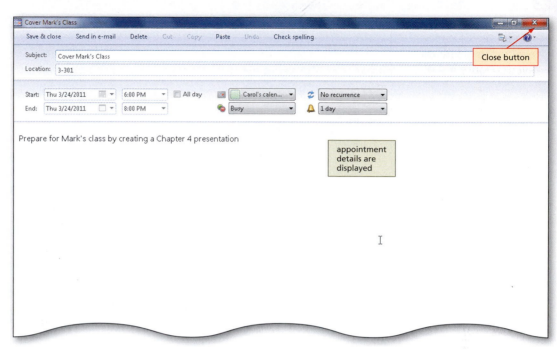

Figure 4–45

Other Ways	
1. Press ALT, click View, click Week, double-click event	2. Press CTRL+ALT+2, double-click event

To Delete an Event

The following steps delete the event for covering Mark's class.

1

- Click the Cover Mark's Class event icon in the Calendar area to select it (Figure 4–46).

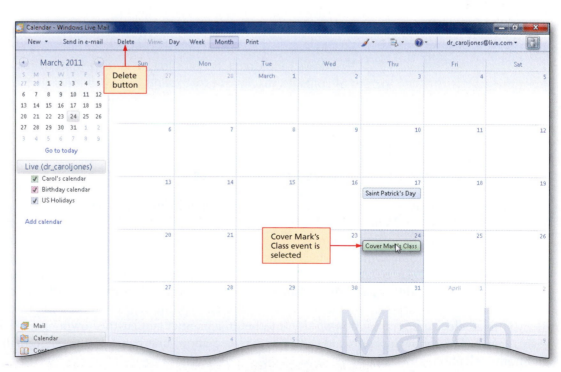

Figure 4–46

2
- Click the Delete button on the Calendar toolbar to delete the event (Figure 4–47).

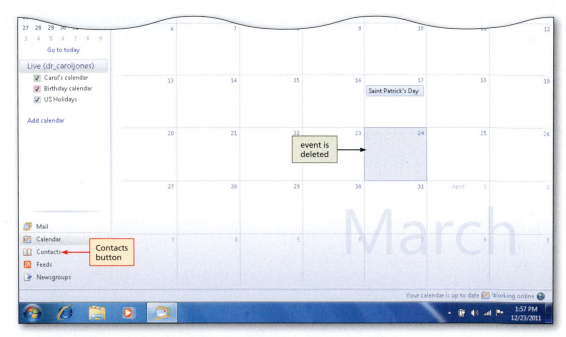

Figure 4–47

Other Ways
1. Select event, press ALT, click Edit, click Delete   2. Select event, press DELETE

Windows Live Contacts

The Windows Live Contacts feature included with Windows Live Mail allows you to store information about your family, friends, colleagues, and others. The information stored in Windows Live Contacts relating to an individual is referred to as a **contact**, and can include e-mail addresses, home and work addresses, telephone and fax numbers, digital IDs, notes, Web site addresses, and personal information such as birthdays or anniversaries.

Windows Live Contacts also allows you to create categories in which to store groups of contacts, making it easy to send an e-mail message to a group of contacts such as business associates, relatives, or friends, because you do not have to remember or type each person's e-mail address.

To Add a Contact to Windows Live Contacts

Before you can use a contact to send an e-mail to an individual, you need to add the contact information to Windows Live Contacts. When you add a contact in Windows 7, the Add a Contact dialog box contains a series of categories. Each category allows you to store different types of information about the contact. If you are entering information for a business contact, you can enter business-related information in the Work category. The Work category allows you to enter business information such as company name, business address, job title, work phone number, work e-mail address, and the company's Web address. The IDs category allows you to view the digital IDs of a selected e-mail address. A digital ID allows you to encrypt messages sent over the Internet and to prove your identity in an electronic transaction on the Internet in a manner similar to showing your driver's license when you cash a check. The following steps add the contact information (first name, last name, e-mail address, home address, and home telephone) for Miriam Winick.

1

- Click the Contacts button to open the Windows Live Contacts window.

- If necessary, maximize the Windows Live Contacts window (Figure 4–48).

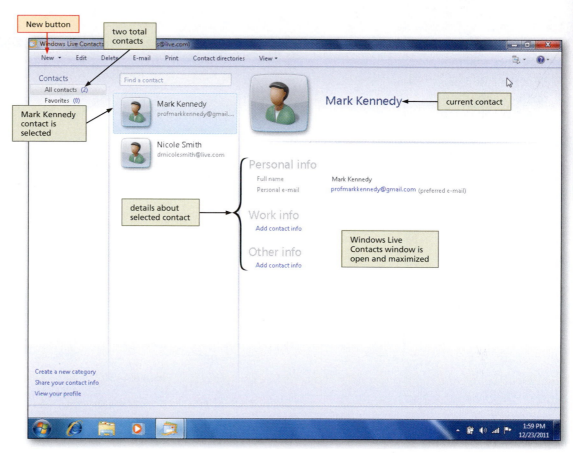

Figure 4–48

2

- Click the New button on the toolbar to display the Add a Contact window (Figure 4–49).

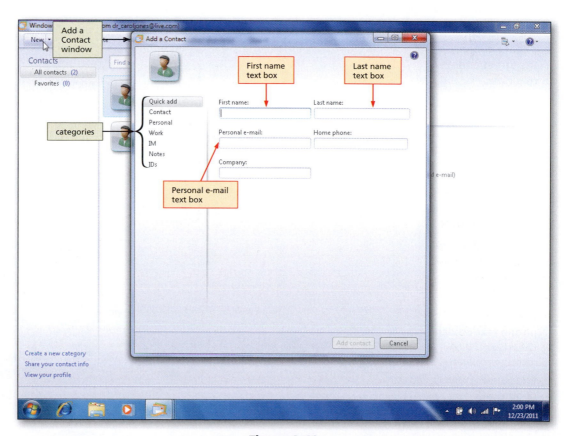

Figure 4–49

3

• Type `Miriam` in the First name text box.

• Click the Last name text box and then type `Winick` in the text box.

• Click the Personal e-mail text box and then type `miriam_winick@hotmail.com` in the text box (Figure 4–50).

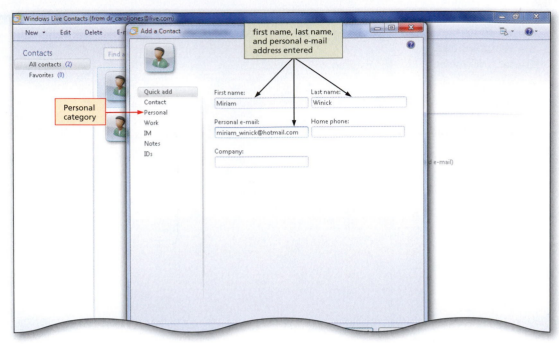

Figure 4–50

4

• Click the Personal category in the Add a Contact dialog box.

• Type `17325 Winding Lane` in the Street address text box.

• Click the City text box and then type `Brea` as the name of the city.

• Click the State/province text box and then type `CA` as the name of the state.

• Click the ZIP/postal code text box and then type `92821` as the postal code.

• Click the Home phone text box and then type `(714) 555-3292` as the telephone number (Figure 4–51).

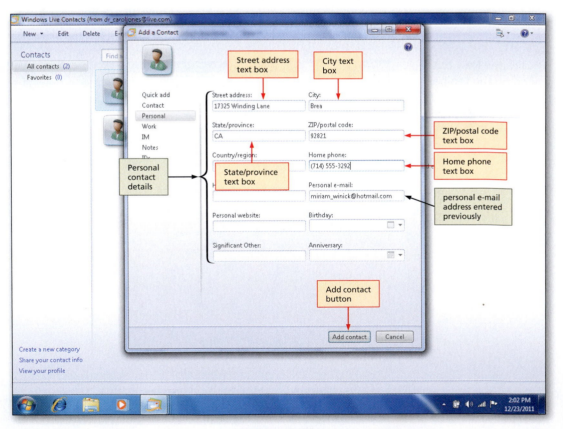

Figure 4–51

5

• Click the Add contact button to add the contact (Figure 4–52).

Figure 4–52

6

• Click the Close button to close the Windows Live Contacts window (Figure 4–53).

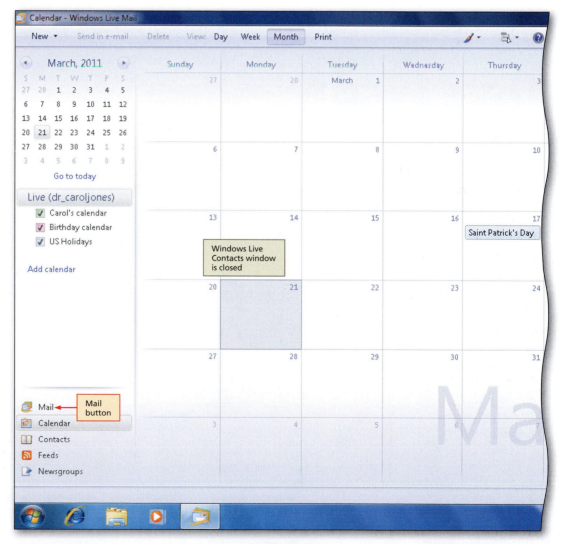

Figure 4–53

To Compose an E-Mail Message Using the Contacts Folder

When you compose an e-mail message, you must know the e-mail address of the recipient of the message. Previously, you addressed an e-mail message by typing the e-mail address in the To text box in the New Message window. You now are able to use the Contacts folder to enter an e-mail address. The following steps compose an e-mail message to Miriam Winick using her e-mail address in the Contacts folder.

- Click the Mail button to switch to Mail view.
- Click the New button to display the New Message window.
- If necessary, maximize the New Message window (Figure 4–54).

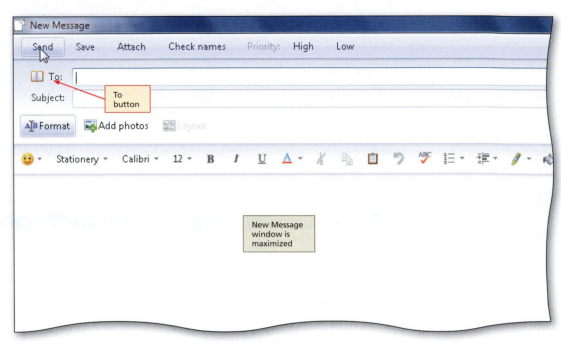

Figure 4–54

- Click the To button in the New Message window to display the Send an E-mail dialog box.
- Click the Miriam Winick contact in the list box to select it (Figure 4–55).

Q&A

What is the difference between the Cc field and the Bcc field?

The names and e-mail addresses of recipients listed in the Cc field will be visible to all recipients. When you use the Bcc field, however, the names and e-mail addresses of recipients will be hidden from all recipients.

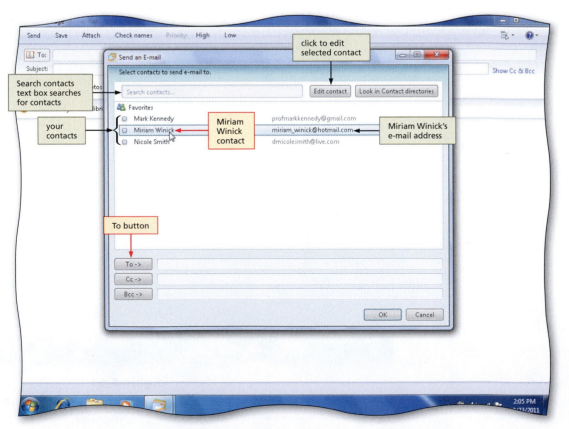

Figure 4–55

3

- Click the To button in the Send an E-mail dialog box to add Miriam Winick to the message recipients list (Figure 4–56).

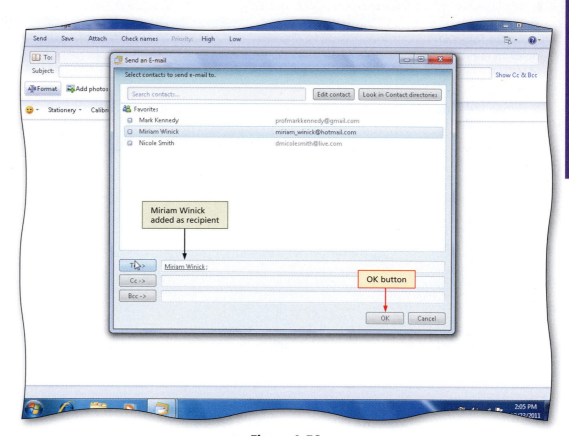

Figure 4–56

4

- Click the OK button in the Send an E-mail dialog box to close the dialog box and add Miriam Winick's name and e-mail address to the To text box in the New Message window.

- Click the Subject text box and then type Contacts list in the text box (Figure 4–57).

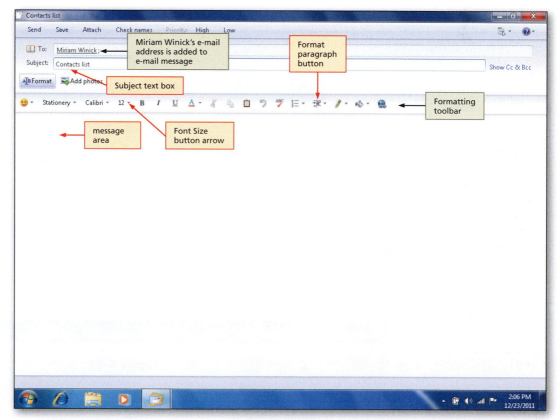

Figure 4–57

- Press the TAB key to move the insertion point to the message area.
- Type Great News! and then press the ENTER key twice.
- Type I have learned to enter an e-mail address using the Contacts list. and then press the ENTER key twice.
- Type your name and then press the ENTER key.

Figure 4–58

- Select the words, Great News!.
- In the message area, click the Format paragraph button on the Formatting toolbar and then select Center to center the text.
- Click the Font Size button arrow on the Formatting toolbar, and then click 36 in the Font Size list to increase the font size to 36 points.
- Click the selected text to remove the highlight (Figure 4–58).

To Send an E-Mail Message

The following step sends the e-mail message.

- Click the Send button on the tool-bar to send the mes-sage (Figure 4–59).

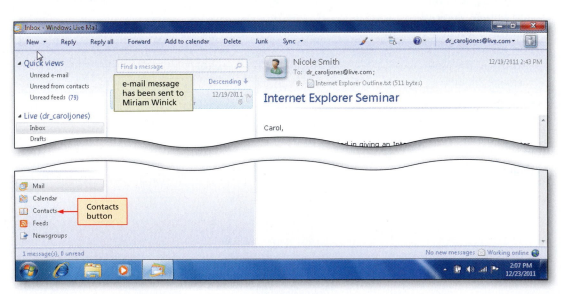

Figure 4–59

To Delete a Contact from the Contacts Folder

Occasionally, you will want to remove a contact from the Contacts folder. The following steps remove the Miriam Winick contact from the Contacts folder.

- Click the Contacts button to display the Windows Live Contacts window.

- If necessary, maximize the Windows Live Contacts window.

- Click the Miriam Winick entry in the Windows Live Contacts window (Figure 4–60).

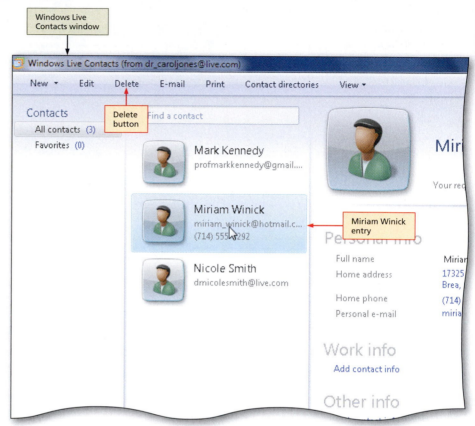

Figure 4–60

- Click the Delete button on the toolbar to display the Windows Live Mail dialog box (Figure 4–61).

Figure 4–61

3

- Click the OK button in the Windows Live Mail dialog box to delete the Miriam Winick contact (Figure 4–62).

- Close the Windows Live Contacts window.

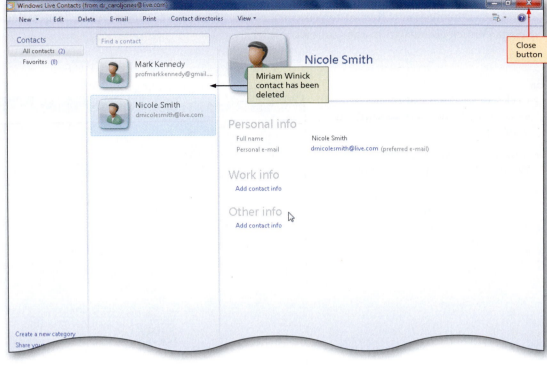

Figure 4–62

Other Ways

1. Right-click contact entry, click Delete Contact on shortcut menu, click OK

Internet Newsgroups

In addition to exchanging e-mail messages, another method of communicating over the Internet is to read and place messages on a newsgroup. A **newsgroup** is a collection of messages posted by many people on a topic of mutual interest that you can access via the Internet. Each newsgroup is devoted to a particular topic. A special computer, called a **news server**, contains related newsgroups.

To participate in a newsgroup, you must use a program called a newsreader. A **newsreader** enables you to access a newsgroup to read a previously entered message, or **article**, and to add a new message, called **posting**. A newsreader also keeps track of which articles you have and have not read. Windows Live Mail includes a newsreader for reading newsgroup articles.

Newsgroups exist to discuss technology and products, such as those from Microsoft and IBM. Other subjects, such as recipes, gardening, and music, are often discussed in blogs, wikis, and social media, such as Facebook, MySpace, and Twitter. A newsgroup name consists of a prefix and one or more subgroup names. For example, the comp.software newsgroup name consists of a prefix (comp), which indicates that the subject of the newsgroup is computers, a period (.), and a subgroup name (software), which indicates that the subject is further narrowed down to a discussion of software.

In addition, some newsgroups are supervised by a moderator, who reads each article before it is posted to the newsgroup. If the moderator thinks an article is appropriate for the newsgroup, the moderator posts the article for all members to read. If the moderator thinks an article is inappropriate, he or she might decide to delete the article without posting it.

BTW

Newsgroup Articles
Many newsgroup articles contain pictures, movies, and sound clips. Check the article name for the words, pictures, video, or audio.

BTW

Local Newsgroups
Some colleges and universities maintain a local newsgroup to disseminate information about school events and answer technical questions asked by students. To locate your local newsgroup, search for the school's name in the list of newsgroup names.

To Subscribe to and Display a Newsgroup on the Microsoft News Server

Before you can access the articles in a newsgroup or post to a newsgroup, you first must establish a news account on your computer. A news account allows access to the news server. Several hundred newsgroups are listed in the Newsgroup Subscriptions dialog box. If you find a newsgroup that you particularly like and want to visit on a frequent basis, you should subscribe to it. Subscribing to a newsgroup adds the newsgroup name to the folder list and allows you to return to the newsgroup quickly instead of searching or scrolling to find the newsgroup name each time you want to visit it. The following steps use Windows Live Mail to subscribe to and view the articles in the microsoft.public.windows.live.mail.desktop newsgroup.

1

- Click the Newsgroups button to display the Newsgroups pane (Figure 4–63).

Q&A Why did a dialog box open asking if I wanted to set Windows Live Mail as my newsgroup client?

Depending on the programs you have installed, you might have another program set as the default newsgroup client (newsreader). Windows 7 is asking if you want to switch the default client to Windows Live Mail.

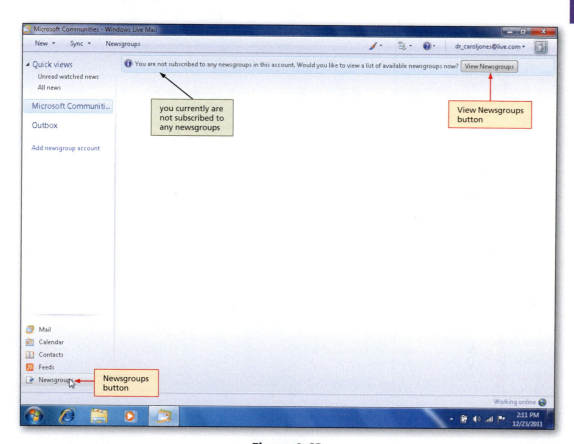

Figure 4–63

2

- Click the View Newsgroups button to download a list of available newsgroups on the Microsoft news server and display the list in the Newsgroup Subscriptions dialog box (Figure 4–64).

Q&A
Why does the View Newsgroups button not appear?

The View Newsgroups button only appears if you are not subscribed to any newsgroups. If the View Newsgroups button does not appear, click the Newsgroups button on the toolbar to display the Newsgroup Subscriptions dialog box.

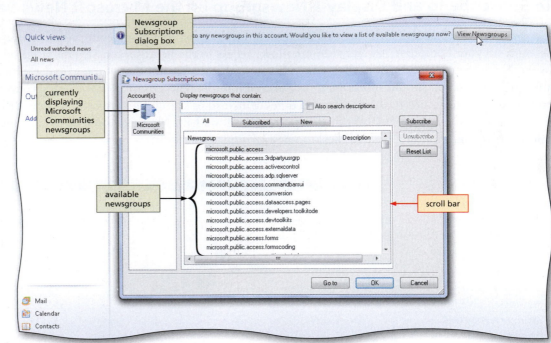

Figure 4–64

3

- Scroll to display the microsoft.public. windows.live.mail. desktop entry in the Newsgroup list (Figure 4–65).

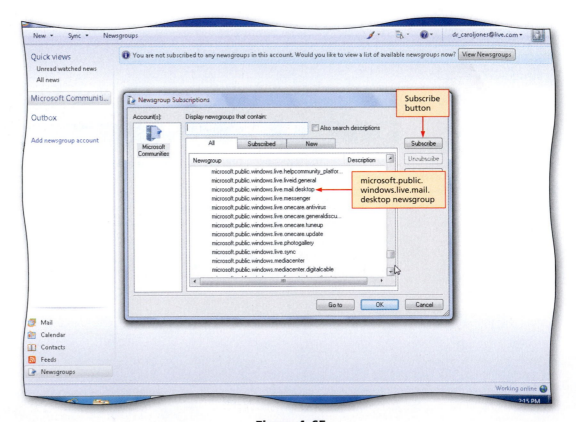

Figure 4–65

4

- Click the microsoft.
  public.windows.live.
  mail.desktop entry in
  the Newsgroup list to
  select it.

- Click the Subscribe
  button to subscribe
  to the newsgroup
  (Figure 4–66).

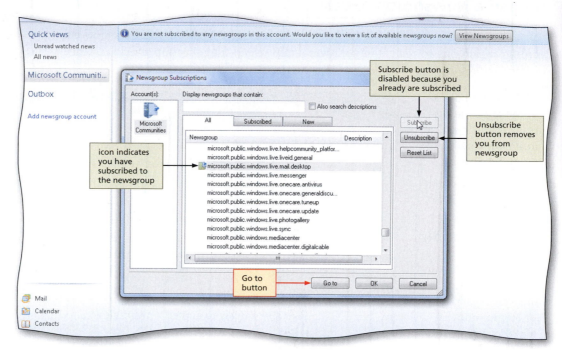

Figure 4–66

5

- Click the Go to
  button to close
  the Newsgroup
  Subscriptions dia-
  log box and display
  the articles in the
  microsoft.public.
  windows.live.mail.
  desktop newsgroup
  (Figure 4–67).

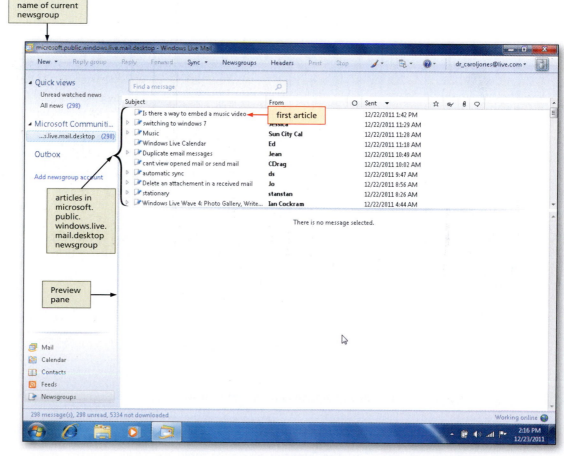

Figure 4–67

To Read a Newsgroup Article

The entries in the Subject column in the message list allow you to review the subjects of a list of articles before deciding which one to read. The following step selects a newsgroup article to read.

1

- Click the first article in the message list to display the article in the Preview pane (Figure 4–68).

Q&A

What do the arrows to the left of an article indicate?

Newsgroup members often post articles in reply to previous postings—either to answer questions or to comment on material in the original posting. These replies often prompt the author of the original article, or other interested members, to post additional articles. This process resembles a conversation. The original article and all subsequent related replies are

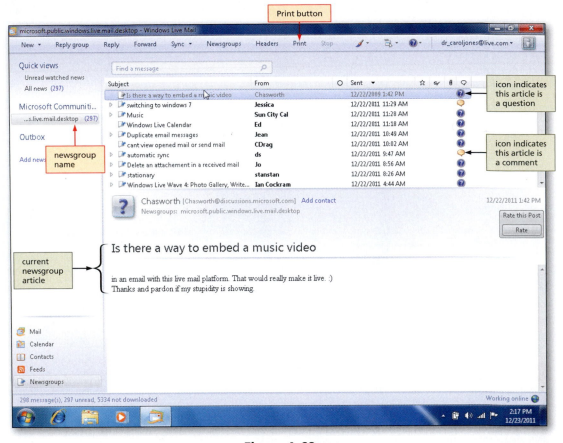

Figure 4–68

called a **thread**, or **threaded discussion**. When an arrow appears to the left of an article in the message list, the article is part of a thread and can be expanded. Expanding the thread displays the replies to the original article indented below the original article and changes the arrow from white to black. Collapsing the thread hides the replies from the thread, displays the original article in the Preview pane, and changes the arrow from black to white.

 **Experiment**

- Click a white arrow to the left of an article to expand the threaded discussion. Click each of the responses in the discussion to view their contents in the Preview pane. Once you are done, click the first article in the message list.

Other Ways	
1. Press CTRL+< to read previous article	2. Press CTRL+> to read next article

To Print a Newsgroup Article

After reading an article, you might want to print it. The method of printing a newsgroup article is identical to how you print an e-mail message, with similar results (see Figure 4–7 on page WIN 210). The following steps print the contents of the first article in the newsgroup.

1 Click the Print button on the toolbar.

2 Click the Print button in the Print dialog box to print the newsgroup article (Figure 4–69).

Page 1 of 1

newsgroup article

From: "Chasworth" <Chasworth@discussions.microsoft.com>
Date: Tuesday, December 22, 2011 1:42 PM
Newsgroups: microsoft.public.windows.live.mail.desktop
Subject: Is there a way to embed a music video
in an email with this live mail platform. That would really make it live. :)
Thanks and pardon if my stupidity is showing.

12/23/2011

Figure 4–69

BTW

Watching Conversations
Windows Live Mail provides a feature that allows you to find all e-mail messages or newsgroup articles that are part of the same conversation. If you are viewing an e-mail message or newsgroup article and quickly want to find the other messages in the conversation, click the Watch conversation command on the Actions menu on the menu bar (which you must display to use).

Posting a Newsgroup Article

Once you become familiar with a newsgroup, you might want to post a reply to a newsgroup article. To be able to post to a newsgroup, you first need to subscribe to it. After subscribing to the newsgroup and displaying the list of articles in the message list, click the Reply group button to display the Reply to article window to compose your newsgroup posting for everyone who has posted on the subject. You can use the Reply button to compose your response for the original poster only, but first you will need to create a profile by using the Mail icon in the Control Panel. You can use the New Message button to open the New Message window to post a message to the entire newsgroup (Figure 4–70). The window looks like a regular e-mail window. Once you type a subject and text for the posting, click the Send button to post the newsgroup article. Because many people will be able to read your posting, make sure that the posting is free from grammatical and spelling errors. If the newsgroup is moderated, postings might not appear immediately after sending them.

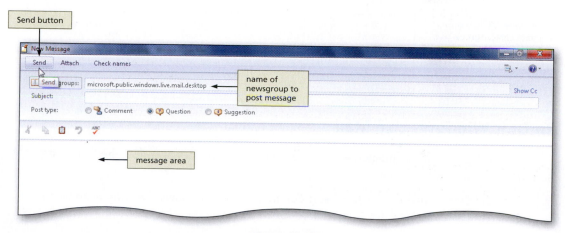

Figure 4–70

To Unsubscribe from a Newsgroup

When you no longer need access to a newsgroup, you can cancel the subscription to the newsgroup, or unsubscribe, and then remove the newsgroup name from the folder list. The next steps unsubscribe from the microsoft.public.windows.live.mail.desktop newsgroup.

- Right-click the microsoft.public. windows.live.mail. desktop news- group name in the Navigation pane to display the shortcut menu (Figure 4–71).

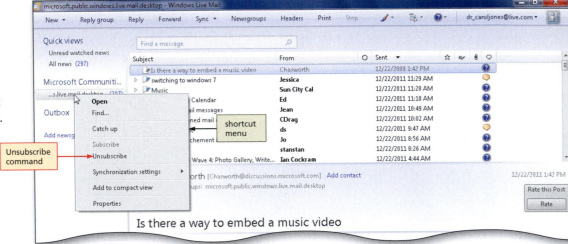

Figure 4–71

- Click the Unsubscribe command on the shortcut menu. If the Windows Live Mail dialog box opens, click the OK button in the dialog box to unsubscribe from the microsoft.public. windows.live.mail. desktop newsgroup.

- Click OK to confirm the unsub- scribing operation (Figure 4–72).

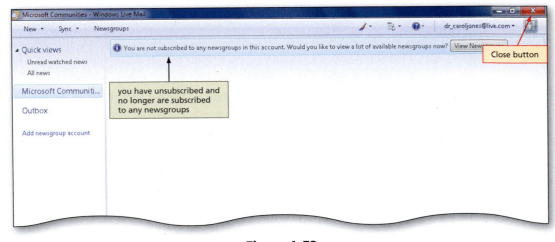

Figure 4–72

Other Ways

1. Select newsgroup name in Newsgroup Subscriptions dialog box, click Unsubscribe
2. Double-click newsgroup name in Newsgroup Subscriptions dialog box

To Quit Windows Live Mail

Now that you have finished working with e-mails and newsgroups, the following step quits Windows Live Mail.

1. Click the Close button in the Microsoft Communities — Windows Live Mail window to quit Windows Live Mail.

Using Internet Explorer to Subscribe to RSS Feeds and Web Slices

In addition to using Windows Live Mail to access information, Internet Explorer provides access to a wealth of information on the Internet. One of the newer technologies on the Internet is **Really Simple Syndication (RSS)**. RSS allows Web page authors to easily distribute, or syndicate, Web content using **RSS feeds**. If you frequently visit multiple Web sites that offer RSS feeds, you can subscribe to their RSS feeds using Internet Explorer, which allows you to quickly review the feed content of all the Web sites in a simple list in your browser window, without having to first navigate to each individual site. For example, the CNN Web site contains two RSS feeds that allow visitors to view top stories and recent stories in one convenient location. By subscribing to an RSS feed, you not only are able to access the feed in Internet Explorer, but also in Windows Live Mail. Although you can subscribe to an RSS feed using Windows Live Mail (using the Feeds button that appears in the Navigation pane above Newsgroups), many people discover RSS feeds while browsing the World Wide Web, and therefore, subscribe to those feeds right from within Internet Explorer. RSS feeds can be found on many Web sites and blogs, particularly those that frequently update their content.

Another way to stay current with content on the Internet, such as weather reports, stock quotes, and news articles, is to use Web Slices. A **Web Slice** is a portion, or slice, of a Web page that can be viewed directly from the Favorites Bar in Internet Explorer. Similar to an RSS feed, Web Slices are found on Web sites that frequently update their content.

To Subscribe to an RSS Feed

Before you can view the contents of an RSS feed, you must subscribe to it. The following steps use Internet Explorer to subscribe to an RSS feed on the PCMag.com Web site.

1

• Click the Internet Explorer button on the taskbar to start Internet Explorer.

• Type www.pcmag.com in the Address bar and then press the ENTER key to display the PCMag.com Web page (Figure 4–73).

Figure 4–73

2

• Click the 'View feeds on this page' button arrow to display a menu containing the available RSS feeds (Figure 4–74).

Figure 4–74

3

• Click the PC Magazine: New Product Reviews command on the list of available RSS feeds to display the PCMag.com: New Product Reviews RSS feed (Figure 4–75).

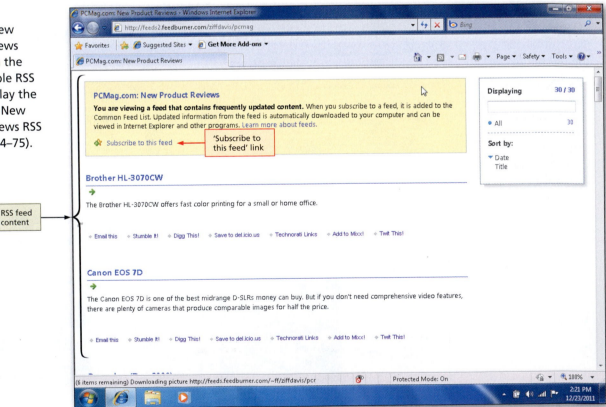

Figure 4–75

4

- Click the 'Subscribe to this feed' link in the PCMag.com: New Product Reviews window to display the Subscribe to this Feed dialog box (Figure 4–76).

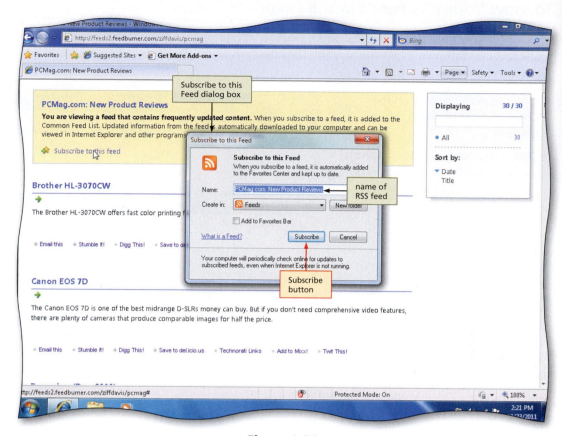

Figure 4–76

5

- Click the Subscribe button in the Subscribe to this Feed dialog box to subscribe to the RSS feed (Figure 4–77).

Figure 4–77

To View Your RSS Feeds in the Favorites Center

After you subscribe to an RSS feed, you are able to view the RSS feeds in the Favorites Center in Internet Explorer. The following steps display the RSS feeds to which you have subscribed in the Favorites Center.

1

- Click the Home button on the Command bar to display your home page.

- Click the Favorites button to display the Favorites Center (Figure 4–78).

Figure 4–78

2

- Click the Feeds tab in the Favorites Center to display the list of RSS feeds to which you have subscribed (Figure 4–79).

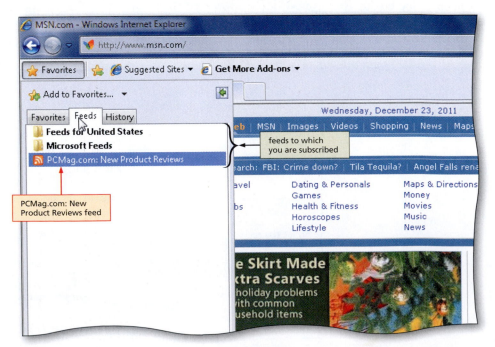

Figure 4–79

3

- Click the PCMag.com: New Product Reviews feed to display the RSS feed.

- If the Favorites Center is pinned, click the Close the Favorites Center button to close the Favorites Center (Figure 4–80).

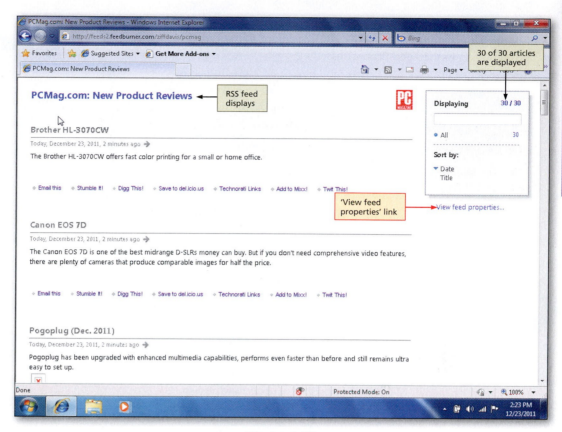

Figure 4–80

To Modify Feed Properties

Because RSS feeds disseminate frequently updated information, Internet Explorer automatically downloads updated RSS content every day. If you want Internet Explorer to download the RSS feeds more frequently so that you are sure that you are viewing the most up-to-date information, you can modify the feed properties. The following steps modify the properties for the PC Magazine: New Product Reviews RSS feed so that the feed will update every four hours.

1

- Click the 'View feed properties' link in the PCMag.com: New Product Reviews - Windows Internet Explorer window to display the Feed Properties dialog box (Figure 4–81).

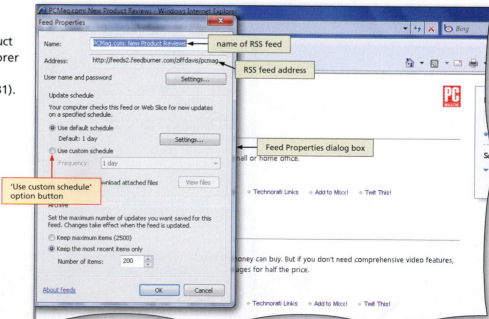

Figure 4–81

2

• Click the 'Use custom schedule' option button in the Feed Properties dialog box to select it (Figure 4–82).

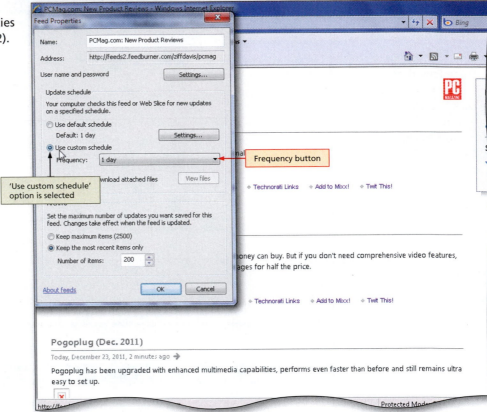

Figure 4–82

3

• Click the Frequency button to display the Frequency list (Figure 4–83).

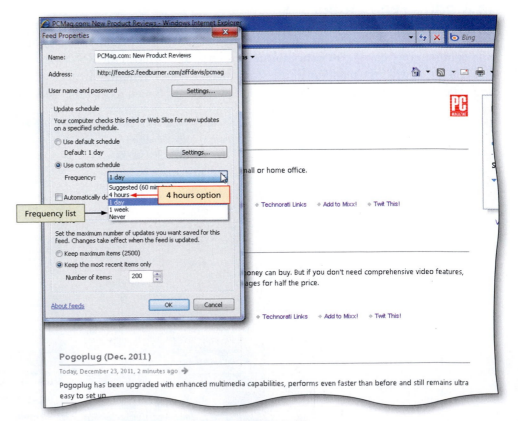

Figure 4–83

4

- Click 4 hours in the Frequency list to set the feed to update every 4 hours (Figure 4–84).

- Click the OK button in the Feed Properties dialog box to save your changes and to close the Feed Properties dialog box.

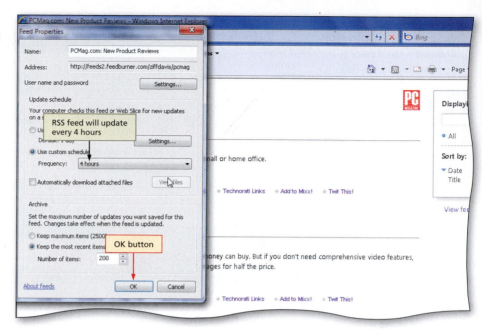

Figure 4–84

To Subscribe to a Web Slice

Similar to an RSS feed, a Web Slice also displays content that is updated frequently; however, Web Slices often display content in graphical format. Before you can view the contents of a Web Slice, you must subscribe to it. The following steps use Internet Explorer to subscribe to a Web Slice on the MSN.com Web site.

1

- Type www.msn.com in the Address bar and then press the ENTER key to display the MSN.com Web page (Figure 4–85).

Figure 4–85

• Click the Web Slice
button to display the
Internet Explorer dia-
log box (Figure 4–86).

Figure 4–86

• Click the Add to
Favorites Bar
button to subscribe
to the MSN.com
Slideshow Web Slice
(Figure 4–87).

Figure 4–87

To View a Web Slice

After you subscribe to a Web Slice, you are able to view the Web Slice in the Favorites Bar. The following steps display the Web Slice to which you have subscribed in the Favorites Bar.

• Click the MSN.com
Slideshow button on
the Favorites Bar to
display the Web Slice
(Figure 4–88).

Figure 4–88

- After viewing the Web Slice, click the MSN.com Slideshow button on the Favorites Bar to close the Web Slice (Figure 4–89).

Figure 4–89

To Delete a Web Slice

When you no longer have need of a Web Slice, you can delete it. The following step deletes the Web Slice to which you have subscribed in the Favorites Bar.

- Right-click the MSN. com Slideshow button on the Favorites Bar to display the shortcut menu (Figure 4–90).

- Click the Delete command to delete the MSN.com Slideshow Web Slice.

- Click the Yes button to confirm the deletion.

- Close Internet Explorer.

Figure 4–90

• Right-click the Nicole contact
to display the shortcut menu
(Figure 4–104).

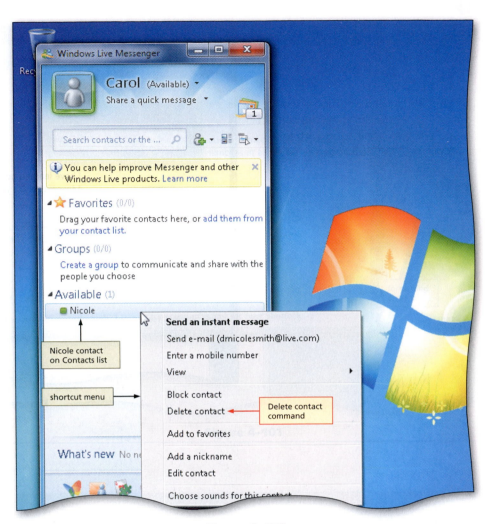

Figure 4–104

• Click the Delete contact command
on the shortcut menu to display the
Windows Live Messenger dialog
box (Figure 4–105).

Figure 4–105

2

- After viewing the Web Slice, click the MSN.com Slideshow button on the Favorites Bar to close the Web Slice (Figure 4–89).

Figure 4–89

To Delete a Web Slice

When you no longer have need of a Web Slice, you can delete it. The following step deletes the Web Slice to which you have subscribed in the Favorites Bar.

- Right-click the MSN. com Slideshow button on the Favorites Bar to display the shortcut menu (Figure 4–90).

- Click the Delete command to delete the MSN.com Slideshow Web Slice.

- Click the Yes button to confirm the deletion.

- Close Internet Explorer.

Figure 4–90

Other Communication Methods

This chapter has so far discussed how to communicate over the Internet by using e-mail, newsgroups, and RSS feeds. In addition to these methods, several other Web applications facilitate communication between individuals over the Internet, including wikis, blogs, online social networks, groups, chat rooms, and instant messaging.

Blogs and wikis are types of Web sites that allow one or more people to publish content easily. A **blog** is a constantly updated commentary on a Web page. For example, you could create a blog about what it is like to attend college. A **wiki** is an online encyclopedia created by its users. Anyone is allowed to edit and add content to a wiki. Some Web sites, such as Google and Yahoo!, allow their visitors to communicate with others via groups. A **group** is a Web application that enables people to form an online community for discussion around specific topics, such as social networking, Windows 7, or your favorite video game. You also can create Web pages inside your group. If you are unable to find a group that matches your interests, you can create a new group. Figure 4–91 shows the Google Groups Web site.

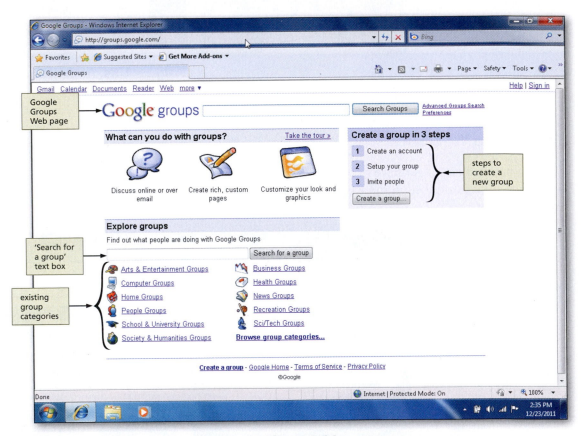

Figure 4–91

Similar to a group, a **chat room** application also allows people to communicate with each other. However, unlike a group, the communication that takes place in a chat room happens in real time. **Real-time communication** means that users participating in the communication must be online at the same time. For example, a phone conversation is one type of communication that takes place in real time. If one person was not on the phone, it would be impossible for the conversation to take place. On the other hand, an e-mail conversation does not take place in real time because you are able to send someone an e-mail regardless of whether or not they are online. When you enter a chat room, messages that you send are viewable by everyone else who is in the same chat room. Some chat rooms are available via Web sites, and others are accessible only by first downloading a special program to your computer that allows you to enter and participate in chat rooms. Figure 4–92 shows a Web site that allows you to download a popular chat program called mIRC.

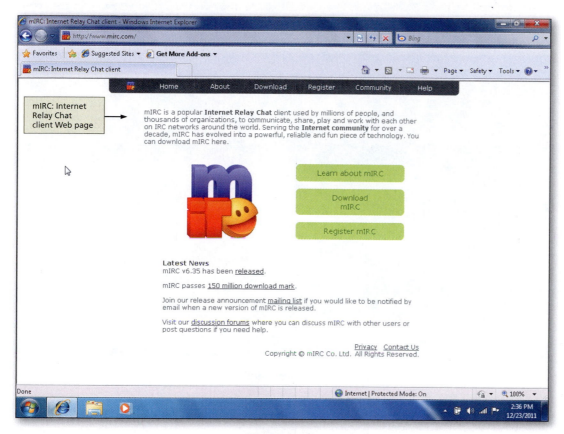

Figure 4–92

Another way by which people on the Internet can communicate is via a mailing list. A **mailing list** allows an individual to send the same e-mail message to multiple recipients at the same time. For example, many colleges and universities allow instructors to communicate with their students outside of class by using a mailing list. At the beginning of the semester, students manually **subscribe** to the mailing list with their e-mail address or the instructor automatically subscribes them. When the instructor needs to disseminate information to the students, he or she sends an e-mail message to the mailing list, which is forwarded to everyone who has subscribed. In addition to schools using mailing lists, many companies also offer mailing lists to update their customers periodically about their products or services. If you have subscribed to a mailing list and no longer want to receive e-mail messages from the list, you can **unsubscribe** from it. Mailing lists offer different methods of unsubscribing, the instructions for which are usually located at the bottom of each e-mail message sent to the list. If you are unable to find instructions for unsubscribing, contact the mailing list administrator. Figure 4–93 on the next page shows a Web page that contains a subscription form for a mailing list that distributes the DivX newsletter.

Many of these options are brought together under a social network. A **social network** is a single Web site from where you can access blogs, wikis, and other communication tools.

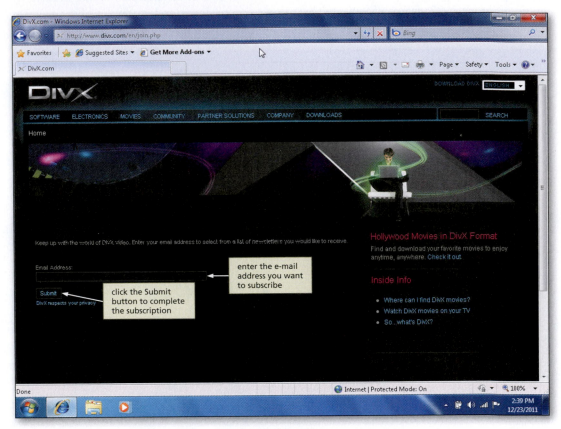

Figure 4–93

Windows Live Messenger and Instant Messaging

Another communication tool is instant messaging (IM). An **instant messaging program** allows two or more people who are online at the same time to exchange messages in real time. Instant messaging differs from a chat room because with instant messaging, only two people are involved in a conversation. In chat rooms, everyone who is in the same chat room can see anything you type. Windows Live Messenger, an instant messaging application, is available for download as part of Windows Live Essentials. One advantage of using Windows Live Messenger instead of e-mail is that once sent, your instant message appears immediately on the recipient's computer and they can reply immediately. A disadvantage is that your recipient must be online and signed in to Windows Live Messenger to receive your message.

Windows Live Messenger users can perform a variety of functions, including adding contacts to the Contacts list, viewing a list of online and offline contacts, performing real-time communication with a single contact or a group of contacts, placing a telephone call from the computer and talking using a microphone and headset, sending files to another computer, sending instant messages to a mobile device, and inviting someone to an online meeting or to play an Internet game.

You sign in to Windows Live Messenger using your Windows Live ID. Your Windows Live ID is a secure way for you to sign in to multiple Microsoft Web sites. If you have a Windows Live Hotmail account, you already have a Windows Live ID. This section assumes that you already have a Windows Live ID and have Windows Live Messenger installed. If you need a Windows Live ID, see your instructor for assistance. Before you will be able to send an instant message, your contact also must have a Windows Live ID and have the Windows Live Messenger software installed on their computer.

To Start Windows Live Messenger and Sign In

Before using Windows Live Messenger, you must start Windows Live Messenger and sign in using your Windows Live ID and password. The following steps, which assume that you have Windows Live Messenger installed on your computer, start and sign in to Windows Live Messenger.

- Display the Start menu.
- Display the All Programs list.
- Click Windows Live, and then click Windows Live Messenger to start Windows Live Messenger. If the Welcome to Windows Live Messenger window is displayed, click the Close button (Figure 4–94).

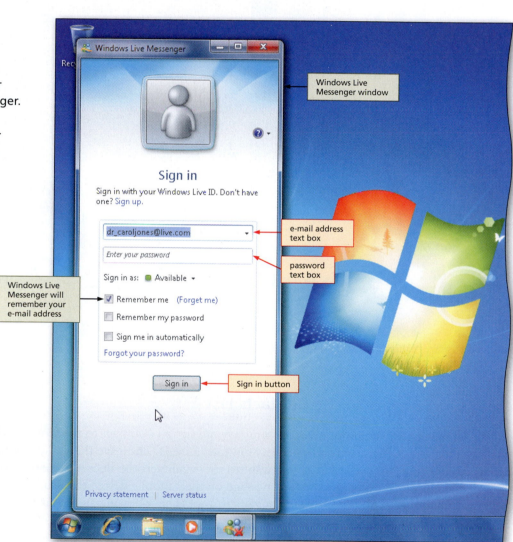

Figure 4–94

2

- If necessary, type your Windows Live ID into the E-mail address text box in the Windows Live Messenger window.

- Type your Windows Live password into the Password text box in the Windows Live Messenger window.

- Click the Sign in button to sign in to Windows Live Messenger and to display your Contacts list (Figure 4–95).

- If the Today window displays, click the Close button to close the window.

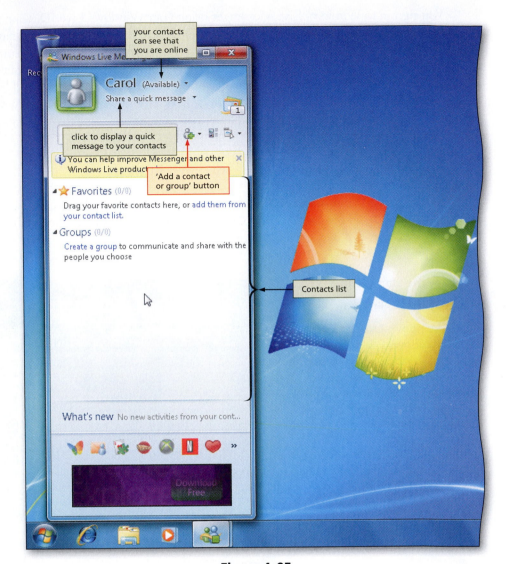

Figure 4–95

To Add a Contact to the Contacts List

After starting Windows Live Messenger, you can add a contact to the Contacts list if you know their instant messaging address. A contact must have a Windows Live ID and have the Windows Live Messenger software installed on his or her computer. If you want to add a contact who does not meet these requirements, you can send the contact an e-mail invitation or text message on their mobile device that explains how to get a Windows Live ID and download the Windows Live Messenger software. The following steps add a contact to the Contacts list using the e-mail address of someone you know who has signed in to Windows Live Messenger.

1

- Click the 'Add a contact or group' button in the Windows Live Messenger window to display a list of options (Figure 4–96).

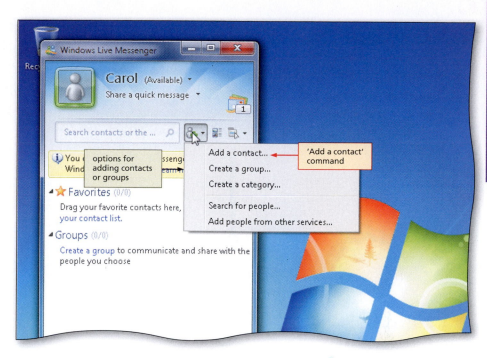

Figure 4–96

2

- Click the 'Add a contact' command to display the Windows Live Messenger dialog box (Figure 4–97).

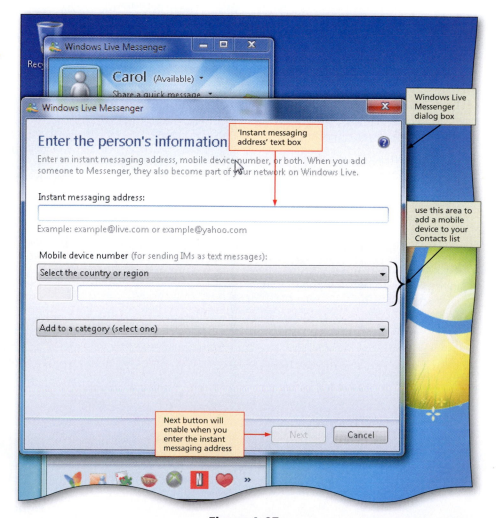

Figure 4–97

3

- Type `drnicolesmith@live.com` in the 'Instant messaging address' text box or enter an instant messaging address specified by your instructor.

- Click the Next button to continue adding the contact (Figure 4–98).

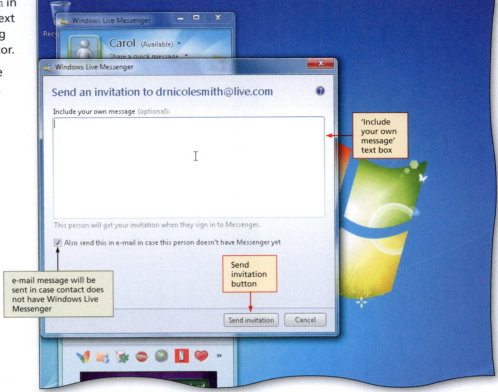

Figure 4–98

4

- Type `Hey Nicole` in the 'Include your own message' text box to enter the first line of your message.

- Press the ENTER key two times to move to the third line of the message.

- Type `I am adding you to my contact list.` to finish the message (Figure 4–99).

- Click the Send invitation button to invite Nicole to become one of your contacts.

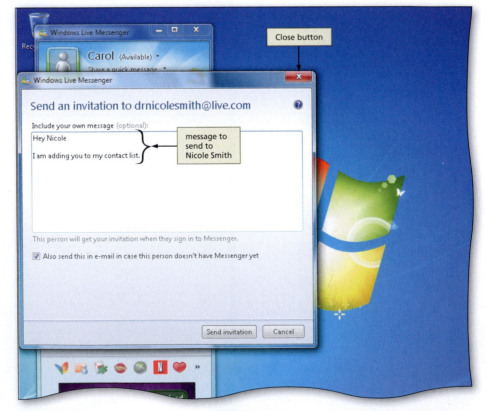

Figure 4–99

5

- Click the Close button to close the dialog box and add the Nicole Smith contact to your Contacts list (Figure 4–100).

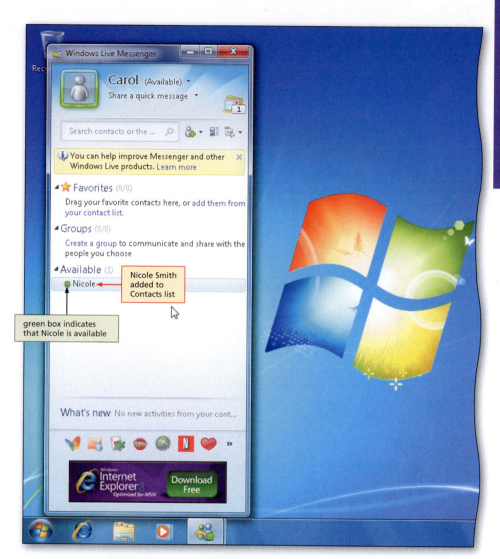

Figure 4–100

To Send an Instant Message

After Nicole has accepted your invitation, you can communicate with her. To use Windows Live Messenger, the person with whom you want to communicate must be online. The Available list shown in Figure 4–100 displays the new contact (Nicole Smith). The steps on the following pages send an instant message to Nicole Smith.

1

- Double-click the Nicole contact to display the Nicole <drnicolesmith@live.com> window (Figure 4–101). If the drnicolesmith@live.com contact is not online, double-click the name of another online contact.

- Type I have learned how to use Windows Live Messenger! Do you have some time to chat? in the Send text box.

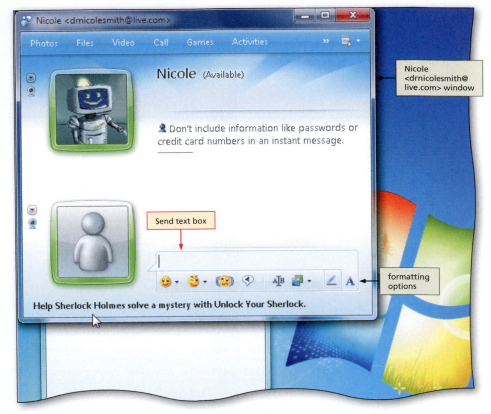

Figure 4–101

2

- Press the ENTER key in the Nicole <drnicolesmith@live.com> window to send the instant message (Figure 4–102).

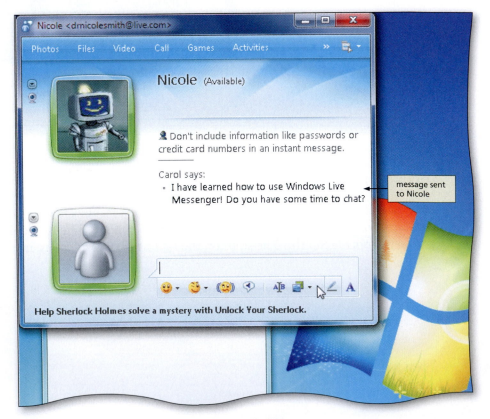

Figure 4–102

3

- The receiver of the message types and then sends a response (Figure 4–103).

Experiment

- Feel free to send additional messages to Nicole Smith or the contact you are communicating with in Windows Live Messenger.

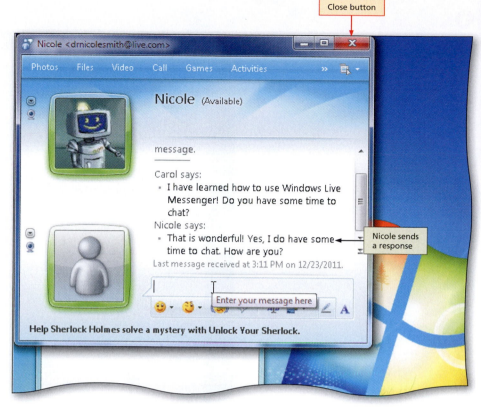

Figure 4–103

Other Ways

1. Right-click contact name, click 'Send an instant message' on shortcut menu

To Close the Instant Messaging Window

When you have finished your conversation, you should close the instant messaging window to end the conversation. The next step closes the drnicolesmith@live.com window.

1 Click the Close button in the Nicole <drnicolesmith@live.com> window to close the instant messaging window.

To Delete a Contact on the Contacts List

The Nicole contact remains on the Contacts list in the Windows Live Messenger window. If you lose touch with a contact, you might want to delete them from your Contacts list. The steps on the following pages delete Nicole Smith from the Contacts list.

1

• Right-click the Nicole contact to display the shortcut menu (Figure 4–104).

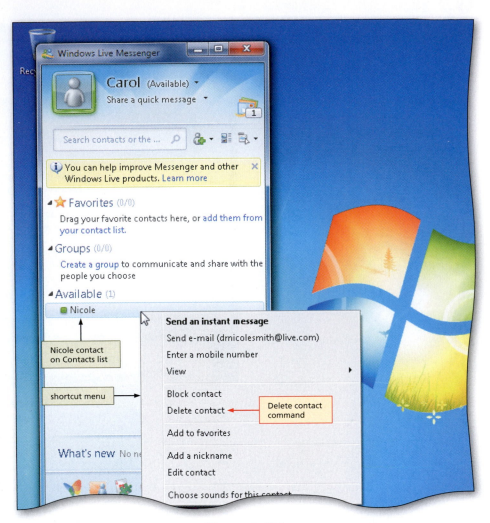

Figure 4–104

2

• Click the Delete contact command on the shortcut menu to display the Windows Live Messenger dialog box (Figure 4–105).

Figure 4–105

3
- Click the Delete contact button in the Windows Live Messenger dialog box to delete Nicole Smith from your Contacts list (Figure 4–106).

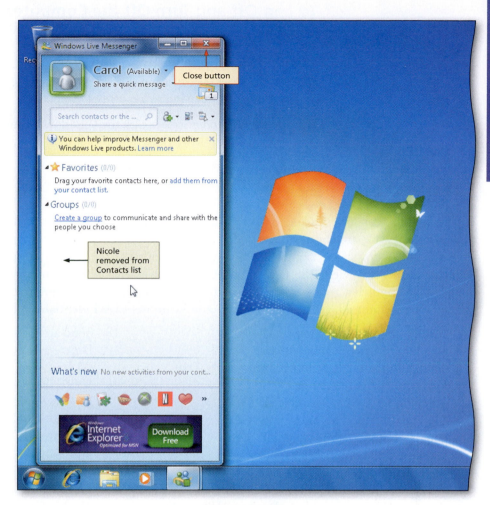

Figure 4–106

To Close and Sign Out from Windows Live Messenger

When you have finished using Windows Live Messenger, close the Windows Live Messenger window. The following steps close the Windows Live Messenger window and sign out from the Windows Live Messenger service.

1
- Close the Windows Live Messenger window (Figure 4–107).

2
- Right-click the Windows Live Messenger icon on the Windows taskbar.

3
- Click the Close window command on the shortcut menu to sign out from Windows Live Messenger.

Figure 4–107

To Log Off and Turn Off the Computer

After completing your work with Windows 7, you first should close your user account by logging off the computer, and then turn off the computer.

1 On the Start menu, click the arrow to the right of the Shut down button, and then click the Log off command to log off the computer.

2 On the Welcome Screen, click the Shut down button to turn off the computer.

Chapter Summary

In this chapter, you have learned to use Windows Live Mail to read, write, format, and send e-mail messages and to attach and view file attachments. You added and removed Calendar appointments and tasks. You added and deleted contacts in Windows Live Contacts. You also used Windows Live Mail to subscribe to and read newsgroups. You used Internet Explorer to view RSS feeds and Web Slices. You learned about other Web applications, including groups, mailing lists, and chat rooms. Finally, you used Windows Live Messenger to send an instant message. The items listed below include all the new Windows 7 and Windows Live Essentials skills you have learned in this chapter.

1. Start Windows Live Mail (WIN 206)
2. Open (Read) an E-Mail Message (WIN 209)
3. Print an Opened E-Mail Message (WIN 210)
4. Close an E-Mail Message (WIN 212)
5. Reply to an E-Mail Message (WIN 212)
6. Delete an E-Mail Message (WIN 213)
7. Open a File Attachment (WIN 214)
8. Compose an E-Mail Message Using Stationery (WIN 216)
9. Format an E-Mail Message (WIN 219)
10. Attach a File to an E-Mail Message (WIN 221)
11. Send an E-Mail Message (WIN 222)
12. Add an Event in Calendar (WIN 223)
13. Add a Reminder and Description to an Event (WIN 226)
14. Change the Calendar View (WIN 227)
15. Delete an Event (WIN 229)
16. Add a Contact to Windows Live Contacts (WIN 230)
17. Compose an E-Mail Message Using the Contacts Folder (WIN 234)
18. Send an E-Mail Message (WIN 236)
19. Delete a Contact from the Contacts Folder (WIN 237)
20. Subscribe to and Display a Newsgroup on the Microsoft News Server (WIN 239)
21. Read a Newsgroup Article (WIN 242)
22. Unsubscribe from a Newsgroup (WIN 244)
23. Subscribe to an RSS Feed (WIN 245)
24. View Your RSS Feeds in the Favorites Center (WIN 248)
25. Modify Feed Properties (WIN 249)
26. Subscribe to a Web Slice (WIN 251)
27. View a Web Slice (WIN 252)
28. Delete a Web Slice (WIN 253)
29. Start Windows Live Messenger and Sign In (WIN 257)
30. Add a Contact to the Contacts List (WIN 258)
31. Send an Instant Message (WIN 261)
32. Delete a Contact on the Contacts List (WIN 263)
33. Close and Sign Out from Windows Live Messenger (WIN 265)

Learn It Online

Test your knowledge of chapter content and key terms.

Instructions: To complete the Learn It Online exercises, start your browser, click the Address bar, and then enter the Web address `scsite.com/win7/learn`. When the Windows 7 Learn It Online page is displayed, click the link for the exercise you want to complete and then read the instructions.

Chapter Reinforcement TF, MC, and SA

A series of true/false, multiple-choice, and short-answer questions that test your knowledge of the chapter content.

Flash Cards

An interactive learning environment where you identify chapter key terms associated with displayed definitions.

Practice Test

A series of multiple-choice questions that test your knowledge of chapter content and key terms.

Who Wants To Be a Computer Genius?

An interactive game that challenges your knowledge of chapter content in the style of a television quiz show.

Wheel of Terms

An interactive game that challenges your knowledge of chapter key terms in the style of the television show *Wheel of Fortune*.

Crossword Puzzle Challenge

A crossword puzzle that challenges your knowledge of key terms presented in the chapter.

Apply Your Knowledge

Reinforce the skills and apply the concepts you learned in this chapter.

Sending an E-Mail Message to Your Instructor

Instructions: You want to send an e-mail message to your instructor stating what you like best about his or her class. Use Windows Live Mail to send the e-mail.

Figure 4–108

Continued >

Apply Your Knowledge *continued*

1. Start Internet Explorer and search for the home page for your college or university. Figure 4–108 on the previous page shows the home page for Valencia Community College.

2. Find and write down the e-mail address of your instructor.

3. Start Windows Live Mail.

4. Click the New button on the Mail toolbar.

5. Using the e-mail address of the instructor you obtained in Step 2, compose a mail message to this instructor stating what you like best about his or her class.

6. Click the Send button to send the e-mail message to your instructor.

Extend Your Knowledge

Extend the skills you learned in this chapter and experiment with new skills. You might need to use Help to complete the assignment.

Posting a Newsgroup Article

Instructions: Locate a newsgroup on Windows Live Messenger, and then compose and post a message to the newsgroup. After posting the article, find your message in the message list pane, and then print the article.

1. Search for and subscribe to a newsgroup that contains articles about Windows Live Messenger.

2. Locate and click the newsgroup name in the folder list.

3. Click the New button to display the New Message window (Figure 4–109).

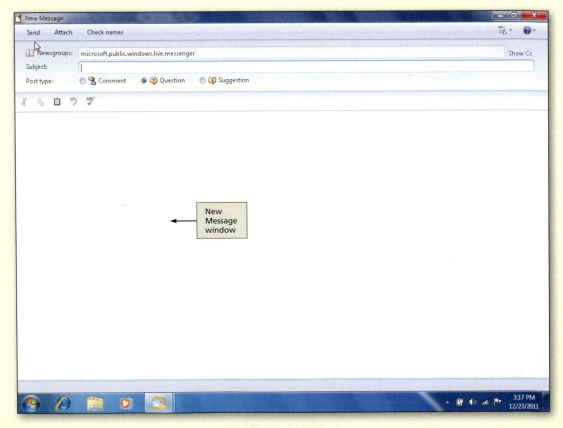

Figure 4–109

4. Compose and then post a message to the newsgroup that either explains your favorite feature of Windows Live Messenger or poses a question about Windows Live Messenger.

5. Find your message in the message list. Print the message, write your name on the printed message, and submit it to your instructor.

In the Lab

Use the guidelines, concepts, and skills presented in this chapter to increase your knowledge of Windows 7. Labs are listed in order of increasing difficulty.

Lab 1: Adding Your Friends to the Contacts Folder

Instructions: You want to use the Contacts feature of Windows Live Mail to keep track of the names, e-mail addresses, home addresses, and home telephone numbers of your friends.

1. Start Windows Live Mail. Click the Contacts button in the Navigation pane to open the Windows Live Contacts window. If necessary, maximize the window (Figure 4–110).

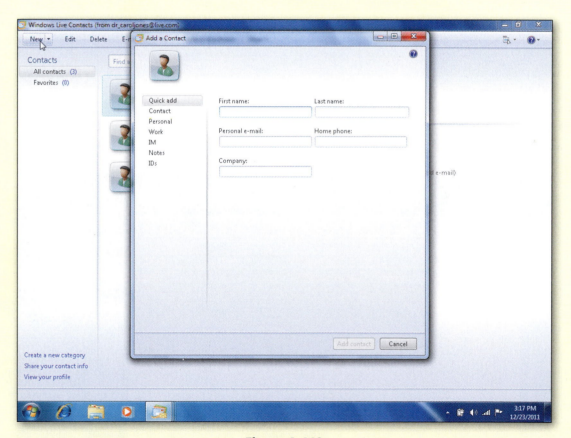

Figure 4–110

Continued >

STUDENT ASSIGNMENTS

In the Lab continued

2. Use the New button on the toolbar to add the contacts listed in Table 4–3 to the Contacts folder.

Table 4–3 Contacts List for Contacts Folder			
Name	**E-Mail Address**	**Address**	**Home Phone**
Pete Alfieris	palfieris@isp.com	8451 Colony Dr., Brea, CA 92821	(714) 555-2831
Theresa Collins	tcollins@isp.com	3544 Clayton Rd., Placentia, CA 92871	(714) 555-1484
Jessica McEwen	jmcewen@isp.com	5689 State St., Fullerton, CA 92834	(714) 555-2318
Tami Newell	tnewell@isp.com	7812 Bennington Dr., Atwood, CA 92811	(714) 555-8622
Cherry Nguyen	cnguyen@isp.com	257 W. Wilson St., Yorba Linda, CA 92885	(714) 555-2782
Amanda Silva	asilva@isp.com	648 Flower Rd., Brea, CA 92821	(714) 555-6495

3. Print the information for all of the contacts by clicking the Print button on the toolbar, selecting All Contacts under the Print range heading, and then clicking the Print button. Write your name on the printout.

4. Delete each contact by selecting the contact name and then clicking the Delete button on the toolbar.

In the Lab

Lab 2: E-Mailing Your Class Schedule as an Attachment

Instructions: You want to send your class schedule to your instructor as an attachment. Type your class schedule into a new Notepad document and save the file. Switch to Windows Live Mail, type an e-mail message to your instructor, and attach the Notepad file containing your class schedule.

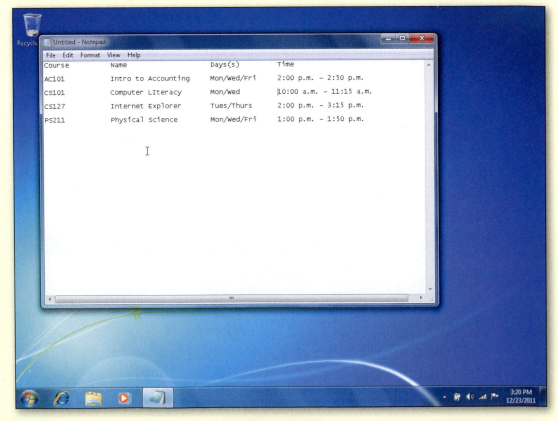

Figure 4–111

1. Start Notepad. Type your class schedule into the Notepad document, organizing your classes using a method of your choosing. A sample Notepad document containing a class schedule is illustrated in Figure 4–111.

2. Using your first and last name as the file name (put a space between your first and last names), save the Notepad document to your Documents library.

3. In Windows Live Mail, compose a new e-mail message to your instructor. Type your instructor's e-mail address into the To text box. Type `My Class Schedule` for the subject. For the body of the e-mail message, type `I have created a document with Notepad that contains my class schedule. The file is attached to this e-mail message.` Sign the e-mail message with your name.

4. Click the Attach button, navigate to the Documents library, and then attach the Notepad file you created to the e-mail message.

5. Send the e-mail message.

6. Display the contents of the Sent items folder to verify that your message was sent.

In the Lab

Lab 3: Using Windows Live Messenger

Instructions: Start and sign in to Windows Live Messenger. Add a new contact to your Windows Live Messenger Contacts list. After adding the contact, send instant messages to each other, and then save and print the entire conversation.

Part 1: Adding a Contact to the Contacts List

1. Click the 'Add a contact or group' button in the Windows Live Messenger window and then click the Add a contact command.

2. Type the Windows Live ID or Windows Live Hotmail e-mail address of a friend in the Instant messaging address text box, click the Next button, and then click the Send invitation button.

Part 2: Sending an Instant Message

1. Double-click the icon of the contact you added in the Contacts list.

2. Type a message in the message area, click the ENTER key, wait for the response, and type your response.

3. Continue conversing in this manner until you have typed at least four messages. Figure 4–112 on the next page shows a sample conversation.

Continued >

In the Lab *continued*

Figure 4–112

Part 3: Saving the Conversation

1. Press the ALT key to display the menu bar.
2. Click File on the menu bar to display the File menu.
3. Click Save as on the File menu. If the Windows Live Messenger dialog box displays, click the OK button.
4. Save the file with the file name Conversation to the Documents library on your computer.
5. Close the instant messaging window.

Part 4: Deleting a Contact on the Contacts List

1. In the Windows Live Messenger window, right-click the contact you want to delete.
2. Click Delete contact on the shortcut menu.
3. Click the Delete contact button in the Windows Live Messenger dialog box.

Part 5: Closing Windows Live Messenger Window and Signing Out from the Windows Live Messenger Service

1. Click the Close button in the Windows Live Messenger window.
2. Right-click the Windows Live Messenger icon on the Windows taskbar.
3. Click Close window on the shortcut menu.
4. Send the Conversation file to your instructor as an e-mail attachment.

Cases and Places

Apply your creative thinking and problem-solving skills to design and implement a solution.

• Easier   •• More Difficult

• 1 Comparing Windows Live Mail and Google Gmail

Using computer magazines, advertising brochures, the Internet, or other resources, compile information about Windows Live Mail and Google Gmail. In a brief report, compare the two programs. Include the differences and similarities, the function and features of each program, and so forth. If possible, test Google Gmail and add your personal comments. Submit your report to your instructor.

• 2 Discussing the Use of False Online Identities

There are concerns that some users will try to disguise their identities by entering false information when signing up for a free e-mail account. In a brief report, summarize the reasons why you should identify yourself correctly on the Internet, what kinds of problems result when users disguise their identities, and offer some suggestions as to how to prevent this problem. Submit your report to your instructor.

•• 3 Researching E-Mail Programs

Using computer magazines, advertising brochures, the Internet, or other resources, compile information about two e-mail programs other than Windows Live Mail or Google Gmail. In a brief report, compare the two programs and the Windows Live Mail e-mail program. Include the differences and similarities, how to obtain the software, the functions and features of each program, and so forth. Submit the report to your instructor.

•• 4 Locating RSS Feeds

Make It Personal
Many Web sites provide their content via an RSS feed. Locate at least two news Web sites and at least two other Web sites that you are interested in that allow you to subscribe to an RSS feed. What are the advantages of subscribing to an RSS feed? Would you rather subscribe to an RSS feed or navigate directly to the Web site to view its content? Why or why not? Submit your answers to your instructor in an e-mail message.

•• 5 Creating a Google Group

Working Together
Groups are a popular way for people to communicate with each other about a certain topic via the Internet. Create a Google Group about a topic of your choice (http://groups.google.com) and have each team member post a message to the group to initiate a conversation. Wait two days to see if anyone outside of your team has signed up for your group. Find one other group that discusses a similar topic. How many people have joined that group? Discuss how you could attract more people to your group. Summarize your findings in a presentation for your class.

5 | Personalizing Your Work Environment

Objectives

You will have mastered the material in this chapter when you can:

- Create, save, and delete a desktop theme
- Change the desktop background
- View sound settings
- Change mouse pointers
- Change the screen saver
- Add icons to the desktop
- Unlock, move, hide, and resize the taskbar

- Pinning programs to and unpinning programs from the taskbar
- Start a program from the taskbar
- Use the Address toolbar to display folder content and search the Internet
- Customize the Start menu and notification area
- Change folder options and restore default folder options

5 | Personalizing Your Work Environment

Introduction

One of the best ways to improve productivity while using the computer is to personalize your work environment. For example, you can add icons for frequently used programs and files to your desktop to save time. If you use many different programs, you might want to modify the Start menu to show additional recently used programs. Similarly, users often personalize their computer by adding unique touches. This includes changing their desktop to display a family photo or changing the appearance and location of the taskbar. By personalizing the work environment, users feel more in tune with their computer, which can put users more at ease and lead to improved productivity.

Overview

As you read this chapter, you will learn how to personalize your work environment by performing these general tasks:

- Opening and changing the desktop settings
- Reviewing your sound and mouse pointer selections
- Changing your screen saver
- Adding additional icons to your desktop
- Unlocking, moving, resizing, locking, and hiding the taskbar
- Pinning programs to and unpinning programs from the taskbar
- Adding and using the Address toolbar
- Customizing Start menu options
- Customizing the notification area

Plan Ahead

Personalizing the Windows 7 Desktop
Customizing and personalizing the Windows 7 desktop requires a basic knowledge of how to use Windows 7, how to access sample files, and how to access the Internet, as well as the appropriate permissions to do so.

1. **Determine the permissions you have on the computer you will be using.** Each user account can have different rights and permissions. Depending on which rights and permissions have been set for your account, you might or might not be able to perform certain operations.

2. **Find out if you have access to the sample files installed with Windows 7.** To complete the steps in this chapter, you will need access to the sample pictures installed with Windows 7.

3. **Determine whether you have Internet access.** For this chapter, you will be accessing the Internet to search for information. You will want to know if your computer has Internet access and if anything is required of you to use it.

Personalizing Your Desktop

Windows 7 provides a variety of methods to modify the desktop with which you work. As introduced in Chapter 1, Windows 7 considers most items on the desktop, including the desktop itself, to be objects. Every object has properties, which are the defining characteristics of an object. In many cases, you can change an object's properties to fit your needs. You might be surprised at the many different preferences people have for their computer desktops. Some like quiet, cool colors whereas others like bright, glittery themes. There is no single correct way to set up your desktop. Preferences are an individual matter, which is why Microsoft and other operating system designers offer many options for customizing your desktop.

To Open the Personalization Window

A starting point for personalizing your work environment is to change the appearance of the desktop. Objects on the desktop that you can modify include the choice of a desktop theme and background, which icons appear on the desktop and their size and color, how windows open on the desktop, and which screen saver to use.

When the Personalization window opens, it displays the current desktop theme. A **desktop theme** is a set of graphical elements that give the desktop a unified and distinctive look. In addition to determining the look of the various graphic elements on the desktop, a desktop theme also can define the sounds associated with events such as opening or closing a program. Unless the desktop already has been modified, the default Windows 7 desktop theme displays when you launch Windows 7.

One method of changing the appearance of the desktop is to change the desktop theme. You can make changes to your desktop using the various options available in the Personalization window. All the changes you make are added to the Unsaved Theme in the My Themes area. After you make changes, you can save the theme with a name of your choice using the Save theme link in the Personalization window.

Before you begin making changes to your work environment, you should view and record which theme currently is in use by Windows 7 so that you can restore it later if you want to do so. In most cases, this will be the Windows 7 theme. The following steps open the Personalization window and allow you to record the current desktop theme.

- Right-click an open area of the desktop to display the shortcut menu (Figure 5–1).

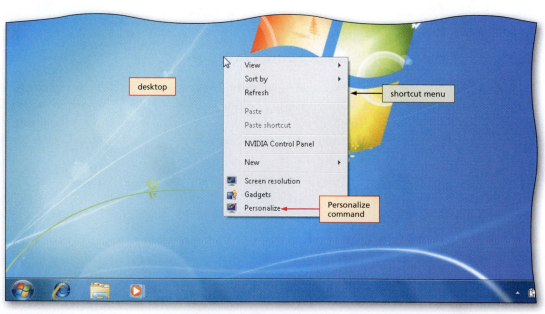

Figure 5–1

2

- Click the Personalize command to open the Personalization window (Figure 5–2).

- Write down the name of the theme being used for future reference.

Q&A

Why is my desktop theme different from the one selected in Figure 5–2?

The desktop theme can be changed after Windows 7 is installed. School computer labs often customize the desktop theme to display school logos and/or colors. This also happens frequently in the workplace environment.

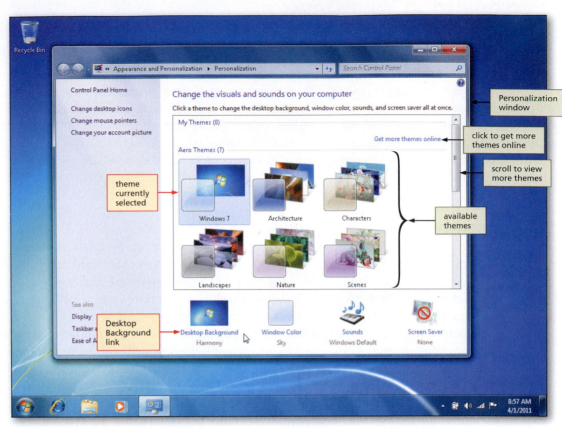

Figure 5–2

Other Ways

1. Open Start menu, click Control Panel, click Appearance and Personalization, click Personalization

To Open the Desktop Background Window

One element of a desktop theme is the desktop background. The **desktop background** is the pattern or picture that displays on the desktop, appearing behind windows and icons. With Windows 7, you even can use videos as your desktop background. To change your desktop background using the Personalization window, you need to open the Desktop Background window. The following step opens the Desktop Background window.

1
- Click the Desktop Background link to open the Desktop Background window (Figure 5–3).

Q&A

Can I use any image as my desktop background?

Yes. If you locate a picture you want to use as the desktop background, right-click the picture, select the 'Set as desktop background' command, and then the picture will be used as your background. You then can open the Desktop Background window and set any additional options you want to use.

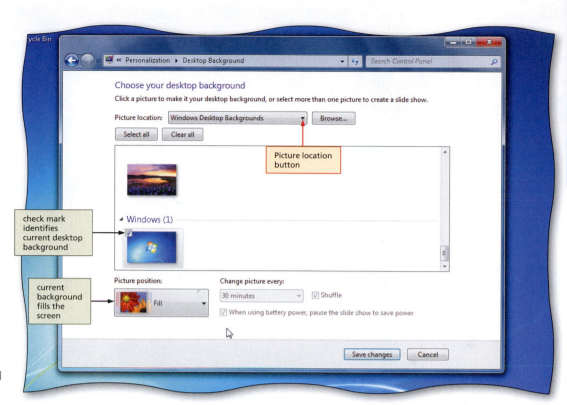

Figure 5–3

Other Ways

1. Press TAB until Desktop Background is selected, press ENTER

To Change the Desktop Background

When you work with Windows 7 and do not maximize the window you are using, the desktop background can be the single most dominant feature of the computer screen. Your choice of background can affect your mood, the ease with which you use your computer, and even others who work nearby. Windows 7 comes with a variety of desktop backgrounds from which you can choose. You also can use any picture that you have saved on your computer. Pictures in your Pictures library can be rated and Windows 7 makes it easy for you to select a top-rated picture as your desktop background. The following steps change the background to the top-rated Penguins picture from the Pictures library.

1
- Click the Picture location button to display the list of location options (Figure 5–4).

Q&A

What file formats are used for desktop backgrounds and pictures?

You can use a photo you took, a picture from the Pictures library, a picture from any other folder on your computer, or an image you found on a Web page as a desktop background. The file can be any of the following formats: bitmap file (.bmp), GIF file (.gif), JPEG file (.jpg), Microsoft PhotoDraw Picture file (.dib), Portable Network Graphics file (.png), or HTML file (.htm).

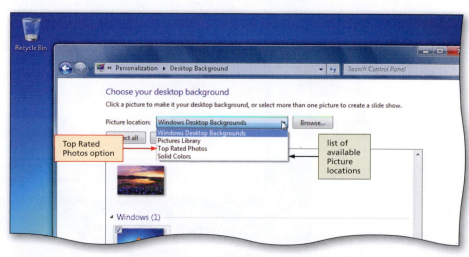

Figure 5–4

2

• Click Top Rated Photos to show the top-rated photos (Figure 5–5).

Q&A

Why do I see a different set of photos?

The top-rated photos shown in Figure 5–5 are those installed with Windows 7. If you do not have Windows 7 Ultimate Edition with the latest updates and extras, you will not see the same photos. Also, some computer labs choose to not install all the extras. **Extras** are enhancements for Windows 7 that you can download from the Internet. In this case, please continue to read the steps without performing them.

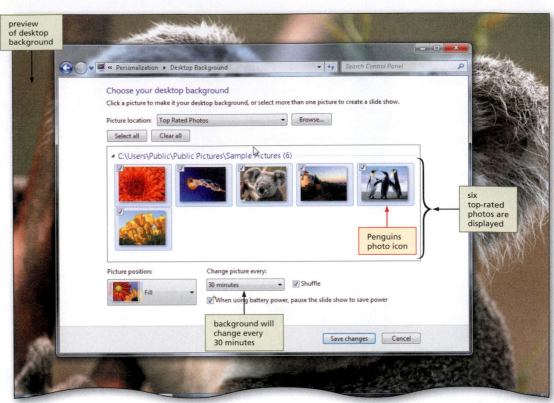

Figure 5–5

Q&A

Why did my desktop background change before I selected anything?

Windows 7 selected every top-rated photo and offers a preview of the new background. This desktop background and background options will be applied if you save the changes.

3

• Click the Penguins photo icon to select the Penguins photo (Figure 5–6).

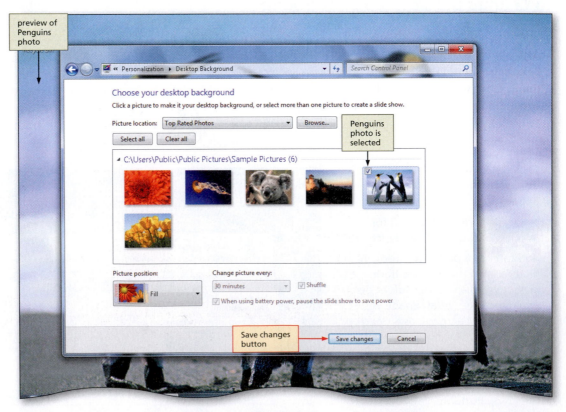

Figure 5–6

4

• Click the Save changes button to set the Penguins photo as the desktop background and return to the Personalization window (Figure 5–7).

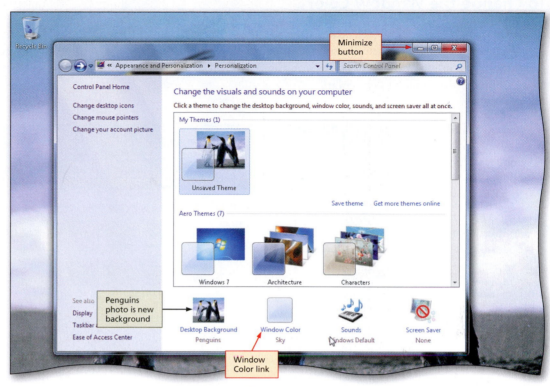

Minimize button

Penguins photo is new background

Window Color link

Figure 5–7

5

• Click the Minimize button to minimize the Personalization window and view the new desktop background (Figure 5–8).

• After viewing the desktop, restore the Personalization window.

new desktop background

click to restore Personalization window

Figure 5–8

To Change the Window Color

One of the easiest ways to customize your desktop is to change the color and appearance of your windows. The Window Color link in the Personalization window allows you to change how your windows look. Windows 7 provides preset color options and gives you the option of turning off the transparency effect. The following steps change the window color to chocolate.

- Click the Window Color link to open the Window Color and Appearance window (Figure 5–9).

Q&A

Why do I see the Window Color and Appearance dialog box instead of the Window Color and Appearance window?

Your computer might not be capable of using Aero or Aero might be turned off. Your computer must be using Aero for the Window Color and Appearance window to appear. To turn on Aero, if available, open the Personalization window and change the theme to Windows 7.

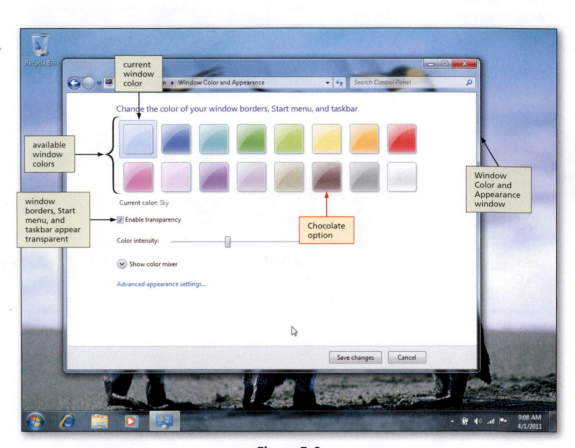

Figure 5–9

2
- Click the Chocolate option (row 2, column 6) to change the color of the window borders, Start menu, and taskbar to chocolate (Figure 5–10).

Experiment

- There are several built-in color schemes for Aero. Click the different color options to see what they look like. After you have changed the color scheme, you also can turn the transparency effect of Aero on and off by clicking the Enable transparency check box. Return to the Chocolate color option and turn on the transparency effect when you are done.

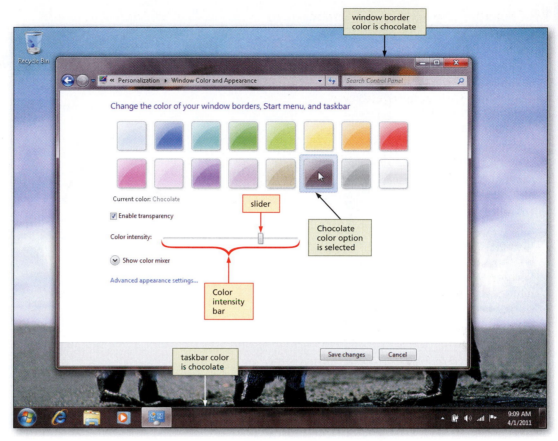

Figure 5–10

Other Ways

1. Press RIGHT ARROW until Chocolate color scheme is selected

To Change the Intensity of the Window Color

Once you have selected a color scheme, you can adjust the intensity using the Color intensity bar. If you move the slider on the Color intensity bar to the left, you make the window appear more transparent by decreasing the amount of color. If you move the slider more to the right, you increase the amount of color and the window appears less transparent. Although changing the color intensity affects how the Chocolate color scheme appears on your desktop, it does not change the default setting of the Chocolate color scheme. If you were to click the Chocolate color scheme, the color intensity would return to the preset value. The step on the following page changes the color intensity to its maximum value.

● Click and drag the slider on the Color intensity bar all the way to the right to increase the color intensity to its maximum value (Figure 5–11).

Experiment

● Move the slider around to see how changing the color intensity can change the appearance of the windows and taskbar. Position the slider all the way to the right when you are finished.

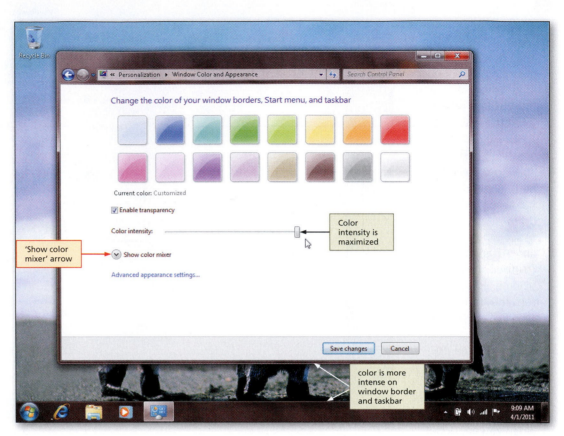

Figure 5–11

Other Ways

1. Press TAB until Color intensity bar is selected, press RIGHT ARROW until slider is at maximum value

To Display the Color Mixer

In addition to altering the color intensity, you also can adjust the color scheme by using the color mixer. The color mixer allows you to change the hue, saturation, and brightness of the color scheme. By changing the hue, you change the color. Changing the **hue** in the color mixer is a way to select a color that is different from the schemes provided by Windows 7. **Saturation** controls whether a color is more or less intense. **Brightness** determines how light or dark the hue and saturation appear.

You can use all three options to create a custom color scheme. When you change these options, you are not changing the default settings of the color scheme. As with changes to the Color intensity bar, if you were to click on the Chocolate color scheme, for example, the color mixer options would change back to the default Chocolate color scheme settings. The following step uses the color mixer to display the hue, saturation, and brightness of your color scheme.

1

- Click the 'Show color mixer' arrow to display the color mixer (Figure 5–12).

🔍 **Experiment**

- Move the sliders for hue, saturation, and brightness to see how changing their values affects the color of your windows. Once you are finished, move the sliders back to their original locations.

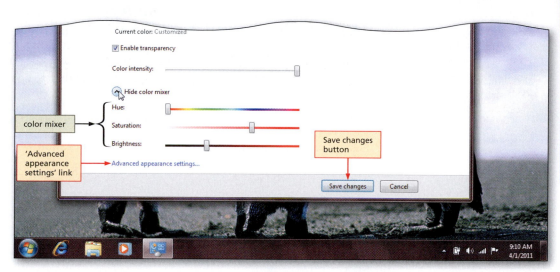

Figure 5–12

To View Advanced Appearance Settings

You can make additional color modifications by using the Window Color and Appearance dialog box. These settings only apply if you are using a Windows 7 Basic theme or a high contrast theme. For example, you can change your color scheme by selecting from a list of preset schemes, or you can change effects such as shadows on menus.

You can use the 'Advanced appearance settings' link to display the Window Color and Appearance dialog box; however, not all of the options can be applied to the Windows Aero scheme. The themes available in the Window Color and Appearance dialog box are similar to familiar desktop colors and appearance found on computers using a previous version of Windows. The following step displays the Window Color and Appearance dialog box.

1

- Click the 'Advanced appearance settings' link to display the Window Color and Appearance dialog box (Figure 5–13).

Q&A What happens if I change one of the settings?

If you are using Aero, none of the changes will be applied, except for the font settings. If you are not using Aero, you can make changes to the sizes and colors of various window features. This includes features such as title bars, buttons, hyperlinks, and icons.

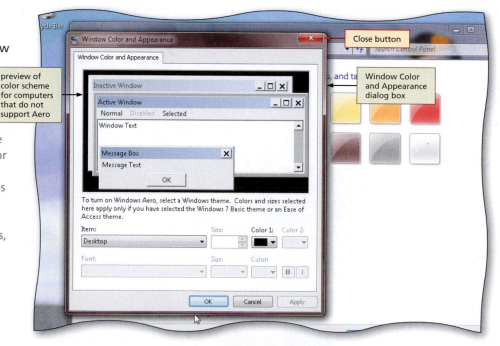

Figure 5–13

To Close the Window Color and Appearance Dialog Box and Window Color and Appearance Window

Now that you have finished exploring the Window Color and Appearance dialog box, you should close it. The following steps close the dialog box and return to the Personalization window.

1 Click the Close button to close the Window Color and Appearance dialog box.

2 Click Save changes button to return to the Personalization window (Figure 5–14).

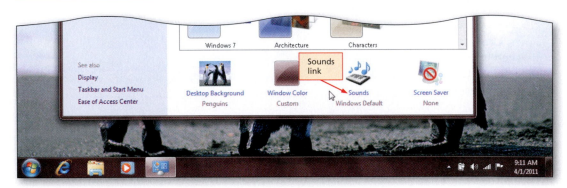

Figure 5–14

To View the Sound Settings

The Sounds link on the Personalization window allows you to view and change the sound settings, including the entire sound scheme, for Windows 7. A **sound scheme** includes all the sounds that are played when Windows events occur, such as when the computer starts up or shuts down, when an error occurs, and when the Recycle Bin is emptied. Many people change the sound scheme so that they can hear clips from songs and movies that they like. You even can use sound schemes that you have created or downloaded from the Internet. The following steps display the Sound dialog box.

1

• Click the Sounds link in the Personalization window to open the Sound dialog box (Figure 5–15).

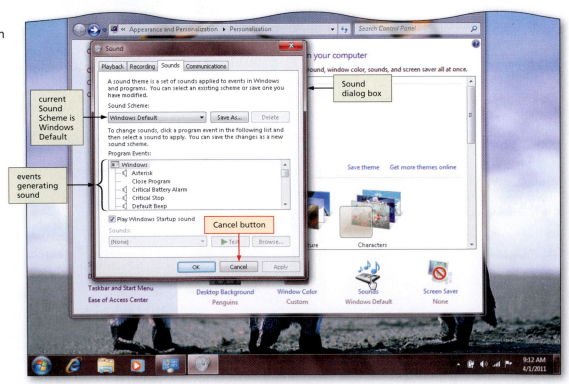

Figure 5–15

2
- After viewing the Sounds settings, click the Cancel button to close the Sound dialog box without making changes (Figure 5–16).

Figure 5–16

To Change the Screen Saver

Another element of a desktop theme that you can modify is the screen saver. A **screen saver** is a moving picture or pattern that displays on the monitor when you have not used the mouse or keyboard for a specified period of time. Originally, screen savers were designed to prevent the problem of **ghosting** (where a dim version of an image would permanently be etched on the monitor if the same image were to be displayed for a long time) by continually changing the image on the monitor. Although ghosting is less of a problem with today's monitors, people still use screen savers. Screen savers can be animations, designs, and other entertaining or fascinating activities that display on the screen after a period of time has passed without any computer activity. You can determine how long this interval should be. Screen savers stop executing when you press a key on the keyboard or move the mouse. Windows 7 provides a variety of screen savers from which you can choose. The steps on the following pages change the screen saver to Photos.

1

• Click the Screen Saver link to display the Screen Saver Settings dialog box (Figure 5–17).

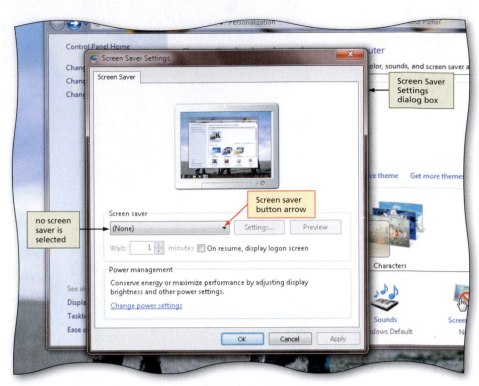

Figure 5–17

2

• Click the Screen saver button arrow to display the list of installed screen savers (Figure 5–18).

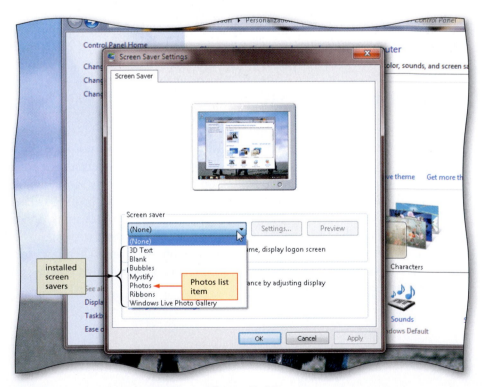

Figure 5–18

3

- Click the Photos list item to select the Photos screen saver (Figure 5–19).

🔍 **Experiment**

- Click the Screen saver button arrow and select other screen savers to see a preview. When you are finished, click the Photos list item to select the Photos screen saver.

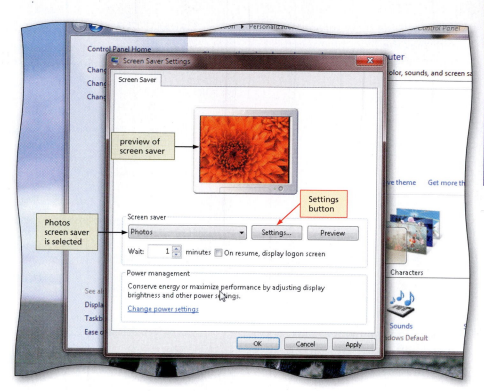

Figure 5–19

To Change the Screen Saver Settings and Preview the Screen Saver

After selecting the Photos screen saver, you can use the Settings button to browse and select pictures you want the screen saver to use. Not all screen savers have settings that you can change. In the Photos Screen Saver Settings dialog box, you can choose to use all pictures from the Pictures library or to select them from a folder on your computer. You also can set the speed of the slide show for the screen saver and whether it shuffles the photos or not. The following steps change the speed to fast and turn on shuffle for the Photos screen saver.

1

- Click the Settings button to display the Photos Screen Saver Settings dialog box (Figure 5–20).

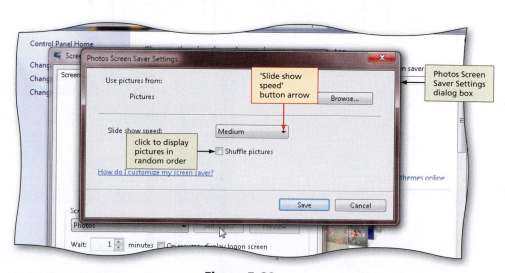

Figure 5–20

2

• Click the 'Slide show speed' button to display the slide show speed options (Figure 5–21).

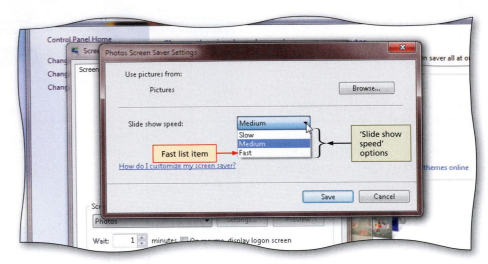

Figure 5–21

3

• Click Fast to change the 'Slide show speed' setting to Fast (Figure 5–22).

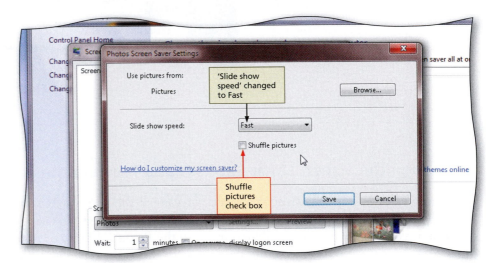

Figure 5–22

4

• Click the Shuffle pictures check box to configure Windows to shuffle the photos (Figure 5–23).

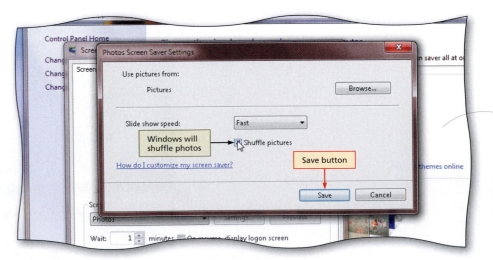

Figure 5–23

5

• Click the Save button to save the changes and return to the Screen Saver Settings dialog box (Figure 5–24).

Q&A

What does changing the Wait or the Power management settings do?

The Wait setting controls how long the computer waits before turning on the screen saver. The default number of minutes to wait is set to 1. If the 'On resume, display logon screen' check box to the right of the Wait box contains a check mark, the Welcome screen will display when you resume using the computer after the screen saver has started running, and you might be required to enter a password to access the desktop. Clicking the 'Change power settings' link in the Power management area allows you to select a power scheme and select the number of minutes or hours of inactivity that you want to elapse before the monitor or hard disk turns off and the system standby or system hibernation feature turns on.

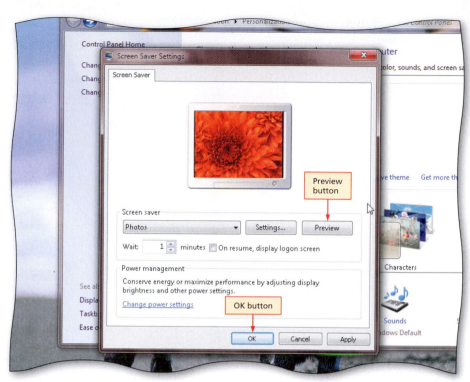

Figure 5–24

6

• Click the Preview button to preview the screen saver (Figure 5–25).

• Move the mouse to exit the preview.

Figure 5–25

7
• Click the OK button to return to the Personalization window (Figure 5–26).

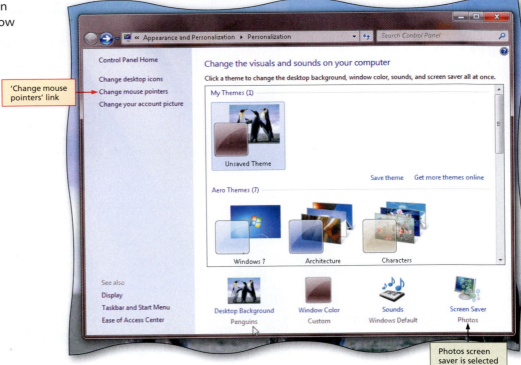

Figure 5–26

To Change the Mouse Pointers

You can change the way the mouse pointers appear by clicking the 'Change mouse pointers' link in the Personalization window. You can customize the mouse pointers by selecting a new scheme or modifying a specific mouse event. After selecting the event, click the Browse button to find mouse pointers that you either have created or downloaded from the Internet. Once you have customized the settings to your satisfaction, you can save the settings as a new scheme. You also can delete schemes that you no longer need. The following steps display the Mouse Properties dialog box and change the mouse pointers scheme to Windows Black (extra large) (system scheme).

1
• Click the 'Change mouse pointers' link in the Personalization window to display the Mouse Properties dialog box (Figure 5–27).

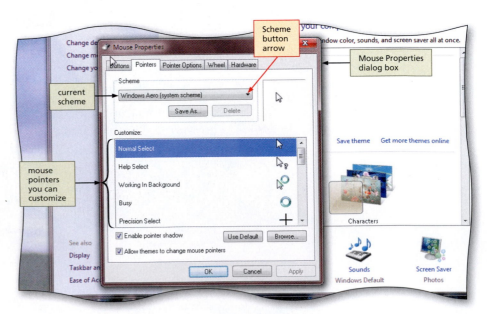

Figure 5–27

2
- Click the Scheme button arrow in the Scheme area to display the list of schemes (Figure 5–28).

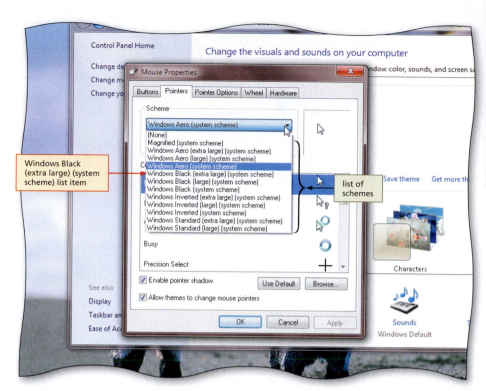

Figure 5–28

3
- Click the Windows Black (extra large) (system scheme) list item to change the mouse pointers to extra large (Figure 5–29).

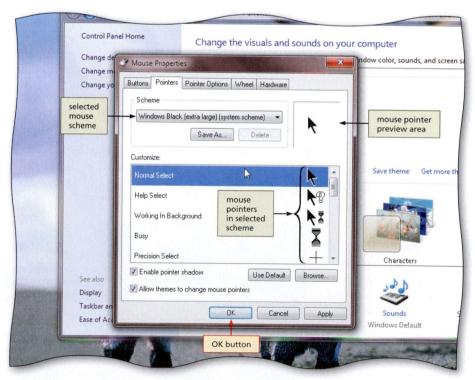

Figure 5–29

● Click the OK button
to save the changes
(Figure 5–30).

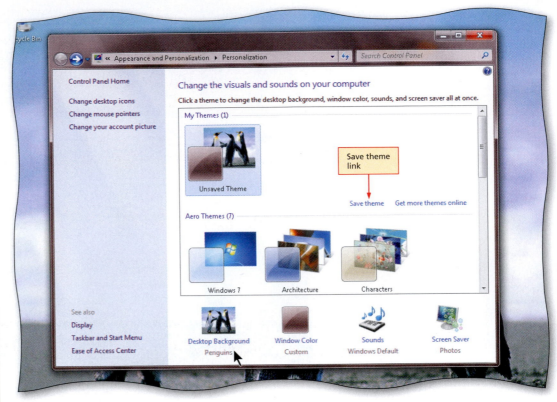

Figure 5–30

To Save a Desktop Theme

Now that you have made all of these changes to your desktop settings, you can save your theme by using the Save theme link in the Personalization window. Up until now, the changes you have made were placed into an Unsaved Theme. If you want to reuse your theme or prevent it from being changed, you should save it. Each user can personalize their Windows 7 environment and can save the themes they create. Some people make themes for holidays or special occasions. The themes you create are saved in the My Themes group in the Personalization window. The following steps save the Unsaved Theme as the SC Theme.

● Click the Save
theme link in the
Personalization win-
dow to display the
Save Theme As dialog
box (Figure 5–31).

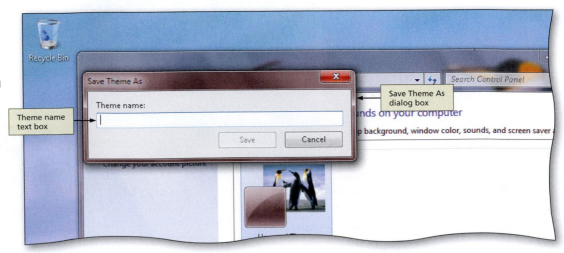

Figure 5–31

2

- Type SC Theme in the Theme name text box to enter the name for the theme (Figure 5–32).

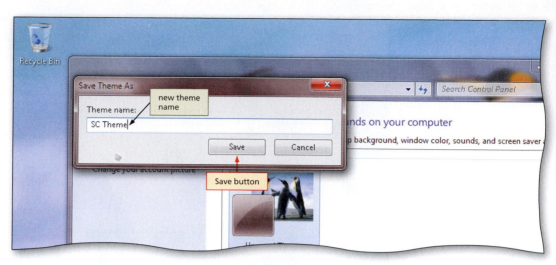

Figure 5–32

3

- Click the Save button in the Save As dialog box to save the SC Theme (Figure 5–33).

Figure 5–33

To Switch to a Different Desktop Theme

You can test your saved desktop theme by switching to another theme and then back again. This lets you see that all your changes were saved properly. The steps on the following page change the desktop theme to Windows 7 and then back to the saved SC Theme.

1

• Click the Windows 7 theme to select the theme (Figure 5–34).

• Notice the changes in the desktop theme.

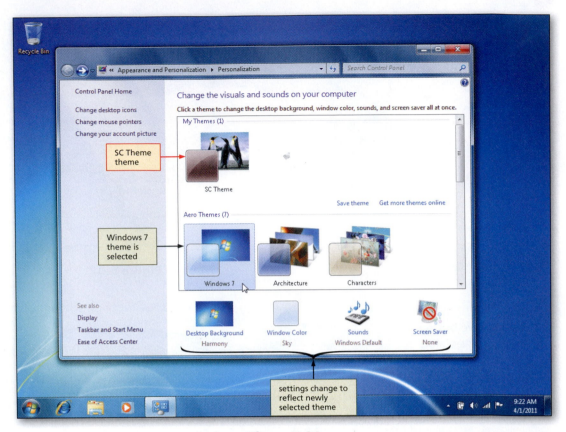

Figure 5–34

2

• Click the SC Theme theme to select the theme (Figure 5–35).

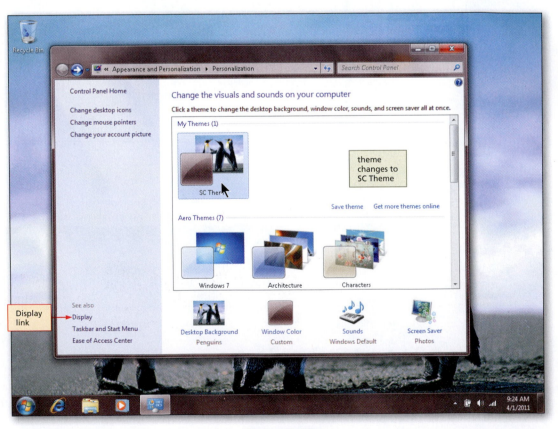

Figure 5–35

To View the Display Window and the Screen Resolution Window

Another way to personalize your computer is to adjust the display settings for your monitor. You can use the Display window to control the display settings for your monitor, such as the size of the desktop or whether more than one monitor is in use. Typically, Windows 7 automatically chooses the best display settings, including screen resolution, orientation, and color, based on your particular monitor and video card. The ability to change the display settings is limited to those supported by your monitor and video card. Only options that are supported by your hardware will appear.

From the Display window, you can change the screen resolution by using the Adjust resolution link. **Resolution** refers to the clarity of the text and images on your screen. The higher the resolution, the sharper and smaller the items will appear on your desktop. At a lower resolution, fewer items fit on the screen, but they are larger and easier to see. The recommended resolution for your monitor will vary based upon the monitor's display size.

Using the Advanced settings link in the Screen Resolution window, you can adjust the adapter settings, adjust the monitor settings such as screen refresh rate (monitor flicker), troubleshoot problems, and configure color management for your display. You only should change these options if necessary. Under normal circumstances, you should let Windows 7 configure these options for you. The following steps display the Display and Screen Resolution windows.

1

- Click the Display link to display the Display window (Figure 5–36).

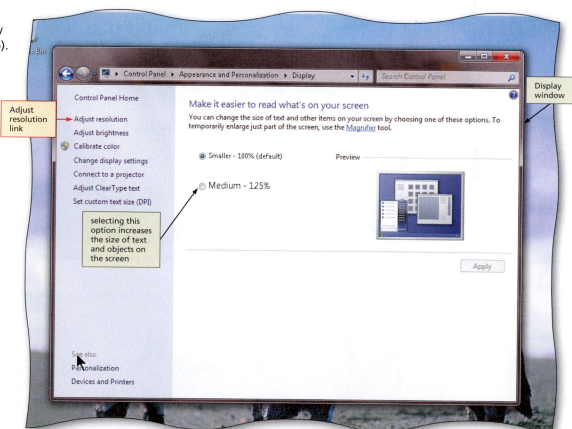

Figure 5–36

2

• After viewing the Display settings, click the Adjust resolution link to display the Screen Resolution window (Figure 5-37).

What screen resolution should I use?

You should use a resolution that provides a maximum amount of room on the screen for windows and other objects but does not make objects and text so small that you are unable to read them. The resolution used to create the figures in this book is 1024 × 768.

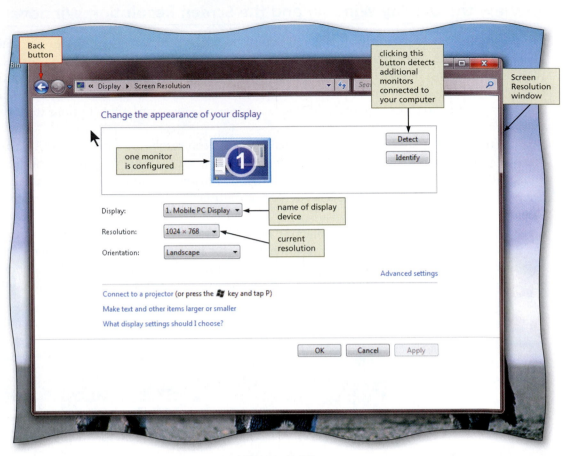

Figure 5–37

3

• After viewing the display settings, click the Back button two times to return to the Personalization window (Figure 5–38).

Figure 5–38

Other Ways

1. Press TAB until Display is selected, press ENTER, press TAB until 'Change display settings' is selected, press ENTER

To Add Desktop Icons

By default, the only icon that appears on the Windows 7 desktop is the Recycle Bin. You can use the 'Change desktop icons' link in the Personalization window to add additional desktop icons such as Computer, User's Files, Network, and Control Panel. The following steps add the Computer icon to the desktop.

1

• Click the 'Change desktop icons' link to display the Desktop Icon Settings dialog box (Figure 5–39).

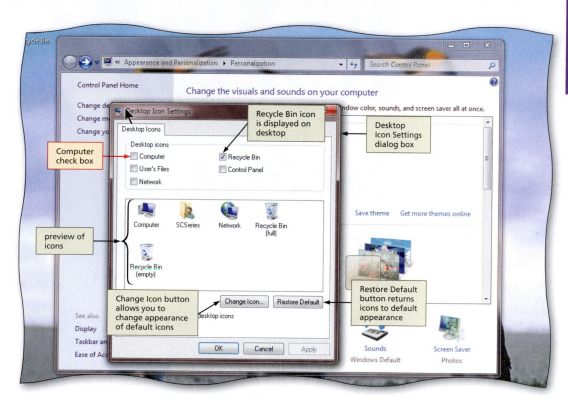

Figure 5–39

2

• Click the Computer check box to configure Windows to display the Computer icon on the desktop (Figure 5–40).

Q&A

Can I change how these icons look?

Yes, you can change the icon image used for each of these icons by clicking the Change Icon button (see Figure 5–39). Click the Restore Default button to change the settings back to their default appearance.

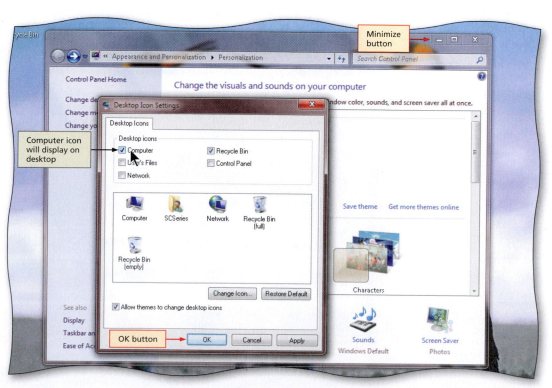

Figure 5–40

3

- Click the OK button to apply the changes and close the Desktop Icon Settings dialog box.

- Click the Minimize button on the Personalization window to minimize the window and view the desktop icon changes (Figure 5–41).

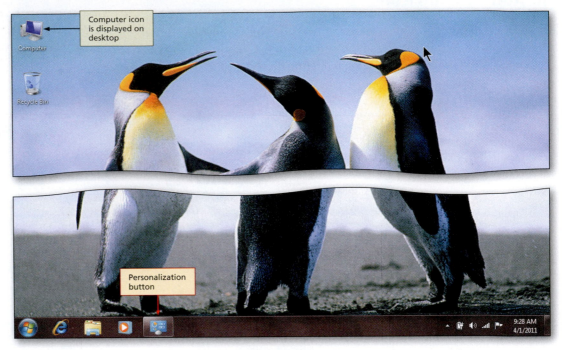

Figure 5–41

To Delete a Saved Desktop Theme

Now that you have finished using the new desktop theme you created and saved, you will remove it. You only can delete desktop themes that you have created and saved, not those provided by Windows 7. The following steps delete the SC Theme and restore the original desktop theme you noted earlier in the chapter.

1

- Click the Personalization button on the taskbar to restore the Personalization window (Figure 5–42).

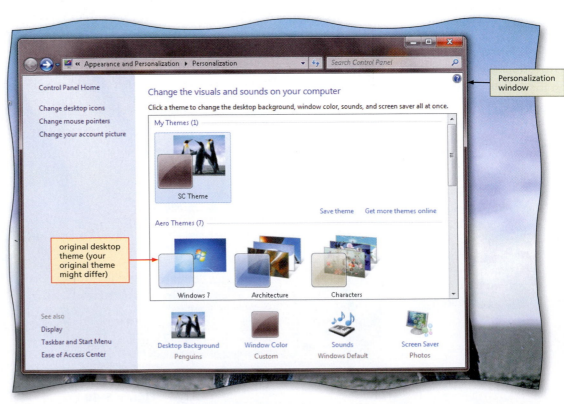

Figure 5–42

• Click the theme that
you wrote down
on page WIN 278 to
restore the original
desktop theme
(Figure 5–43).

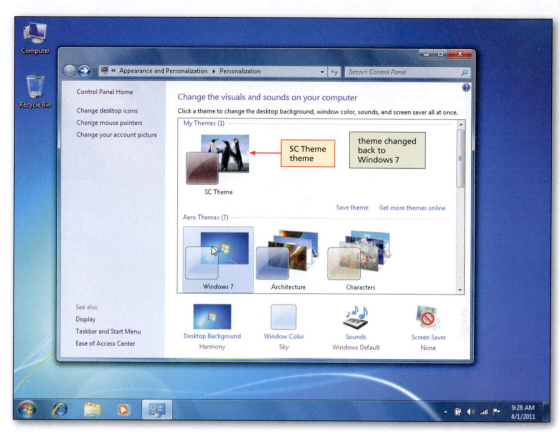

Figure 5–43

❸

• Right-click the SC
Theme theme to
display a shortcut
menu (Figure 5–44).

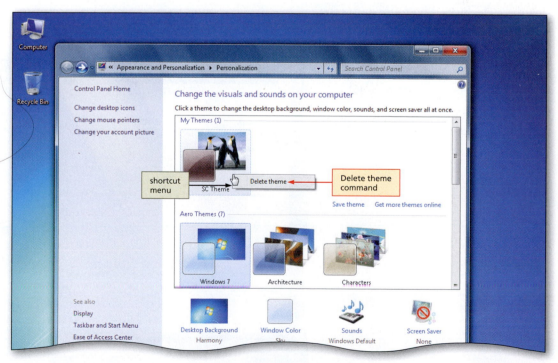

Figure 5–44

4

- Click the Delete theme command to delete the SC Theme from the My Themes group (Figure 5–45).

- Click the Yes button in the Delete File dialog box to confirm deletion of the SC Theme.

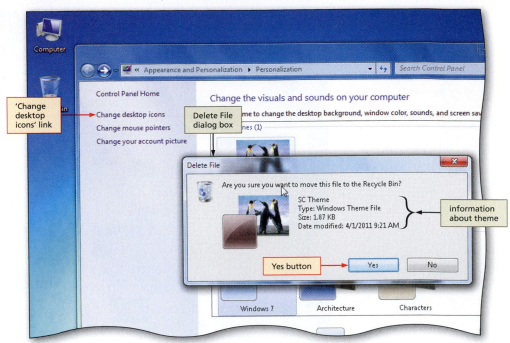

Figure 5–45

To Remove a Desktop Icon

Because you are restoring the desktop back to its original state, you also should remove the Computer icon from the desktop. The following steps remove the Computer icon.

1

- Click the 'Change desktop icons' link to display the Desktop Icon Settings dialog box (Figure 5–46).

Figure 5–46

2

- Click the Computer check box to remove the check mark (Figure 5–47).

Figure 5–47

3

- Click the OK button to remove the Computer icon from the desktop.

- Click the Close button in the Personalization window to close the Personalization window and to view the desktop icon changes (Figure 5–48).

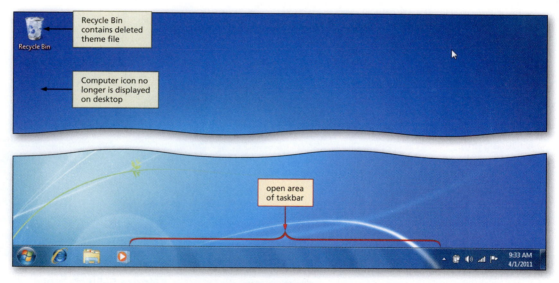

Figure 5–48

Customizing the Taskbar

Another method of modifying the desktop work environment is to customize the taskbar at the bottom of the desktop. For example, you can move, resize, and hide the taskbar; add toolbars to the taskbar; change the appearance of the taskbar; and change the taskbar properties. The next sections illustrate how to customize the taskbar and the toolbars on the taskbar.

To Unlock the Taskbar

By default, the taskbar is locked into position at the bottom of the desktop. Locking the taskbar prevents the taskbar from inadvertently being moved to another location on the desktop and also locks the size and position of any toolbars displayed on the taskbar. Prior to moving or resizing the taskbar, you must unlock the taskbar. After moving or resizing the taskbar, you might want to lock it in its new location so that you do not accidentally change its size and position. The following steps unlock the taskbar.

1

- Right-click an open area of the taskbar to display a shortcut menu (Figure 5–49).

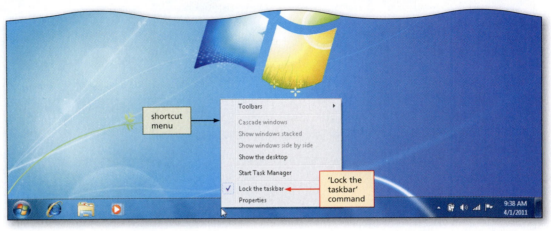

Figure 5–49

2

- Click the 'Lock the taskbar' command on the shortcut menu to remove the check mark and unlock the taskbar (Figure 5–50).

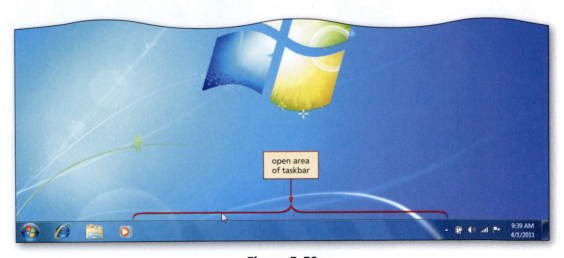

Figure 5–50

Other Ways

1. Right-click open area of taskbar, click Properties, click 'Lock the taskbar', click OK

2. Right-click Start, click Properties, click Taskbar tab, click 'Lock the taskbar', click OK

To Move the Taskbar

When the taskbar is unlocked, you can move it to different locations. By default, the taskbar is docked at the bottom edge of the desktop, but it can be dragged to any of the four edges of the desktop. The following steps move the taskbar to the top, left, and right edge of the desktop and then back to the bottom.

1
● Click an open area on the taskbar to select the taskbar (Figure 5–51).

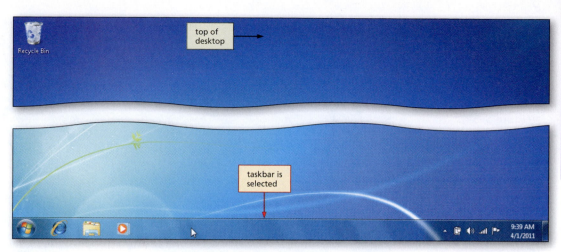

top of desktop

taskbar is selected

Figure 5–51

2
● Drag the taskbar to the top of the desktop to position the taskbar at the top of the desktop (Figure 5–52).

Q&A Why am I unable to drag the taskbar?

If you cannot drag the taskbar, the taskbar is still locked.

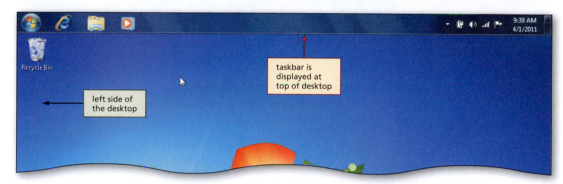

taskbar is displayed at top of desktop

left side of the desktop

Figure 5–52

3
● Drag the taskbar to the left side of the desktop to position the taskbar on the left side of the desktop (Figure 5–53).

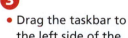

taskbar is displayed on left side of desktop

right side of the desktop

Figure 5–53

● Drag the taskbar to the right side of the desktop to position the taskbar on the right side of the desktop (Figure 5–54).

taskbar is displayed on right side of desktop

bottom of desktop

Figure 5–54

● Drag the taskbar back to the bottom of the desktop to return the taskbar to its original location (Figure 5–55).

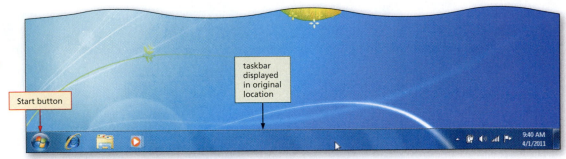

Start button

taskbar displayed in original location

Figure 5–55

To Pin an Item to the Taskbar

As introduced in Chapter 1, a shortcut is defined as a link to any object on the computer or a network, such as a program, file, folder, disk drive, Web page, printer, or another computer. By default, three shortcuts are displayed on the taskbar when Windows 7 is installed: Internet Explorer, Windows Explorer, and Windows Media Player. You can place additional shortcut icons on the taskbar to make starting other programs easier. For example, you might want to add a shortcut icon for WordPad on the taskbar to make it quicker to start the WordPad program. The following steps place a shortcut icon to the WordPad program on the taskbar.

1

- Display the Start menu.

- Type `wordpad` in the Search box to display the WordPad search result (Figure 5–56).

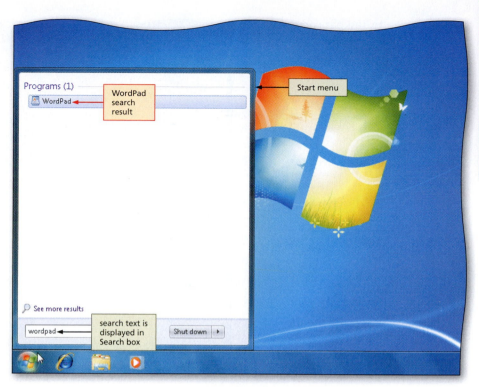

Figure 5–56

2

- Right-click the WordPad search result to display a shortcut menu (Figure 5–57).

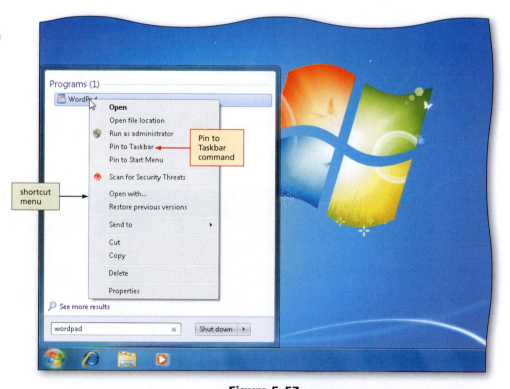

Figure 5–57

3
● Click the Pin to Taskbar command to add the WordPad shortcut to the taskbar (Figure 5–58).

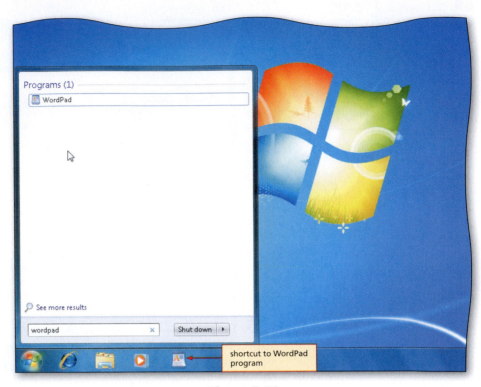

Figure 5–58

Other Ways

1. Right-drag program icon to taskbar, release mouse button

To Start a Pinned Program

Once a program is pinned to the taskbar, you can launch it just as you do the other pinned programs. The following step starts WordPad using the pinned program icon.

1 Click the WordPad icon on the taskbar to start WordPad (Figure 5–59).

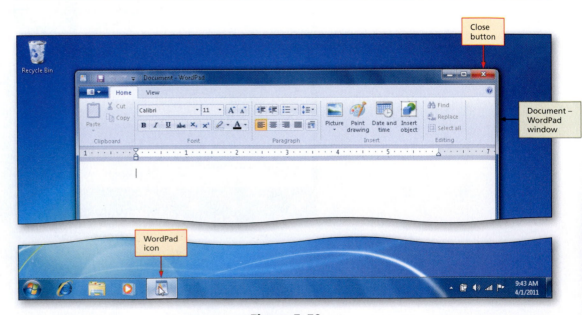

Figure 5–59

To Unpin a Program from the Taskbar

When you no longer use a pinned program frequently, you should remove it from the taskbar to keep the taskbar from becoming cluttered. The following steps unpin WordPad from the taskbar.

1
- Click the Close button in the Document – WordPad window to close WordPad.

- Right-click the WordPad icon on the taskbar to display a shortcut menu (Figure 5–60).

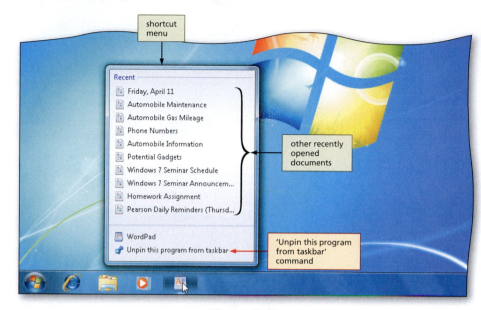

Figure 5–60

2
- Click the 'Unpin this program from taskbar' command to delete the WordPad icon from the taskbar (Figure 5–61).

Figure 5–61

To Enable Auto-Hide

Another way to customize the desktop is to hide the taskbar so that only its top edge is visible at the bottom of the desktop. When the taskbar is hidden, you must point to the bottom of the desktop to display the taskbar. The taskbar will remain on the desktop as long as the mouse pointer hovers on the taskbar. The taskbar does not have to be unlocked to enable Auto-hide. The steps on the following pages hide and then redisplay the taskbar.

- Right-click an open area on the taskbar to display the shortcut menu (Figure 5–62).

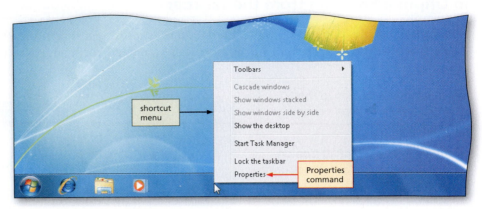

Figure 5–62

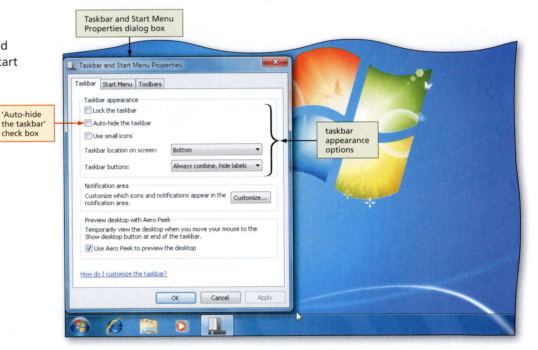

- Click the Properties command to display the Taskbar and Start Menu Properties dialog box (Figure 5–63).

Figure 5–63

- Click the 'Auto-hide the taskbar' check box to select it (Figure 5–64).

Figure 5–64

4
- Click the Apply button to apply the Auto-hide feature (Figure 5–65).

Figure 5–65

5
- Point to the bottom of the screen to display the taskbar (Figure 5–66).

 Q&A

Is there another way to display the hidden taskbar?

In addition to pointing to the bottom of the screen to display the taskbar, you can display the taskbar and the Start menu at any time by pressing the WINDOWS key or pressing CTRL+ESC.

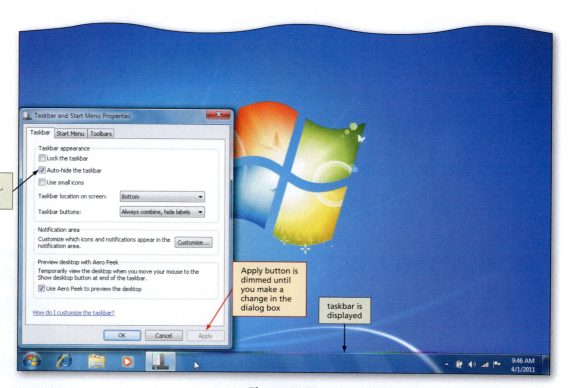

Figure 5–66

6

- Click the 'Auto-hide the taskbar' check box in the Taskbar and Start Menu Properties dialog box to remove the check mark and deselect the option.

- Click the Apply button to turn off the Auto-hide feature (Figure 5–67).

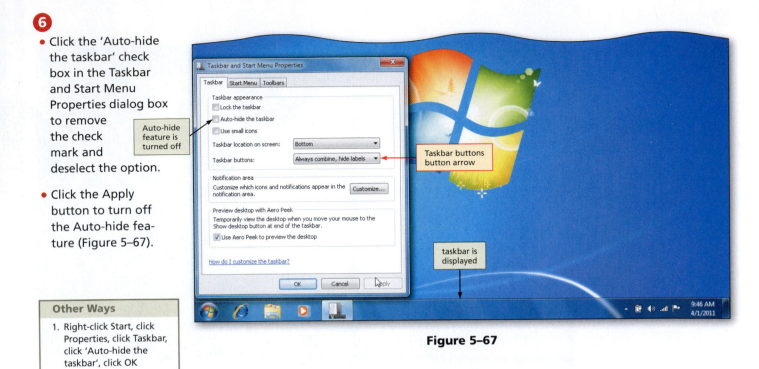

Figure 5–67

Other Ways

1. Right-click Start, click Properties, click Taskbar, click 'Auto-hide the taskbar', click OK

To Change Taskbar Buttons

Some people prefer that the taskbar display buttons with descriptive labels and that each open window be assigned its own button on the taskbar. By default, Windows 7 hides button labels and combines buttons when multiple windows are open in the same program. Windows 7 provides options for changing these button settings in the Taskbar and Start Menu Properties dialog box. The following steps change the taskbar button settings.

1

- Click the Taskbar buttons button arrow to display a list of taskbar button options (Figure 5–68).

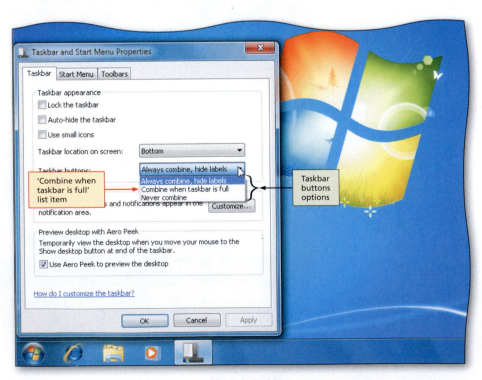

Figure 5–68

2

- Click the 'Combine when taskbar is full' list item to configure Windows to display a taskbar button for each window and to show labels for each button.

- Click the Apply button to apply the changes to buttons on the taskbar (Figure 5–69).

Q&A

Why do the pinned icons not display labels?

Labels only are displayed if the pinned program is running. If it is not running, no label is shown.

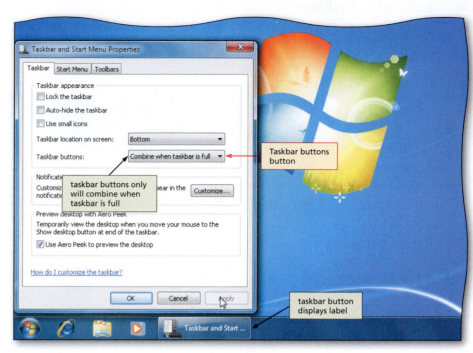

Figure 5–69

3

- After viewing the changes in the taskbar, click the Taskbar buttons button to display the list of taskbar button options (Figure 5–70).

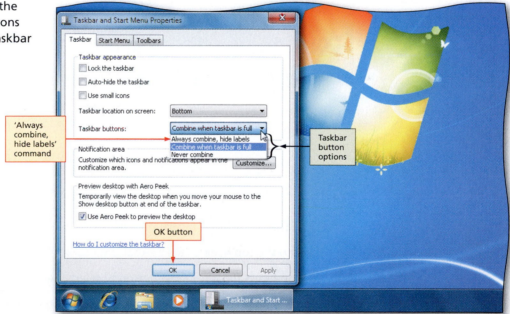

Figure 5–70

4

- Click the 'Always combine, hide labels' command to cause the buttons to combine and hide the labels.

- Click the OK button to close the Taskbar and Start Menu Properties dialog box and apply the changes to the buttons on the taskbar (Figure 5–71).

Figure 5–71

To Resize the Taskbar

Sometimes, you might have so many items on the taskbar that it becomes difficult to view everything at once. You can resize the taskbar to make it easier to view everything. The following steps resize the taskbar.

• Point to the top edge of the taskbar until a two-headed arrow displays.

• Click and hold the left mouse button to select the taskbar (Figure 5–72).

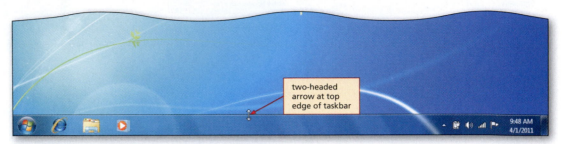

two-headed arrow at top edge of taskbar

Figure 5–72

Q&A What if the taskbar is on the left, right, or top edge of the desktop?

If the taskbar is located elsewhere on your desktop, point to the taskbar border closest to the center of the desktop until a two-headed arrow displays.

2

• Drag the top edge of the taskbar toward the top of the desktop until the taskbar on your desktop is about twice its current size (Figure 5–73).

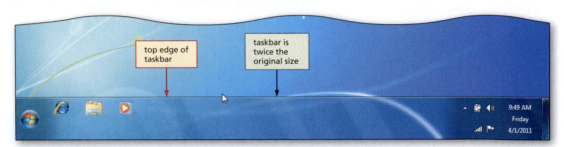

top edge of taskbar

taskbar is twice the original size

Figure 5–73

To Return the Taskbar to Its Original Size

The following steps return the taskbar to its original size.

1 Point to the top edge of the taskbar until a two-headed arrow displays.

2 Click and hold the left mouse button to select the taskbar.

3 Drag the top edge of the taskbar downward until the taskbar is back to its original size (Figure 5–74).

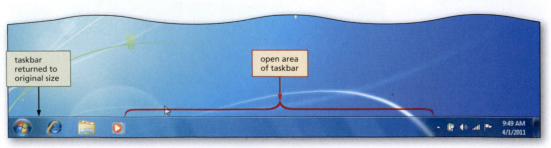

taskbar returned to original size

open area of taskbar

Figure 5–74

Working with Toolbars on the Taskbar

Windows 7 offers other toolbars that you can add to the taskbar. The Address toolbar allows you to open a document, open a folder, start a program, and even search for a Web page. The Links toolbar allows you to go to selected Web sites without first having to launch Internet Explorer. The Tablet PC Input Panel toolbar allows you to get input from a tablet pen instead of from the keyboard, and primarily is designed to be used with a Tablet PC. The Desktop toolbar contains links to your libraries, user folders, Computer folder, Network folder, Control Panel, and Recycle Bin.

In addition to adding one of these toolbars provided by Windows 7, you also can create a custom toolbar and add it to the taskbar using the New Toolbar option. For example, you might create a Current Projects toolbar containing the icons for all the programs and files with which you currently are working. In addition, some programs that you have installed on your computer will provide additional toolbars that you can display on the taskbar. For example, if you were to download Google Desktop from the Internet, a Google Desktop toolbar would be added to the list of available toolbars that you can place on the taskbar.

BTW

Custom Toolbars
To create a custom toolbar on the taskbar, right-click the taskbar, point to Toolbars on the shortcut menu, and then click New toolbar. When the New Toolbar – Choose a folder dialog box is displayed, navigate to a folder containing contents you want to display on this new toolbar, and then click the Select Folder button.

To Add a Toolbar to the Taskbar

You can add other toolbars (Address toolbar, Links toolbar, Tablet PC Input Panel toolbar, and Desktop toolbar) to the taskbar. The function of the Address toolbar is multifaceted: It allows you to search for a Web page, start a program, open a document, and open a folder. The following steps add the Address toolbar to the taskbar.

- Right-click an open area of the taskbar to display a shortcut menu.

- Point to the Toolbars command to display the Toolbars submenu (Figure 5–75).

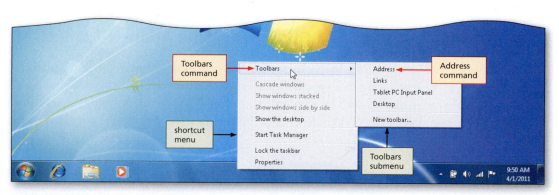

Figure 5–75

- Click the Address command to add the Address toolbar to the taskbar (Figure 5–76).

Q&A

Can I change the toolbar's appearance?

You can change the appearance of a toolbar by removing the toolbar title. Right-click the toolbar label to display a shortcut menu and then click the Show title command to remove or display the toolbar title.

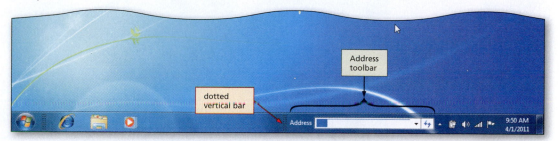

Figure 5–76

To Expand a Toolbar

When you add toolbars to the taskbar, the toolbars display in a collapsed form depending upon the available space on the taskbar. The following step expands the Address toolbar to its full size.

- Double-click the dotted vertical bar on the left side of the Address toolbar to expand the Address toolbar (Figure 5–77).

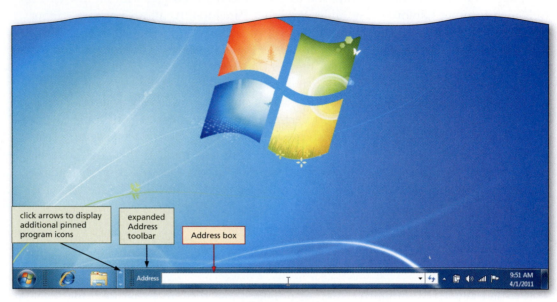

Figure 5–77

To Display the Contents of a Folder Using the Address Toolbar

To display the contents of a folder using the Address toolbar, enter the path of the folder in the Address box. A **path** is the means of navigating to a specific location on a computer. To specify a path to a folder on a computer, you must type the drive letter, followed by a colon (:), a backslash (\), and the folder name. For example, the path for the Windows folder on drive C is: c:\Windows. The following steps display the contents of the Windows folder.

- Type `c:\windows` in the Address box to specify the folder to be opened (Figure 5–78).

Q&A

Is capitalization important when typing the folder name?

No. The Windows operating system ignores inconsistencies with capitalization when typing folder names in the Address toolbar.

Figure 5–78

2
- Press the ENTER key to open the folder.

- If necessary, click the Maximize button to maximize the Windows folder window (Figure 5–79).

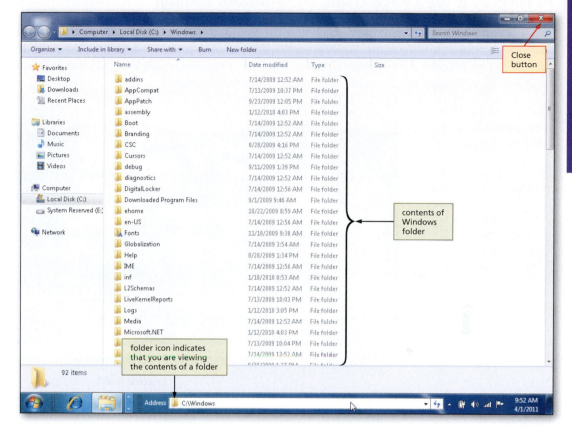

Figure 5–79

3
- After viewing the folder, click the Close button to close the window (Figure 5–80).

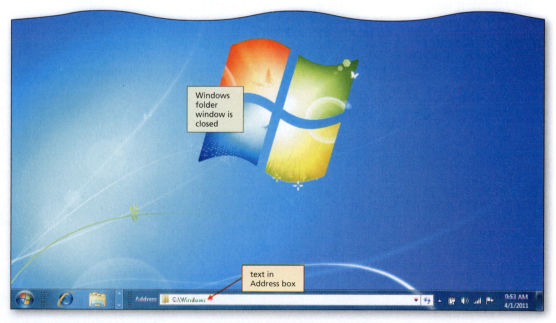

Figure 5–80

Other Ways
1. Click Address box, type path until Address list box is displayed, click path in Address list

To Display a Web Page Using the Address Toolbar

To search for and display a Web page using the Address toolbar, you enter a Web address, or Uniform Resource Locator (URL), in the Address box. A Web address provides a unique identifier for every Web page and Web site. The following steps enter the Web address of the Microsoft Web page in the Address box, launch Internet Explorer, and display the Microsoft Web page in a browser window.

- Click the text in the Address box to select it.

- Type www.microsoft.com in the Address box to enter the address for the Microsoft Web page (Figure 5–81).

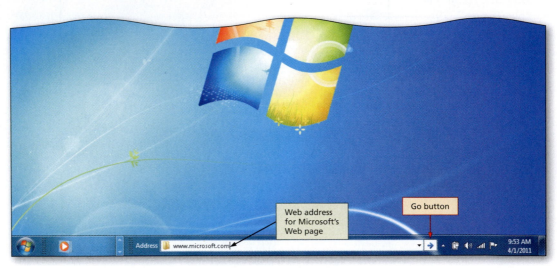

Figure 5–81

❷

- Click the Go button to open the Microsoft Web page in the Internet Explorer window. If necessary, maximize the window (Figure 5–82).

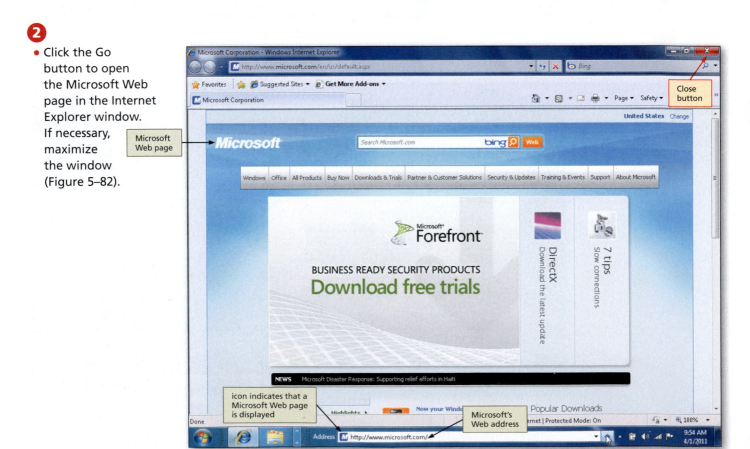

Figure 5–82

- After viewing the Web page, click the Close button to close Internet Explorer (Figure 5–83).

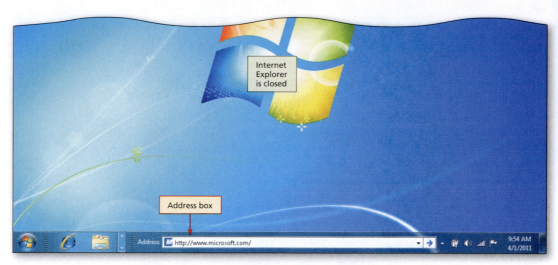

Figure 5–83

To Search for Information on the Internet Using the Address Toolbar

To search for information on the Internet using the Address toolbar, you enter a keyword or phrase in the Address box and then click the Go button. The following steps enter the phrase *national weather* in the Address box and display links to Web pages containing the phrase *national weather*.

- Click the Address box.

- Type national weather in the Address box to specify the search keywords (Figure 5–84).

Figure 5–84

• Click Search for "national weather" in the list box to search the Internet and display the search results (Figure 5–85).

Q&A

Do all search engines process search requests the same way?

Search engines that process search requests have their own rules for entering a search inquiry. Some might require that you place the word *AND* between two words to find Web pages containing both words. With other search engines, you might have to select a check box (any of the words, all the words, and so on) to perform a search. To learn the rules for a search engine, look for a Tips or Help link and then click the link.

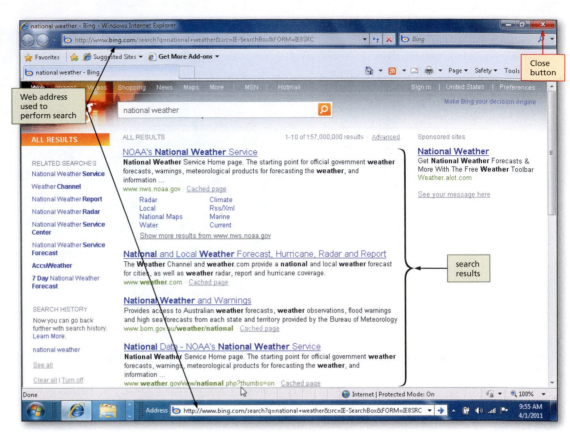

Figure 5–85

• After viewing the search results, close Internet Explorer (Figure 5–86).

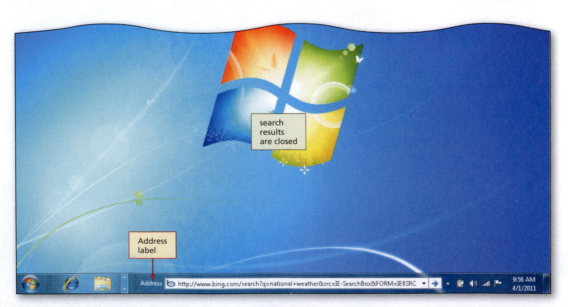

Figure 5–86

To Remove a Toolbar from the Taskbar

When you no longer want the Address toolbar, or any toolbar, to appear on the taskbar, you can remove it. The following steps remove the Address toolbar from the taskbar.

1 Right-click the Address label on the taskbar to display a shortcut menu.

2 Point to Toolbars on the shortcut menu to display the Toolbars submenu.

3 Click Address on the Toolbars submenu to remove the Address toolbar from the taskbar (Figure 5–87).

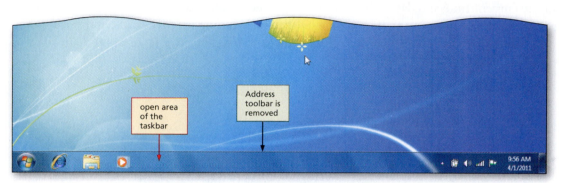

Figure 5–87

To Lock the Taskbar

Now that you are done customizing and manipulating the taskbar, you will lock the taskbar so that the taskbar is fixed and cannot be changed. The following steps lock the taskbar.

1

- Right-click an open area of the taskbar to display the shortcut menu (Figure 5–88).

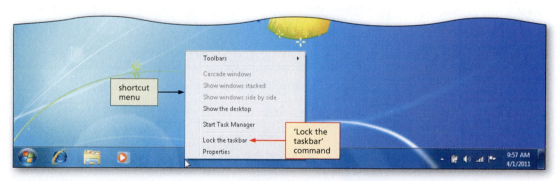

Figure 5–88

2
- Click the 'Lock the taskbar' command on the shortcut menu to lock the taskbar (Figure 5–89).

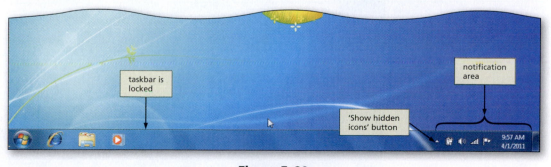

Figure 5–89

Customizing the Notification Area

Another method of modifying the desktop work environment is to customize the notification area. The **notification area** displays the time and also can contain shortcuts that provide quick access to programs that run in the background on your computer, such as Windows Live Messenger and Volume Control. Other shortcuts in the notification area provide information about the status of activities. For example, the Printer icon is displayed when a document is sent to the printer and is removed when printing is complete.

To Set the Notification Behavior of a Notification Item

The notification area shown in Figure 5–89 on the previous page contains the 'Show hidden icons' button, four notification icons, and the current time and date. The contents of the notification area might be different on your computer. You can customize the notification area by removing the clock, hiding inactive icons, and setting the behavior for the items in the notification area. By default, the clock is displayed and inactive icons are hidden from view. The following steps set the behavior for the Volume icon.

• Right-click an open area in the notification area to display a shortcut menu (Figure 5–90). (*Hint*: Click just above the 'Show hidden icons' button.)

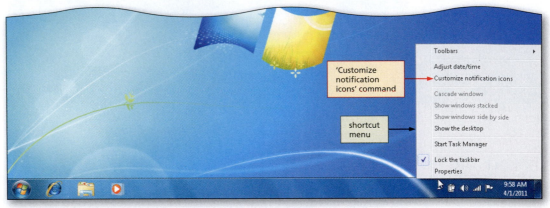

Figure 5–90

• Click the 'Customize notification icons' command to display the Notification Area Icons window (Figure 5–91).

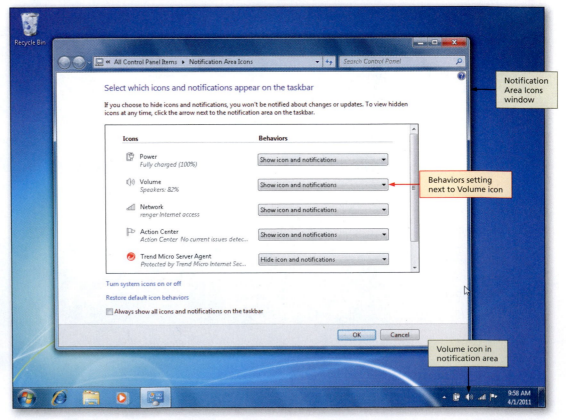

Figure 5–91

3

- Click the Behaviors button to the right of the Volume icon to display a list of behaviors (Figure 5–92).

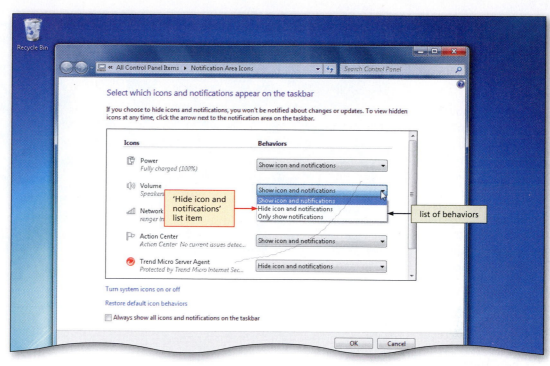

Figure 5–92

4

- Click the 'Hide icons and notifications' option in the Behaviors list to hide the Volume icon all of the time (Figure 5–93).

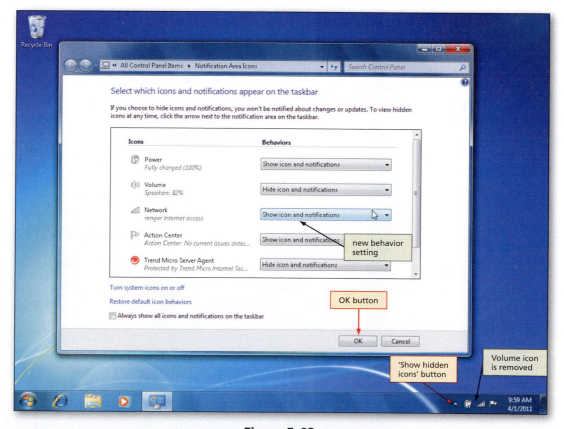

Figure 5–93

5

• Click the OK button in the Notification Area Icons window to close the window (Figure 5–94).

• Click the 'Show hidden icons' button in the notification area to view the hidden icons, including the Volume icon.

• Click the 'Show hidden icons' button in the notification area to hide the icons.

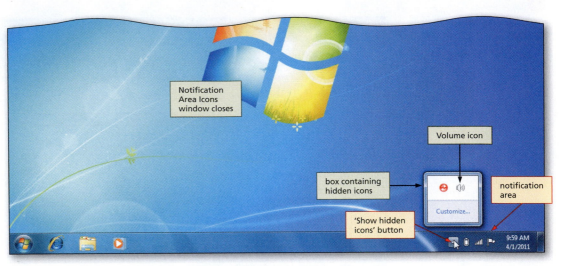

Figure 5–94

To Restore the Default Notification Behaviors

The following steps restore the original notification behavior for the Volume icon.

1

• Right-click an open area in the notification area to display a shortcut menu.

• Click the 'Customize notification icons' command on the shortcut menu to display the Notification Area Icons window (Figure 5–95).

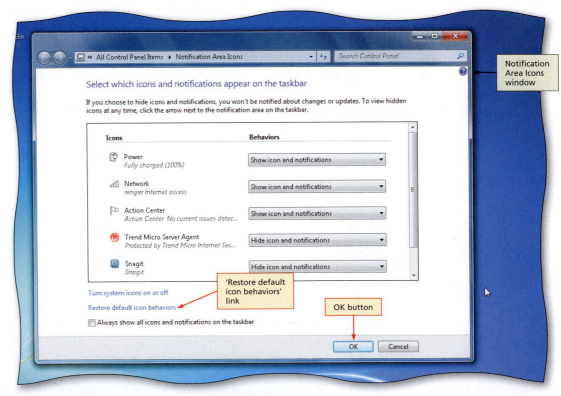

Figure 5–95

2

- Click the 'Restore default icon behaviors' link in the Notification Area Icons window to revert the Volume icon to its default behavior (Figure 5–96).

- Click the OK button to close the Notification Area Icons window.

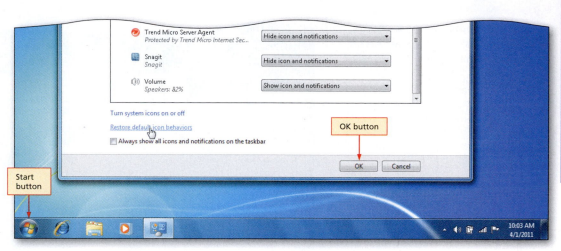

Figure 5–96

Customizing the Start Menu

You also can modify the appearance of the Start menu as a means of personalizing your desktop. Recall that in Chapter 2, you customized the Start menu by adding a shortcut to the Daily Reminders folder. In addition to adding a shortcut, you change the number of recent programs to display or alter the look and behavior of menu items.

To Display the Computer Command as a Menu

By default, the Computer command is shown on the Start menu. This command serves as a link to open the Computer window. Using the Customize Start Menu dialog box, you can change the behavior of the Computer command from a button to a menu. By changing the behavior of the Computer command to a menu, instead of opening the Computer window, it will display the items normally appearing in the Computer window as menu items for you to select. The following steps change the look and behavior of the Computer command to a menu and display the new menu.

1

- Right-click the Start button to display a shortcut menu (Figure 5–97).

Figure 5–97

● Click the Properties command to open the Taskbar and Start Menu Properties dialog box (Figure 5–98).

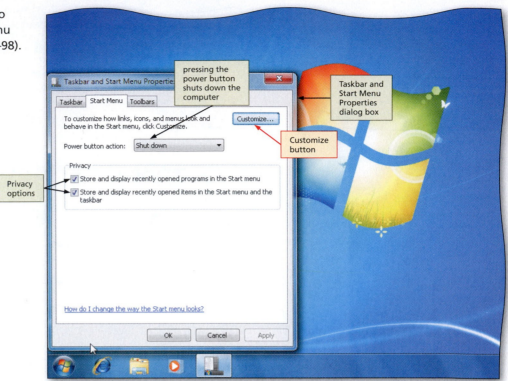

Figure 5–98

● Click the Customize button to open the Customize Start Menu dialog box (Figure 5–99).

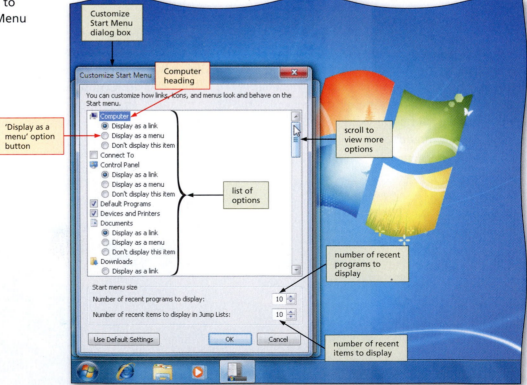

Figure 5–99

4

- In the customize list, click the 'Display as a menu' option button under the Computer heading to change the Computer command to look and behave like a menu (Figure 5–100).

- Click the OK button in the Customize Start Menu dialog box to close the dialog box.

- Click the OK button in the Taskbar and Start Menu Properties dialog box to close the dialog box.

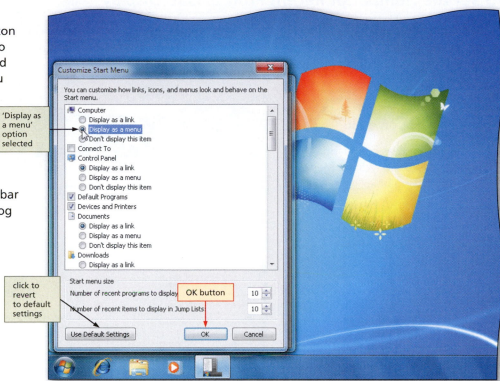

Figure 5–100

5

- Display the Start menu.

- Point to the Computer command to display the Computer menu (Figure 5–101).

- Click an open area of the desktop to close the Start menu.

Figure 5–101

To Set the Number of Recent Programs to Display

By default, the maximum number of programs that can appear on the 'Number of recent programs to display' list on the Start menu is 10. The following steps set the maximum number of programs that appear on the 'Number of recent programs to display' list to 12.

- Right-click the Start button to display the shortcut menu.

- Click the Properties command to open the Taskbar and Start Menu Properties dialog box.

- Click the Customize button to open the Customize Start Menu dialog box (Figure 5–102).

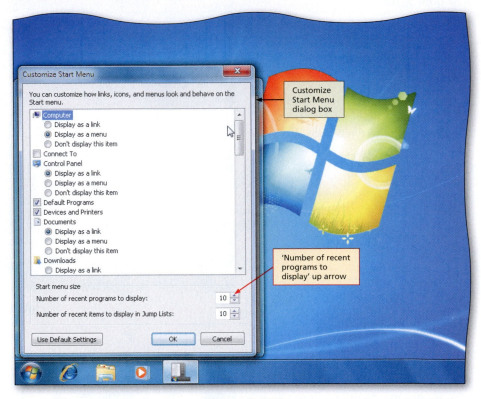

Figure 5–102

- Click the 'Number of recent programs to display' up arrow until the number 12 is displayed (Figure 5–103).

- Click the OK button in the Customize Start Menu dialog box to close the dialog box.

- Click the OK button in the Taskbar and Start Menu Properties dialog box to close the dialog box.

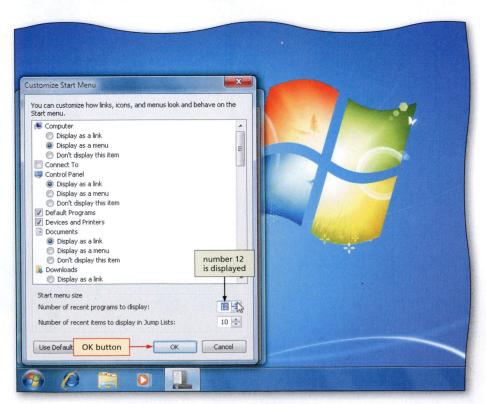

Figure 5–103

3

- Display the Start menu (Figure 5–104).

- Close the Start menu.

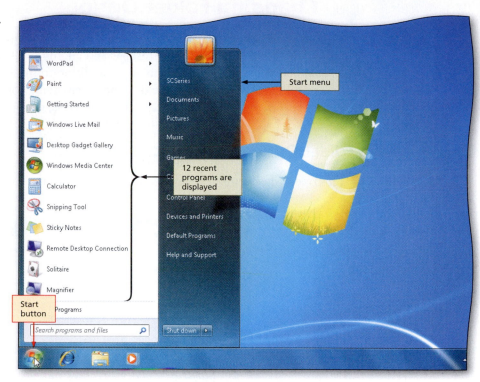

Figure 5–104

To Reset the Default Settings of the Start Menu

After changing the Computer command and the 'Number of recent programs to display' settings, you revert to the original settings. The following steps reset the Start menu settings.

1

- Right-click the Start button to display a shortcut menu.

- Click the Properties command to open the Taskbar and Start Menu Properties dialog box.

- Click the Customize button to open the Customize Start Menu dialog box.

- Click the Use Default Settings button to reset the Start menu to default settings (Figure 5–105).

2

- Click the OK button in the Customize Start Menu dialog box to close the dialog box.

- Click the OK button in the Taskbar and Start Menu Properties dialog box to close the dialog box.

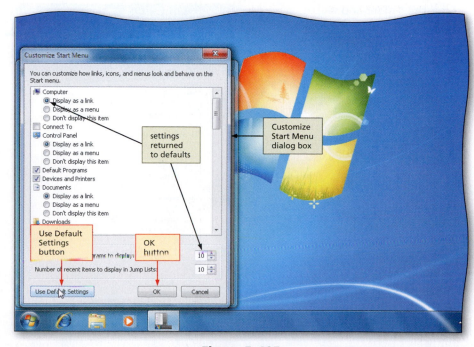

Figure 5–105

Changing Folder Options

In this chapter, you modified the desktop work environment by changing the desktop properties, customizing the taskbar and adding toolbars, customizing the notification area, and customizing the Start menu. In addition to these changes, you also can make changes to folders, windows, and the desktop by changing folder options. Folder options allow you to specify how you open and work with icons, windows, folders, and files on the desktop.

To Display the Folder Options Dialog Box

The following steps open the Computer window and then display the Folder Options dialog box.

1

- Display the Start menu.

- Click the Computer command to display the Computer window.

- Click the Organize button in the Computer window to display the Organize menu (Figure 5–106).

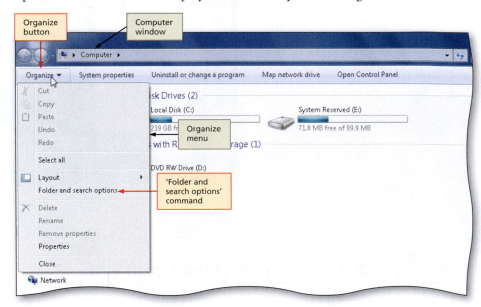

Figure 5–106

2

- Click the 'Folder and search options' command to display the Folder Options dialog box (Figure 5–107).

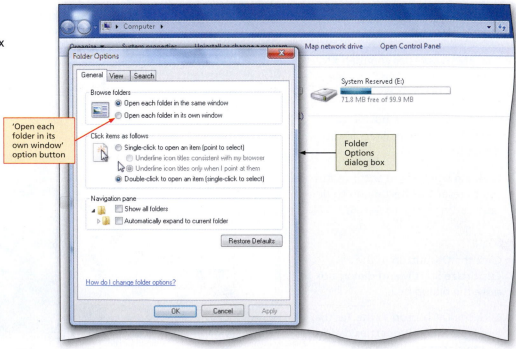

Figure 5–107

To Select the Open Each Folder in Its Own Window Option

In previous chapters, each time you double-clicked a folder icon in an open window, the new folder opened in the same window where the previously opened folder was displayed. The process of opening a folder in the same window as the previously opened folder is referred to as opening a folder in the same window, and is the default setting in Windows 7. Selecting the 'Open each folder in its own window' option causes each folder to open in its own window, so that you easily can view the contents of each open folder at the same time. The following step enables the 'Open each folder in its own window' option.

1

• Click the 'Open each folder in its own window' option button to select it (Figure 5–108).

• Click the OK button to apply the changes and close the Folder Options dialog box.

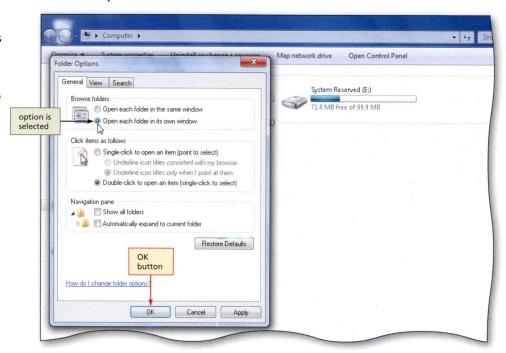

Figure 5–108

To Open a Folder in Its Own Window

The following steps open the Local Disk (C:) folder in its own window.

1

• Double-click the Local Disk (C:) icon in the Computer window to display the Local Disk (C:) folder in its own window (Figure 5–109).

• Click the Close button in the Local Disk (C:) window to close the window.

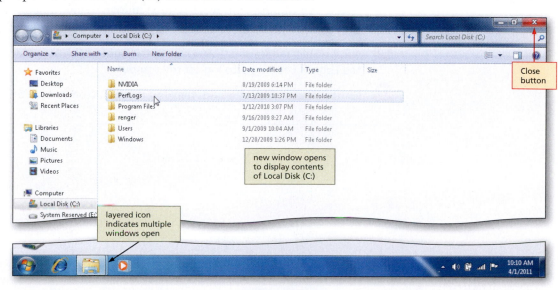

Figure 5–109

To Restore the Folder Options to the Default Folder Options

After changing one or more folder options, you can restore the default folder options you changed by manually resetting each option you changed, or you can restore all the folder options to their default options by using the Restore Defaults button. The following step restores the changed folder options to their default folder options.

- Click the Organize button in the Computer window to display the Organize menu.

- Click the 'Folder and search options' command to display the Folder Options dialog box.

- Click the Restore Defaults button to restore the folder defaults (Figure 5–110).

- Click the OK button to close the Folder Options dialog box, and then click the Close button to close the Computer window.

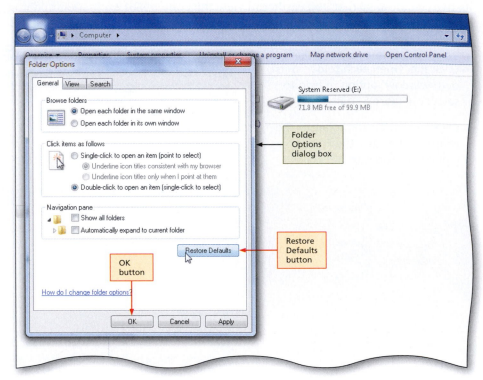

Figure 5–110

To Log Off and Shut Down the Computer

After completing your work with Windows 7, you first should close your user account by logging off the computer, and then shut down the computer.

1 On the Start menu, click the arrow to the right of the Shut down button, and then click the Log off command to log off the computer.

2 On the Welcome screen, click the Shut down button to turn off the computer.

Chapter Summary

In this chapter, you learned to customize and personalize the Windows 7 desktop. You selected a desktop theme, and then created a new desktop theme by changing the desktop background, the window color, the mouse pointers, and the screen saver. You personalized the taskbar by moving, resizing, and hiding the taskbar; adding toolbars to the taskbar; and pinning a program to the taskbar. You customized the notification area by changing the behavior of a notification icon and customized the Start menu by changing the behavior of commands on the Start menu. Finally, you changed and restored folder options. The items listed below include all the new Windows 7 skills you have learned in this chapter.

1. Open the Personalization Window (WIN 277)
2. Open the Desktop Background Window (WIN 278)
3. Change the Desktop Background (WIN 279)
4. Change the Window Color (WIN 282)
5. Change the Intensity of the Window Color (WIN 283)
6. Display the Color Mixer (WIN 284)
7. View Advanced Appearance Settings (WIN 285)
8. View the Sound Settings (WIN 286)
9. Change the Screen Saver (WIN 287)
10. Change the Screen Saver Settings and Preview the Screen Saver (WIN 289)
11. Change the Mouse Pointers (WIN 292)
12. Save a Desktop Theme (WIN 294)
13. Switch to a Different Desktop Theme (WIN 295)
14. View the Display Window and the Screen Resolution Window (WIN 297)
15. Add Desktop Icons (WIN 299)
16. Delete a Saved Desktop Theme (WIN 300)
17. Remove a Desktop Icon (WIN 302)
18. Unlock the Taskbar (WIN 304)
19. Move the Taskbar (WIN 304)
20. Pin an Item to the Taskbar (WIN 306)
21. Unpin a Program from the Taskbar (WIN 309)
22. Enable Auto-hide (WIN 309)
23. Change Taskbar Buttons (WIN 312)
24. Resize the Taskbar (WIN 314)
25. Add a Toolbar to the Taskbar (WIN 315)
26. Expand a Toolbar (WIN 316)
27. Display the Contents of a Folder Using the Address Toolbar (WIN 316)
28. Display a Web Page Using the Address Toolbar (WIN 318)
29. Search for Information on the Internet Using the Address Toolbar (WIN 319)
30. Lock the Taskbar (WIN 321)
31. Set the Notification Behavior of a Notification Item (WIN 322)
32. Restore the Default Notification Behaviors (WIN 324)
33. Display the Computer Command as a Menu (WIN 325)
34. Set the Number of Recent Programs to Display (WIN 328)
35. Reset the Default Settings of the Start Menu (WIN 329)
36. Display the Folder Options Dialog Box (WIN 330)
37. Select the Open Each Folder in Its Own Window Option (WIN 331)
38. Open a Folder in Its Own Window (WIN 331)
39. Restore the Folder Options to the Default Folder Options (WIN 332)

Learn It Online

Test your knowledge of chapter content and key terms.

Instructions: To complete the Learn It Online exercises, start your browser, click the Address bar, and then enter the Web address scsite.com/win7/learn. When the Windows 7 Learn It Online page is displayed, click the link for the exercise you want to complete and then read the instructions.

Chapter Reinforcement TF, MC, and SA
A series of true/false, multiple-choice, and short-answer questions that test your knowledge of the chapter content.

Flash Cards
An interactive learning environment where you identify chapter key terms associated with displayed definitions.

Practice Test
A series of multiple-choice questions that test your knowledge of chapter content and key terms.

Who Wants To Be a Computer Genius?
An interactive game that challenges your knowledge of chapter content in the style of a television quiz show.

Wheel of Terms
An interactive game that challenges your knowledge of chapter key terms in the style of the television show *Wheel of Fortune*.

Crossword Puzzle Challenge
A crossword puzzle that challenges your knowledge of key terms presented in the chapter.

Apply Your Knowledge

Reinforce the skills and apply the concepts you learned in this chapter.

Creating and Saving a Desktop Theme

Instructions: Your friend owns a tropical fish store and showed you the creative desktop theme she created for the computers in her store. The desktop looked like an aquarium. You own a comic book store and want to create a unique desktop theme for the computers in your business, instead of using the default Windows 7 desktop theme.

Part 1: Determining the Existing Desktop Theme
1. Right-click the desktop and then click Personalize on the shortcut menu to open the Personalization window.
2. In the space provided, write down the desktop theme name that currently is selected.

Part 2: Changing the Desktop Background
1. Click the Desktop Background link.
2. Change the Picture location to the Windows Desktop Backgrounds, scroll until the Characters heading is visible, and then select the third Character desktop background. If the Character desktop backgrounds are not available, select another background and use this background for the remainder of this assignment.
3. Change the Picture position to Center and then click the Save changes button to close the Desktop Background window.

Part 3: Adding Icons to the Desktop

1. Click the 'Change desktop icons' link to display the Desktop Icon Settings dialog box.
2. Click the Computer and User's Files check boxes in the Desktop icons area.
3. Click the OK button in the Desktop Icon Settings dialog box.

Part 4: Changing the Color Scheme

1. Click the Window Color link to open the Window Color and Appearance window.
2. Click the Lavender color option.
3. Click the Save changes button to save and apply the color scheme (Figure 5–111).

Figure 5–111

Part 5: Changing the Screen Saver

1. Click the Screen Saver link to display the Screen Saver Settings dialog box.
2. Click the Screen Saver button arrow and then click the Bubbles option.
3. Click the Preview button to display the screen saver on the desktop. Move the mouse to end the screen saver.
4. Click the OK button in the Screen Saver Settings dialog box.

Continued >

Apply Your Knowledge *continued*

Part 6: Saving the Desktop Theme

1. Click the Save theme link.

2. Type `Anime Comics for` in the Theme name text box, and then type your first and last name.

3. Click the Save button to save the new desktop theme.

4. Click the Close button in the Personalization window.

Part 7: Printing the Desktop

1. Double-click the Computer icon on the desktop to display the Computer window. Resize the Computer window so that the Computer window and the desktop icons (Computer and User's Files) are visible on the desktop.

2. Press the PRINT SCREEN key on the keyboard to place an image of the desktop on the Clipboard, a temporary Windows storage area.

3. Display the Start menu, click All Programs, click Accessories, and then click Paint.

4. Maximize the Untitled – Paint window.

5. Click the Paste button on the Ribbon to copy the image from the Clipboard to the Paint window.

6. Click the Paint button, click Print on the Paint menu, and then click the Print button in the Print dialog box to print the Paint document.

7. Click the Close button in the Untitled – Paint window and then click the Don't Save button in the Paint dialog box to quit the Paint program.

8. Click the Close button in the Computer window to close the window.

Part 8: Deleting the Desktop Theme

1. Right-click an open area on the desktop and then click Personalize on the shortcut menu.

2. Verify that the name of the desktop theme (Anime Comics) you created earlier displays in the Theme box.

3. Click the Windows 7 theme in the Aero Themes group to change the theme to Windows 7.

4. Right-click the Anime Comics theme, and then click Delete theme on the shortcut menu. Click the Yes button in the Delete File dialog box.

Part 9: Deleting the Icons on the Desktop

1. Click the 'Change desktop icons' link in the Personalization window.

2. Click the Computer and User's Files check boxes to remove the check marks.

3. Click the OK button in the Desktop Icon Settings dialog box.

4. Click the Close button in the Personalization window.

5. Submit the printed Paint document with your new desktop theme to your instructor.

Extend Your Knowledge

Extend the skills you learned in this chapter and experiment with new skills. You might need to use Help to complete the assignment.

Researching Power Plans and Folder Options

Instructions: Your friend has asked for your input about how best to personalize the power plan and folder options on her computer to meet her needs. Not knowing much about these two topics, you decide to research them further.

Part 1: Learning about Power Options

1. Right-click the desktop and then click Personalize on the shortcut menu to display the Personalization window.

2. Click the Screen Saver link. Click the 'Change power settings' link to display the Power Options window (Figure 5–112).

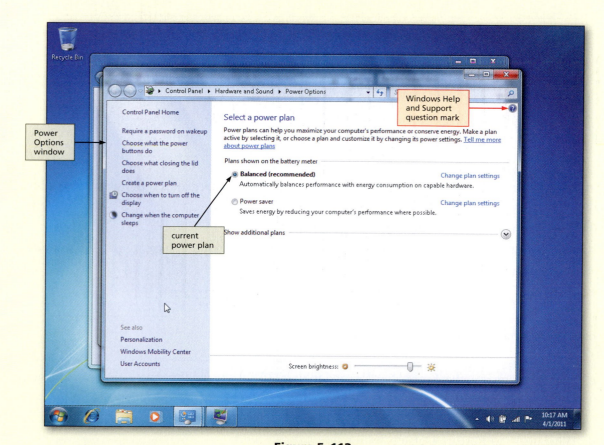

Figure 5–112

3. Answer the following questions about energy management using the Windows Help and Support question mark button in the Power Options window.

   a. What is a power plan?

Continued >

Extend Your Knowledge *continued*

   b. Which plans are available on your computer?

_____

_____

   c. Which plans are listed in the Windows Help and Support window? Do these differ from those that are available on your computer?

_____

_____

   d. Which plan is the best for a laptop?

_____

_____

4. Answer the following questions about power plans using the figure and Windows Help and Support.

   a. Click the 'Change plan settings' link for the Balanced power plan. What do the entries for the 'Turn off the display' options indicate?

_____

   b. Click the 'Change advanced power settings' link. What does the entry for Hard disk indicate? (*Hint:* You might have to scroll or expand menu items to view this entry.)

_____

   c. What options can you set under the Sleep heading?

_____

5. Close all open windows without saving any changes.

Part 2: Learning about Folder Options

1. Display the Start menu, click the Computer command, click the Organize button, and then click the 'Folder and search options' command.

2. Click the View tab in the Folder Options dialog box.

3. Answer the following questions about the advanced settings. You might have to use Windows Help and Support to find the answers.

   a. What does the Apply to Folders button do?

_____

   b. How many advanced settings are selected?

_____

   c. Which setting is active for hidden files and folders? (A selected option button indicates an active setting.)

_____

   d. What does the Restore Defaults button do?

_____

4. Click the Cancel button in the Folder Options dialog box, and then click the Close button in the Computer window.

In the Lab

Use the guidelines, concepts, and skills presented in this chapter to increase your knowledge of Windows 7. Labs are listed in order of increasing difficulty.

Lab 1: Working with Folder Options

Instructions: You recently took an operating system course at school. The instructor spent an entire hour demonstrating how to change folder options, but there was no time left at the end of the class to practice in the computer lab. You want to practice changing folder options on your home computer.

Part 1: Recording the Current Folder Options

1. Display the Start menu and then click the Computer command.

2. Click the Organize button on the toolbar and then click the 'Folder and search options' command.

3. In the space provided, record which option buttons on the General tab of the Folder Options dialog box are selected.

_____

_____

4. Click the Cancel button in the Folder Options dialog box.

5. Close the Computer window.

Part 2: Displaying Icons on the Desktop

1. Right-click an open area of the desktop and then click Personalize.

2. Click the 'Change desktop icons' link.

3. Click the User's Files and Network check boxes in the Desktop Icon Settings dialog box. Change the User's Files and Network icons to different icons of your choosing, and then click the OK button (Figure 5–113).

Figure 5–113

Continued >

In the Lab *continued*

4. Click the OK button in the Desktop Icon Settings dialog box.

5. Close the Personalization window.

Part 3: Turning on the Single-click to Open an Item (Point to Select) Option

1. Double-click the User File's icon on the desktop to open the User File's window.

2. Click the Organize button and then click the 'Folder and search options' command.

3. Select the 'Single-click to open an item (point to select)' option in the 'Click items as follows' area. If necessary, click 'Underline icon titles consistent with my browser'.

4. Click the OK button in the Folder Options dialog box.

Part 4: Opening a Folder by Single-Clicking

1. Click the My Pictures link in the User File's window.

   a. Does the My Pictures folder open in its own window?

   _____

2. Close the My Pictures window.

Part 5: Printing the Desktop

1. Click the User File's icon on the desktop, and then click the My Documents icon in the User File's window.

2. Press the PRINT SCREEN key on the keyboard to place an image of the desktop on the Clipboard.

3. Display the Start menu, type `paint` in the Search box, and then click Paint in the results list under Programs.

4. Maximize the Untitled – Paint window.

5. Click the Paste button on the Ribbon to copy the image from the Clipboard to the Paint window.

6. Click the Paint button on the Ribbon, click Print on the Paint menu, and then click the Print button in the Print dialog box to print the Paint document.

7. Click the Close button in the Untitled – Paint window and then click the Don't Save button in the Paint dialog box to quit the Paint program.

8. Close all open windows.

Part 6: Removing the Icons on the Desktop

1. Right-click an open area on the desktop and then click Personalize.

2. Click the 'Change desktop icons' link.

3. Change the desktop icon images back to their original settings.

4. Click the User's Files and Network check boxes to remove the check marks.

5. Click the OK button in the Desktop Icon Settings dialog box.

6. Close the Personalization window.

Part 7: Resetting the Folder Options

1. Display the Start menu, click the Computer command, click the Organize button, and then click the 'Folder and search options' command.

2. Click the option buttons in the Folder Options dialog box that correspond to the settings you recorded in Step 3 of Part 1 and then click the OK button.

3. Close the Computer window.

4. Submit the printed Paint document illustrating the open windows on the desktop to your instructor.

In the Lab

Lab 2: Using the Address Toolbar to Search the Internet

Instructions: You decide to use your newly acquired Internet searching skills to earn money during your summer vacation. You take a part-time job in the Information Technology Department to assist an instructor doing research on searching techniques. You decide to use the Address toolbar on the taskbar as a means of searching the Internet.

Part 1: Unlocking the Taskbar and Adding the Address Toolbar to the Taskbar

 1. Right-click an open area of the taskbar.

 2. Click the 'Lock the taskbar' command on the shortcut menu to unlock the taskbar.

 3. Right-click an open area of the taskbar, point to Toolbars, and then click Address.

 4. Double-click the dotted vertical bar to the left of the Address title.

Part 2: Locking the Taskbar

 1. Right-click an open area of the taskbar.

 2. Click the 'Lock the taskbar' command on the shortcut menu to lock the taskbar (Figure 5–114).

Figure 5–114

Part 3: Using the Address Toolbar to Display Folder Content

 1. Type c:\users in the Address box and then press the ENTER key.

   a. What contents display in the Users folder?

   _____

 2. Type videos in the Address box and then press the ENTER key.

   a. What window displays on the desktop?

   _____

 3. Type pictures in the Address box and then click the Go button.

   a. What window displays on the desktop?

   _____

 4. Close all open windows.

Part 4: Using the Address Toolbar to Display a Web Page

 1. Type www.cengagebrain.com in the Address box and then click the Go button. Print the Web page using the Print button.

 2. Type www.facebook.com in the Address box and then click the Go button. Print the Web page using the Print button.

Continued >

In the Lab *continued*

3. Type www.youtube.com in the Address box and then click the Go button. Print the Web page using the Print button.

Part 5: Using the Address Toolbar to Search for Information

1. Type university of cincinnati in the Address box and then click the 'Search for "university of cincinnati"' link in the list box. A list of search results displays in the Web browser. Click an appropriate link to display the associated Web page, and print the Web page using the Print button.

2. Type hybrid cars in the Address box and then press the ENTER key. A list of search results displays in the Web browser. Click an appropriate link to display the associated Web page, and print the Web page using the Print button.

3. Type social networking in the Address box and then click the Go button. A list of search results displays in the Web browser. Click an appropriate link to display the associated Web page, and print the Web page using the Print button.

Part 6: Removing the Address Toolbar from the Taskbar

1. Right-click an open area of the taskbar, point to Toolbars on the shortcut menu, and then click Address on the submenu.

2. Close all open windows.

3. Submit the printed Web pages to your instructor.

In the Lab

Lab 3: Using the Personalization Window

Instructions: Your boss appoints you to design a desktop that all employees within your company will use. Experiment with the options in the Personalization window (Figure 5–115) until you have decided on the perfect desktop theme, background, desktop icons, mouse pointers, screen saver, color scheme, and display options. Write down all settings. Make sure after this exercise that you reset the computer to its original settings.

1. Select a picture from the Windows Desktop Backgrounds, from the Sample Pictures folder, from the Internet, or from your own photos for the background.

2. Add at least two new desktop icons and change their icons.

3. Change the theme of the mouse pointers.

4. Change the screen saver to an appropriate choice and change the wait time to 20 minutes.

5. Change the display of text on your screen to a larger size.

6. Save this as the Company Desktop theme.

Figure 5–115

Personalization window

Cases and Places

Apply your creative thinking and problem-solving skills to design and implement a solution.

• EASIER   •• MORE DIFFICULT

• 1 Finding Screen Savers

Although several screen savers are included with Windows 7, many more are available for download online, and various organizations give them away. Using your favorite search engine, locate five free screen savers from different Web sites. In a brief report, describe each screen saver, state the source from which you can obtain the screen saver, the contents of the screen saver, and whether you would install this screen saver.

• 2 Finding Desktop Themes

Besides screen savers, themes for the desktop often are available for download and purchase online. Using the 'Get more themes online' link and your favorite search engine, find three Web sites that have Windows 7 desktop themes available. How much do the themes for sale cost? For both the free and for sale themes, how much hard disk space do they require? Which ones would you consider using? Is creating your own theme better than purchasing one? Write a brief report containing your findings.

Continued >

Cases and Places *continued*

•• 3 Researching Advanced Search Techniques

In this chapter, you typed a keyword or phrase in the Address toolbar to search for information on the Internet. In addition, you can perform advanced searches using compound search criteria in which the words *AND*, *OR*, and *NOT* control how individual keywords are used. You also can specify which keywords are more important and can cause multiple keywords to be treated as a phrase. Use the Internet, Windows Help and Support, computer articles, and your own opinions to find out as much information as you can about advanced search techniques. Summarize your findings in a brief report and provide examples of some advanced searches that you created. Include sample output from running the advanced searches.

•• 4 Customizing the Taskbar

Make It Personal

The taskbar is a central part of the Windows 7 desktop. As such, it is important to organize the taskbar, and the toolbars on the taskbar, to best fit your individual needs. Make a list of items you would like to have appear on your desktop and on the taskbar. Design the taskbar and toolbars to meet your needs. Write a brief report summarizing your experience.

•• 5 Constructing the Optimal Desktop for Workplace Efficiency

Working Together

Colors, patterns, and the arrangement of the workplace can have a significant effect on worker productivity. These factors might draw attention to some objects, de-emphasize others, speed the completion of tasks, or even promote desirable moods and attitudes. Working with classmates, visit the Internet, a library, or other research facility to find out how colors, patterns, and arrangements can impact a work environment. Using what you have learned, together with the concepts and techniques presented in this chapter, create the Windows 7 desktop that you think would help workers be more efficient. Write a report describing your desktop and explaining why you feel it would enhance productivity.

6 | Customizing Your Computer Using the Control Panel

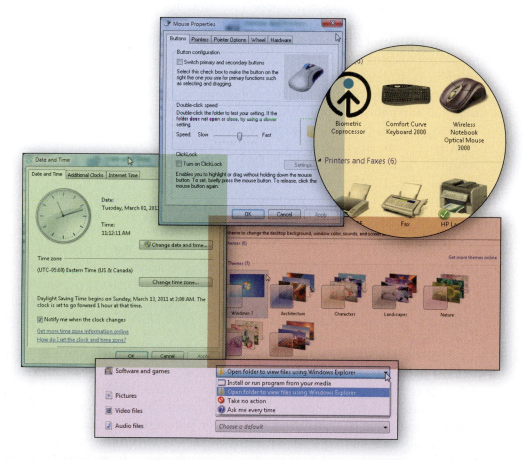

Objectives

You will have mastered the material in this chapter when you can:

- Open Control Panel and switch views

- View system information and hardware properties

- Add and remove a printer

- Customize the mouse configuration

- Install and uninstall a program

- Explain account privileges and view account information

- Create and configure a new user account

- View and change the date, time, and time zone

- Adjust Ease of Access Center settings

6 | Customizing Your Computer Using the Control Panel

Introduction

As you have learned, personalizing your work environment can lead to improved productivity. In Chapter 5, you modified desktop properties by creating a new desktop theme, personalizing the taskbar, and customizing folder options. However, there are other ways to customize Windows 7 so that you can get the most from your computer. Technology works best when it supports our lifestyles, providing the tools we need to accomplish the tasks set before us.

The Control Panel window contains categories that allow you to change the properties of an object and, thus, customize the Windows 7 environment (Figure 6–1). In addition, Control Panel provides links to other windows that contain settings, allowing you to further customize your computer. In this chapter, you will learn how to install and uninstall a program, make the computer more usable for physically challenged individuals, add a printer to the computer, use a troubleshooter to solve a hardware problem, and view the properties of the hardware devices attached to the computer. In addition, you will use Control Panel to customize the mouse, keyboard, date and time, and time zone.

You will not be able to perform some tasks in this chapter unless you have proper User Account Control access. **User Account Control** (**UAC**) controls the access granted to each user. A **user account** is a collection of information that Windows 7 needs to know about a computer user. This information includes the user name, password, picture, work-groups in which the user has membership, and rights and permissions the user has for accessing a computer or network resources. User accounts make it possible for each user to perform tasks, such as log on to the computer, keep information confidential and com-puter settings protected, customize Windows 7, store files in unique folders, and maintain a personal list of favorite Web sites.

Normally, user accounts operate in standard user mode, which allows you to use most of the capabilities of the computer. A standard user cannot install software that affects other users or change system settings that affect security. An **administrator account** has full control of the computer and operating system, and can change user permissions, install software that affects all users, and change system settings that affect security. When a task requires administrator access, depending on the User Account Control setting, you might be prompted to authorize the task. By default, you only are asked for permission when programs attempt to make a change to the computer. Once authorized, the user has temporary administrator privileges. After the task is finished, the user returns to standard user mode. User Access Control is designed to prevent malicious software from being installed inadvertently, even by administrators. For standard user accounts, the user needs to know an administrator account user name and password to authorize User Account Control. Only administrators are prompted to continue without requiring a user name and password.

In the Control Panel window, a shield displays next to tasks requiring User Account Control access. Some of the steps in this chapter require administrative privileges. If you do not have administrative privileges, read the steps instead of performing them.

Figure 6–1

Overview

As you read this chapter, you will learn how to customize your computer by performing these general tasks:

- Viewing and monitoring your system
- Adding and removing a hardware device
- Customizing your mouse functionality
- Installing and uninstalling software
- Creating, using, and deleting a user account
- Accessing and configuring Ease of Access features

Customizing Your Computer Using Control Panel

Customizing your computer using the Control Panel window requires the appropriate permissions to make changes to your computer.

1. **Determine the permissions you have on the computer you will be using.** Each user account can have different rights and permissions. Depending on which rights and permissions have been set for your account, you might or might not be able to perform certain operations.

2. **Identify the type of keyboard and mouse you will be using.** Sections in this chapter will make changes to your keyboard and mouse settings. If you are using a touch pad or a mouse with a scroll wheel, different options might be available to you. If your keyboard lacks a numeric keypad, you will be instructed not to perform certain steps.

3. **Determine if you have Internet access.** For this chapter, you will be accessing the Internet to search for infomation. You will want to know if your computer has Internet access and if anything is required of you to use it.

The System and Security Window

You can use the System and Security window to open the Action Center, change Windows Firewall settings, view and change system settings, configure Windows Update, change your energy-saving settings, schedule backups (covered in Appendix D), encrypt the contents on your hard disk, and use other administrator tools. Each option provides different opportunities for you to fine-tune your computer. However, be aware that some of the advanced system and maintenance options require User Account Control authorization. If you are using an administrative account, Windows will not require you to enter a user name and password.

To Open the Control Panel Window

The following step opens the Control Panel window.

- Display the Start menu.

- Click the Control Panel command to display the Control Panel window (Figure 6–2).

Q&A

Why do some of the links display a shield icon?

Links leading to an action that requires administrative access appear with a shield icon so that you can identify them easily. Standard account users must enter a user name and password to proceed with those actions.

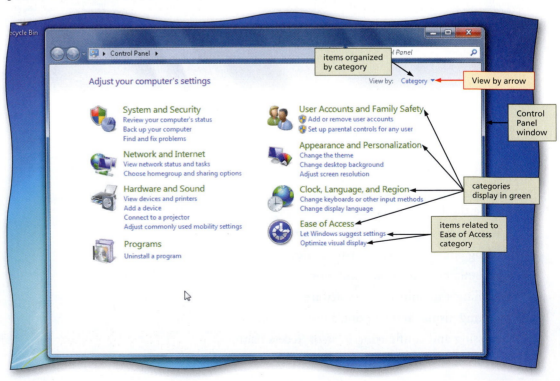

Figure 6–2

To Switch Control Panel Views

By default, the Control Panel window displays in Category view. Category view offers the various Control Panel options organized into eight functional categories. Links to common tasks are provided below each category name. The View by arrow in the Control Panel window allows you to display the items as large or small icons. When changed to icons, all of the individual Control Panel icons display in alphabetical order instead of organized into categories. The following steps switch to Large icons view and then back to Category view.

- Click the View by arrow in the Control Panel window to display a list of view options (Figure 6–3).

Q&A Why might I want to use Large or Small icons view?

Some users prefer icons view, large or small, because they feel that it makes commands in the Control Panel easier to find. In addition, individuals who are familiar with previous versions of Windows might be more comfortable using icons view.

Figure 6–3

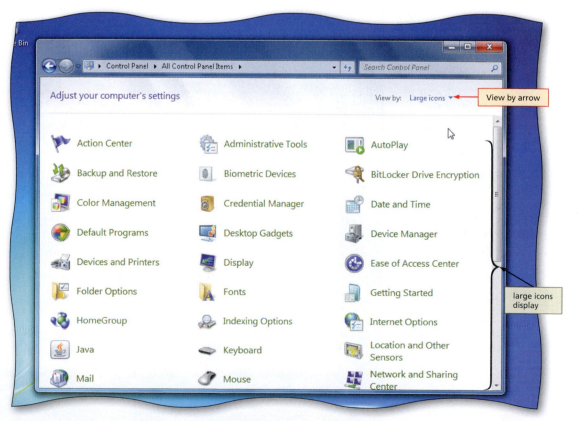

- Click the Large icons command to display the Control Panel in Large icons view (Figure 6–4).

Figure 6–4

3

- Click the View by arrow in the Control Panel window to display a list of view options.

- Click Category to return the Control Panel window to Category view (Figure 6–5).

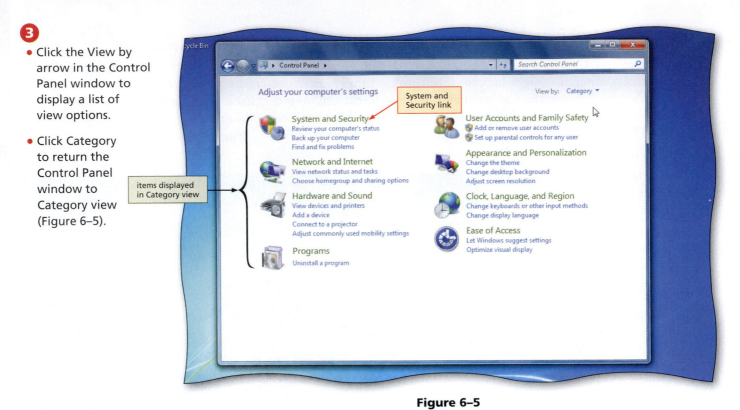

Figure 6–5

To Open the System and Security Window

The following step opens the System and Security window.

1

- Click the System and Security link to open the System and Security window (Figure 6–6).

Q&A Why do my links differ from those shown in the figure?

Depending upon the configuration and the devices installed, you might see different links within the System and Security window.

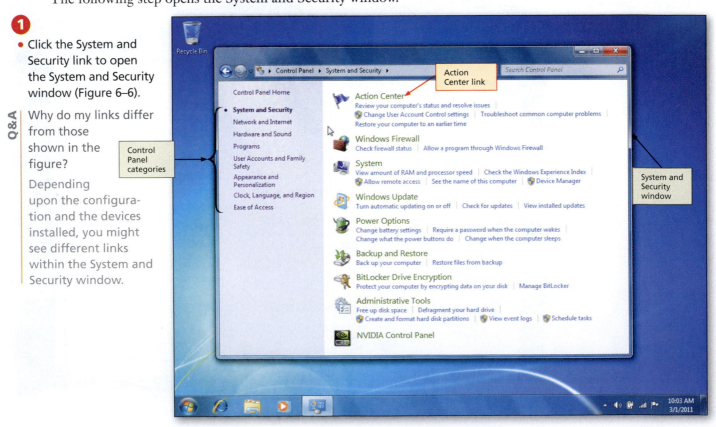

Figure 6–6

To Display the Action Center

The **Action Center** can help you to manage your computer's security by monitoring the status of several essential security features on your computer, including firewall settings, Windows automatic updating, virus protection, spyware and unwanted software protection, Internet security settings, User Account Control settings, and Network Access Protection. The following step displays the Action Center.

- Click the Action Center link in right pane of the Control Panel window to display the Action Center.

- If necessary, maximize the Action Center window (Figure 6–7).

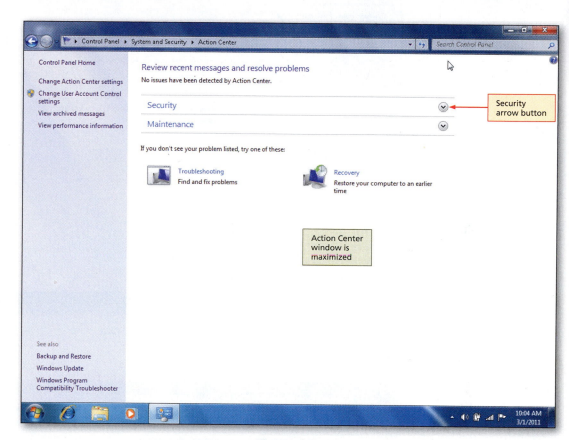

Figure 6–7

To View Security and Maintenance Settings in the Action Center

The Action Center allows you to view and monitor your security and maintenance settings. The steps on the following pages display the security and maintenance settings in the Action Center.

1

- Click the Security arrow button to expand the Security section to view the security settings (Figure 6–8).

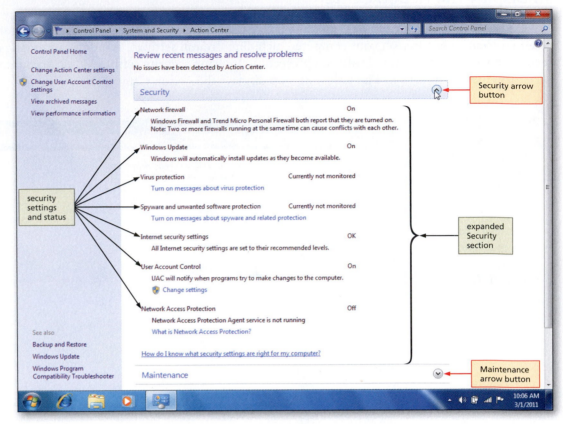

Figure 6–8

2

- Click the Security arrow button to collapse the Security section.

- Click the Maintenance arrow button to expand the Maintenance section to view the maintenance settings (Figure 6–9).

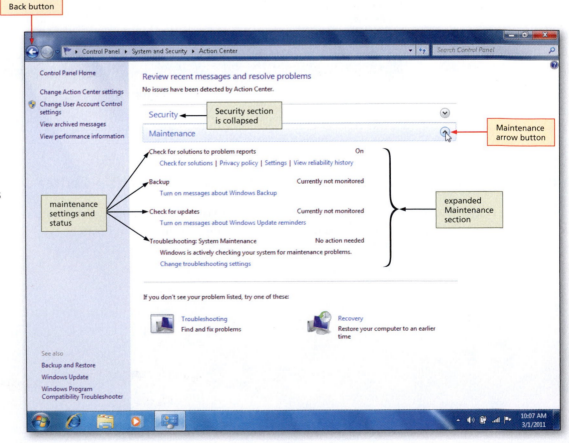

Figure 6–9

3
- Click the Maintenance arrow button to collapse the Maintenance section.

- Click the Back button to return to the System and Security window (Figure 6–10).

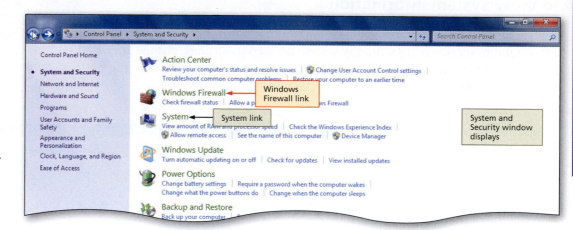

Figure 6–10

To View Windows Firewall Settings

Windows Firewall is a program that protects your computer from unauthorized users by monitoring and restricting information that travels between your computer and a network or the Internet. Windows Firewall also helps to block computer viruses and worms from infecting your computer. Windows Firewall is automatically turned on when Windows 7 is launched. It is recommended that Windows Firewall remain on.

1
- Click the Windows Firewall link to display the Windows Firewall window (Figure 6–11).

- After viewing the settings, click the Back button to return to the System and Security window.

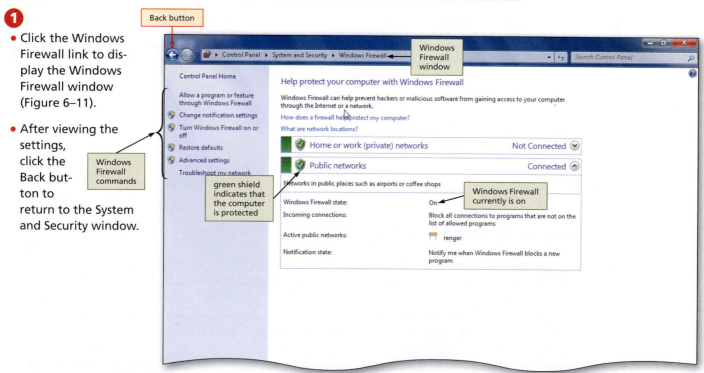

Figure 6–11

To View System Information

The System window displays summary information about your computer. You can access Device Manager, adjust remote access settings, modify system protection settings, change advanced system settings, view the Windows Experience Index, and update Windows 7 registration information using the System window. The following step opens the System window.

1

- Click the System link to open the System window. If necessary, click the Maximize button to maximize the window (Figure 6–12).

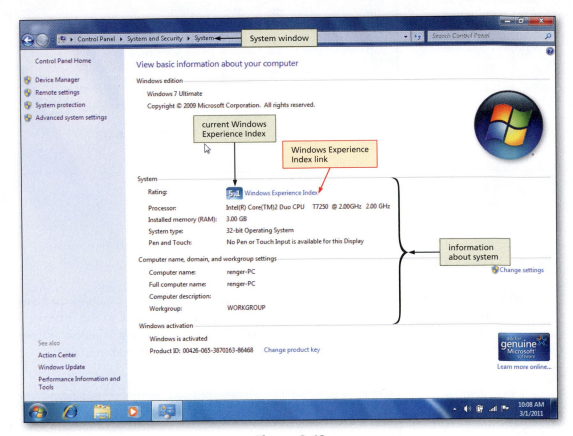

Figure 6–12

Other Ways

1. Open Control Panel, change to Large or Small icons, click System
2. Open Computer window, click System properties

To View the Windows Experience Index

The **Windows Experience Index** measures the capability of your computer's hardware and software configuration and assigns a base score to your system. Computers with higher base scores perform complex tasks more easily than computers with lower scores. To calculate the Windows Experience Index, each hardware component is scored, and the lowest score becomes your base score. When buying software, you can use the base score to determine if your computer can support the new software. Changing your hardware components requires you to recalculate your Windows Experience Index. Microsoft says that for now, the base scores can range from 1 to 7.9; however, this range might expand in the future as technology advances. You can view the complete details of your score or update your score in the Performance Information and Tools window. The following steps display the complete Windows Experience Index information.

1

• Click the Windows Experience Index link to open the Performance Information and Tools window (Figure 6–13).

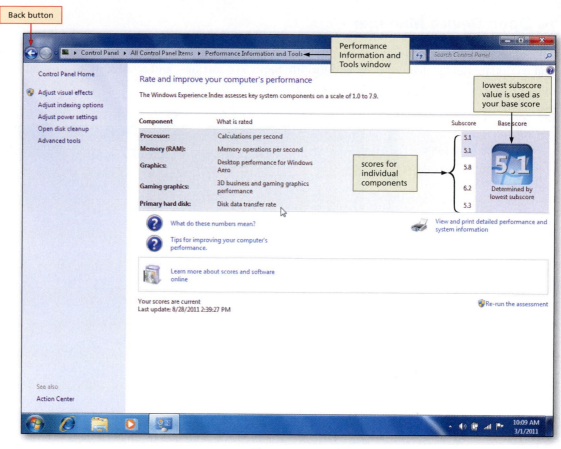

Figure 6–13

2

• After viewing your score information, click the Back button two times to return to the System and Security window (Figure 6–14).

Figure 6–14

To Open Device Manager

Device Manager allows you to display a list of the hardware devices installed on your computer and also allows you to update device drivers, view and modify hardware settings, and troubleshoot problems. The following step opens Device Manager.

1

- Click the Device Manager link to open Device Manager (Figure 6–15).

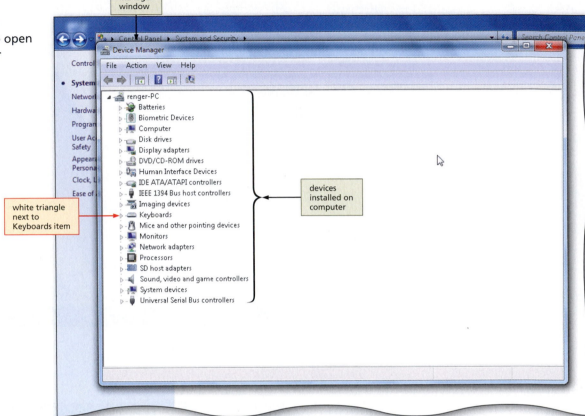

Figure 6–15

Other Ways

1. Open Control Panel, change to Large or Small icons, click Device Manager icon

To View the Properties of a Device

You can use Device Manager to see the properties of the devices installed on your computer. Normally, device drivers are downloaded and installed automatically when Windows 7 is installed and Windows Update runs. A **device driver** is a program used by the operating system to control the hardware. You can view the driver details in the Device Properties dialog box for the particular device. If necessary, you can update the device driver manually. You also can roll back the driver to a previous working version if the current driver fails to work properly, or disable the device if you want to prevent users from accessing it. The following steps display the properties and driver information for the keyboard.

1

- Click the white triangle next to Keyboards to expand the list of installed keyboards (Figure 6–16).

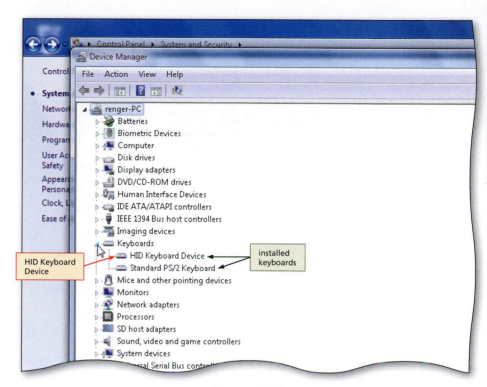

Figure 6–16

2

- Double-click the installed HID Keyboard Device to open the HID Keyboard Device Properties dialog box. If you do not have an HID Keyboard Device listed, double-click the keyboard device displayed on your computer (Figure 6–17).

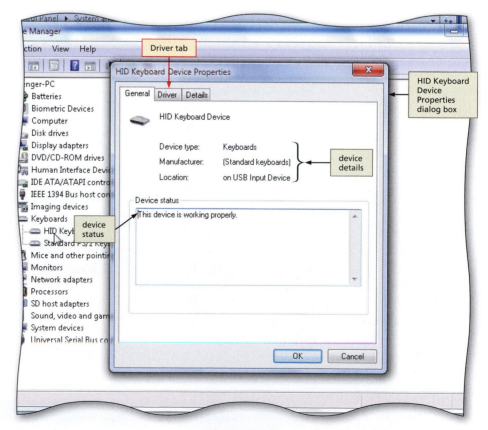

Figure 6–17

3

- Click the Driver tab to display the Driver sheet (Figure 6–18).

- After viewing the driver information, click the OK button to close the dialog box.

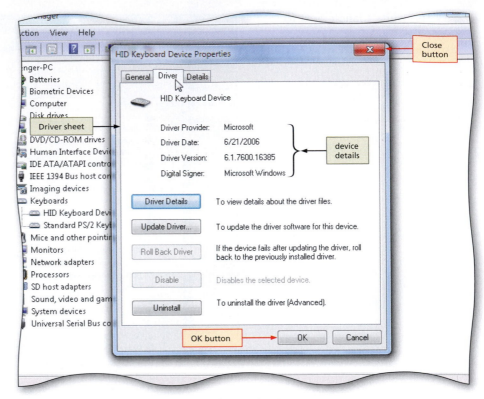

Figure 6–18

4

- Close Device Manager (Figure 6–19).

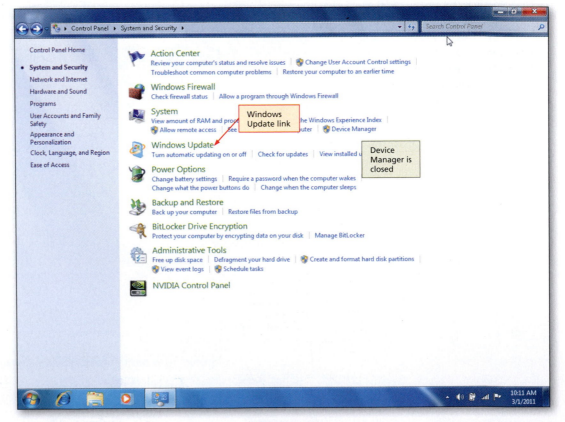

Figure 6–19

To View Installed Updates

Windows Update is turned on by default when Windows 7 is installed. Windows Update automatically searches online for updates to your computer while you are connected to the Internet. These updates are then routinely installed. Although this process occurs without your involvement, you should be aware of the updates that are installed on your computer, and from time to time, review the list. The following steps open Windows Update and display the update history.

- Click the Windows Update link to open the Windows Update window (Figure 6–20).

Figure 6–20

- Click the 'View update history' link to open the 'View update history' window (Figure 6–21).

Q&A

Why are there different levels of importance given to updates?

Microsoft offers three different levels of updates based upon how critical the update is. An update that is identified as Important is a critical update and usually is a security update, a bug fix, or both. Recommended updates are noncritical updates, but can improve performance. Optional updates also are noncritical and are not installed automatically.

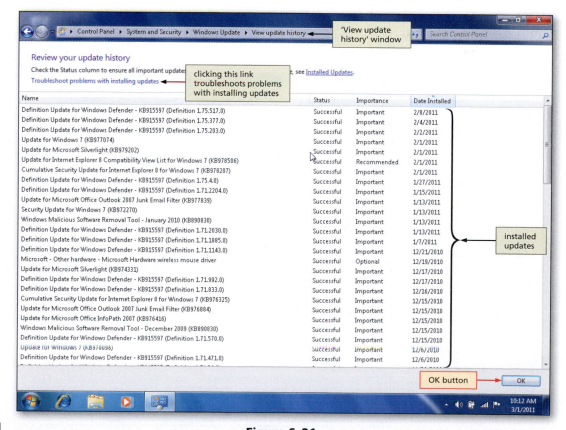

Figure 6–21

3

- Click the OK button to return to the Windows Update window (Figure 6–22).

Q&A What happens if an update fails?

If the automatic update feature is turned on, Windows 7 continues trying to install the update. If the update still fails, you can use the 'Troubleshoot problems with installing updates' link to find solutions to the installation problems.

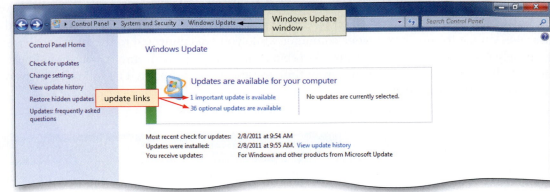

Figure 6–22

Other Ways
1. Open Control Panel, change to Large or Small icons, click Windows Update, click 'View update history'	2. Open Control Panel, open System and Security window, click 'View installed updates'

To View Available Updates

In the Windows Update window, you might see links for available important, recommended, and optional updates. Clicking any of the provided links takes you to the 'Select updates to install' window where you can select and install the updates of your choosing. You always should install important updates. The following steps display the 'Select updates to install' window.

1

- Click one of the available update links to display the 'Select updates to install' window (Figure 6–23).

Q&A Why do I not see any available update links?

If your computer is up to date and requires no updates at the present time, the links do not appear.

Q&A Why do I see a different list of available updates?

The list of available updates is determined by your edition of Windows 7, the software that you have installed, and the updates you already have installed.

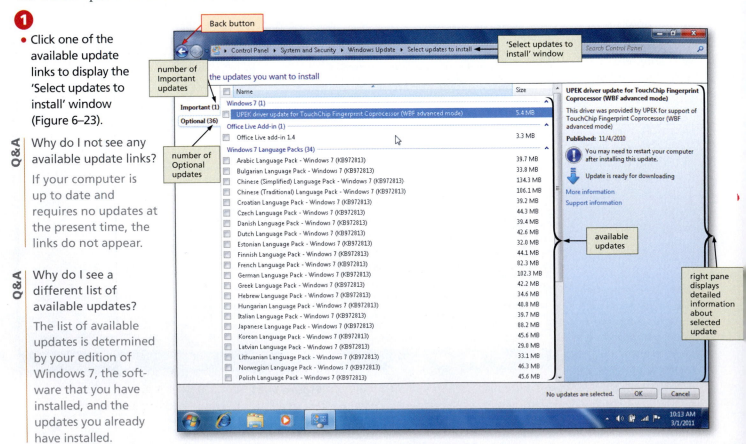

Figure 6–23

2

• After viewing the available updates, click the Back button to return to the Windows Update window (Figure 6–24).

Q&A

How do I install an update?

Click the 'View available updates' link, and then select the updates that you want to install. After selecting the updates, click the Install updates button to install them. Depending on the update, you might be instructed to restart your computer.

Figure 6–24

3

• Click the Control Panel Home link to return to the Control Panel window (Figure 6–25).

Figure 6–25

Other Ways

1. Open Control Panel, change to Large or Small icons, click Windows Update, click one of the available update links

The Hardware and Sound Window

You can install printers, configure AutoPlay (**AutoPlay** refers to the default action that occurs when you connect a device such as a USB flash drive or an optical disc), configure the mouse, configure scanners and cameras, connect to a projector, adjust Tablet PC settings, and more, from the Hardware and Sound window.

When you add a printer, scanner, camera, keyboard, mouse, or any other hardware device, Windows 7 usually installs and configures it automatically. If you want to install it manually or configure it after it is installed, you can use the Hardware and Sound window to access the appropriate controls.

To Add a Printer

The procedure to add a printer to a computer depends upon whether the printer is a local printer or network printer. A **local printer** is a printer directly attached to the computer. A **network printer** is a printer attached to another computer or directly attached to the network. New printers generally support the **Plug and Play** standard, which makes adding a new printer easy because Windows 7 automatically finds the correct driver to use and adds the printer to your list of printers. Older printers might not support Plug and Play.

Windows 7 also allows you to add printers manually. To add a local printer, you must know to which port the printer is connected, and then decide whether the printer should be designated as the default printer. A **port** is a socket on the back of a computer used to connect a hardware device to the computer. The **default printer** is the printer to which all printed documents are sent. Most likely, a printer already is attached to the computer on which you are working and that printer is designated as the default printer. Therefore, you should not designate the printer you add to the computer in the following steps as the default printer. The following steps use the Add Printer Wizard to add the HP Officejet Pro 8000 A809 printer to the computer as a local printer.

- Click the Hardware and Sound link to open the Hardware and Sound window (Figure 6–26).

Figure 6–26

- Click the Devices and Printers link to open the Devices and Printers window (Figure 6–27).

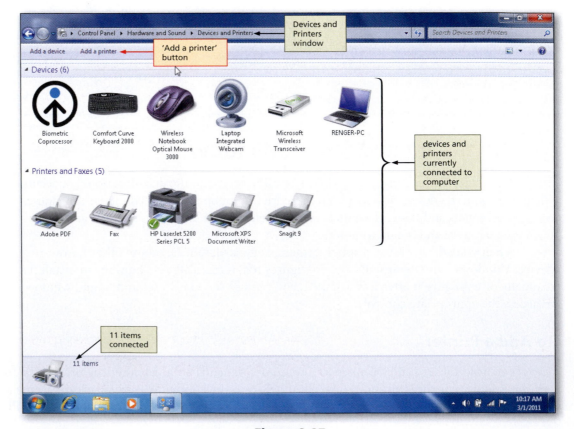

Figure 6–27

3

- Click the 'Add a printer' button to start the Add Printer Wizard (Figure 6–28).

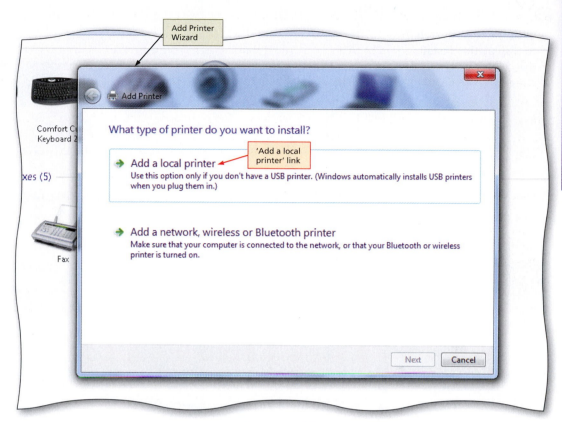

Figure 6–28

4

- Click the 'Add a local printer' link.

- If necessary, click the 'Use an existing port' option button to select it. Verify that the LPT1 port is selected. If necessary, change the port to LPT1 (Figure 6–29).

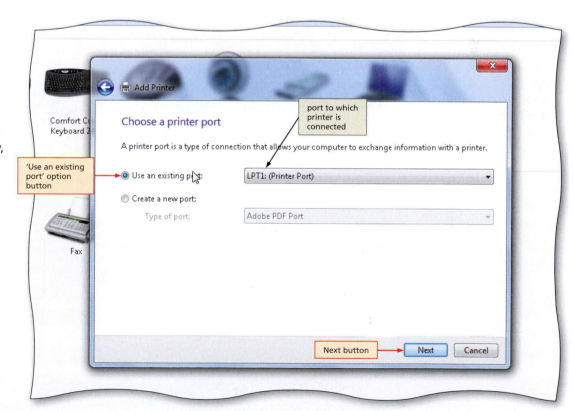

Figure 6–29

• Click the Next button
to display the 'Install
the printer driver'
screen (Figure 6–30).

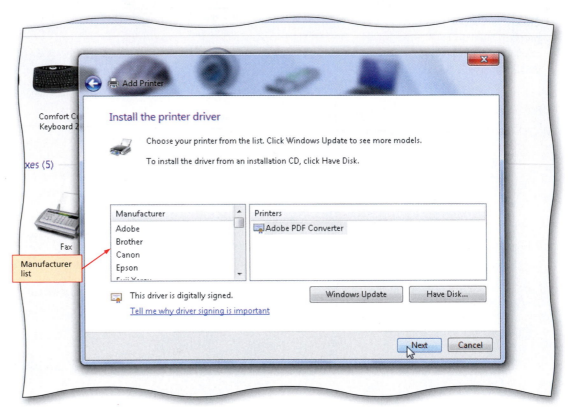

Figure 6–30

• Scroll down in the
Manufacturer list to
display HP.

• Click HP to display
a list of HP printers
in the Printers list
(Figure 6–31).

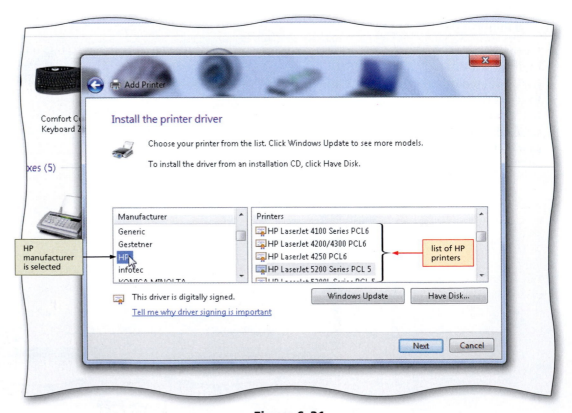

Figure 6–31

7

- Scroll down in the Printers list until the HP Officejet Pro 8000 A809 Series appears.

- Click HP Officejet Pro 8000 A809 Series to select it (Figure 6–32).

- Click the Next button to continue.

- Click the Next button to accept the default Printer name.

- The Installing printer message appears, indicating the progress of the installation.

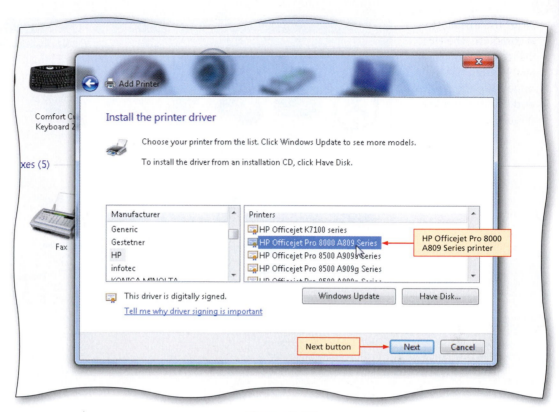

Figure 6–32

8

- If the Add Printer dialog box displays asking if you wish to share the printer, click the 'Do not share this printer' option button, and then click the Next button.

- If necessary, click the 'Set as the default printer' check box to remove the check mark (Figure 6–33).

- Click the Finish button to complete the printer addition.

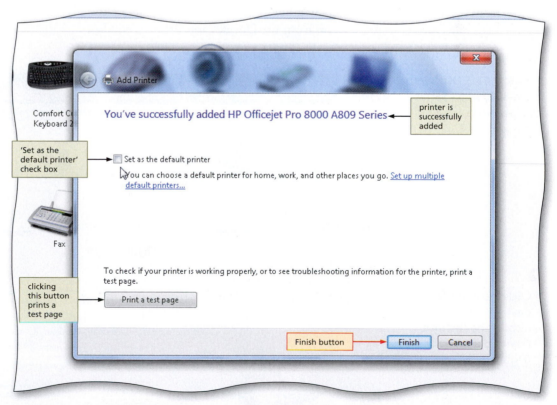

Figure 6–33

● After the installation is complete, the HP Officejet Pro 8000 A809 Series printer appears in the Devices and Printers window (Figure 6–34).

Figure 6–34

Other Ways

1. Open Control Panel, click 'View devices and printers', click 'Add a printer'

2. Open Control Panel, change to Large or Small icons, click Devices and Printers, click 'Add a printer'

To Delete a Printer

When you disconnect a printer and have no plans to reconnect the printer in the future, you should delete the printer from the Devices and Printers window. The following steps delete the HP Officejet Pro 8000 A809 Series printer from the computer and its icon from the Devices and Printers window.

● Click the HP Officejet Pro 8000 A809 Series printer icon to select it (Figure 6–35).

Figure 6–35

● Click the Remove device button to display the Remove Device dialog box (Figure 6–36).

Figure 6–36

3

- Click the Yes button in the Remove Device dialog box to confirm that you want to delete the printer (Figure 6–37).

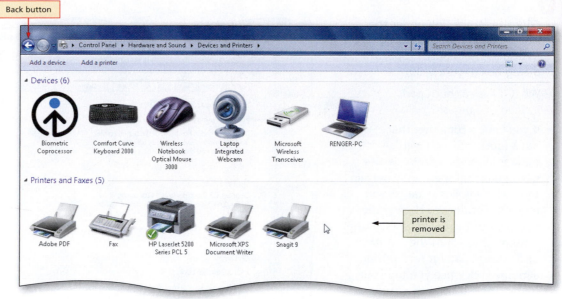

Figure 6–37

 4

- Click the Back button to return to the Hardware and Sound window (Figure 6–38).

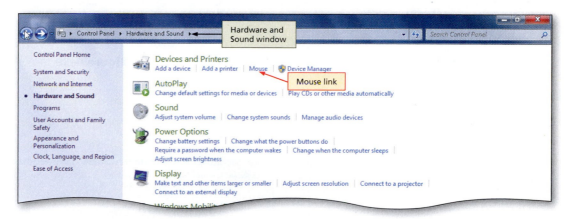

Figure 6–38

To Change the Mouse Button Configuration

The mouse is another hardware device that Windows 7 allows you to customize. In Chapter 5, you changed the mouse pointers scheme to Windows Black (extra large) (system scheme), which increased the size of the mouse pointers. Among the other mouse properties you can customize are the functions of the left and right mouse buttons, the double-click speed, and the pointer speed. You also can turn on ClickLock and Snap To functionality, as well as add pointer trails. If you have a mouse with a scroll wheel, you can adjust how far a page scrolls each time you move the mouse wheel one notch. You use the Mouse Properties dialog box to change all of these properties.

Typically, the left mouse button is the primary button, which performs the operations of selecting and dragging, and the right mouse button is the secondary button, which performs the aptly named right-clicking and right-dragging. If you are left-handed, you might find it more convenient to change the button configuration, by switching the selecting and dragging operations to the right mouse button and the right-clicking and right-dragging operations to the left mouse button. The steps on the following pages switch the primary and secondary buttons and then change the buttons back to the original configuration.

1

- Click the Mouse link under the Devices and Printers heading to display the Mouse Properties dialog box (Figure 6–39).

Q&A

What if I use a touch pad instead of a mouse?

If you have a computer that has a touch pad, you will see options in the Mouse Properties dialog box that specifically pertain to touch pads. For instance, you might see options to change the functions of the touch pad's mouse buttons or to adjust the sensitivity of the touch pad for recognizing a mouse click when you tap your finger. Some touch pad programs, as well as other custom mouse software, can completely change the appearance of the Mouse Properties dialog box. Once this software is installed, the only way to return the Mouse Properties dialog box to its original state might be to uninstall the touch pad or custom mouse software.

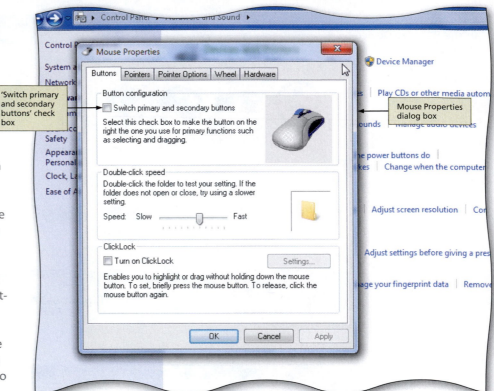

Figure 6–39

2

- Click the 'Switch primary and secondary buttons' check box to select it (Figure 6–40).

🔍 **Experiment**

- Experiment with the left and right mouse buttons until you are comfortable with this configuration. Return to the Mouse Properties dialog box when you are done.

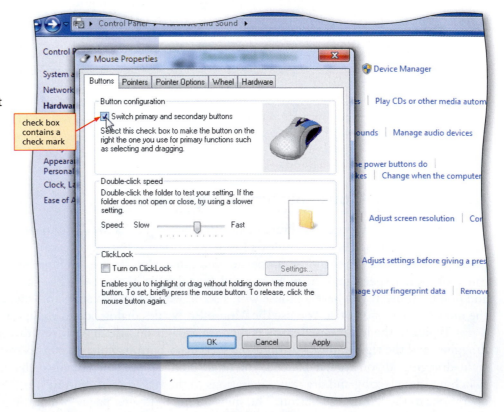

Figure 6–40

- Using the right mouse button, click the 'Switch primary and secondary buttons' check box to deselect it (Figure 6–41).

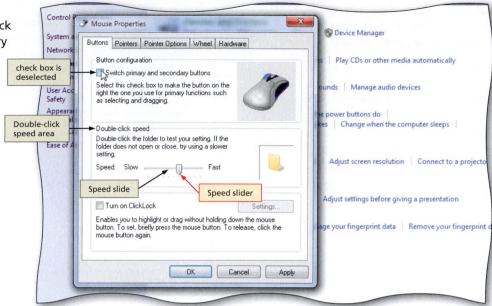

Figure 6–41

To Adjust the Double-Click Speed

Windows 7 measures the amount of time that occurs between clicking the mouse button once and then clicking the same button again. This time interval, called **double-click speed**, determines whether Windows 7 recognizes when a mouse button is clicked twice as a double-click or two single clicks. If you click a mouse button twice, and the second click does not fall within the double-click time interval, Windows 7 treats the action as two single clicks, not as a double-click. The following steps adjust and test the double-click speed.

- Drag the Speed slider in the Double-click speed area to the right end of the slide to select the fastest Double-click speed (Figure 6–42).

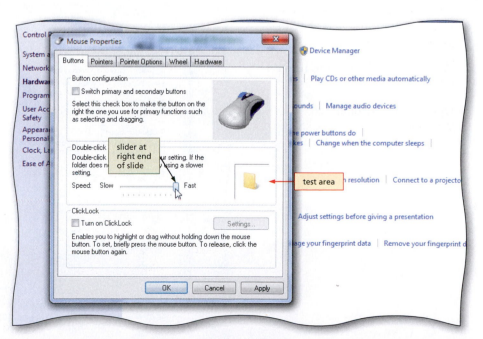

Figure 6–42

2

- Double-click the test area until the folder opens (Figure 6–43).

- If the folder does not open, drag the speed slider to the left until the folder opens when you double-click the test area.

Q&A Why was I unable to open the folder when the speed slider was set all the way to the right?

Setting the double-click speed to its fastest speed might make it impossible for you to double-click an object. The speed at which individuals can double-click a mouse can vary.

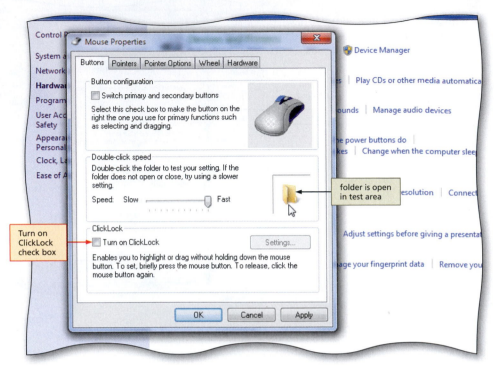

Figure 6–43

To Turn On and Use ClickLock

The ClickLock feature allows you to select or drag text without continuously holding down the mouse button. Once the ClickLock feature is turned on, you activate it by holding the mouse button down for a few seconds to "lock" the mouse click. You simply click the mouse button again to "unlock" the button. The following steps turn on ClickLock, create a simple text document, lock the mouse click, and then highlight text in the document.

1

- Click the Turn on ClickLock check box in the ClickLock area in the Mouse Properties dialog box to select it (Figure 6–44).

- Click the Apply button to turn on ClickLock.

- Open a new document in WordPad.

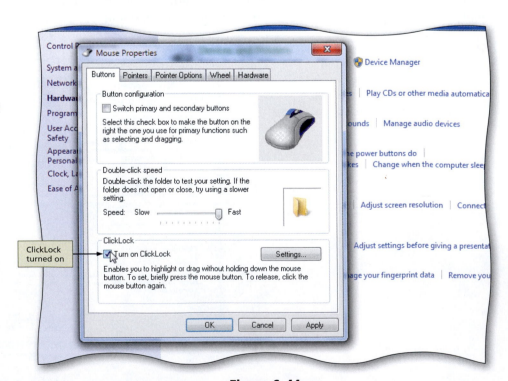

Figure 6–44

2

- **Type** `ClickLock allows you to lock a mouse button and select or drag text.` in the Document - WordPad window (Figure 6–45).

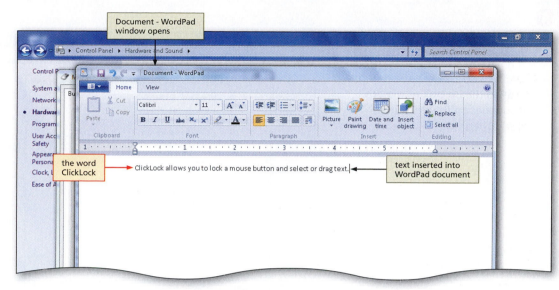

Figure 6–45

3

- Position the insertion point to the left of the word, ClickLock, in the document, hold down the left mouse button for several seconds, release the mouse button, move the insertion point to the right to highlight the word, ClickLock, and then click the left mouse button to select the word, ClickLock (Figure 6–46).

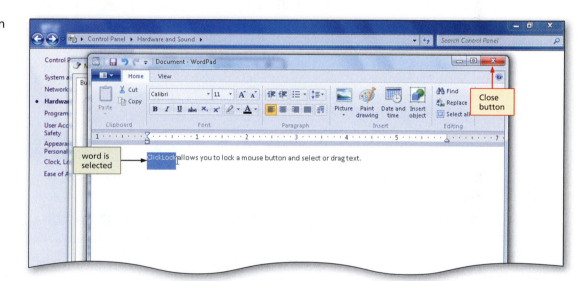

Figure 6–46

Other Ways

1. Open Control Panel, change to Large or Small icons, click Mouse, click Turn on ClickLock

To Close the Document and Turn Off ClickLock

The steps on the following page close the Document - WordPad window and turn off ClickLock.

1

- Close the Document - WordPad window.

- Click the Don't Save button in the WordPad dialog box to discard the changes to the document (Figure 6–47).

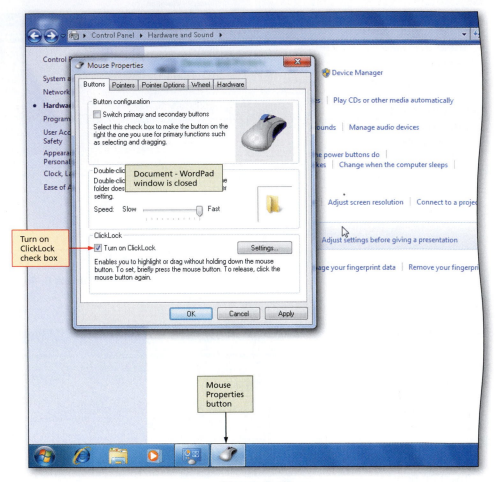

Figure 6–47

2

- If necessary, click the Mouse Properties button on the taskbar to make the Mouse Properties dialog box active.

- Click the Turn on ClickLock check box to remove the check mark (Figure 6–48).

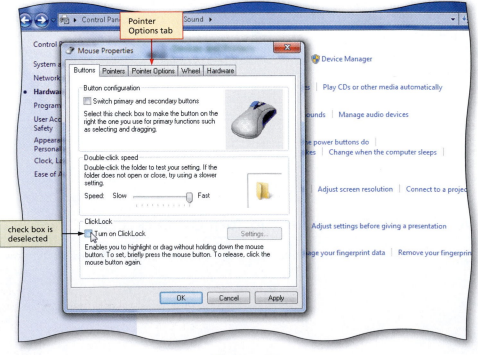

Figure 6–48

To Adjust the Pointer Speed

You can adjust the pointer speed from the Pointer Options sheet in the Mouse Properties dialog box. The **pointer speed** is the speed at which the mouse pointer travels across the desktop when you move the mouse. The following steps adjust the pointer speed.

1

- Click the Pointer Options tab in the Mouse Properties dialog box to display the Pointer Options sheet (Figure 6–49).

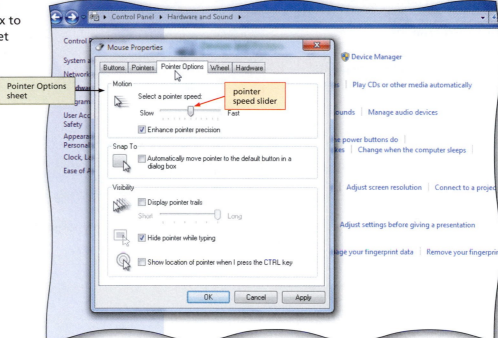

Figure 6–49

2

- Drag the pointer speed slider in the Motion area to the left end of the slide to select the slowest setting (Figure 6–50).

- Move the mouse pointer around the desktop and notice the difference in the pointer speed.

Q&A

Do I need to click the Apply button?

Because moving the slider adjusts the pointer speed immediately, it is not necessary to click the Apply button.

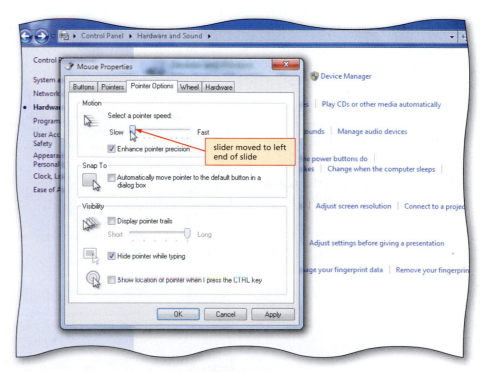

Figure 6–50

3

- Drag the pointer speed slider to the right end of the slide to select the fastest setting (Figure 6–51).

- Move the mouse pointer around the desktop and notice the difference in the pointer speed.

 Experiment

- Experiment with the pointer speed until you find the pointer speed that works best for you.

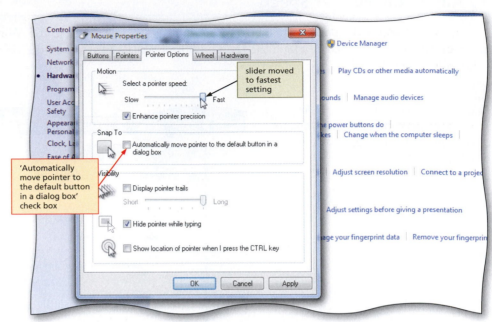

Figure 6–51

Other Ways

1. Open Control Panel, change to Large or Small icons, click Mouse, click Pointer Options, drag pointer speed slider

To Turn On Snap To

Normally when a dialog box appears on the desktop, the mouse pointer remains where it was before the dialog box appeared. However, you can change the settings so that the mouse pointer automatically "snaps to" the default button in any dialog box. The following steps turn on Snap To and cause the mouse pointer to point to the default (OK) button in the Mouse Properties dialog box.

1

- Click the 'Automatically move pointer to the default button in a dialog box' check box in the Snap To area to select it (Figure 6–52).

- Apply the changes, and then close the Mouse Properties dialog box.

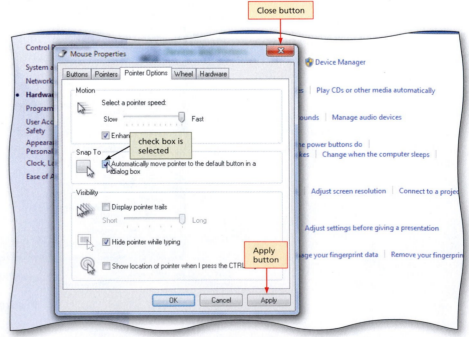

Figure 6–52

2

• In the Hardware and Sound window, click the Mouse link to open the Mouse Properties dialog box (Figure 6–53).

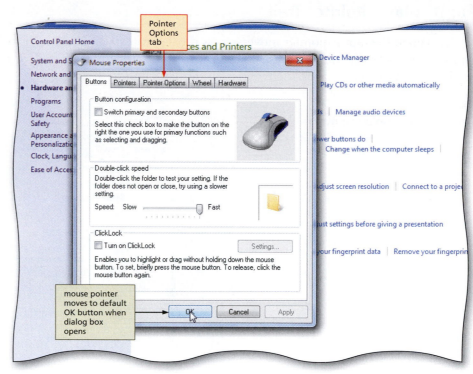

Figure 6–53

3

• Click the Pointer Options tab to display the Pointer Options sheet.

• Click the 'Automatically move pointer to the default button in a dialog box' check box to remove the check mark (Figure 6–54).

• Click the Apply button to apply the changes.

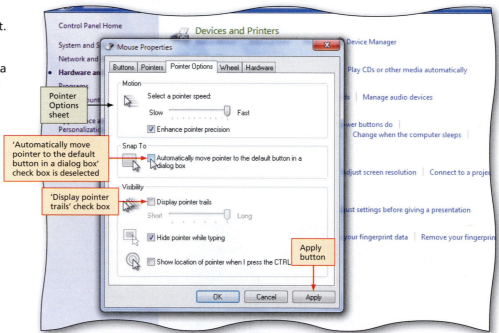

Figure 6–54

Other Ways

1. Open Control Panel, change to Large or Small icons, click Mouse, click Pointer Options, click 'Automatically move pointer to the default button in a dialog box', click Apply

To Display a Pointer Trail

When the mouse pointer moves across the desktop, it can be difficult to see where it is on the desktop. To improve the visibility of the mouse pointer, you can display a pointer trail, or trail of mouse pointers, on the desktop as you move the mouse. The following steps display a pointer trail.

1
- Click the 'Display pointer trails' check box in the Visibility area to select it (Figure 6–55).

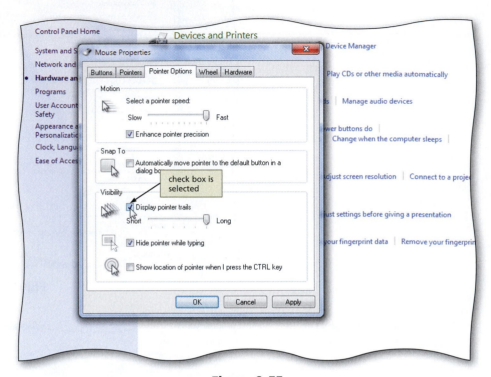

Figure 6–55

2
- Move the mouse and then watch the trail of mouse pointers that appears as the mouse moves across the desktop (Figure 6–56).

 Experiment

- Experiment with the length of the pointer trail by dragging the pointer trails slider until you find the best length for you.

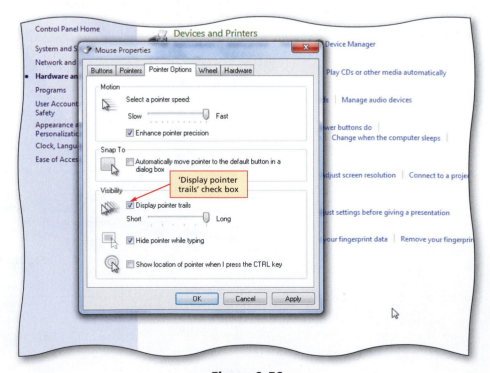

Figure 6–56

3

- When you have finished viewing the pointer trails, click the 'Display pointer trails' check box to deselect the pointer trails option (Figure 6–57).

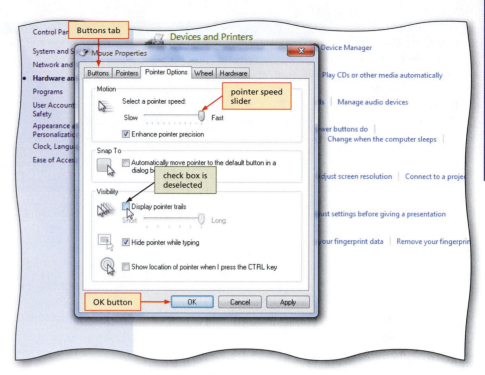

Figure 6–57

To Restore Double-Click and Pointer Speed

The following steps restore the mouse functionality back to its original settings.

1 Drag the pointer speed slider back to its original position.

2 Click the Buttons tab.

3 Drag the Speed slider in the Double-click speed area back to its original position.

4 Click the OK button to save the changes and close the Mouse Properties dialog box.

To Adjust AutoPlay Settings

Windows 7 allows you to customize the AutoPlay features for your computer. As mentioned previously, AutoPlay refers to the default action that occurs when media and devices are connected to your computer. You already have seen AutoPlay in action when you used a USB flash drive. In that case, Windows 7 asked you what you would like to do. Using the AutoPlay window, you can view and modify the settings for all media and devices inserted into your computer. Once set, the new action will be used the next time you insert the media or device. The steps on the following pages open the AutoPlay window and change the action for the 'Software and games' setting to the 'Open folder to view files using Windows Explorer' action.

1
● From the Hardware and Sound window, click the AutoPlay link to open the AutoPlay window (Figure 6–58).

types of media

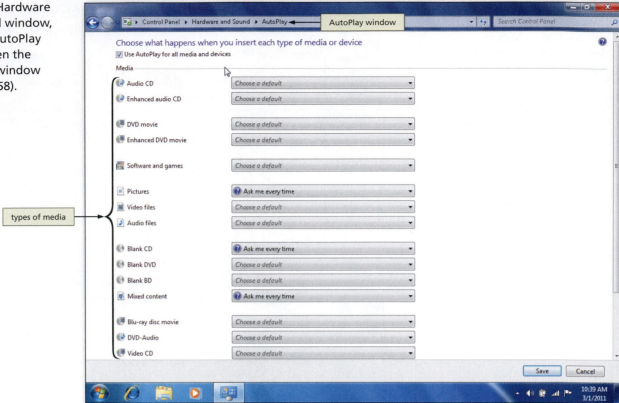

Figure 6–58

2
● Scroll down to view the remaining AutoPlay settings (Figure 6–59).

remaining AutoPlay settings

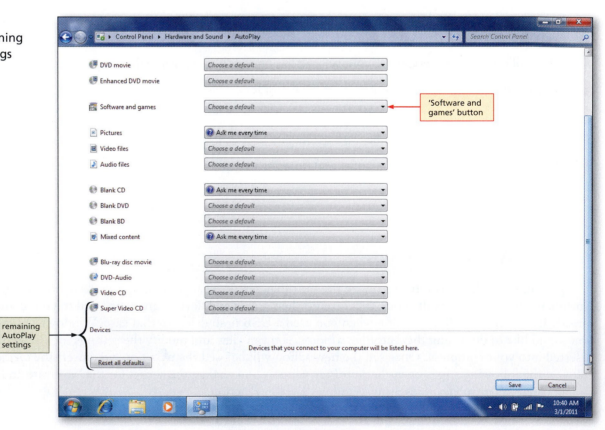

Figure 6–59

3

- If necessary, scroll up until the 'Software and games' media type is visible.

- Click the 'Software and games' button to see a list of available actions (Figure 6–60).

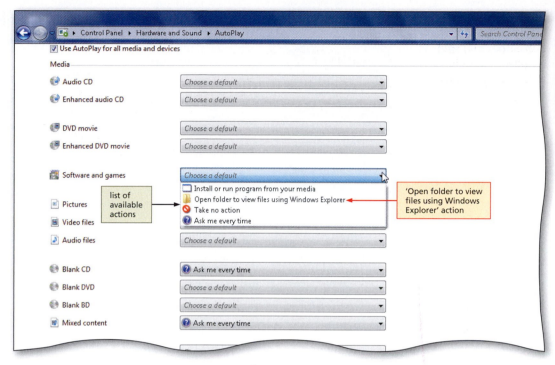

Figure 6–60

4

- Click the 'Open folder to view files using Windows Explorer' action to change the action for Software and games (Figure 6–61).

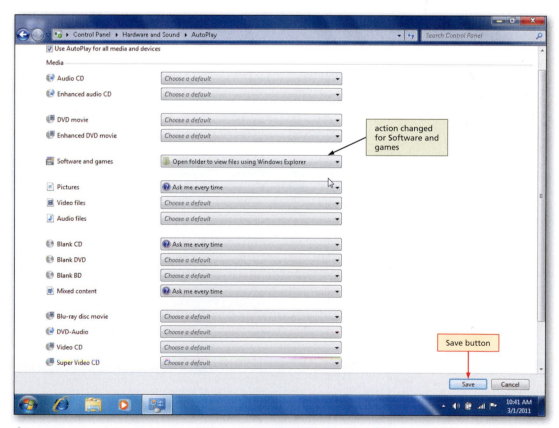

Figure 6–61

5

- Click the Save button to save the changes and return to the Hardware and Sound window (Figure 6–62).

Figure 6–62

Other Ways

1. Open Control Panel, change to Large or Small icons, click AutoPlay

To Revert an AutoPlay Setting

The following steps open the AutoPlay window and change the action of the 'Software and games' media type to 'Ask me every time'.

1

- Click the 'Change default settings for media or devices' link to open the AutoPlay window.

- Click the 'Software and games' button to display a list of available actions (Figure 6–63).

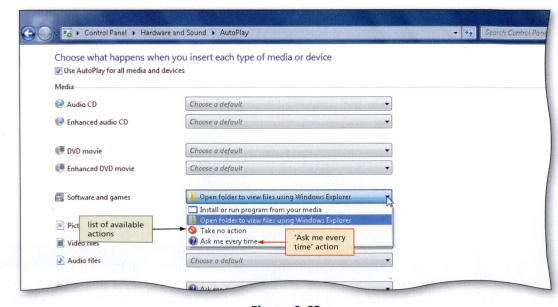

Figure 6–63

2

- Click the 'Ask me every time' action to change the default action (Figure 6–64).

- Save the changes and return to the Hardware and Sound window.

What if 'Ask me every time' was not the original action set for 'Software and games' on my computer?

Click the action that was selected before you changed the action. Your lab administrators might have set a different default action for 'Software and games' or might have set no action at all. If no action at all is set, you will see the message 'Choose a default'.

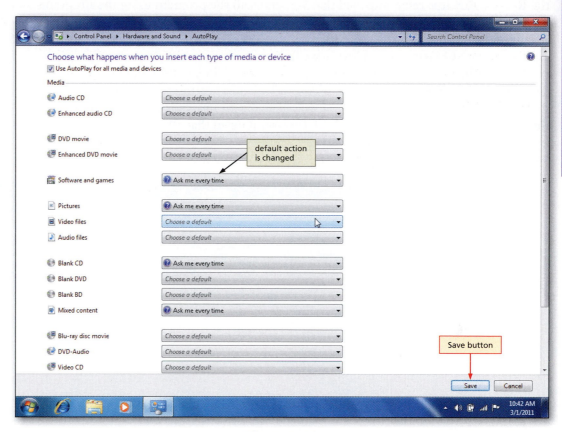

Figure 6–64

The Programs Window

The Programs window brings together all of the tools you need when working with the various programs on your computer. From the Programs window, you can uninstall programs, configure older programs to run in Windows 7, and turn a variety of Windows features on and off. You also can access Windows Defender (covered in Appendix B), set your default programs, configure a second display device using SideShow, work with the desktop gadgets (which you learned about in Chapters 1 and 2), and access the Personalization Gallery online. In this section, you will install and uninstall a program as these are among the most common program tasks that users perform.

To Uninstall a Program

Some programs include uninstall options as a part of their installation. For example, some programs, when installed, add a folder to the Start menu which includes an uninstall command that you can use to run the uninstall program. Other programs do not offer an uninstall option or a folder on the Start menu. Instead, a menu command is available during the installation process to uninstall the software. Other programs must be removed by deleting the files that compose the program. Although you can remove programs by dragging the program's folder to the Recycle Bin, it is recommended that you uninstall the program using the Programs and Features window. This ensures that the program is completely removed from the system without leaving any miscellaneous files to potentially interfere with the normal processes of the computer. Most of the programs you install can be uninstalled from the Programs and Features window as well.

When installing or uninstalling programs, you will be required to provide the proper User Account Control authorization. If you are not using an account with administrator privileges or do not have the user name and password of an administrator account, you will be unable to install or uninstall a program. The following steps uninstall the Microsoft Silverlight plug-in, a Web browser plug-in that allows you to view high-definition media files on the Internet, using the Programs and Features window.

- Click the Programs link in the left pane to display the Programs window (Figure 6–65).

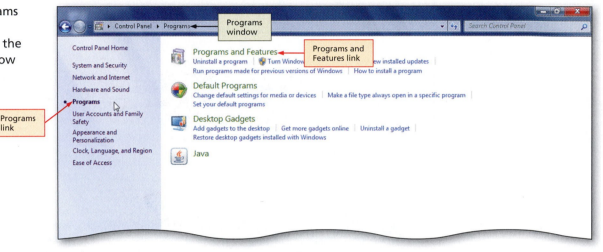

Figure 6–65

2

- Click the Programs and Features link to open the Programs and Features window (Figure 6–66).

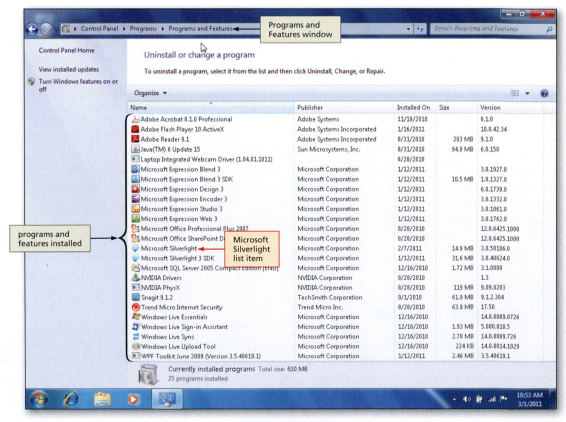

Figure 6–66

3

- Click the Microsoft Silverlight list item to select it (Figure 6–67).

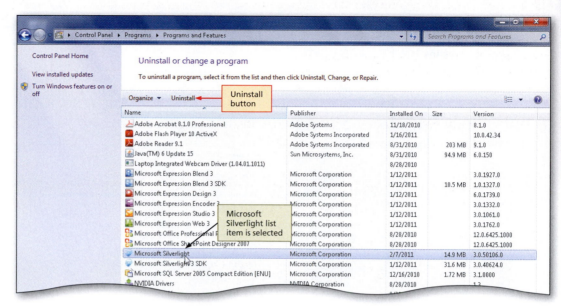

Figure 6–67

4

- Click the Uninstall button to display the Programs and Features dialog box (Figure 6–68).

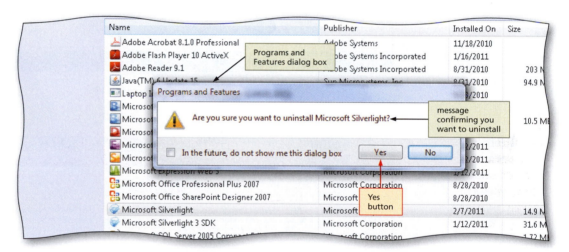

Figure 6–68

5

- Click the Yes button to confirm that you want to uninstall Microsoft Silverlight, display the Windows Installer dialog box, and begin the uninstall process (Figure 6–69). If the User Account Control dialog box displays, click the Yes button.

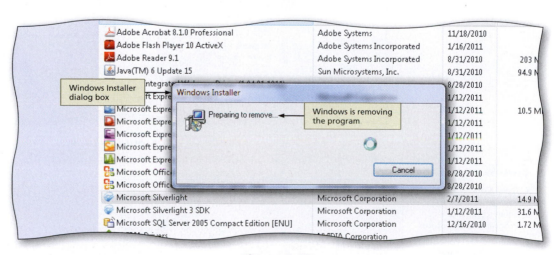

Figure 6–69

6

- After a short amount of time, the uninstall process finishes (Figure 6–70).

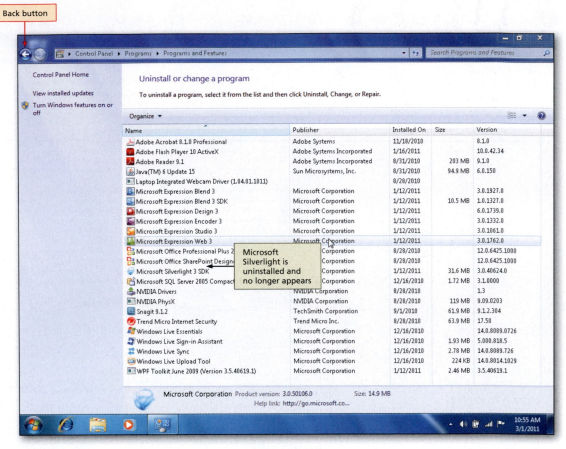

Figure 6–70

7

- Return to the Control Panel window (Figure 6–71).

Figure 6–71

Other Ways

1. Open Control Panel, change to Large or Small icons, click Programs and Features
2. Open Control Panel, click 'Uninstall a program'

To Install a Program

In previous versions of Windows, you could install a program using Control Panel. In Windows 7, you install a program by inserting the optical disc or USB flash drive that has the program you want to install and running its install program, or you can download and install a program from the Internet.

The following steps reinstall Microsoft Silverlight. It is important to note that due to different computer configurations, and because Web sites on the Internet frequently change, the steps required to download Microsoft Silverlight might vary slightly from the following steps. If you are having difficulty locating the Microsoft Silverlight program online, contact your instructor. If you do not have administrative privileges or you do not have access to administrative logon information, read the following steps without performing them.

1 Start Internet Explorer.

2 If necessary, maximize the Windows Internet Explorer window.

3 Type `microsoft.com/silverlight/` in the Address bar and then press the ENTER key to display the Microsoft Silverlight Web page.

4 Click the 'Experience this in Silverlight Install the free Plug-in' link to display the Microsoft Silverlight download dialog box.

5 Click the Run button in the File Download dialog box to download Microsoft Silverlight.

6 Click the Run button in the Internet Explorer dialog box to run the installation program. If necessary, click the Yes button in the User Account Control dialog box to continue installation.

7 Click the Install now button in the Install Silverlight dialog box to install Microsoft Silverlight.

8 Click the Close button to close the Installation successful dialog box.

9 Close the Internet Explorer window.

The User Accounts and Family Safety Window

From the User Accounts and Family Safety window, you can create and manage user accounts, set up parental controls for accounts, configure Windows CardSpace, and set up Mail profiles. The three types of user accounts (Administrator, Standard, and Guest) have different levels of access to the computer. The privileges of the Administrator, Standard, and Guest user accounts are summarized in Table 6–1 on the next page. For Standard accounts that will be used by children, you also can set up parental controls so that the child is restricted from performing certain actions such as playing games with certain ratings or browsing the Internet for too long.

BTW

Windows CardSpace
Windows CardSpace is used to create and manage a set of digital identities, similar to phone book entries, that can be shared with Web sites that support the technology. These cards can be used to replace the user names and passwords you use to register and log on to Web sites.

Table 6–1 User Accounts and Privileges	
User Accounts	**Privileges**
Administrator	• Creates, changes, and deletes user accounts and groups • Installs programs • Sets folder sharing • Sets permissions • Accesses all files • Takes ownership of files • Grants rights to other user accounts and to themselves • Installs or removes hardware devices • Logs on in safe mode
Standard	• Changes the password and picture for their own user accounts • Uses programs that have been installed on the computer • Views permissions • Creates, changes, and deletes files in their libraries • Views files in shared document folders
Guest	• Same as Standard account, but cannot create a password • Is turned off by default, and must be turned on before it can be used

To View Account Information

If you have administrative privileges, you can do more than simply view account information for all user accounts. You also can change a user account, create a new user account, and change the way users log on or off. You also can turn User Account Control on and off; however, it is not recommended that you turn it off. If you do not have administrative privileges, only information about your account will be visible. The following steps display your account information.

• Click the User Accounts and Family Safety link in the Control Panel window to display the User Accounts and Family Safety window (Figure 6–72).

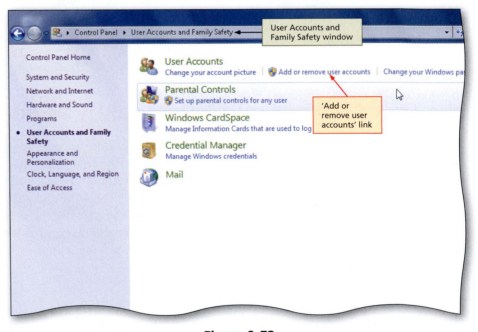

Figure 6–72

- Click the 'Add or remove user accounts' link to display the Manage Accounts window (Figure 6–73).

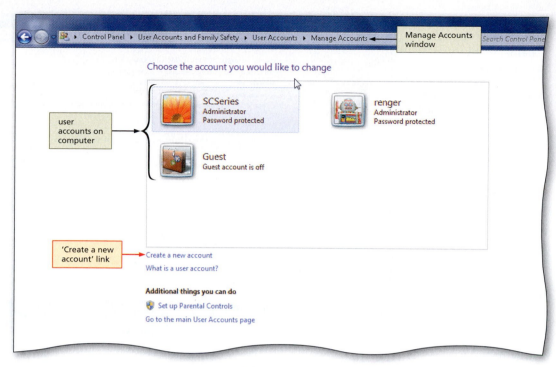

Figure 6–73

To Create a User Account

If you have administrative privileges, you can create a new user account. When you create a new user account and use the default settings, Windows 7 creates a standard account with no password. To make the account more secure after you create it, you can view the account information and add a password. The steps on the following page create the SCStudent user account as a standard account and display its information.

- Click the 'Create a new account' link to display the Create New Account window (Figure 6–74).

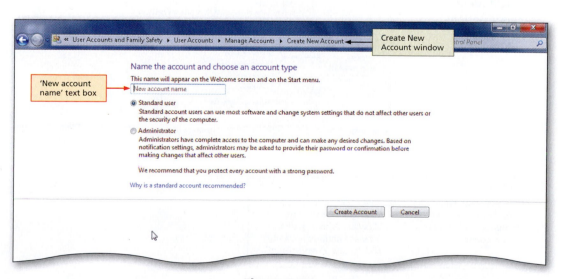

Figure 6–74

2

- Type SCStudent in the 'New account name' text box (Figure 6–75).

- If necessary, click the Standard user option button.

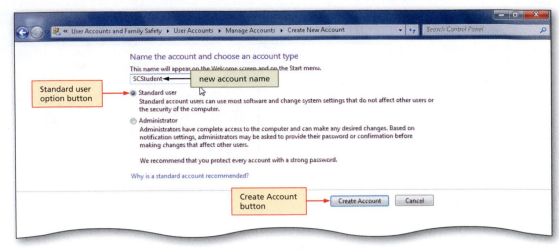

Figure 6–75

3

- Click the Create Account button to create the SCStudent user account (Figure 6–76).

Figure 6–76

4

- Click the SCStudent icon to view the SCStudent account options (Figure 6–77).

Figure 6–77

Other Ways

1. Open Control Panel, click 'Add or remove user accounts,' click 'Create a new account'

2. Open Control Panel, change to Large or Small icons, click User Accounts, click 'Manage another account,' click 'Create a new account'

To Switch to a Different User

Even though you currently are logged on with your own user account, you can switch to a different user account without logging off of your account. In fact, you do not even have to close any open windows when switching to a different user account, as Windows 7 maintains separate desktops for each user. The following steps switch to the SCStudent account, and then log off and return to your user account.

- Display the Start menu.

- Point to the arrow to the right of the Shut down button to display the 'Shut down options' menu (Figure 6–78).

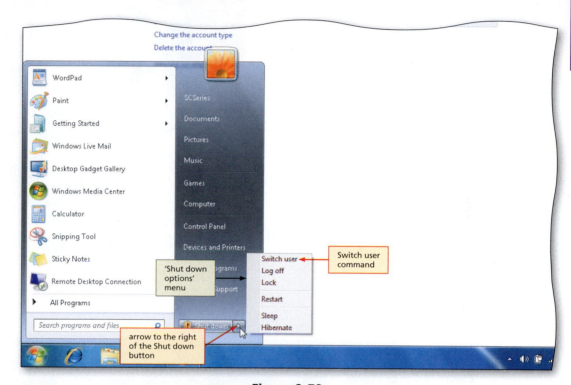

Figure 6–78

- Click the Switch user command to display the Welcome Screen (Figure 6–79).

- Click the SCStudent icon to log on.

- After the Preparing Your Desktop message disappears, the SCStudent desktop is displayed.

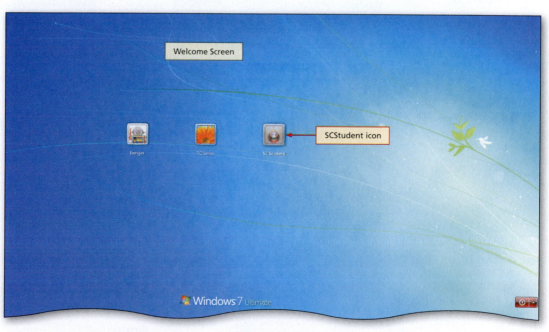

Figure 6–79

4

- After reviewing the desktop for SCStudent, display the Start menu.

- Point to the arrow to the right of the Shut down button to display the 'Shut down options' menu (Figure 6–80).

Figure 6–80

5

- Click the Log off command to log off the SCStudent account and display the Welcome Screen (Figure 6–81).

- Click SCSeries icon (or your icon) to switch back to your user account.

- If necessary, enter your password.

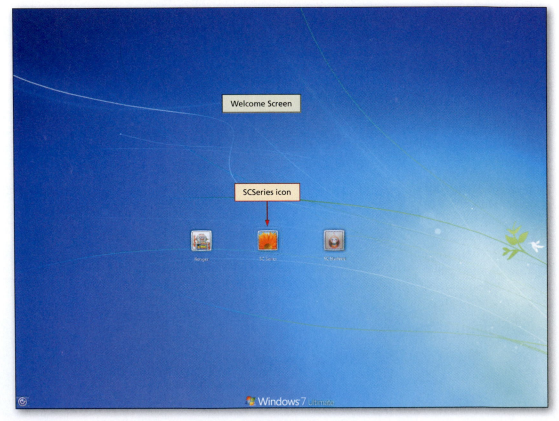

Figure 6–81

6

- Click the arrow button to display your user account (Figure 6–82).

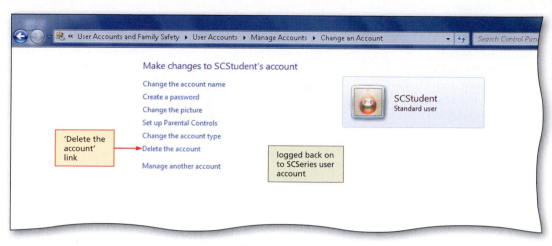

Figure 6–82

To Delete a User Account

When you no longer have a need for a particular user account, you should delete it from your computer. The following steps delete the SCStudent account.

1

- If necessary, make the Change an Account window the active window.

- Click the 'Delete the account' link to display the Delete Account window (Figure 6–83).

Figure 6–83

2

- Click the Delete Files button to delete the files associated with the SCStudent user account and display the Confirm Deletion window (Figure 6–84).

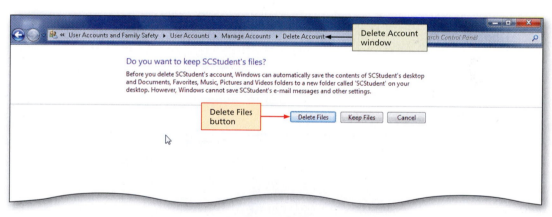

Q&A

Do I have to delete the files?

You can keep a copy of the files associated with the user account you are deleting, but because the SCStudent account was created for demonstration purposes, there is no need to keep the files.

Figure 6–84

3

- Click the Delete Account button to confirm that you want to delete the user account and return to the Manage Accounts window (Figure 6–85).

Figure 6–85

4

- Click the Control Panel button to return to the Control Panel window (Figure 6–86).

Figure 6–86

Time Servers

If you always want the date and time on your computer to be correct and you have an Internet connection, you might consider retrieving this information from an Internet time server. When you configure Windows 7 to synchronize the date and time with a time server (the default time server is time.windows. com), your computer periodically will check its date and time against the time server to make sure that it is correct.

The Clock, Language, and Region Window

The Clock, Language, and Region window includes the controls for setting the date and time and adjusting the Region and Language options. The Date and Time dialog box is where you can change the date, time, and time zone; add additional clocks; and alter Internet time settings. You can use the Internet time settings to automatically synchronize the time and date on the computer with the time and date on an Internet time server. The Region and Language dialog box is where you can change and customize date formats, change the country programs used when providing localized information, change keyboards and languages, and make other administrative changes related to the language you choose to use with Windows 7.

To Change the Date and Time

Changes to the date and time are made in the Date and Time Settings dialog box. Administrative privileges are required to change the date and time. The following steps change the date and time, and then cancel the changes. If you do not have administrative privileges, read the following steps without performing them.

1

- Click the Clock, Language, and Region link in the Control Panel window to display the Clock, Language, and Region window (Figure 6–87).

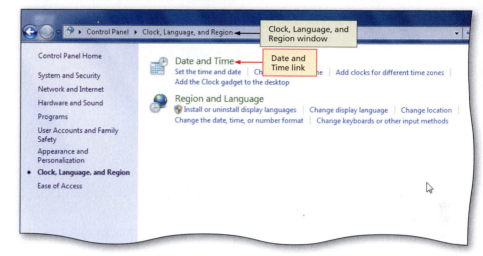

Figure 6–87

2

- Click the Date and Time link to display the Date and Time dialog box (Figure 6–88).

Q&A Do I need to manually adjust the clock for daylight savings time?

No. Windows 7 automatically changes the time for daylight savings time.

Q&A Should I change the time or the time zone if I travel?

If you travel to a different time zone, you can use the 'Change time zone' button to update the day and time on your computer so that the clock displays the correct time, or you can configure an additional clock to display the time and date of your destination.

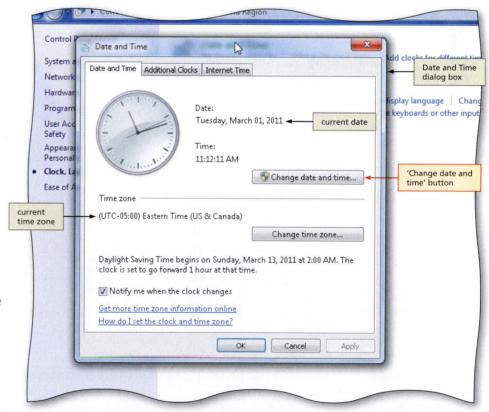

Figure 6–88

- Click the 'Change date and time' button to display the Date and Time Settings dialog box (Figure 6–89).

- If necessary, click the Continue button in the User Account Control dialog box.

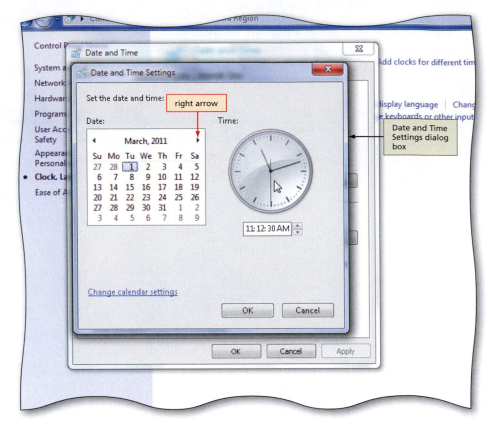

Figure 6–89

- Click the right month arrow until the month changes to November (Figure 6–90). If November already is the current month, you do not need to click the right arrow.

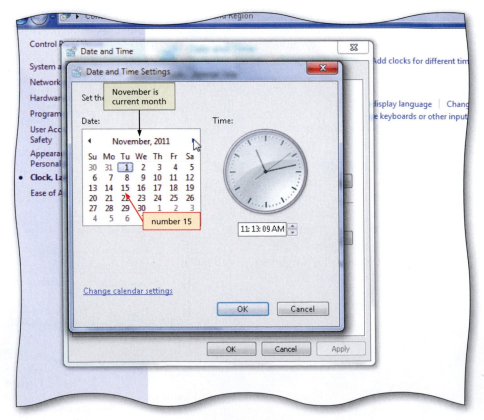

Figure 6–90

5

- Click the number 15 in the monthly calendar to select November 15 (Figure 6–91).

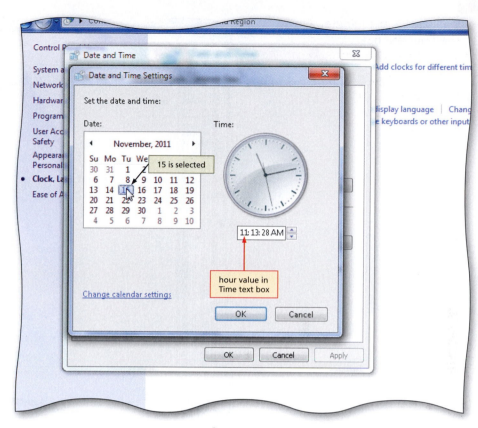

Figure 6–91

6

- Double-click the hour value in the Time text box, and then type 9 as the new value to change the hour (Figure 6–92).

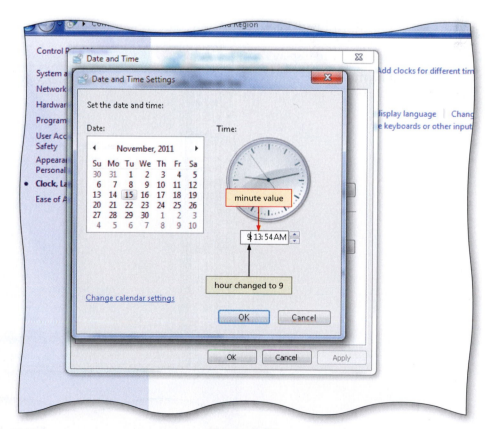

Figure 6–92

7

• Double-click the minute value in the Time text box.

• Type 00 as the new value to change the minute (Figure 6–93).

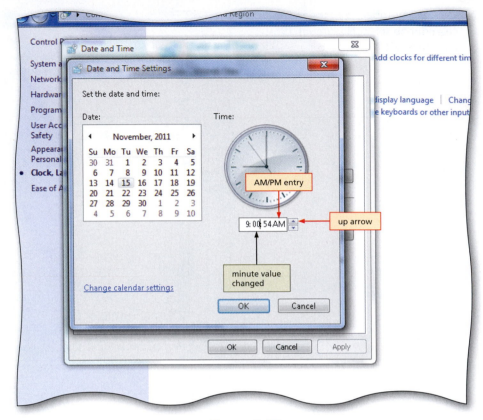

Figure 6–93

8

• If the PM entry displays in the time text box, click the PM entry and then click the up arrow to display the AM entry (Figure 6–94).

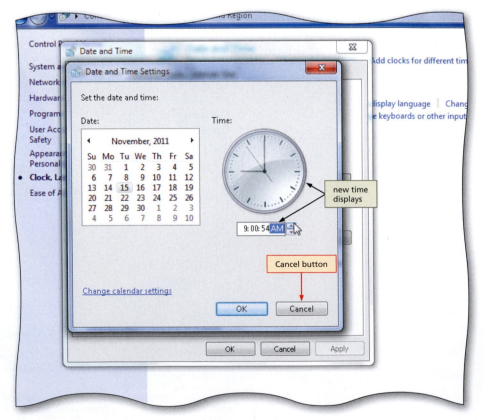

Figure 6–94

9

- Click the Cancel button to cancel the changes and return to the Date and Time dialog box (Figure 6–95).

Q&A

What if I want to save the date and time changes?

If you want to save the date and time changes, you should click the OK button instead of the Cancel button.

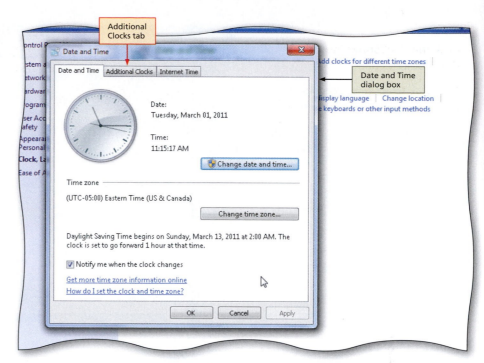

Figure 6–95

Other Ways

1. In notification area, right-click time, click 'Adjust date/time'

2. Open Control Panel, change to Large or Small icons, click Date and Time

To Add a Second Clock

Windows 7 can display several clocks besides the default clock in the notification area. Each clock that you add can show the time for a different time zone. International students, business travelers, and tourists might find it useful to have a clock to show the time in the location they are visiting, as well as the time in their home location. The following steps add a second clock to show Hawaii time, display it in the notification area, and then delete it.

1

- Click the Additional Clocks tab to display the Additional Clocks sheet (Figure 6–96).

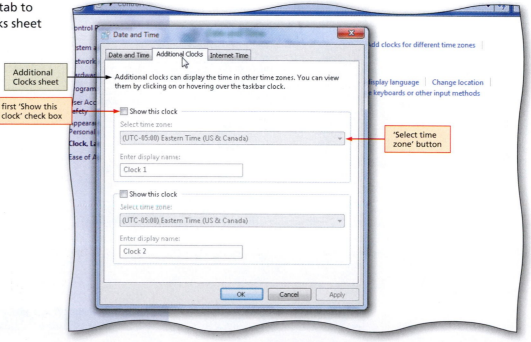

Figure 6–96

2

- Click the first 'Show this clock' check box to enable it.

- Click the Select time zone button to display a list of time zones.

- If necessary, scroll until you see the Hawaii list item (Figure 6–97).

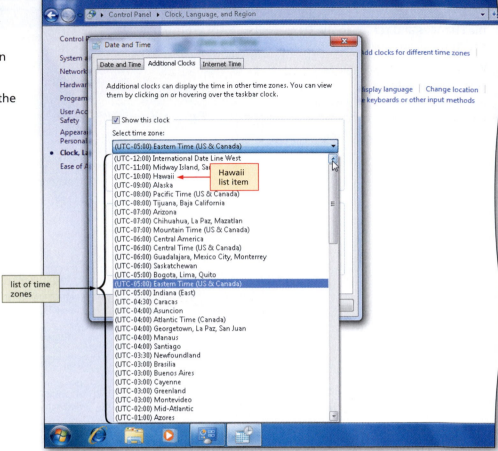

Figure 6–97

3

- Click the Hawaii list item to select it. If your time zone already is set for Hawaii, select another time zone.

- Type Hawaii in the 'Enter display name' text box to name the clock (Figure 6–98). If you selected a different time zone, enter an appropriate name for the clock.

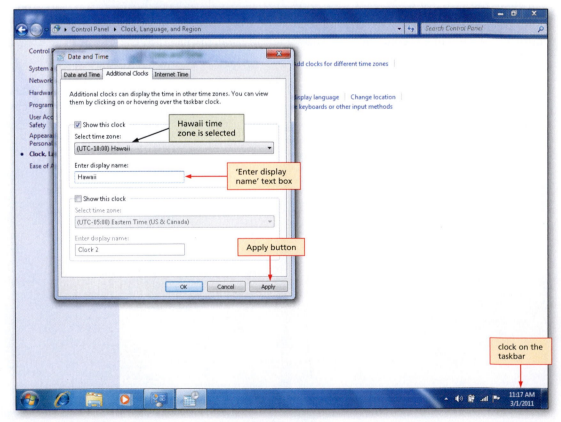

Figure 6–98

4

- Click the Apply button to apply the changes.

- Point to the clock on the taskbar to display the additional clock (Figure 6–99).

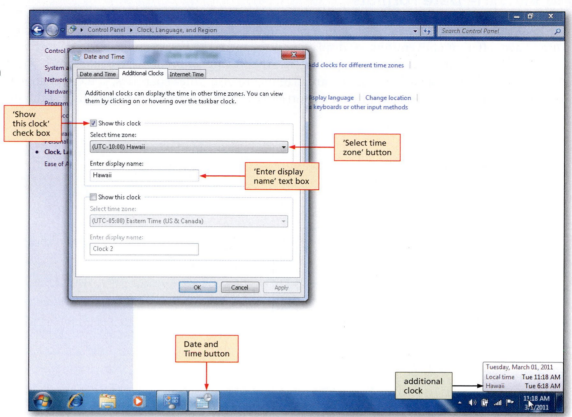

Figure 6–99

5

- Click the Date and Time button on the taskbar to activate the Date and Time dialog box.

- Type Clock 1 in the 'Enter display name' text box.

- Change the time zone back to the Eastern Time (US & Canada) setting, or your original time zone.

- Click the 'Show this clock' check box to deselect it (Figure 6–100).

- Click the OK button to apply the changes and close the Date and Time dialog box.

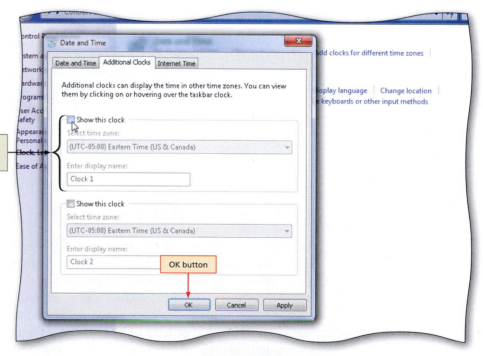

Figure 6–100

Other Ways	
1. Right-click time on taskbar, click 'Adjust date/time', click Additional Clocks	2. Open Control Panel, change to Large or Small icons, click Date and Time, click Additional Clocks

To View the Date Formats

Windows 7 is designed to work in many regions of the world and in many different languages. Other countries often have different conventions for displaying dates and time. For example, many countries in Europe use the 24-hour clock when displaying time. You can use the Region and Language dialog box to view the formats that Windows 7 uses to display dates. If you are planning to visit other countries, you can change the date formats so that they will match the formats used by the countries you visit. The following steps display the Region and Language dialog box.

1

- Click the Region and Language link to display the Region and Language dialog box (Figure 6–101).

- After viewing the date formats, click the Cancel button to close the dialog box.

Experiment

- Try changing the current format selection and review the various date formats used by other countries that Windows 7 supports.

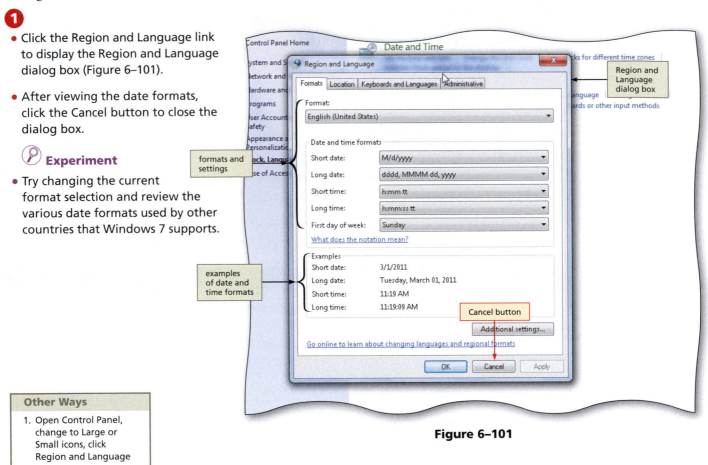

Figure 6–101

Other Ways

1. Open Control Panel, change to Large or Small icons, click Region and Language

---

BTW

Windows 7 Accessibility Features
For more information about the accessibility features of Windows 7, visit the Windows 7 Accessibility Web Page (scsite.com/win7/access).

The Ease of Access Center

Windows 7 provides customization tools for people who are mobility, hearing, or vision impaired, which are known as **accessibility features**. All of the accessibility features can be found in the Ease of Access Center. People who have restricted movement and cannot move the mouse (mobility impaired) have the option of using Mouse Keys that allow them to use the numeric keypad to move the mouse pointer, click, double-click, and drag. People who are deaf or hard of hearing (hearing impaired) can enable Sound Sentry, which generates visual warnings when the computer makes a sound and can turn on captions when a program speaks or makes sounds, if captions are available. People who have difficulty seeing the screen (vision impaired) can select a High Contrast theme. High Contrast themes rely on a black or white background and bold colors to create a greater contrast between objects on the screen, which improves an individual's ability to read the text. Windows 7 also offers Narrator, which translates text to speech, and Magnifier, which creates a separate window to display a magnified part of the screen.

These are just a few of the accessibility features that are available in Windows 7. From the Ease of Access Center, you also can access a questionnaire that allows Windows 7 to determine the right accessibility features for you. If you are unsure of where to begin, start with the questionnaire. The following section demonstrates some of the accessibility features.

To View Accessibility Options

The following steps open the Ease of Access Center.

1

- Click the Ease of Access link in the left pane of the Clock, Language, and Region window to open the Ease of Access window (Figure 6–102).

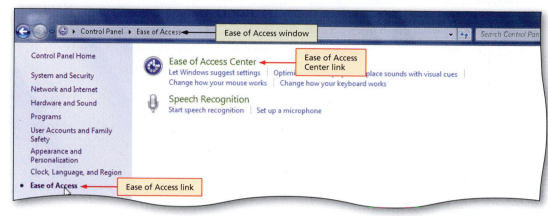

Figure 6–102

2

- Click the Ease of Access Center link to open the Ease of Access Center window.

- If necessary, maximize the Ease of Access Center window (Figure 6–103).

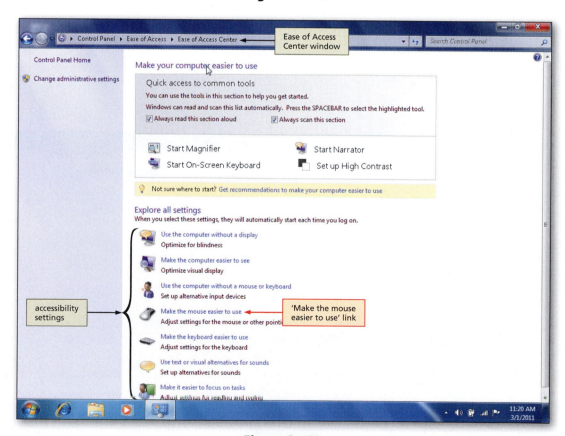

Figure 6–103

Other Ways
1. Press WINDOWS+U
2. Open Control Panel, change to Large or Small icons, click Ease of Access Center

To Use Mouse Keys

Mouse Keys allows you to use the numeric keys on the keypad, instead of a mouse, to move the pointer across the desktop. For example, pressing the 2, 4, 6, or 8 key moves the mouse pointer down, left, right, or up, respectively, while the 5 key is used to select an object. To illustrate the use of an accessibility option, the following steps turn on Mouse Keys, and then turn off Mouse Keys.

- Click the 'Make the mouse easier to use' link to open the 'Make the mouse easier to use' window (Figure 6–104).

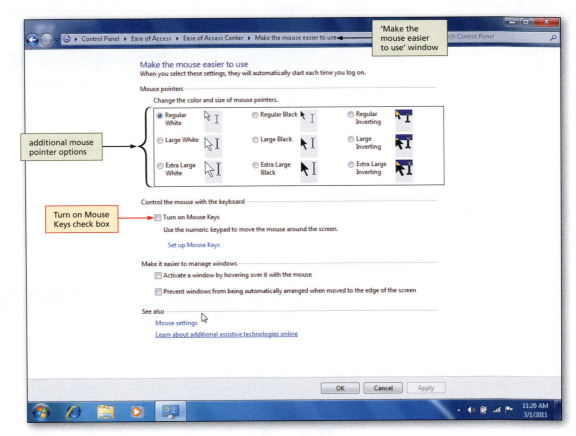

Figure 6–104

2

- Click the Turn on Mouse Keys check box to turn on Mouse Keys (Figure 6–105).

- Click the Apply button to apply the changes.

Q&A

What if I do not have a numeric keypad on my keyboard?

Mouse Keys requires that the keyboard have a numeric keypad. If you do not have a numeric keypad, you will not be able to use Mouse Keys.

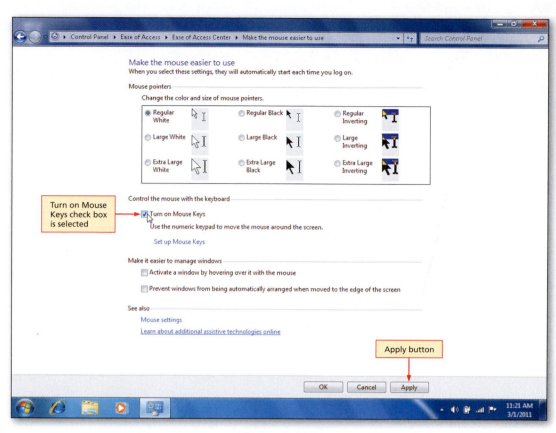

Figure 6–105

3

- Use the 1, 2, 3, 4, 6, 7, 8, and 9 keys on the numeric keypad to move the mouse pointer to the Turn on Mouse Keys check box.

- Press the 5 key to remove the check mark from the Turn on Mouse Keys check box (Figure 6–106).

- Use the numeric keys on the numeric keypad to move the mouse pointer to the Apply button.

- Press the 5 key to click the Apply button to turn off Mouse Keys.

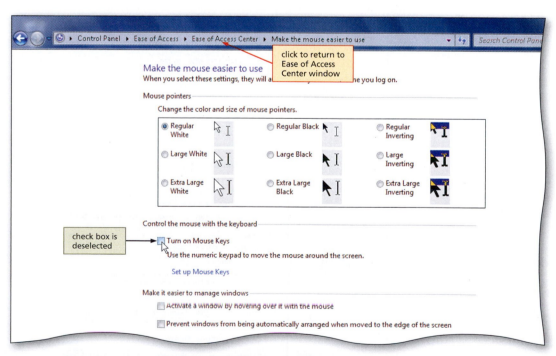

Figure 6–106

4

- Return to the Ease of Access Center window (Figure 6–107).

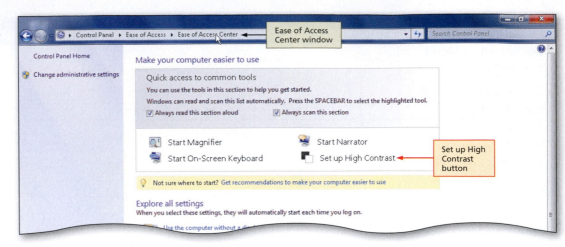

Figure 6–107

Other Ways

1. Open Control Panel, change to Large or Small icons, click Ease of Access Center, click 'Make the mouse easier to use', click
Turn on Mouse Keys, click Apply
2. Press LEFT ALT+LEFT SHIFT+ NUM LOCK

To Turn On High Contrast

High Contrast themes are designed for individuals who are visually impaired. The following steps turn on a High Contrast theme.

1

- Click the Set up High Contrast button to display the 'Make the computer easier to see' window (Figure 6–108).

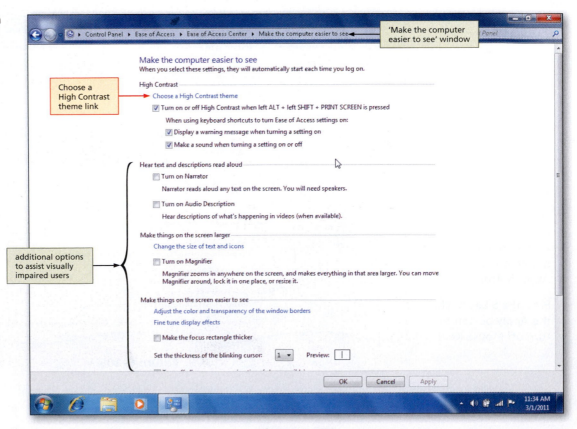

Figure 6–108

2

- Click the Choose a High Contrast theme link to display the Personalization window.

- Make note of the current color scheme being used.

- Scroll down to display the High Contrast themes (Figure 6–109).

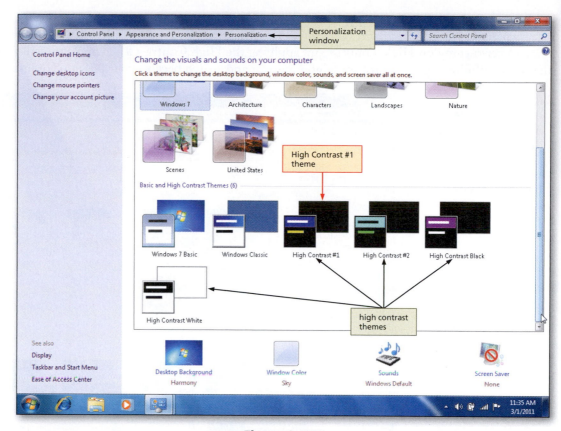

Figure 6–109

3

- Click the High Contrast #1 theme to select and use it (Figure 6–110).

Figure 6–110

Other Ways

1. Press LEFT ALT+LEFT SHIFT+PRINT SCREEN

To Turn Off High Contrast

After turning on High Contrast and applying the High Contrast #1 theme, you will return to the previous theme. The following steps turn off High Contrast and switch back to your previous theme.

1

- Click the theme you noted earlier to select it (Figure 6–111).

- Close the Personalization window.

Figure 6–111

2

- Close the Ease of Access Center window (Figure 6–112).

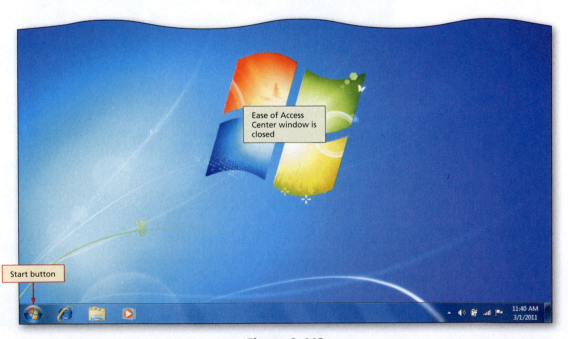

Figure 6–112

Other Ways
1. Press LEFT ALT+LEFT SHIFT+PRINT SCREEN

To Log Off and Turn Off the Computer

After completing your work with Windows 7, you first should close your user account by logging off the computer, and then turn off the computer.

1 On the Start menu, click the Shut down options button, and then click the Log off command to log off the computer.

2 Click the Shut down button to turn off the computer.

Chapter Summary

In this chapter, you have learned how to customize Windows 7 using various links from the Control Panel window. You customized the keyboard, mouse, and date and time. You installed and removed a program, added and deleted a printer, viewed installed updates, and viewed the properties of the hardware devices attached to the computer. Using the Ease of Access Center, you made adjustments to the computer for mobility impaired and visually impaired users. You also created a new user account, switched users while logged on to an account, and deleted a user account. The items listed below include all of the new Windows 7 skills you have learned in this chapter.

1. Open the Control Panel Window (WIN 348)
2. Switch Control Panel Views (WIN 349)
3. Open the System and Security Window (WIN 350)
4. Display the Action Center (WIN 351)
5. View Security and Maintenance Settings in the Action Center (WIN 351)
6. View Windows Firewall Settings (WIN 353)
7. View System Information (WIN 354)
8. View the Windows Experience Index (WIN 354)
9. Open Device Manager (WIN 356)
10. View the Properties of a Device (WIN 356)
11. View Installed Updates (WIN 359)
12. View Available Updates (WIN 360)
13. Add a Printer (WIN 361)
14. Delete a Printer (WIN 366)
15. Change the Mouse Button Configuration (WIN 367)
16. Adjust the Double-Click Speed (WIN 369)
17. Turn On and Use ClickLock (WIN 370)
18. Close the Document and Turn Off ClickLock (WIN 371)
19. Adjust the Pointer Speed (WIN 373)
20. Turn On Snap To (WIN 374)
21. Display a Pointer Trail (WIN 376)
22. Adjust AutoPlay Settings (WIN 377)
23. Revert an AutoPlay Setting (WIN 380)
24. Uninstall a Program (WIN 381)
25. View Account Information (WIN 386)
26. Create a User Account (WIN 387)
27. Switch to a Different User (WIN 389)
28. Delete a User Account (WIN 391)
29. Change the Date and Time (WIN 393)
30. Add a Second Clock (WIN 397)
31. View the Date Formats (WIN 400)
32. View Accessibility Options (WIN 401)
33. Use Mouse Keys (WIN 402)
34. Turn On High Contrast (WIN 404)
35. Turn Off High Contrast (WIN 406)

Learn It Online

Test your knowledge of chapter content and key terms.

Instructions: To complete the Learn It Online exercises, start your browser, click the Address bar, and then enter the Web address scsite.com/win7/learn. When the Windows 7 Learn It Online page is displayed, click the link for the exercise you want to complete and then read the instructions.

Chapter Reinforcement TF, MC, and SA

A series of true/false, multiple-choice, and short-answer questions that test your knowledge of the chapter content.

Flash Cards

An interactive learning environment where you identify chapter key terms associated with displayed definitions.

Practice Test

A series of multiple-choice questions that test your knowledge of chapter content and key terms.

Who Wants To Be a Computer Genius?

An interactive game that challenges your knowledge of chapter content in the style of a television quiz show.

Wheel of Terms

An interactive game that challenges your knowledge of chapter key terms in the style of the television show *Wheel of Fortune*.

Crossword Puzzle Challenge

A crossword puzzle that challenges your knowledge of key terms presented in the chapter.

Apply Your Knowledge

Reinforce the skills and apply the concepts you learned in this chapter.

Adding a Printer

Instructions: You decide to add a Lexmark T650 (MS) printer using the Add Printer Wizard. You must have administrative privileges for this exercise.

Part 1: Installing the Lexmark T650 (MS)Printer
1. Display the Start menu and then click Devices and Printers (Figure 6–113).
2. Click the 'Add a printer' button to run the Add Printer Wizard.
3. Add Lexmark T650 (MS) as a local printer on the LPT1 port.

Part 2: Printing the Contents of the Printers Window
1. Maximize the Devices and Printers window.
2. Press the PRINT SCREEN key on the keyboard to place an image of the desktop on the Clipboard.
3. Display the Start menu, click All Programs, click Accessories, and then click Paint.
4. Maximize the Untitled – Paint window.
5. Paste the image from the Clipboard to the Paint window.
6. Print the Paint document.
7. Quit the Paint program, and do not save the file.

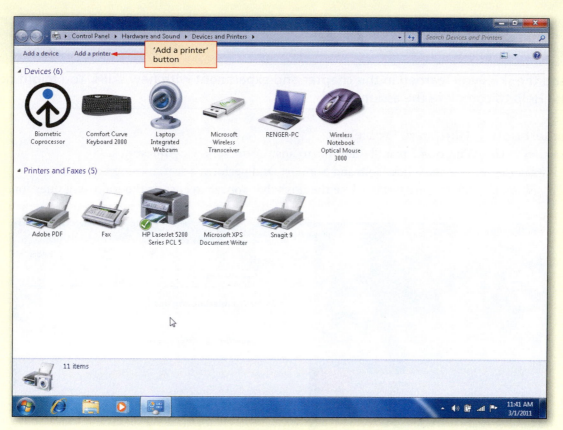

Figure 6–113

Part 3: *Displaying the Properties of the Lexmark T650 (MS) Printer*

1. Right-click the Lexmark T650 (MS) icon and then click Printing preferences on the shortcut menu to display the Lexmark T650 (MS) Printing Preferences dialog box. Using the tabs in the dialog box, answer the following questions.

   a. What is the orientation of the paper?

   _____

   b. What is the page order?

   _____

   c. What is the print quality?

   _____

2. Close the Lexmark T650 (MS) Printing Preferences dialog box.

Part 4: *Deleting the Lexmark T650 (MS) Printer*

1. Right-click the Lexmark T650 (MS) icon and then click Remove device on the shortcut menu.

2. Click the Yes button in the Remove Device dialog box to remove the Lexmark T650 (MS) printer.

3. Close the Devices and Printers window.

4. Submit the printed Paint document and the answers to the questions to your instructor.

Extend Your Knowledge

Extend the skills you learned in this chapter and experiment with new skills. You might need to use Help to complete the assignment.

Troubleshooting Hardware Problems

Instructions: Use Windows 7 troubleshooters to answer the following questions.

1. Display the Start menu, click Help and Support, and perform a search using keywords *Troubleshooting tips* (Figure 6–114). Use the links that appear to answer the following questions.

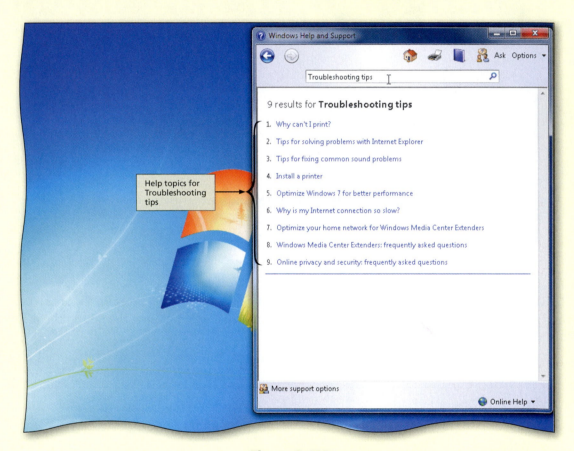

Help topics for Troubleshooting tips

Figure 6–114

   a. Your document does not print at all. How do you troubleshoot it? What suggestions does Windows offer that might help fix your printing problem?

   _____

   b. You are having trouble with your Internet connection being slow. What should you do?

   _____

   c. You are having trouble with Internet Explorer. What should you do?

   _____

   d. You are having sound problems. You decide to see what Windows 7 recommends. What are some of the tips that Windows 7 gives you?

   _____

2. Close the Windows Help and Support window.

In the Lab

Use the guidelines, concepts, and skills presented in this chapter to increase your knowledge of Windows 7. Labs are listed in order of increasing difficulty.

Lab 1: Developing a Control Panel Guide

Instructions: Although most people like to use the Category view when working with Control Panel, your boss favors the Small icons view (Figure 6–115). Your boss asks you to create a Control Panel guide so that other employees can familiarize themselves with the Small icons view and the Control Panel icons. Using WordPad, create a guide with a title and description of the following icons in the Control Panel window: Network and Sharing Center, Windows CardSpace, Performance Information and Tools, and Windows Mobility Center.

Part 1: Launching the WordPad Application
1. Open the Control Panel window and change to Small icons view (Figure 6–115).
2. Open WordPad and maximize the Document - WordPad window.

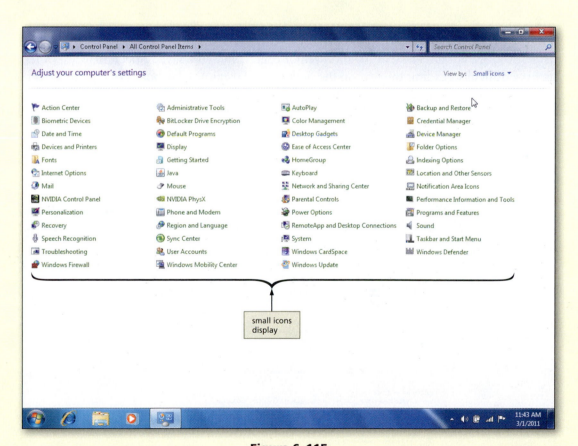

Figure 6–115

Part 2: Creating the Control Panel Guide
1. Type `The Control Panel Window (Small icons view)` as the title.
2. Type a brief statement about how Small icons view is different from the normal Windows 7 Control Panel.
3. Type `Network and Sharing Center` and then type a brief description of the Network and Sharing Center.

Continued >

In the Lab *continued*

4. Type `Windows CardSpace` and then type a brief description of Windows CardSpace.

5. Type `Performance Information and Tools` and then type a brief description of how Performance Information and Tools can be used.

6. Type `Windows Mobility Center` and then type a brief description of the various Windows Mobility Center Settings.

Part 3: Saving and Printing the Control Panel Guide

1. Save the completed document on a USB flash drive using the file name, Control Panel Guide.

2. Print the completed document.

3. Close WordPad and the Control Panel window.

4. Eject the USB flash drive.

5. Submit the Control Panel Guide to your instructor.

In the Lab

Lab 2: Customizing the Computer Using the Ease of Access Center

Instructions: You are volunteering at the local senior center, and you have noticed that a number of the residents have difficulty reading the text on the desktop and using the keyboard to type text. You decide to change the settings to help them access the computer more easily. You will make the screen easier to read and make it easier to type in WordPad. After seeing how these changes helped some of the seniors to use the computer, you decide to explore additional accessibility options.

Part 1: Using Magnifier

1. Open the Ease of Access Center (Figure 6–116).

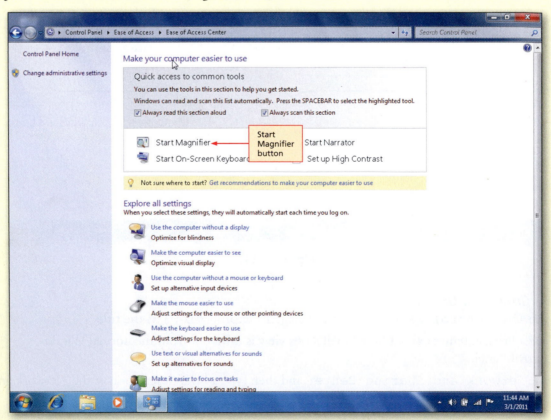

Figure 6–116

2. Click the Start Magnifier button to start the Magnifier and open the Magnifier dialog box.

3. Point to the text in the Magnifier dialog box. What is displayed in the Magnifier dialog box?

_____

4. Click the Help button in the Magnifier dialog box. What Help topic appears? What are the three modes?

_____

5. Click the Minimize button in the Magnifier dialog box. What is displayed in the window at the top of the desktop?

_____

6. Close Magnifier.

Part 2: Using the On-Screen Keyboard
1. Click the Start On-Screen Keyboard link in the Ease of Access Center. The On-Screen Keyboard allows you to type text in a document window using the mouse.

2. If necessary, drag the On-Screen Keyboard window to position the window at the bottom of the desktop.

3. Open WordPad. Resize and position the WordPad window at the top of the desktop.

4. Using the mouse pointer and On-Screen Keyboard, type the following sentence: It is easy to type using the On-Screen Keyboard. and then click the ENTER key on the On-Screen Keyboard two times. (*Hint:* To type using the On-Screen Keyboard, click the key on the On-Screen Keyboard corresponding to the character you want to type. Click the SHIFT key on the On-Screen Keyboard to capitalize text. Click the SPACEBAR on the On-Screen Keyboard to insert a blank space.)

5. Use the On-Screen Keyboard to type your first and last name and then click the ENTER key.

6. Print the document.

7. Close the On-Screen Keyboard window and then close WordPad without saving your changes.

Part 3: Letting Windows Help You Configure Settings
1. Open the Personalization window from the Control Panel window, and write down the name of the current theme:

_____

2. Return to the Ease of Access Center and click the 'Get recommendations to make your computer easier to use' link. As you answer the questions in the accessibility questionnaire, select the appropriate options as if you had a visibility and hearing impairment.

3. After you complete the questionnaire, turn on the suggested options.

Part 4: Working with Accessibility Settings
1. Display the Start menu.

   a. What color is the background color on the Start menu?

   _____

   b. Did the size of the commands on the Start menu change? If so, how?

   _____

   c. Is each icon on the Start menu fully visible?

   _____

Continued >

In the Lab *continued*

2. Open and maximize the Control Panel window.

   a. Are the icons in the Control Panel window easy to see?

   _____

3. Close the Control Panel window.

Part 5: Restoring the Default Settings

1. Restore the Theme to the original theme you noted in Part 3, Step 1.

2. Turn off the options you turned on in the Ease of Access Center.

3. Submit the printed WordPad document and the answers to the questions to your instructor.

In the Lab

Lab 3: Creating an Account with Parental Controls

Instructions: Your skills with Windows 7 are becoming well known. Your neighbor asks for help in setting up Parental Controls for her children. Before you make changes to your neighbor's computer, you decide to research how to use Parental Controls, and then you create an account to test them.

Part 1: Understanding Parental Controls

1. Open Windows Help and Support.

2. Answer the following questions concerning Parental Controls.

   a. Can you control when and how long a child can use the computer? If so, how?

   _____

   b. What can you adjust concerning games that a child can play on the computer?

   _____

   c. Can you limit the programs that a child can use? If so, how?

   _____

Part 2: Creating a User Account and Turning on Parental Controls

1. Open User Accounts and Family Safety and click the 'Add or remove user accounts' link.

2. Click the 'Create a new account' link and create a new standard user account with kidFriendly as the user name.

3. Change the user icon to the robot icon. (*Hint:* Click the icon assigned to the kidFriendly account and then click the 'Change the picture' link.)

4. After creating the account, return to the User Accounts and Family Safety window, and then click the Parental Controls link (Figure 6–117). If the Windows Live Family Safety Filter dialog box is displayed, click the Close button on the title bar.

5. Click kidFriendly to set up Parental Controls for the kidFriendly account from the User Controls window.

6. Click the 'On, enforce current settings' option to turn on Parental Controls., and then click OK.

7. Click the Off link to the right of Time Limits to activate this control. Restrict the kidFriendly account to three hours a day.

8. Click the Off link to the right of Game Ratings to activate this control. Click the 'Set game ratings' link. Select the 'Block games with no rating' and the Early Childhood options.

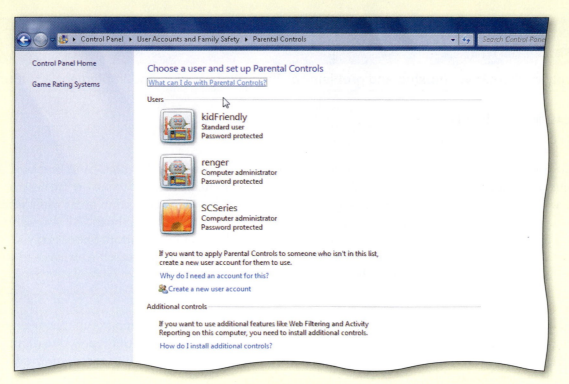

Figure 6–117

9. In addition to setting time limits and controlling which games a user account can play, what other programs on your computer might you consider blocking children from accessing?

_____

Part 3:   Testing Parental Controls
  1. Switch to the kidFriendly account. Can you access the account or is this time blocked?

  _____

  2. Open the Games folder on the Start menu. What games do you see?

  _____

  3. In the User Controls window for kidFriendly, click View activity reports. What does the activity report display?

  _____

  4. What content, if any, was blocked?

  _____

Part 4:   Restoring Default Settings
  1. Return to the User Controls window.
  2. Turn off Parental Controls.
  3. Return to the Manage Accounts window. Delete the kidFriendly user account.
  4. Submit your answers for this lab to your instructor.

Cases and Places

Apply your creative thinking and problem-solving skills to design and implement a solution.

• EASIER   •• MORE DIFFICULT

• 1 Helping a Friend

Your friend recently purchased a new computer. She wants to customize the mouse and keyboard. She wants to change the mouse pointer to add a pointer shadow to make it easier to see on the desktop, and she wants to slow down the cursor blink rate, to make it easier to see the insertion point while word processing. (*Hint:* Cursor blink rate appears in the keyboard properties dialog box.) She also wants to see a pointer trail. She is left-handed and has trouble using the left mouse button. She asks if you would write down the instructions for these changes so she can make the changes herself. You agree to write the instructions and print a copy for her.

• 2 Researching Wireless USB Devices

Windows 7 supports the use of wireless USB devices. Using the Internet, computer magazines, or other resources, collect information about wireless USB devices. Prepare a brief report describing how wireless USB devices work, and the problem these devices solve. Include a list of three wireless USB devices currently available for sale, their cost, and where you can purchase them.

•• 3 Configuring Accessibility Options

One of your close friends has physical limitations that interfere with his use of the computer. He asks you to help him customize the keyboard to his specific needs. He is unable to hold down the ALT, CTRL, or SHIFT key while pressing another key and would prefer to use the keyboard instead of the mouse. He also would like to control the mouse pointer using the keys on the numeric keypad. List two accessibility options you can use to help your friend. Summarize each accessibility option, including how you use the keyboard with and without the option.

•• 4 Troubleshooting Installation Problems

Make It Personal

On a Monday night, you purchase and install a new DVD burner and video card on the computer. The process involves installing the devices and their device drivers. Tuesday morning, you turn on the computer and nothing happens. The Windows 7 operating system will not launch. You assume it must be a problem resulting from the installation last night. Instead of calling technical support, your friend suggests you investigate the problem using safe mode to launch the computer. Windows Help and Support contains information about safe mode and other features that allow you to repair a system. Write a brief report explaining these features.

•• 5 Researching Networking Usage Standards

Working Together

Many companies maintain a Standards and Procedures manual to outline the standards for using a computer on their network. Topics often include the procedures for adding new hardware, adding and removing applications, and customizing a company computer. Working with classmates, research a small, medium, and large company online to find out if, and how, each company handles computer standards and procedures. Prepare a brief report summarizing the standards and procedures developed for each company. In the report, make recommendations for best practices based on what you found.

7 | Advanced File Searching

Objectives

You will have mastered the material in this chapter when you can:

- Understand advanced searching techniques
- Find a file by using Boolean operators
- Search for a file by specifying properties
- View and modify the index

- Search for media files using specialized properties
- Save a search and find a file using a saved search
- Expand Start menu searches

7 | Advanced File Searching

Introduction

In addition to the search techniques you learned in previous chapters, other methods for searching are available in Windows 7. Searching for files and folders can be an everyday activity. If you want to work with your budget, you need your budget files. If you want to edit some photos, you need to locate your photos. If you want to send an important document to a colleague, you need to know where the document is located.

Windows 7 provides a variety of methods for searching. The easiest method is to use the Search box in the folder or library where the files you are searching for should be located. You performed this basic type of search in earlier chapters. Another way is to use file list headings to organize your files so that you can find items faster. You can use file list headings to organize the contents of folders by filtering or sorting items, after which you can search to find what you want. If you are unable to find your files in one folder, you can use the customize option to change the search location without having to completely re-create the search. Finally, you can search from the Start menu to locate your programs and files. The Start menu offers efficient searching without first having to open a folder.

In this chapter, you will learn how to use these search tools and how indexing decreases search times. You will search for files on the local hard disk by specifying the date, file type, or word or phrase that appears in the file. You also will learn techniques for searching for digital media files (photos, music, and video files) as well as document files (Figure 7–1).

Overview

As you read this chapter, you will learn how to use file and folder search options by performing these general tasks:

- Understanding Boolean operators
- Searching using natural language
- Modifying and limiting searches
- Adding a folder to and removing a folder from the index
- Using advanced search options
- Searching for media files using specialized properties
- Saving and reusing searches
- Expanding searches using the Start menu

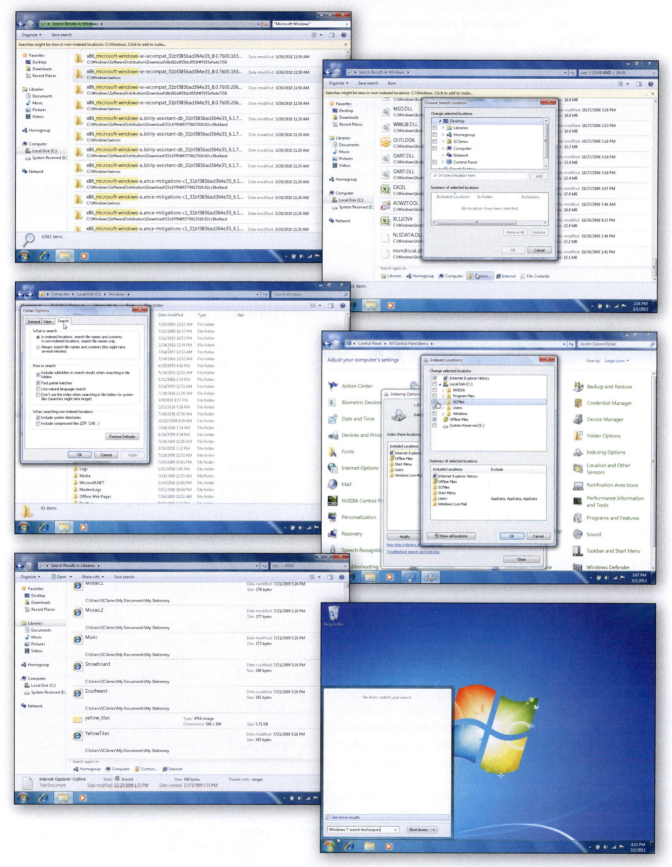

Figure 7–1

Plan Ahead

Advanced File Searching

Advanced file searching requires a basic knowledge of how to open the Search folder window and open personal folders.

1. **Determine the permissions you have on the computer you will be using.** Each user account can have different rights and permissions. Depending on which rights and permissions have been set for your account, you might or might not be able to perform certain operations.

2. **Determine if you have Internet access.** For this chapter, you will be accessing the Internet to search for infomation. You will want to know if your computer has Internet access and if anything is required of you to use it.

3. **Find out if you have access to the sample files installed with Windows 7.** To complete the steps in this chapter, you will need access to the sample pictures, videos, and sounds installed with Windows 7.

Advanced Searching Techniques

As you learned in earlier chapters, you can perform searches in any folder by using the Search box. This works well if the files you want to find are in the folder you are searching. When using the Search box, you simply type a keyword, and Windows 7 searches for matches. Search results can include all or part of a file name, a file type, a tag for a file, or any other file property. For example, if you enter the word, text, into the Search box, all files with *text* in the title will be found along with all files of type text, with a tag value of text, or any other file property with the value of text.

When designing a search, it can be helpful to consider what you know as well as what you do not know. Try to think of keywords or parts of keywords that you can use in your search. The more specific the keywords, the more likely that you will locate the files you want. The keywords can be any part of the file name or located in tags or properties. Keywords also do not have to be complete words. Recall that in Chapter 3, you used an * (asterisk) as part of your searches. Known as a wildcard, the * takes the place of one or more characters when part of your keyword is unknown. For example, searchng for *rd would result in matches for all words that end in rd, such as word, board, and herd, whereas *.bmp would match all files that have a file name extension of .bmp. If you know that a file you want to find begins with the letter, h, and ends with the letter, o, you can use the wildcard to create the search keyword, h*o. Perhaps you know that the file is an MP3, but you only know that the name has the word, hey, as part of it. You are unsure if it begins with hey, has hey in the middle, or ends with hey. You would use *hey*.mp3 to find all MP3 files with the word, hey, in the file name.

You also can design a **Boolean search**, which is a type of search that uses Boolean operators. A **Boolean operator** is used to expand or narrow a search. Table 7–1 lists the Boolean operators with examples and explanations. If you know that a photo you want to find was taken on vacation and you added the tag, our vacation, to your photos as well as saved them as JPEG files; you could structure your search as follows: *.jpg AND tag: our vacation. Be aware that the Boolean operators AND, NOT, and OR must be typed in all capital letters. If you type them in lowercase, Windows 7 will not treat the word as a Boolean operator. Also, you only can use one Boolean operator in a search at a time.

Table 7–1 Boolean Operators

Boolean Operator	Example	Search Results
AND '+' (plus)	text AND type: TXT	Finds all files with text as part of a property with a file type of TXT
OR '-' (hyphen)	text OR WordPad	Finds all files with either text or WordPad as part of a property (name, tag, file type, etc.)
NOT	June NOT bug	Finds all files with June as part of a property but they will not have bug as part of any property
<	date: < 11/11/2012	Finds all files with a date property value of before 11/11/2012
>	size: > 20 MB	Finds all files with a size property value of greater than 20 MB
" "	"Sunny day"	Finds all files with the exact phrase "Sunny day" as part of a property
( )	(Sunny day)	Finds all files with both Sunny and day as part of a property; the order of the keywords does not matter

BTW

Years
When you type numbers in the Search box, Windows 7 searches for files that match the number. If you type a four-digit number such as 2012, the search results will include files that have any of their date properties matching the year 2012. This is convenient if the only fact you can recall about a file you want to find is that it was created in a particular year.

To Search Using Boolean Operators

The following steps use the Boolean operator, AND, to find all files that have the keywords koala and jpg.

1

- Open the Computer window.

- Display the contents of the Local Disk (C:).

- Maximize the Computer window.

- Double-click the Windows folder in the right pane to open the Windows folder (Figure 7–2).

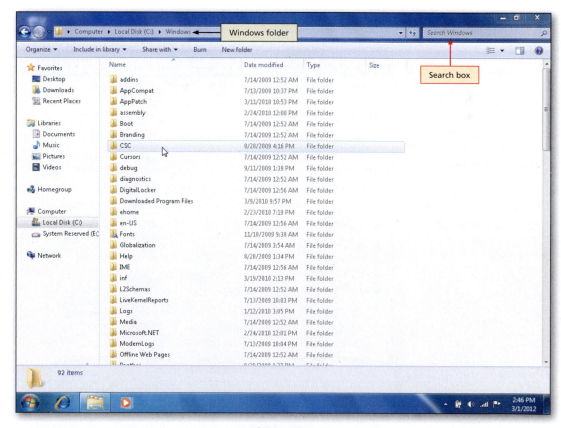

Figure 7–2

2

- Type `koala AND jpg` into the Search box to specify what you want to find and press the ENTER key (Figure 7–3).

Q&A

Why do my results differ from the figure?

Depending upon your computer's configuration, you might have different files appear or none at all.

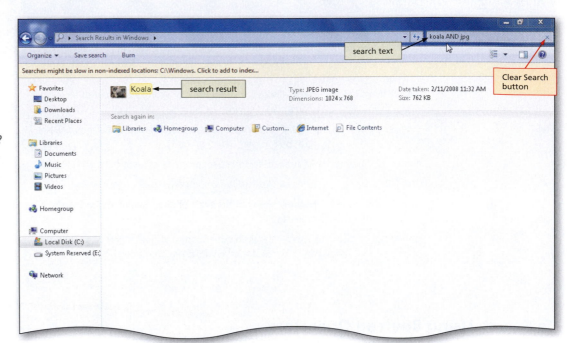

Figure 7–3

3

- After viewing the results, click the Clear Search button in the Search box to end the search and display the contents of the Windows folder.

- Click an open area of the window to close the filter list (Figure 7–4).

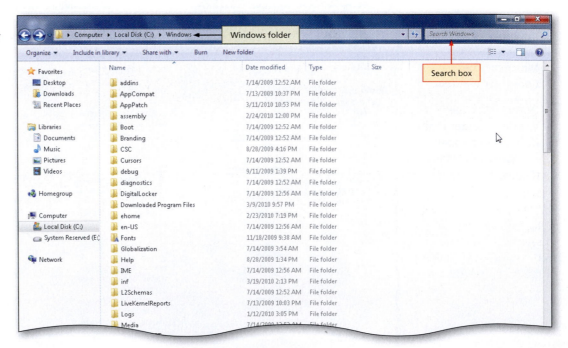

Figure 7–4

To Search for an Exact Phrase

You can search for files that match an exact phrase as part of its properties using double quotation marks. The following steps begin searching for all files that have the exact phrase, Microsoft Windows, in the file name and then modify the search to reduce the number of results.

1

• Type `"Microsoft Windows"` into the Search box as your search criteria and to begin searching for results (Figure 7–5).

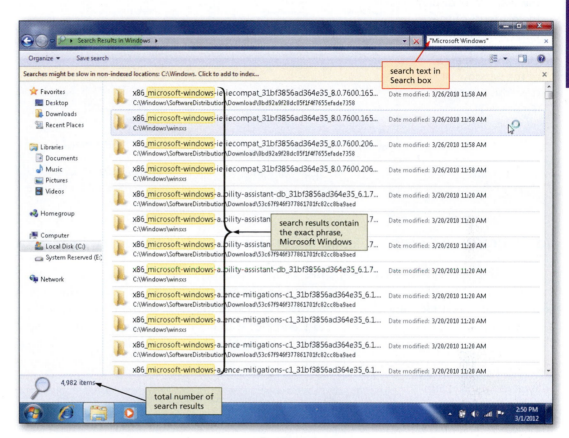

Figure 7–5

2

• Type `NOT x86` in the Search box, following "Microsoft Windows", to narrow your search and reduce the number of search results and press the ENTER key (Figure 7–6).

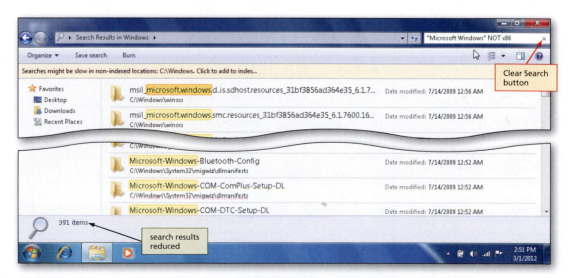

Figure 7–6

3

- After viewing the results, click the Clear Search button in the Search box to end the search and display the contents of the Windows folder.

- Click an open area of the window to close the filter list (Figure 7–7).

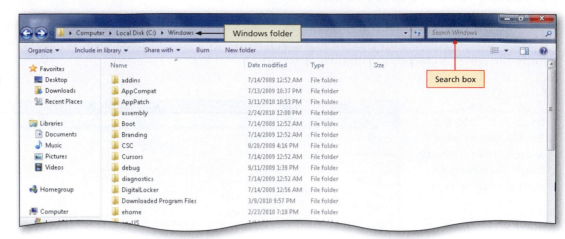

Figure 7–7

To Structure a Complex Search Combining a File Property and a Range

As you recall, all files have properties. When searching a folder, you can be more specific by adding a property to your search such as file name, type, tag, or author. For example, when you search using type: text as the search text, the search will find text files only. Any property can be used in this fashion. You need to type the colon (:) after the property name for the search to work. You can create complex searches by combining searches for specific property values with Boolean operators. The following step searches for all files that range in size between 10 and 30 megabytes (MB).

1

- Type `size: > 10MB AND < 30MB` into the Search box to specify that you want to see all files that are between 10 and 30 MB in size and press the ENTER key (Figure 7–8).

Q&A

Can I specify size in kilobytes (KB) or gigabytes (GB)?

Yes, when working with the Search box to search using file size, you can specify kilobytes (KB), megabytes (MB), or gigabytes (GB).

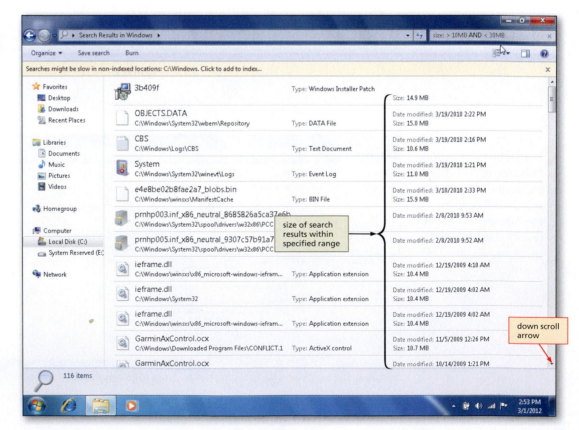

Figure 7–8

To Search a Custom Scope

At the bottom of the search results is a list of options for redoing your search in common locations, which might include Libraries, Homegroup, Computer, Internet, and File Contents. Windows 7 also provides a Custom option that allows you to change the search by using the Choose Search Location dialog box to create a custom scope. In a custom scope, you select the locations you want to search and then apply the current search to the locations. The following steps change the scope of the search to the Videos library.

- Scroll down until the end of the results list displays (Figure 7–9).

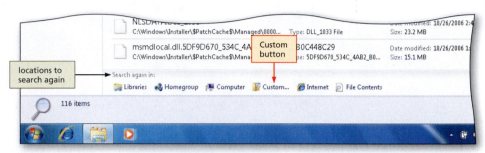

Figure 7–9

- Click the Custom button to display the Choose Search Location dialog box (Figure 7–10).

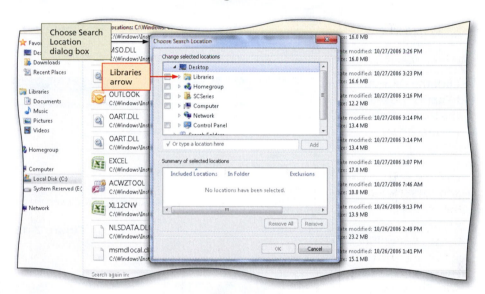

Figure 7–10

- Click the Libraries arrow to expand the Libraries list (Figure 7–11).

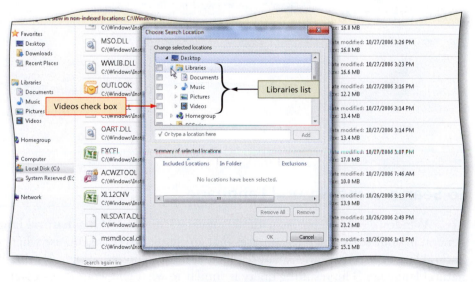

Figure 7–11

4

- Click the Videos check box to select the Videos library (Figure 7–12).

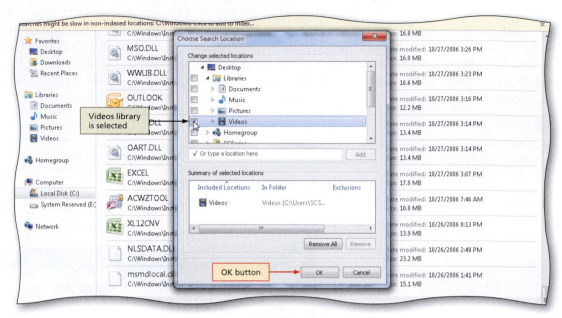

Figure 7–12

5

- Click the OK button to apply the search to the Videos library (Figure 7–13).

Figure 7–13

6

- Click the Back button to return to the Windows folder (Figure 7–14).

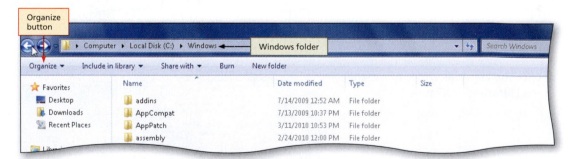

Figure 7–14

To Search Using Natural Language

Windows 7 also supports natural language searching. When **natural language** is turned on, you can be more general in your search, and use phrases that are similar to those you use when you write or speak. When using natural language, Windows 7 analyzes what you have entered using rules that it has constructed for processing natural language. The resulting query is similar to what you would have created without natural language. This can be helpful if you have a hard time remembering Boolean operators and property names.

For example, you can enter the phrase, music files, to find any music file in the folder. If you wanted to find all music files from when you recorded a piano recital, you could enter, `music piano recital`. If you wanted to find a research paper you made for your English class on Shakespeare, you could enter, `William Shakespeare document`. Although not complete sentences, the phrases are much more natural because you are not specifying the file type or using Boolean operators. Windows 7 constructs the search based upon the text you have entered. The following steps search for all flower pictures using natural language.

1

- Click the Organize button to display the Organize menu.

- Click the 'Folder and search options' command to display the Folder Options dialog box (Figure 7–15).

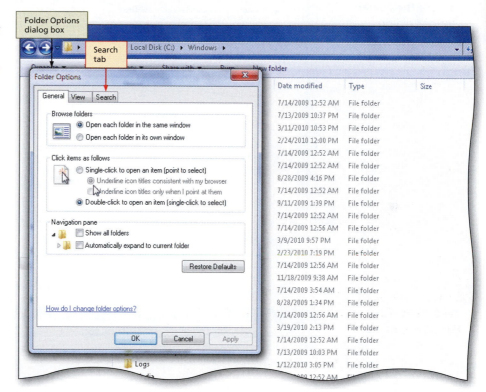

Figure 7–15

2

- Click the Search tab to display search options (Figure 7–16).

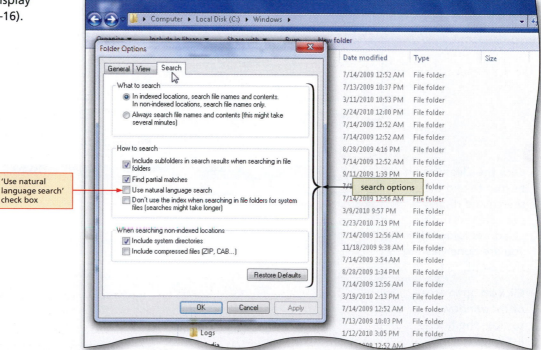

Figure 7–16

3

● Click the 'Use natural language search' check box to select it (Figure 7–17).

● Click the OK button to close the Folder Options dialog box and apply the changes.

check box is selected

OK button

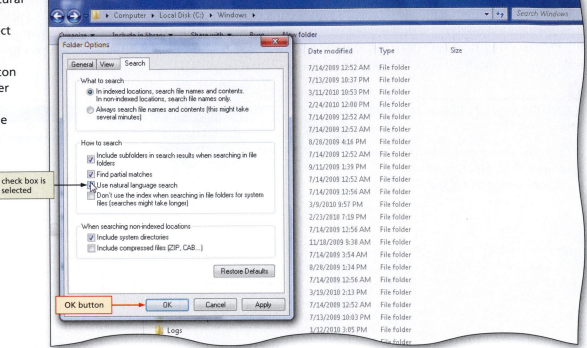

Figure 7–17

4

● Type flower pictures in the Search box to find all pictures of flowers and press the ENTER key (Figure 7–18).

search results contain pictures of flowers

natural language search text

Clear Search button

dialog box closes and natural language search is enabled

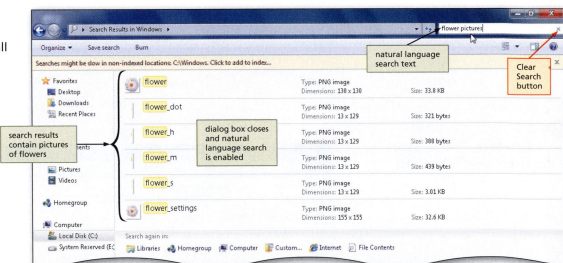

Figure 7–18

5

● Click the Clear Search button to end the search and display the contents of the Windows folder after you are done viewing the results.

● Click an open area of the window to close the filter list (Figure 7–19).

Organize button

Windows folder

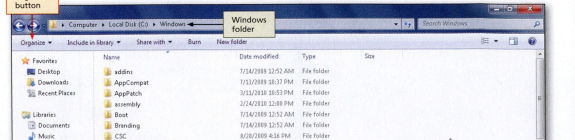

Figure 7–19

6

- Click the Organize button, and then click the 'Folder and search options' command to display the Folder Options dialog box.

- Click the Search tab to display search options.

- Click the 'Use natural language search' check box to deselect it (Figure 7–20).

- Click the OK button to apply the changes and close the Folder Options dialog box.

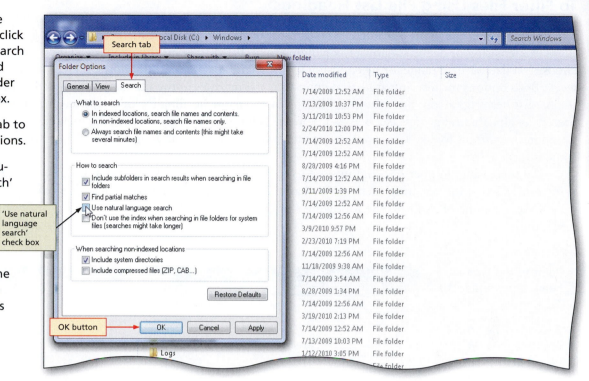

Figure 7–20

7

- Click in the Search box.

- Click the flower pictures entry in the Search list box to perform the same search with natural language search turned off and press the ENTER key (Figure 7–21).

Figure 7–21

8

- After you are done viewing the results, clear the search and display the contents of the Windows folder (Figure 7–22).

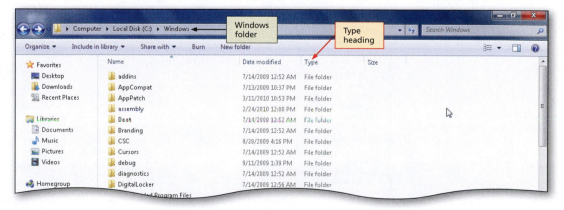

Figure 7–22

To Filter Files Using File List Headings

When using the file list headings, you can sort or filter files according to their headings. **Sorting** files arranges them in increasing or decreasing order depending upon the file list heading you select. You also can filter files by choosing a date or date range, or by choosing a time frame specified by Windows, such as today, yesterday, or last week. Both options for filtering are based upon the existing titles of the files and folders and are available by clicking the file list headings arrow. For example, filtering by the name heading includes options for organizing the files and folders by alphabetical groups (such as A–H), whereas filtering by the type heading includes a list of the file types found in the current folder. These options are most helpful when searching for files about which you already have some information.

An increasing number of programs are using XML (Extensible Markup Language) files. One reason for using XML is that the resulting files can be shared more easily over networks. For that reason, Windows 7 also uses XML for some of its files. The following steps filter the Windows folder on the Local Disk (C:) to display only XML files.

- Point to the Type heading to display the Type arrow.

- Click the Type arrow to display the list of filter options for file types (Figure 7–23).

Q&A Can I change which file list headings are displayed in the window?

Yes, by right-clicking a list heading, you can select which file list headings are displayed. You can add or subtract file list headings based on your needs.

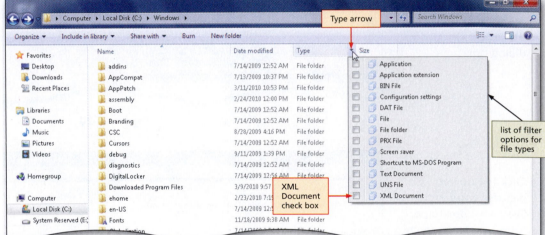

Figure 7–23

- Click the XML Document check box to filter the Windows folder for XML files only (Figure 7–24).

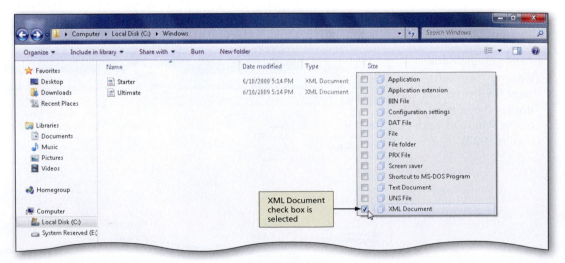

Figure 7–24

3

- Click any open space in the folder window to close the list of filter options (Figure 7–25).

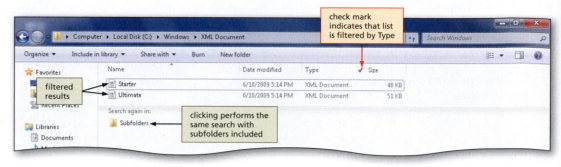

Figure 7–25

4

- After viewing the results, click the Type check mark to display the list of filter options for file types (Figure 7–26).

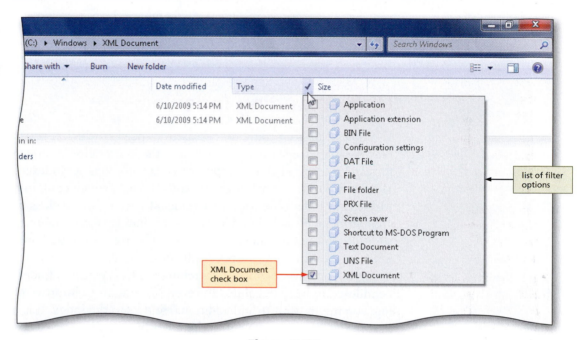

Figure 7–26

5

- Click the XML Document check box to remove the filter (Figure 7–27).

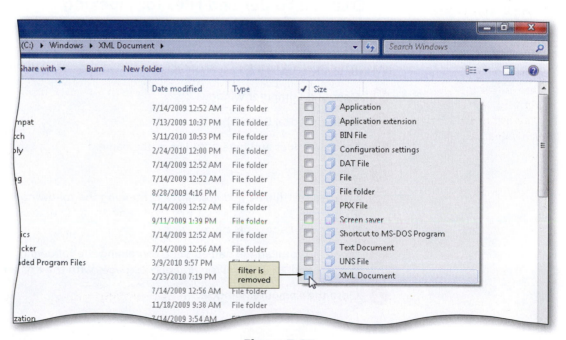

Figure 7–27

6
- Click any open space to close the filter list (Figure 7–28).

- Close the Windows folder window.

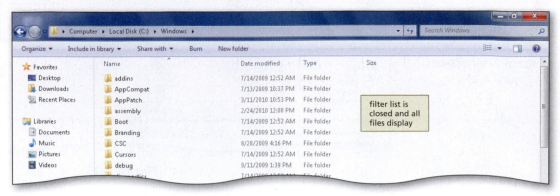

Figure 7–28

Understanding Indexing

Windows 7 uses indexing to increase the speed at which it searches selected folders and files. As you have learned in Chapter 3, the index helps Windows 7 keep track of those files and folders on your computer that are stored in an indexed location. By default, Windows 7 indexes each user's personal folders, which contain the Documents, Pictures, Music, and Videos libraries. Program and system files, such as the C:\Windows folder, are not included as indexed locations. Excluding these folders keeps the index small. In addition, to keep the index at a manageable size, Windows 7 prevents you from indexing network locations, unless specifically designated.

As you have seen while searching the C:\Windows folder, a folder does not have to be indexed to be searchable. However, if you want to improve performance when searching, you might want to add additional folders to the index. It is important to note that the Search folder window relies on the index by default.

To Create a Folder and Files for Indexing

First, you will create a new folder and some files that you will then add to the index. The following steps create a folder named SCFiles and create both a text file and a WordPad file within it.

1 Open the Computer window.

2 Open the Local Disk (C:).

3 Create a folder and type SCFiles as the name.

4 Open the SCFiles folder.

5 Create a text file named homework containing the following lines: 1) Must read 15 pages from my Chemistry book and 2) Write summary about Save the Planet's Facebook page.

6 Create a WordPad file named ToDo containing the following two lines: 1) Answer my E-mail and 2) Update my Facebook page with the Koala exhibit photos.

7 Close the Computer window.

To Add a Folder to the Index

You can add any folders to the index, but remember that the index will not perform well if it grows too large. It is recommended that you only add locations that contain personal files, and never add program or system files. The following steps add the SCFiles folder to the Search Index by using the Indexing Options dialog box.

1
- Open the Control Panel.
- Change the view to Large icons (Figure 7–29).

Figure 7–29

2
- Click the Indexing Options link to display the Indexing Options dialog box (Figure 7–30).

Q&A
Why is my list of indexed locations different?

Your index might have been modified by the administrator. Also, the number of files you have installed in various indexed locations might be different.

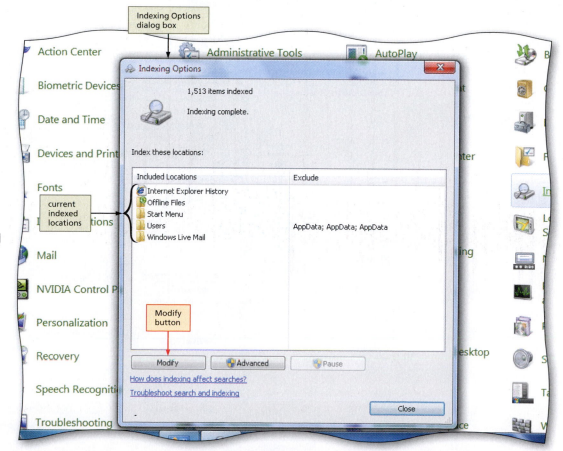

Figure 7–30

3
- Click the Modify button to display the Indexed Locations dialog box (Figure 7–31).

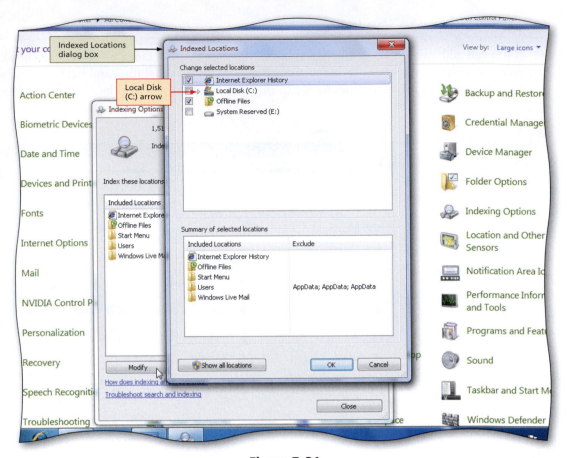

Figure 7–31

4
- Click the Local Disk (C:) arrow to display the list of folders (Figure 7–32).

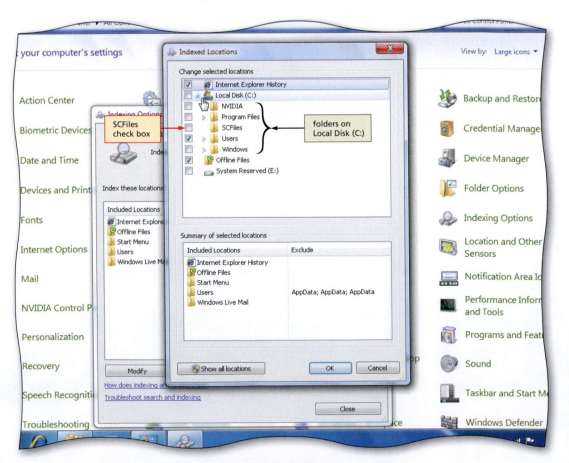

Figure 7–32

5

- If necessary, click the down scroll arrow until the SCFiles folder is displayed.

- Click the SCFiles check box to select it (Figure 7–33).

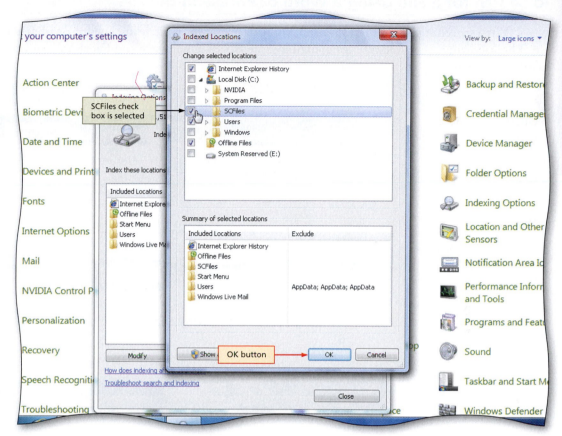

Figure 7–33

6

- Click the OK button to add the SCFiles folder to the Search Index (Figure 7–34).

- Click the Close button to close the Indexing Options dialog box.

- Change the view to Category in the Control Panel window.

- Close the Control Panel window.

Figure 7–34

To Search for a File Using a Word or Phrase in the File

When searching an indexed location, you can search for a file using a word or phrase that appears within the file. The following steps find all files containing the words, Chemistry and Facebook, and the phrase, Answer my E-mail.

 1

- Open the Computer window.
- Open the Local Disk (C:) drive.
- Open the SCFiles folder.
- If necessary, maximize the SCFiles folder window.

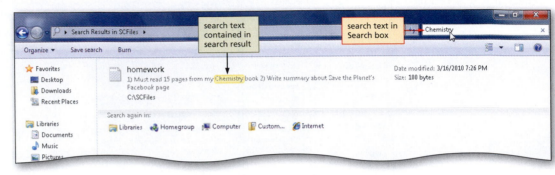

Figure 7–35

- Type `Chemistry` in the Search box to search for all files containing the word, Chemistry and press the ENTER key (Figure 7–35).

2

- After viewing the results, clear the Search box.
- Type `Answer my E-mail` in the Search box to search for all files containing the phrase, Answer my E-mail, and press the ENTER key (Figure 7–36).

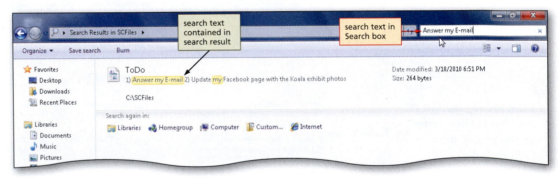

Figure 7–36

 3

- After viewing the results, clear the Search box.
- Type `Facebook` in the Search box to search for all files containing the word, Facebook, and press the ENTER key (Figure 7–37).

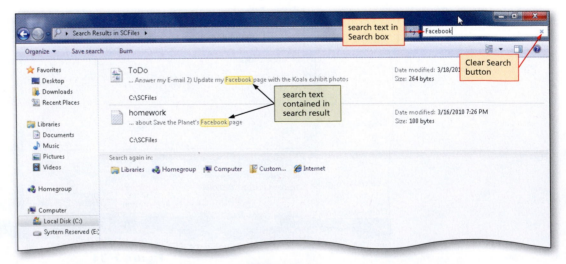

Figure 7–37

4

- After viewing the results, clear the search results (Figure 7–38).

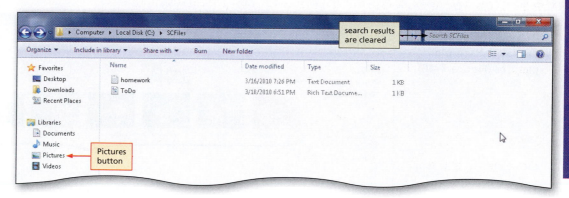

Figure 7–38

Using File Properties to Refine Your Search

You can search for files using any of the file properties, as discussed earlier in this chapter, such as the file's name, author, size, and type. However, media files often have additional specialized properties that are searchable. These specialized properties often are assigned values by the file's creators. For example, if you want to find all the photos taken using your Kodak camera, you can enter, camera make: Kodak, in the Search box to find these pictures. You also can search for a file based on when you last worked with the file or search for files containing specific text. Additionally, if you have edited the properties of a file or folder and added tags, you then will be able to find those files and folders using the tags you assigned.

If your search results are not satisfactory, you can refine your search by changing the search keywords, looking in other locations, or changing whether hidden and system files are included in the search. If no files were found, a message (No items match your search) will appear in the Search Results window. In this case, you might want to double-check the search criteria you entered or select different parameters with which to continue your search.

To Add a Tag to a File

To search for files using tags, you must first add the tags to the files. The following steps add a tag, landscape, to the desert picture in the Pictures library.

1

- Click Pictures in the Navigation pane to switch to the Pictures library (Figure 7–39).

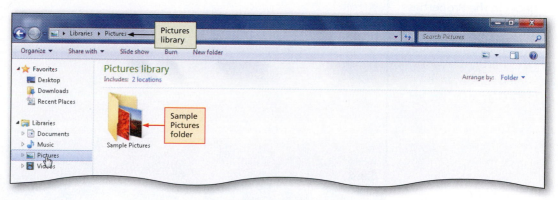

Figure 7–39

2

- Open the Sample Pictures folder to display the sample pictures (Figure 7–40).

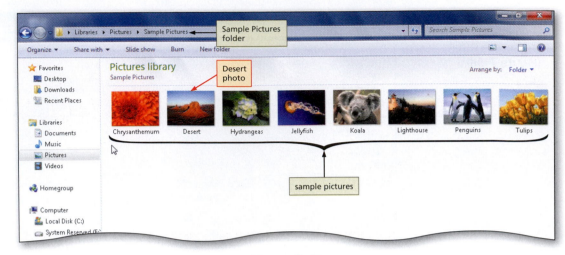

Figure 7–40

3

- Click the Desert picture to select it (Figure 7–41).

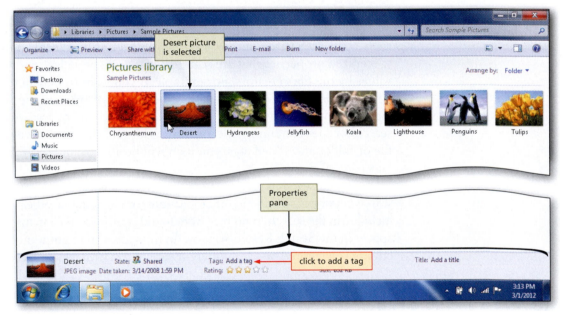

Figure 7–41

4

- Click the 'Add a tag' label in the Properties pane to display a text box (Figure 7–42).

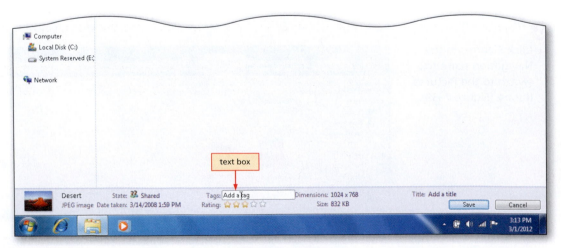

Figure 7–42

5

- Type landscape in the text box to assign the tag to the picture (Figure 7–43).

Q&A

Why does a semicolon appear at the end of the tag?

Because files can have multiple tags, Windows 7 places semicolons between each tag.

Figure 7–43

6

- Click the Save button to save the change (Figure 7–44).

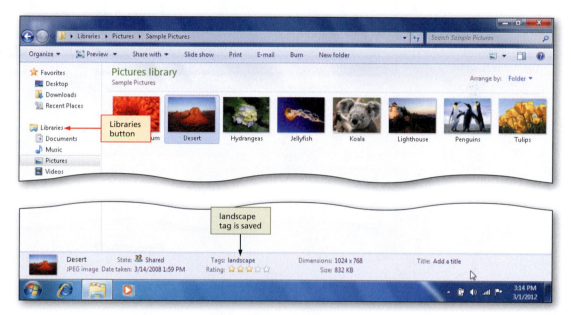

Figure 7–44

To Search Using the Tags Property

If you have added tags to your files, you can search for files by using the tags property in your search. The following steps find all files in the Libraries folder with a tag containing the word, landscape.

1

- Click Libraries in the Navigation pane to display the libraries (Figure 7–45).

Figure 7–45

2

- Type `tags:`
  `landscape` in the
  Search box to enter
  the search criteria and
  press the ENTER key
  (Figure 7–46).

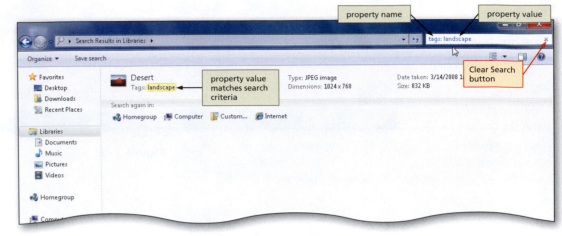

Figure 7–46

3

- After viewing
  the results, clear
  the search results
  (Figure 7–47).

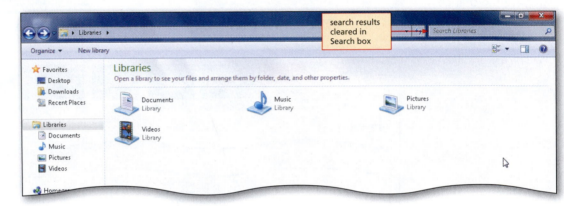

Figure 7–47

To Search Using the Authors Property

When you know the author of a file, you can search for the file by using the authors property in your search.
The following steps find all files authored by Corbis, a company that licenses stock photography.

1

- Type `authors:`
  `Corbis` in the Search
  box to enter the
  search criteria and
  press the ENTER key
  (Figure 7–48).

Figure 7–48

2

● After viewing the search results, clear the search results (Figure 7–49).

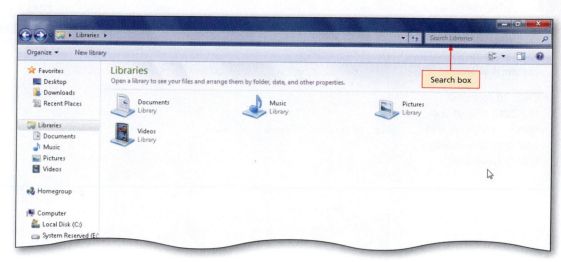

Figure 7–49

To Search Using the Date Property

When searching for a file, Windows 7 allows you to search using the date property. This can be helpful if you are searching for a photo you took two years ago, but you do not want to search through each photo in your library. You can select to find files by using the creation date (using the datecreated: property) or modification date (using the datemodified: property) for a file. The following steps find all files modified after the 20th of the previous month.

1

● Type `datemodified:` in the Search box to display a list of date options (Figure 7–50).

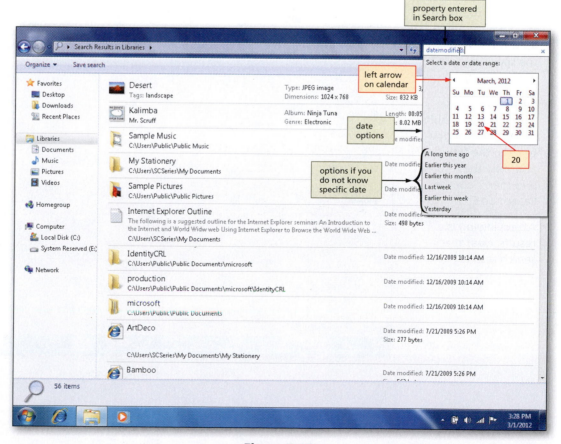

Figure 7–50

2

- Click the left arrow on the calendar to change to the previous month.

- Click 20 to select the 20th day of the previous month and add it to the Search box (Figure 7–51).

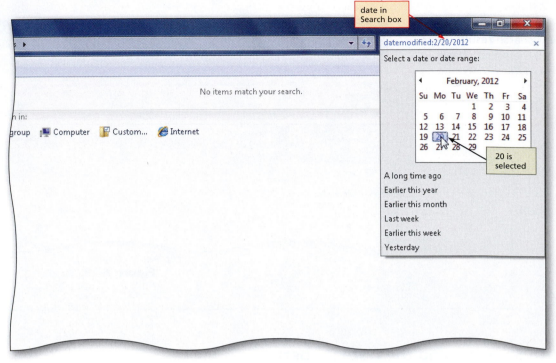

Figure 7–51

3

- Type > before the date showing in the Search box to indicate that you want to search for items modified after (greater than) the specified date (Figure 7–52).

- Click an open area of the Search Results in Libraries window to close the filter list and view the results, and then clear the Search box.

- After viewing the results, clear the search results.

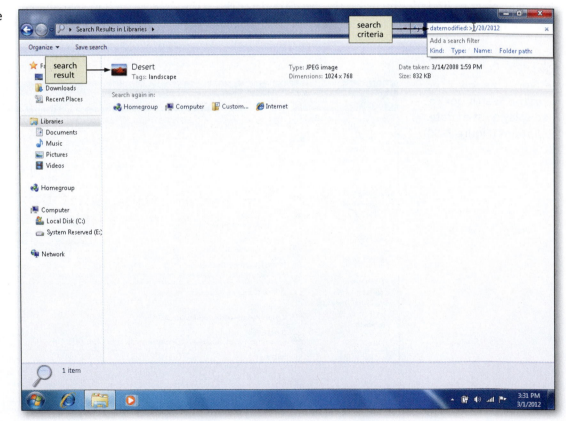

Figure 7–52

To Search for a File by File Size

If you only can remember a file's approximate size, you can specify the file size in your search. You can find files that are equal to, smaller than, or greater than a particular size. When specifying a file size, you can specify a measurement such as megabytes (MB), kilobytes (KB), or gigabytes (GB). You also can exclude the measurement and Windows 7 will assume you are specifying size in KB. The following steps find all files smaller than 10000 KB.

1

• Type `size: < 10000` in the Search box and press the ENTER key (Figure 7–53).

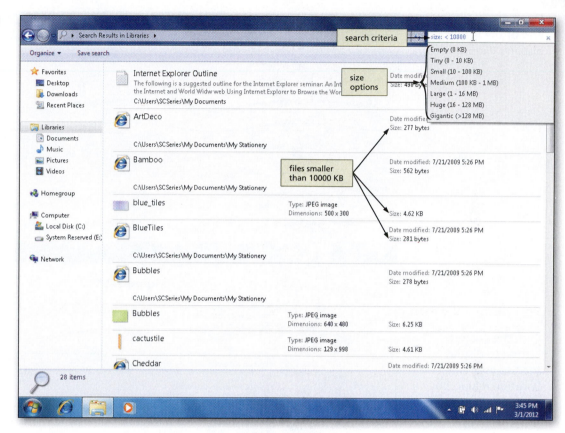

Figure 7–53

2

• Click an open area of the window to close the filter list (Figure 7–54).

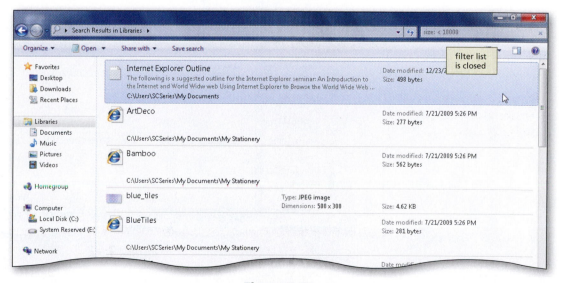

Figure 7–54

To Search Non-Indexed Locations

Even though you currently are viewing your libraries (an indexed location), you can redo the search using non-indexed locations, such as other hard disks, optical discs, USB flash drives, or network locations. The following steps search the Windows folder on Local Disk (C:) for all files with size less than 10000 KB and with the keyword, pen, in the file name.

- Scroll down until the end of the results list displays (Figure 7–55).

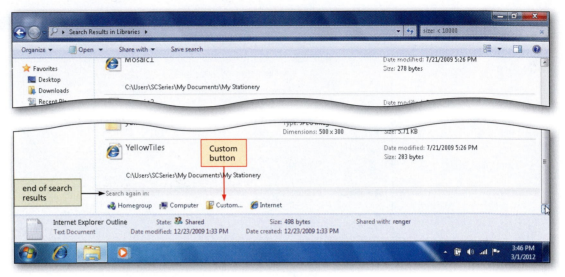

Figure 7–55

2

- Click the Custom button to display the Choose Search Location dialog box (Figure 7–56).

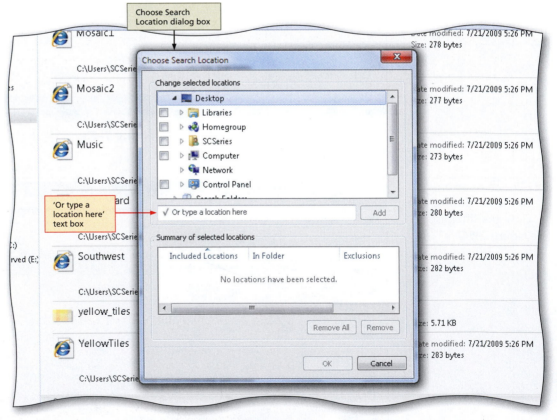

Figure 7–56

3

- Type C:\Windows in the 'Or type a location here' text box to enter a non-indexed search location (Figure 7–57).

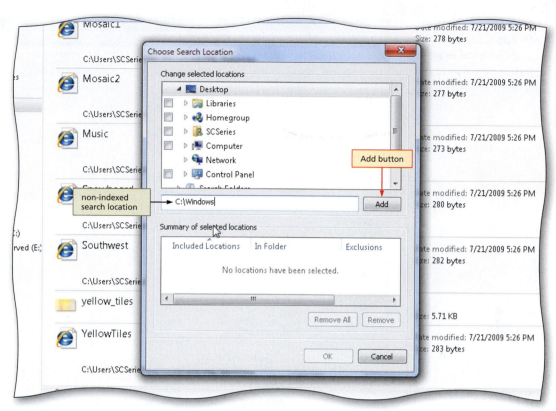

Figure 7–57

4

- Click the Add button to add C:\Windows to the list of selected locations (Figure 7–58).

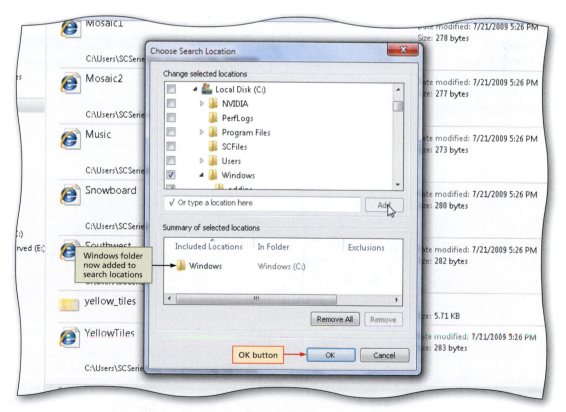

Figure 7–58

5

• Click the OK button to apply the changes and redo the search in the new location (Figure 7–59).

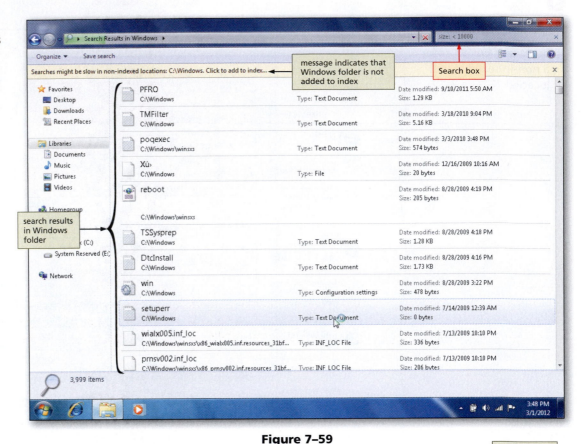

Figure 7–59

6

• Type AND pen in the Search box after the text, size: < 10000, and press the ENTER key (Figure 7–60).

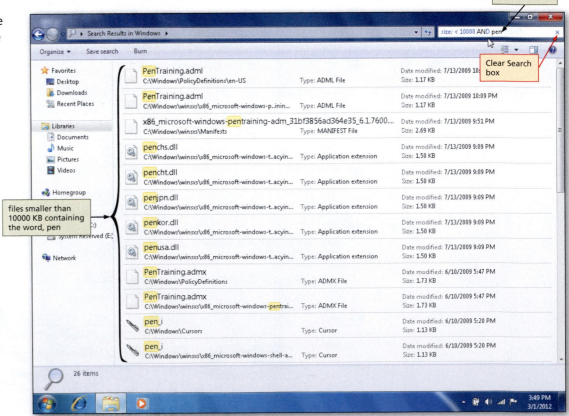

Figure 7–60

- After viewing the results, clear the search results (Figure 7–61).

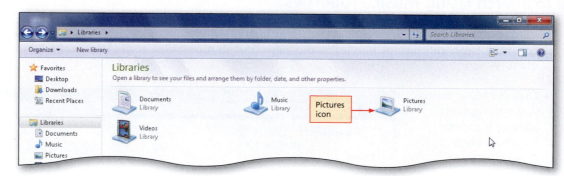

Figure 7–61

To Search Using Picture Properties

Specialized properties of picture files in Windows 7 include camera make, camera model, dimensions, orientation, date taken, width, height, flash mode, and rating. The following steps find all pictures with a three-star rating. Computer users typically assign their own ratings, where five stars indicates the highest rating and fewer stars indicate lower ratings.

- Double-click the Pictures icon in the Libraries window to switch to the Pictures library (Figure 7–62).

Figure 7–62

- Type `rating:` in the Search box, and then click the 3 Stars list item on the filter list to search for photos with a three-star rating (Figure 7–63).

Figure 7–63

To Search Using Music Properties

Music files in Windows 7 may have additional properties, such as bit rate, artist, year, duration, album, genre, lyrics, track, year, and rating. The following steps find all music files in the Jazz genre.

- Click the Music button in the Navigation pane to switch to the Music library (Figure 7–64).

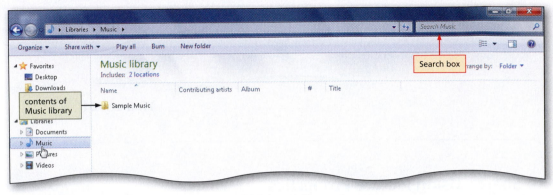

Figure 7–64

- Type `genre: jazz` in the Search box to search for jazz music files and press the ENTER key (Figure 7–65).

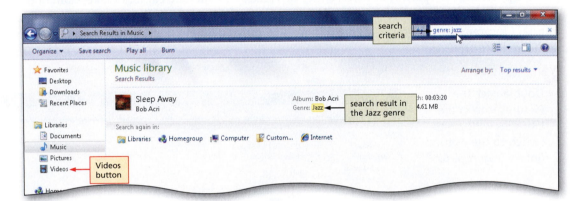

Figure 7–65

To Search Using Video Properties

The properties of video files typically contain the combined properties of music and picture files because they include both audio and visual components. Video properties also may have specialized properties, such as title, length, frame width, frame height, data rate, total bit rate, and frame rate. Videos acquired from sources such as television, the Internet, and other producers often will contain comments that identify the original producer of the video. The following steps find all videos with the acronym, HD, in their titles.

- Click Videos in the Navigation pane to switch to the Videos library (Figure 7–66).

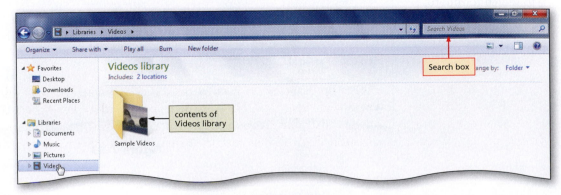

Figure 7–66

2
- Type `title:HD` in the Search box to search for videos with HD in their titles and press the ENTER key (Figure 7–67).

Q&A

Is the title the same as the file name?

No. To view the title of a video, click the video's icon to select it, and then refer to the Properties pane.

Figure 7–67

Working With Saved Searches

Every user has a Searches folder that is created by Windows 7 when their user account is created. The Searches folder is the default location for all saved searches. Any searches that you have saved will appear in your Searches folder. It is important to note that a **saved search** is a set of instructions about how to conduct a particular search, and not the actual search results themselves. Different search results might appear each time you execute a saved search.

Microsoft provides you with two saved searches by default: Everywhere and Indexed Locations. These searches were designed, based upon research by Microsoft, to quickly provide access to files that users typically want to find. The **Everywhere search** displays all files on your computer. This allows you to then conduct searches on those files in indexed and non-indexed locations. The **Indexed Locations search** searches all files from indexed locations. This allows you to conduct searches of all the indexed locations on your computer. Any search you perform in these search windows can then be saved as their own searches. For example, you could start with the Indexed Locations search and then search for all files you modified today and then save it so that you can run it at any time to find the files you modified recently.

Be aware that saved searches are not history lists. Some people mistakenly believe that some searches, such as a recently modified file search, are history lists, like those found when working with a browser. They believe that if they delete the search results, they will clear the history on the computer, which is not the case. Deleting search results deletes the files from your computer, so be very careful when choosing to delete search results.

To Search Using Boolean Operators in the Music Library

Just like you can use Boolean operators when performing an advanced search in a folder, you also can use Boolean operators when performing an advanced search in the Search window. For example, you only can remember parts of the names of your favorite artists, but you want to find all music files on your computer that might reference them. The step on the following page finds all files with the words, Scruff or Symphony, in the artists list.

1

- Click Music in the Navigation pane to switch to the Music library.

- Type `artist:Scruff OR artist: Symphony` in the Search box to enter the search criteria and press the ENTER key (Figure 7–68).

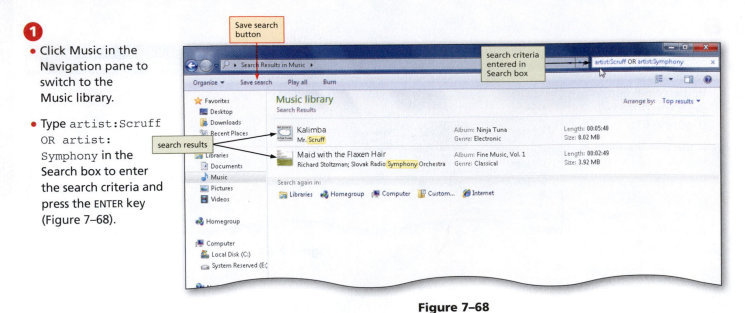

Figure 7–68

To Save a Search

After defining search criteria, you can save the search. By using a saved search, you can repeatedly perform the same search without having to re-create the search each time. The next time you execute a saved search, the search results might differ from the results you received when the search was first performed. Because you often download new music files, you decide to save the search. The following steps save the current search as My Music Search.

1

- Click the Save search button to display the Save As dialog box (Figure 7–69).

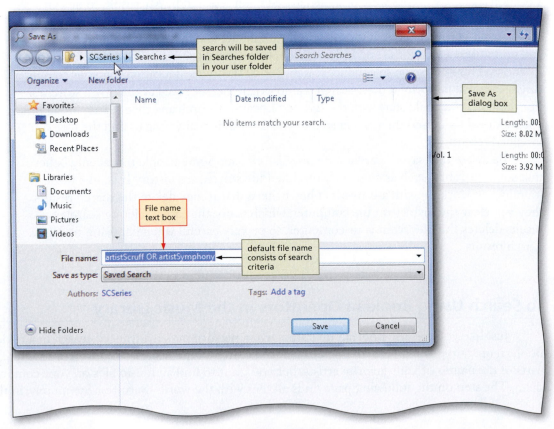

Figure 7–69

2

• Type `My Music Search` in the File name text box to enter a name for the search (Figure 7–70).

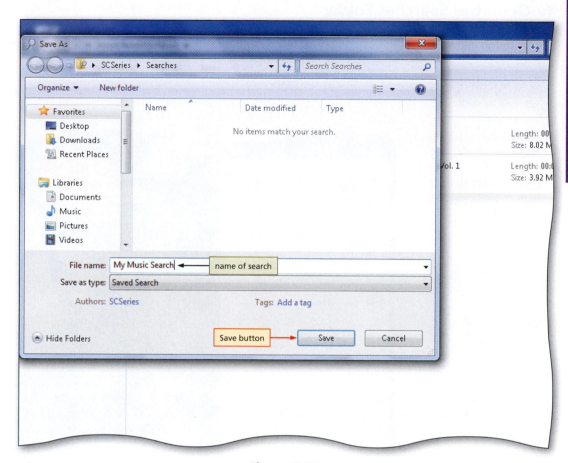

Figure 7–70

3

• Click the Save button to save the search (Figure 7–71).

• Close the My Music Search window.

Q&A

Can I save searches that I create in folder windows other than the Music library?

In addition to saving searches created using the Music library, any search you perform can be saved. If you are viewing the Pictures library and search using the Search box, Windows offers the option to save the search just as you would if you searched using the Music library.

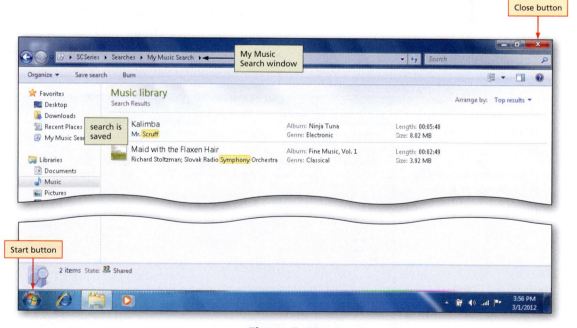

Figure 7–71

To Open the Searches Folder

To access saved searches you have created, you can find them in the Navigation pane under the Favorites listing. To see all of the available saved searches including the ones provided by Windows 7, you must open the Searches folder. The Searches folder can be accessed from the personal folder that Windows 7 creates for your user account. You can access your personal folder from the Start menu. The following steps open the Searches folder.

- Display the Start menu (Figure 7–72).

Figure 7–72

- Click your user name (SCSeries, in this case) to open your personal folder.

- If necessary, maximize your personal folder (Figure 7–73).

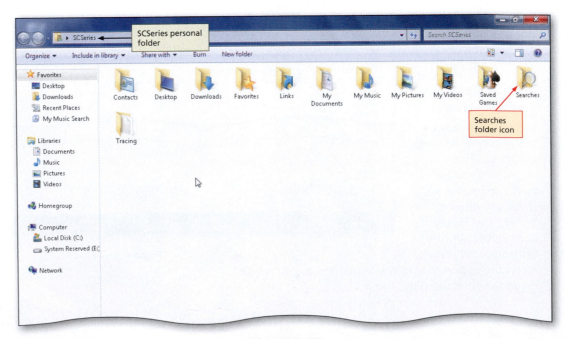

Figure 7–73

3

- Double-click the Searches folder icon to open the Searches folder (Figure 7–74).

Figure 7–74

To Create a Search from a Saved Search

You can use the Everywhere and Indexed Locations saved searches as a basis for more searches. This is handy when you want to create a search that will use all the indexed locations as a starting point. The following steps search for results using the keyword, Koala, in the Indexed Locations search folder, and then save the search using the name Koala Search.

1

- Double-click Indexed Locations in the Searches folder to display the Indexed Locations search folder (Figure 7–75).

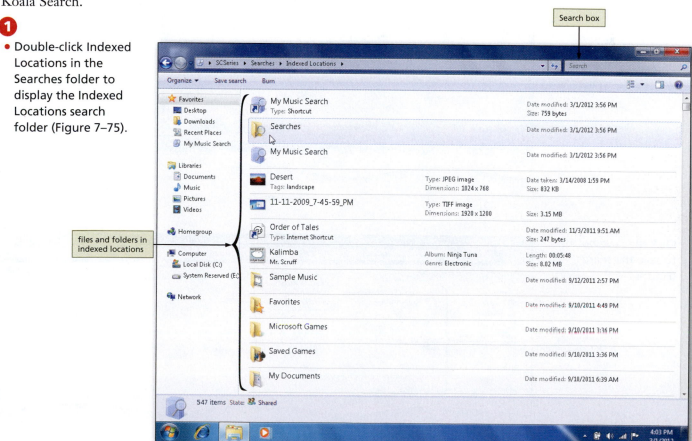

Figure 7–75

2

- Type `Koala` in the Search box to enter the search criteria and press the ENTER key (Figure 7–76).

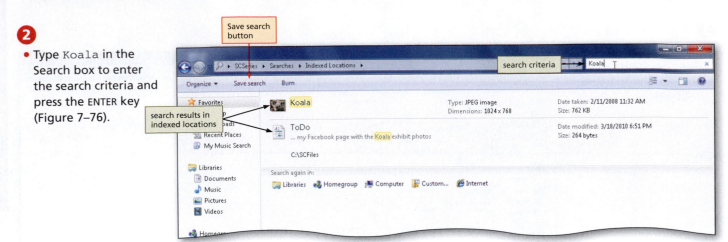

Figure 7–76

3

- Click the Save search button to display the Save As dialog box.

- Type `Koala Search` in the File name text box to enter a name for the search (Figure 7–77).

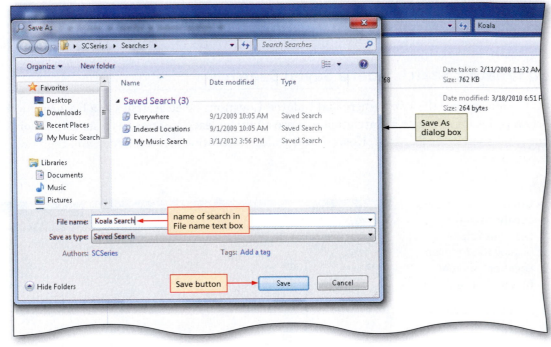

Figure 7–77

4

- Click the Save button to save the search (Figure 7–78).

Figure 7–78

To Search for Files Using a Saved Search

Now that you have saved searches, you can perform them easily using the links in the Favorites section of the Navigation pane. The following steps execute the My Music Search and the Koala Search from the Navigation pane.

- Click My Music Search in the Navigation pane to execute the search and display the results (Figure 7–79).

Figure 7–79

- Click Koala Search in the Navigation pane to execute the search and display the results (Figure 7–80).

Q&A

Why does the Koala Search show in the search results?

By default, Windows 7 considers all of the folders in your user folder to be indexed locations, including the Searches folder. Because of this, the Koala Search, which searches for the keyword, Koala, results in the saved search itself appearing in the results.

Figure 7–80

- After viewing the search results, click Searches in the Address bar to return to the Searches folder (Figure 7–81).

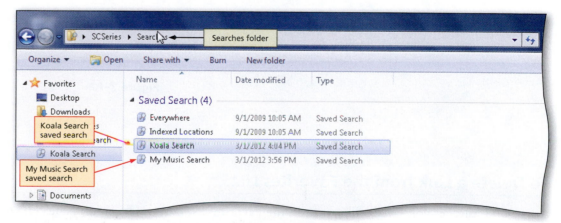

Figure 7–81

To Delete a Saved Search

You can delete any saved search in your Searches folder, including the saved searches provided by Microsoft. Before deleting a saved search, you should be sure that you no longer need it. The following steps delete the My Music Search and Koala Search saved searches.

1 Right-click the My Music Search saved search to display the shortcut menu.

2 Click the Delete command to display the Delete Folder dialog box.

3 Click the Yes button to delete the saved search.

4 Right-click the Koala Search saved search to display the shortcut menu.

5 Click the Delete command to display the Delete Folder dialog box.

6 Click the Yes button to delete the saved search (Figure 7–82).

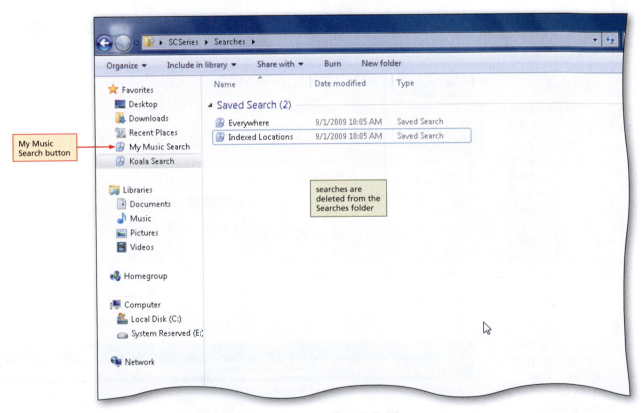

Figure 7–82

To Delete a Link from the Favorites List

The searches you saved still appear in the Favorites list in the Navigation pane. The following steps remove the My Music Search and the Koala Search from the Favorites list.

1
• Right-click My Music Search in the Navigation pane to display a shortcut menu (Figure 7–83).

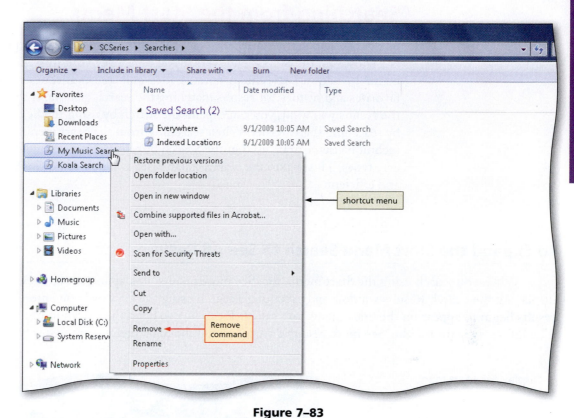

Figure 7–83

2
• Click Remove to remove My Music Search from the Favorites list (Figure 7–84).

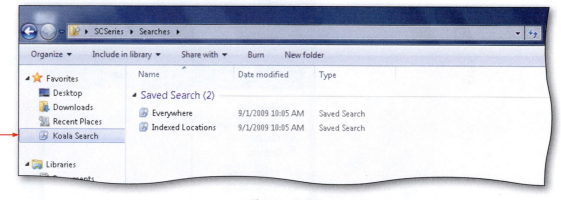

Figure 7–84

3
• Right-click Koala Search in the Navigation pane to display a shortcut menu.

• Click Remove to remove Koala Search from the Favorites list (Figure 7–85).

• Close the window.

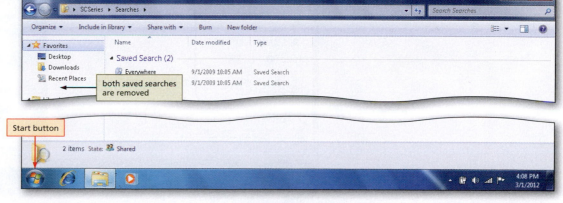

Figure 7–85

Searching from the Start Menu

As discussed in earlier chapters, you can search using the Search programs and files text box shown on the Start menu. When you type a keyword into the Search box on the Start menu, Windows 7 searches programs, files, and communications as well as Web browser favorites and history for results matching the search criteria. If the search does not display the results you want, you can expand the search by using the Search Results window or by searching the Internet. When searching from the Start menu, you can use any search technique that can be used in the Search box, from Boolean operators to specifying property types. This makes the search capabilities available from the Start menu powerful and efficient.

To Expand the Start Menu Search to See All Results

When you search using the Start menu, the 'See more results' link appears, which expands the search by displaying the Search Results window and executing a search using the keyword you entered. In fact, as soon as results begin to appear on the Start menu, you can click this link to open the search in the Search Results window. The following steps use the 'See more results' link to expand the Start menu search after typing in the letter, m.

1
- Display the Start menu.

- Type m in the Search box to start finding all items that match (Figure 7–86).

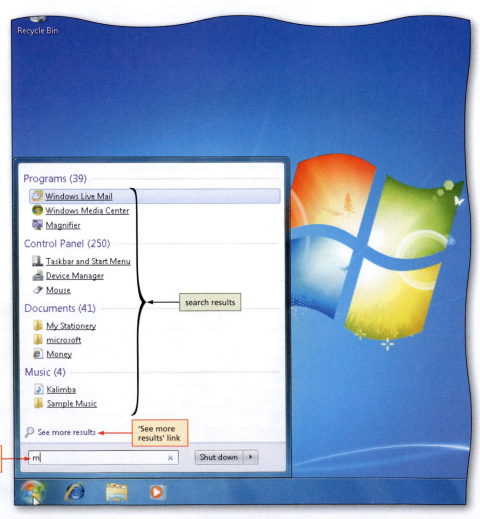

Figure 7–86

2
- Click the 'See more results' link to expand the Start menu search to view more results in the Search Results window (Figure 7–87).

- After viewing the results, close the Search Results window.

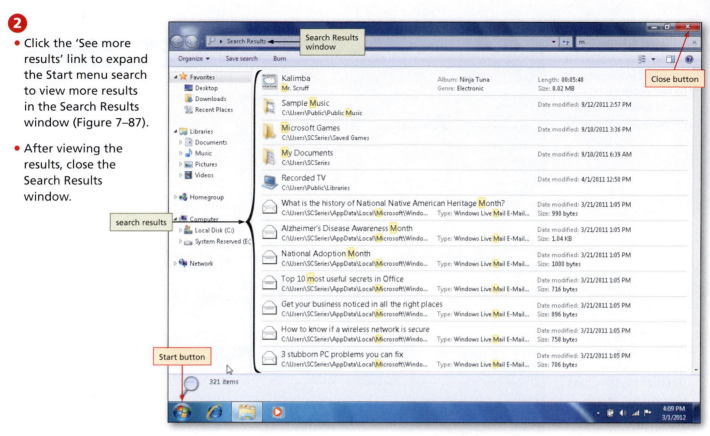

Figure 7–87

To Expand the Start Menu Search to the Internet

If your search returns no items, you can expand the search to the Internet by using the Search Results window. In fact, any search can be expanded to the Internet using the Internet link displayed when you perform a search. The following steps expand the Start menu search for the phrase, Windows 7 search techniques, to the Internet.

1
- Display the Start menu.

- Type `Windows 7 search techniques` in the Search box to find all items that match the search criteria (Figure 7–88).

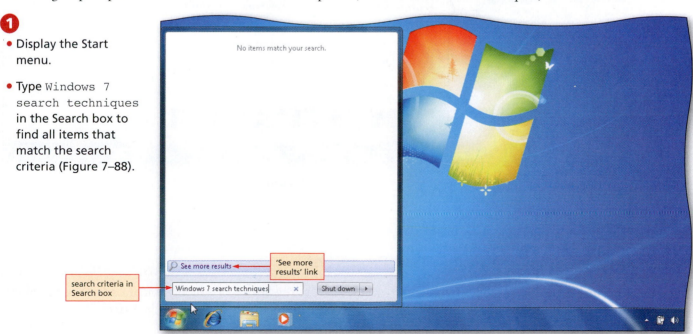

Figure 7–88

2

- Click the 'See more results' link to expand the Start menu search to see more results in the Search Results window (Figure 7–89).

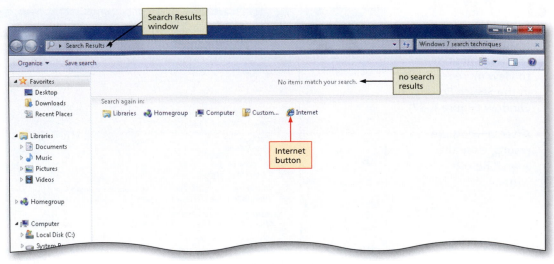

Figure 7–89

3

- Click the Internet button to open Internet Explorer and execute the search using the Bing search engine (Figure 7–90). (Your search engine might differ.)

- After viewing the results, close the Windows Internet Explorer window.

- Close the Search Results window.

Figure 7–90

To Search from the Start Menu Using Properties

Because the Search box on the Start menu works the same as the Search box in any folder or the Search folder window, you can find files using properties. The following step searches for all files with today's date.

1

- Display the Start menu.

- Type `date:today` in the Search box to find all items that were created or modified today (Figure 7–91).

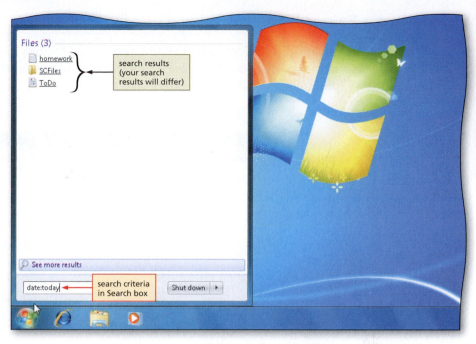

Files (3)

homework
SCFiles
ToDo

search results (your search results will differ)

See more results

date:today ← search criteria in Search box

Shut down ▶

Figure 7–91

To Search from the Start Menu Using Boolean Operators

When you enter a keyword in the Search box on the Start menu, your results not only include files where the keywords are part of the file name, but also include files that contain the keyword. This is possible because the Start menu search searches both indexed and non-indexed locations. Recall that when using the Search box in a folder window, your initial search is restricted to that folder, and that folder would need to be included in the list of indexed locations to search file contents. You also can use Boolean operators when searching using the Start menu. The following step searches for all files containing the keyword, read, or the keyword, photos.

1

- Delete the previous search from the Search box on the Start menu.

- Type `read OR photos` in the Search box to find all items that match either keyword (Figure 7–92).

- After viewing the results, close the Start menu.

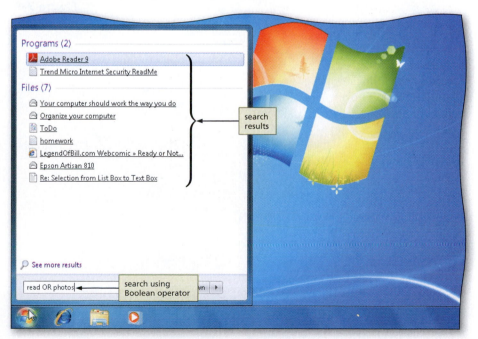

Programs (2)

Adobe Reader 9
Trend Micro Internet Security ReadMe

Files (7)

Your computer should work the way you do
Organize your computer
ToDo
homework
LegendOfBill.com Webcomic » Ready or Not...
Epson Artisan 810
Re: Selection from List Box to Text Box

search results

See more results

read OR photos ← search using Boolean operator

Figure 7–92

To Remove a Folder from the Index

When you no longer need a folder to be indexed, you should remove it from the index. This means that if you search the folder at a later time, the search might be slower, depending upon the size of the folder. The following steps remove the SCFiles folder from the Search Index.

1

- Open the Control Panel.

- Change the view to Large icons (Figure 7–93).

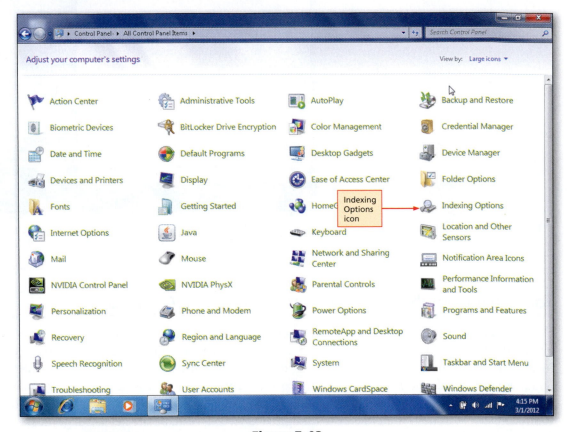

Figure 7–93

2

- Click the Indexing Options icon to display the Indexing Options dialog box (Figure 7–94).

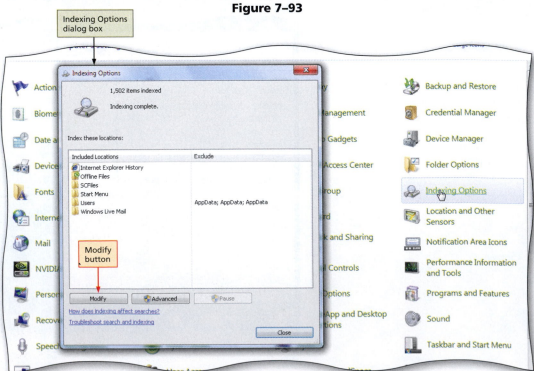

Figure 7–94

3

- Click the Modify button to display the Indexed Locations dialog box (Figure 7–95).

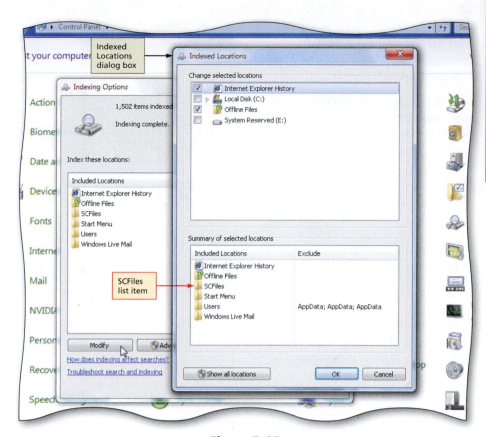

Figure 7–95

4

- Click the SCFiles list item in the 'Summary of selected locations' list to select it (Figure 7–96).

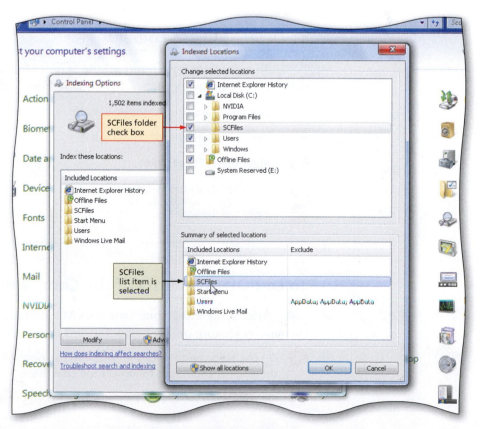

Figure 7–96

5

- Click the SCFiles folder check box in the 'Change selected locations' list to remove the check mark (Figure 7–97).

- Click the OK button to remove the SCFiles folder from the Search Index and to close the Indexed Locations dialog box.

6

- Close the Indexing Options dialog box.

- Change the Control Panel view to Category.

- Close the Control Panel window.

 **Experiment**

- Use the Search box to perform a search for the keyword, chemistry. Notice the increased amount of time it takes for the search results to display when the file for which you are searching is not stored in an indexed location.

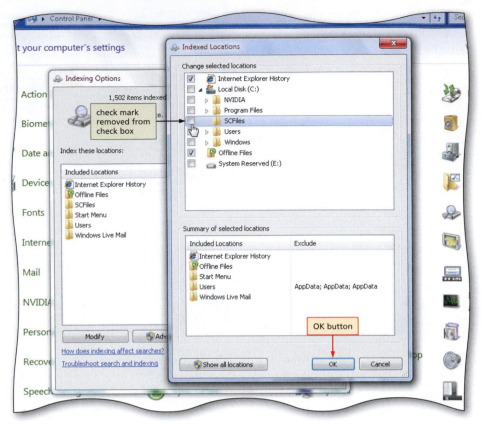

Figure 7–97

To Delete SCFiles Folder

Now that you have removed the SCFiles folder from the Search Index, you can delete it. The following steps delete the SCFiles folder and the files it contains.

1 Open the Computer window.

2 Display the contents of Local Disk (C:).

3 Delete the SCFiles folder.

4 Close the Computer window.

5 Empty the Recycle Bin.

To Log Off and Turn Off the Computer

After completing your work with Windows 7, you first should close your user account by logging off the computer, and then turn off the computer.

1 On the Start menu, click the arrow to the right of the Shut down button, and then click the Log off command to log off the computer.

2 On the Welcome screen, click the Shut down button to turn off the computer.

Chapter Summary

In this chapter, you have learned how to use advanced search techniques. Using the Search box, you have learned how to search a folder using keywords, Boolean operators, and property data. You filtered files using the file list headings. You added a location to the index and learned the differences between using indexed and non-indexed locations when searching. You have learned how each file type has different properties and that you can search using those properties. Using the advanced search options of the Search box, you found files based on name, tags, authors, file size, dates, and locations. You also learned that you can apply all the search techniques when searching from the Start menu. Additionally, you learned how to expand your search from the Start menu to the Search Results window and to the Internet using your Web browser. Above all else, you now know that Windows 7 provides powerful search tools that allow you to find your files quickly and efficiently, based on little information. The items listed below include all of the new Windows 7 skills you have learned in this chapter.

1. Search Using Boolean Operators (WIN 421)
2. Search for an Exact Phrase (WIN 423)
3. Structure a Complex Search Combining a File Property and a Range (WIN 424)
4. Search a Custom Scope (WIN 425)
5. Search Using Natural Language (WIN 426)
6. Filter Files Using File List Headings (WIN 430)
7. Add a Folder to the Index (WIN 433)
8. Search for a File Using a Word or Phrase in the File (WIN 436)
9. Add a Tag to a File (WIN 437)
10. Search Using the Tags Property (WIN 439)
11. Search Using the Authors Property (WIN 440)
12. Search Using the Date Property (WIN 441)
13. Search for a File by File Size (WIN 443)
14. Search Non-Indexed Locations (WIN 444)
15. Search Using Picture Properties (WIN 447)
16. Search Using Music Properties (WIN 448)
17. Search Using Video Properties (WIN 448)
18. Search Using Boolean Operators in the Music Library (WIN 449)
19. Save a Search (WIN 450)
20. Open the Searches Folder (WIN 452)
21. Create a Search from a Saved Search (WIN 453)
22. Search for Files Using a Saved Search (WIN 455)
23. Delete a Link from the Favorites List (WIN 456)
24. Expand the Start Menu Search to See All Results (WIN 458)
25. Expand the Start Menu Search to the Internet (WIN 459)
26. Search from the Start Menu Using Properties (WIN 460)
27. Search from the Start Menu Using Boolean Operators (WIN 461)
28. Remove a Folder from the Index (WIN 462)

Learn It Online

Test your knowledge of chapter content and key terms.

Instructions: To complete the Learn It Online exercises, start your browser, click the Address bar, and then enter the Web address `scsite.com/win7/learn`. When the Windows 7 Learn It Online page is displayed, click the link for the exercise you want to complete and then read the instructions.

Chapter Reinforcement TF, MC, and SA

A series of true/false, multiple-choice, and short-answer questions that test your knowledge of the chapter content.

Flash Cards

An interactive learning environment where you identify chapter key terms associated with displayed definitions.

Practice Test

A series of multiple-choice questions that test your knowledge of chapter content and key terms.

Who Wants To Be a Computer Genius?

An interactive game that challenges your knowledge of chapter content in the style of a television quiz show.

Wheel of Terms

An interactive game that challenges your knowledge of chapter key terms in the style of the television show *Wheel of Fortune*.

Crossword Puzzle Challenge

A crossword puzzle that challenges your knowledge of key terms presented in the chapter.

Apply Your Knowledge

Reinforce the skills and apply the concepts you learned in this chapter.

Exploring Different Search Techniques

Instructions: You know that searching is an important feature of Windows 7. You decide to use the Search box to search for a variety of pictures on your hard disk, and then store them in the Pictures folder.

Part 1: Searching for Picture Files
1. Open the Computer window and navigate to the Windows folder. If necessary, maximize the window.
2. Search for pictures with the file name, img22.
3. Select each search result and copy it to the Pictures library.
4. Search for pictures containing the word, tulip, in the file name (Figure 7–98).
5. Select each search result and copy it to the Pictures library.

Figure 7–98

Part 2: Searching for Pictures Using Boolean Operators
1. In the Windows folder, search for all files with names that contain the word, sleep, or the word, jellyfish, using the Boolean OR operator.
2. Select each picture search result and copy it to the Pictures library.
3. Search for all files with names that contain the keyword, baby, but not the keyword, rectangle.
4. Select each picture search result and copy it to the Pictures library.

Part 3: Searching for Pictures Using Properties
1. Search for pictures in the JPEG file format that contain the keyword, wmp.
2. Select each search result and copy it to the Pictures library.
3. Search for pictures that begin with the letters, co, have a file size of less than 1 KB, and do not contain the keyword, settings.
4. Select each search result and copy it to the Pictures library.
5. Record the list of the files that you have copied to the Pictures library in this exercise, and then submit the list to your instructor.

Part 4:   Deleting the Pictures

1. Open the Pictures library.

2. Select all the picture icons. Do not select the Sample Pictures folder icon.

3. Right-click one of the picture icons to display a shortcut menu, and then click the Delete command.

4. Click the Yes button in the Delete Multiple Items dialog box.

5. Close the Pictures library.

Extend Your Knowledge

Extend the skills you learned in this chapter and experiment with new skills. You might need to use Help to complete the assignment.

Researching Windows 7 Searches

Instructions: Use Windows Help and Support to answer the following questions.

1. Open Windows Help and Support, and if necessary, maximize the window.

2. Answer the following question by searching Help and Support for tips for working with files (Figure 7–99).

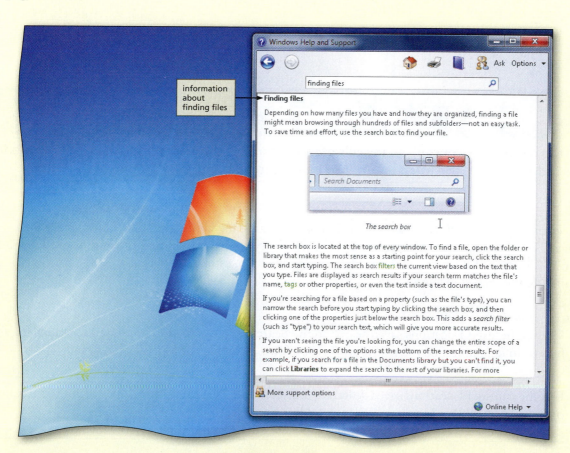

Figure 7–99

Continued >

Extend Your Knowledge *continued*

    a. Where does Help suggest you start first when searching?

      _____

3. Answer the following questions after reviewing the Help and Support topic 'Find a file or folder.'
    a. List three ways to search for files or folders.

      _____

    b. What does Windows recommend if you cannot find a file?

      _____

4. Answer the following questions after reviewing the Help and Support topics on advanced tips for searching in Windows.
    a. What are the different ways you can search using dates?

      _____

    b. How can you find saved e-mail messages?

      _____

    c. How do you find pictures that are not stored in the Pictures folder?

      _____

5. Using the Help and Support topic on using the index, answer the following question.
    a. Should you index your whole computer?

      _____

6. Close the Help and Support Center window.

In the Lab

Use the guidelines, concepts, and skills presented in this chapter to increase your knowledge of Windows 7. Labs are listed in order of increasing difficulty.

Lab 1: Using the Windows 7 Saved Searches to Search for Files and Folders

Instructions: In the past, you used the Search box to search for files when all you knew were their file names. Now you have learned that you can use the Everywhere and Indexed Locations saved searches from the Searches folder to search for files. You decide to investigate how to use these saved searches for finding files and folders.

Part 1:   Searching for Files Based on Date
1. Use the Indexed Locations saved search in the Searches folder to search indexed locations for all files or folders modified today (Figure 7–100). How many files or folders were found?

    _____

2. Use the Indexed Locations saved search to search indexed locations for all files or folders modified on your last birthday. How many files or folders were found?

    _____

Figure 7–100

3. Use the Indexed Locations saved search to search indexed locations for all files or folders modified within the past month. How many files or folders were found?

_____

Part 2:   Searching for Files Based on File Type
1. Use the Everywhere saved search to search all locations for JPEG files.
2. List the first three JPEG files found during the search.

_____

_____

_____

3. Scroll to make the first icon visible and then double-click the first icon. Which image displays on the desktop?

_____

4. Scroll to make the last icon visible and then double-click the last icon. Which image displays on the desktop?

_____

5. Use the Everywhere saved search to search all locations for music files in the WAV file format using the keyword, WAV.
   a. How many files or folders were found?

   _____

   b. Double-click one of the files that was found. What do you hear?

   _____

6. Use the Everywhere saved search to search all locations for video files.
   a. How many files or folders were found?

   _____

   b. Double-click one of the videos. What displays?

   _____

Continued >

In the Lab *continued*

Part 3:   Searching for Files Based on Content or File Name

1. Use the Indexed Locations saved search to search for all text documents containing the keyword, homework.

   a. How many files or folders were found?

   _____

2. Use the Indexed Locations saved search to search for files or folders with the .bat extension. (*Hint:* Type `*.bat` in the Search box.)

   a. What type of files were found?

   _____

3. Close the Search Results window.

In the Lab

Lab 2: Using the Start Menu to Search for Information

Instructions: While attending a one-day Internet seminar, you discover multiple methods of using the Start menu to search your computer. You decide to learn more about this method of searching. You will conduct keyword searches using the Start menu and then expand it as needed.

Part 1:   Searching for Information on the Internet

1. Design a search statement for each of the following topics, and then type the statement into the Search box on the Start menu (Figure 7–101). Expand each search to the Internet; find and print an appropriate Web page for each statement.

Figure 7–101

a. You want to find out more about the scripts that are available in the UCLA library. Write your search statement on the following line.

_____

b. You want current temperature readings for major cities in the United States. Write your search statement on the following line.

_____

c. You need information to write a report about the senators that represent your state in the United States Senate. Write your search statement on the following line.

_____

d. You want to shop for the best prices for a new SLR digital camera. You already know that you do not want to buy a Pentax or an Olympus camera. Write your search statement on the following line.

_____

Part 2:   Searching for Information on Your Computer

1. Design a set of search keywords for each of the following topics, type the keywords you come up with into the Search box in the Start menu to test them (expand if necessary), and then write a summary of your results in WordPad.

a. You want to know how many files you have that contain information about creating a movie. Write the search keywords on the following line.

_____

b. You know that you have saved Web pages about buying a new hybrid car. Write your search keywords on the following line.

_____

c. You have applied for admission to the University of Central Florida and have received e-mail messages from the University. Write your search keywords on the following line.

_____

2. Submit your answers and printouts to your instructor.

In the Lab

Lab 3: Searching for Files Based on Content

Instructions: You want to test the way Windows 7 can find files based on content. You plan on creating four files using WordPad and then practicing your search techniques to list files based on content.

Continued >

In the Lab *continued*

Part 1:   Creating the Files

1. Create a folder in the Documents library titled `Lab3`.

2. Create the four documents shown in Figure 7–102 using WordPad and save them to the Lab3 folder.

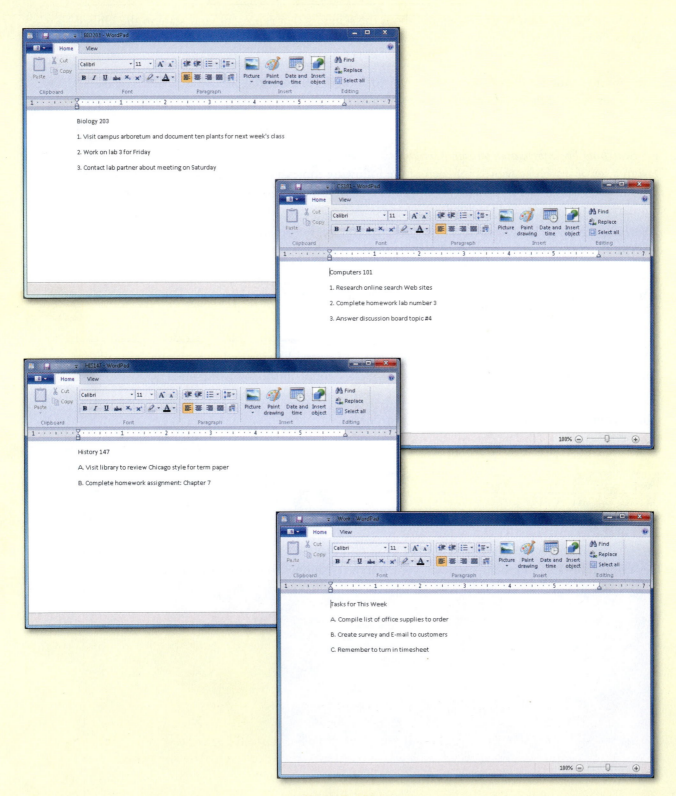

Figure 7–102

Part 2:   *Searching for File Content*

  1. Search for your classes using the keyword, class. How many results appear?

  _____

  2. Search for homework assignments using the keyword, Lab 3. How many results appear?

  _____

  3. Search for your work task list using the keyword, work. How many results appear?

  _____

Part 3:   *Removing Files and Folders*

  1. Submit your answers to your instructor.
  2. Delete the folder and files that you added to the Documents library.

Cases and Places

Apply your creative thinking and problem-solving skills to design and implement a solution.

• Easier   •• More Difficult

•1: Searching by Content

You help your friend Sharon buy a new computer. Late one night, she calls and is frantic because she cannot find a document on the computer. The document contains a big project for her Science class that she created using Microsoft Word that she last worked on two days ago. She cannot remember what file name she used to save the file, but does remember that the document contains her teacher's name, Ms. Lipton. Using WordPad, write steps to help her find her document, given that you know the file type, when it was modified, and possible keywords the file might contain.

•2: Searching Music Files Using Keywords

You want to move music files you accidentally saved in the Documents library to the Music library. You know that you listen to a variety of music files by different artists. Using WordPad, write down the steps to find the various music files using your favorite artists as part of the search criteria. Be sure to list the type of keyword searches you would perform and what results you would expect to see. Copy some music files to the Documents library and then try your searches to make sure that they will work.

••3: Understanding Wildcards

Wildcard characters often are used in a file name to locate a group of files while searching. For example, to locate all files with the Business file name regardless of the file extension, an entry (Business.*) containing the asterisk wildcard character would be used. Using the Internet, computer magazines, or any other resources, develop a guide to using wildcards. Summarize what a wildcard character is, what the valid wildcard characters are, and give several examples to explain their use.

••4: Adding Folders to the Search Index

Make It Personal

You would like to experiment with adding folders that are not part of the normal indexed locations to the Search Index. Create a folder to hold your files. Put some of your music, documents, and other files into the folder you created. Run searches for your files and write down the amount of time it takes for the searches to execute. Add the folder to the list of indexed locations. Perform the same searches as before and write down the amount of time it takes for the searches to execute. Write a brief report about your experience. Include descriptions of the files, as well as the time that it takes to find them.

Continued >

Cases and Places *continued*

••5: Privacy Concerns

Working Together

The amount of information available on the Internet about an individual is amazing. Identity theft is increasingly common. Credit card fraud affects thousands monthly. Information about an individual that used to take days to find can be found in minutes with only a few mouse clicks. When there is more than one account on a computer, all the information can be accessed by other users. Should we be concerned about our privacy? Use magazine articles, personal experience, and the Internet to understand the problem of identity theft. Prepare a brief report summarizing the methods used to obtain personal information, the problems arising from the unauthorized use of this information, and then recommend preventive measures including those offered by Windows 7.

8 | Mastering Digital Pictures and Music

Objectives

You will have mastered the material in this chapter when you can:

- Open and work with Windows Live Photo Gallery

- Add pictures to the gallery

- Organize and view pictures in the gallery

- Modify pictures

- Understand how to order pictures online

- Create and burn a DVD using Windows DVD Maker

- Open and work with Windows Media Player

- View media files in the Player library

- Rip music from a CD

- Burn a playlist to a CD

8 | Mastering Digital Pictures and Music

Introduction

Digital media includes pictures, audio, and video, and is stored in picture files, audio files, and video files. Windows DVD Maker and Windows Media Player are two programs that allow you to work with digital media in Windows 7.

In addition to these programs, you can download Windows Live Essentials, which provides additional programs to let you work with digital media. For more information about installing Windows Live Essentials, review the steps on page WIN 205. As you learned, Windows Live Photo Gallery can be used to view and edit pictures. You also can use Windows Live Photo Gallery to organize your video clips, although you cannot edit your videos using this program. Windows Live Essentials includes a separate program, Windows Live Movie Maker, expressly for editing video. Windows Live Movie Maker will be covered in detail in Chapter 9.

Windows DVD Maker allows you to create a DVD from your pictures and video. You can select a layout, add your media, and then burn your files to a DVD. You can import content from both Windows Live Photo Gallery and Windows Movie Maker to create DVDs (Figure 8–1).

Windows Media Player allows you to view digital media that is playing, organize and play audio and video files, download audio and video files from the Internet, copy (or rip) songs from audio CDs to the computer, and copy (or burn) audio files to a CD or portable media player. Recall that in Chapter 3, you launched the Windows Media Player program using an icon on the taskbar and played one of the sample music files included in Windows 7.

Overview

As you read this chapter, you will learn how to use Windows Live Photo Gallery, Windows DVD Maker, and Windows Media Player by performing these general tasks:

- Importing pictures to the Pictures library
- Viewing and editing pictures in Windows Live Photo Gallery
- Creating a DVD using Windows DVD Maker
- Ripping music from a CD and adding music to Windows Media Player
- Burning an audio and data CD

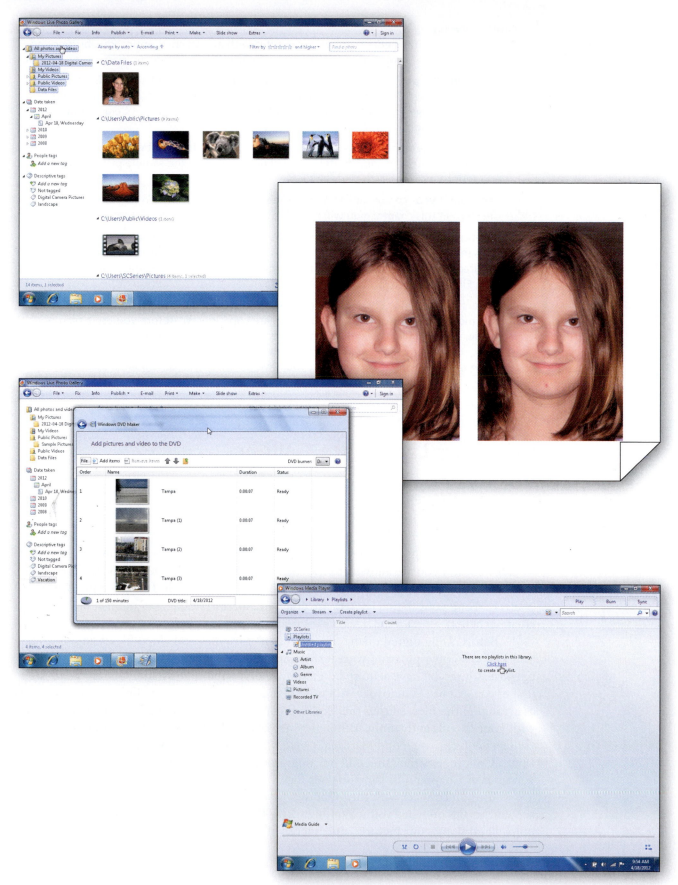

Figure 8–1

**Plan
Ahead**

Digital Media

Working with digital media requires a computer with an attached optical disc burner and basic knowledge of how to use a computer and navigate the Windows 7 operating system.

1. **Determine the permissions you have on the computer you will be using.** Each user account can have different rights and permissions. Depending on which rights and permissions have been set for your account, you might or might not be able to perform certain operations.

2. **Determine whether you have access to the sample files installed with Windows 7.** To complete the steps in this chapter, you will need access to the sample pictures, videos, and sounds installed with Windows 7.

3. **Ascertain if your computer has an attached optical disc burner.** To be able to complete the steps in this chapter, you will need the ability to create optical discs.

4. **Determine if you are allowed to connect a digital camera.** To be able to complete the steps in this chapter, you will need the ability to connect a digital camera and download pictures. If you do not have access to a digital camera, verify that you have access to the Data Files for this chapter.

5. **Understand copyright issues.** When working with digital media, you should be aware that most pictures, movies, and music files are copyrighted. Before you use a picture, movie, or music file, you should make sure that you are not violating any copyrights. Just because you can download a picture, video, or music file from the Internet does not mean that it belongs to you or that you have permission to download and use it.

Windows Live Photo Gallery

Windows 7 allows you to import pictures and videos from your digital camera. You also can acquire pictures from a scanner or download them from the Internet. When working with pictures, you should be aware that most pictures that you did not create yourself, like other digital media files, are copyrighted. When a work is copyrighted, it means that the work belongs to its creator. The pictures that come with Windows 7 are part of Windows 7 and you are allowed to use them, but they are not your property. You only can use them according to the rights given to you by Microsoft. However, pictures that you take using your digital camera are yours to edit, distribute, and publish because you created them.

Before using digital media files such as picture files and video files, you should be aware of any copyrights and whether you are allowed to use the files for your intended purpose. Once you have acquired digital media files and understand your rights to their usage, you can use Windows Live Photo Gallery to manage them. This includes such tasks as arranging the files, editing the files, and compiling them onto a DVD that you can share with your friends and family. Although you cannot edit videos in Windows Live Photo Gallery (you can use Windows Live Movie Maker to edit your videos), Windows Live Photo Gallery uses the same CD burning process to store pictures and videos on CD that you used in Chapter 3 to back up your files.

You can connect with the Windows Live community if you use your Windows Live account to sign in when using Windows Live Photo Gallery. Using this feature, you can upload and share your pictures and videos with others in the Windows Live community.

To Copy Pictures from a Digital Camera to the Computer

A digital camera has many advantages over a traditional camera that uses film. One advantage is that you can print pictures on your own printer and avoid paying a photo-processing lab to develop and print them. Another advantage is that digital cameras store pictures on a reusable storage medium, thus eliminating the costs of purchasing film. Digital cameras also allow you to preview pictures, delete unwanted pictures, and retake pictures prior to copying the pictures to a computer. In addition, digital pictures can be shared easily with friends in e-mail messages or by publishing the pictures to the World Wide Web.

Once you have digital pictures, you can transfer them to Windows 7. Although most digital camera manufacturers include a program designed to transfer pictures from the camera to the computer easily, Windows 7 also can access the pictures stored on the camera or on a memory card within the camera. If Windows 7 has a driver installed for your camera, the AutoPlay feature will provide you with the option to import the pictures using the Import Pictures and Videos dialog box. If AutoPlay is turned off, you can access the Import Pictures and Videos dialog box from within Windows Live Photo Gallery by selecting the Import from Camera or Scanner command from the File enu.

Because AutoPlay is turned on, you will import your pictures by connecting the camera to your computer and allowing AutoPlay to initiate the import process. The following steps import the pictures from a Canon PowerShot SD1100 IS digital camera. If you do not have a digital camera to attach to import pictures, you can copy the 2012-04-18 Digital Camera Pictures folder from the Data Files for this chapter to the Pictures library on your computer following the steps shown on page WIN 482.

1

- Connect the digital camera to an available USB port on the computer.

- If necessary, turn on the digital camera.

- After a moment, the AutoPlay dialog box is displayed (Figure 8–2).

Q&A How can I import pictures taken with a traditional film camera onto the computer?

You can have pictures that are taken from a film camera converted to digital pictures on an optical disc when you get your pictures developed at a photo-processing lab. Then you can copy the pictures from the optical disc to your computer and work with them using Windows Live Photo Gallery. You also can scan in pictures using a scanner.

Q&A What is the difference between importing with Windows 7 and with Windows Live Photo Gallery?

When you import pictures using Windows Live Photo Gallery, the program opens after importing and you can begin working with your pictures. Importing with Windows 7 copies the pictures to the My Pictures folder on the computer without opening Windows Live Photo Gallery.

Figure 8–2

2

- Click the Import pictures and videos using Windows option to display the Import Pictures and Videos dialog box (Figure 8–3).

What happens if I try to import pictures that I already imported?

When Windows 7 imports pictures from the digital camera, it checks to see if the pictures have been downloaded from the camera previously. If Windows determines that it has already downloaded the pictures, a message will display saying that there are no new pictures to import.

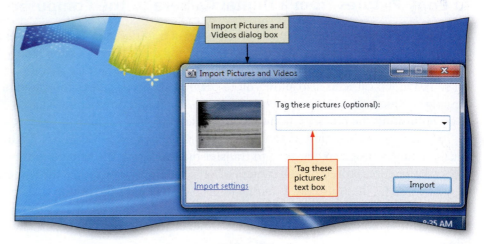

Figure 8–3

3

- Type Digital Camera Pictures in the 'Tag these pictures' text box (Figure 8–4).

Why should I tag my pictures?

Tagging your pictures will make it easier for you to organize them and to find them when you search the gallery.

Figure 8–4

4

- Click the Import settings link in the Import Pictures and Videos dialog box to display a complete list of import settings in the Import Settings dialog box (Figure 8–5).

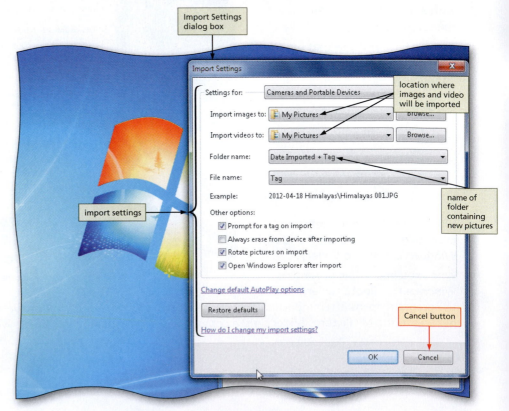

Figure 8–5

5

- After viewing the available options, click the Cancel button to close the Import Settings dialog box without making changes (Figure 8–6).

 Q&A What happens if I change a setting?

If you change the settings and then click the OK button, the Import Pictures dialog box will be displayed with the changes you made in place. All future imports will use the new settings, until you change the settings again.

Figure 8–6

6

- Click the Import button to import the pictures (Figure 8–7).

 Q&A Why did the Import Pictures and Videos dialog box not appear on my screen?

If you are importing a small number of pictures, the Import Pictures and Videos dialog box might only display for a few seconds.

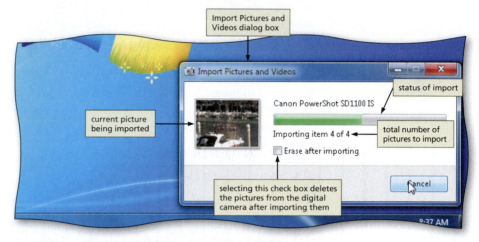

Figure 8–7

7

- After the images are imported, Windows 7 will display your images in a new window (Figure 8–8).

- Turn off your camera and disconnect it from the computer.

- Close the window.

Q&A Why should I turn off and disconnect my camera?

Because you have imported all of the pictures, you no longer

Figure 8–8

need your camera connected to the computer. Most cameras will shut off automatically after a few minutes of inactivity; however, turning your camera off manually will preserve the battery.

Other Ways

1. Open Windows Live Photo Gallery, click File, click 'Import from camera or scanner'

To Copy the Data Files

Because you might not have a picture of a person displaying the red-eye effect in your gallery, one is provided with the Data Files for this chapter. If you have a picture with red-eye, you can use it instead of copying this file. If computer lab restrictions prevent you from creating a folder on the Local Disk (C:), create the folder elsewhere on the hard disk or USB flash drive outside of the Pictures library.

1 Create a folder called `Data Files` on the Local Disk (C:) hard disk.

2 Navigate to the location containing the Data Files.

3 Copy the redeye.jpg picture to the Data Files folder you created.

4 If necessary, close the Local Disk (C:) folder window.

To Open Windows Live Photo Gallery

Because you will be using Windows Live Photo Gallery to work with your pictures, you need to open the program. When you start Windows Live Photo Gallery, you might be prompted to sign in to your Windows Live account. We will not be using the account, so you do not need to sign in.

1 Display the Start menu.

2 Display the All Programs list.

3 Click the Windows Live command to display the Windows Live list.

4 Click the Windows Live Photo Gallery command to open Windows Live Photo Gallery. Click the Cancel button if the 'Sign in to Windows Live' dialog box displays. If necessary, maximize the Windows Live Photo Gallery window.

To Add a Folder to Windows Live Photo Gallery

When you import pictures from your digital camera, they are saved in the My Pictures folder in the Pictures library by default. Additionally, any pictures that you choose to save while working in a Windows 7 program will be saved to the Pictures library. In fact, any files saved in the Pictures library or Videos library will appear in Windows Live Photo Gallery. However, you might have pictures stored on the network or you might use pictures in a program that does not default to the Pictures library. When you have pictures in other locations, you can add them to Windows Live Photo Gallery by adding the folders that contain them to the gallery. The following steps add the Data Files folder to the gallery.

1

- If necessary, make Windows Live Photo Gallery the active window.

- Click the File button to display the File menu (Figure 8–9).

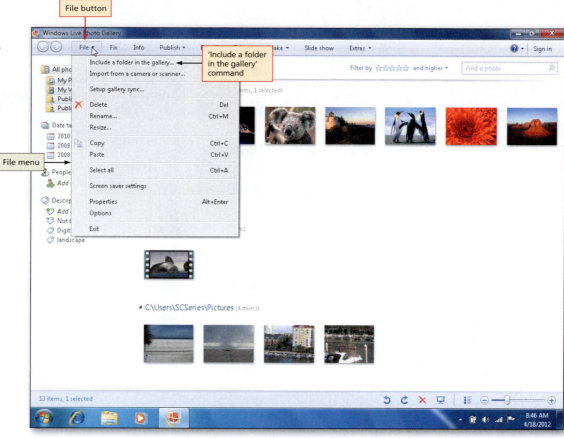

Figure 8–9

2

- Click the 'Include a folder in the gallery' command to display the Include a Folder in the Gallery dialog box (Figure 8–10).

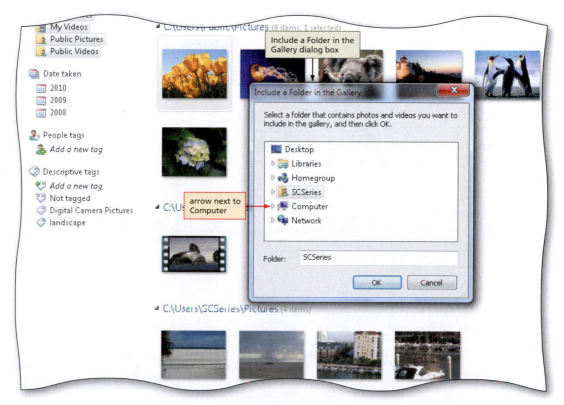

Figure 8–10

3

- Click the arrow next to Computer to expand it.

- Click the arrow next to Local Disk (C:) to expand it.

- Click Data Files to select the folder (Figure 8–11).

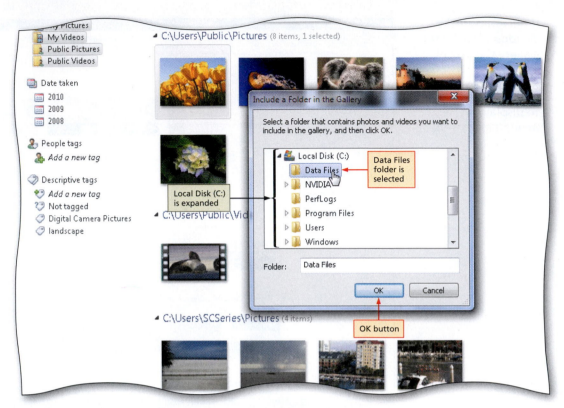

Figure 8–11

4

- Click the OK button to include the folder in the gallery (Figure 8–12).

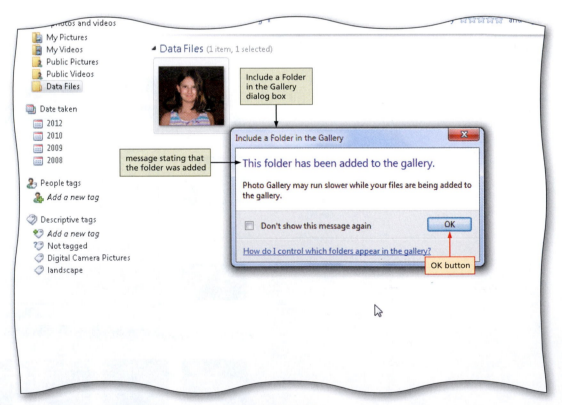

Figure 8–12

5

- Click the OK button to acknowledge that the folder was added (Figure 8–13).

Q&A

Why does the gallery display the Data Files folder?

To demonstrate that the folder was added successfully, Windows Live Photo Gallery opens the new folder and displays its contents.

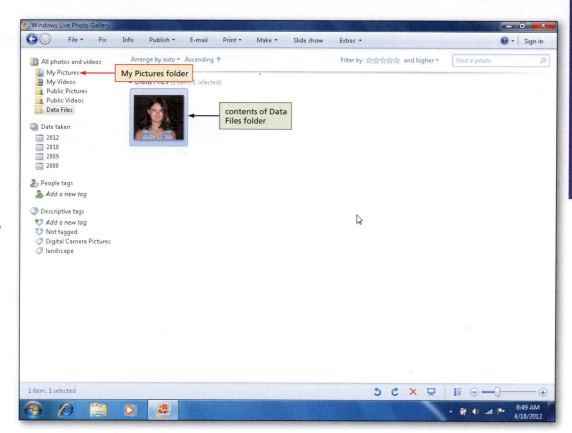

Figure 8–13

Other Ways
1. Right-click 'All photos and videos' folder in the Navigation pane, click 'Include a folder in the gallery'

Viewing Pictures in Windows Live Photo Gallery

Once you start using Windows Live Photo Gallery, you can accumulate a large collection of pictures and videos in the gallery. This can make it difficult to view the gallery in an efficient manner. For this reason, Windows Live Photo Gallery offers many different ways to organize your pictures and videos. You can view your files according to file type, date taken, tags, ratings, or storage location; or by using the thumbnail view or details view; or with an accompanying table of contents. Using these views can save you time and effort when you want to look at the pictures and videos stored on your computer.

To View the My Pictures Folder in the Gallery

By default, Windows Live Photo Gallery displays both pictures and videos. If you only want to view your pictures, you can restrict Windows Live Photo Gallery to display your My Pictures folder. The step on the following page limits your view to the My Pictures folder located in the gallery.

1

- Click the My Pictures folder in the Navigation pane to restrict the view to the My Pictures folder located in the gallery (Figure 8–14).

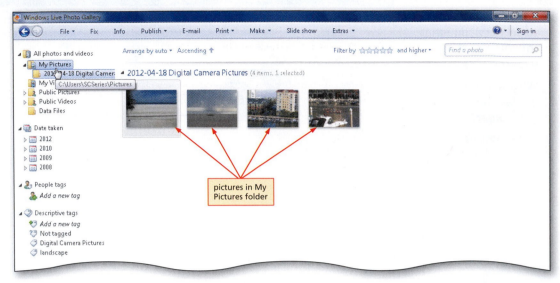

Figure 8–14

To View a Live Preview of a Picture

When you hover your mouse over a picture in the gallery, a live preview of the picture will display. The following step displays a live preview.

1

- Hover your mouse over one of the pictures to display its live preview (Figure 8–15).

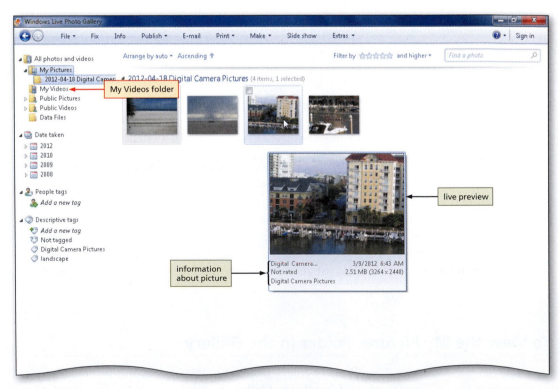

Figure 8–15

To View Videos in the Gallery

As with pictures, you can restrict the view to only show your videos in Windows Live Photo Gallery. The following step displays only the My Videos folder in the gallery.

1

• Click the My Videos folder in the Navigation pane to view only videos in the gallery (Figure 8–16).

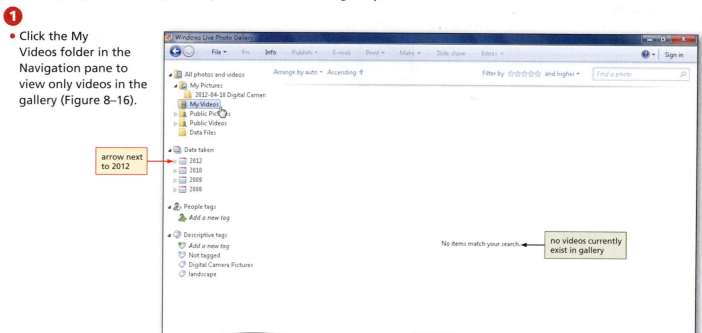

Figure 8–16

To View Pictures by Date Taken

You can view pictures and videos by date. By default, Windows Live Photo Gallery groups pictures by year, but you can expand these categories to view pictures grouped by month and day. The following steps display the pictures taken in April of 2012.

1

• Click the arrow next to 2012 to expand it. If 2012 is not an available option, click another year that is displayed (Figure 8–17).

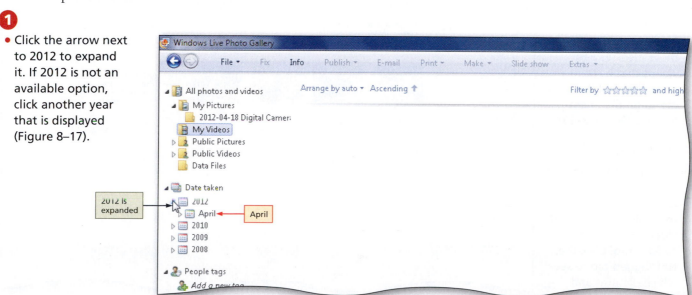

Figure 8–17

- Click April to view pictures taken in April 2012 (Figure 8–18).

 Experiment

- Click a different year to view pictures taken in that year. Expand the year and select a month to view the pictures that were taken in that month.

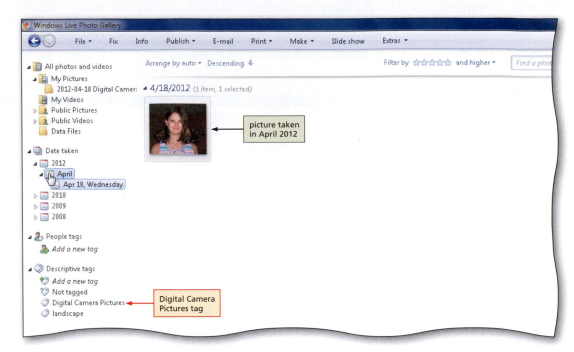

Figure 8–18

To View Pictures by Tags

You can use tags to organize and display pictures and videos. When Windows Live Photo Gallery displays pictures, it generates a list of all of the tags used in the pictures and then displays that list in the Descriptive tags area of the Navigation pane. By clicking on a tag, you can display pictures and videos that contain the tag in their properties. If your pictures have been tagged using People tags, you can use those tags to group pictures by the people in them. The following step displays only those pictures and videos that contain the tag, Digital Camera Pictures.

- In the Navigation pane, click the Digital Camera Pictures tag to display only those pictures and videos that have been assigned the tag, Digital Camera Pictures (Figure 8–19).

 Experiment

- Click the other tags displayed in the Navigation pane to see which pictures and videos are assigned to each tag. Click the Not tagged tag to see which pictures and videos have not been assigned any tags.

Figure 8–19

To View Pictures as Thumbnails with Date Taken

Windows Live Photo Gallery offers several ways to display your pictures and videos. All of the views include small versions of the pictures, known as **thumbnails**. In Windows Live Photo Gallery, thumbnails can be displayed with specific properties of the picture or video appearing underneath the thumbnail, including date taken, file size, rating, or file name. The following steps display pictures and videos in the gallery as thumbnails with the date the picture or video was taken.

1

- Click the 'All photos and videos' folder in the Navigation pane to display all of the pictures and videos in the gallery (Figure 8–20).

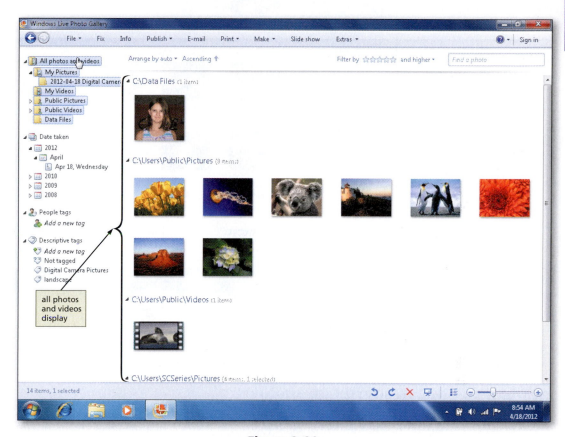

Figure 8–20

2

- Right-click an open area to the right of the pictures and video to display a shortcut menu.

- Point to the View command to display a list of the available views in the gallery (Figure 8–21).

- Write down which view currently is being used.

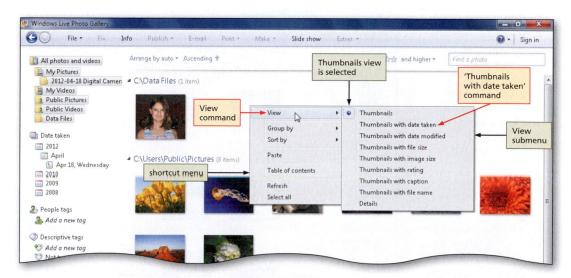

Figure 8–21

3

- Click the 'Thumbnails with date taken' command to display thumbnails with the date and time the picture or video was taken (Figure 8–22).

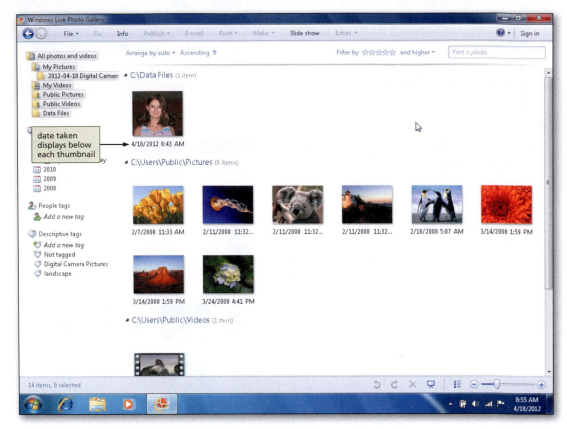

Figure 8–22

To View Pictures Using Details View

You can display all of the details for each picture and video next to its thumbnail using Details view. The following steps display pictures and videos in the gallery in Details view.

1

- Right-click an open area of the window to display the shortcut menu.

- Point to the View command to display the View submenu (Figure 8–23).

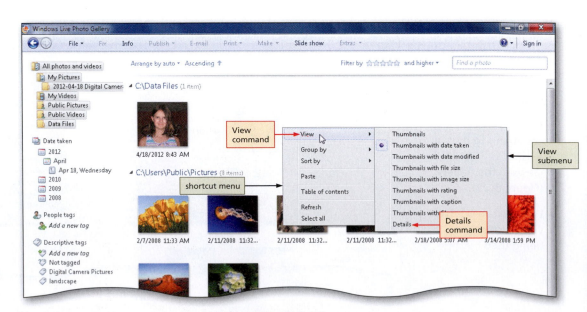

Figure 8–23

2

• Click the Details command to display the pictures and videos in Details view (Figure 8–24).

Q&A

Can I use this view to modify the properties of pictures and videos?

Yes, you can modify the properties by first selecting the property you want to change, and then making your changes.

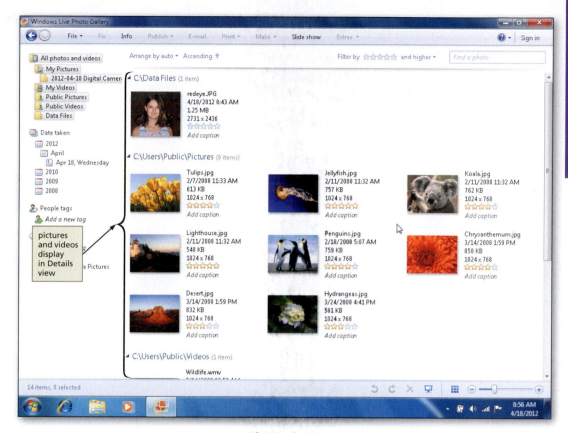

Figure 8–24

To View the Table of Contents

You can view your pictures and videos with the aid of a table of contents. When displayed, the table of contents allows you to peruse your gallery by file location. If you select a tag, rating, folder, or other option in the Navigation pane, the table of contents will change to reflect the option you selected. The table of contents appears to the left of the pictures, and your pictures and videos will continue to display in their current view. The following steps display the table of contents.

1

• Right-click an open area of the window to display a shortcut menu (Figure 8–25).

Figure 8–25

2

• Click the 'Table of contents' command to display the table of contents (Figure 8–26).

 Experiment

• Click the entries in the table of contents to peruse the gallery. Then click the various options in the Navigation pane to see how the table of contents changes to reflect what you have selected.

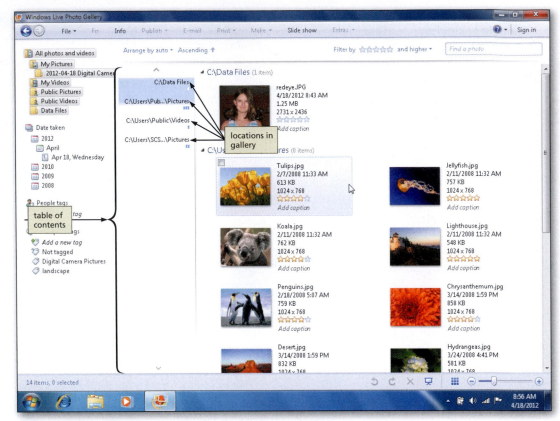

Figure 8–26

3

• After viewing the table of contents, right-click an open area to the right of the pictures to display a shortcut menu.

• Click the 'Table of contents' command to remove the table of contents.

• Right-click an open area of the window to display a shortcut menu.

• Point to View to display a list of available views in the gallery.

Figure 8–27

• Click the option that you wrote down earlier in Step 2 on page WIN 489 to return the pictures to their original display setting (Figure 8–27).

To Sort Pictures

When you use the Navigation pane to view your pictures and videos, the pictures and videos are sorted by the link you select. If you select a folder, the items will appear in alphabetical order. If you select a month, they will be shown for that month sorted by date. You also can sort pictures in ascending or descending order. The following step changes the sort order of the pictures.

- Click the Ascending button to change the sort order of the gallery to descending (Figure 8–28).

- Click the Descending button to change the sort order back to ascending.

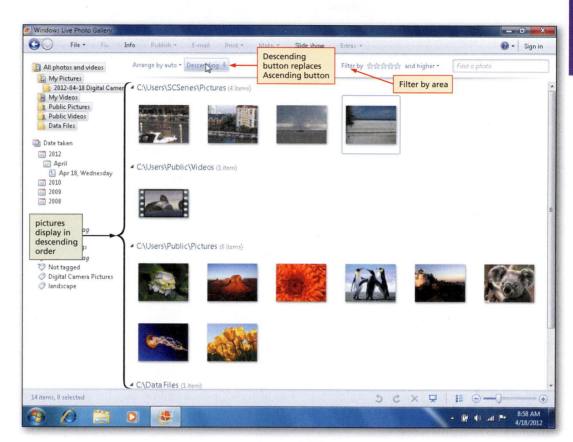

Figure 8–28

To Filter Pictures by Rating

You can rate your pictures as you view them, and then you can restrict your view to only those pictures that match a particular rating. You also can view pictures and videos that have not been assigned a rating. The step on the following page displays all the pictures and videos that have been given a five-star rating.

1

- Click the fifth star in the Filter by area of the gallery to display pictures and videos rated five stars (Figure 8–29).

- Click the Clear filter button to clear the ratings filter.

🔍 **Experiment**

- Click the other stars to see the ratings of the various pictures and videos in the gallery.

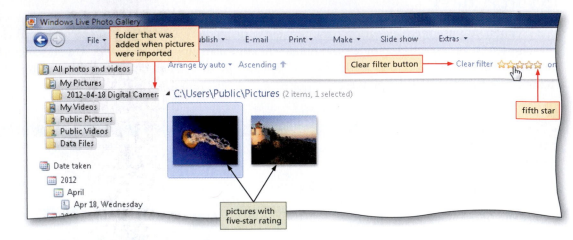

Figure 8–29

Q&A | What is the purpose of the list box to the right of the ratings filter?

The list box lets you select three options for customizing the ratings filter: 'and higher,' 'and lower,' and 'only.' Selecting 'and higher' will find all those pictures that match the specified number of stars as well as any pictures that have more stars than specified. Similarly, 'and lower' will display all pictures that match the specified number of stars as well as any pictures that have fewer stars than specified. Choosing 'only' in the list box restricts the filter to display only those pictures that are rated with the specified number of stars.

To Rename Groups of Pictures

When you imported the pictures from your camera, Windows Live Photo Gallery created file names for the pictures using the tag you entered followed by a number. The first picture was given the name Digital Camera Pictures 001, the second was named Digital Camera Pictures 002, and so on. Although you could rename each picture individually, Windows Live Photo Gallery allows you to rename an entire group of pictures at once. When you rename a group, Windows Live Photo Gallery uses the name you supply for the first picture, and then uses the name followed by a number for the remaining pictures. The following steps rename the pictures in the Digital Camera Pictures folder.

1

- In the Navigation pane, click the folder that was added when you imported the pictures from your camera or copied from the Data Files (Figure 8–30).

Figure 8–30

2

- Select multiple pictures by clicking the first picture, pressing and holding the SHIFT key, and then clicking the last picture.

- Right-click the last picture to display the shortcut menu (Figure 8–31).

Q&A Can I rotate my pictures?

If your pictures are not displayed in the correct orientation, you can use the shortcut menu or the Rotate counterclockwise and Rotate clockwise buttons at the bottom of the window to rotate them. Click the desired direction until the picture is positioned properly.

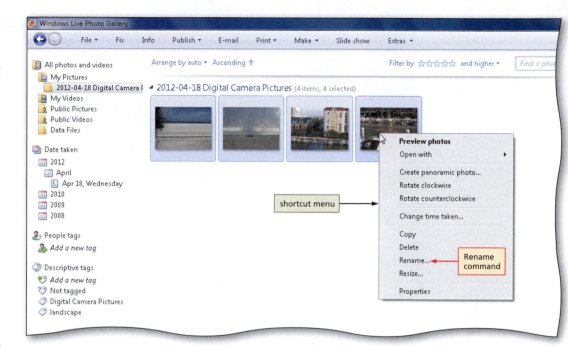

Figure 8–31

3

- Click the Rename command to display the Info pane (Figure 8–32).

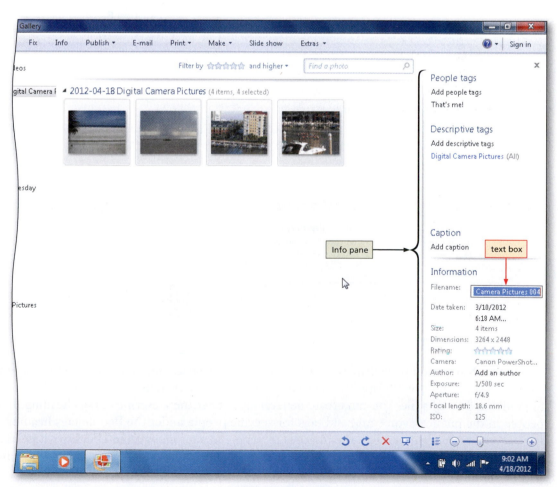

Figure 8–32

4

- Type Tampa in the text box, and then press the ENTER key to rename the pictures (Figure 8–33).

 **Experiment**

- Click the other pictures to view their new names in the Info pane.

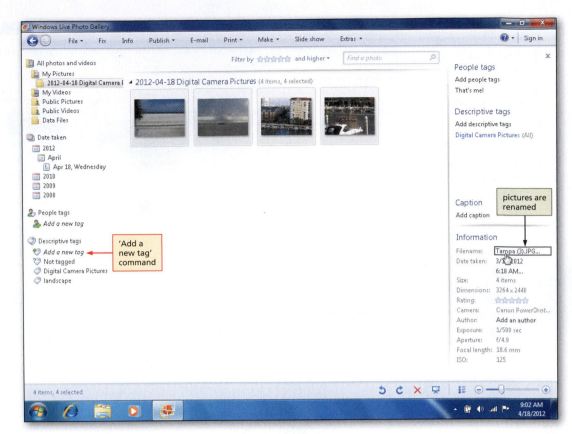

Figure 8–33

Q&A

What is a caption?

A caption is a brief description of a picture. It is longer and more descriptive than a tag. You can add a caption by clicking the Add caption link in the Info panel.

Q&A

Can I rate my pictures using the Info panel?

Yes, besides adding a caption, you can use the Info panel to change the rating of your pictures. You can rate an entire group (in this case) by clicking on the rating star of your choosing.

Other Ways

1. Select files, click Info on toolbar, click file name in Info pane, type new name, press ENTER

2. Select files, click File on toolbar, click Rename, type new name, press ENTER

To Create a Tag

The Navigation pane displays a list of tags that have been applied to the pictures and videos in the gallery. As you recall, you normally apply a tag to a specific file. However, in Windows Live Photo Gallery, you can create a tag independent of a file. You can create general tags under the Descriptive tags heading. If you want to identify the people in the pictures, you could add tags for specific people under the People tags heading. If you have a Windows Live account, you can even link the pictures to people in your contacts in Windows Live. Using Descriptive tags, you can create tags for organizing your pictures and videos before importing them. The following steps create the tag, Vacation.

1

- In the Navigation pane, click the 'Add a new tag' command below the Descriptive tags heading to create a new descriptive tag (Figure 8–34).

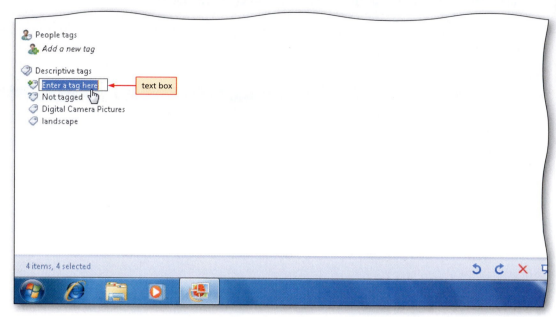

Figure 8–34

2

- Type Vacation in the text box.

- Press the ENTER key to add the tag.

- Click the Descriptive tags command to show all pictures and videos organized by tag (Figure 8–35).

Q&A

Can I add a tag using the Info pane?

Yes. First select a picture (or pictures), click the 'Add descriptive tags' command in the Info panel, and then type a new tag or select from the list of existing tags. The tag is applied to the files that are selected when you add the tag. You cannot enter a tag in the Info pane without first selecting a picture or video.

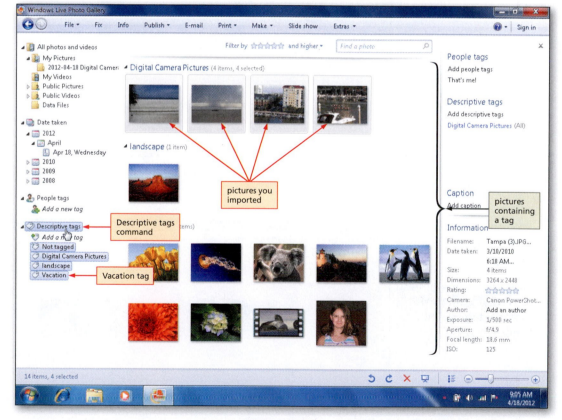

Figure 8–35

To Add Pictures and Videos to a Preexisting Tag

Once you have added your tag, you can assign the tag to pictures by dragging the pictures to the tag. The following steps add the pictures you imported to the Vacation tag.

- Select the pictures you imported.

- Drag the selected files to the Vacation tag (Figure 8–36).

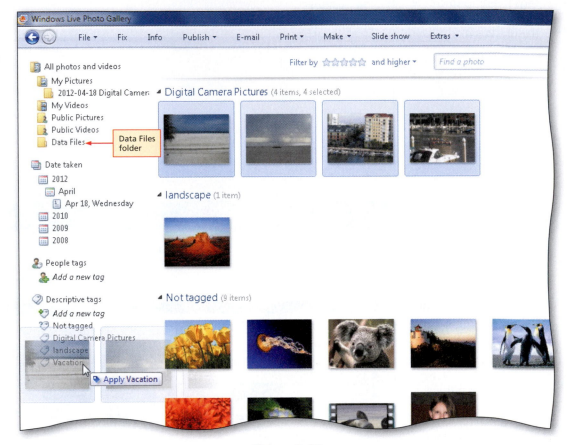

Figure 8–36

- Drop the files on the Vacation tag to assign the tag.

- Click the Vacation tag to view your files with the new tag assigned (Figure 8–37).

Figure 8–37

Editing Pictures

Although you can take great pictures using a digital camera, not all of your pictures will be perfect. For instance, using a flash might cause people's eyes in the picture to reflect light and appear red, known as the **red-eye effect**. You can remove the red-eye effect from a picture by using the editing tools included in Windows Live Photo Gallery.

You also can use Windows Live Photo Gallery to crop the picture to fit standard photo printing sizes. When you **crop** a picture, you trim it to a smaller size, either to improve the composition of the picture or to fit a standard photo printing size. With the cropping tool, you can crop the picture using a preset proportion rectangle so that only the portion that you want to keep is selected, or resize the rectangle by using its control points.

Additionally, you can adjust the exposure and color of a picture manually or by using the auto adjust feature in Windows Live Photo Gallery. When you adjust the exposure, you change the amount of light in the picture, which has the effect of increasing or decreasing the amount of contrast in the picture. Adjusting the color involves altering the color temperature, tint, and saturation. For example, if you set the saturation to its lowest value, you can make a picture look as if it was taken with black and white film. Auto adjusting is best used when you are unsure of how to modify the exposure and color and want Windows Live Photo Gallery to make the adjustments for you. When you are done editing your pictures, you can print them, upload them to a photo-sharing site on the Web, or send them as an attachment to an e-mail message.

To Make a Copy of a Picture

Before editing, it is recommended that you make a backup copy of your picture by using the Make a Copy command on the File menu. Once you have made a copy, you can make changes to the original picture until you are satisfied with your edits, without fear of making an irretrievable mistake. When you are sure that you no longer need or want the copy, you can delete it. The following steps make a copy of the red-eye picture included in the Data Files.

1

- If necessary, scroll the Navigation pane until the Data Files folder is visible.

- Click the Data Files folder to select it (Figure 8–38).

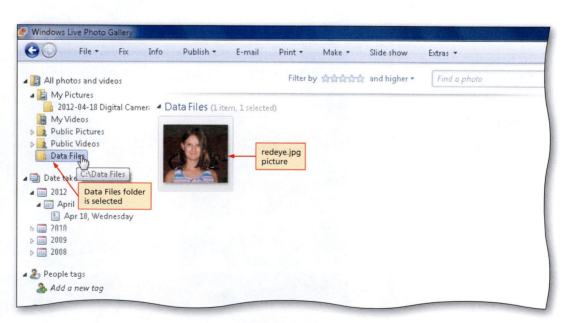

Figure 8–38

2

- Double-click the picture with the file name redeye.jpg to display the edit view of the picture (Figure 8–39).

Q&A

How can I see the picture's file name?

When the mouse hovers over a thumbnail, a live preview of the picture is displayed. In the live preview, the image is shown at a larger size along with its basic properties, including its file name.

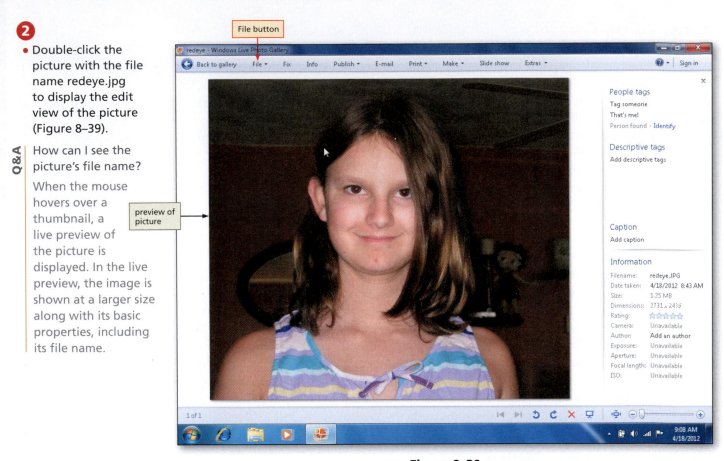

Figure 8–39

3

- Click the File button to display the File menu (Figure 8–40).

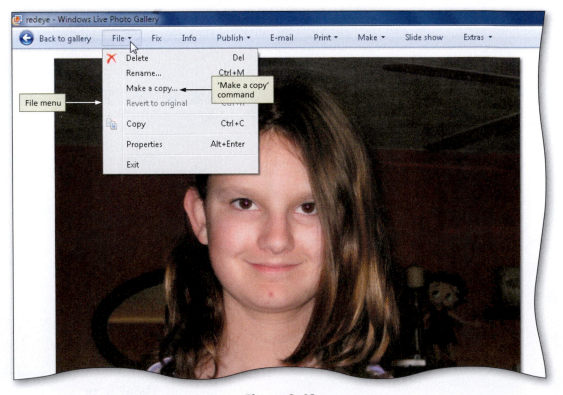

Figure 8–40

4

• Click the 'Make a copy' command to display the 'Make a copy' dialog box (Figure 8–41).

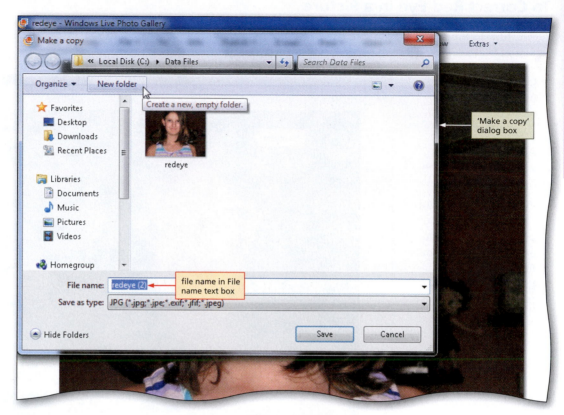

Figure 8–41

5

• Change the file name in the File name text box to redeye – Backup (Figure 8–42).

• Click the Save button to save the copy.

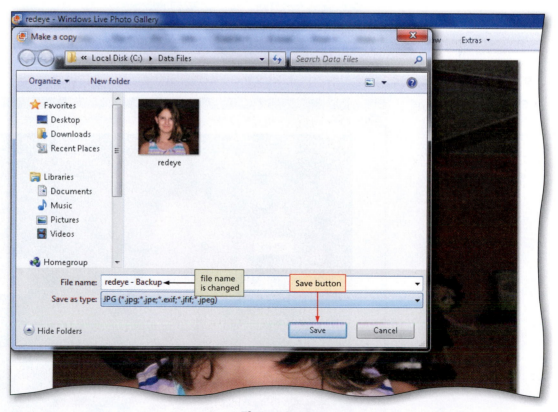

Figure 8–42

To Correct Red-Eye in a Picture

The following steps remove the red-eye effect from the picture.

1

• Click the Fix button on the toolbar to open the Fix pane (Figure 8–43).

Q&A

Am I now working with the copy or the original?

You are working with the original file; the previous steps made a copy of the original file but did not display the copy.

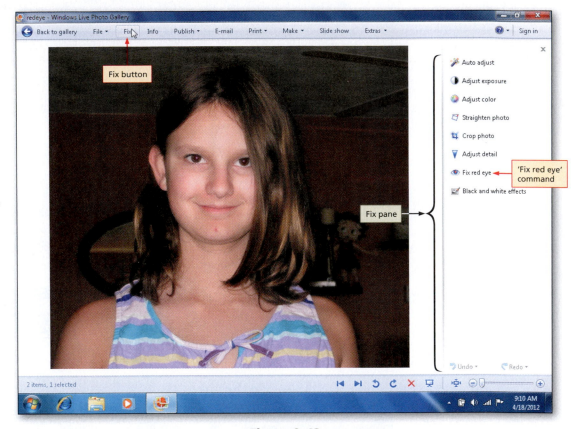

Figure 8–43

2

• Click the 'Fix red eye' command to begin fixing the red-eye effect (Figure 8–44).

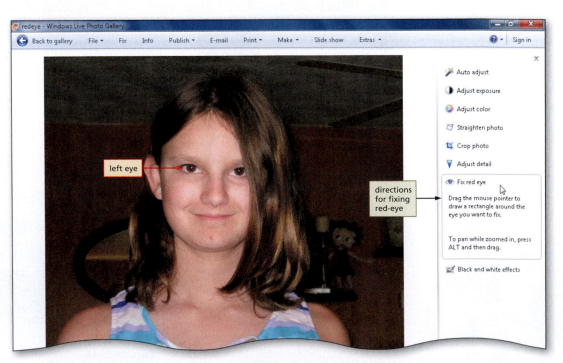

Figure 8–44

3

- Drag the pointer to position a rectangle around the eye on the left (Figure 8–45).

- Release the mouse button to finish fixing the red-eye effect.

Q&A What if I make a mistake?

You can use the Undo button at the bottom of the Fix pane to undo the change you made, and then you can try again.

Q&A Can I zoom in to view the picture in more detail?

Yes. You can use the zoom controls at the bottom of the screen to change the zoom level. You might find it easier to draw the rectangle by enlarging the picture. However, if the rectangle covers more than the eye, Windows Live Photo Gallery still will recognize and correct the red-eye effect; the eye just needs to be within the rectangle.

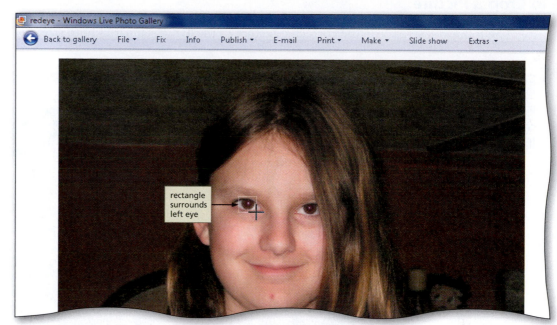

Figure 8–45

4

- Drag the pointer to position a rectangle around the eye on the right (Figure 8–46).

- Release the mouse button to finish fixing the eye.

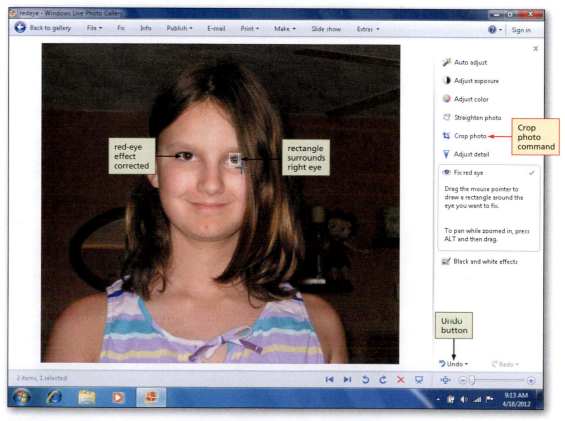

Figure 8–46

To Crop a Picture

The following steps crop the corrected picture to the 4 × 6 standard photo size.

1
- Click the Crop photo command in the Fix pane to display cropping options (Figure 8–47).

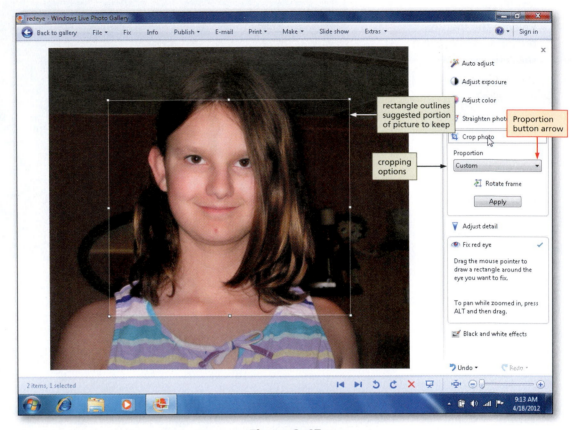

Figure 8–47

2
- Click the Proportion button arrow to display the list of proportion options (Figure 8–48).

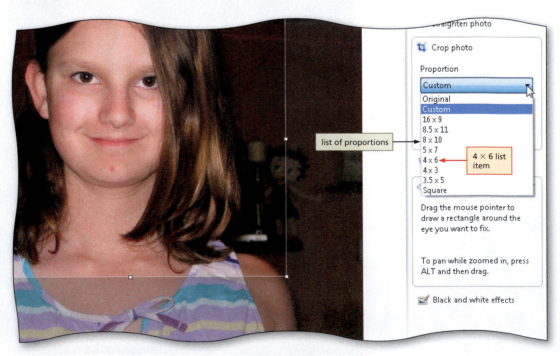

Figure 8–48

- Click the '4 × 6' item to select the 4 × 6 cropping rectangle.

- If necessary, click the Rotate frame command to rotate the 4 × 6 cropping rectangle to portrait view (Figure 8–49).

Q&A

What does the Rotate frame command do?

Use the Rotate frame command to change the orientation of the cropping rectangle from portrait to landscape. This can help when you want the picture to be cropped with a longer width than height.

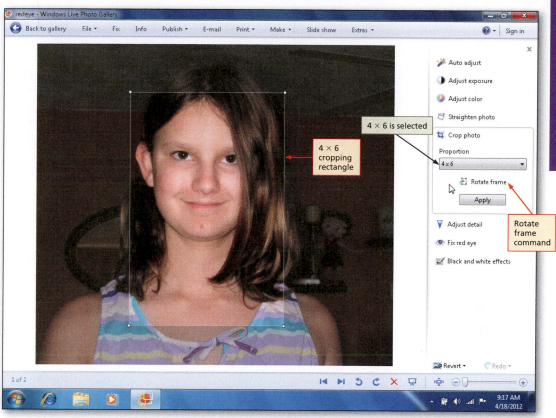

Figure 8–49

- Drag the rectangle over the top of the head so that the head is positioned in the rectangle (Figure 8–50).

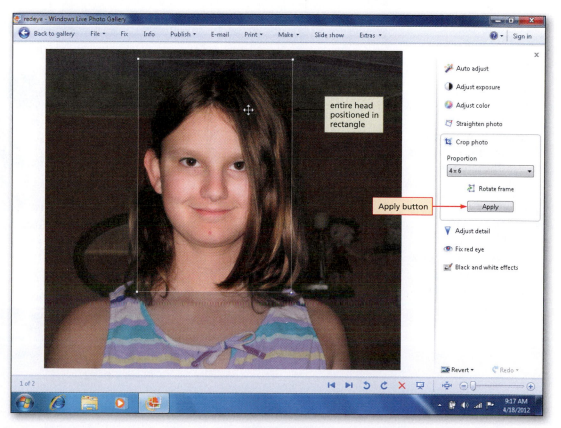

Figure 8–50

- Click the Apply button to crop the picture (Figure 8–51).

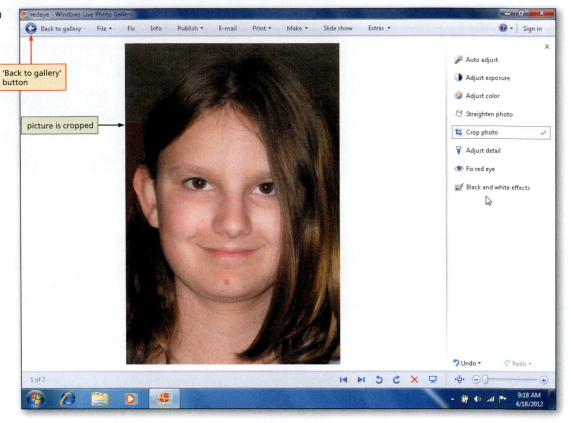

'Back to gallery' button

picture is cropped

Figure 8–51

- Click the 'Back to gallery' button on the toolbar to save the changes and return to the gallery (Figure 8–52).

- Click the OK button to close the Windows Live Photo Gallery dialog box.

Q&A

Do I need to save my changes to the picture?

Windows Live Photo Gallery saves the changes you make automatically.

Print button

message indicating changes automatically saved

Windows Live Photo Gallery

Your changes were automatically saved. You can undo your changes at any time by clicking Revert.

☑ Don't show this message again   OK

Windows Live Photo Gallery dialog box

OK button

Figure 8–52

To Print a Picture

Windows Live Photo Gallery allows you to print pictures directly from the gallery. Using the Print Pictures dialog box, you can select the number of copies, the printing options, and the type of paper to be used, among other options. For best results when printing a picture, you should use high-quality glossy paper designed specifically for printing pictures and select the highest resolution setting on the printer. Although higher resolution settings will increase the time that it takes to print a picture, it will result in a higher-quality printed image. The following steps print two 4 × 6 prints of the picture you just fixed.

- Click the Print button on the toolbar to display the Print menu (Figure 8–53).

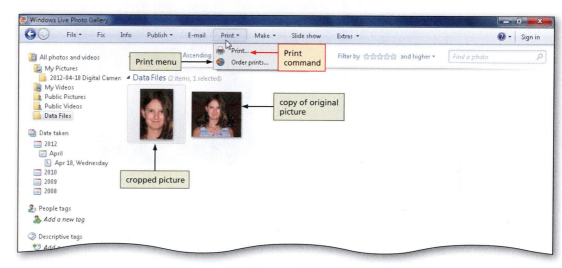

Figure 8–53

- Click the Print command to display the Print Pictures dialog box (Figure 8–54).

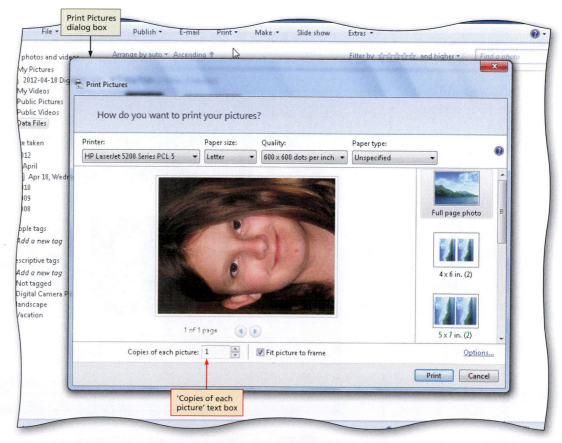

Figure 8–54

3

• Type 2 in the 'Copies of each picture' text box (Figure 8–55).

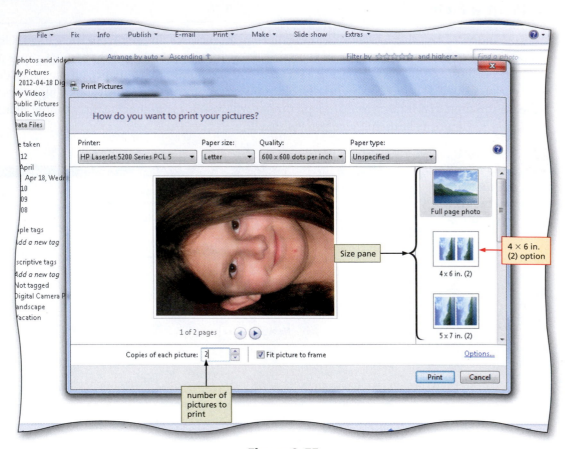

Figure 8–55

4

• Click the '4 × 6 in. (2)' option in the Size pane to select the two 4 × 6 pictures on one page option (Figure 8–56).

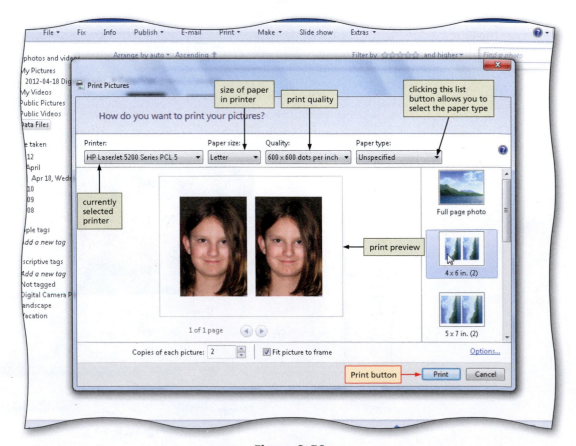

Figure 8–56

5
- Click the Print button to print the pictures (Figure 8–57).

printout

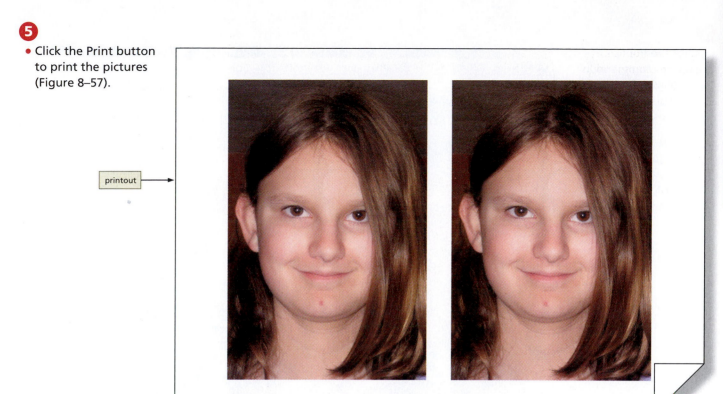

Figure 8–57

Other Ways

1. Select files, press CTRL+P, select options, click Print

To Create a Black-and-White Picture

Windows Live Photo Gallery allows you to adjust the color of your pictures. When adjusting the color, you can change the color temperature, tint, and saturation. Altering the **color temperature** can make the image appear warmer (by adding more red tones) or cooler (by adding more blue tones). Changing the **tint** adjusts the amount of green in a picture. If the colors in your picture look too vivid or dull, adjust the saturation, which determines the amount of color in an image. If you change the saturation level to its lowest setting, you remove the color from the picture. This allows you to convert a color picture into a black-and-white picture. To further adjust the effect, you can experiment with the other color options.

Windows Live Photo Gallery provides a set of black-and-white effects that you can use to create a black-and-white picture more easily than manually adjusting the color options. Options for the black-and-white effects include a choice of filters: none, orange, sepia tone, yellow, red, or cyan. The steps on the following pages transform the Tulips sample picture into a black-and-white picture using a black-and-white effect.

1

- Click the Public Pictures command in the Navigation pane to display the sample pictures.

- Double-click the Tulips.jpg picture to display the edit view of the picture (Figure 8–58).

Figure 8–58

2

- Click the 'Black and white effects' command to display the 'Black and white effects' options (Figure 8–59).

Figure 8–59

3

- Click the Sepia tone effect to apply the Sepia effect to the Tulips picture (Figure 8–60).

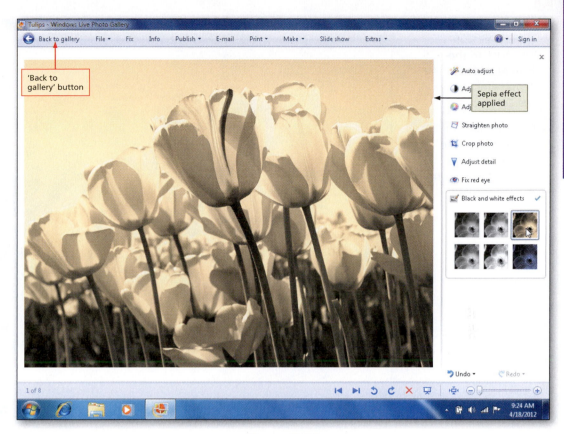

Figure 8–60

To Revert Back to the Original Picture

If you now return to the gallery, the changes you have made will be saved. Up until the changes are saved, you can undo the changes by using the Undo options in the Fix pane. Once saved, you can undo the changes by reverting back to the original. When you revert back to the original picture, all of the changes you have made are undone. Windows Live Photo Gallery keeps a backup of pictures that you edit so that you can revert back to the original as long as the originals have not been deleted. The steps on the following pages revert the Tulips sample picture back to its original.

1

- Click the 'Back to gallery' button to return to the gallery and save the Sepia effect on the Tulips picture.

- Double-click the Tulips.jpg picture to display a preview of the picture (Figure 8–61).

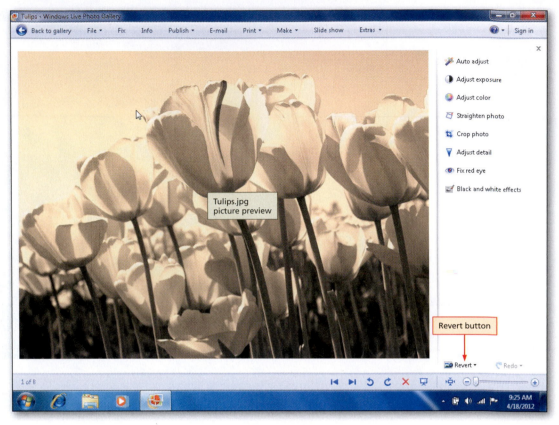

Figure 8–61

2

- Click the Revert button to display the 'Revert to original' dialog box (Figure 8–62).

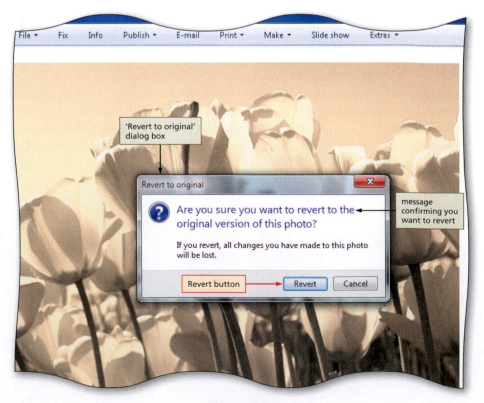

Figure 8–62

- Click the Revert button to revert the picture to its original state (Figure 8–63).

- Click the 'Back to gallery' button to return to the gallery and save the reverted picture.

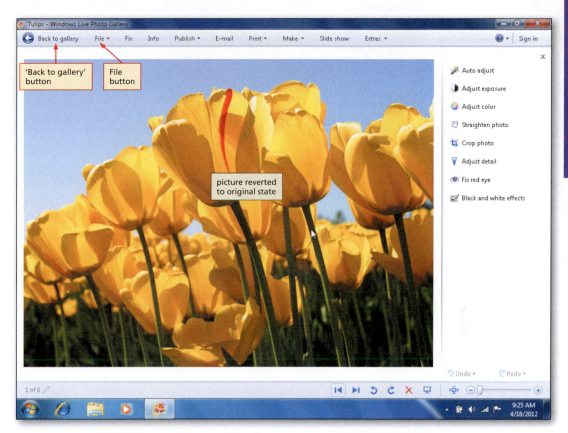

Figure 8–63

To View Windows Live Photo Gallery Options

The reason you can revert back to the original picture after making changes is that a copy of the picture is saved by Windows Live Photo Gallery automatically. Although you cannot access this original except by reverting, you can adjust the Windows Live Photo Gallery options so that these originals are deleted to save space. In the Windows Live Photo Gallery Options dialog box, you can set the import settings used when importing pictures and adjust tag settings when publishing pictures as well as cleaning up unused tags. The steps on the following page display the Windows Live Photo Gallery options without making changes.

1

- Click the File button to display the File menu.

- Click the Options command to display the Windows Live Photo Gallery Options dialog box (Figure 8–64).

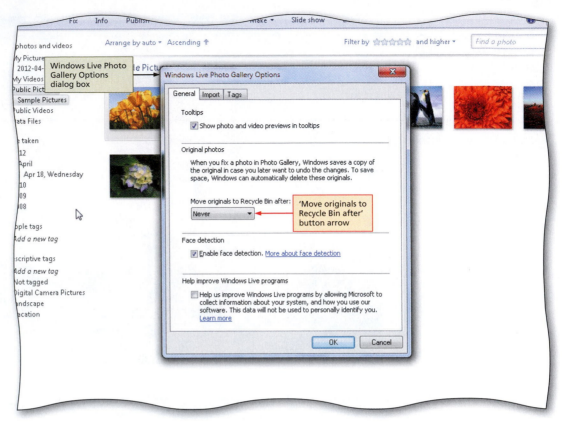

Figure 8–64

2

- Click the 'Move originals to Recycle Bin after' button arrow to display a list of deletion options (Figure 8–65).

- After viewing the options, click the button arrow again to close the list.

- Click the Cancel button to close the dialog box without making changes.

Experiment

- Click the Import and Tags tabs to see which settings you can configure in the gallery.

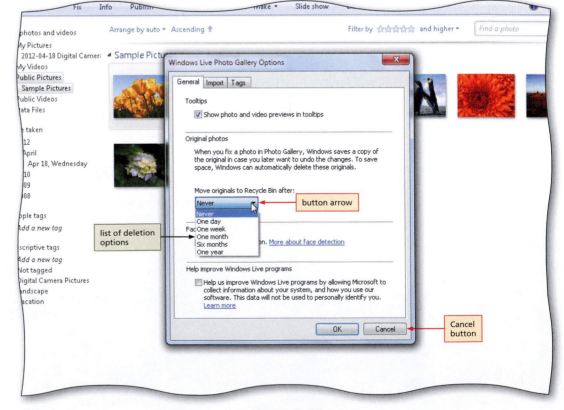

Figure 8–65

To Order Pictures Online

Another way to obtain printed copies of your pictures is to order prints online. Using Windows Live Photo Gallery, you can order prints using the Order Prints dialog box. The Order Prints dialog box allows you to select the company you want to use to print the picture, select the quantity and print size, and pay using available payment options. Sometimes, the printer's Web site will recommend settings for your pictures based upon the quality of your pictures. Depending upon the quality of the picture, you might only be able to select certain print sizes. You then can choose to pick up the pictures at a local store or have them mailed to you. The following steps begin the process of ordering prints of the vacation pictures.

- Click the Vacation tag to display the vacation pictures.

- Select all of the pictures to prepare to order the prints (Figure 8–66).

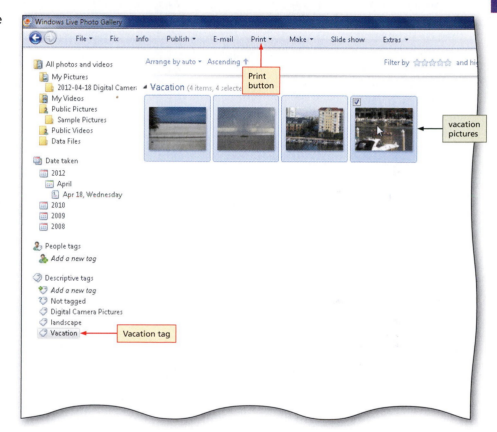

Figure 8–66

- Click the Print button on the toolbar to display the Print menu (Figure 8–67).

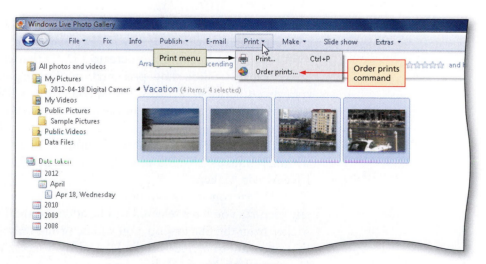

Figure 8–67

3

● Click the Order prints command to display the Order Prints dialog box (Figure 8–68).

4

● If you decide to order prints, you first select a print-ing company, and then click the Send Pictures button. Follow the on-screen prompts to order your prints. If you decide not to order prints, click the Cancel button.

Q&A

What can I expect when ordering prints?

Expect to be prompted to upload your files to the printing company's Web site. Once your files are uploaded, you will select the size and number of prints you want for each file. Next, you will be prompted to enter your billing information, including your credit card details. Many printing companies will give you the option to have your prints mailed to you or to pick them up at a local store.

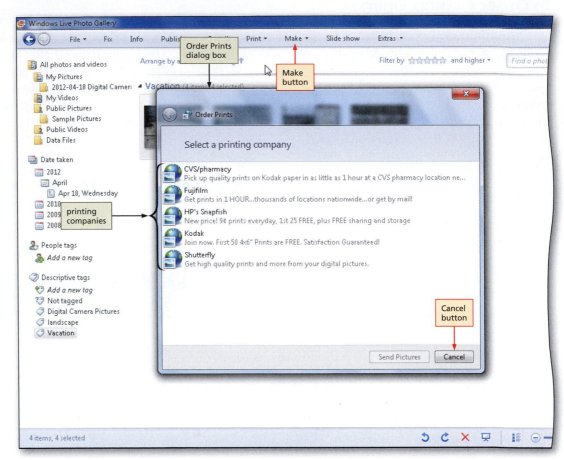

Figure 8–68

Windows DVD Maker

Windows DVD Maker allows you to create a DVD of your files either as a backup or to share with other people. Any DVD player can play the DVDs that you make using Windows DVD Maker. If you create a DVD that contains pictures, Windows DVD Maker creates a slide show presentation of your pictures, complete with fade and cut transitions between pictures. When you create a DVD, you can customize the text and style of the DVD menu, add music, change the timing and transition style of the slide show, and add pan and zoom effects. If you add music to your DVD, it will play in the background while the slide show is running. You can access Windows DVD Maker from within Windows Live Photo Gallery, from the Start menu, or from within Windows Live Movie Maker.

When you access Windows DVD Maker from within Windows Live Photo Gallery, any pictures you have selected will be added to the DVD. If you run Windows DVD Maker from the Start menu, you will be prompted to select the pictures and videos that you want to include on the DVD. If you access Windows DVD Maker from within Windows Live Movie Maker, the movies you have selected will be added. In this section, you will create a DVD by opening Windows DVD Maker from within Windows Live Photo Gallery.

To Open Windows DVD Maker

When you are ready to create your DVD, you first need to select the desired pictures or videos, and then open Windows DVD Maker. Once you have opened Windows DVD Maker, you can continue to add pictures and videos before proceeding. By default, the title will be the date that the DVD is created, but you can change the title to one of your choosing. The following steps select your vacation pictures and then open Windows DVD Maker.

1

- If necessary, select all of the vacation pictures.

- Click the Make button on the toolbar to display the Make menu (Figure 8–69).

Figure 8–69

2

- Click the Burn a DVD command to open Windows DVD Maker (Figure 8–70).

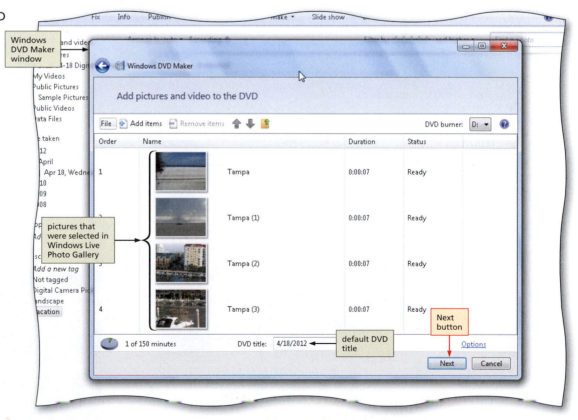

Figure 8–70

To Change the DVD Title

Now you can change the title of the DVD from the default of today's date. The following steps change the title to Vacation Photos.

 1

- Click the Next button to view the DVD burning options (Figure 8–71).

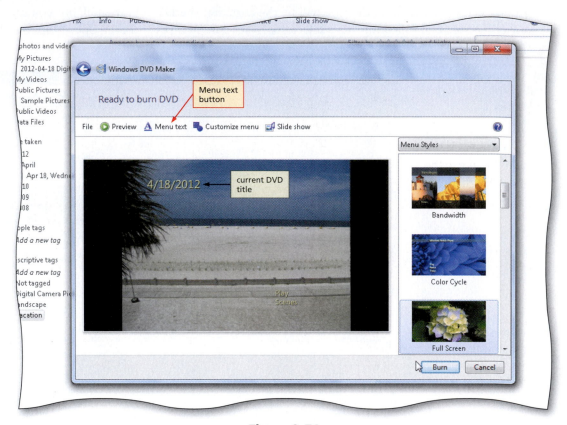

Figure 8–71

2

- Click the Menu text button to display Menu text settings (Figure 8–72).

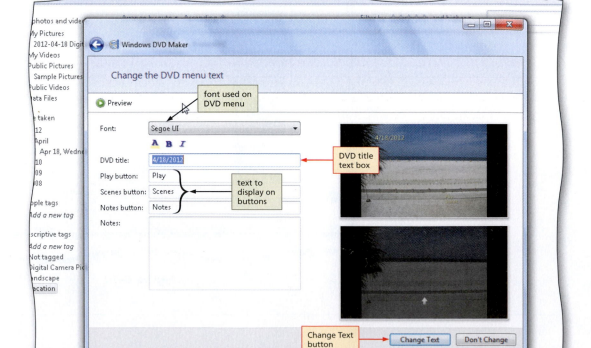

Figure 8–72

3

- Type Vacation Photos in the DVD title text box.

- Click the Change Text button to apply the changes (Figure 8–73).

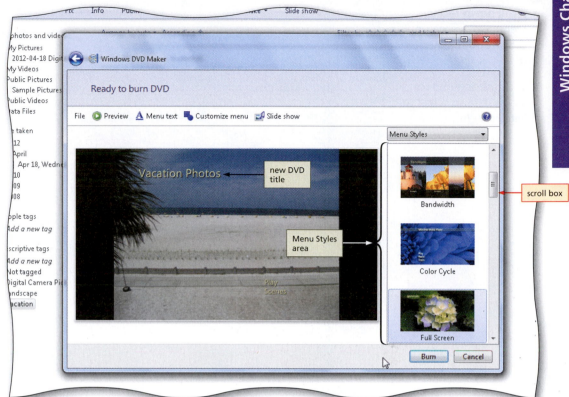

Figure 8–73

To Select a DVD Menu Style

Windows DVD Maker will create a menu for navigating your DVD automatically. You can select a layout for the menu in the Menu Styles area. If the menu style options are not to your liking, you can click the Customize menu button and then add a foreground or background video to the menu, add music to be played while the menu is displayed, or adjust the menu button style. The step on the following page selects the Scrapbook menu style from the list of included layouts.

1

- Scroll down in the Menu Styles area until the Scrapbook menu style is visible.

- Click the Scrapbook menu style to select it (Figure 8–74).

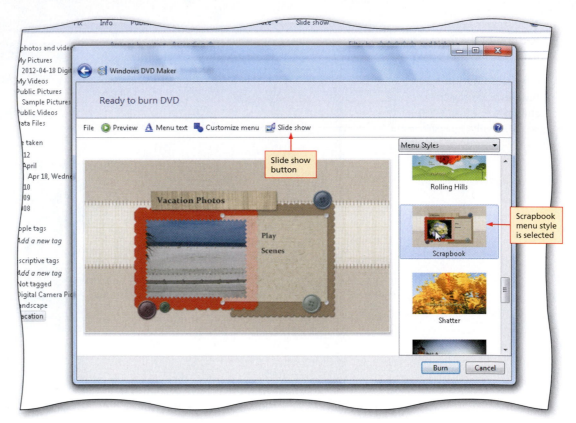

Figure 8–74

To Change Slide Show Settings

Windows DVD Maker provides other options for customizing your DVD slide show. To enliven your DVD, you can add music to be played during the slide show. You can modify other aspects of the slide show, such as selecting the types of transitions and pan and zoom effects. The following steps select the Sleep Away sample music file to play in the background of your DVD, and then change the transition type to Flip.

1

• Click the Slide show button to view slide show settings (Figure 8–75).

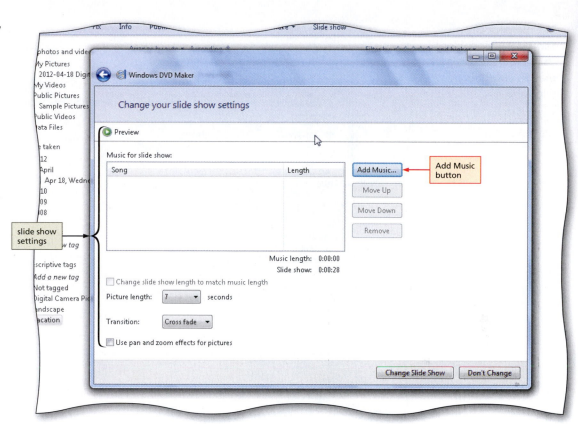

Figure 8–75

2

• Click the Add Music button to display the Add Music to Slide Show dialog box (Figure 8–76).

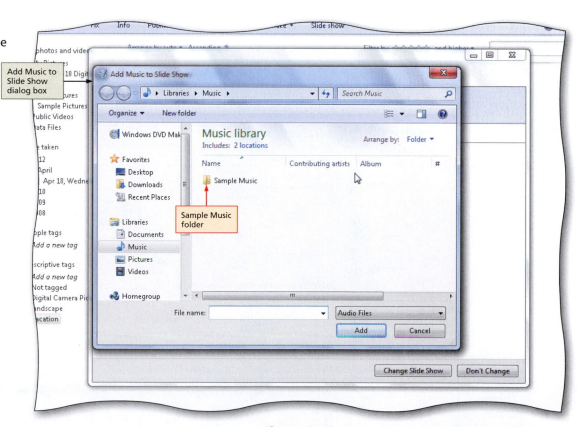

Figure 8–76

- Double-click the Sample Music folder to open it and display its contents (Figure 8–77).

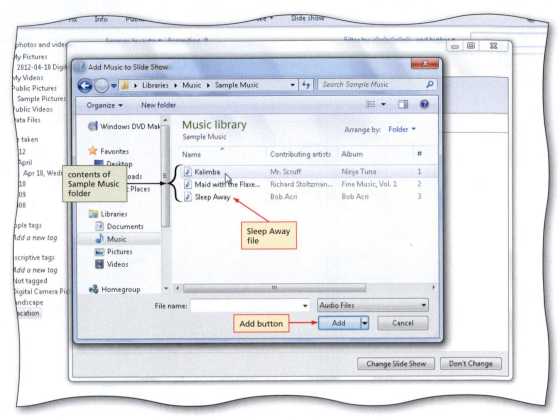

Figure 8–77

- Select the Sleep Away file.

- Click the Add button to add the music file to the slide show (Figure 8–78).

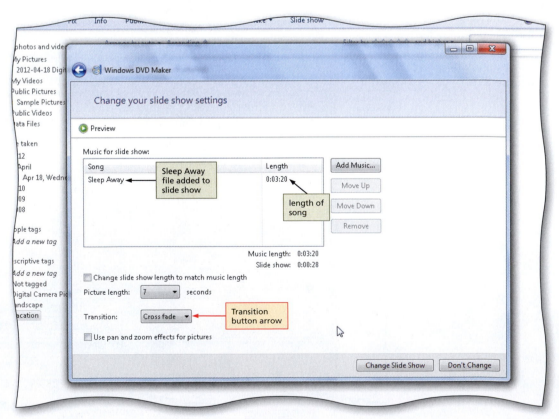

Figure 8–78

5
- Click the Transition button arrow to display a list of transition options (Figure 8–79).

- Click the Flip option to change the transition to the Flip effect.

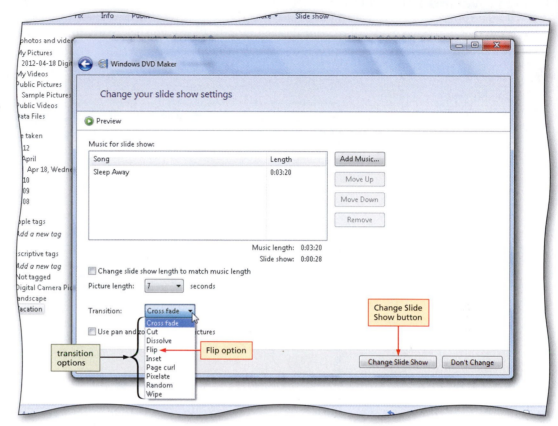

Figure 8–79

6
- Click the Change Slide Show button to apply the changes (Figure 8–80).

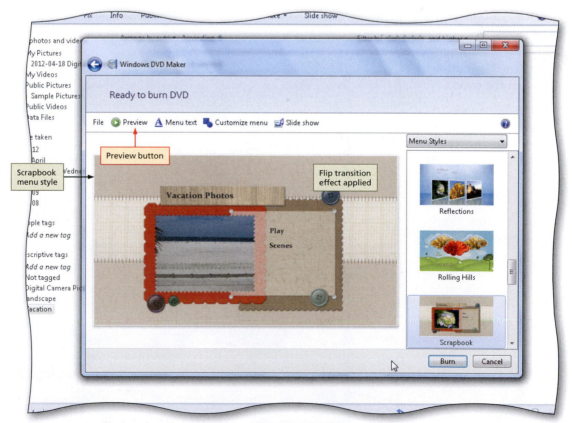

Figure 8–80

To Preview and Burn a DVD

Now that you have made all of your desired modifications, you are ready to preview the slide show and then burn the DVD. The following steps preview and burn the DVD.

• Click the Preview button to preview the DVD (Figure 8–81).

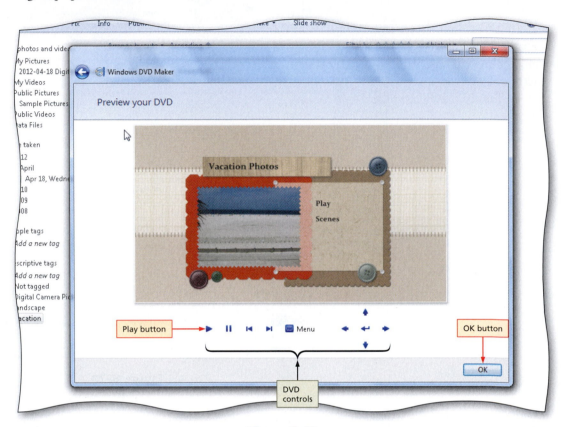

Figure 8–81

2

• Click the Play button to start the preview.

• After viewing the preview, click the OK button to close the preview (Figure 8–82).

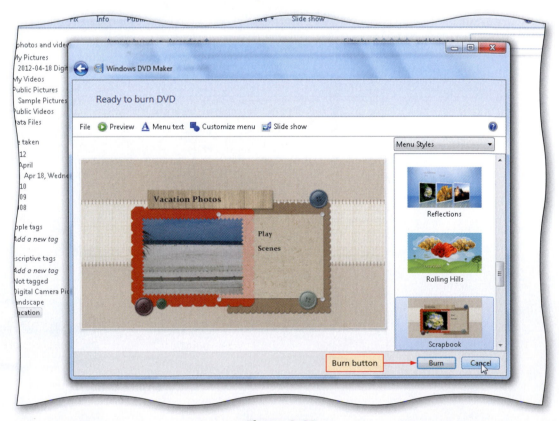

Figure 8–82

3

- Click the Burn button to burn the DVD.

- When prompted, insert a blank DVD.

- A Windows DVD Maker dialog box displays an animated progress bar while the slide show is burned to the DVD.

- After the DVD is complete, a confirmation message is displayed (Figure 8–83).

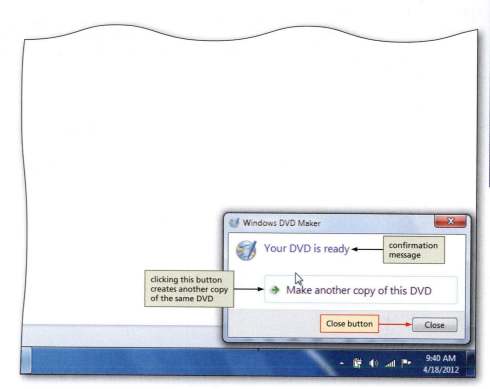

Figure 8–83

4

- Click the Close button to return to Windows DVD Maker (Figure 8–84).

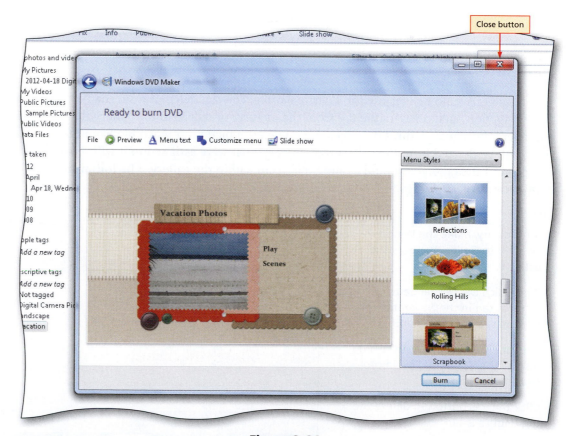

Figure 8–84

- Close Windows DVD Maker.

- Click the No button to return to Windows Live Photo Gallery without saving the project (Figure 8–85).

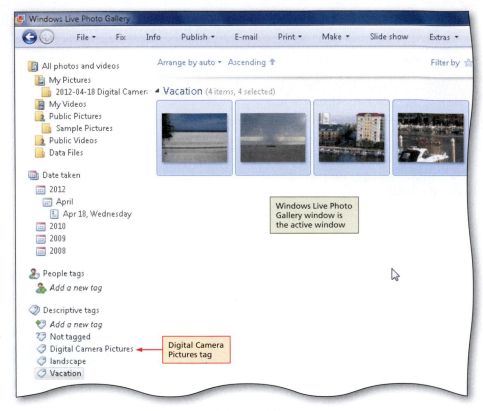

Figure 8–85

To Delete Tags

If you have no further use for a particular tag, you can delete it from the Navigation pane. Deleting a tag from the Navigation pane removes the tag from the pictures or videos in the gallery that contained the tag, but it does not delete the actual pictures or videos. If you delete a picture or video file from the Pictures library, that picture or video will be deleted from the gallery, but any tags that were assigned to it will remain in the Navigation pane. If you do not need the tags, you should delete them from within the gallery. The following steps delete the Digital Camera Pictures and Vacation tags.

- If necessary, make the Windows Live Photo Gallery window the active window.

- Right-click the Digital Camera Pictures tag in the Navigation pane to display a shortcut menu.

- Click the Delete command to display the Windows Live Photo Gallery dialog box.

- Click the Yes button to delete the tag (Figure 8–86).

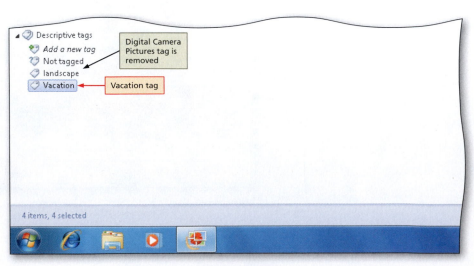

Figure 8–86

2

- Right-click the Vacation tag in the Navigation pane to display a shortcut menu.

- Click the Delete command to display the Windows Live Photo Gallery dialog box.

- Click the Yes button to delete the tag (Figure 8–87).

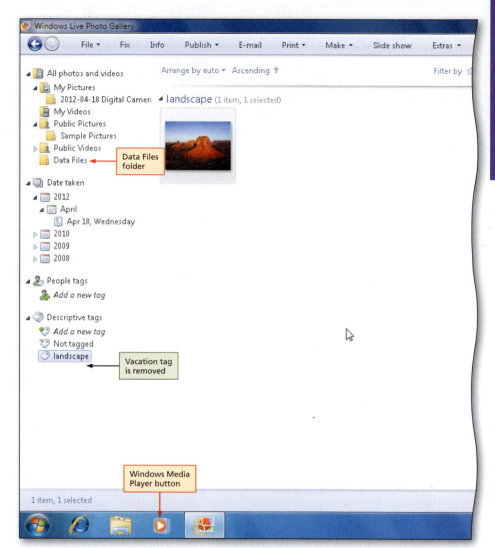

Figure 8–87

To Delete the Data Files and Imported Pictures

Now that you are finished using Windows Live Photo Gallery and Windows DVD Maker, you can delete the Data Files folder and associated pictures. Windows Live Photo Gallery gives you two options for folders: you can remove them from the gallery, which only removes the reference from the gallery, or you can delete the folder, which removes the reference from the gallery and deletes it from the computer. The following steps delete the pictures and folders you added to the computer.

1 If necessary, scroll to view the Data Files folder in the Navigation pane.

2 Right-click the Data Files folder and click the Delete command.

3 Click the Yes button in the Delete Folder dialog box.

4 Delete the Digital Camera Pictures folder in the Navigation pane.

5 Close Windows Live Photo Gallery.

Windows Media Player

Windows Media Player allows you to play CDs and DVDs, view any currently playing digital media, organize and play audio and video files, download audio and video files from the Internet, rip music from an audio CD to the computer, listen to Internet radio stations, and copy audio files to a CD or portable media player. You can play music and videos stored in a Windows Media format, such as Windows Media Audio (wma) and Windows Media Video (wmv), as well as MP3, MPG, and WAV music files. Microsoft Update keeps Windows Media Player up to date automatically by downloading and installing any updates as they are available.

To Open Windows Media Player

The following step opens Windows Media Player.

1 Click the Windows Media Player button on the taskbar to open Windows Media Player. If necessary, maximize the Windows Media Player window (Figure 8–88).

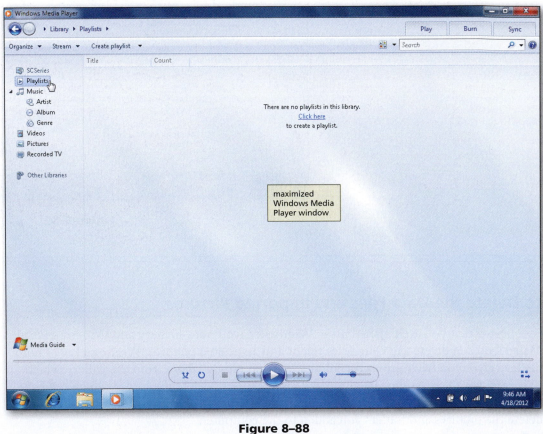

Figure 8–88

Other Ways

1. Click Start, click All Programs, click Windows Media Player

To View the Player Library Categories

Windows Media Player scans your computer automatically and includes any media files that it finds in your libraries. (You also can manually add folders to the Windows Media Player library.) These media files are organized into a Player library maintained by Windows Media Player. The Windows Media Player library is organized into categories based upon media type: music, pictures, videos, recorded TV, and other media. For each type, you can view and organize your digital files based upon the properties for that category. When you play a media file, it will be added to the Player library automatically as long as it is not located on removable media, such as a USB flash drive, an optical disc, or a network drive. When you have a set of songs that you like, you can create a playlist for the set. Windows Media Player includes a Playlists category that allows you to view all of your playlists.

When Windows Media Player first opens, it displays the Music category. If you switch to a different category and then close Windows Media Player, the new category will be displayed the next time you open Windows Media Player. The following steps explore the different Player library categories.

1
• Click Playlists in the Navigation pane to switch to the Playlists category (Figure 8–89).

 Why are no playlists listed?

If there are no files in that category, nothing will display. This could be due to files being deleted or not yet added to the Player library.

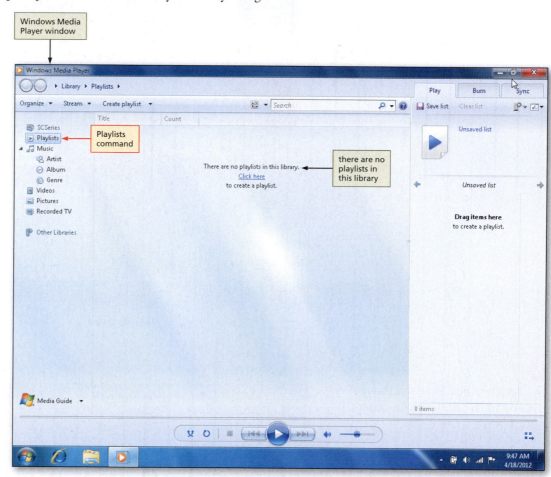

Figure 8–89

2
• Click Videos in the Navigation pane to switch to the Videos category (Figure 8–90).

 Are these the same files displayed in Windows Live Photo Gallery?

Yes and no. Windows Live Photo Gallery and Windows Media Player both display pictures and videos from the same personal and public folders in the Pictures and Videos libraries. Windows Media Player also will include any picture that you have viewed using Windows Media Player even if the picture is not located in the Pictures or Videos library.

Figure 8–90

● Click Pictures in the
Navigation pane
to switch to the
Pictures category
(Figure 8–91).

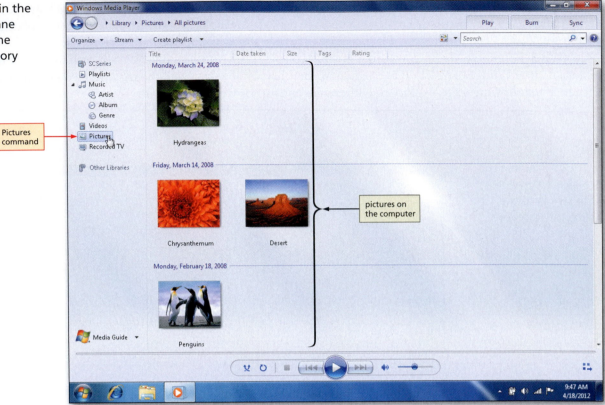

Figure 8–91

● Click Recorded TV in the Navigation
pane to switch to the Recorded TV
category (Figure 8–92).

Figure 8–92

5
- Click Music in the Navigation pane to return to the Music category (Figure 8–93).

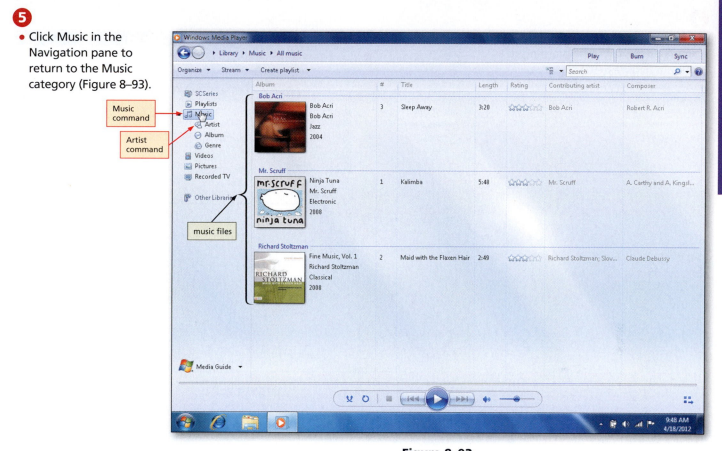

Music command

Artist command

music files

Figure 8–93

Other Ways

1. Click Library arrow on Player navigation bar, click desired category

To Filter Player Library Listings

You can use the Navigation pane to filter the Player library listings according to artist, album, and genre. You also can choose to view songs by rating and filter songs that are one-, two-, three-, four-, or five-star rated. The following steps display songs organized by artist, by album, and, finally, by genre.

1
- Click Artist in the Navigation pane to display files according to artist (Figure 8–94).

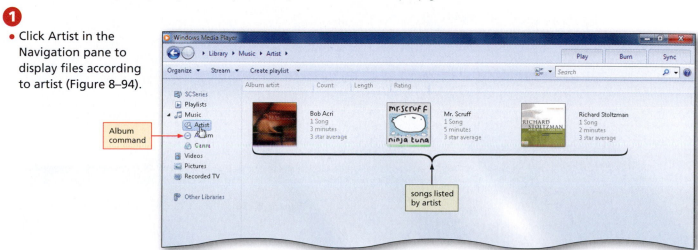

Album command

songs listed by artist

Figure 8–94

2

● Click Album in the Navigation pane to display files according to album (Figure 8–95).

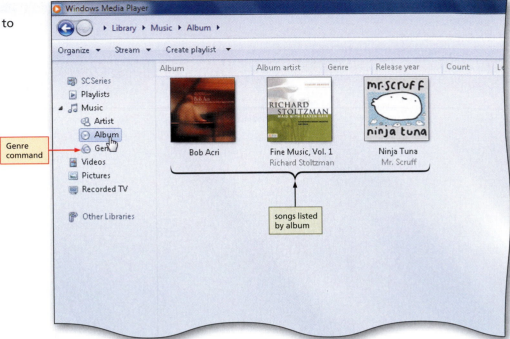

Figure 8–95

3

● Click Genre in the Navigation pane to display files according to genre (Figure 8–96).

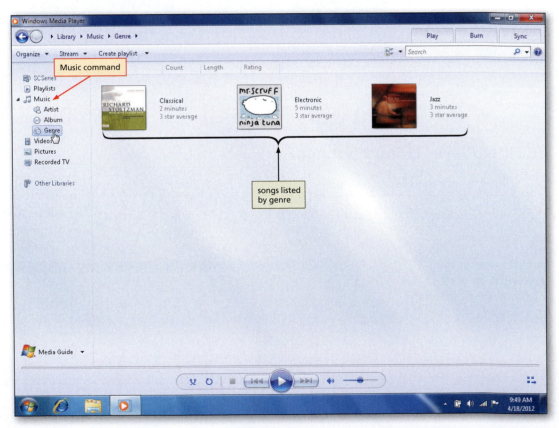

Figure 8–96

4
- Click Music in the Navigation pane to display all songs in the Player library using the expanded tile view (Figure 8–97).

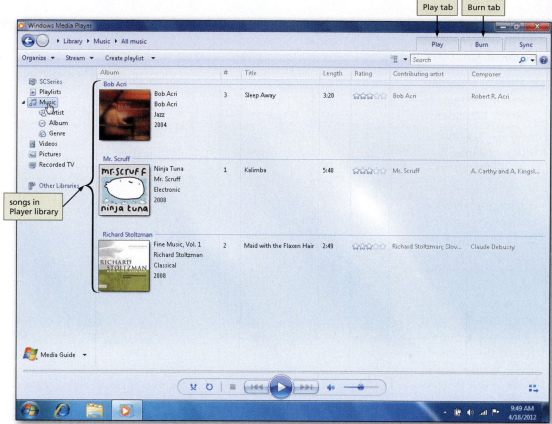

Figure 8–97

To Rip a Song from a CD

Windows Media Player can import (or rip) music from your audio CDs and add them to your Player library. You need to be mindful of copyright rules before you rip music from a CD. If you insert a CD when the Burn tab is active, the rip process will start automatically, and the contents of the CD will be added to the Player library. While Windows Media Player is ripping the music, it also will play the CD. Alternatively, you can insert the CD while the Play tab is active, which simply plays the CD. If you then want to rip the CD, you can switch to the Burn tab, select the desired tracks, and Windows 7 will rip the songs and add them to the Player library. The steps on the following pages rip one song from a CD.

❶

- Insert a music CD in the optical disc drive (Figure 8–98).

- If another program opens and begins to play the CD, close it.

Q&A Why did the CD I inserted display as unknown?

Not all music CDs have album cover or track information on them that can be displayed in Windows Media Player. In that case, a musical note is shown, and the CD properties are listed as unknown. The tracks will be displayed as Track 1, Track 2, and so on. After you have ripped the tracks, you can enter the artist, album, and song data manually.

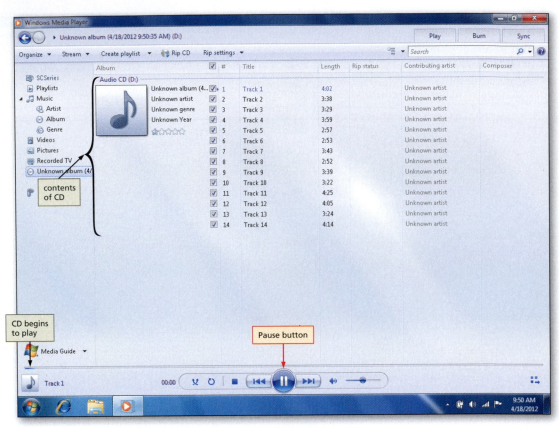

Figure 8–98

❷

- Click the Pause button to pause the playing of the CD (Figure 8–99).

Q&A Why did the CD information just now appear?

Windows Media Player can take a few seconds to read and display the CD information. If Windows Media Player cannot read the track information from the CD, the CD will remain identified as unknown.

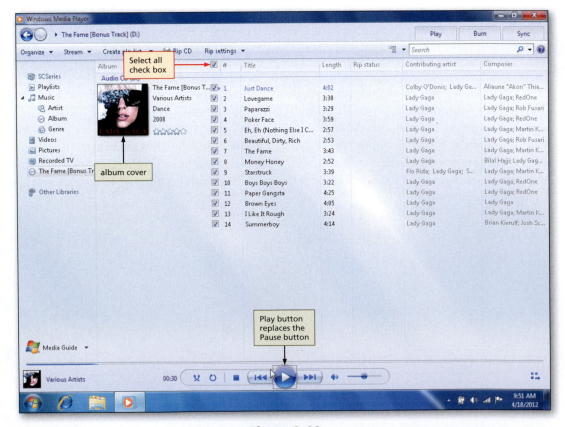

Figure 8–99

- Click the Select all check box to deselect all the tracks (Figure 8–100).

Q&A

Why am I deselecting all of the tracks?

You only are ripping one track right now. You either can deselect one track at a time, leaving the selected track checked, or you can deselect all of the tracks at once and then select the track that you want to rip. By using the Select all check box, you can make your selection quickly.

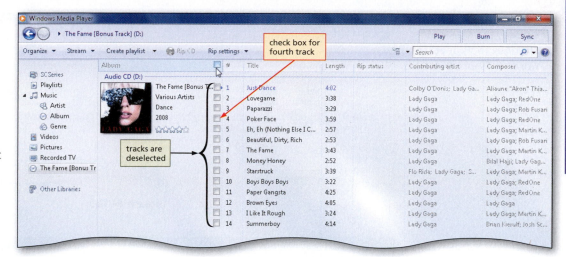

Figure 8–100

- Click the check box next to the fourth track to select it (Figure 8–101).

Figure 8–101

5

- Click the Rip CD button to start the rip process (Figure 8–102).

Figure 8–102

- After the song is ripped, the rip status changes to 'Ripped to library' (Figure 8–103).

Figure 8–103

- Click Music in the Navigation pane to switch to the Music category.

- If necessary, scroll the Player library to verify that the song was added to the library (Figure 8–104).

- Remove the CD from the optical disc drive.

Q&A Can Windows Media Player eject the CD?

Yes. If you select the 'Eject CD after ripping' option from the Rip settings menu before you rip your CD, then Windows Media Player will automatically eject the CD when it has finished ripping the CD. Or you can right-click the CD in the Navigation pane and select Eject.

Figure 8–104

To Create a Playlist

Most people have a set of favorite media files. With Windows Media Player, you can create playlists of media files, where you select sets of files and play them as a sequence. People often create multiple playlists around themes, such as to help them study or to play at a party. You can create a holiday playlist, an easy listening playlist, or even a kids-only playlist. You can save a playlist and listen to it over and over again.

You double-click your playlist in the Navigation pane to play it. You can burn the playlist to a CD or download it to a portable media player. You also can let Windows Media Player create a playlist by using the auto playlist option. Windows Media Player selects the music for your playlist based upon criteria you set such as rating and library location.

The following steps create a playlist called SCPlaylist, and then add the newly ripped song to it.

● Click Playlists in the Navigation pane to display the Playlists category (Figure 8–105).

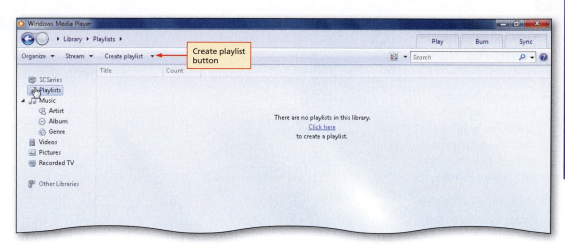

Figure 8–105

● Click the Create playlist button to create a playlist (Figure 8–106).

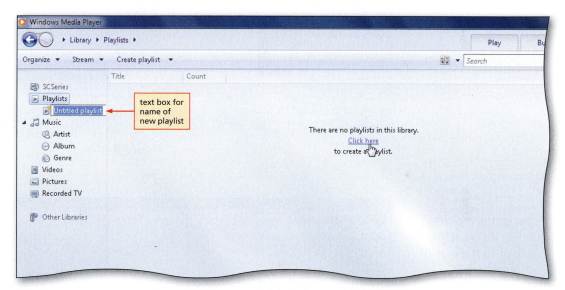

Figure 8–106

3

● Type SCPlaylist in the text box and press the ENTER key to assign a name to the playlist (Figure 8–107).

Figure 8–107

4

- Click Music in the Navigation pane to switch to the Music category.

- Click and drag the ripped song to the SCPlaylist playlist in the Navigation pane to add it to the playlist (Figure 8–108).

- If necessary, click the Pause button to stop the song from playing.

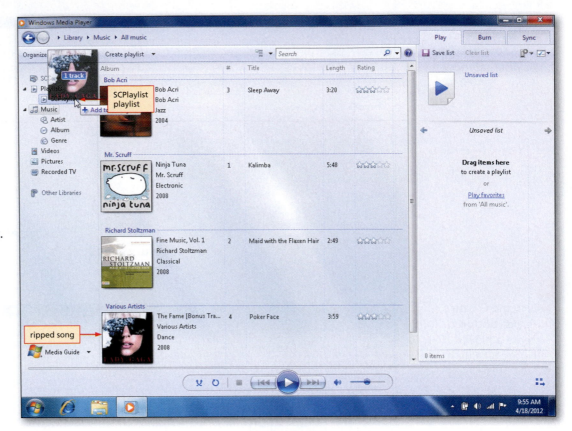

Figure 8–108

5

- Click SCPlaylist in the Navigation pane to verify the song was added to the playlist (Figure 8–109).

Figure 8–109

Other Ways

1. Click Play tab, drag song to 'Drag items here' area, click Save list, enter playlist name, press ENTER

To Burn a Playlist to an Audio CD

Windows Media Player provides three tabs for your use with managing your media files. The Play tab allows you to play your media files and work with your playlists. The Sync tab allows you to sync Windows Media Player with a portable media player. The Burn tab provides you with options for burning your media files to CD. When you click one of the tabs, the List pane updates with information that corresponds to the tab chosen.

With Windows Media Player, you can save (or burn) your playlist to a CD to play in other stereo systems or the CD player in your car using the Burn tab options. Windows Media Player can burn optical discs, including audio CDs, data CDs, or DVDs. When burning a music playlist to play in a standard CD player, you should burn the CD as an audio CD. When you want to include media files such as pictures and videos on your CD or DVD, you should burn a data CD or DVD. If you burn a playlist that contains pictures or videos along with music to an audio CD, only the music files will be burned. The following steps burn the SCPlaylist to an audio CD.

1

• Click the Burn tab to display the burn options in the List pane (Figure 8–110).

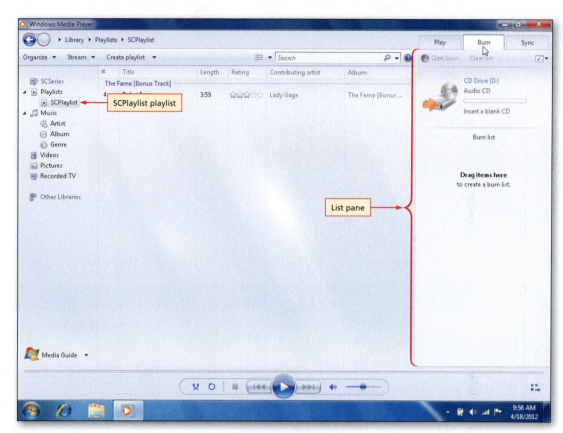

Figure 8–110

2

• Drag the SCPlaylist playlist to the 'Drag items here' area in the List pane to add the playlist to the Burn list (Figure 8–111).

Figure 8–111

- Insert a blank audio CD.

- If necessary, close the AutoPlay dialog box by clicking the Close button.

- Click the Start burn button to begin burning the playlist on to the CD (Figure 8–112).

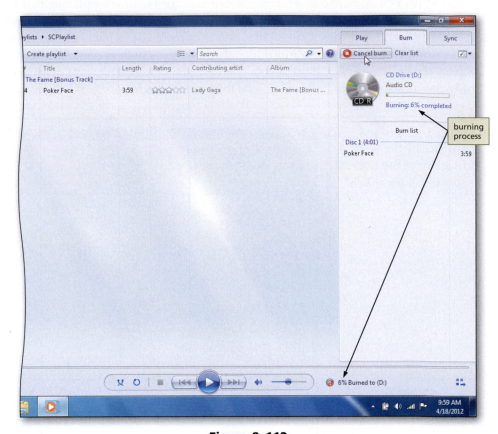

Figure 8–112

- After the CD has been burned, the CD is ejected and the Burn pane is available to burn another CD (Figure 8–113).

- Remove the CD from your optical disc drive, and using a felt-tip pen or marker, label your CD with an appropriate title and date.

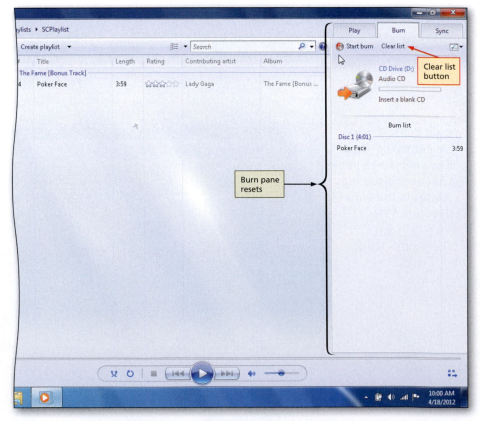

Figure 8–113

5

- Click the Clear list button to clear the Burn list (Figure 8–114).

Figure 8–114

To Add a Picture to a Playlist

Playlists can contain more than just music files. You can add other media files to the playlist by selecting them and then dragging them to the playlist. The following steps add a picture to the playlist.

1 Click Pictures to switch to the picture category.

2 Drag a picture of your choice to the SCPlaylist.

3 Click SCPlaylist to display the SCPlaylist containing the song and the picture.

4 Drag the SCPlaylist to the 'Drag items here' area to add it to the Burn list (Figure 8–115).

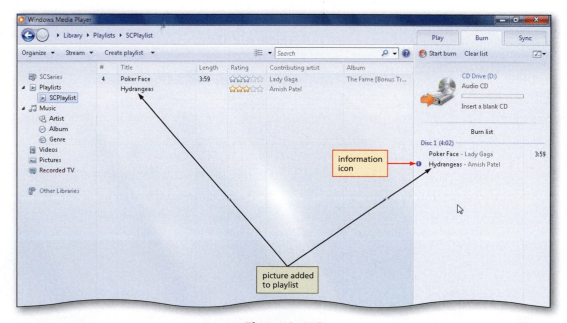

Figure 8–115

To Burn a Playlist to a Data CD

When you have media files other than music files in a playlist, you need to burn a data CD instead of an audio CD. The following steps burn the SCPlaylist to a data CD.

- Click the information icon next to the picture in the Burn list to display a list of options (Figure 8–116).

Figure 8–116

2

- Click the Change Burn Format to Data Disc command to switch the burn mode to Data disc (Figure 8–117).

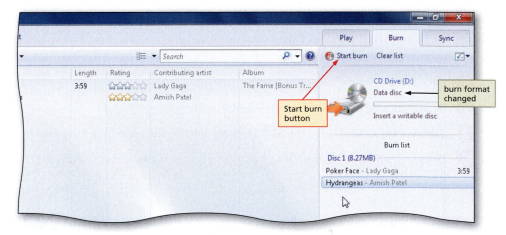

Figure 8–117

3

- Insert a blank CD, and if necessary, close the AutoPlay dialog box.

- Click the Start burn button to burn the CD (Figure 8–118).

Figure 8–118

4

- After the CD has been burned, the CD is ejected from the optical disc drive.

- Click the Clear list button to clear the Burn list (Figure 8–119).

Figure 8–119

To Delete a Playlist

Now that you are done working with this playlist, you can delete it. The following steps delete the SCPlaylist.

1

- Right-click SCPlaylist in the Navigation pane to display a shortcut menu (Figure 8–120).

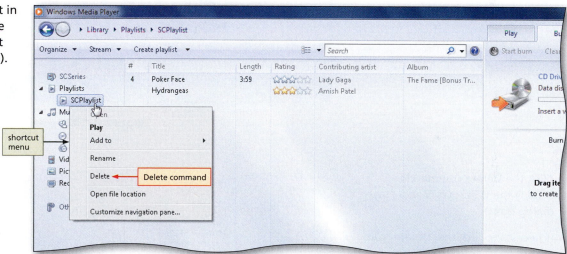

Figure 8–120

2

- Click the Delete command to display the Windows Media Player dialog box.

- Click the OK button to delete the playlist (Figure 8–121).

Q&A

Why are there two options for deletion?

Windows Media Player allows you to delete entries from the Player library only or from both the Player library and your computer. If you delete a file from the Player library, it will remain on your computer in the location where it is stored.

Figure 8–121

To Delete a Song from the Player Library

Now that you are done listening to and working with the song you ripped, you can delete it. The following steps delete the ripped song from the Player library.

- Click Music in the Navigation pane to switch to the Music category.

- Right-click the ripped song to display a shortcut menu (Figure 8–122).

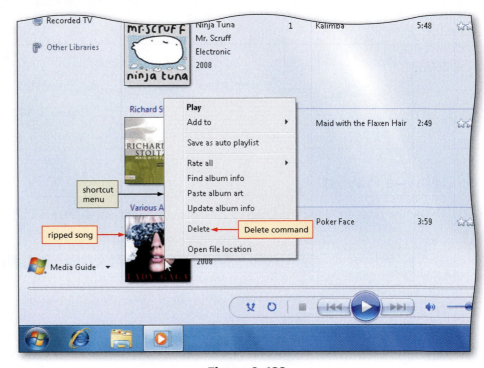

Figure 8–122

- Click the Delete command to display the Windows Media Player dialog box.

- If necessary, click the 'Delete from library only' option button to select it.

- Click the OK button to delete the song from the Player library only (Figure 8–123).

- Close Windows Media Player.

- Empty the Recycle Bin.

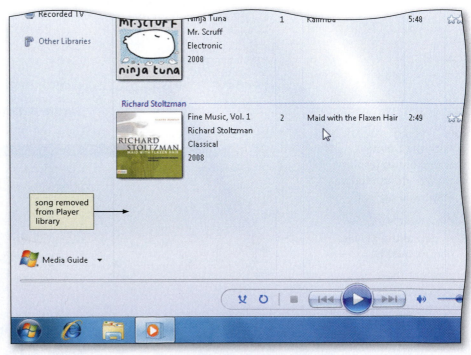

Figure 8–123

To Log Off and Turn Off the Computer

After completing your work, you should exit your user account by logging off the computer, and then turn off the computer.

1 On the Start menu, click the arrow to the right of the Shut down button, and then click the Log off command to log off the computer.

2 On the Welcome Screen, click the Shut down button to turn off the computer.

Chapter Summary

In this chapter, you have learned about the features of Windows Live Photo Gallery. You imported pictures from your digital camera and added folders containing pictures to your gallery. Using the Navigation pane, you discovered how to switch gallery views. You learned how to create tags independent of pictures and videos, and how to add pictures and videos to those tags. You removed the red-eye effect from a picture, cropped and printed your pictures, and learned about ordering prints online. You also applied a black-and-white effect to a picture. Using Windows DVD Maker, you created a DVD for sharing your pictures and videos. Using Windows Media Player, you browsed the media files in the Player library, ripped music from an audio CD to the Player library, created a playlist, and burned the playlist to both an audio and a data CD. The items listed below include all of the new Windows 7 skills you have learned in this chapter.

1. Copy Pictures from a Digital Camera to the Computer (WIN 479)
2. Add a Folder to Windows Live Photo Gallery (WIN 482)
3. View Pictures in the Gallery (WIN 485)
4. View a Live Preview of a Picture (WIN 486)
5. View Videos in the Gallery (WIN 487)
6. View Pictures by Date Taken (WIN 487)
7. View Pictures by Tags (WIN 488)
8. View Pictures as Thumbnails with Date Taken (WIN 489)
9. View Pictures Using Details View (WIN 490)
10. View the Table of Contents (WIN 491)
11. View Pictures in Sorted Order (WIN 493)
12. Filter Pictures by Rating (WIN 493)
13. Rename Groups of Pictures (WIN 494)
14. Create a Tag (WIN 496)
15. Add Pictures and Videos to a Preexisting Tag (WIN 498)
16. Make a Copy of a Picture (WIN 499)
17. Correct Red-Eye in a Picture (WIN 502)
18. Crop a Picture (WIN 504)
19. Print a Picture (WIN 507)
20. Create a Black-and-White Picture (WIN 509)
21. Revert Back to the Original Picture (WIN 511)
22. View Windows Live Photo Gallery Options (WIN 513)
23. Order Pictures Online (WIN 515)
24. Open Windows DVD Maker (WIN 517)
25. Change the DVD Title (WIN 518)
26. Select a DVD Menu Style (WIN 519)
27. Change Slide Show Settings (WIN 520)
28. Preview and Burn a DVD (WIN 524)
29. Delete Tags (WIN 526)
30. View the Player Library Categories (WIN 528)
31. Filter Player Library Listings (WIN 531)
32. Rip a Song from a CD (WIN 533)
33. Create a Playlist (WIN 536)
34. Burn a Playlist to an Audio CD (WIN 538)
35. Burn a Playlist to a Data CD (WIN 542)
36. Delete a Playlist (WIN 543)
37. Delete a Song from the Player Library (WIN 544)

Learn It Online

Test your knowledge of chapter content and key terms.

Instructions: To complete the Learn It Online exercises, start your browser, click the Address bar, and then enter the Web address scsite.com/win7/learn. When the Windows 7 Learn It Online page is displayed, click the link for the exercise you want to complete and then read the instructions.

Chapter Reinforcement TF, MC, and SA
A series of true/false, multiple-choice, and short-answer questions that test your knowledge of the chapter content.

Flash Cards
An interactive learning environment where you identify chapter key terms associated with displayed definitions.

Practice Test
A series of multiple-choice questions that test your knowledge of chapter content and key terms.

Who Wants To Be a Computer Genius?
An interactive game that challenges your knowledge of chapter content in the style of a television quiz show.

Wheel of Terms
An interactive game that challenges your knowledge of chapter key terms in the style of the television show *Wheel of Fortune*.

Crossword Puzzle Challenge
A crossword puzzle that challenges your knowledge of key terms presented in the chapter.

Apply Your Knowledge

Reinforce the skills and apply the concepts you learned in this chapter.

Creating a Custom DVD
Instructions: Use Windows Live Photo Gallery, Windows Media Player, and Windows DVD Maker to perform the following tasks.

Part 1: Acquiring Pictures
1. Open the Pictures library, and then create a subfolder titled Scavenger Hunt.
2. Select one or more of the following options — digital camera, scanner, CD, Internet, or Paint — to acquire six pictures.
   a. Digital Camera option: If a digital camera is available, take a variety of pictures, select six of them, and then import the pictures to the computer using the steps in this chapter or the software included with the camera.
   b. Scanner option: Find six printed pictures, and following the manufacturer's directions, use a scanner to scan the pictures into your computer.
   c. CD option: Take pictures with a traditional film camera and have them developed and put onto a CD.
   d. Internet option: Find free pictures — or pictures with copyrights that allows you to use them — on the Internet. (*Hint:* Try morguefile.com or flickr.com/creativecommons.)
   e. Paint option: Use the Paint program to create six pictures.
3. Save the pictures in the Scavenger Hunt folder (Figure 8–124).

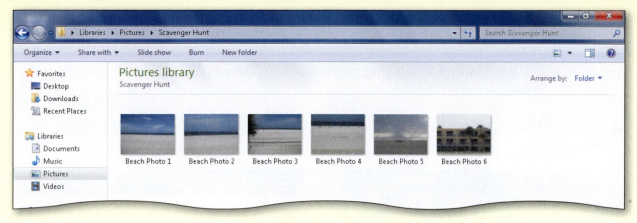

Figure 8–124

Part 2: Printing the Pictures

1. Open Windows Live Photo Gallery.

2. Select the six pictures in the Scavenger Hunt folder.

3. Click the Print button to display the Print menu, and then click the Print command to display the Print Pictures dialog box.

4. Print a copy of the six pictures to your printer, using the 3.5 × 5 in. layout. (*Hint:* This will result in two pages of pictures.)

Part 3: Acquiring Background Music

1. Open Windows Media Player.

2. Insert one of your favorite audio CDs.

3. Click the select all check box to deselect all the songs.

4. Click the check box for the song you like the most.

5. Click the Rip CD button to rip the music from the CD.

6. Click Music to see the music you just ripped.

7. Double-click a song to play it to make sure that it ripped properly.

Part 4: Creating a DVD

1. In Windows Live Photo Gallery, select the six pictures in the Scavenger Hunt folder.

2. Click the Make button and then click the Burn a DVD command to open Windows DVD Maker.

3. Click the Next button, click the Menu text button, and then enter a new title of your choosing for the slide show.

4. Select the Reflections menu style.

5. Click the Slide show button, add the song you ripped in the previous steps as the music for the slide show, and then select the transition of your choice.

6. Click the Preview button to preview the slide show.

7. Insert a blank DVD in the optical disc drive and click the Burn button to burn the DVD.

Part 5: Removing the Pictures and Song from the Computer

1. If necessary, delete the Scavenger Hunt folder from Windows Live Photo Gallery.

2. If necessary, delete the song you ripped in Part 3 from Windows Media Player.

3. Close Windows Media Player and Windows Live Photo Gallery.

Extend Your Knowledge

Extend the skills you learned in this chapter and experiment with new skills. You might need to use Help to complete the assignment.

1. Open Windows Help and Support and search for Windows Media Player (Figure 8–125).

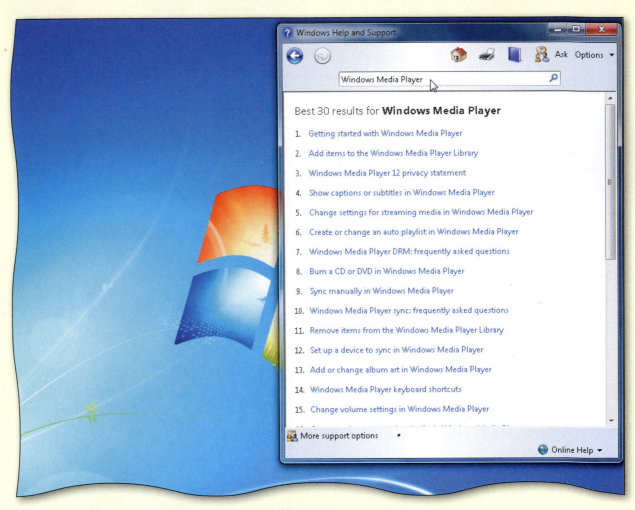

Figure 8–125

2. Answer the following questions using information from the search results.

   a. What are Windows Media Player's modes of operation?

   _____

   b. How do you change the volume settings in Windows Media Player?

   _____

   c. How do you play DVDs?

   _____

   d. How do you edit album information for an individual track in the Player library?

   _____

   e. How do you rearrange items in a playlist?

   _____

3. Answer the following questions about how to sync a portable device in Windows Media Player.

   a. How do you set up your device using Windows Media Player?

   _____

   b. What conditions have to be met for Windows Media Player to default to automatic sync?

   _____

   c. How do you manually sync a portable device? Why would you have to do this?

   _____

   d. How can you customize what playlists will sync automatically?

   _____

In the Lab

Use the guidelines, concepts, and skills presented in this chapter to increase your knowledge of Windows 7. Labs are listed in order of increasing difficulty.

Lab 1: Acquiring Pictures and Ordering Prints Online

Instructions: You want to search for pictures on the Internet. Once you locate the pictures, you want to print the pictures on your own printer, send the pictures to a friend in an e-mail message, and then order prints online.

Part 1: Searching for Free Pictures of Cars on the Internet

1. Create a new folder titled `Internet Pictures` in the Pictures library.

2. Open Internet Explorer, type `free hybrid car pictures` in the Bing search box. Press the ENTER key to search the Internet for Web sites containing free pictures of hybrid cars (Figure 8–126).

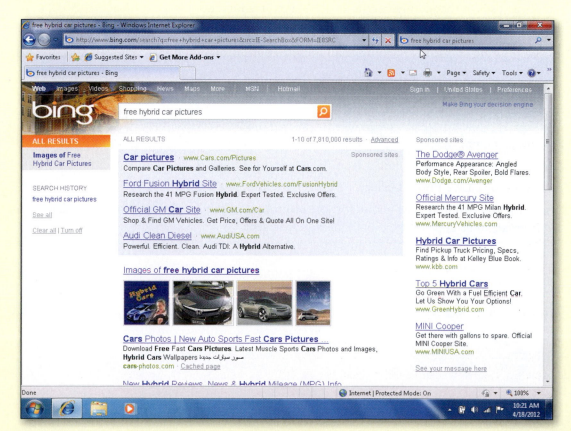

Figure 8–126

Continued >

In the Lab *continued*

3. Locate four pictures and then save each picture to the Internet Pictures folder by right-clicking the picture and then clicking the Save Picture As command.

4. Close Internet Explorer (all windows).

Part 2: Editing and Printing the Pictures

1. Open Windows Live Photo Gallery.

2. Crop each picture to 5 × 7.

3. Select the four pictures.

4. Open the Print Pictures dialog box and then select the 5 × 7 inch print layout.

5. Select the highest print quality available and then print the pictures.

Part 3: Sending the Pictures in an E-mail Message

1. With the pictures selected, click the E-mail button.

2. Select the Small Photo size, and then click the Attach button to attach the pictures to an e-mail message.

3. Type your instructor's e-mail address in the To text box. Type I searched the Internet to find these pictures. in the message area.

4. Click the Send button.

5. Print a copy of the e-mail message.

Part 4: Ordering Prints Online

If you do not have a valid credit card, are unable to pick up the prints, or are not willing to accept the terms of service of the company printing the pictures, skip the following steps. Otherwise, perform the following steps:

1. If necessary, select the pictures in the Internet Pictures folder.

2. Click the Print button, and then click the Order prints command to display the Order Prints dialog box.

3. Select a printing company, click the Send Pictures button, and then select the quantity and print size of your choosing.

4. Enter your billing information and then finalize your purchase.

5. Pick up your pictures from the store you selected.

Part 5: Deleting the Pictures

1. Delete the Internet Pictures folder from Windows Live Photo Gallery.

2. Close Windows Live Photo Gallery.

3. Submit the following to your instructor: the printouts of the four pictures you printed, the print(s) you ordered, and a copy of the e-mail message you sent.

In the Lab

Lab 2: Using Windows Media Player

Instructions: You want to import two audio CDs to the Windows Media Player library, create a playlist containing tracks from both albums, and then burn the playlist to a CD.

Part 1: Launching Windows Media Player
  1. Select two audio CDs from your CD collection.
  2. Insert the first audio CD into the optical disc drive (Figure 8–127).
  3. Click the 'Switch to library' button.

Figure 8–127

Part 2: Printing a Copy of the Windows Media Player Screen
  1. Press the PRINT SCREEN key to place a picture of the desktop on the Clipboard.
  2. Open Paint and if necessary, maximize the window.
  3. Click Edit on the menu bar and then click the Paste command to copy the picture from the Clipboard to the Paint window.
  4. Click File on the menu bar, click the Print command, and then click the Print button in the Print dialog box to print the picture.
  5. Close Paint without saving the picture.

Part 3: Copying Tracks from Two CDs to the Computer
  1. Using the first CD, click the Rip CD button to add the songs to the Player library.
  2. While ripping the CD, write down the album title and the artist on the following line. Does Windows Media Player display the titles of each song or the album cover?

_____

Continued >

In the Lab *continued*

3. When the process is complete, eject the CD from the optical disc drive, and then insert the second audio CD.

4. While ripping the second CD, summarize the album and artist information for the second CD.

_____

5. Eject the second CD.

Part 4: Creating a Playlist

1. Click the Library button to return to the Player library.

2. Click Create playlist on the menu bar. Use your first name and the words, Party Mix, to name the new playlist (for example, Ray's Party Mix).

3. Click the Album button in the Navigation pane.

4. Double-click the album cover of the first album you ripped and drag five tracks from the album to the new playlist.

5. Click the Album button, double-click the album cover of the second album you ripped, and then drag five tracks to the new playlist.

6. Arrange the titles in the playlist so that the tracks alternate between the two albums.

Part 5: Burning a CD Containing a Playlist

1. Click the Burn tab to display the Burn pane.

2. Drag the new playlist to the 'Drag items here' area in the Burn pane, click the Burn options button, and then select the Audio CD option.

3. Insert a blank CD in the optical disc drive.

4. Answer the following questions:

   a. How many MB is the playlist?

   _____

   b. How many MB or GB are available on the CD?

   _____

5. Click the Start burn button to burn your playlist to the CD. When you are finished burning the CD, click the Clear list button to clear the Burn pane.

Part 6: Removing Your Media Files from the Player Library

1. Click the Library button.

2. Delete the Party Mix playlist from the Player library and the computer.

3. Click the Album button and delete the albums you ripped.

4. Close Windows Media Player.

5. Submit the Paint document you printed and the CD you burned to your instructor. Be sure to write your name on the CD before submitting it.

In the Lab

Lab 3: Creating a Family Album

Instructions: You would like to make a CD of pictures of your family accompanied by their favorite songs.

Part 1: Acquiring the Files

1. Using a digital camera, take pictures of your family members.

2. Create a folder in Windows Live Photo Gallery, name the folder, My Family, and import the pictures into the My Family folder. Close Windows Live Photo Gallery.

3. Have each family member select songs from their favorite CDs.

4. Launch Windows Media Player. Rip the songs into Windows Media Player.

Part 2: Creating the Playlist

1. Create a playlist with the title, My Family Album (Figure 8–128).

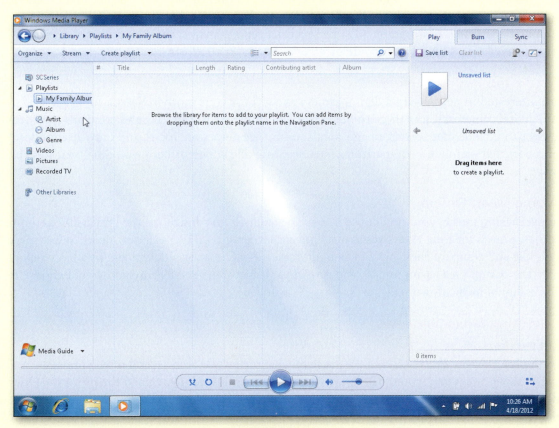

Figure 8–128

2. Repeat the following steps for each family member.

   a. Add the family member's picture to the playlist.

   b. Add the songs the family member picked to the playlist.

Part 3: Creating the CD

1. Switch to the Burn tab, and verify that you are burning a data CD or DVD.

2. Insert a blank CD or DVD.

3. Burn the My Family Album playlist to the CD or DVD.

Continued >

In the Lab *continued*

Part 4: Removing the Pictures and Songs from the Computer
1. Delete the My Family Album folder from Windows Live Photo Gallery.
2. Delete the ripped songs from Windows Media Player.
3. Submit the CD to your instructor.

Cases and Places

Apply your creative thinking and problem-solving skills to design and implement a solution.

● Easier ●● More Difficult

● 1 Understanding the Difference Between DVDs and CDs

You can play an audio CD or DVD in a DVD drive but you cannot play a DVD disc in a CD drive. To understand this statement, investigate how music (audio) is stored on an audio CD and how a movie (audio and video) is stored on a DVD. In a brief report, answer the question as to why a DVD cannot be played on a CD drive. Include pictures as necessary to illustrate how the data is stored.

● 2 Comparing Digital Cameras

You are interested in purchasing a digital camera as a gift for your mother. Search for three Web sites that sell digital cameras, select three cameras that you think she would like, and compare their features. Remember to include megapixels, image stabilization, face detection, focus, and exposure modes. Write a brief report that includes a comparison of features. Include which camera would be your top choice and why.

● 3 Buying Music Online

When purchasing music, you can choose to buy an actual CD or download the entire CD as digital media files. Search for four Web sites that sell music, either as a CD or as a download. Select three CDs that you like and compare their prices when purchased as a CD or as a download. In a brief report, compare the cost of purchasing music, and provide at least three reasons why you would choose to buy a CD or a digital music download.

●● 4 Watching Movie Previews

Make It Personal

Search the Internet for Web sites that advertise movie previews. Watch several movie previews, and then select four movies that you would like to see when they are released. Download the previews. Open Windows DVD Maker and create a DVD of these previews that you can share with your friends. Create a presentation that demonstrates how to find Web sites that have movie previews, how to create a DVD of the movies from Windows DVD Maker, and any other interesting information about the movie previews and Web sites.

●● 5 Creating Digital Music and Pictures

Working Together

As a team, visit a music recording studio to learn how musicians and music producers use computers to play and record music. Learn how musical instruments have changed because of computers and how the process of recording music on audio CDs has affected music and the music industry. Working together, research two businesses that use different drawing programs to create pictures. Interview an individual at each business who uses a digital drawing program. Have each individual demonstrate how they use the drawing program, what they like or dislike about the drawing program, and any other comments. Summarize your findings in a brief report.

9 | Mastering Digital Video

Objectives

You will have mastered the material in this chapter when you can:

- Launch Windows Live Movie Maker
- Import media files into Windows Live Movie Maker
- Play and rename video items
- Add and edit video items in the storyboard

- Add a title and credits to a project
- Preview and save a project
- Publish a movie onto your computer, the Web, or an optical disc

9 | Mastering Digital Video

Introduction

Windows 7 offers several programs that allow you to work in the digital world. In Chapter 8, you used Windows DVD Maker and Windows Media Player. Windows Live Essentials added Windows Live Photo Gallery, which you also used in Chapter 8. In this chapter, you will use Windows Live Movie Maker. Windows Live Movie Maker further expands the digital media experience that Windows 7 provides. With these tools, you can enhance your life and make using a computer even more worthwhile. Today, people want to view their pictures, manage their music, create their own videos, and, overall, have their computer do more of the work so that they can be more productive.

Windows Live Movie Maker allows you to transfer recorded digital media from an analog or digital video camera to the computer, import pre-existing audio and video files, combine audio and video items to create a movie, edit a movie, send a movie to someone via an e-mail message, and publish the movie to your computer or the Web (Figure 9–1). You also can capture videos with your digital camera and download them in a similar manner to how you downloaded your pictures in Chapter 8. Then using Windows Live Movie Maker, you can edit the videos and prepare them for posting online.

In this chapter, you will use Windows Live Movie Maker to import media files, rearrange and edit your media items to create a project, preview and save a project, and save the final movie.

Overview

As you read this chapter, you will learn how to use Windows Live Movie Maker by performing these general tasks:

- Transferring videos from a digital video camera to your computer
- Importing media files
- Rearranging and editing items in Windows Live Movie Maker
- Creating a title and credits for a movie
- Publishing a movie

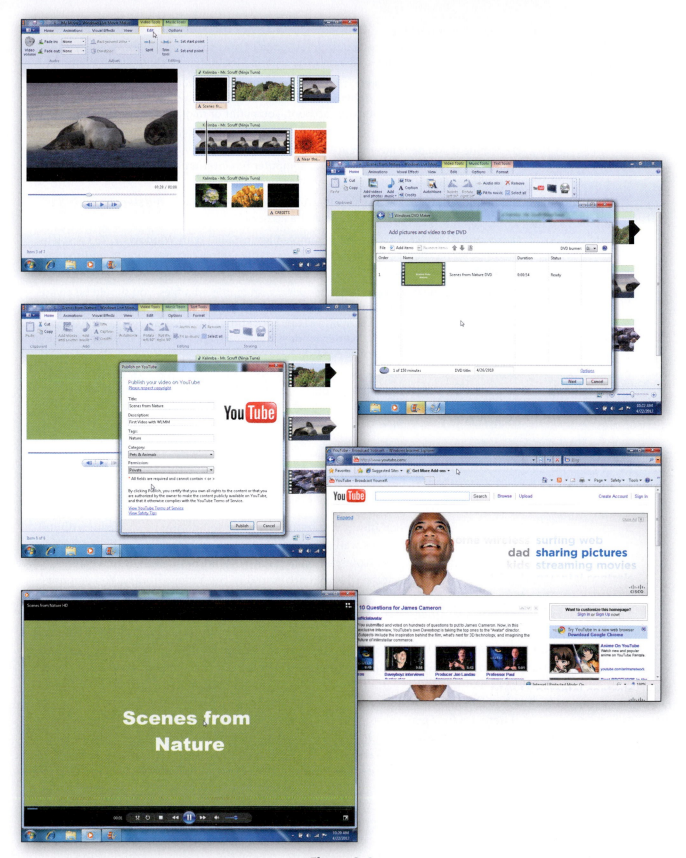

Figure 9–1

> **Mastering Digital Video**
>
> Mastering digital video requires a basic knowledge of how to work with Windows 7, attach hardware, access the Internet, and access the sample files that are included with Windows 7.
>
> 1. **Determine the permissions you have on the computer you will be using.** Each user account can have different rights and permissions. Depending on which rights and permissions have been set for your account, you might or might not be able to perform certain operations.
>
> 2. **Determine if you have Internet access.** For this chapter, you will be accessing the Internet. You will want to know if your computer has Internet access and if anything is required of you to use it.
>
> 3. **Determine if you have access to a YouTube account.** To complete the steps in this chapter, you will need access to a YouTube account.
>
> 4. **Determine if you have access to the sample files installed with Windows 7.** To complete the steps in this chapter, you will need access to the sample pictures, videos, and sounds installed with Windows 7.
>
> 5. **Understand copyright issues.** When working with multimedia files, you should be aware that most pictures, movies, and music files are copyrighted. Before you use them, you should make sure that you are aware of any copyrights. Just because you can download a picture or music file from the Internet does not mean that it belongs to you or that you have permission to download and use it.
>
> 6. **Verify that you have the appropriate ports on your computer.** To transfer videos from a video camera to your computer, your computer will need either a USB or FireWire port. In addition, to add narration to your movie, you will need to have a microphone connected to your computer.

Windows Live Movie Maker

Windows Live Movie Maker allows you to import recorded digital media from a digital video camera to the computer as well as to import pre-existing picture, audio, and video files. When you import videos from your camera into Windows Live Movie Maker, Windows 7 creates digital media files that are stored in the Videos library. You can use Windows Live Photo Gallery to manage your videos. These movies can then be added in to Windows Live Movie Maker.

Movies inform people of news events, entertain people, advertise and sell products, and train employees. You can create home movies to share with your family and friends. For instance, you can create a homemade movie of a child's dance recital or of a class project that shows how hummingbirds gather nectar. You can post the movies you create on Web sites such as YouTube or Facebook, or simply send them in e-mail messages to your friends.

There are four general steps to follow when creating a movie. The first step is to import the digital media files. Once all your digital media files are imported, the second step is to edit the project. In Windows Live Movie Maker, a **project** is the file that is created once you save the results of adding various items to the storyboard. Essentially, a project can be considered a rough draft of a movie. The **storyboard** is the area in Windows Live Movie Maker where you create your movie. Editing a project involves rearranging the order of items, splitting items into two or more segments, trimming items to hide unwanted portions, adding effects, creating transitions between items, and adding music.

The third step in creating a movie is to preview the project. As you develop a project, you might want to preview the project multiple times as you split and rearrange items. Windows Live Movie Maker allows you to preview a single item in the project to verify that you recorded the source materials correctly, or to preview the entire project to check the results of the overall editing.

File Formats
You can import video files with the following file formats: .asf, .avi, dvr-ms, .m1v, .mp2, .mp2v, .mpe, .mpeg, .mpg, .mpv2, .wm, and .wmv. The audio file formats you can import include aif, .aifc, .aiff, .asf, .au, .mp2, .mp3, .mpa, .snd, .wav, and .wma. Finally, you can import pictures in the .bmp, .dib, .emf, .gif, .jfif, .jpe, .jpeg, .jpg, .png, .tif, .tiff, and .wmf file formats.

The fourth step in creating a movie is to publish and distribute the project as a movie. When the project is finished, you can publish the project as a movie file. The **movie file** is the file created by combining the audio, video, and pictures contained in the project. You can publish the movie to the computer, an optical disc, an e-mail message, or even YouTube.

Importing Digital Media Files

You have several options when importing digital media files. First, you can import items directly from a digital video camera. To import from a digital video camera, you need a camera that uses DV (Digital Video) tape and connects to the computer using either a USB connection or an IEEE 1394 connection. **IEEE 1394** is a standard specification for high-speed connections and data transfer. It is sometimes known by the brand names FireWire or i.Link. Most new notebook and desktop computers include an IEEE 1394 port. Using the IEEE 1394 port, you can import your movies into either the .avi or .wmv formats. Imported videos are always placed into Windows Live Photo Gallery. The files then are available for use in Windows Live Movie Maker.

You also can import videos from cell phones, digital cameras, portable media players, and other mobile devices. Windows 7 does not include import software for these devices; therefore, you need to install software that allows you to import from your device. Windows Live Essentials does include software for video importing, so if you install Windows Live Essentials, you can import videos. Without Windows Live Essentials, you would need to install other software, such as the import program provided with your device. For example, you can use iTunes to import video from your iPod Nano. Even if you have other software installed, Windows Live Movie Maker usually can import from the device without requiring the other software. If you plug in your iPod Nano and then import media using Windows Live Movie Maker, Windows Live Movie Maker will access your iPod and copy the video to Windows Live Photo Gallery.

Videos imported using the IEEE 1394 port will be placed in the Videos section of Windows Live Photo Gallery. Videos imported using the USB port will be placed in the Pictures section of Windows Live Photo Gallery. Recall that you use Windows Live Photo Gallery to manage your media files, and can easily move a video from the Pictures section to the Videos section.

You also can import digital media files that you have created using other programs, downloaded from the Internet, or received from someone else. As always, when you acquire digital media files that you have not created yourself, you should review the copyright and make sure you have permission to use the files.

To Import from a Digital Video Camera

Windows Live Movie Maker allows you to import video from your digital video camera using the Import Video dialog box. As mentioned earlier, your camera connects to the computer through an IEEE 1394 or USB port. If your computer does not have the proper port to connect your camera, you will not be able to import the video unless you upgrade your computer. Remember that your digital video camera has to use DV tape to be able to take advantage of the Import Video dialog box. You can import videos from other types of digital video cameras, but you will have to use the software provided by those cameras to import your video.

You can access the Import Video dialog box from the AutoPlay dialog box when you connect your camera to the computer, or from within Windows Live Movie Maker. When you use AutoPlay, you also have the options of saving and burning your video directly to DVD using Windows DVD Maker, or saving and opening your video in Windows Live Photo Gallery. If you import your video from within Windows Live Movie Maker, you only will be given the option of saving the video to your computer in Windows Live Photo Gallery. You can later choose to burn your video to a DVD from within Windows Live Movie Maker if you prefer.

You can import live video or recorded video. If your camera is in playback mode, where you are able to view your recorded video, you will import video you already have recorded. If your camera is in camera mode, where you

BTW

Webcams and Other Cameras
You cannot import directly from a Web cam into Windows Live Movie Maker. A Web cam is a camera that plugs into your computer and feeds video directly to the computer. You can use the software provided with your Web cam to record and save the videos and pictures. Once the files have been saved, you can import them into Windows Live Movie Maker. The same goes for digital video cameras that use media other than DV tape. You can use the software provided with your camera to record and save your videos, and then you can import the files into Windows Live Movie Maker.

are actively recording video with the camera, you will import live video as it is recorded. You can use the Import Video dialog box to control your camera during playback so that you only import the portions of the video that you want. Once imported, the video is saved to the Videos folder, unless you change the default location, and an item of the newly saved video is added to Windows Live Movie Maker.

The following steps open Windows Live Movie Maker and import a video from a digital video camera. If you do not have a digital video camera, you should copy the Birds movie from the Data Files for this chapter to the Videos library on your computer, and then follow the steps in the To Preview and Add Videos section on page WIN 564 to import the Data Files into Windows Live Movie Maker.

- Display the Start menu and then click the All Programs command to display the All Programs list.

- Click the Windows Live command to display the Windows Live list.

- Click the Windows Live Movie Maker command to open Windows Live Movie Maker.

- If necessary, maximize the Windows Live Movie Maker window (Figure 9–2).

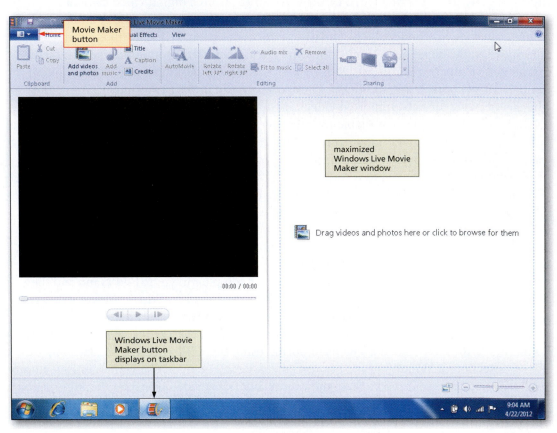

Figure 9–2

- Connect the digital video camera to an available port on the computer and turn it on in playback mode.

- Click the Movie Maker button to display the Movie Maker menu (Figure 9–3).

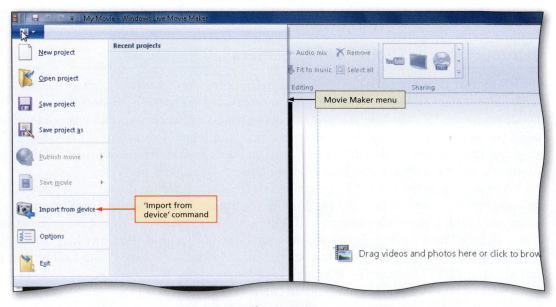

Figure 9–3

3

- Click 'Import from device' to display the Import Photos and Videos dialog box.

- If necessary, click OK in the Windows Live Movie Maker dialog box to acknowledge that you understand the videos will be placed in Windows Live Photo Gallery.

- If necessary, click the icon representing your digital video camera to select it (Figure 9–4).

Q&A Why did I not see a message about Windows Live Photo Gallery?

The dialog box displaying the message that your videos will be put into Windows Live Photo Gallery provides an option for not displaying the message again. If you or someone else on your computer selected not to show the message again, the message will not appear.

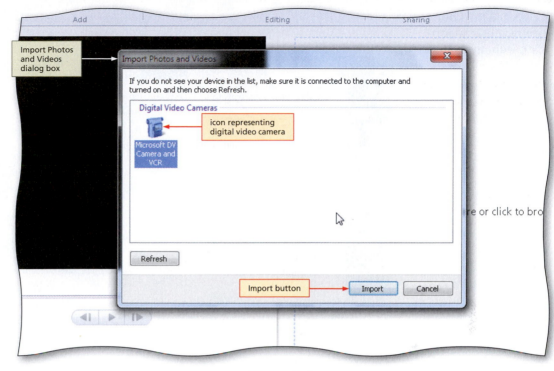

Figure 9–4

4

- Click the Import button to display the Import video dialog box (Figure 9–5).

- Type `Birds` in the Name text box to enter a name for the video.

- Click the 'Choose parts of the video to import' option button to only import part of the videotape.

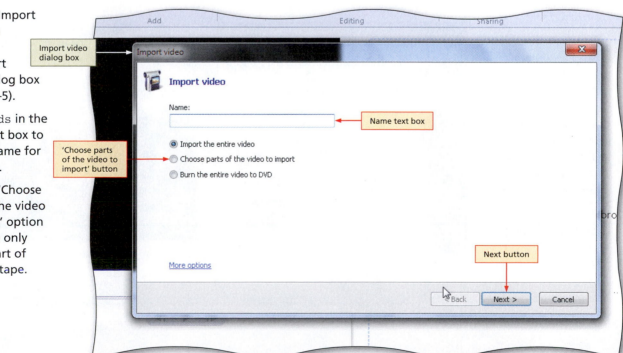

Figure 9–5

5

• Click the Next button to continue importing from the camera (Figure 9–6).

How long can it take to import an entire DV tape?

The time required depends upon the size of the tape and how much video you have recorded. The rule of thumb is that every minute of tape takes one minute to import. If it is a one-hour tape, then it will take one hour to import the full tape.

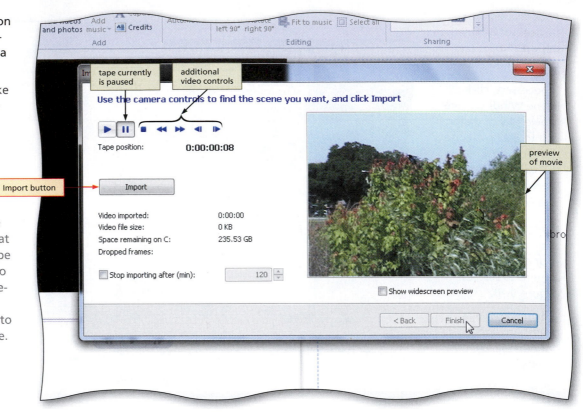

Figure 9–6

6

• Click the Import button to import the video from the tape (Figure 9–7).

Can I set the import to stop automatically after a certain number of minutes?

Yes. Otherwise, you can watch the tape position and manually stop the import when the meter displays the time at which you want the import to end.

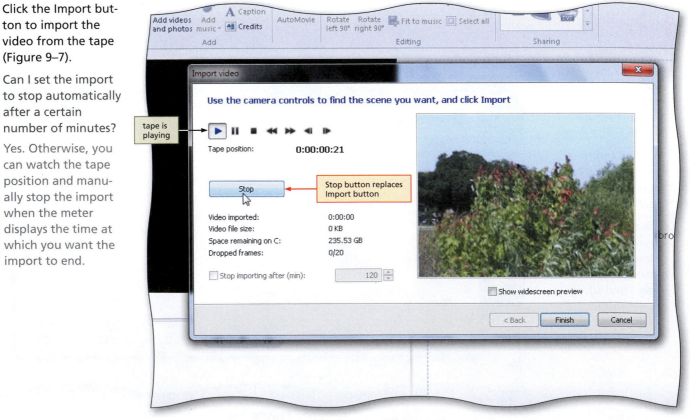

Figure 9–7

7

- Click the Stop button when the tape position reaches 15 seconds to stop the import (Figure 9–8).

Q&A

I was not able to stop the import at exactly 15 seconds. Will this be a problem?

To stop at exactly 15 seconds, you would have to be very quick when clicking the mouse. Remember that you will be able to edit the item after it is imported into Windows Live Movie Maker.

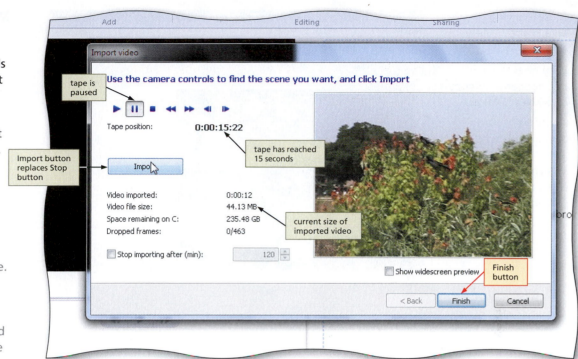

Figure 9–8

8

- Click the Finish button to complete the import process (Figure 9–9).

- Turn off the digital video camera and disconnect it from the computer.

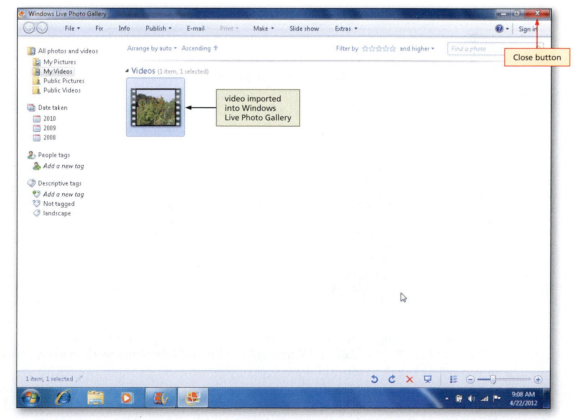

Figure 9–9

9

- Close Windows Live Photo Gallery (Figure 9–10).

Why does the video not appear in Windows Live Movie Maker?

You only imported it into Windows Live Photo Gallery. You now need to add it to Windows Live Movie Maker to be able to use it in creating your movie.

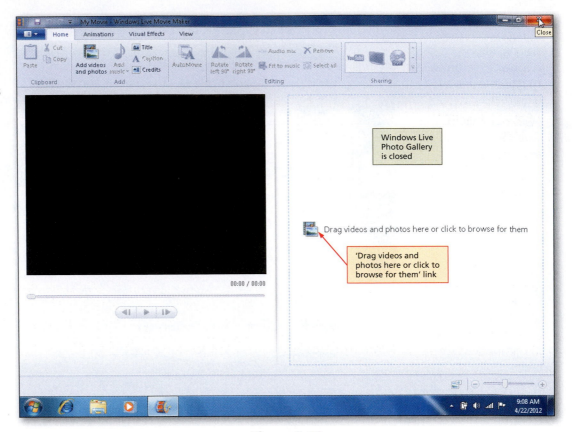

Figure 9–10

To Copy the Data Files

Because you might not have a digital camera, the Birds video is provided with the Data Files for this chapter. If you have a digital video camera, you can use the video you imported.

1 Open the Videos library.

2 Copy the Birds video to the Videos library.

3 If necessary, close the Videos library.

To Preview and Add Videos

In addition to importing videos recorded with your digital video camera, you also can add videos that are on your computer already. Remember that videos you import do not appear in Windows Live Movie Maker — they appear in Windows Live Photo Gallery. Windows Live Photo Gallery places the videos into the appropriate libraries on your computer. You then can add the videos to your project in Windows Live Movie Maker by browsing for the videos. Once you have selected a video, you can preview it before adding it, to make sure that it is the video you intend to import. The following steps add the Birds video, which you imported earlier, and the Wildlife video, from the sample videos included with Windows 7, to Windows Live Movie Maker.

1

- Click the 'Drag videos and photos here or click to browse for them' link to display the Add Videos and Photos dialog box (Figure 9–11).

- If necessary, click Videos in the Navigation pane to select the Videos library.

Q&A

Do I have to preview the video?

No, you can just add it and then preview it later in Windows Live Movie Maker. Previewing a video before adding it allows you to make sure that you are adding the correct one.

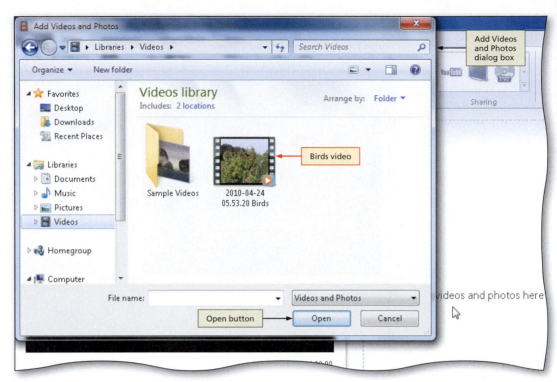

Figure 9–11

2

- Right-click the Birds video to display a shortcut menu.

- Click the Play command to preview the video using Windows Media Player (Figure 9–12).

- After previewing the movie, close Windows Media Player.

Figure 9–12

• Click the Open button to add the video to the project (Figure 9–13).

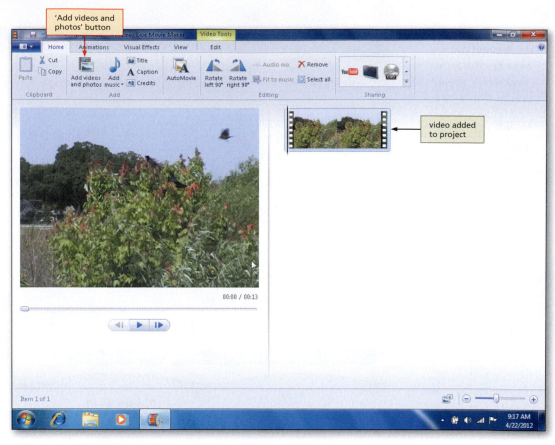

Figure 9–13

• Click the 'Add videos and photos' button on the Ribbon to display the Add Videos and Photos dialog box (Figure 9–14).

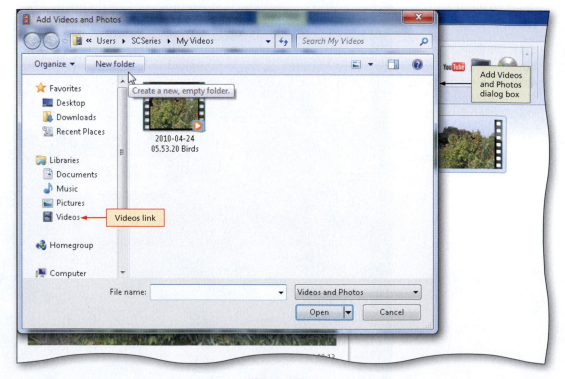

Figure 9–14

5

- Click Videos in the Navigation pane to open the Videos library.

- Double-click the Sample Videos folder to open it (Figure 9–15).

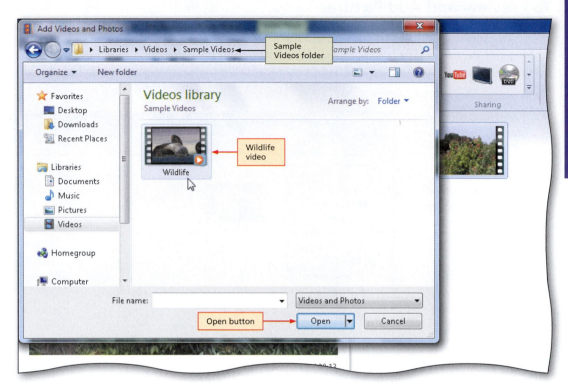

Figure 9–15

6

- If necessary, click the Wildlife video to select it.

- Click the Open button to add the video to the project (Figure 9–16).

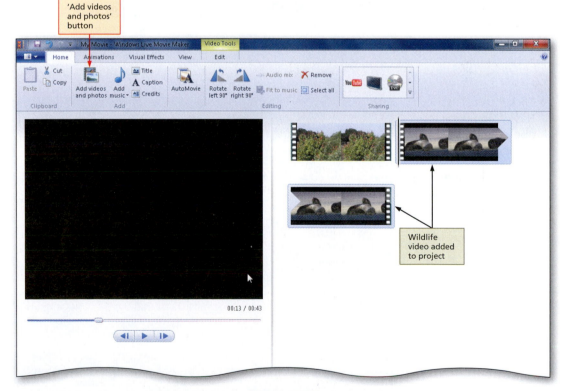

Figure 9–16

To Preview and Add Pictures

You can add pictures to your movie the same way you added videos. By changing the view in the Add Videos and Photos dialog box, you can preview the pictures before you add them. The following steps add the Chrysanthemum, Hydrangeas, and Tulips pictures from the sample pictures included with Windows 7.

- If necessary, click Home on the Ribbon to display the Home tab.

- Click the 'Add videos and photos' button in the Add tab on the Ribbon to display the Add Videos and Photos dialog box (Figure 9–17).

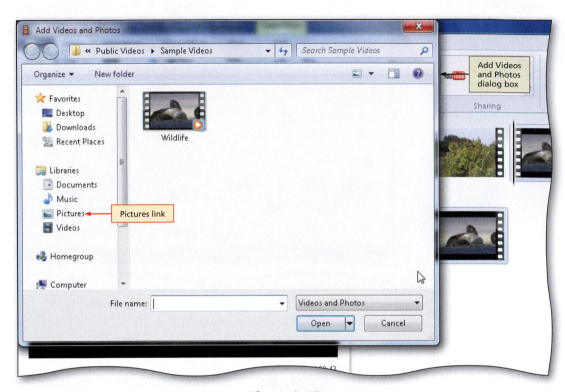

Figure 9–17

- Click Pictures in the Navigation pane to open the Pictures library.

- Double-click the Sample Pictures folder to display its contents (Figure 9–18).

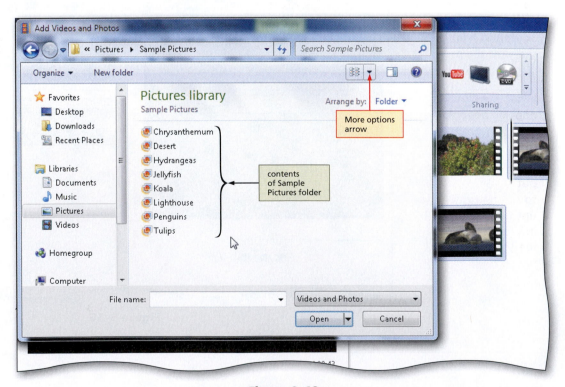

Figure 9–18

3

- Click the More options arrow on the toolbar to display a list of views.

- If necessary, click Large Icons to switch views so that you can preview the pictures (Figure 9–19).

Figure 9–19

4

- Press the CTRL key and click the Chrysanthemum, Hydrangeas, and Tulips pictures to select them.

- Click the Open button to add the pictures (Figure 9–20).

Q&A

What if my picture appears sideways?

You can use the Rotate left 90° or the Rotate right 90° button on the Ribbon to rotate the picture until it looks right. In fact, you also can use these buttons for videos.

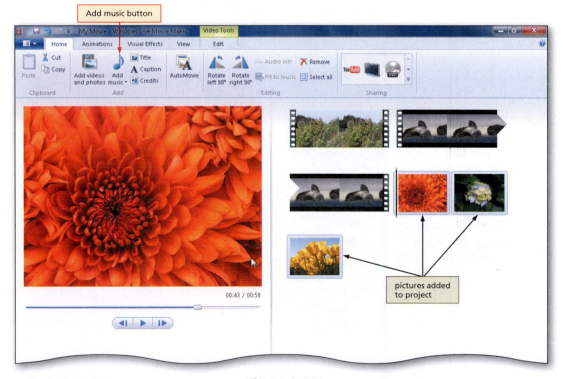

Figure 9–20

To Preview and Add Music

Although videos usually are recorded with their own sound, you might want to add additional music to your movie. This is useful when you have items in your movie that do not include sound, such as pictures or image-only videos (one of the options on most digital video cameras is the ability to record video with the sound turned off), or when you want to provide an overall theme for the movie. Alternatively, you could add multiple music files to use a different music at appropriate times for dramatic effect, as in professionally produced movies.

Similar to pictures and videos, you can preview a music file before you add it. The following steps import the Kalimba music file from the sample music included with Windows 7.

• Click the Add music button on the Ribbon to display the Add Music dialog box (Figure 9–21).

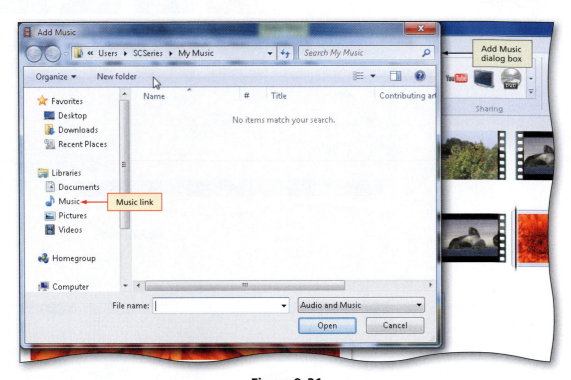

Figure 9–21

2

• Click Music in the Navigation pane to open the Music library.

• Double-click the Sample Music folder to display its contents (Figure 9–22).

Figure 9–22

3

- Right-click the Kalimba music file to display a shortcut menu.

- Click the Play command to preview it using Windows Media Player (Figure 9–23).

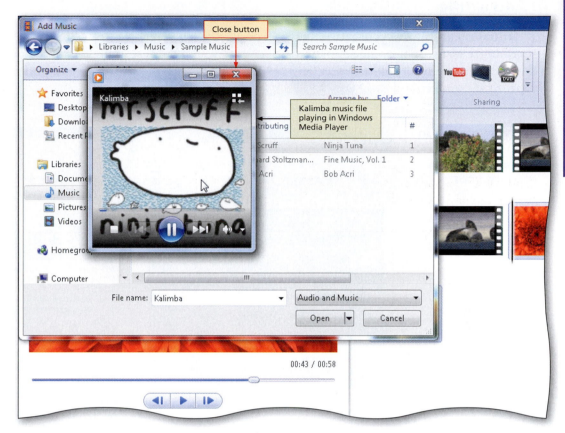

Figure 9–23

4

- After previewing the music, close Windows Media Player.

- Click the Open button to add the music to the project (Figure 9–24).

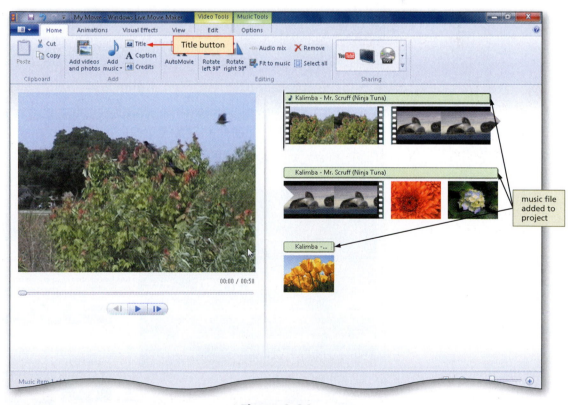

Figure 9–24

To Add a Title

You can add a title to your movie so that it displays when the movie first starts. When you add a title, you can customize its text, color, and animation style. For now, you only are going to add the title text. You will edit the color of the title item and add an effect later in this chapter. The following steps add the opening title, Scenes from Nature, to the project.

- Click the Title button on the Ribbon to add a title to the movie (Figure 9–25).

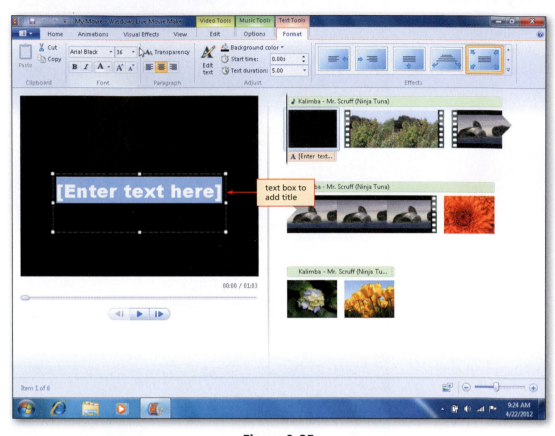

text box to add title

Figure 9–25

- Type Scenes from Nature in the text box to enter a title (Figure 9–26).

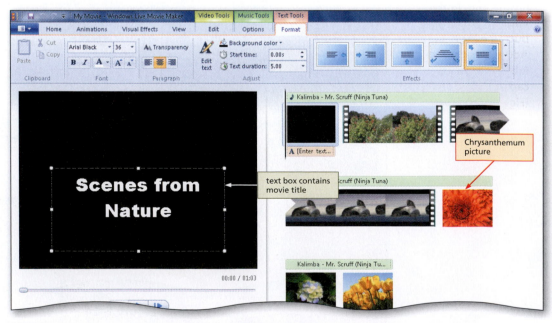

Chrysanthemum picture

text box contains movie title

Figure 9–26

To Add a Caption

Besides adding a title to the beginning of the movie, you can add captions to the other items in your movie. This is especially handy if the item is being used to introduce a following segment. In this movie, the picture items will introduce the video items that follow. The following steps add a caption to the Chrysanthemum picture.

1
- Click the Chrysanthemum picture to select it (Figure 9–27).

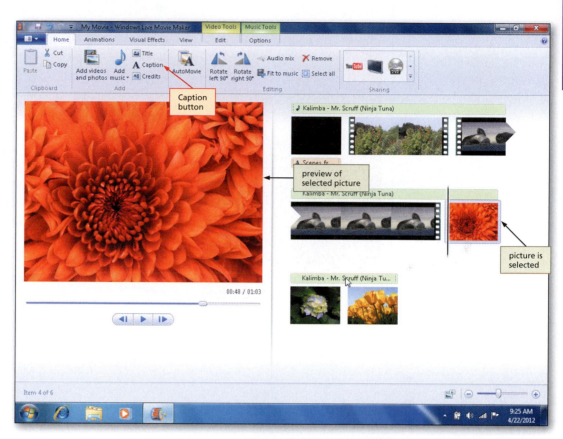

Figure 9–27

2
- Click the Caption button in the Add group on the Ribbon to add a caption to the picture (Figure 9–28).

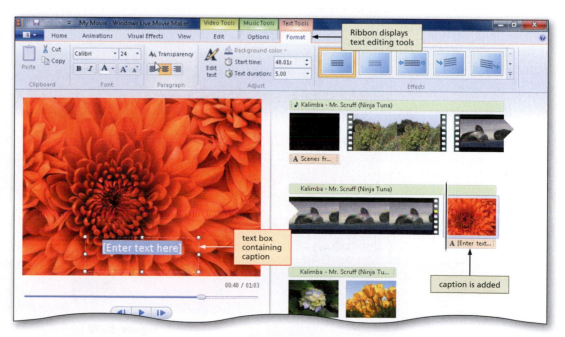

Figure 9–28

3

- Type Near the Lake in the text box to enter a caption (Figure 9–29).

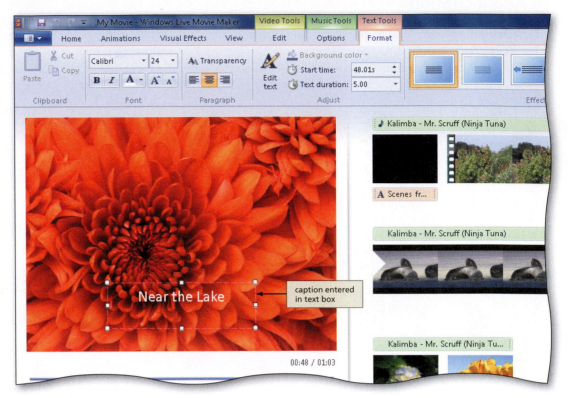

Figure 9–29

To Add Credits

Now that you have added the title and caption, you will add the closing credits to the end of the movie. The following steps add closing credits to the project.

1

- Click Home on the Ribbon to display the Home tab (Figure 9–30).

Figure 9–30

2

• Click the Credits button on the Ribbon to display the credits item (Figure 9–31).

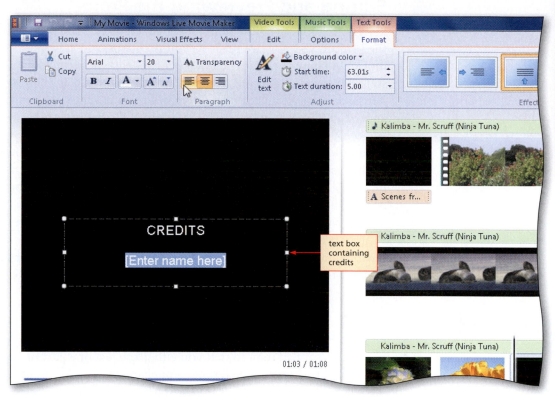

Figure 9–31

3

• Type Created by Your Name (substitute your name for *Your Name*) in the text box to enter the credits (Figure 9–32).

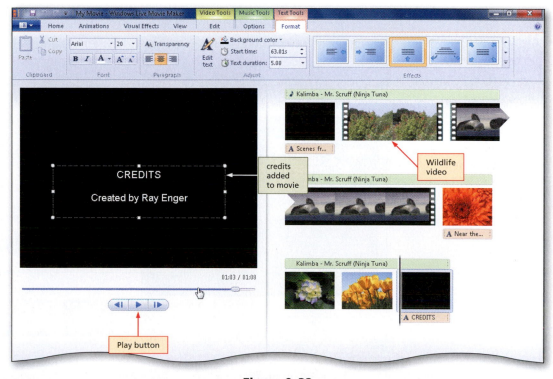

Figure 9–32

Editing and Previewing the Project

After adding all the items — video, pictures, music, title, caption, and credits — to the project, you now are ready to edit the items, which is the second step in creating a movie. When you edit an item, you only change how the item appears in the project; the source files are unaffected. Windows Live Movie Maker's editing tools allow you to add an item before or after an existing item, split an item into two items, remove an item, resize an item, and rearrange the items. You can add a **transition** between two items to move smoothly from one item to another, add an **effect** to change how an item appears, and add a **pan and zoom** to change how an item plays. For example, you can use a fade transition so that as one item fades away, the next item fades in. An effect is used while the entire item is playing. For example, using a black-and-white effect, you can have an item display in black and white even though it was recorded in color.

As you edit your movie, remember to preview the changes to the project in the Preview Monitor. If you remember from the beginning of the chapter, the third step in creating a movie is to preview the project. As you develop a project, you might want to preview the project multiple times as you split and rearrange items.

To Split an Item

Sometimes, you might want to split an item so that you either use just one part of it or remove an unneeded portion. Only the item will be split; the source file will remain unchanged.

Windows Live Movie Maker offers two methods of resizing a video item: splitting and trimming. When you split an item, the result is two separate items that can be manipulated separately. When you trim an item, you hide part of the item, either from the beginning or from the end of the item, which results in a single, shorter item. The following steps split the Wildlife video twice so that there are three items on the storyboard.

- Select the Wildlife video.

- Click the Play button to advance the playback indicator (Figure 9–33).

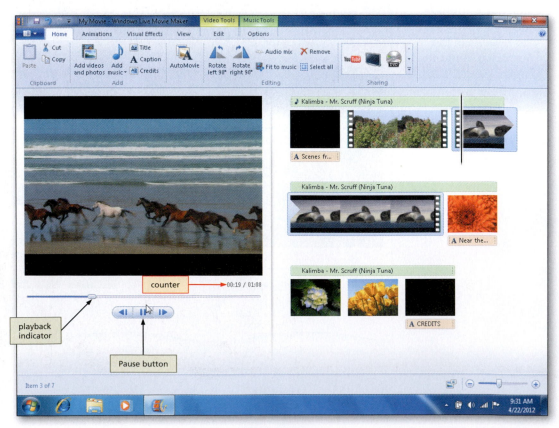

Figure 9–33

2

- Click the Pause button when the counter reaches 28 seconds (Figure 9–34).

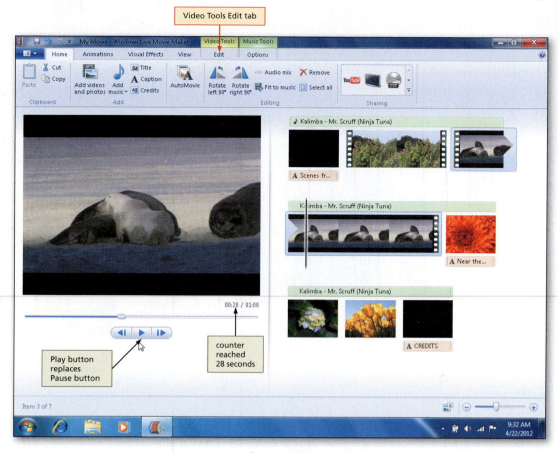

Figure 9–34

3

- Click Video Tools Edit on the Ribbon to display the Video Tools Edit tab (Figure 9–35).

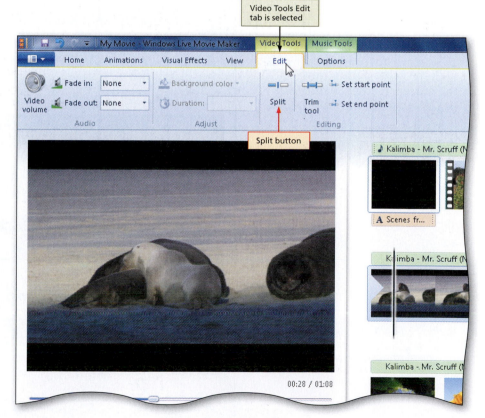

Figure 9–35

● Click the Split button to split the Wildlife video (Figure 9–36).

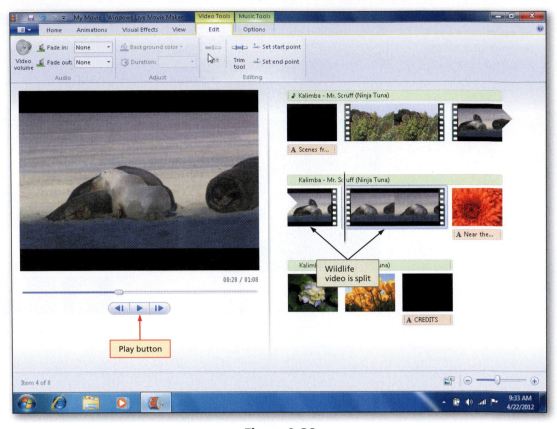

Figure 9–36

● Click the Play button to advance the playback indicator in the second Wildlife video.

● Click the Pause button when the counter reaches 30 seconds (Figure 9–37).

Figure 9–37

6

- Click the Split button to split the Wildlife video (Figure 9–38).

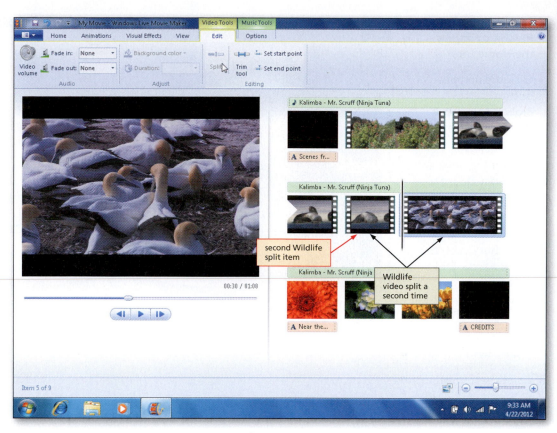

second Wildlife split item

Wildlife video split a second time

Figure 9–38

To Remove an Item

Now that you have split the Wildlife video, you can remove any portion you no longer need. The following steps remove the section split from the middle of the Wildlife video, from the storyboard.

- Click the section split from the middle of the Wildlife video item to select it (Figure 9–39).

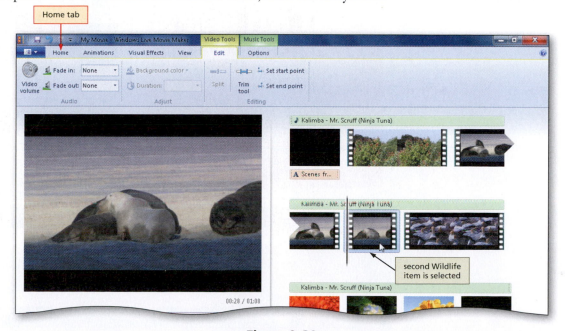

Home tab

second Wildlife item is selected

Figure 9–39

2

- Click Home on the Ribbon to display the Home tab.

- Click the Remove button on the Ribbon to remove the selected item (Figure 9–40).

Q&A

What if I remove an item by accident?

If you remove an item by accident, you can click the Undo button on the Quick Access Toolbar to restore it.

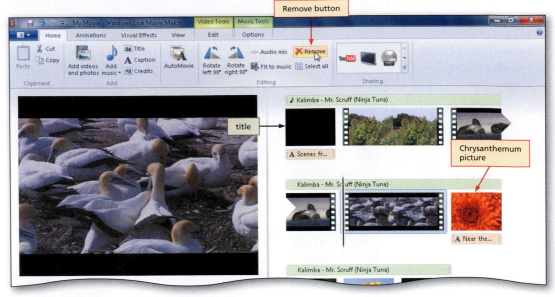

Figure 9–40

Other Ways

1. Select item, right-click item, click Remove

To Reposition an Item on the Storyboard

You easily can move an item to a new position in the storyboard by dragging the video or picture to the desired position. The following steps move the pictures in the storyboard to the desired locations.

1

- Click and drag the Chrysanthemum picture to position it after the title (Figure 9–41).

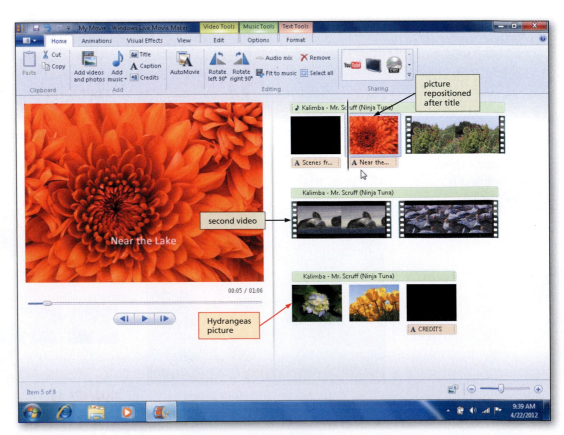

Figure 9–41

2

- Click and drag the Hydrangeas picture to position it before the second video (Figure 9–42).

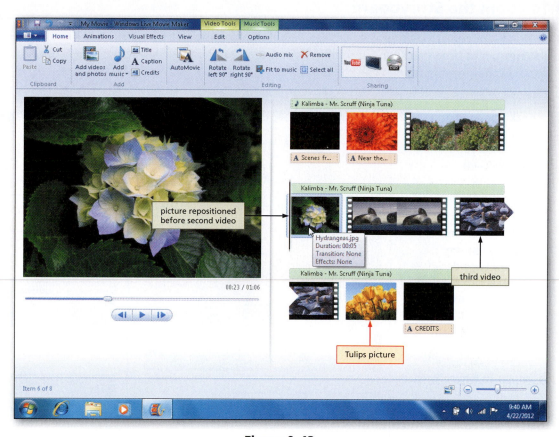

Figure 9–42

3

- Click and drag the Tulips picture to position it before the third video (Figure 9–43).

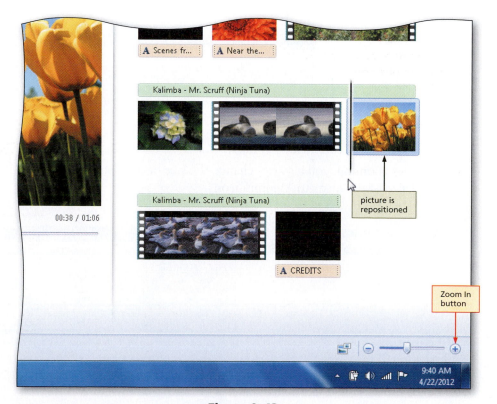

Figure 9–43

To Zoom the Storyboard

When you are editing items, it can be helpful to zoom in and out as necessary. Zooming out can help reduce the amount of time you spend scrolling. Zooming in can help you see more details of each item. The following steps zoom in the storyboard.

- Click the Zoom In button to zoom in to the storyboard (Figure 9–44).

🔍 **Experiment**

- Click the Zoom In button a few more times to see the different appearances as you zoom. Click the Zoom out button an appropriate number of times to return the zoom level so that your screen looks similar to Figure 9–44.

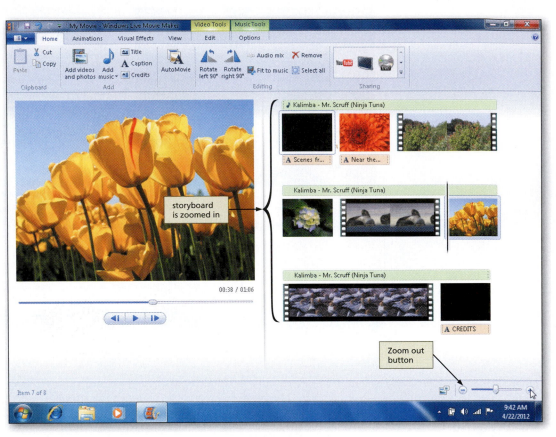

Figure 9–44

Other Ways
1. Click View tab on Ribbon, click Zoom in

To Change the Size of the Items

Besides zooming, you also can change the size of the items on the storyboard. The following steps change the thumbnail size of the icons to Medium icons.

- Click View on the Ribbon to display the View tab (Figure 9–45).

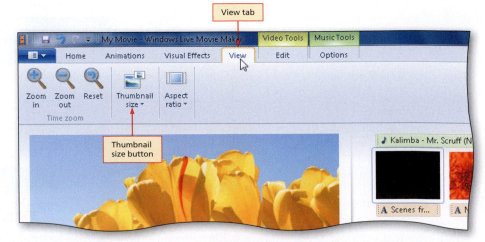

Figure 9–45

2

• Click the Thumbnail size button on the Ribbon to display the list of options (Figure 9–46).

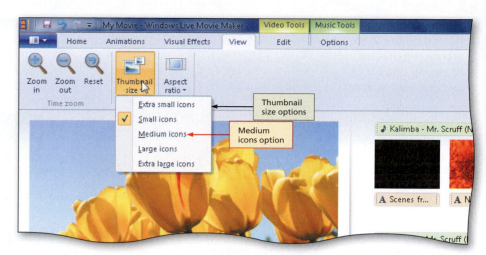

Figure 9–46

3

• Click Medium icons to increase the size of the icons (Figure 9–47).

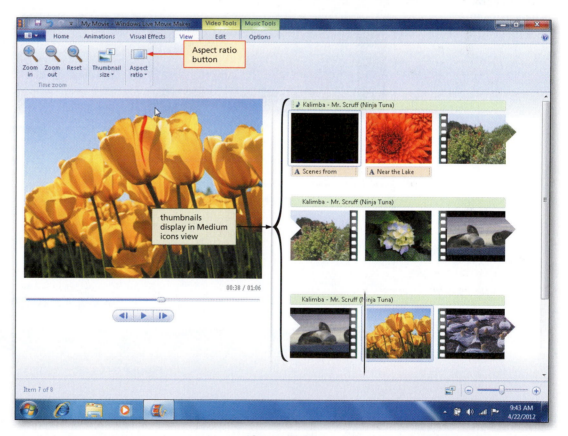

Figure 9–47

Other Ways
1. Click 'Change thumbnail size' on status bar, click Medium icons

To Change the Aspect Ratio

The aspect ratio defines the proportion of screen width to screen height. By default, the aspect ratio is set to standard; however, once you change it, Windows Live Movie Maker remembers the setting. You can change the aspect ratio from standard to widescreen. This is great for widescreen televisions and other display devices that support widescreen. The steps on the following page change the aspect ratio to widescreen.

• Click the Aspect ratio button on the View tab on the Ribbon to display the list of options (Figure 9–48).

Figure 9–48

• Click the Widescreen button to change the aspect ratio to widescreen (Figure 9–49).

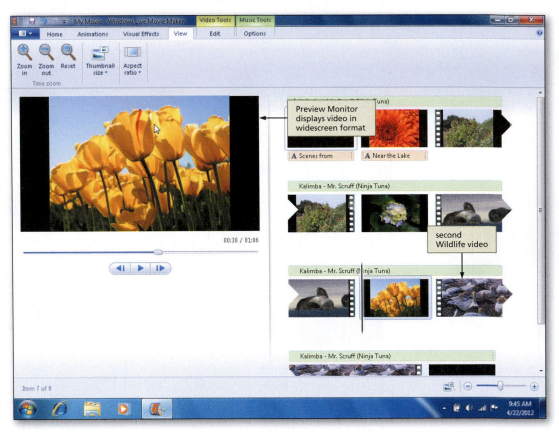

Figure 9–49

To Trim an Item Using the Playback Indicator

One way to resize an item is to trim the item. When you trim an item, you select part of the item to hide. There are two ways to trim an item. The first way is to play the video until the playback indicator reaches your desired start or end point, and then click the 'Set start point' or 'Set end point' button on the Ribbon. The second way to trim an item is to use the Trim tool. If you trim from the beginning, the item will be modified so that the portion before the playback indicator is hidden. If you trim from the end, the item will be modified so that the portion after the playback indicator is hidden.

Because the second Wildlife video is too long, you will trim it to 10 seconds in length. The following steps trim the second Wildlife video to 10 seconds by positioning the playback indicator 10 seconds after the start of the item and then trimming the end of the item.

1

- Click the second Wildlife video on the storyboard to position the playback indicator at the start of the item (Figure 9–50).

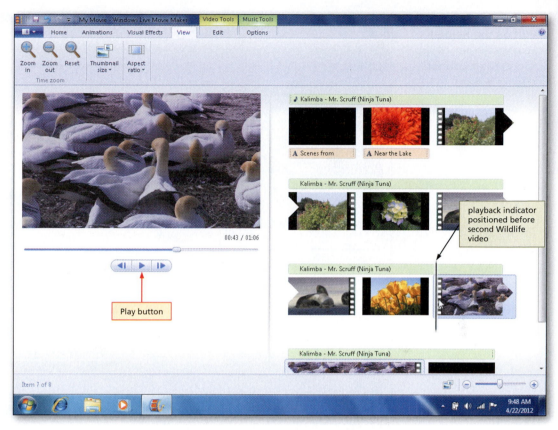

Figure 9–50

2

- Click the Play button to move the Playback indicator.

- Click the Pause button after 10 seconds have passed (Figure 9–51).

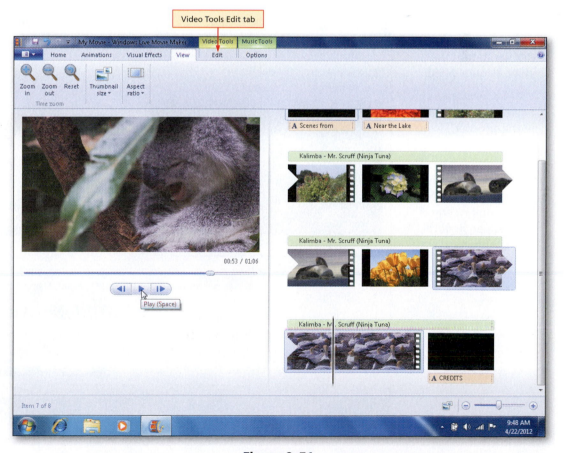

Figure 9–51

3

● Click Video Tools
Edit on the Ribbon
to display the
Video Tools Edit tab
(Figure 9–52).

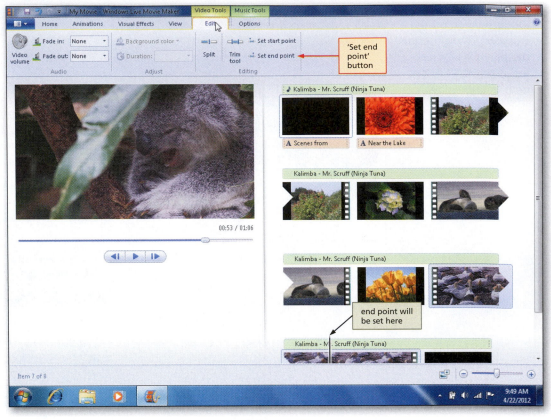

Figure 9–52

4

● Click the 'Set end
point' button on the
Ribbon to trim the
video (Figure 9–53).

Q&A

What if I make a
mistake at any point
in this process?

You can undo an
edit by clicking the
Undo button on the
Quick Access Toolbar.
Then, you can edit
the item again until
you are happy with
your results.

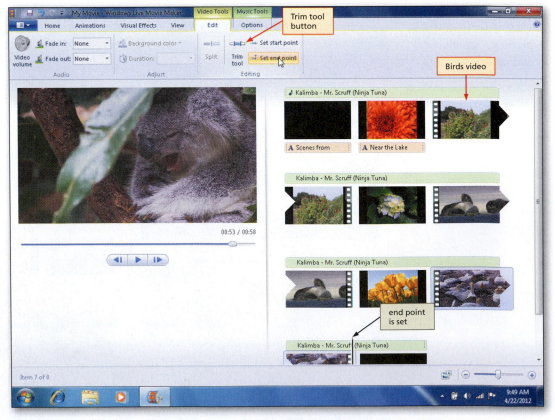

Figure 9–53

To Trim an Item Using the Trim Tool

The second way to trim is to use the Trim tool. When you use the Trim tool, you can set the start and end points by typing the number of seconds into the Start point and End point text boxes or by dragging the Trimming duration sliders to the desired start and end points. The Birds video needs to be trimmed to 10 seconds. The following steps trim the Birds video by using the Trim tool.

- Click the Birds video to select it.

- Click the Trim tool button on the Ribbon to display the Trim tab on the Ribbon and the Trimmed duration sliders below the preview window (Figure 9–54).

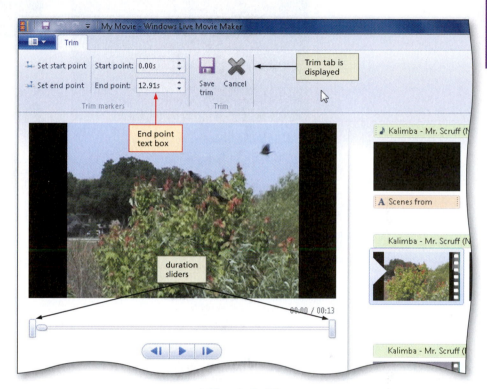

Figure 9–54

2

- Type `10.00s` in the End point text box to change the end point of the item to 10 seconds (Figure 9–55).

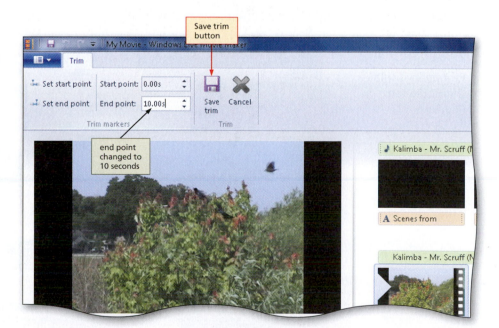

Figure 9–55

● Click the Save trim
  button on the
  Ribbon to save
  the trim settings
  (Figure 9–56).

Figure 9–56

Other Ways	
1. Display Trim tab, click end point text box down arrow until 10.00s displays	2. Display Trim tab, move right Trim slider until 10.00s displays

To Modify the Audio Mix

Because you will have a music item playing for the duration of the movie, you need to mute the audio that accompanies the video items. You can use the Audio mix slider to use the music you have added to the project and not the audio that accompanies each video. Or you can edit each video individually to mute the audio. The following steps set Kalimba as the only background music that will be played during the movie.

● Click Home on the
  Ribbon to display
  the Home tab
  (Figure 9–57).

Figure 9–57

• Click the Audio mix button to display the Audio mix slider (Figure 9–58).

Q&A What would happen if I did not adjust the Audio mix?

If you do not turn off the audio associated with the video items, both the video's audio track and the music item will play simultaneously.

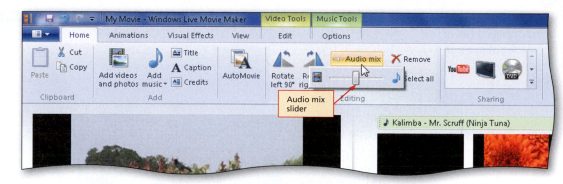

Figure 9–58

• Drag the slider all the way to the right to set Kalimba as the background music and mute the video item's audio (Figure 9–59).

• Click a blank area of the Ribbon to hide the slider.

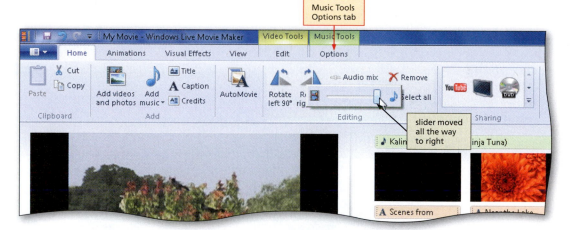

Figure 9–59

To Adjust Audio Fade

Now you would like to adjust the way the music fades in and out. You can do that using the Options tab of the Music Tools Ribbon. The following steps change the fade in to slow and the fade out to medium for the background music.

1

• Click Music Tools Options on the Ribbon to display the Music Tools Options tab (Figure 9–60).

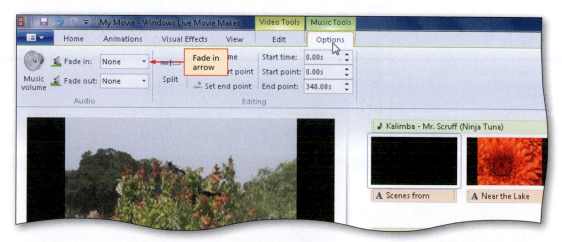

Figure 9–60

● Click Fade in arrow to display a list of options (Figure 9–61).

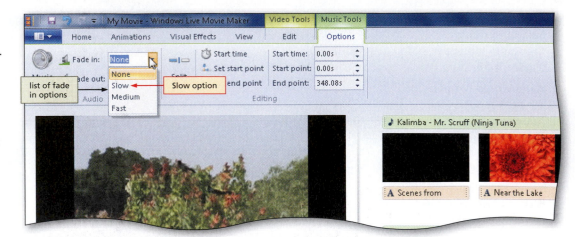

Figure 9–61

● Click Slow to configure the music to fade in at a slow rate (Figure 9–62).

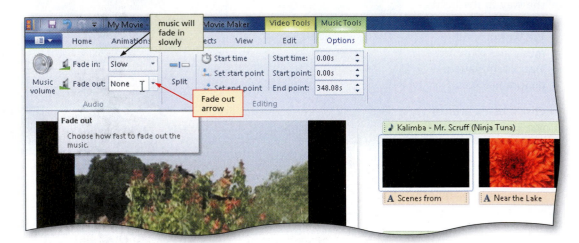

Figure 9–62

● Click the Fade out arrow to display a list of options.

● Click Medium to configure music to fade out at a medium rate (Figure 9–63).

Figure 9–63

To Edit a Title Item

Because the whole movie involves nature scenes, you decide to change the background color of the title item to Olive green. You also decide to change the effect used when displaying the title to use the Swing down effect. The following steps change the background color of the title item and apply the Swing down effect.

- Click the Title item to select it.

- Click Text Tools Format on the Ribbon to display the Text Tools Format tab (Figure 9–64).

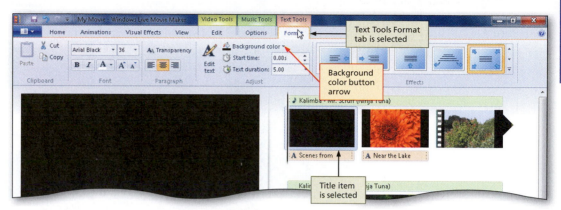

Figure 9–64

- Click the Background color button arrow to display the color options (Figure 9–65).

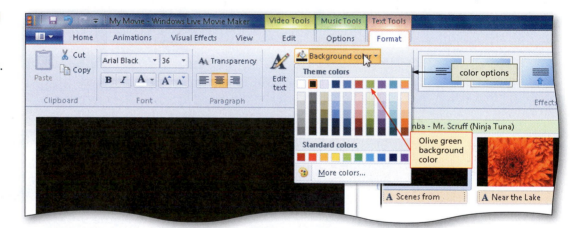

Figure 9–65

3

- Click the Olive green color swatch (row 1, column 7) to change the background color to Olive green (Figure 9–66).

Figure 9–66

4

● If necessary, click the More button in the Effects group to display the Gallery.

● Click the Swing down effect in the Effects group on the Ribbon to apply the to Swing down effect (Figure 9–67).

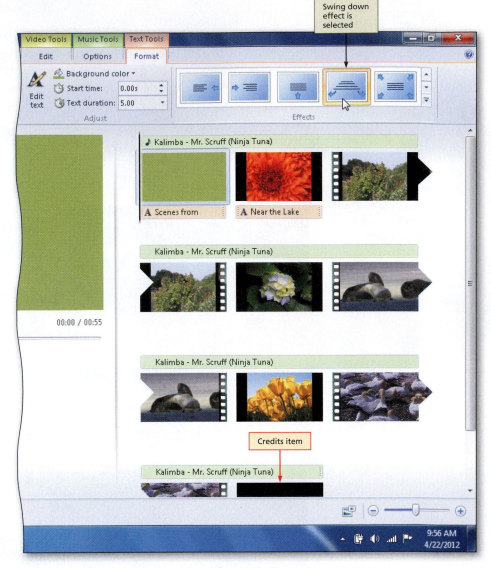

Figure 9–67

To Edit the Credits

Now you will change the background color of the credits item to Olive green, but you will keep the current effect. The following steps edit the credits item.

1 Click the Credits item to select it.

2 Click the Background color button arrow on the Ribbon to display the color options.

3 Click the Olive green color swatch to change the background color to Olive green (Figure 9–68).

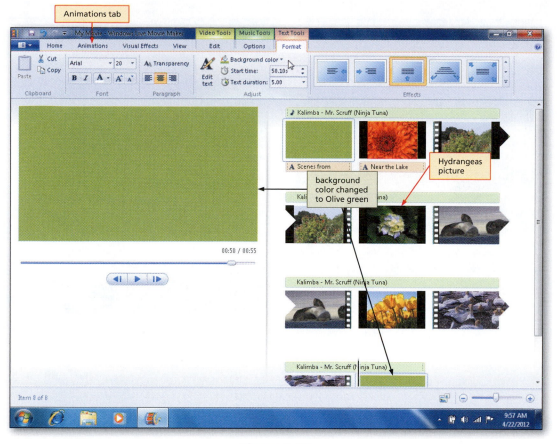

Animations tab

background color changed to Olive green

Hydrangeas picture

Figure 9–68

To Add a Transition

Transitions control how your movie plays from one item to the next, and are designed to enhance scene changes. Windows Live Movie Maker offers many transitions, including fades, dissolves, spins, flips, and wipes. You can add transitions between pictures, video items, or titles in any combination, and you can use the same or different transitions between each item. You decide to use the Diagonal - box out transition before the Hydrangeas picture. The following steps add the Diagonal - box out transition before the Hydrangeas picture.

- Click the Hydrangeas picture to select it.

- Click Animations on the Ribbon to display the Animations tab (Figure 9–69).

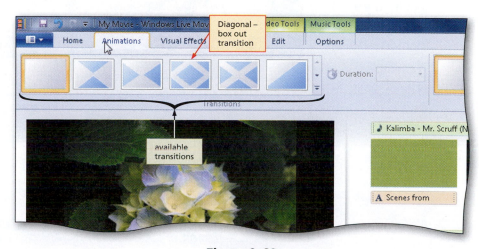

Diagonal – box out transition

available transitions

Figure 9–69

2

● Click the Diagonal — box out transition in the Transitions group to add the effect to the storyboard before the Hydrangeas picture (Figure 9–70).

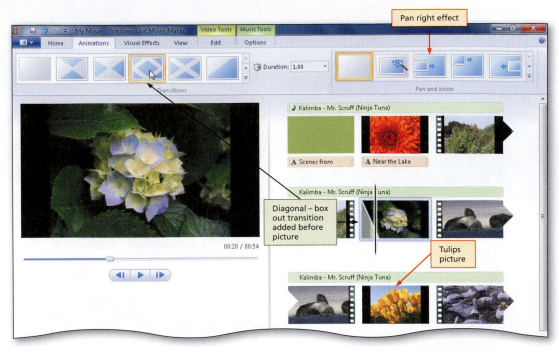

Figure 9–70

To Configure Pan and Zoom

From the Animations tab, you also can configure the pan and zoom for an item. The following step changes the pan and zoom of the Tulips picture.

1

● Click the Tulips picture to select it.

● Click the Pan right effect in the 'Pan and zoom' group on the Ribbon to change the pan and zoom effect of the Tulips picture to Pan right (Figure 9–71).

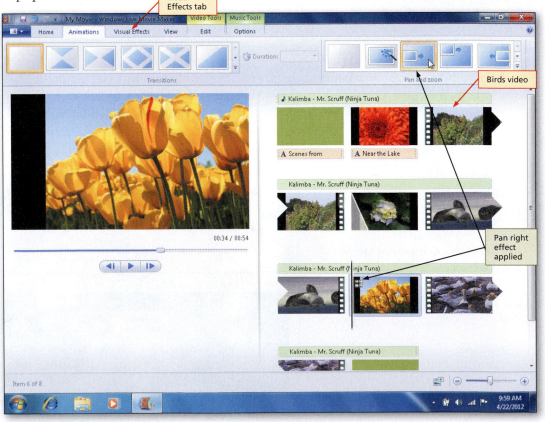

Figure 9–71

To Add an Effect

You can add many different special effects to your items. For example, you could modify an item to appear in black and white to give the effect of an old movie, or you could add a mirror effect that makes the action flow in the opposite direction. The following steps add the Mirror horizontal effect to the Birds video.

- Click the Birds video to select it.

- Click Visual Effects on the Ribbon to display the Visual Effects tab (Figure 9–72).

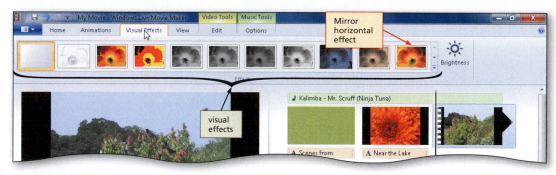

Figure 9–72

- Click the Mirror horizontal effect to add the effect to the Birds video (Figure 9–73).

Q&A

What if I apply the wrong effect to the item?

Click the Undo button to undo the effect, and then apply the correct one.

Figure 9–73

To Adjust Brightness

Sometimes a picture or a video needs to have its brightness adjusted. Perhaps too much — or not enough — light shows in the picture or video. The following steps adjust the brightness of the Birds video to make the video slightly darker.

- Click the Brightness button on the Ribbon to display the Brightness slider (Figure 9–74).

Figure 9–74

2

● Click left of the slider
to move the slider
one click to the left
to make the Birds
video slightly darker
(Figure 9–75).

● Click an open area of
the Ribbon to hide
the slider.

Figure 9–75

To Preview a Project

Now that you are finished editing your movie, you will preview it to make sure that you are happy with the
results. The following steps preview the entire movie.

1

● Click the Title item
to move to the
beginning of the
movie (Figure 9–76).

Figure 9–76

2

- Click the Play button to play the movie in the Preview Monitor (Figure 9–77).

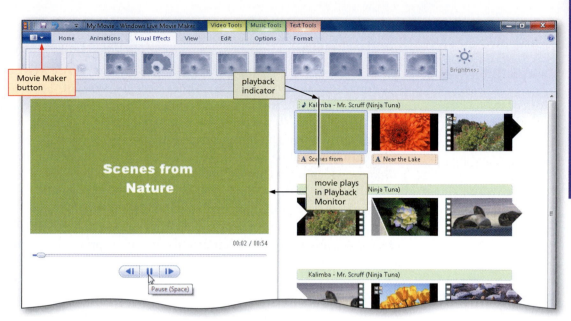

Figure 9–77

To Save a Project

You are now ready to save your project. Windows Live Movie Maker projects are saved to the My Documents folder by default. You always can reopen your project at a later time if you decide to make changes or republish it. The following steps save the project.

1

- Click the Movie Maker button to display the Movie Maker menu.

- Click the Save project command to display the Save Project dialog box.

- Type Scenes from Nature in the File name text box (Figure 9–78).

- Click the Save button to save the project.

Q&A

What file extension does Windows Live Movie Maker give to projects? Is it different from published movies?

Projects receive the .wlmp file extension. Files with this extension contain information about how the items are ordered in the storyboard and only can be used by Windows Live Movie Maker. Published movies can be played using Windows Media Player or any compatible movie player. Published movies are saved with the .wmv or .avi extension and do not contain information about the individual items that make up the movie, just the finished movie itself.

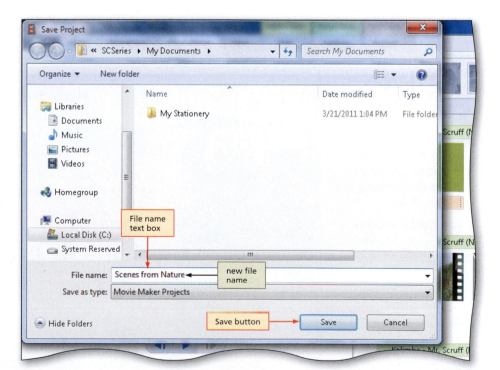

Figure 9–78

Saving and Publishing a Movie

The fourth step in creating a movie is to publish and distribute the project as a movie. When you publish a movie in Windows Live Movie Maker, you can publish it to the computer, an optical disc, an e-mail message, or YouTube. Depending upon which option you use, you will be given different choices that affect how the movie will be published. If you publish to an optical disc, Windows DVD Maker will open and you will be given the same burning options that were presented in Chapter 8. If you publish to your computer, you will be given choices that differ from the Windows DVD Maker options. To know which settings you should use, you need to know how you will be using the movie.

If you publish your movie to an e-mail message, the movie will be created using settings that are more appropriate for sending via e-mail programs, including smaller file sizes and lower bit rates. If you publish your movie in high definition, the movie will be created automatically using settings that are appropriate for high-definition movies such as larger file sizes and higher bit rates.

To Publish a Movie to YouTube

Nowadays, many people use YouTube for sharing their movies. Windows Live Movie Maker can create your movie and then post it to your YouTube account. To publish to YouTube, you first must have a YouTube account. If you do not have one, visit the YouTube Web site and create an account. A copy of the video also will be saved to the My Videos folder on the computer. The following steps publish the movie to YouTube.

1
- Click Home on the Ribbon to display the Home tab (Figure 9–79).

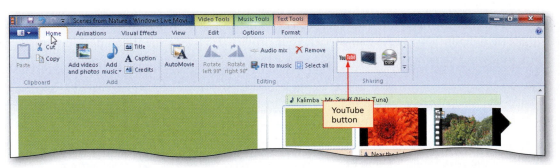

Figure 9–79

2
- Click the YouTube button on the Ribbon to display the Publish on YouTube dialog box (Figure 9–80).

Q&A
What other sharing options are available?

The Sharing group provides options allowing you to share the movie in various formats, such as high-definition, standard definition, and a size suitable to be displayed on smart phones and other mobile devices. An option also is available that enables you to distribute a movie as an e-mail attachment.

Figure 9–80

3

- Enter your YouTube user name and password in the Publish on YouTube dialog box (Figure 9–81).

Q&A

What if I do not have a YouTube account?

If you do not have one, click the 'Don't have an account? Create one.' link. This link will open the YouTube Web site in your browser where you can create an account. You cannot upload a video without an account.

Figure 9–81

4

- Click the Sign In button to sign in to YouTube (Figure 9–82).

Figure 9–82

- Type `First Video with WLMM` in the Description text box.

- Type `Nature` in the Tags text box.

- Click the Category list box to change the Category to Pets & Animals.

- Click the Permission list box to change the permission to Private (Figure 9–83).

Figure 9–83

- Click the Publish button to publish the movie to YouTube (Figure 9–84).

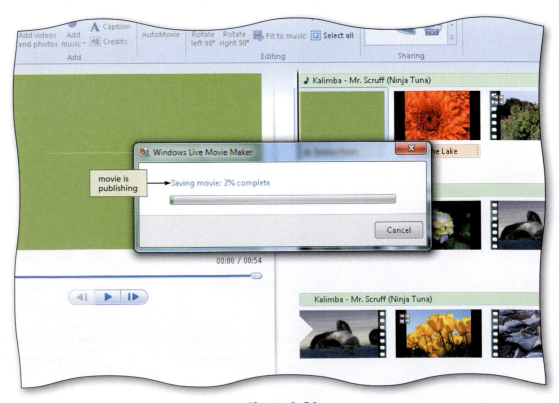

Figure 9–84

7

- After the movie is published, the Publish on YouTube dialog box reappears (Figure 9–85).

- Click the View online button to view the movie in your Web browser.

- After viewing the movie, close the Web browser.

Q&A What if my movie did not publish successfully?

If your movie did not publish, you can try to publish your movie again after you verify that you have a good Internet connection and that the YouTube Web site is working correctly. Also, because your movie has been saved to the computer, you could upload it directly to YouTube following the directions for uploading files on the YouTube Web site.

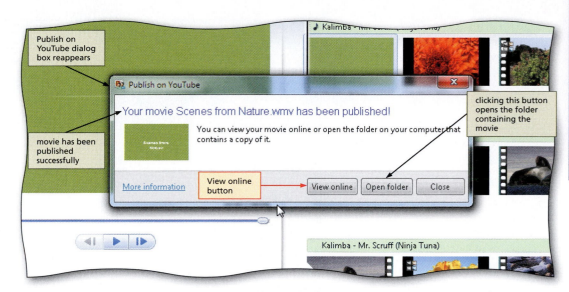

Figure 9–85

To Save a Movie to the Computer

If you are unsure of what you want to do with your movie, you simply can save it to your computer. You can then decide at a later time whether to burn it to an optical disc using Windows DVD Maker or to attach it to an e-mail message to send to a friend. Saving the movie to the computer also is a good option if you want to post the movie on the Internet to a Web site other than YouTube. The following steps save the movie to the computer.

1

- Click the High-definition (1080p) button in the Sharing group on the Ribbon to display the Save Movie dialog box (Figure 9–86).

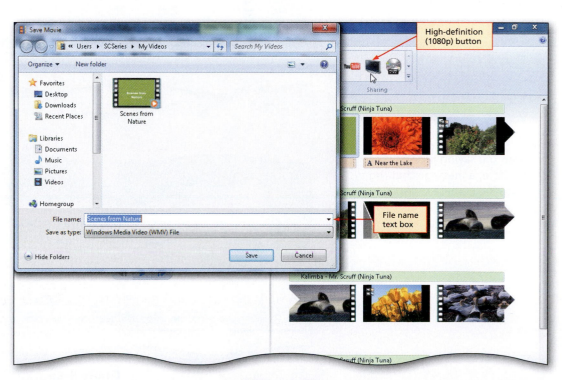

Figure 9–86

2

- Type HD after Scenes from Nature in the File name text box to indicate the movie is HD (high definition) (Figure 9–87).

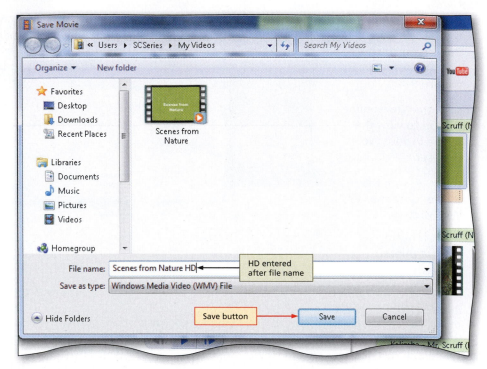

Figure 9–87

3

- Click the Save button to save the movie (Figure 9–88).

Q&A

Can I save to formats other than HD?

Yes, by clicking the More button in the Sharing group, you can select other options such as widescreen or standard definition.

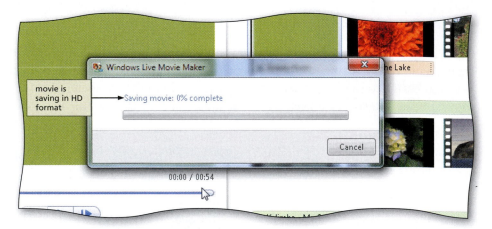

Figure 9–88

4

- When the saving process is complete, a message that the movie is complete is displayed (Figure 9–89).

Figure 9–89

5

- Click the Play button to complete the publishing process and play the published movie in Windows Media Player (Figure 9–90).

- After viewing the movie, close Windows Media Player.

Q&A

Do I have to play the movie?

No. If you click the Close button, the Publish Movie dialog box will close without playing the movie.

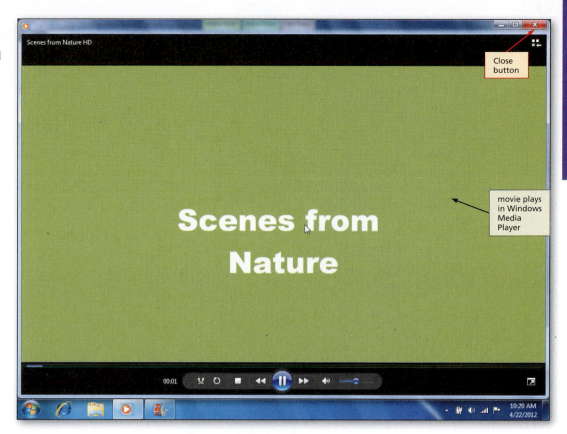

Figure 9–90

To Publish a Movie to DVD

Finally, you might want to save your movie on a DVD, which allows you to play your movie on any standard DVD player. When you choose this option, Windows DVD Maker is used to make your DVD. Before Windows DVD Maker is launched, a copy of the video will be saved to the My Videos folder. The following steps publish your movie to DVD.

1

- Click the DVD button in the Sharing group on the Ribbon to display the Save Movie dialog box.

- Type DVD after Scenes from Nature in the File name text box to indicate that this is the DVD version of the movie (Figure 9–91).

- Click the Save button to save the movie.

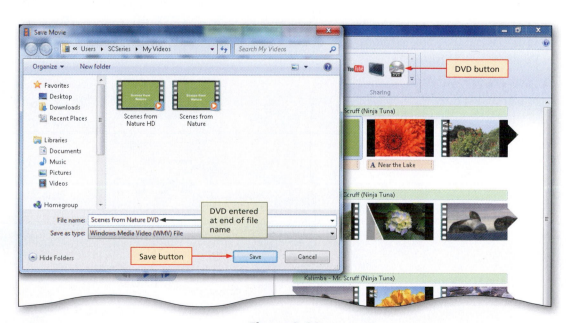

Figure 9–91

2

• After the movie has been saved, Windows DVD Maker opens (Figure 9–92).

• Click the Next button to continue making the DVD with the default settings.

• Click the Burn button to burn the DVD (insert a blank DVD when prompted).

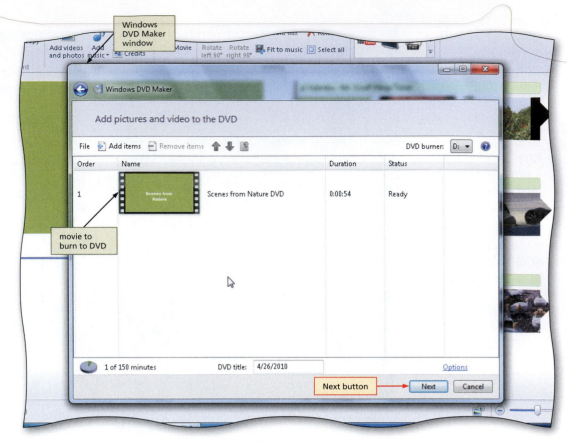

Figure 9–92

3

• After the DVD has been burned, a confirmation message is displayed (Figure 9–93).

• Close the dialog box.

• Close Windows DVD Maker.

• Click the No button in the Windows DVD Maker dialog box to return to Windows Live Movie Maker.

• Close the Windows Live Movie Maker dialog box.

Figure 9–93

To Create an AutoMovie

You might know which items you want to include in a movie, but you might not be confident about the order in which they should appear. In that case, you can have Windows Live Movie Maker create the movie automatically. Windows Live Movie Maker will ask you to confirm that you want to use AutoMovie and then create the movie for you. To see how this works, you will use the AutoMovie command to rearrange the project. The following steps use the AutoMovie command to create a movie.

- Click the AutoMovie button on the Ribbon to display a Windows Live Movie Maker dialog box that explains the AutoMovie feature (Figure 9–94).

Figure 9–94

- Click the OK button to confirm that you want to use AutoMovie to generate a new movie (Figure 9–95).

- Close the dialog box.

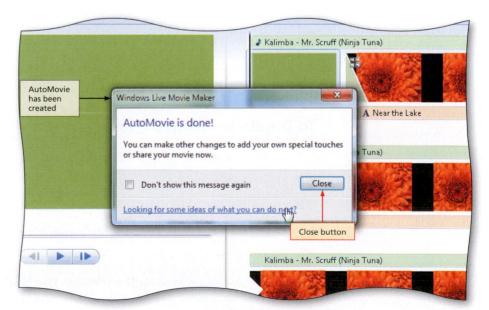

Figure 9–95

● Click the Play button to preview the AutoMovie (Figure 9–96).

Figure 9–96

To Close Windows Live Movie Maker

Now that you have finished making your movies, you can close Windows Live Movie Maker. There is no need to save changes that were made when you created the AutoMovie as you will not be reusing the project.

1 Close Windows Live Movie Maker without saving any changes.

To Delete Unneeded Files

Now you will delete the files you created.

1 Open the Videos library.

2 Delete the Scenes from Nature videos from the Videos library.

3 Delete the Birds video from the My Videos folder.

4 Open the Documents library.

5 Delete the Scenes from Nature Windows Live Movie Maker project file from the My Documents folder.

6 Empty the Recycle Bin.

To Log Off and Turn Off the Computer

After completing your work with Windows 7, you first should close your user account by logging off the computer, and then turn off the computer.

1 On the Start menu, click the arrow to the right of the Shut down button, and then click the Log off command to log off the computer.

2 On the Welcome Screen, click the Shut down button to turn off the computer.

Chapter Summary

In this chapter, you have learned how to use Windows Live Movie Maker. Using Movie Maker, you imported video from a digital video camera, added a variety of media files, played and edited video items, added transitions and effects, previewed and saved a project, and published a movie. You now know how to create a movie and publish it in a format that you can share and enjoy with your friends and family. You learned that Windows Live Movie Maker is an easy tool to use to create movies. The items listed below include all of the new Windows 7 skills you have learned in this chapter.

1. Import from a Digital Video Camera (WIN 559)
2. Preview and Add Videos (WIN 564)
3. Preview and Add Pictures (WIN 568)
4. Preview and Add Music (WIN 570)
5. Add a Title (WIN 572)
6. Add a Caption (WIN 573)
7. Add Credits (WIN 574)
8. Split an Item (WIN 576)
9. Remove an Item (WIN 579)
10. Reposition an Item on the Storyboard (WIN 580)
11. Zoom the Storyboard (WIN 582)
12. Change the Size of the Items (WIN 582)
13. Change the Aspect Ratio (WIN 583)
14. Trim an Item Using the Playback Indicator (WIN 584)
15. Trim an Item Using the Trim Tool (WIN 587)
16. Modify the Audio Mix (WIN 588)
17. Adjust Audio Fade (WIN 589)
18. Edit a Title Item (WIN 591)
19. Add a Transition (WIN 593)
20. Configure Pan and Zoom (WIN 594)
21. Add an Effect (WIN 595)
22. Adjust Brightness (WIN 595)
23. Preview a Project (WIN 596)
24. Save a Project (WIN 597)
25. Publish a Movie to YouTube (WIN 598)
26. Save a Movie to the Computer (WIN 601)
27. Publish a Movie to DVD (WIN 603)
28. Create an AutoMovie (WIN 605)

Learn It Online

Test your knowledge of chapter content and key terms.

Instructions: To complete the Learn It Online exercises, start your browser, click the Address bar, and then enter the Web address `scsite.com/win7/learn`. When the Windows 7 Learn It Online page is displayed, click the link for the exercise you want to complete and then read the instructions.

Chapter Reinforcement TF, MC, and SA

A series of true/false, multiple-choice, and short-answer questions that test your knowledge of the chapter content.

Flash Cards

An interactive learning environment where you identify chapter key terms associated with displayed definitions.

Practice Test

A series of multiple-choice questions that test your knowledge of chapter content and key terms.

Who Wants To Be a Computer Genius?

An interactive game that challenges your knowledge of chapter content in the style of a television quiz show.

Wheel of Terms

An interactive game that challenges your knowledge of chapter key terms in the style of the television show *Wheel of Fortune*.

Crossword Puzzle Challenge

A crossword puzzle that challenges your knowledge of key terms presented in the chapter.

Apply Your Knowledge

Reinforce the skills and apply the concepts you learned in this chapter.

Making a Movie for YouTube

Instructions: Now that you have learned that you can publish movies to YouTube using Windows Live Movie Maker, you want to make more movies to publish to YouTube.

Part 1: Creating a YouTube Account (if necessary)
1. Launch your Web browser and navigate to `youtube.com` (Figure 9–97).
2. Click the Create Account link to display the Create Account Web page.
3. Follow the instructions to create a YouTube account.
4. Close the Web browser window.

Part 2: Creating your Movie
1. Launch Windows Live Movie Maker.
2. Click the 'Add videos and photos' button to add a picture of your choice either from the sample pictures that are installed with Windows 7 or one of your own pictures.
3. Click the 'Add videos and photos' button to either add the sample video that is installed with Windows 7 or a video you created.
4. Click the Title button to add a title to the movie. Type `My Second YouTube Video` as the title.
5. Preview the video. Write down a description that describes the video:

_____

6. Click the Credits button and enter your name to add closing credits to your movie.
7. Click the Movie Maker button, and then click Save project to save your project. Type `My Second YouTube Video` in the File name text box.

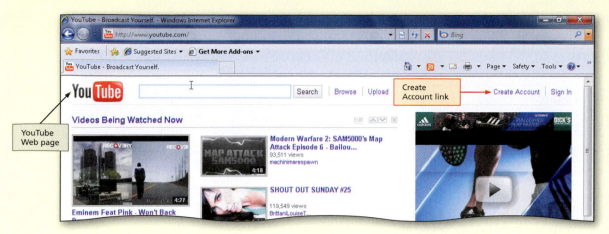

Figure 9–97

Part 3: Publishing your Movie to YouTube

1. Click the Publish on YouTube button in the Sharing group on the Home tab.

2. Sign in to YouTube using your user name and password.

3. Type My Second YouTube Video in the Title text box.

4. Enter the description you wrote in Step 5 from Part 2 in the Description text box. Add tag(s) of your choosing.

5. Select a category that fits your video and select Private from the Permission list.

6. Click the Publish button.

7. Click the View online button to watch your video on YouTube.

8. Submit the YouTube URL of your video to your instructor.

Part 4: Backing Up and Deleting Files

1. Close Windows Live Movie Maker.

2. Open the Videos library, and save a copy of your movie to your USB device.

3. Delete the movie from the Videos library.

4. Open the Documents library, and save a copy of your project to your USB device.

5. Delete the project from the Documents library.

Extend Your Knowledge

Extend the skills you learned in this chapter and experiment with new skills. You might need to use Help to complete the assignment.

Using Windows Live Movie Maker Help

Instructions: Use Windows Live Movie Maker Help and a computer to perform the following tasks and answer the questions.

1. Launch Windows Live Movie Maker. If necessary, maximize the Windows Live Movie Maker window.

2. Click the Help button on the Ribbon to open Windows Live Movie Maker Help in your Web browser. If necessary, maximize the Web browser window.

3. Click the 'Table of contents' link (Figure 9–98 on the next page). Use the Table of contents to answer the following questions.

Continued >

STUDENT ASSIGNMENTS

Extend Your Knowledge *continued*

Figure 9–98

a. What are the basic steps to create a movie?

_____

b. How do you capture video?

_____

c. How do you burn an entire videotape to DVD?

_____

d. Can you publish to Web sites other than YouTube?

_____

e. How do you change the duration of pictures in a movie?

_____

f. What can you do after using AutoMovie?

_____

g. What is a transition? An effect?

_____

4. Close Windows Live Help and close your browser.

In the Lab

Use the guidelines, concepts, and skills presented in this chapter to increase your knowledge of Windows 7. Labs are listed in order of increasing difficulty.

Lab 1: Showcase Progress in Movie Making Technology

Instructions: You want to create a movie that illustrates how movie technology has advanced since the early days of moviemaking. You decide to apply different effects to a sample video to illustrate how moviemaking has changed.

Part 1: Launching Windows Live Movie Maker
1. Launch Windows Live Movie Maker.
2. Select and add a sample video.
3. Select and add a sample picture to accompany the sample video.

Part 2: Adding a Title Item
1. Insert a title item.
2. Type Movie Making Progress as the title (Figure 9–99).
3. Change the title effect to Scroll. If necessary, move the title to the beginning of the movie.

Figure 9–99

Part 3: Duplicating Items on the Storyboard
1. Copy the picture you added to the storyboard and paste it after your video.
2. Copy the video you added to the storyboard and paste it after the second picture.
3. Copy the picture you added to the storyboard and paste it after the second video.
4. Copy the video you added to the storyboard and paste it after the third picture.

Part 4: Adding Captions to the Picture Items
1. Add the caption, First there were black and white movies, to the first picture item.
2. Add the caption, Along came color movies, to the second picture item.
3. Add the caption, Finally, movies with modern effects, to the third picture item.

Part 5: Adding Transitions and Effects
1. Click the Animations tab, and then add the 'Filled V down' transition to the first video item.
2. Add the 'Filled V right' transition to the second video item. (*Hint:* You might need to click the More button to view additional transitions.)
3. Add the 'Filled V up' transition to the third video item.
4. Click the Visual Effects tab, and then add the 'Black and white' effect to the first video item.
5. Add the '3D ripple' effect to the third video item.

Continued >

STUDENT ASSIGNMENTS

In the Lab *continued*

Part 6: Adding and Adjusting Audio
1. On the Home tab, click the Add music button to add a sample music file that complements the video item.
2. Adjust the audio mix so that only the background music plays.
3. Change the Fade In to slow and the Fade out to fast.

Part 7: Burning a DVD
1. Save the project and type Movie Progress as the file name.
2. Click the 'Burn a DVD' button to publish the movie to DVD.
3. What style did you choose for the movie?

_____

4. What is the length of the movie?

_____

5. What are your options for movie settings?

_____

6. Type Movie Progress as the title of the movie.
7. Burn the DVD.

Part 8: Backing Up and Deleting the Files
1. Submit the DVD you burned to your instructor.
2. Back up the files you created to your USB device.
3. Delete any files you created from the computer.

In the Lab

Lab 2: Creating a Home Movie

Instructions: You want to create a movie to share with your friends. You decide that you are going to create a movie of people doing funny things.

Part 1: Recording the Movie
1. Use your digital video camera (or find some free videos on the Internet) to record you and your friends or family acting out five humorous scenes of your choice.

Part 2: Importing a Video into Windows Live Movie Maker
1. Launch Windows Live Movie Maker.
2. Import the video you took (Figure 9–100), naming the items as follows: Funny Video 1, Funny Video 2, Funny Video 3, Funny Video 4, and Funny Video 5.
3. Add the videos you imported or the videos you found into Windows Live Movie Maker.

Figure 9–100

Part 3: Editing the Project

1. Rearrange the items on the storyboard in the following order:

   a. First item on the storyboard: Funny Video 1

   b. Second item on the storyboard: Funny Video 4

   c. Third item on the storyboard: Funny Video 2

   d. Fourth item on the storyboard: Funny Video 3

   e. Fifth item on the storyboard: Funny Video 5

Part 4: Previewing and Saving the Project

1. Click Play to preview the movie. Are the video items in order according to the instructions given in Part 3?

2. Save the project using the name, Edited Funny Project, as the title.

Part 5: Printing a Copy of the Storyboard

1. Press the PRINT SCREEN key on the keyboard to place an image of the desktop on the Clipboard.

2. Start Paint. If necessary, maximize the Untitled — Paint window.

3. Paste a copy of the image in the Paint window.

4. Print the Paint document.

5. Close the Untitled — Paint window without saving the file.

Continued >

In the Lab *continued*

Part 6: Saving the Movie

1. Publish the movie to your computer using standard-definition movie settings.

2. Type `Edited Funny Movie` in the Title text box.

3. Choose to play the movie after publishing.

4. After viewing the movie, close Windows Media Player.

Part 7: Backing Up and Deleting Files

1. Submit the printed Paint document and a copy of your movie to your instructor.

2. Back up the files you created to your USB device.

3. Delete any files you created from the computer.

In the Lab

Lab 3: Creating a Campus Tour

Instructions: You would like to create a video for your cousin who is thinking of attending your school. You decide to use Windows Live Movie Maker to make a campus tour.

Part 1: Recording your Video and Taking Pictures

1. Using a digital video camera, make a video of your three favorite places at your school.

2. Using your digital camera, take a picture of the three locations.

Part 2: Importing your Video

1. Launch Windows Live Movie Maker.

2. Import your video into Windows Live Movie Maker.

3. Type `Campus Location 1` into the Name text box. Select the 'Choose parts of the video to import' option (Figure 9–101).

4. Click the Import button to import the first location video. Click the Stop button at the point where you leave that location. Click the Finish button to import the video.

5. Follow the previous three steps to import the two other campus locations, naming them as Campus Location 2 and Campus Location 3, respectively.

6. Add the three videos to Window Live Movie Maker.

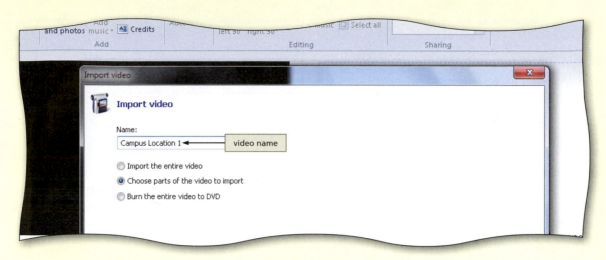

Figure 9–101

Part 3: Importing your Pictures

1. Import the pictures from your digital camera. Close Windows Live Photo Gallery after it opens.

2. Add the three pictures into Windows Live Movie Maker.

Part 4: Creating your Movie

1. Add the items to the storyboard in order of location, with the pictures appearing first, followed by the videos.

2. Add an appropriate title, captions, and credits to your movie.

3. Add any special effects or transitions that you think will add to the movie.

4. Save your project.

Part 5: Publishing your Movie

1. Change the aspect ratio of the movie to Widescreen.

2. Publish the movie to your computer in a High-definition (1080p) format.

3. After viewing the movie, close Windows Media Player.

Part 6: Backing Up and Deleting Files

1. Submit a copy of your movie to your instructor.

2. Back up the files you created to your USB device.

3. Remove the collections from Windows Live Movie Maker and close it.

4. Delete any files you created from the computer.

Cases and Places

Apply your creative thinking and problem-solving skills to design and implement a solution.

• EASIER   •• MORE DIFFICULT

• 1 Researching Online Video Web Sites

There are many Web sites that allow users to share their videos with the world. To understand how these Web sites operate, you will investigate three of them. Using your Web browser, use your search engine to find three Web sites that allow you to share videos. Write a one-page report that summarizes which video file types can be used on each Web site, what content restrictions exist, and what type of copyright laws apply to the videos once posted.

• 2 Creating a Video Editing Presentation

Windows Live Movie Maker allows you to edit video items on the storyboard using editing features such as trimming, splitting, adding an effect, and creating a transition. In a class presentation, explain the steps needed to perform three editing operations and demonstrate each one.

•• 3 Buying Movies Online

Many Web sites allow you to purchase and download movies. Using your Web browser, find three or more Web sites that allow you to purchase and download movies, and read the rules and prices for downloading movies. Prepare a demonstration showing how to buy and download a movie from a Web site, and include any information regarding the usage and viewing of the downloaded movies. Include answers to these questions: How much does it cost to download a movie? What are the restrictions concerning these movies? Do the movie downloads expire after a specified amount of time? Can you burn them to DVD?

•• 4 Making Music

Make It Personal

You are interested in creating custom music for your videos. Search online and in magazines to find music authoring software that work with Windows 7. Research how you can create your own custom music and effects. Can you save and then import these effects into Windows Live Movie Maker? Summarize your findings in a brief report.

•• 5 Creating a Movie

Working Together

Working as a team, write a short movie script for team members to act out. Have one person record the scenes using a video recording device. Import the video into Windows Live Movie Maker and then as a team, edit the movie until you all like the results. Publish the movie to the computer and share with the rest of the class.

Appendix A

Comparison of the New Features of Windows 7 Editions

The Microsoft Windows 7 operating system is available in a variety of editions. The six editions that you most likely will encounter are Windows 7 Starter, Windows 7 Home Basic, Windows 7 Home Premium, Windows 7 Professional, Windows 7 Enterprise, and Windows 7 Ultimate. Because not all computers have the same hardware or are used for the same functions, Microsoft provides these various editions so that each user can have the edition that meets his or her needs. Table A–1 compares features in the various editions. Windows 7 Ultimate, the most complete version of Windows 7, is used as a baseline for clarifying the features of the other editions. Windows 7 Starter and Windows 7 Home Basic are not included in this table as they are more limited in their offerings.

Table A–1 Comparison of Windows 7 Editions

Ultimate Features	Home Premium	Professional	Enterprise
64-bit Support	✓	✓	✓
Action Center	✓	✓	✓
Aero Peek	✓	✓	✓
Aero Shake	✓	✓	✓
Backup and Restore	✓	✓	✓
BitLocker			✓
DirectX 11	✓	✓	✓
Domain Join		✓	✓
HomeGroup	✓	✓	✓
Internet Explorer 8	✓	✓	✓
Jump Lists	✓	✓	✓
Libraries	✓	✓	✓
Location Aware Printing		✓	✓
Maximum RAM (32-bit)	4 GB	4 GB	4 GB
Maximum RAM (64-bit)	16 GB	192 GB	192 GB
Minimum RAM (32-bit)	1 GB	1 GB	1 GB
Minimum RAM (64-bit)	2 GB	2 GB	2 GB
Multiplayer Games	✓	✓	✓

Table A–1 Comparison of Windows 7 Editions *(continued)*			
Ultimate Features	**Home Premium**	**Professional**	**Enterprise**
Parental Controls	✓	✓	✓
Pin	✓	✓	✓
Play To	✓	✓	✓
Power Management	✓	✓	✓
ReadyBoost	✓	✓	✓
Remote Media Streaming	✓	✓	✓
Sleep and Resume	✓	✓	✓
Snap	✓	✓	✓
Sticky Notes	✓	✓	✓
Supports 35 Languages			✓
System Restore	✓	✓	✓
Tablet PC	✓	✓	✓
User Account Control	✓	✓	✓
View Available Networks	✓	✓	✓
Windows Connect Now	✓	✓	✓
Windows Defender	✓	✓	✓
Windows Easy Transfer	✓	✓	✓
Windows Experience Index	✓	✓	✓
Windows Fax and Scan	✓	✓	✓
Windows Firewall	✓	✓	✓
Windows Media Center	✓	✓	✓
Windows Media Player 12	✓	✓	✓
Windows Search	✓	✓	✓
Windows Taskbar	✓	✓	✓
Windows Touch	✓	✓	✓
Windows Troubleshooting	✓	✓	✓
Windows Update	✓	✓	✓
Windows XP Mode		✓	✓
WordPad	✓	✓	✓
XPS	✓	✓	✓

Appendix B

Windows 7 Security

Windows 7 Security Features

According to Microsoft, Windows 7 has been engineered to be the most secure version of Windows ever. It includes a number of updated security features that help you accomplish three important goals: to enjoy a computer free from malware, including viruses, worms, spyware, and other potentially unwanted software; to have a safer online experience; and to understand when a computer is vulnerable and how to protect it from external threats.

Malware, short for malicious software, are computer programs designed to harm your computer, whether displaying inappropriate Web sites to facilitating identity theft. Examples of malware include viruses, worms, and spyware. A **virus** is a program that attaches itself to another program or file so that it can spread from computer to computer, infecting programs and files as it spreads. Viruses can damage computer software, computer hardware, and files. A computer **worm** copies itself from one computer to another by taking advantage of the features that transport data and information between computers. A worm is dangerous because it has the ability to travel without being detected and to replicate itself in great volume. For example, if a worm copies itself to every person in your e-mail address book and then the worm copies itself to the names of all the e-mail addresses of each of your friends' computers, the effect could result in increased Internet traffic that slows down business networks and the Internet. **Spyware** is a program that is installed on your computer that monitors the activity that takes place to gather personal information and send it secretly to its creator. Spyware also can be designed to take control of the infected computer.

A **hacker** is an individual who uses his or her expertise to gain unauthorized access to a computer with the intention of learning more about the computer or examining the contents of the computer without the owner's permission.

To Display the Windows Action Center

The **Action Center** can help you to manage your computer's security by monitoring the status of several essential security features on your computer, including firewall settings, automatic updating, virus protection, spyware and unwanted software protection, Internet security settings, User Account Control settings, and Network Access Protection. The following steps display the Action Center.

- Click the Start button on the taskbar to display the Start menu (Figure B–1).

Figure B–1

- Click the Control Panel command to open the Control Panel (Figure B–2).

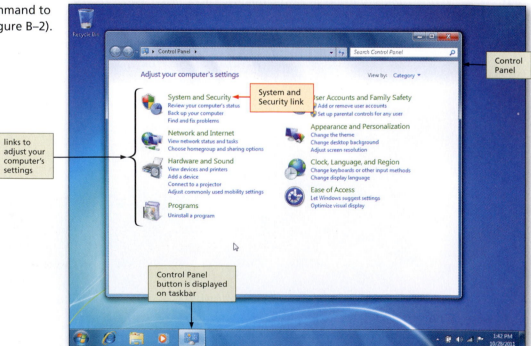

Figure B–2

3

● Click the System and Security link to display the System and Security window (Figure B–3).

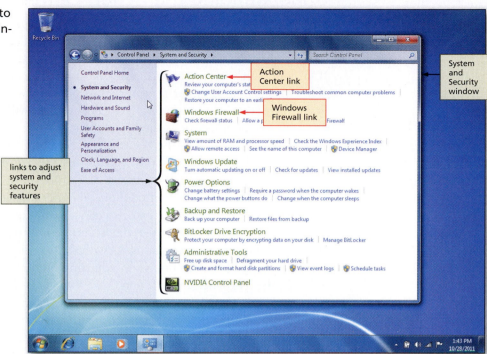

Figure B–3

4

● Click the Action Center link in the right pane of the System and Security window to display the Action Center (Figure B–4).

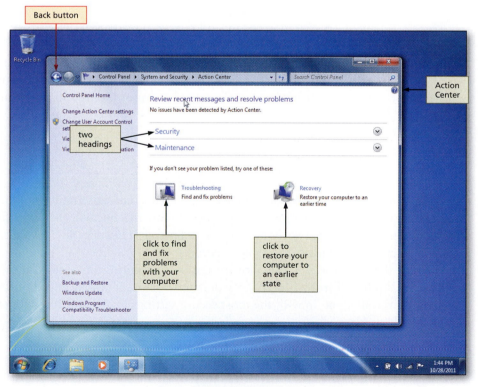

Figure B–4

Understanding the Action Center

The right pane displays options to let you review messages and resolve problems. There are two expandable sections. The first is the Security section. Clicking the arrow to the right of the Security heading expands the section and displays security features. "On" and "OK" mean that the security feature is turned on and working properly. "Off" means that the security feature is turned off and you should turn it on, if appropriate. For features that have settings you can change, you will see options for adjusting them.

The second section is the Maintenance section, which allows you to view maintenance features. Similar to the Security section, "On" means that the maintenance feature is turned on and working, and "Off" means that the feature is turned off and you should turn it on, if appropriate. Not all maintenance features have the same options. For example, if troubleshooting features are turned on, you only will see the message "No action needed." For some of the features, you can also choose whether you want to monitor the messages that pop up when an issue arises. If you choose not to monitor a feature, you will see a "Currently not monitored" status. As with the security features, if there are settings you can change, you will see options for adjusting them.

In the left pane of the Action Center window are links to Control Panel Home, Change Action Center settings, Change User Account Control settings, View archived messages, and View performance information. At the bottom of the left pane are links to related areas of the Control Panel that you might want to visit.

Managing Windows Firewall

Windows Firewall is a program that protects your computer from unauthorized users by monitoring and restricting data that travels between your computer and a network or the Internet. Windows Firewall also helps to block, but does not always prevent, computer viruses and worms from infecting your computer. Windows Firewall automatically is turned on when Windows 7 is launched. It is recommended that Windows Firewall remain on, unless you have another firewall program actively protecting your computer.

To Open Windows Firewall

From the Windows Firewall window's right pane, you can monitor and manage the firewall settings for any network to which you are connected. Connected networks normally are classified as home, work, and public networks. Home and work networks are considered private networks and have settings that are different from public networks that are not considered to be as secure.

From the left pane, you can allow programs or features through Windows Firewall, change notification settings, turn Windows Firewall off, restore default settings, adjust advanced settings, and troubleshoot your network. Windows Firewall is set up with the most secure settings by default, according to Microsoft. The following step opens Windows Firewall.

1

- Click the Back button in the Action Center window to return to the System and Security window.

- Click the Windows Firewall link to display the Windows Firewall window (Figure B–5).

Q&A

Why does my window show a different network?

You can connect to different types of networks. The type of network connection you have will determine whether your home or a public network is displayed.

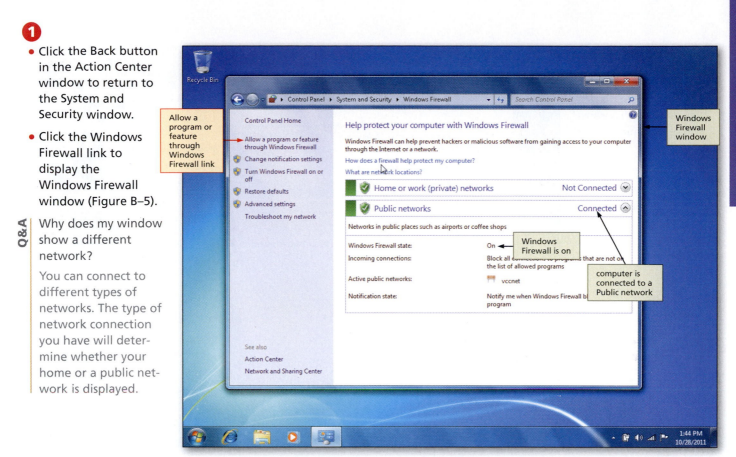

Figure B–5

To Allow a Feature Through the Firewall

You can adjust Windows Firewall settings as needed. For example, if you have a program or feature that you want to allow to communicate through the firewall, you can allow it using the 'Allow a program or feature through Windows Firewall' link. Caution should be used as each program or feature allowed through the firewall carries the risk of making your computer less secure; that is, the computer becomes easier to access and more vulnerable to attacks by hackers. The more programs and features you allow, the more vulnerable is the computer. To decrease the risk of security problems, only allow programs or features that are necessary and recognizable, and promptly remove any program or feature that no longer is required.

One feature that is sometimes allowed for home and work networks is File and Printer Sharing. This feature allows other computers access to files and printers that you choose to share with the network. The steps on the following pages allow File and Printer Sharing through the firewall for home and work networks only.

1
- Click the Allow a program or feature through Windows Firewall link to display the Allowed Programs window (Figure B–6).

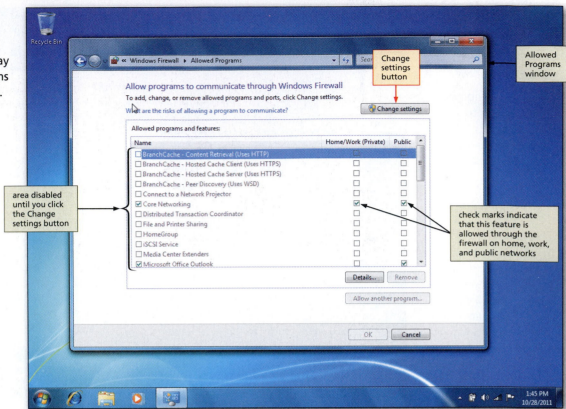

Figure B–6

2
- Click the Change settings button to enable the 'Allowed programs and features' area (Figure B–7).

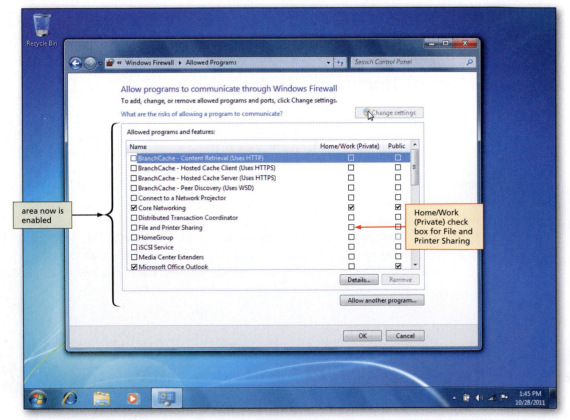

Figure B–7

3

- Click the Home/Work
(Private) check box
for File and Printer
Sharing to allow the
feature through the
firewall (Figure B–8).

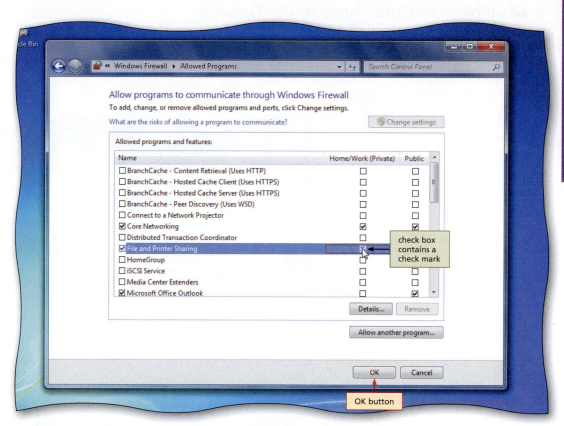

Figure B–8

4

- Click the OK button
to accept the
changes and return
to the Windows
Firewall window
(Figure B–9).

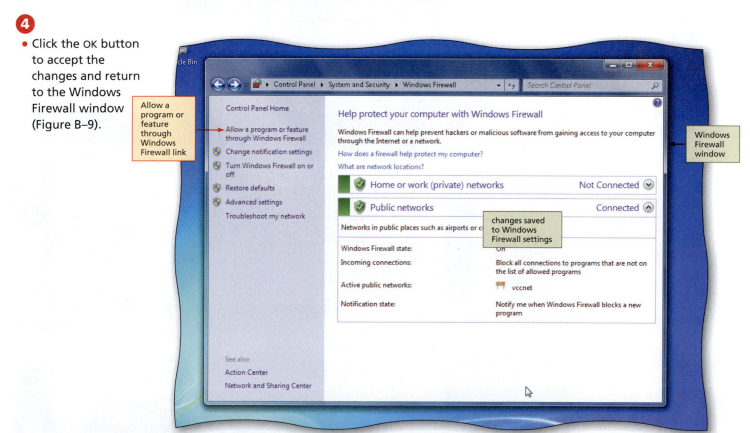

Figure B–9

To Disallow a Feature Through the Firewall

If you later decide that you do not want to allow a program or feature through the Windows Firewall, you should disallow it. The following steps disallow File and Printer Sharing through the firewall for Home/Work networks only.

1

• Click the Allow a program or feature through Windows Firewall link to display the Allowed Programs window (Figure B–10).

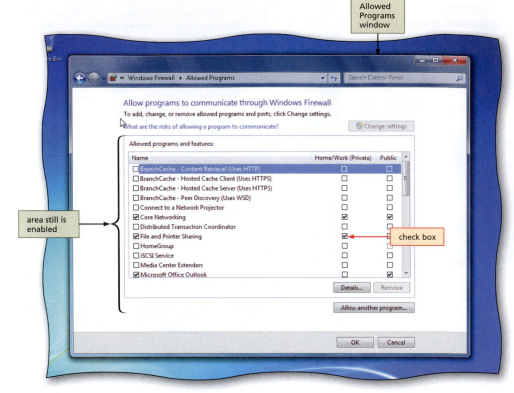

Figure B–10

2

• If necessary, click the Change settings button to enable the 'Allowed programs and features' area.

• Click the Home/Work (Private) check box for File and Printer Sharing to disallow the feature through the firewall (Figure B–11).

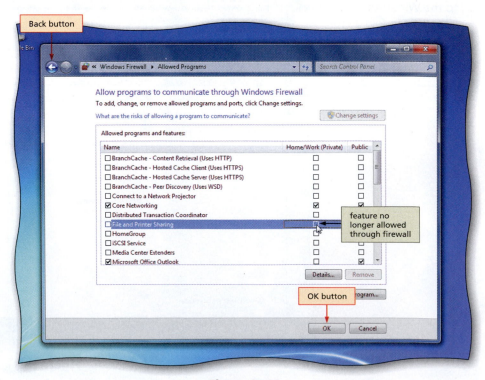

Figure B–11

3
- Click the OK button to accept the changes and return to the Windows Firewall window (Figure B–12).

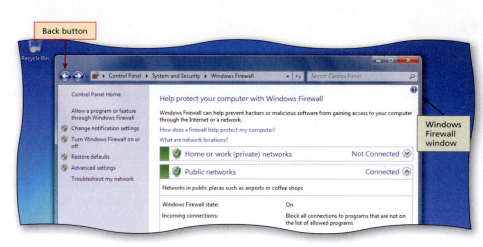

Figure B–12

Windows Update

Windows Update helps to protect your computer from viruses, worms, and other security risks. When Windows Update is turned on and the computer is connected to the Internet, Windows 7 periodically checks with Microsoft to find updates for your computer, and then automatically downloads them. If the Internet connection is lost while downloading an update, Windows 7 resumes downloading when the Internet connection becomes available.

To Set an Automatic Update

You want to make sure that Windows Update runs once each week, so you decide to set it to run on a specific day and at a specific time. Once you set the day and time, Windows 7 will check with Microsoft to find updates, automatically download any available updates, and install them at the specified day and time. The followings steps configure an automatic update for a day (Friday) and time (6:00 AM).

1
- Click the Back button to return to the System and Security window.
- Click the Windows Update link in the System and Security window to display the Windows Update window (Figure B–13).

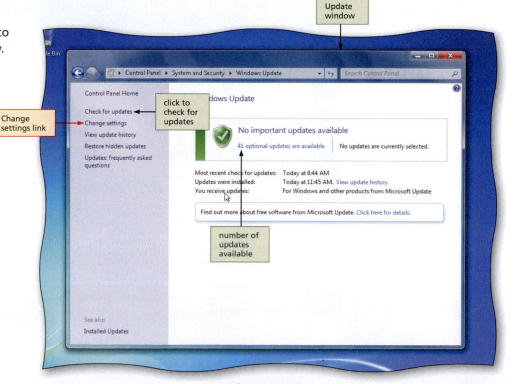

Figure B–13

2

• Click the Change settings link to display the Change settings window (Figure B–14).

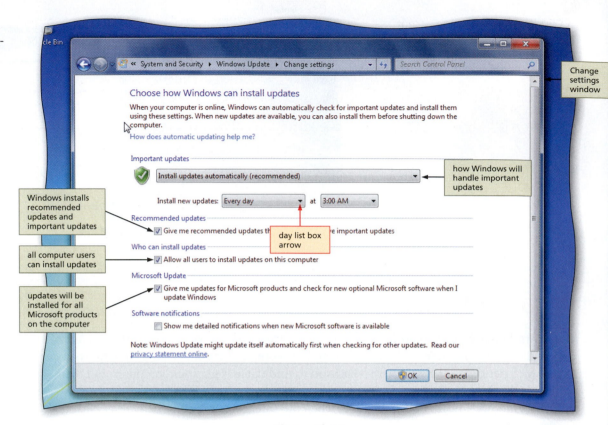

Figure B–14

3

• Click the day list box arrow to display a list of day options (Figure B–15).

Figure B–15

4

• Click the Every Friday list item to set the day to Every Friday.

• Click the time list box arrow to show the list of time options (Figure B–16).

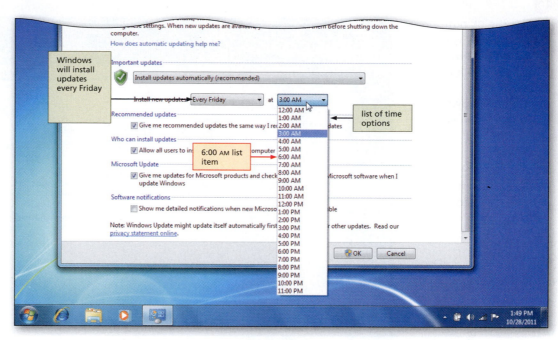

Figure B–16

5

• Click the 6:00 AM list item in the time list box to set the time to 6:00 AM (Figure B–17).

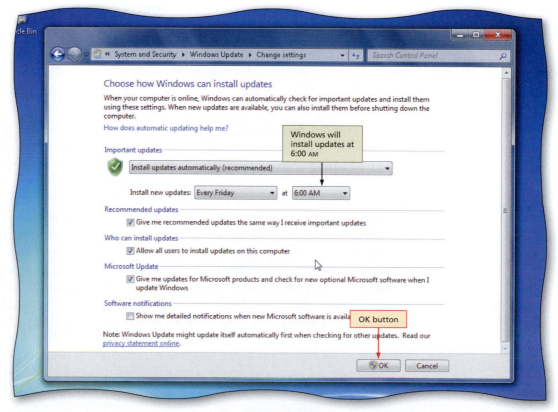

Figure B–17

• Click the OK button in the Windows Update window to save the changes and return to the Windows Update window (Figure B–18).

• Close the Windows Update window.

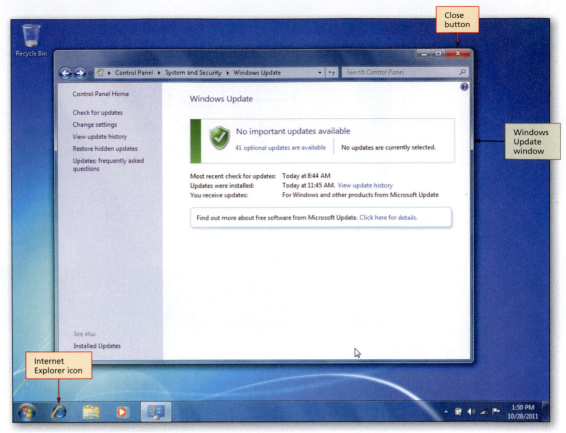

Figure B–18

Protecting Against Computer Viruses

Most computer magazines, daily newspapers, and even the nightly news channels warn of computer virus threats. Although these threats sound alarming, a little common sense and a good antivirus program can ward off even the most malicious viruses.

A computer can be protected against viruses by following these suggestions. First, educate yourself about viruses and how they spread. Downloading a program from the Internet, accessing a Web site, or receiving an e-mail message can cause a virus to infect your computer. Second, learn the common signs of a virus. Observe any unusual messages that appear on the computer screen, monitor system performance, and watch for missing files and inaccessible hard disks. Third, recognize that programs on removable media might contain viruses, and scan all removable media before copying or opening files.

Finally, Windows 7 does not include an antivirus program. You should purchase and install the latest version of an antivirus program and use it regularly to check for computer viruses. Many antivirus programs run automatically and display a dialog box on the screen when a problem exists. If you do not have an antivirus program installed on your computer, you can search online for antivirus software vendors to find a program that meets your needs.

To Search for Antivirus Software Vendors

The following steps go online to display a list of Microsoft-approved consumer security providers.

1

• Click the Internet Explorer icon on the taskbar to open Internet Explorer (Figure B–19).

Figure B–19

2

• Type www.microsoft.com/ windows/antivirus-partners/ windows-7.aspx in the Address bar and press the ENTER key to display the Windows 7 Consumer security software providers Web page (Figure B–20).

3

• Scroll to review the list of providers and visit a few links to learn more about some of the providers and their products.

4

• Close Internet Explorer.

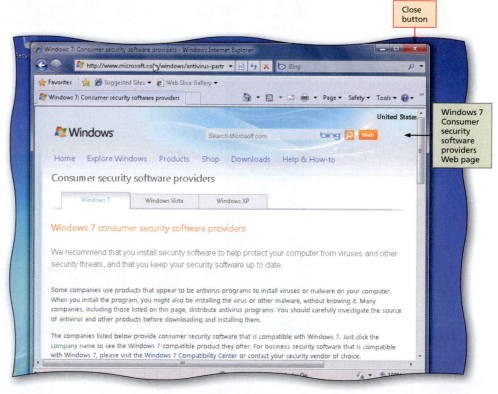

Figure B–20

Protecting Against Malware

It is important to run anti-malware software whenever you are using your computer. Malware and other unwanted software can attempt to install itself on your computer any time you connect to the Internet. It also can infect your computer when you install some programs using an optical disc or other removable media. Potentially unwanted or malicious software also can be programmed to run at unexpected times, not just when it is installed.

Windows Defender is installed with Windows 7. Windows Defender uses definitions similar to those used by antivirus programs. A **definition** is a rule for Windows Defender that identifies what programs are malware and how to deal with them. Windows Defender scans your computer regularly to find and remove malware.

To keep up with new malware developments, Windows Defender uses Windows Update to regularly check for definition updates. This helps you to ensure that your computer can handle new threats. It is recommended to allow Windows Defender to run using the default actions. Windows Defender is not a replacement for antivirus software; it is important that in addition to using Windows Defender, you also have current antivirus software installed.

To View the Windows Defender Settings for Automatic Scanning

The following steps display the automatic scanning settings in Windows Defender.

- Display the Start menu.

- Type windows defender in the Search box.

- Click the Windows Defender link to open Windows Defender (Figure B–21).

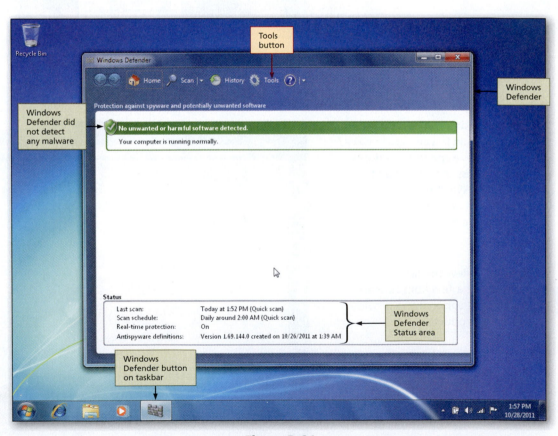

Figure B–21

2

• Click the Tools button on the toolbar to display the Windows Defender Tools and Settings (Figure B–22).

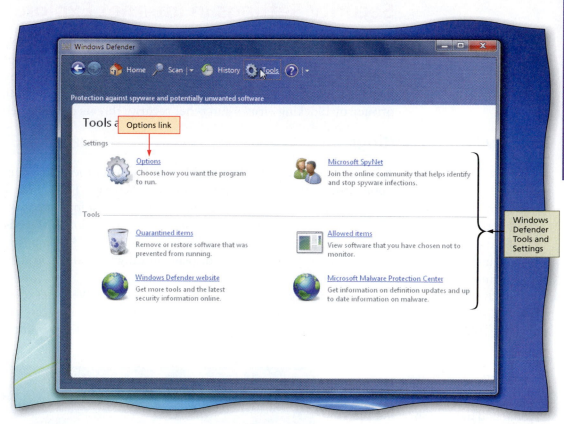

Figure B–22

3

• Click the Options link to view the Windows Defender settings for Automatic scanning (Figure B–23).

• Close the Windows Defender window.

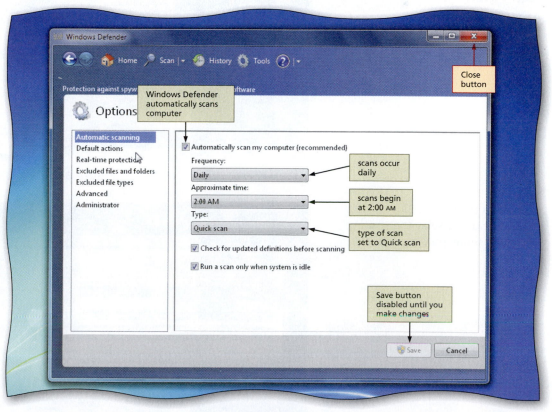

Figure B–23

Security Settings in Internet Explorer

In addition to the security features shown earlier in this appendix, you can configure the security features of Internet Explorer. These security features protect the computer while you browse the Internet or send and receive e-mail messages. The Internet Explorer security settings protect the computer, the computer's contents, and the computer's privacy by blocking viruses and other security threats on the Internet.

To View Pop-Up Settings

One security feature in Internet Explorer is the Pop-up Blocker. **Pop-up Blocker** prevents annoying **pop-up windows**, also referred to as **pop-ups**, from appearing while you view a Web page. Pop-up windows typically advertise products or services. They can be difficult to close, often interrupt what you are doing, and can download spyware, which secretly gathers information about you and your computer, and sends the information to advertisers and other individuals.

By default, Pop-up Blocker is turned on by Internet Explorer and set to a Medium setting, which blocks most pop-up windows. Pop-up Blocker also plays a sound and displays an Information Bar in Internet Explorer when a pop-up window is blocked.

In the Pop-up Blocker Settings dialog box, if you want to allow certain Web sites to display pop-up windows when you visit the site, you can add the site's Web address to the list of allowed sites. Internet Explorer adds the Web site to the Allowed sites list. The following steps display the Pop-up Blocker settings in Internet Explorer.

- Open Internet Explorer.

- Click the Tools button on the Command bar to display the Tools menu (Figure B–24).

Figure B–24

- Point to the Pop-up Blocker command to display the Pop-up Blocker submenu (Figure B–25).

Figure B–25

3

- Click Pop-up Blocker Settings to display the Pop-up Blocker Settings dialog box (Figure B–26).

Q&A

How do I block all pop-ups?

If you want to block all pop-ups, click the Blocking level list box arrow, and then click High: Block all pop-ups in the Blocking level list box. If you want to allow more pop-ups, click the Blocking level box arrow, and then click Low: Allow pop-ups from secure sites in the Blocking level list box.

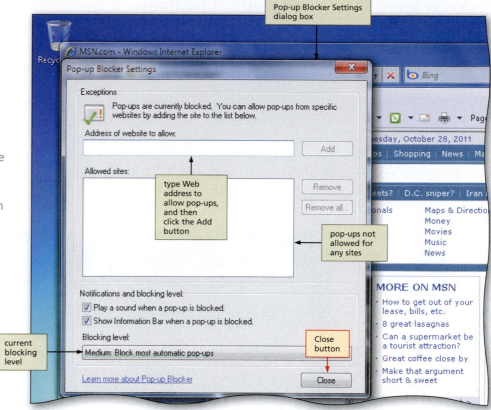

Figure B–26

4

- After viewing the Pop-up Blocker Settings dialog box, close the Pop-up Blocker Settings dialog box (Figure B–27).

Figure B–27

To View Internet Explorer Add-On Settings

Internet Explorer **add-ons** add functionality to Internet Explorer by allowing different toolbars, animated mouse pointers, and stock tickers. Although some add-ons are included with Windows 7, thousands are available from Web sites on the Internet. Most Web site add-ons require permission before downloading the add-on, whereas others are downloaded without your knowledge, and some add-ons do not need permission at all.

Add-ons usually are safe to use, but some might slow down your computer or shut down Internet Explorer unexpectedly. This usually happens when an add-on is poorly built or created for an earlier version of Internet Explorer. In some cases, spyware is included with an add-on and might track your Web browsing habits. The Manage Add-ons window allows you to display add-ons that have been used by Internet Explorer or that run without permission, enable or disable add-ons, and remove downloaded ActiveX controls.

The following steps illustrate how to view the Add-on settings.

1
- Click the Tools button to display the Tools menu.
- Click the Manage Add-ons command to display the Manage Add-ons dialog box (Figure B–28).

2
- When finished viewing the add-ons, close the dialog box.
- Close Internet Explorer.

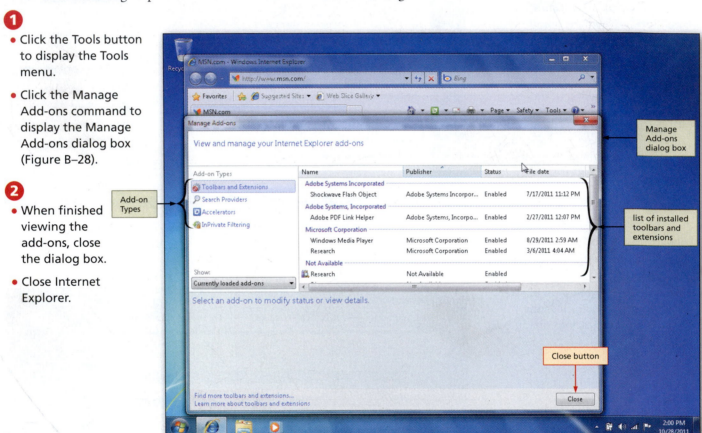

Figure B–28

Summary

Security is an important issue for computer users. You need to be aware of the possible threats to your computer as well as the security features that can be used to protect your computer. The Action Center, along with other security features in Windows 7, allows you to configure the security settings that will help you keep your computer safe.

Exercises

1. Researching Antivirus Software

1. Visit www.microsoft.com/windows/antivirus-partners/windows-7.aspx (Figure B–29) in Internet Explorer.

2. Follow the link to Avast. Answer the following questions regarding their antivirus software.

   a. How much does the home antivirus software cost?

   _____

   b. Does Avast offer other malware protection? Spyware protection?

   _____

3. Return to the Windows 7 Consumer security software providers Web page. Follow the link to Trend Micro. Answer the following questions regarding their home antivirus software.

   a. How much does the antivirus software cost?

   _____

   b. Does Trend Micro offer other malware protection? Spyware protection?

   _____

   c. Compare the home version with the other versions offered. How much difference is there between the versions in price? In features?

   _____
   _____

Figure B–29

Continued >

Exercises *continued*

2. Viewing Windows Update

1. Open Windows Update (Figure B–30).

2. It is important to know what has been updated on your computer. You should view your installed updates on a regular basis. Click the 'View update history' link.

3. For Windows Defender, answer the following questions.

a. What is the definition number of the latest Windows Defender update installed?

_____

b. When was the latest update installed?

_____

c. Was the latest update successful?

_____

d. What was the level of importance of the update?

_____

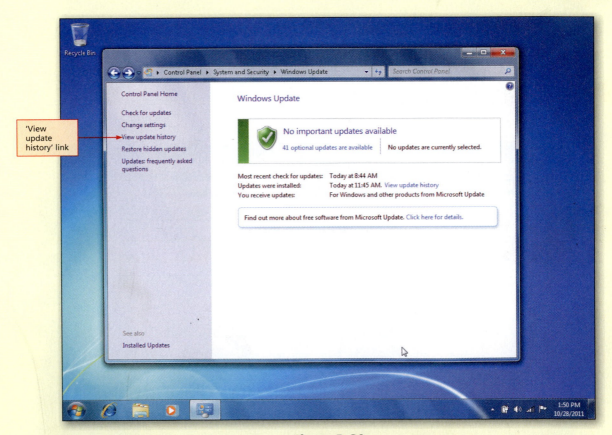

Figure B–30

4. For Windows 7, answer the following questions.

a. What is the ID number of the latest Windows 7 update installed?

_____

b. When was the latest update installed?

_____

STUDENT ASSIGNMENTS

   c. Was the latest update successful?

   _____

   d. What was the level of importance of the update?

   _____

5. For Security Updates, answer the following questions.
   a. What is the ID number of the latest Security update installed?

   _____

   b. When was the latest update installed?

   _____

   c. Was the latest update successful?

   _____

   d. What was the level of importance of the update?

   _____

6. Sometimes updates fail to install. Can you find an instance of an update that failed to install? What was it?

   _____

   _____

   _____

Appendix C

Introduction to Networking

A **network** is a group of computers and other devices connected by a communications link, which enables the devices to interact with each other. The advantages of using a network include simplified communications between users (such as e-mail systems, instant messenging, chat rooms, newsgroups, and video and voice conversations) as well as the ability to share resources easily across the network. Shared resources can include hardware (such as printers, scanners, and cameras), data and information (such as files, folders, and databases), and programs.

Setting Up a Network

Computers on a network connect to each other using a communication channel. A **communication channel** is the means by which information is passed between two devices. Communication channels include cable (twisted-pair, coaxial, and fiber-optic) and wireless communication (broadcast radio, cellular radio, microwaves, communications satellites, Bluetooth, and infrared). Communication channels are measured in **bandwidth**. The higher the bandwidth, the more data and information the channel can transmit at one time.

Computer networks can be classified either as local area networks or wide area networks. A **local area network (LAN)** is a network that connects computers and devices in a limited geographical area, such as a home, school computer lab, office building, or closely positioned group of buildings. A LAN enables people in a small geographic area to communicate with one another and to share the computer resources connected to the network. Each device on the network, such as a computer or printer, is referred to as a **node**. Nodes can be connected to the LAN via cables; however, a **wireless LAN** is a LAN that uses no physical wires. Instead of wires or cables, WLANs use wireless media, such as radio waves. A **wide area network (WAN)** is a network that covers a large geographic area (such as a city or state) and uses many types of media, such as telephone lines, cables, and airwaves. A WAN can be one large network or consist of two or more LANs that are connected together. The Internet is the world's largest WAN.

If you have multiple computers in your home or small office, you can create a home or small office network using Windows 7. The advantages of a home or small office network include sharing a single Internet connection, sharing hardware devices, sharing files and folders, and communicating with others. Today, because of competition in the hardware industry and lower computer prices, many homes have one or more computers and a connection to the Internet. Three types of networks that are suitable for home or small office use include Ethernet networks, telephone-line networks, and wireless networks.

Understanding Wired Networks

Wired networks use cables to connect devices together (Figure C–1). Ethernet is the most popular type of network connection because it is relatively inexpensive and fast. There are two types of Ethernet cables: **coaxial cable**, which resembles the cable used for televisions and rarely is used, and **unshielded twisted pair (UTP) cable**, which looks like telephone cable but with larger connectors at each end. Category 5 (CAT 5) or Category 6 (CAT 6) UTP cable typically is used for networking. A network based on CAT 5 UTP cable requires an additional piece of hardware, called a hub, to which all computers on the network connect.

Another type of wired network is a telephone-line network. A **telephone-line network** takes advantage of the existing telephone wiring to connect the computers on a network. This technology is supported by a group of industry experts called the Home Phoneline Networking Alliance (HomePNA). The network takes advantage of the unused bandwidth of the telephone lines, while still allowing them to be used for telephone conversations. The only equipment needed for this type of network is a telephone-line network adapter for each computer, as well as telephone cable long enough to connect each computer to a telephone jack.

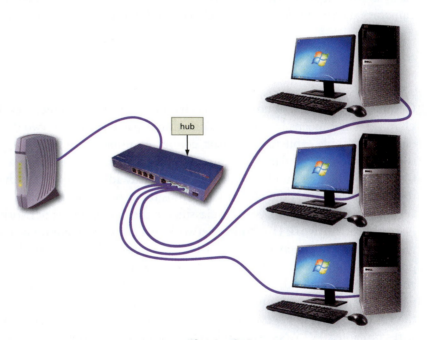

hub

Figure C–1

Understanding Wireless Networks

A wireless network is the easiest type of network to install. Each computer uses a special network adapter that sends wireless signals through the air (Figure C–2). Any computer located within range that also has a network adapter can send and receive through floors, ceilings, and walls. The distance between computers limits this connection, and the hardware required for the system is relatively inexpensive. Most hardware devices implement the Wi-Fi (Wireless Fidelity) standard, which was developed by the Wi-Fi Alliance to improve the interoperability of wireless products.

Several companies and industry groups have come together to create standards for wireless networking. The leader is the Wi-Fi Alliance, which certifies the interoperability of Wi-Fi (IEEE 802.11) products, offers speeds of more than 100 Mbps

(Megabits per second), with that speed increasing as technology advances. The two types of Wi-Fi networks are ad hoc and infrastructure. In an **ad hoc network**, every computer with a wireless network adapter communicates directly with every other computer with a wireless network adapter. Although the range varies by manufacturer, ad hoc networks work best when connecting computers are within 100 feet of each other.

Figure C–2

An **infrastructure network** is based on an access point connected to a high-speed Internet connection. An **access point** functions as a bridge between two different types of networks, such as a wireless network and an Ethernet network. The access point allows for a much greater range than an ad hoc network because a computer needs to be within range of the access point and not within range of the other computers. This network is best when connecting more than two computers that are more than 100 feet apart and commonly is used in wireless networks that simultaneously share a single Internet connection.

Some infrastructure networks use a router to share an Internet connection between computers on the network. A **router** is a hardware device that can connect two networks together. Home users typically use routers to connect a cable or DSL modem to a network, allowing several computer users to simultaneously use the same Internet connection. Some network hardware manufacturers combine the access point and router in a device called a **wireless router**. A wireless router can function as a bridge between two different types of networks and allows all computers on the network to access the same Internet connection.

Putting It All Together

Each computer on a network must have a **network adapter** to connect to the network. Both internal network adapters and external network adapters are available. Most computers come with internal network adapters. An **internal network adapter** plugs into an expansion slot inside the computer. Before purchasing an internal network adapter, check to be sure that the computer has an available slot that can accept the adapter (also called an expansion card). An **external network adapter** plugs into a port on the system unit. In most cases, external network adapters connect to a USB port.

A **modem** is used to connect to an Internet access provider. Common Internet access providers include cable service providers, phone service providers, and satellite service providers. The modem is connected to the router, which is then used to connect to the nodes on the network. A USB, CAT 5, or CAT 6 cable connects the modem to wired computers. If the network is wireless, the computers connect using wireless network adapters and an access point. Many home networks use a wireless router and support wired and wireless connections (Figure C–3).

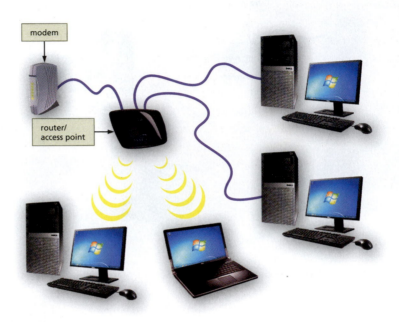

Figure C–3

Wireless Security Issues

Whether you connect a single computer to the Internet or connect multiple computers on a home or small office network to the Internet, problems can develop if you do not protect computers from external threats. Hackers scan the Internet looking for unprotected computers. When an unprotected computer is found, a hacker can access and damage files on the computer and release harmful computer viruses that can render the computer unusable.

You can protect computers on a network from hackers, viruses, and other malicious attacks by using a firewall. As mentioned previously, a firewall is a security system intended to protect a network from external threats. A firewall commonly is a combination of hardware and/or software that prevents computers on the network from communicating directly with computers that are not on the network and vice versa. Many routers come with integrated firewalls. Windows 7 also comes with a built-in firewall (see Appendix B).

Setting Up Wireless Security

Wireless networks require extra thought as they introduce some security concerns that wired networks do not. Because the signal travels through the air, anyone with the proper equipment can intercept the signal. As a result, a wireless network should use extra precautions to prevent unauthorized access. When you purchase a wireless router, it might include a program that allows you to set up security on your wireless network.

If the wireless router does not include a program that can set up security, Windows 7 can configure it using the Set Up a Connection or Network Wizard, accessible from the Network and Sharing Center window.

The key to securing a wireless network successfully is to use a multipronged defense. For best results, use more than one of the following recommended security measures. First, make sure that the wireless router's user name and password are changed from the defaults so that the hacker is unable to use the default user name and password found in the device's documentation (often kept on the manufacturer's Web site for public access). Second, you can turn on wireless encryption. This can include Wired Equivalent Privacy (WEP), Wi-Fi Protected Access (WPA), or 802.1X authentication. **Encryption** protects your data by ensuring that only those with the correct encryption key will be able to understand the information being sent across the network. Third, you can set up the wireless router to not broadcast its **SSID** (**service set identifier**), the network name for the wireless router. This makes it more difficult for hackers to see your router. Next, you can change the SSID from its default setting. The most secure SSIDs are a combination of letters and numbers, and do not include any part of your name or location. Finally, you can turn on MAC Address Control, so that only devices with authorized MAC addresses are allowed to connect. A **MAC address** is an address that uniquely identifies each device that is connected to a network.

Using the Network and Sharing Center

Normally when you turn on your computer, Windows 7 detects available networks and prompts you to set up a connection. However, you can set up a connection manually by using the Network and Sharing Center. The Network and Sharing Center is designed to provide you with the tools you need to connect to a network and share information. From the Network and Sharing Center, you can view available connections, connect to a network, manage a network, set up a network, and diagnose and repair network problems.

To Open the Network and Sharing Center

When first opened, the Network and Sharing Center shows your current network connection and the properties for that connection. If you are not connected to a network, you are shown which networking options are available to you. The following steps open the Network and Sharing Center.

1

- Right-click the networking icon in the notification area on the taskbar to display a shortcut menu (Figure C–4).

Q&A What if the networking icon does not display in the notification area?

You either are not connected to a network, your computer does not have a network adapter installed, or the notification area is not configured to display the networking icon. If this is the case, open Control Panel, click the Network and Internet link, and then click the Network and Sharing Center link.

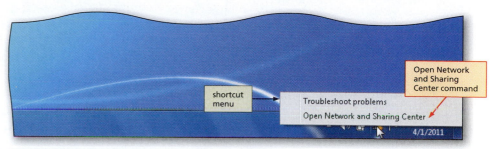

Open Network and Sharing Center command

shortcut menu

Troubleshoot problems

Open Network and Sharing Center

4/1/2011

Figure C–4

2

- Click the Open Network and Sharing Center command to open the Network and Sharing Center (Figure C–5).

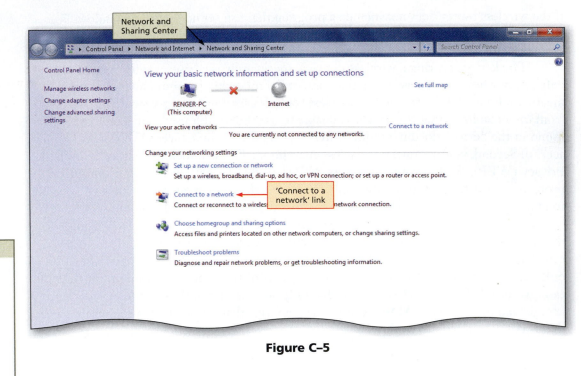

Network and Sharing Center

'Connect to a network' link

Figure C–5

Other Ways

1. Open Control Panel, click Network and Internet, click Network and Sharing Center
2. Open Control Panel, change to Small or Large icons view, click Network and Sharing Center

To View Available Wireless Networks

If there are wireless networks available, the Network and Sharing Center displays a message stating that they are available. The following step displays the list of available wireless networks.

1

- Click the 'Connect to a network' link to display a list of available wireless networks (Figure C–6).

Q&A

Why do I see a different list of networks?

Because your computer shows the wireless networks that are near your physical location, the list of available wireless networks will be different from those shown in Figure C–6.

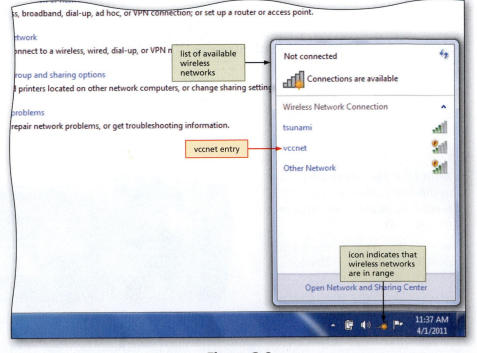

list of available wireless networks

vccnet entry

icon indicates that wireless networks are in range

Figure C–6

Other Ways

1. Right-click networking icon in notification area on the taskbar, click 'Connect to a network'
2. Open Control Panel, change to Small or Large icons view, click Network and Sharing Center, click 'Connect to a network' link

To Connect to a Public Network

When connecting to a network, you need to know what information is necessary to connect. You first should determine whether the network is secure or unsecure. Secure wireless networks typically use WPA or WEP encryption, whereas unsecured networks are not encrypted. Second, you should know whether the network location should be classified as home, work, or public. For public locations, **network discovery**, which is the capability of network devices to identify your computer when connected, is turned off. With your computer hidden, hackers will have a more difficult time locating it. The following steps connect the computer to a wireless network and allow Windows 7 to configure all the settings.

1
- Click the vccnet entry, or the entry corresponding to a wireless network available in your area, to select the wireless network (Figure C–7).

How can I locate public wireless networks?

When you view network connections, any public wireless networks should display. Some cities and towns sponsor public Wi-Fi; many public libraries, schools, hotels, and airports offer Wi-Fi; and, occasionally, cafés and coffeehouses offer free Wi-Fi.

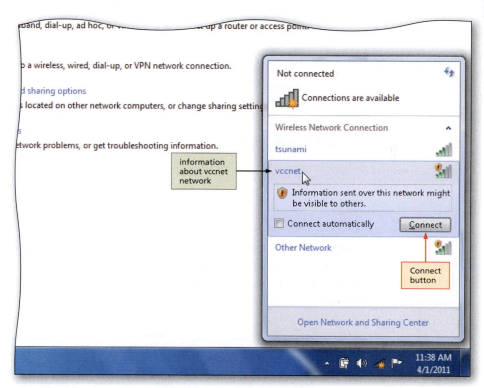

Figure C–7

2
- Click the Connect button to connect to the network (Figure C–8).

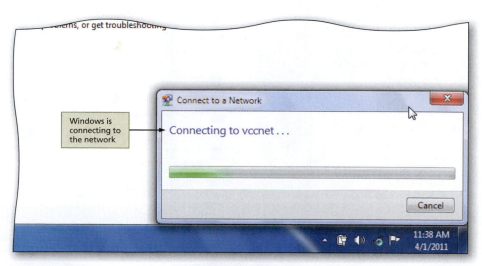

Figure C–8

- After the connection is established, the connection appears in the Network and Sharing Center (Figure C–9).

Q&A

What if Windows prompts me to select whether this is a Home network, Work network, or Public network?

Select a setting that corresponds to your current location. If you are unsure of which setting you should select, contact your instructor. If an instructor is not available, select Public network.

Figure C–9

To View the Status of a Connection

You can view the status of the connection from the Network and Sharing Center. The Wireless Network Connection Status dialog box displays the properties of the connection and allows you to adjust the properties of the connection manually, disable the connection, and diagnose problems with the connection. The following steps display the connection status.

- Click the Wireless Network Connection link to display the Wireless Network Connection Status dialog box (Figure C–10).

Q&A

Why does a homegroup appear?

Homegroups automatically can be set up when Windows 7 is installed, especially if Windows detects that the computer already is connected to a network.

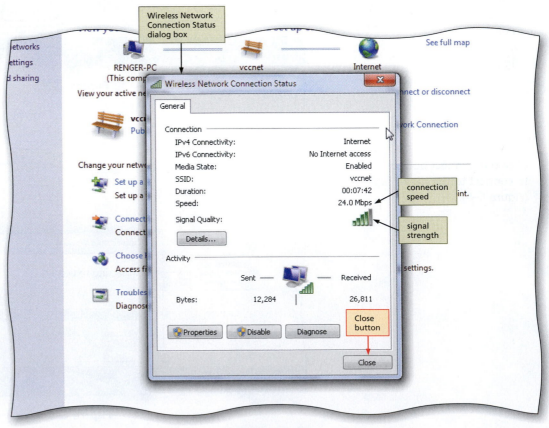

Figure C–10

- After viewing the connection status, click the Close button to close the dialog box (Figure C–11).

Figure C–11

To Disconnect from a Network

The following step disconnects the computer from the public network.

- Click the 'Connect or disconnect' link to display a list of wireless networks (Figure C–12).

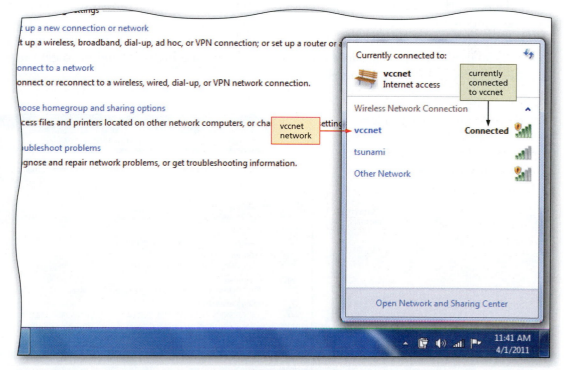

Figure C–12

- Click vccnet to select the wireless network (Figure C–13).

- Click the Disconnect button to disconnect from the public network.

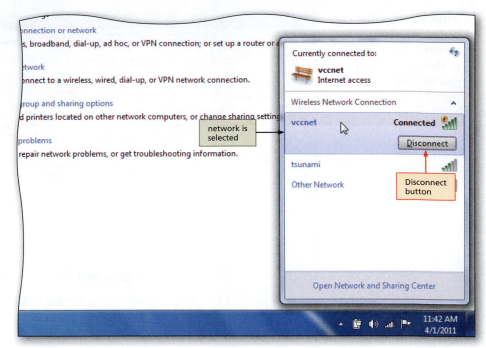

Figure C–13

To Troubleshoot a Problem

If a network connection is not functioning properly, you can use the Troubleshoot problems – Network and Internet window to allow Windows 7 to detect problems and suggest solutions to you. If Windows cannot determine a solution, a message is displayed. If there are no problems, Windows also displays an appropriate message. The following steps use the Troubleshoot problems – Network and Internet window to get suggestions from Windows 7 about how to fix an Internet connection.

- Click the Troubleshoot problems link to display the 'Troubleshoot problems – Network and Internet' window (Figure C–14).

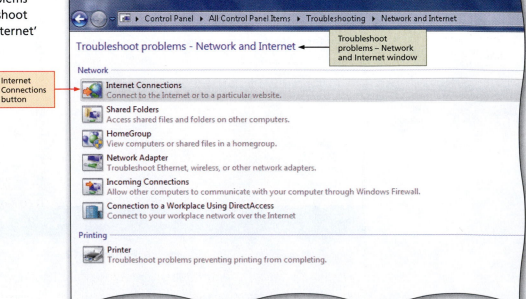

Figure C–14

2
- Click the Internet Connections button to display the Internet Connections dialog box (Figure C–15).

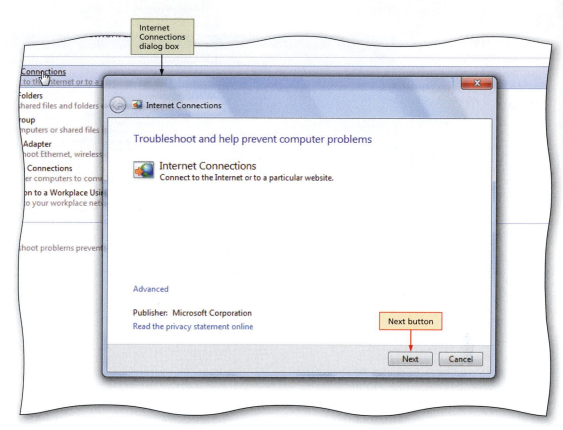

Figure C–15

3
- Click the Next button to display a list of troubleshooting options (Figure C–16).

- After viewing the options, click the Cancel button to close the Internet Connections dialog box.

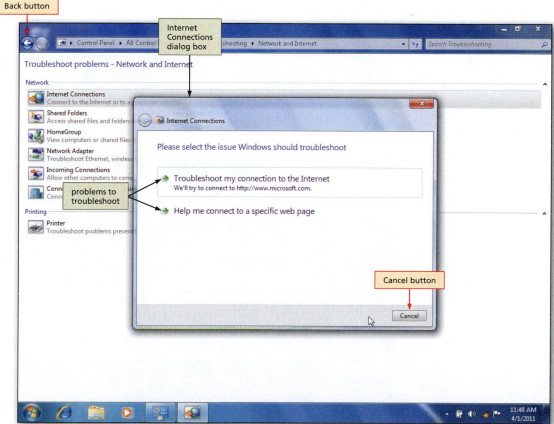

Figure C–16

4

- Click the Back button to return to the Network and Sharing Center (Figure C–17).

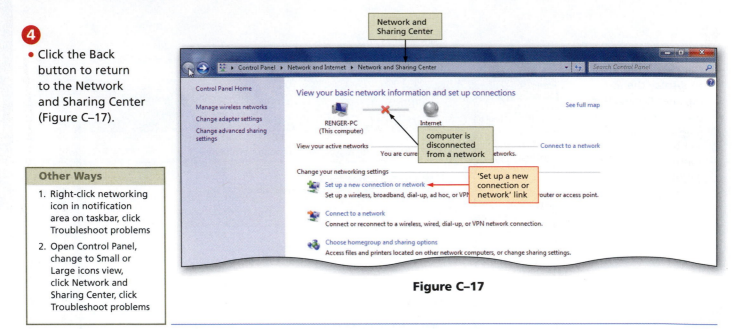

Figure C–17

To Connect to a Home Network

When connecting to a network, you also can use the Set Up a Connection or Network Wizard. In this case, because the network is a home network, the location type should be set to Home network. The following steps connect the computer to a wireless network and change the location type to Home network.

1

- Click the 'Set up a new connection or network' link to run the Set Up a Connection or Network Wizard (Figure C–18).

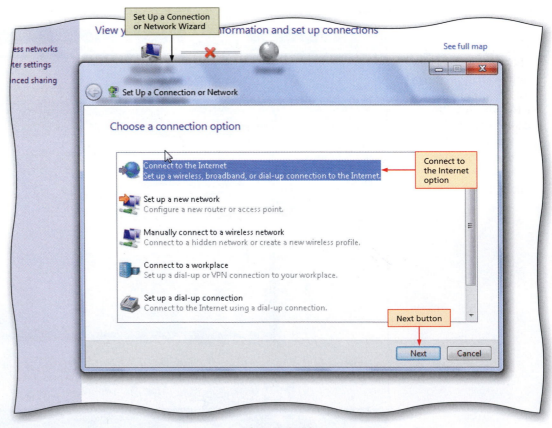

Figure C–18

2
- If necessary, click the Connect to the Internet option to select it.

- Click the Next button to view a list of connection options (Figure C–19).

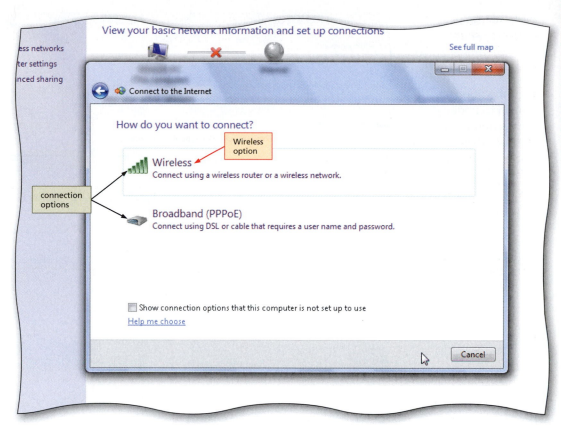

Figure C–19

3
- Click the Wireless option to view a list of available wireless networks (Figure C–20).

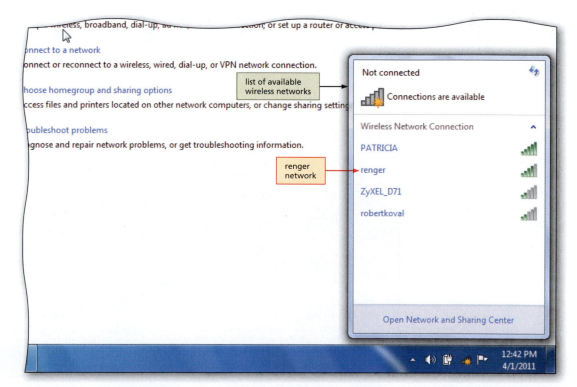

Figure C–20

4
- Click the renger network, or your local security-enabled network, to select it.
- Click the Connect button to begin connecting to the network (Figure C–21).

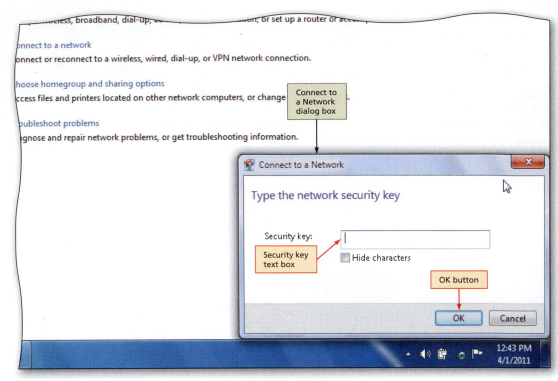

Figure C–21

5
- Type your security key into the Security key text box.
- Click the OK button to connect to the network (Figure C–22).

Q&A

What is my security key?

The security key will be provided either by your network administrator (if at school or at work) or by your wireless router software (if at home).

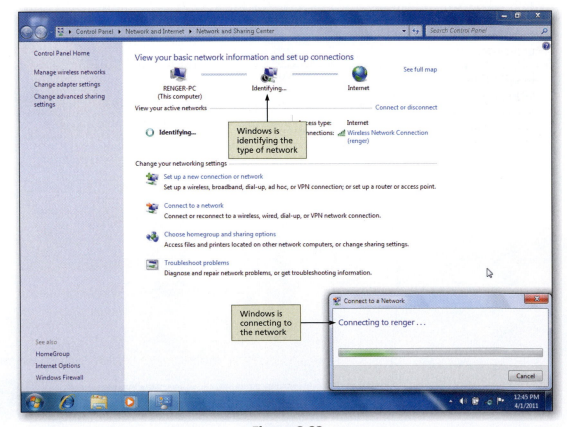

Figure C–22

6

- After the connection is established, the connection appears in the Network and Sharing Center (Figure C–23).

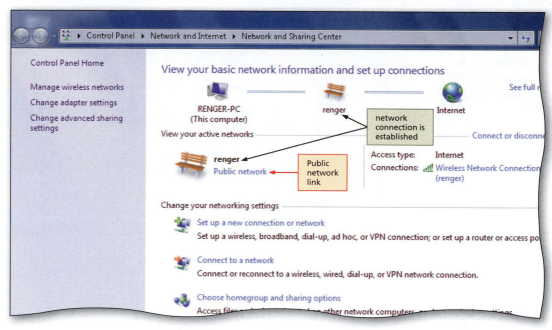

Figure C–23

7

- Click the Public network location to configure this network connection as a connection to a public network.

- Click the Public network link in the Network and Sharing Center to display the Set Network Location dialog box (Figure C–24).

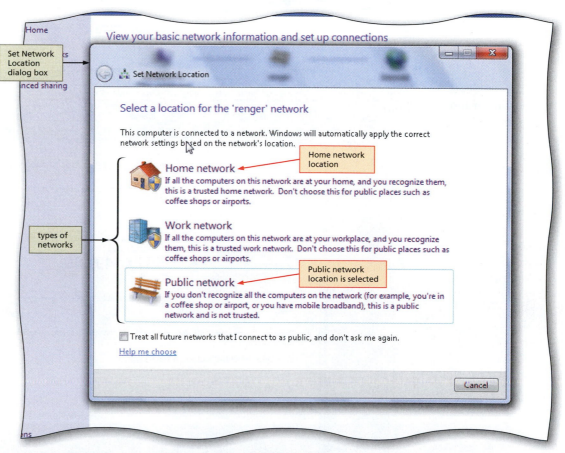

Figure C–24

8

• Click the Home network location to configure the network as a home network (Figure C–25).

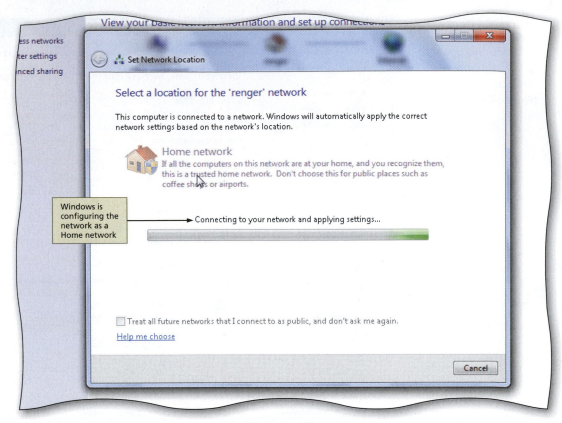

Figure C–25

9

• Click the Next button to create the Homegroup (Figure C–26).

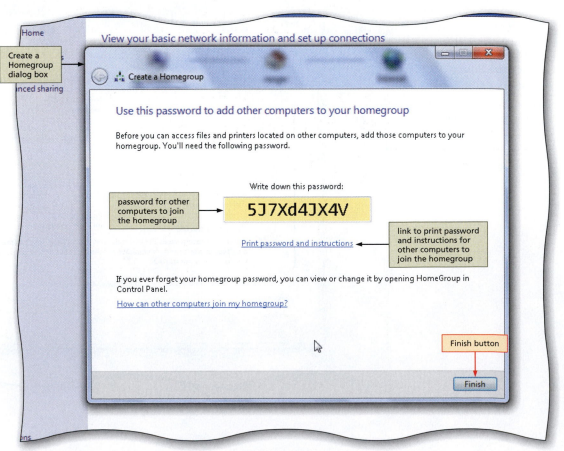

Figure C–26

10
• Click the Finish button to close the dialog box (Figure C–27).

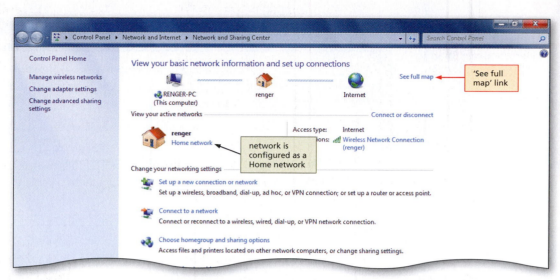

Figure C–27

Other Ways

1. Right-click networking icon in notification area on the taskbar, click 'Connect to a network', click 'Set up a connection or network'

To View Network Computers and Devices

Now that the location type of the network is set to Home network, you can see the other computers and devices that are connected to the network. The following steps display the computers and devices that are connected to the home network, and then return to the Network and Sharing Center.

1
• Click the 'See full map' link to open the Network Map window (Figure C–28).

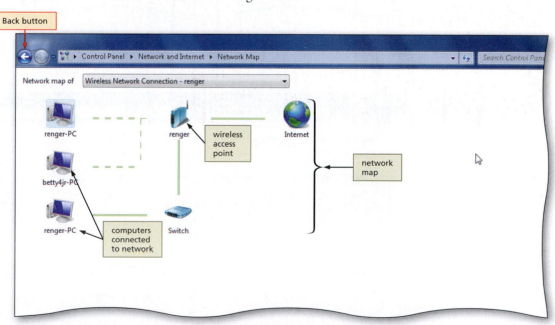

Figure C–28

- Click the Back button to return to the Network and Sharing Center (Figure C–29).

Figure C–29

To Remove a Wireless Network Connection

If you no longer will be connecting to a particular wireless network, you should delete the wireless network connection. The following steps remove the Home network wireless connection you just created.

- Click the 'Manage wireless networks' link to open the Manage Wireless Networks window (Figure C–30).

Figure C–30

- Click the renger network, or your local network, to select it (Figure C–31).

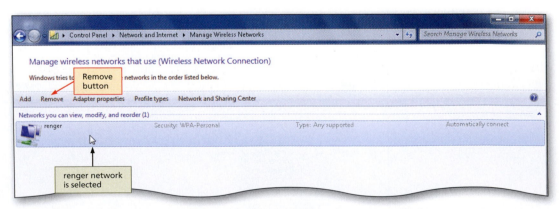

Figure C–31

- Click the Remove button to display the Manage Wireless Networks dialog box, verifying that you want to remove the network (Figure C–32).

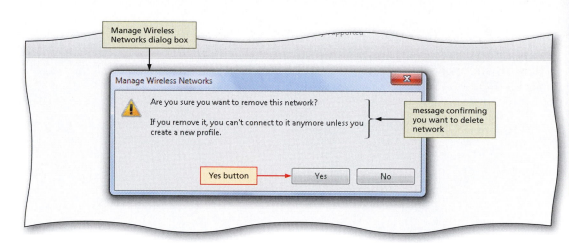

Figure C–32

- Click the Yes button to confirm that you no longer want to connect to this wireless network automatically (Figure C–33).

- Close the Manage Wireless Networks window.

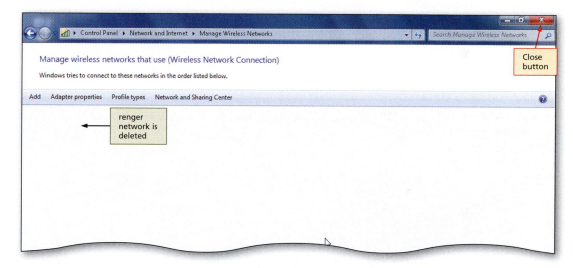

Figure C–33

Summary

Being able to connect to a network is essential in today's society where people use notebook computers more often and in more locations. Once connected, you should be aware of the type of network you are accessing and how secure it is, so that you and your computer are protected whether at home or in public.

Maintaining Your Computer

It can be frustrating to lose data. Almost everyone has heard a story about someone who lost a file and spent hours trying to recover it. In addition, hard disks fail more often than any other component on a computer. When a hard disk fails, it is extremely difficult to recover the data without obtaining professional help at a hefty price.

Even if a hard disk never fails, errors made while using the computer can result in the loss of a file or group of files. If you are not careful when you save a file, you could lose the file by saving a new file with the original file's name, or by clicking the wrong button in a dialog box and wiping out the contents of the file accidentally. In either case, you most certainly are going to lose some data. If a hard disk failure occurs, all of the files you have created or saved since the last backup might be gone for good. To avoid the loss of data, you should get into the habit of backing up the data on a regular basis.

Backing Up and Restoring Files

Although Windows 7 cannot prevent you from losing data on your hard disk, taking proper steps will ensure that you can recover lost data when an accident happens. To protect data on a hard disk, you should use a backup program. A typical **backup program** copies and then automatically compresses the files and folders from the hard disk into a single file, called a **backup file**. The backup program stores the backup file on a **backup medium**, which can be a hard disk, optical disc, shared network folder, USB flash drive, or even another computer on the network.

To Open Backup and Restore

Windows 7 includes powerful backup utilities. Backup and Restore allows you to back up selected files or your entire computer, restore selected files or your entire computer, create a restore point, and use the restore options to repair Windows 7. The steps on the following page open the Backup and Restore windows.

1

- Display the Start menu, and then open the Control Panel window.

- Click the System and Security link to open the System and Security window (Figure D–1).

Figure D–1

2

- Click the Backup and Restore link to open the Backup and Restore window (Figure D–2).

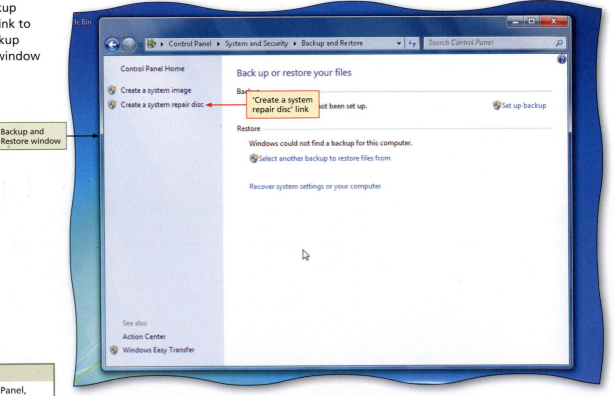

Other Ways

1. Open Control Panel, change to Large or Small icons, click Backup and Restore link

Figure D–2

To Create a System Repair Disc

Before backing up your data or system files, you should create a system repair disc. A **system repair disc** can be used to repair and restore your operating system to a working state when a serious system error has occurred. The following steps create a system repair disc.

- Click 'Create a system repair disc' in the left pane to display the 'Create a system repair disc' dialog box (Figure D–3).

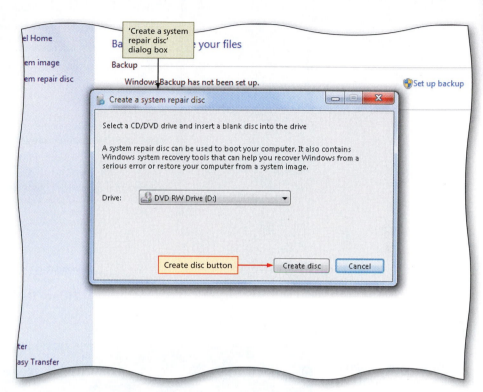

Figure D–3

2

- Insert a blank, recordable DVD into the DVD burner.

- Click the Create disc button to create the system repair disc. When the system repair disc is ready, a message will display about how you can use the disc (Figure D–4). If necessary, close the AutoPlay dialog box.

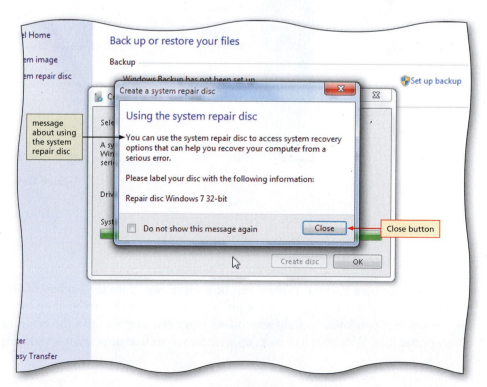

Figure D–4

3

- Click the Close button to return to the 'Create a system repair disc' dialog box (Figure D–5).

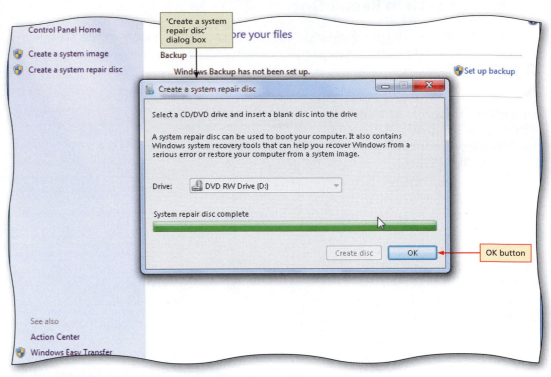

Figure D–5

4

- When the system repair disc is complete, click the OK button to close the 'Create a system repair disc' dialog box (Figure D–6).

- Eject the DVD from the computer.

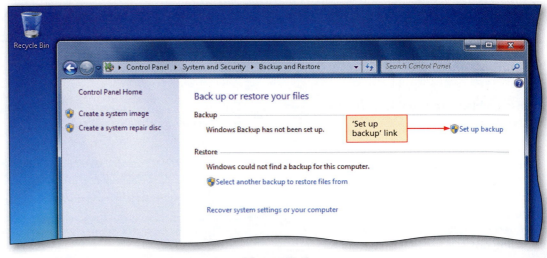

Figure D–6

To Configure a Backup

The 'Set up a backup' Wizard can be used to configure the backup of your computer. You either can choose to let Windows 7 decide what to back up or choose which files to back up by yourself. Only choose to select the files yourself if you know exactly which files you need to recover in the event of a system failure. When Windows 7 chooses the files, Windows will back up data files as well as important system files in a system image. A **system image** is a copy of the state of the computer, complete with system settings and operating system restore data as well as data files. You cannot use the system image to restore individual files; it is used for restoring your entire computer.

If you decide to choose the files yourself, you can select to back up files without a system image as well as select which files and folders you back up on a one-by-one basis. If you choose, you can back up files regularly and then use the 'Create a system image' link in the Backup and Restore window to make a system image. Although a system image takes time to create, it can be a great comfort to have when you need to restore the entire computer; therefore, you should create one at regular intervals. You could make one system image per week or per month, for example. Many people choose to make one each week, especially if they are doing quite a lot with their computer that might involve risks, such as installing many new programs on their computer. Alternatively, some people choose to only back up individual files, such as their data files. This can be useful if one or more files become lost or corrupt. In the event of a system failure requiring the entire computer to be restored, people who backed up individual files will have to install the operating system and programs manually, before being able to restore the individual files.

Once you have selected which files and folders you will back up, you then decide where to back up your files — on an optical disc, a hard disk (internal or external), or a network location. You also can choose the frequency, day, and time the backups occur. It is recommended that you back up your files weekly. The first time that you use the 'Set up backup' Wizard, you will be asked these questions, after which an initial backup will be created. The amount of time a backup takes to run depends upon the options you choose. It can take from a few minutes to one hour or more. The following steps schedule a backup to an external hard disk that will occur weekly on Saturday at 11:00 P.M., and then the steps create the first backup file.

1

- Click the 'Set up backup' link to briefly display the 'Set up backup' dialog box, and then display the 'Select where you want to save your backup' page of the 'Set up backup' Wizard (Figure D–7).

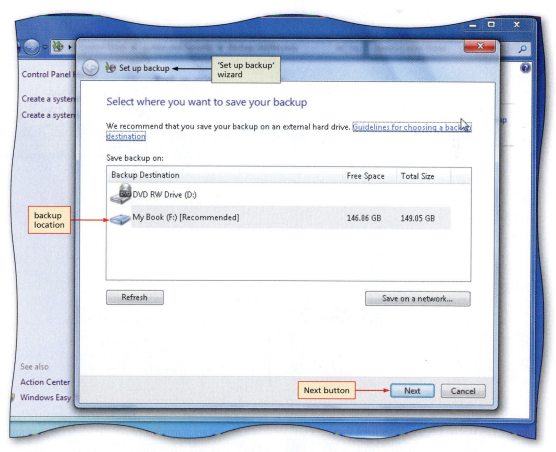

Figure D–7

2

- Select the hard disk My Book (F:) as the location for the backup. If the My Book (F:) drive does not appear, choose the desired drive where you want to back up your files.

- Click the Next button to display the 'What do you want to back up?' page of the wizard.

- Select the 'Let Windows choose (recommended)' option if it is not selected already (Figure D–8).

Q&A

Why did I get a warning message about using my drive?

Depending upon the storage device you use, Windows 7 might display warning messages if the drive is not secure. For example, if you share a drive with more than one user, Windows 7 might warn you that other people could have access to your backup.

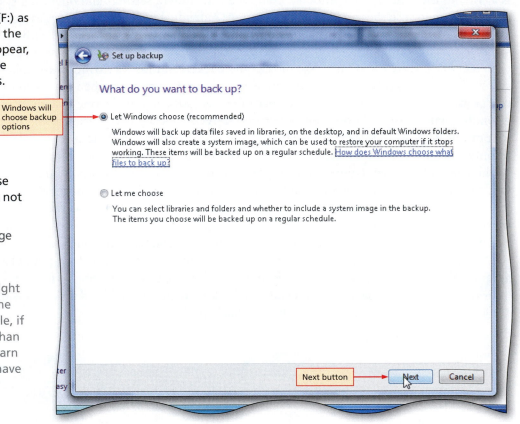

Windows will choose backup options

What do you want to back up?

○ Let Windows choose (recommended)

Windows will back up data files saved in libraries, on the desktop, and in default Windows folders. Windows will also create a system image, which can be used to restore your computer if it stops working. These items will be backed up on a regular schedule. How does Windows choose what files to back up?

○ Let me choose

You can select libraries and folders and whether to include a system image in the backup. The items you choose will be backed up on a regular schedule.

Next button → Next   Cancel

Figure D–8

3

- Click the Next button to display the 'Review your backup settings' page of the wizard (Figure D–9).

Q&A

Why does Windows display a warning regarding a system repair disc?

Windows requires that you have a system repair disc before it allows you to restore the backed-up system image.

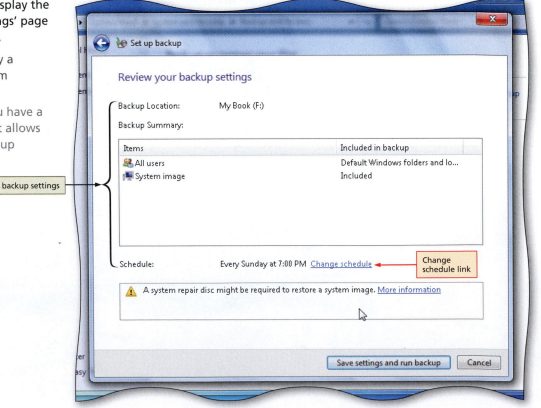

Set up backup

Review your backup settings

Backup Location: My Book (F:)

Backup Summary:

Items	Included in backup
All users	Default Windows folders and lo...
System image	Included

backup settings

Schedule: Every Sunday at 7:00 PM Change schedule ← Change schedule link

⚠ A system repair disc might be required to restore a system image. More information

Save settings and run backup   Cancel

Figure D–9

4

- Click the Change schedule link to display the 'How often do you want to back up' page of the wizard with scheduling options (Figure D–10).

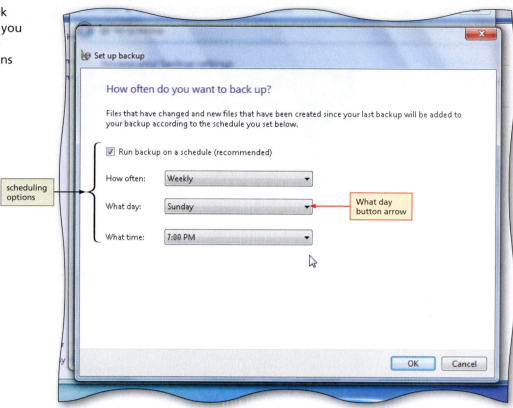

Figure D–10

5

- Click the What day button arrow to display the list of days (Figure D–11).

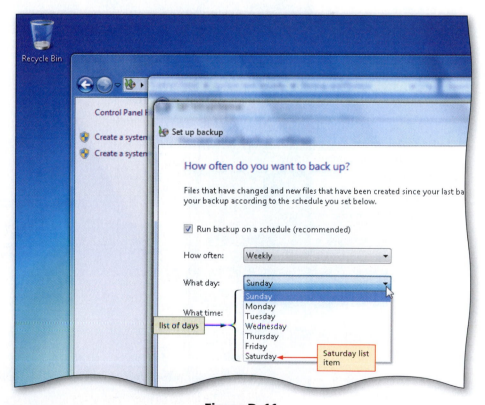

Figure D–11

- Click the Saturday
list item to change
the backup day
to Saturday
(Figure D–12).

Figure D–12

- Click the What time
button arrow to
display the list of
times (Figure D–13).

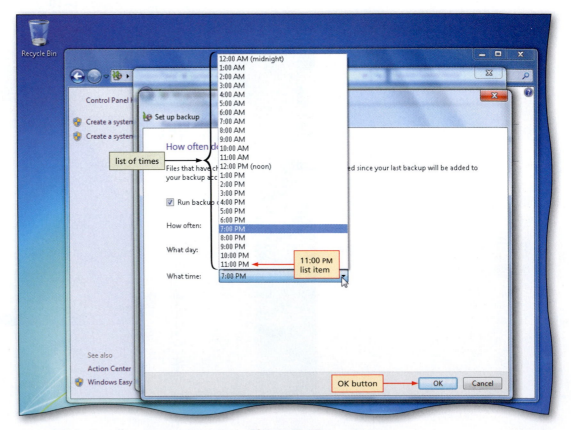

Figure D–13

8

- Click the 11:00 PM list item to change the backup time to 11:00 P.M.

- Click the OK button to close the dialog box and return to the 'Review your backup settings' page of the wizard (Figure D–14).

 Q&A How do I change the backup schedule once it has been created?

After the wizard runs for the first time, you can use the Change settings link on the Backup and Restore window to open the 'Set up backup' Wizard. You then can change the backup schedule as well as which files are backed up.

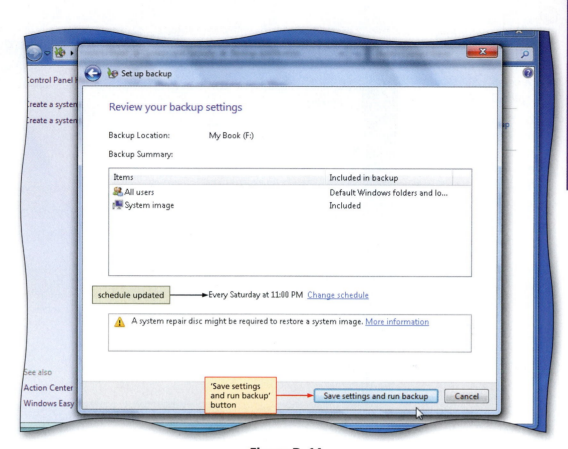

Figure D–14

9

- Click the 'Save settings and run backup' button to save the backup settings and start the backup process (Figure D–15).

 Q&A How long does it take to create the backup?

Time spent creating a backup depends on the backup media as well as the amount of information being backed up. If you have a USB drive and few files, it might take only a few minutes. For a larger set of files, it could take more than an hour.

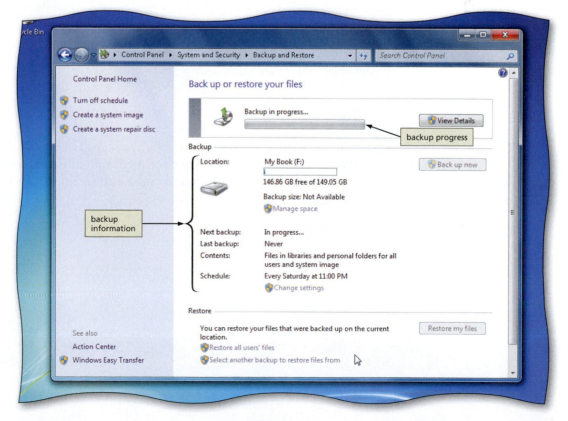

Figure D–15

• After the backup is created, the results of the backup are displayed (Figure D–16).

Do I have to use the 'Set up backup' Wizard every time I want to create a backup?

No, you do not have to run the 'Set up backup' Wizard. After the wizard creates the initial backup, simply clicking the 'Back up now' button in the Backup and Restore window will initiate a new backup file. If you want to change which files and folders are backed up, you will need to use the 'Set up backup' Wizard or click the Change settings link.

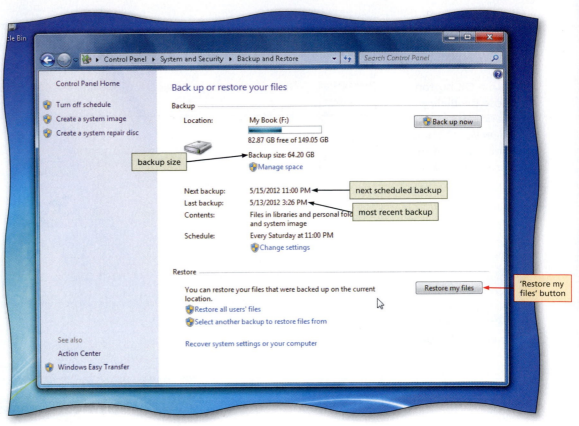

Figure D–16

To Restore Files from a Backup

There might be occasions when you need to restore files from a backup. The Restore Files Wizard will allow you to restore individual files and folders from a backup you have created. You only can restore individual files from a backup that is not a system image. (System images are discussed in the next section.) The following steps restore the Penguins.jpg file from the most recent backup.

1

• Click the 'Restore my files' button to start the Restore Files Wizard (Figure D–17).

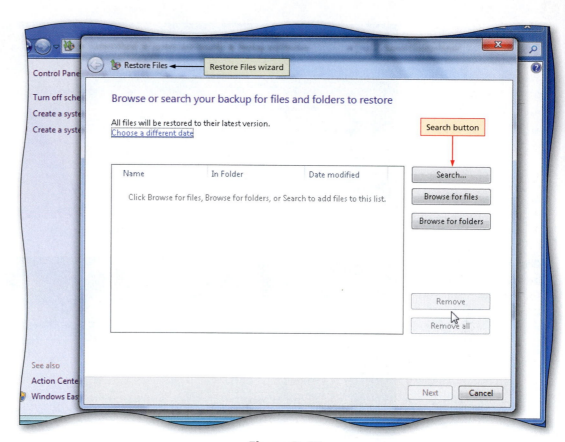

Figure D–17

2

• Click the Search button to open the 'Search for files to restore' dialog box (Figure D–18).

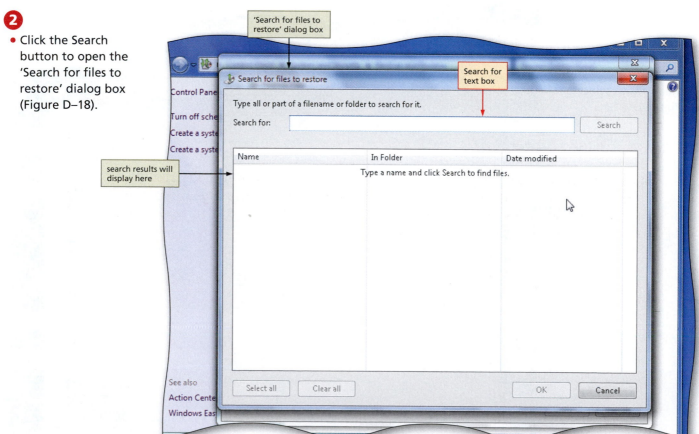

Figure D–18

3

- Type Penguins.jpg in the Search for text box (Figure D–19).

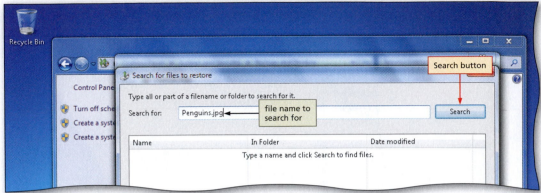

Figure D–19

4

- Click the Search button to search for the file (Figure D–20).

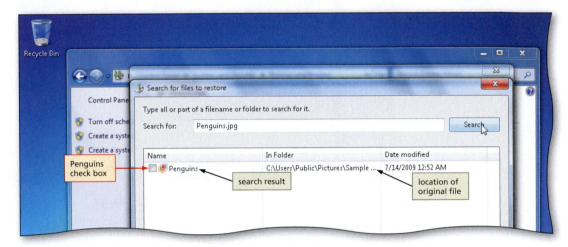

Figure D–20

5

- Click the Penguins check box to select it (Figure D–21).

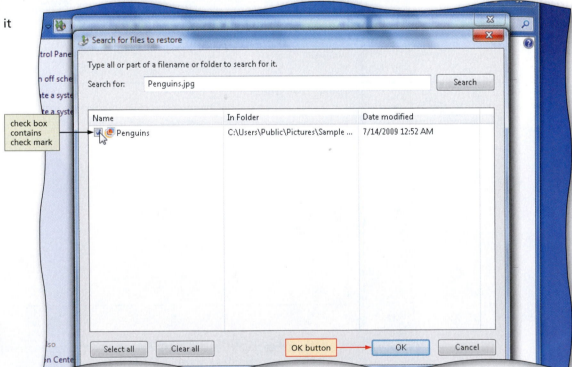

Figure D–21

6

- Click the OK button to add the file to the restore list (Figure D–22).

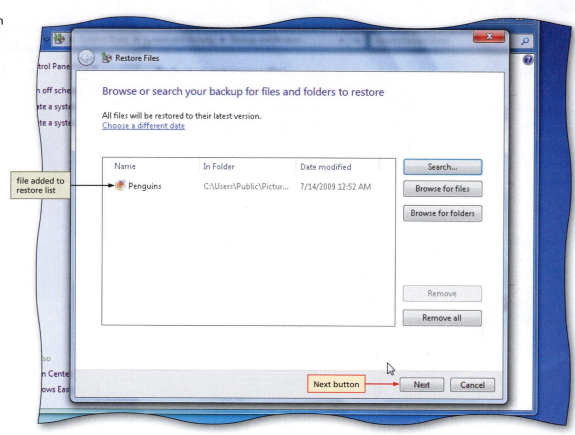

Figure D–22

7

- Click the Next button to continue the restoration.

- Verify that the 'In the original location' option is selected (Figure D–23).

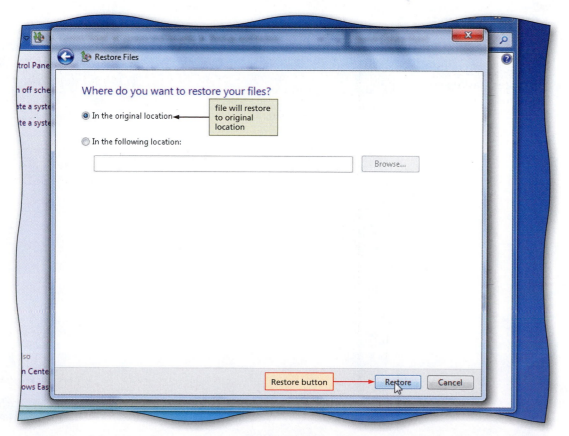

Figure D–23

8

- Click the Restore button to start the restoration (Figure D–24).

Why does the Copy File dialog box appear?

The Copy File dialog box appears because there is a file in the same location with the same name in Windows 7. From this dialog box, you can choose to replace the existing file with the file from the backup, keep the original file, or keep both files.

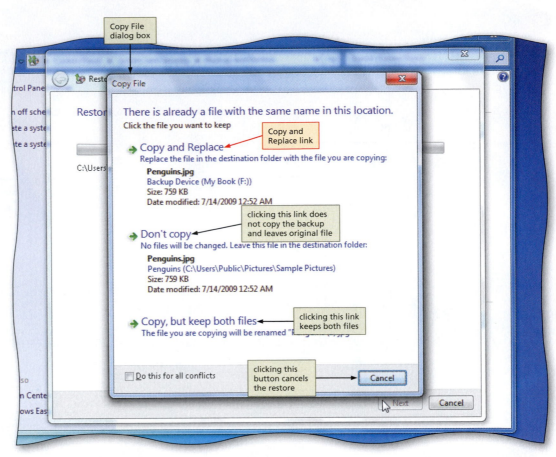

Figure D–24

9

- Click the Copy and Replace link to replace the existing Penguins.jpg with the restored backup copy (Figure D–25).

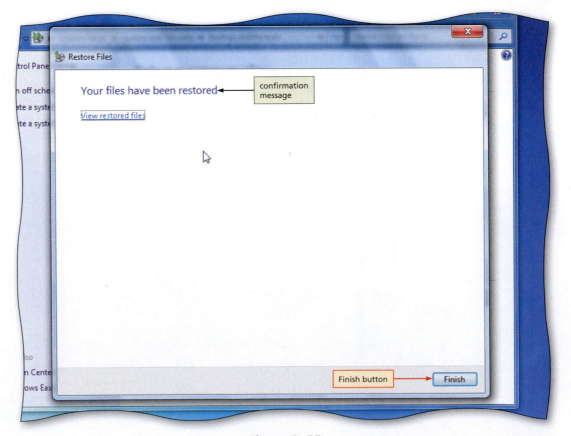

Figure D–25

10
- Click the Finish button to exit the Restore Files Wizard (Figure D–26).

- Close the Backup and Restore window.

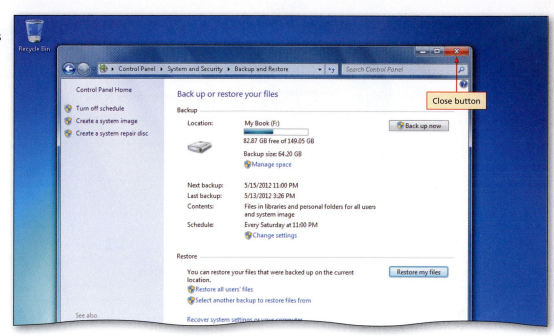

Figure D–26

To Create a Restore Point

Another safeguard for preventing damage to a computer is System Restore. **System Restore** is a tool that tracks changes to the computer and automatically creates a restore point when it detects the beginning of a change. A **restore point** is a representation of a stored state of the computer. System Restore automatically runs in the background and monitors changes to files, folders, and settings that are essential to the correct operation of the operating system.

System Restore creates an initial restore point when you install or upgrade to Windows 7. At regular intervals, System Restore creates a restore point to capture the current configuration of the computer and stores the configuration in the Registry. Restore points are created when you install an unsigned device driver, install a program using an installer program that is compatible with System Restore, install a Microsoft Update or patch, restore a prior configuration using System Restore, or restore data from a backup set created with the Backup program and store the configuration in the Registry.

Using a system image to restore your computer can help correct problems that occur when you install device drivers or programs that conflict with other device drivers or programs on the computer, when you update device drivers that cause performance or stability problems, or when the computer develops performance or stability problems for an unknown reason. System Restore cannot protect the computer from viruses, worms, and Trojan horse programs. An antivirus program is your best defense against these malicious threats. System Restore does not back up personal files: Use the backup features of the Backup and Restore window for personal files.

In addition to creating restore points automatically, Windows 7 allows you to create and name a restore point manually. Restore points commonly are set prior to making changes to the computer, such as when you install new hardware, install software, or install new or updated device drivers. If, after setting a restore point, you install hardware, software, or device drivers that cause your computer to function improperly, you can reset the computer to the state it was in when you set the restore point. This prevents you from losing personal files (documents, Internet favorites, e-mail messages, and so on) that would have been lost if you needed to reformat the hard disk and reinstall Windows 7. The steps on the following pages manually set a restore point with the name, Restore Point – May 13, and then display the System Restore dialog box.

1

• Display the Start menu.

• Right-click Computer to display a shortcut menu.

• Click the Properties link to display the System window (Figure D–27).

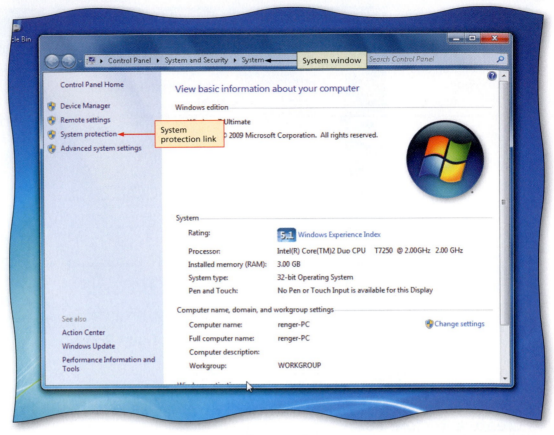

Figure D–27

2

• Click the System protection link to display the System Properties dialog box with the System Protection tab active (Figure D–28).

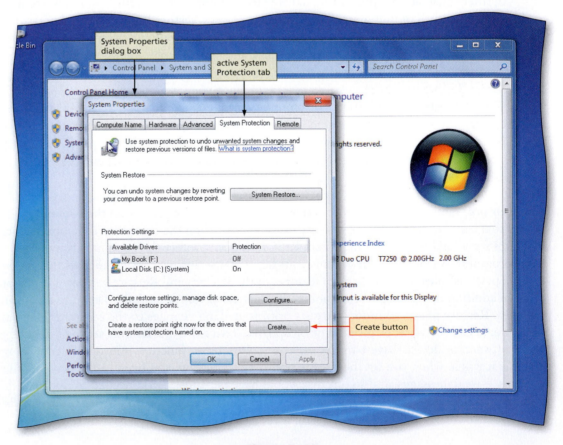

Figure D–28

3

- Click the Create button to create a restore point manually (Figure D–29).

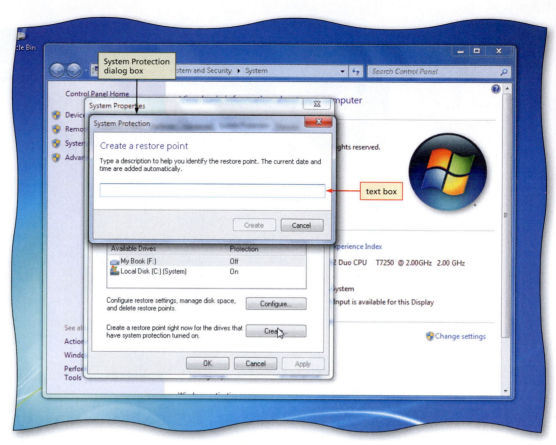

Figure D–29

4

- Type `Restore Point – May 13` in the text box to enter a description of the restore point (Figure D–30).

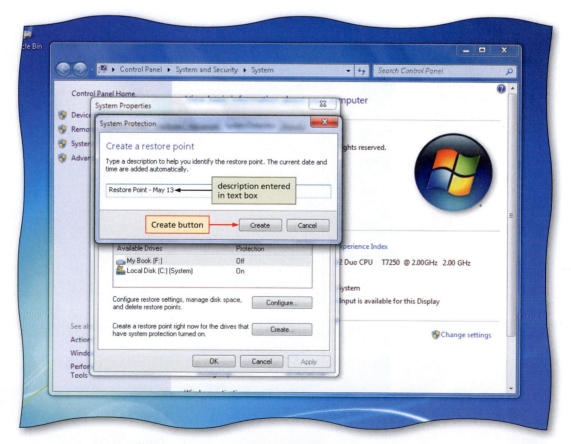

Figure D–30

5

• Click the Create button to create the restore point (Figure D–31).

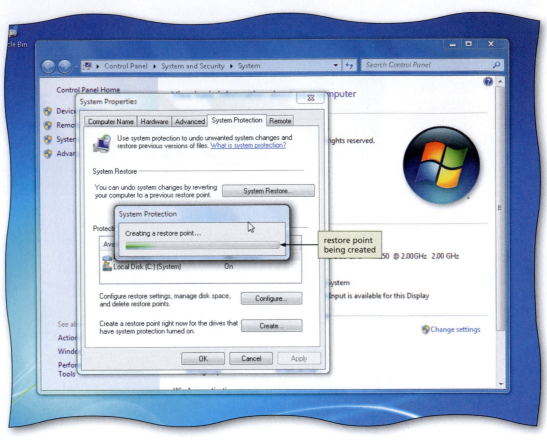

Figure D–31

6

• The System Protection progress indicator animates. When the restore point has been created, the System Protection dialog box displays a message stating that the restore point was created successfully (Figure D–32).

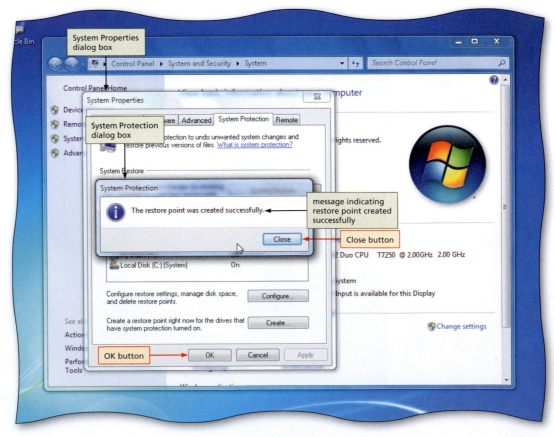

Figure D–32

7

- Click the Close button to close the System Protection dialog box.

- Click the OK button to close the System Properties dialog box (Figure D–33).

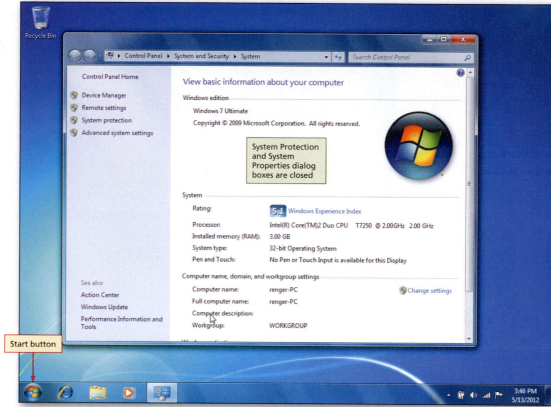

Figure D–33

8

- Display the Start menu.

- Type System Restore in the Search box.

- Click the System Restore link to start the System Restore Wizard (Figure D–34).

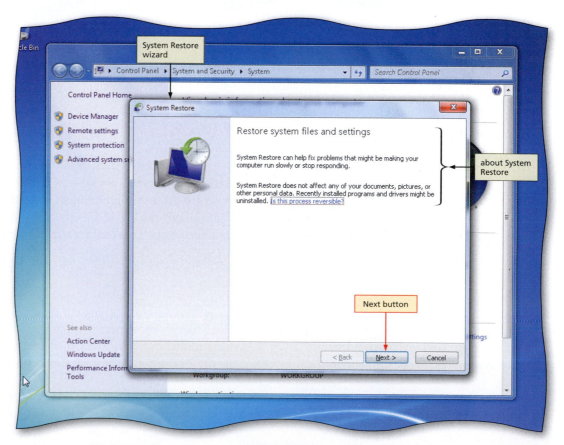

Figure D–34

- Click the Next button to see the list of restore points (Figure D–35).

- After viewing the dialog box options, click the Cancel button to close the dialog box without making changes.

- Close the System window.

Q&A

Why do my restore points differ?

Depending on the number of restore points that your system has made, the number of restore points on your computer might differ from those in the figure.

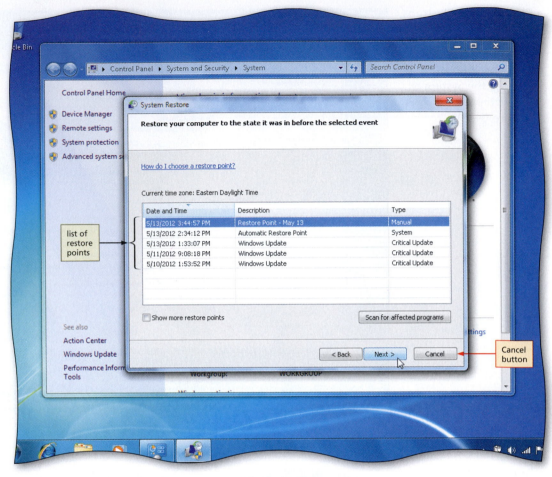

Figure D–35

Performance Information and Tools

After a long period of usage — and especially after installing programs and saving and deleting files — you might notice changes in your system performance. Your computer might not do what it is supposed to do or it might run slower than usual. These changes mean that your computer is not functioning as it did when Windows 7 was first installed. By performing some system maintenance, you can greatly improve the performance of your computer.

To Open the Performance Information and Tools Window

The Performance Information and Tools window contains the links to most of the tools that you will need to improve system performance. The following step opens the Performance Information and Tools window.

1

- Display the Start menu.

- Type `Performance` in the Search box.

- Click the Performance Information and Tools link to open the Performance Information and Tools window (Figure D–36).

Figure D–36

Other Ways

1. Open Control Panel, change to icons view, double-click Performance Information and Tools

To Run Disk Cleanup

Whenever you launch a program, delete a file using the Recycle Bin, view a Web page, or download a file from a Web site, files are stored on the hard disk. As a result, the hard disk contains many unnecessary files that reduce the amount of free space. If the free space falls too low for the operating system, error messages might display when you run programs. Removing the unnecessary files and increasing the amount of free space on the hard disk will increase the performance of your computer.

The easiest method to delete unnecessary files and make more free space available is to use Disk Cleanup. **Disk Cleanup** searches the hard disk, lists the files that you can delete safely, allows you to select the type of files to delete, and then deletes those files from the hard disk. Files you can select for deletion include temporary Internet files, downloaded program files, temporary files, and files in the Recycle Bin. The steps on the following pages run Disk Cleanup.

1
- Click the 'Open disk cleanup' link to open the Disk Cleanup: Drive Selection dialog box (Figure D–37).

Why does the Disk Cleanup: Drive Selection dialog box not appear on my computer?

The dialog box will only appear if you have more than one hard disk installed. If you only have one hard disk, your screen will match Figure D–38.

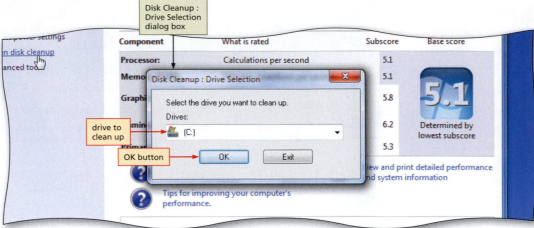

Figure D–37

2
- Verify that the (C:) drive is selected, and then click the OK button to search for files to clean up (Figure D–38).

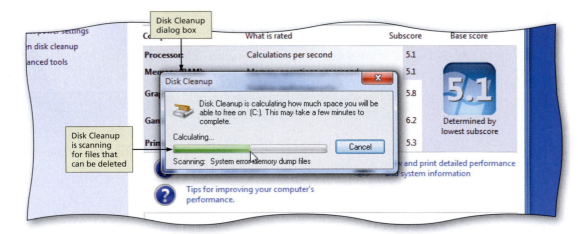

Figure D–38

3
- When Disk Cleanup finishes scanning the computer, the Disk Cleanup for (C:) dialog box appears (Figure D–39).

Experiment
- Scroll the 'Files to delete' area to view the additional types of files Disk Cleanup can delete.

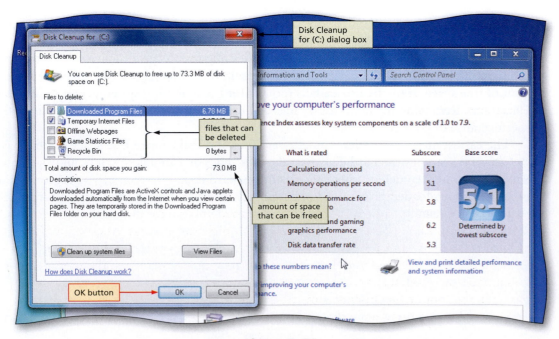

Figure D–39

4

- Click the OK button to display the Disk Cleanup dialog box where you will confirm that you want to delete the selected file types (Figure D–40).

Q&A

Which files should I remove?

Normally, you should only delete the downloaded program files and temporary Internet files (these are selected by default); however, you also can delete other files if you scroll and find that they are using a lot of storage space. If you are performing these steps in a computer lab, ask your instructor before deleting any files.

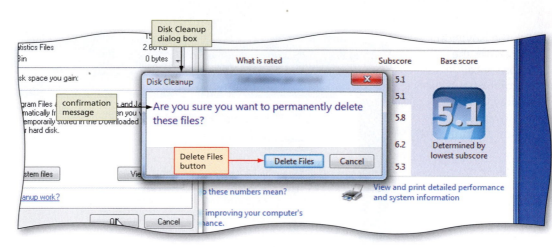

Figure D–40

5

- Click the Delete Files button to remove the files marked for deletion (Figure D–41).

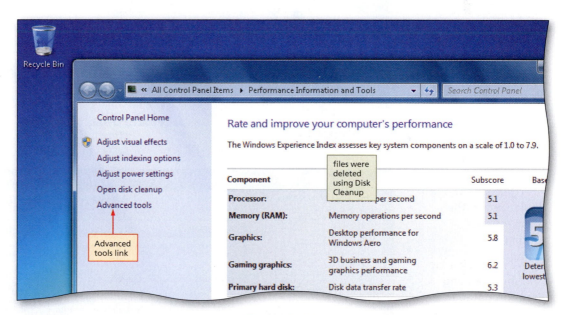

Figure D–41

To Open the Performance Monitor Window and View the Performance Monitor

It often is unclear what is making your computer or program run slowly. To research this problem, you can open the Performance Monitor window. The Performance Monitor allows you to view data logs that detail the performance of your computer. The Performance Monitor displays the processor utilization over time. This can be helpful to see if the processor is being tasked too hard during a particular time period. This can help shed light on why system performance might be slow. If there are particular times when the processor is extremely busy, you can then examine what programs were running at that time. Also, if the processor always is busy, this can be a sign that a program might not be functioning properly or that you might need to add more memory to your computer. The steps on the following pages open the Performance Monitor window and display the Performance Monitor.

1

• Click the Advanced tools link in the Performance Information and Tools window to open the Advanced Tools window (Figure D–42).

Figure D–42

2

• Click the Open Performance Monitor link to open the Performance Monitor window (Figure D–43).

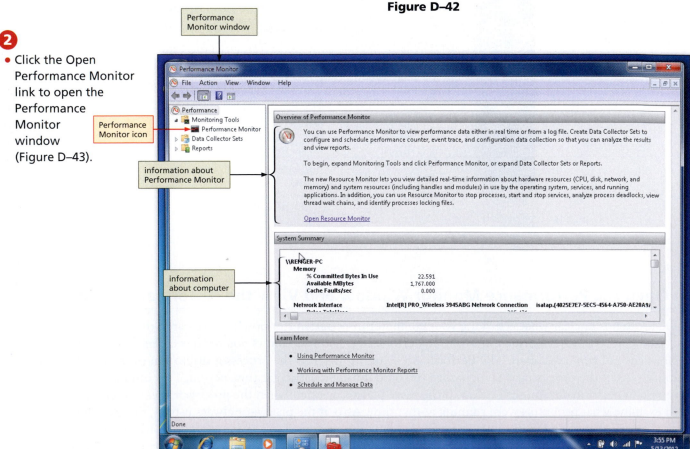

Figure D–43

3

• Click Performance Monitor in the left pane to view Performance Monitor data (Figure D–44).

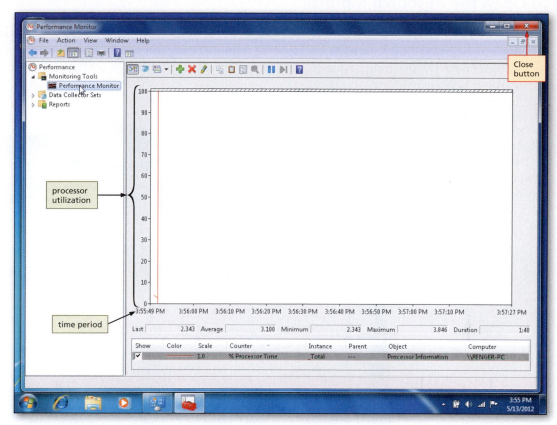

Figure D–44

4

• After viewing the monitor data, close the Performance Monitor window (Figure D–45).

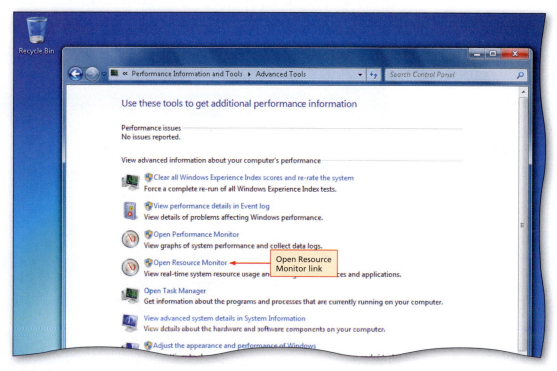

Figure D–45

Other Ways

1. Type Performance in Search box, then click Performance Monitor link

To Open the Resource Monitor

The Resource Monitor displays system usage in real time. From here, you can view which programs are running and how much of the resources are being used. If a program is taking too much of a resource, you will be able to identify the program and then attempt to reinstall, repair, or remove the program. The following steps display the Resource Monitor.

1

• Click the Open Resource Monitor link to view the Resource Monitor data (Figure D–46).

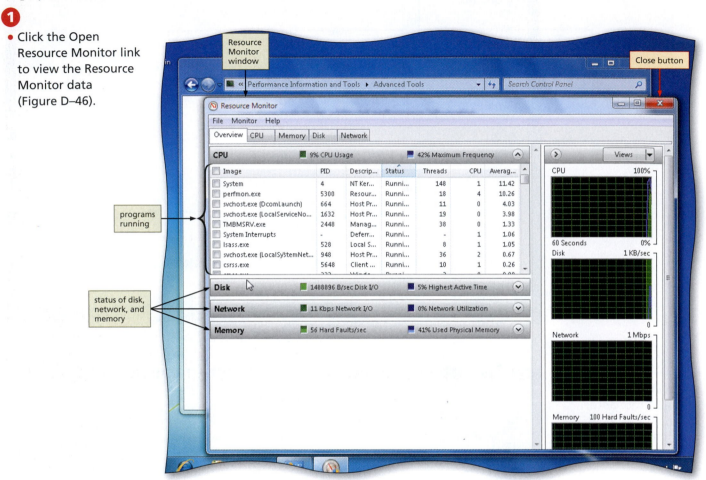

Figure D–46

2

● After viewing the resource data, close the Resource Monitor window (Figure D–47).

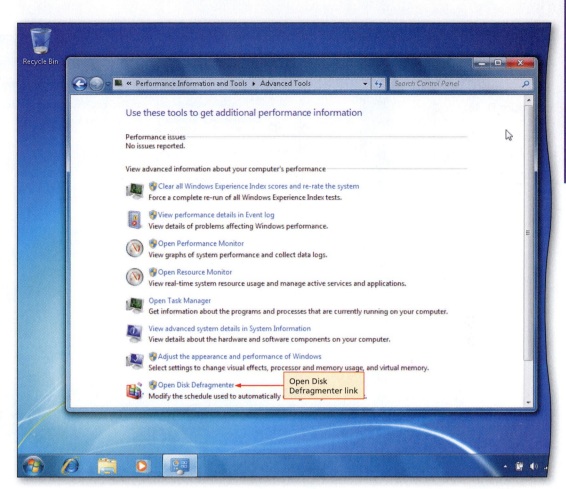

Figure D–47

Other Ways

1. Type `Resource` in Search box, then click Resource Monitor link

To Open the Disk Defragmenter

When you delete a file from a disk, the locations on the disk used by the deleted file become free disk space on the disk, and the next file stored by the operating system might use all or part of those locations. When new files are repeatedly added and deleted, the disk locations for a single file, called **clusters**, not always are located together on the hard disk, which creates a **fragmented file**. For your computer to run more efficiently, these clusters need to be periodically rearranged so that each file's clusters are located together. This process is called **disk defragmentation**. Disk Defragmenter, an administrative tool included with Windows 7, rearranges the files on the hard disk in contiguous blocks with no fragmentation. In Windows 7, disk defragmentation is scheduled to occur on a regular basis. You can change the schedule, but you should leave automatic disk defragmentation enabled. The steps on the following page open the Disk Defragmenter to allow you to view the settings.

- Click the Open Disk Defragmenter link in the Advanced Tools window to open the Disk Defragmenter (Figure D–48).

- After viewing the options, close the Disk Defragmenter.

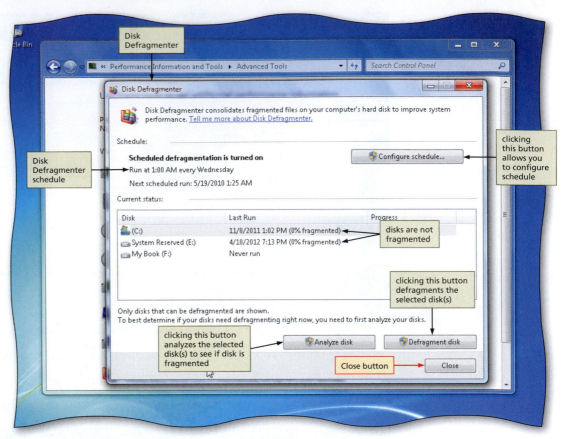

Figure D–48

To Generate a System Health Report

Windows 7 allows you to generate system health reports that detail the status of your resources, response times, and processes on your computer, along with system information and configuration data. Windows 7 analyzes the computer system for 60 seconds to generate the report. In the report, suggestions are provided to help you improve your system. The following steps generate a system health report.

- Scroll down the Advanced Tools window to display the 'Generate a system health report' link (Figure D–49).

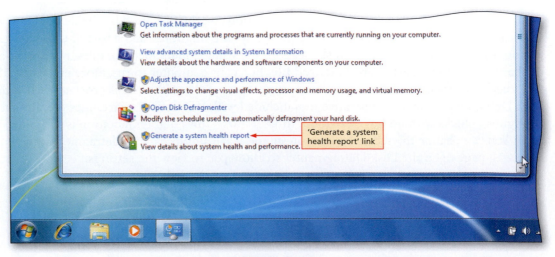

Figure D–49

2

- Click the 'Generate a system health report' link to open the Resource and Performance Monitor and generate and display a system health report (Figure D–50).

- After viewing the system health report, close the Resource and Performance Monitor window.

- Close the Advanced Tools window.

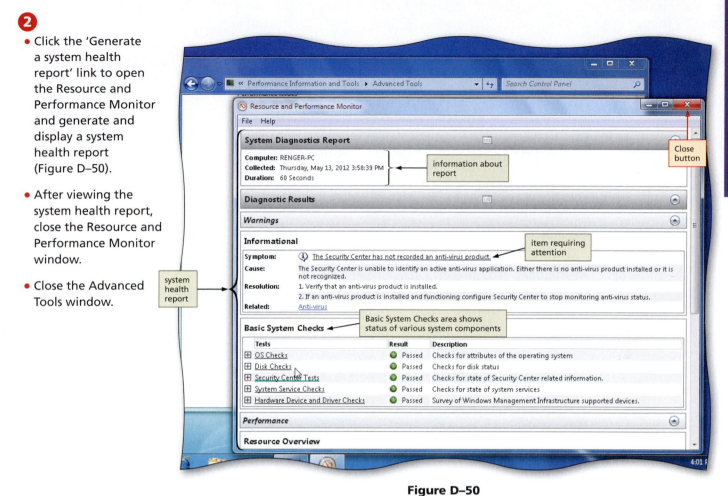

Figure D–50

Summary

Being able to maintain your computer is very important. An essential part of computer security is making sure that your computer functions properly. Part of the process of maintenance that people often overlook is making proper backups. By using backups, you protect yourself and your computer from valuable data loss.

Index

Note: **Boldfaced** page numbers refer to pages where key terms are defined.